AN EYEWITNESS HISTORY

WORKING IN AMERICA

Catherine Reef

■®
Facts On File, Inc.

Working in America

Copyright © 2000 by Catherine Reef

Facts On File, Inc.
11 Penn Plaza
New York NY 10001

Library of Congress Cataloging-in-Publication Data
Reef, Catherine
    Working in America : eyewitness history / Catherine Reef.
        p. cm.
    Includes bibiliographical references and index.
    ISBN 0-8160-4022-2
    1. Working class—United States—History. 2. Labor supply—United States—History. I. Title

    HD8066 .R44 2000
    305.5'62'0973—dc21   00-021058

Facts On File books are available at special discounts when purchased in bulk quantities for businesses, associations, institutions or sales promotions. Please call our Special Sales Department in New York at 212/967-8800 or 800/322-8755.

You can find Facts On File on the World Wide Web at
http://www.factsonfile.com

Text design by Joan M. Toro

Jacket design by Cathy Rincon

Printed in the United States of America.

VB FOF 10 9 8 7 6 5 4 3 2 1

This book is printed on acid-free paper.

I hear America singing, the varied carols I hear,
Those of mechanics, each one singing his as it should be blithe and strong,
The carpenter singing his as he measures his plank or beam,
The mason singing his as he makes ready for work, or leaves off work,
The boatman singing what belongs to him in his boat, the deckhand singing on
the steamboat deck,
The shoemaker singing as he sits on his bench, the hatter singing as he stands,
The wood-cutter's song, the ploughboy's on his way in the morning, or at noon
intermission or at sundown,
The delicious singing of the mother, or of the young wife at work, or of the girl
sewing or washing. . . .

—Walt Whitman, "I Hear America Singing"

NOTE ON PHOTOS

Many of the illustrations and photographs used in this book are old, historical images. The quality of the prints is not always up to modern standards, as in many cases the originals are from glass negatives or the originals are damaged. The content of the illustrations, however, made their inclusion important despite problems in reproduction.

For my father

CONTENTS

ACKNOWLEDGMENTS

I wish to thank my son, John S. Reef, for his good-natured help, and to acknowledge the important role played by Nicole Bowen, an insightful editor, in the development of this book. I hereby express my appreciation as well to the many librarians and collection curators who assisted me in large and small ways, particularly those at the Library of Congress and the University of Maryland libraries.

INTRODUCTION

"The greatest of all workers," preached the Reverend Henry Ward Beecher on a Sunday morning in 1875, "is God." Diligent New Englander that he was, Beecher found it impossible to imagine a Supreme Being who avoided labor. "He is the *Husbandman* of the universe," Beecher announced. "He tills, and he toils."

The association of work with virtue or godliness has been a singularly American construct since English settlers first came to the New World in the 1600s. The Puritans taught that all work was noble, that one labored on Earth for the glory of Heaven. "God sent you not into this world as into a Play-house, but a Work-house," they chided. Their work ethic had a dark side as well: that if labor was the business of God's people, then idleness was the province of the Devil. Too much leisure gave rein to the baser instincts. It was their lack of industry, after all, that had made Adam and Eve vulnerable to the serpent's temptations.

This mindset took root in the soil of North America and flourished as it never was to do in Europe. As long ago as the first half of the 19th century, Europeans visiting American shores remarked on the odd industriousness of nearly everyone they encountered. "Whoever goes to the United States for the

Workers at the McCormick Harvesting Machine Company, Chicago, circa 1902 (State Historical Society of Wisconsin; Whi[X3]30648)

purpose of settling there must resolve in his mind to find pleasure in business, and business in pleasure; or he will be disappointed, and wish himself back to the social idleness of Europe," warned Francis J. Grund, an Englishman who toured the United States in the 1830s. It must be remembered, though, that building a nation in the wilderness required a great deal of work. America could not afford an aristocracy like Europe's—every hand was needed. The Puritan ethic, then, had practical as well as religious value.

It is no wonder that working people figure prominently among the heroes of U.S. history. Paul Revere was a silversmith, for example, while Benjamin Franklin was a printer. Americans feel a special admiration for leaders who worked their way up from humble laboring origins. The fact that Abraham Lincoln once split rails earns him an extra measure of respect; similarly, Harry Truman's time spent as a haberdasher is viewed as an asset, an experience that helped him understand the needs of common people.

Evidence that the work ethic endured in the 20th century abounds. In 1905, the socialist and labor organizer Eugene V. Debs called workers "the saviors of society; the redeemers of the race." On March 4, 1933, when the newly inaugurated Franklin D. Roosevelt spoke about "the joy and moral stimulation of work," a vast audience of hungry and unemployed Americans understood the emotions to which he referred. Thirty-eight years later, on Labor Day, 1971, another president, Richard M. Nixon, stated that "America's competitive spirit, the 'work ethic' of this people is alive and well. . . ."

Of course, there have been critics of the work ethic in all eras. Perhaps none was more eloquent or offered a more refreshing viewpoint than Henry David Thoreau. This self-appointed "inspector of snow storms and rain storms" observed in the mid-19th century:

> If a man walk in the woods for love of them half of each day, he is in danger of being regarded as a loafer; but if he spends his whole day as a speculator, shearing off those woods and making earth bald before her time, he is esteemed as an industrious and enterprising citizen. As if a town had no interest in its forests but to cut them down!

THE OCCUPATIONS DESCRIBED IN THIS BOOK

Americans have engaged in many lines of work since 1776, and most have interesting histories. It is beyond the scope of any one book, however, to give accounts of them all. The occupations described in this volume reflect major trends in employment in the United States—how large numbers of people earned their livings at different times in the nation's history. Some of these occupations illustrate the effects of technology on the American worker. Those of us living at the dawn of the 21st century, so accustomed to rapidly advancing technology, are often surprised to learn that technological change was virtually an alien concept to the farmers and craftspeople plying their trades 200 or more years ago. Their farming methods and means of transportation had undergone little modification since biblical times, while artisans practiced their crafts as others had done for many generations. The Industrial Revolution, which began in the United States in 1790 with the establishment of the first mechanized textile mill in New England, broke the chains of tradition as it brought science and engineering to bear on the methods of work.

Many 19th-century Americans found the changes they witnessed exhilarating. They wondered at Robert Fulton's steamboat, which clipped along at 4.5 miles per hour; at a factory turning out a pair of women's high-button shoes in half a day; at trains inching like caterpillars along the steep sides of mountains. Yet the United States needed still further development "in products, in agriculture, in commerce, in networks of intercommunication," and in "materialistic prosperity in all its varied forms," proclaimed Walt Whitman, one of technology's greatest champions, in 1879.

The developments that Whitman called for came—but at a price. In order for millions to enjoy material prosperity, millions of others had to abandon the fields and artisans' shops for the factory and to sacrifice the satisfaction of a worthwhile task well done, accepting instead mistreatment and meager wages. Much of the history recounted in this book is the story of working people's subsequent efforts to regain their dignity.

THE AMERICAN WORKER IN THE 18TH CENTURY

When the United States was a new nation, 90 percent of the population farmed. Thomas Jefferson and others envisioned a future in which most U.S. citizens would continue to live off their own land. "Cultivators of the earth are the most valuable citizens. They are the most vigorous, the most independent, the most virtuous," Jefferson argued. The farmer's way of life may have been idealized, but it was a hard one that required maximum effort from every family member. Although land was abundant and cheap, labor was in short supply. There were fields to be cleared of trees; there was soil to be turned over. Crops needed to be planted, tended, and harvested, through the use of crude tools, simple methods, and strong arms and backs. Human beings were the chief source of power on early American farms.

Isolated farm families had to be self-sufficient, to provide food for themselves and their livestock, to make their own clothing, and to build shelters for humans and animals. They were at the mercy of drought, floods, insect infestations, and other forces of nature to a greater degree than farmers are today. Even if farmers were capable of producing a surplus, most, living impossibly far from markets, lacked any incentive to do so. Farmers constituted the first wave of settlement as the nation pushed west. In 1785, when the Mississippi River marked the western boundary of the United States, the federal government first provided for the sale of land in the public domain.

Towns and cities were home to the tradespeople, to the shoemakers, coopers, smiths, tailors, and carpenters who had spent long apprenticeships honing their skills. They did business in small shops, worked with their hands, and could perform every step in the manufacturing process and do it well.

THE INDUSTRIAL REVOLUTION

Although Americans of the 18th century were living in the New World, in a young and growing country, most expected their manner of living and working to remain stable. But changes they never could have imagined were about to transform their world. Issues that would confront the Americans of the 19th century were already taking shape.

The Industrial Revolution began in Great Britain when inventors mechanized the making of cloth. The flying shuttle, which made it possible to weave cloth more rapidly, was invented in 1733. With the arrival in 1769 of the spinning frame, a machine that spun thread for weaving, cloth making moved out of the home and into the factory. The first U.S. textile mill to employ British technology was established at Pawtucket, Rhode Island, in 1790 by Samuel Slater, an English immigrant. James Watt and Matthew Boulton produced their first steam engine in 1776. Once perfected, it would power steamboats and locomotives as well as factories.

In 1794, Eli Whitney patented the cotton gin, one of the most important technological innovations in the history of American agriculture. Whitney's machine removed seeds from the fibers of short-staple cotton and made that crop profitable to grow. The spread of cotton culture gave rise to an economy based on agriculture in the South and led to an enormous increase in the number of African slaves, as growers relied on unpaid labor to grow and pick

Enslaved workers leaving for the fields, James Hopkinson Plantation, Edisto Island, South Carolina *(New Hampshire Historical Society; Moore 512)*

their cotton. In 1790, 700,000 enslaved African Americans lived south of the Mason-Dixon Line and the Ohio River.

THE 1800s: CENTURY OF CHANGE

The first years of the 19th century saw a greater push westward. The Louisiana Purchase in 1803 increased the area of the United States by 828,000 square miles and extended the nation's western border to the Rocky Mountains. Settlers rushing in to claim their portions of the new territory caused the population west of the Appalachians to top 1 million in 1810. Technological advances, such as improved plows and the mechanical reaper, permitted farmers to cultivate more acres, and many profit-minded farmers set their sights on virgin land still farther west.

A revolution in transportation was under way as well. Fulton's steamboat appeared in 1807. Construction of the National Road, which connected Maryland with the Ohio River, began in 1811, and digging of the Erie Canal commenced in 1817. These innovations in land and water transport facilitated the movement of people and goods. Once western farmers had ways to get crops and livestock to market, they had reason to produce a surplus.

Canals, steamboats, and macadamized roads could not compete with the railroads, though. The first railway line in the United States began operation in 1831. Over the next 30 years, railroads connected communities throughout the East, profoundly altering the social and economic life of the nation. Departing from Chicago, they carried the bounty of the Mississippi and Ohio River valleys to eastern markets. Southern growers shipped their crops of cotton, tobacco, and rice northward by train and brought in food and factory-made goods.

At the same time, factories were rapidly replacing the artisan's shop and the home as centers of production. By 1800, Eli Whitney had put into practice a method of manufacturing firearms with interchangeable parts. This development gave rise to the assembly line and demonstrated that each worker need only master a single step in the manufacturing process. Skilled craftspeople saw their business slip away, and the apprenticeship system broke down. Manufacturers increasingly relied on cheap, unskilled labor, including young women from rural communities and children.

The profit motive ruled the workplace. With no legislation to govern hours of work, wages, schooling, or factory conditions, plant owners squeezed as much labor as possible from their employees for the smallest possible expenditure. Fourteen-hour days were not uncommon—and neither were work-related injuries and illnesses. Whether society benefited more from child literacy or child productivity was an open question. Some workers formed unions and expressed their discontent by striking. Laborers in Philadelphia, for example, successfully struck for a 10-hour day in 1835. But economic downturns ended most early efforts at worker organization.

By the end of the Civil War, in 1865, manufacturers had the necessary equipment to produce shoes in factories. Clothing sizes had been standardized, facilitating the sale of ready-made garments, and growing numbers of foreign-born workers were finding employment on the factory floor. Relieved of the need to make wartime munitions, factories could now produce the nails, spikes, and equipment essential to the expanding railroads. The continental United States had

Dynamite blasts away rock, clearing the path for a railroad to Deadwood, South Dakota, in 1890. *(Library of Congress)*

assumed its present dimensions in 1853, and the population was impatient for a noisy, smoke-emitting, tangible link between the East and the West—a transcontinental railroad line. Construction of the Central Pacific Railroad had begun in San Francisco in 1863 and was moving east; work started in Omaha, Nebraska, on a connecting line, the Union Pacific, in 1865. Four short years later, locomotives of the two railroads stood on a single track in the Utah wilderness, touching noses—"Half a world behind each back," as the poet Hart Crane observed.

THE MINING PIONEERS

Following the discovery of gold in California in 1848, the miner had joined the farmer as an opener of the West. Forty thousand miners were sifting soil in the Sierra Nevada range by the end of 1849. The California mining population exceeded 100,000 by late 1852, which was the year of peak production.

California may have been "El Dorado on the Pacific," according to the *New York Tribune,* but the Washoe Mountains of Nevada promised even greater wealth in the form of "blue stuff": a vein of decomposed quartz buried 2,000 feet below the summit of Mt. Davidson. Known as the Comstock Lode, this rich deposit yielded $300 million in silver and gold over the next 20 years. Again, speculative easterners crossed mountains and deserts to claim their share of hidden wealth. When an act of Congress created the Nevada Territory in 1861, the region's population was approaching 20,000.

Railroads not only brought hopeful miners west, but as additional mineral wealth was discovered in Colorado, South Dakota, Montana, Idaho, and elsewhere, the railroads transported tools and equipment to the mines and carried out the unprocessed ore. They provided passage for the merchants, saloon keepers, and women who followed the miners to siphon off their profits. Numerous settlements were established and soon abandoned, but some flourished and became permanent towns and cities.

The railroads also permitted the growth of the cattle industry in the second half of the 19th century, which made the cowboy one of the most celebrated American workers. In the 1860s, abundant herds of longhorn cattle grazed on the Texas plains, while a burgeoning population in the East hungered for beef. Once railroads linked eastern cities with Kansas and other western states and territories, cattle ranching underwent explosive growth. Texas ranchers hired young men—the cowboys—to round up herds that were grazing on the range and drive them north to Abilene, Kansas, and other booming cattle towns. Between 1867 and the mid 1880s, as many as 10 million cattle journeyed out of Texas on the Chisholm Trail and other routes in the greatest movement of domestic animals known to have occurred anywhere, at any time.

Thoughts of spending days crossing the open country, passing nights under the stars, facing the constant danger of thieves and predators, and knowing how to ride and rope and shoot appealed to the imaginations of easterners, who fashioned a myth of romance and adventure centered on the cowboy. In reality, his work was hard and dirty, his pay was poor, and his glory days were brief. As railroad lines branched farther into western lands and cattle ranchers put up fences, roundups and trail drives took place with far less frequency. Demoted to the duties of ranch hands, the cowboys dwindled in number.

The cattle industry supported 35,000 cowboys between 1866 and 1895. A larger segment of the workforce, one that received far less public attention during these years, was the population of formerly enslaved African Americans. Approximately 4 million slaves had been living in the Confederate states at the outbreak of the Civil War. Once peace was established, they began a long struggle to gain their rightful place in society and to perform meaningful work that provided an adequate income. Most had been kept illiterate by southern Slave Codes and had acquired no employable skills other than those needed for farming. The majority therefore continued to tend cotton, tobacco, and other crops as hired hands or, more likely, as sharecroppers. New restrictive laws known as Black Codes and white-supremacist terrorists, such as the Ku Klux Klan, kept them living in poverty and submission.

Approximately 100 labor unions had been organized along craft lines by 1860, but most restricted their membership to white workers or shunted blacks into segregated local auxiliaries. The first major U.S. labor organization, the Knights of Labor, which was founded in 1869, permitted African Americans to join its assemblies. The American Federation of Labor (AFL), established in 1886, prohibited its member unions from barring blacks but almost never enforced that rule.

The history of the American labor movement in the late 19th century is punctuated by episodes of violence, as employers opposed workers' efforts to organize and press their demands. Rioting broke out in Pittsburgh, Philadelphia, St. Louis, and other cities during a widespread railroad strike in 1877. A bomb killed several police officers attempting to break up a workers' rally in Chicago's Haymarket Square in May 1886. Four local anarchists were hanged in retaliation, although no evidence linked them to the bombing. Blood was shed in Homestead, Pennsylvania, in 1892, when striking steel workers did battle with 300 armed Pinkerton detectives who had been hired by their employer, the Carnegie Steel Company. Three detectives and seven strikers died. The workers defeated the Pinkertons and sent them packing, but the powerful Carnegie Company nonetheless put down the strike.

During the second half of the 19th century, a time known as the Gilded Age, newly minted tycoons such as Andrew Carnegie dominated American industry, and massive corporations cast powerful shadows across the economic landscape. Just as Carnegie rose from humble origins to control most U.S. steel production, John D. Rockefeller used ruthless tactics and an extraordinary aptitude for business to build an empire in oil. Other robber barons created monopolies in various industries as well. The challenges these individuals posed to the validity of the free-market economy forced Congress to pass such laws as the Sherman Anti-Trust Act of 1890, limiting the power of corporations.

The robber barons lived in opulence on their newly acquired wealth. Far less glamorous was the life of millions of laborers who toiled in factories and tenement sweatshops and faced poverty every day. Men, women, and children, many of them immigrants, worked and lived in an environment in which disease thrived and the likelihood of an accident or fire was high.

Millions of European immigrants arrived in the United States in the 19th and early 20th centuries. In the record year, 1907, 1.5 million people entered the United States. Before 1890, the majority came from Great Britain, Ireland, Germany, and after 1860, Scandinavia. Most who came after 1890 were from southern and eastern Europe, especially Austria, Hungary, Italy, and Russia. The immigrants came to escape political upheaval, famine in the case of the Irish, and religious persecution in the case of eastern European Jews. The principal reason that most came, though, was to work, to make a life and a living.

BOUNDLESS OPTIMISM

American industry exploited the continent's abundant natural resources and the cheap labor made available by large-scale immigration to build the United States into the world's leading manufacturing nation. In 1900, manufacturing, transportation, and communications contributed twice the dollar value to the

U.S. economy as agriculture, forestry, and fishing combined. The decline in agriculture's contribution to the gross national product (GNP) that had begun before 1900 would continue throughout the 20th century. Industry, meanwhile, would increase its share of the GNP through the 1960s.

Looking ahead to the 20th century, few political leaders in 1900 were inclined to listen to pessimists like Senator Chauncey Depew of New York, who warned that widespread mechanization "endangers the health, happiness and lives of the people of Europe and America." Instead, some politicians redefined the concept of manifest destiny, envisioning now a single nation of 118 states spanning North and South America. In his second inaugural address, on March 4, 1901, President William McKinley predicted that the new century would be a kind of Aquarian Age, an era free of wars in which humanity gained "a keener realization of the brotherhood of man."

To an increasing number of laborers in the first years of the 20th century, brotherhood—or sisterhood—meant banding together to demand better working conditions. One of the most militant organizations in the history of U.S. labor, the Industrial Workers of the World (IWW), was founded in 1905. Known as the Wobblies, these activists aspired to do nothing less than bring down the capitalist system. They sang, "Workers of the world, awaken! / Break your chains, demand your rights," and they resorted to strikes, violence, or sabotage as they thought the situation required. The Wobblies participated most famously in a textile workers' strike in Lawrence, Massachusetts, in 1912. IWW strike leaders kept more than 20,000 factory hands, most of them immigrants from diverse cultural backgrounds, focused on a common objective in the face of police attacks, attempted bombings, and the arrest of two IWW organizers, Joseph J. Ettor and Arturo Giovannitti, on a false charge of murder.

In 1909, garment workers had struck in New York and Philadelphia after a seamstress announced in a union meeting that she was tired of listening to speeches. That young woman, Clara Lemlich, cried out, "I offer a resolution that a general strike be called—now!"

The strikes called attention not only to low wages and long hours of work but also to the deplorable conditions that many people endured on the job, which included noise, extreme heat, fire hazards, unsafe machinery, locked windows and doors, and exposure to toxic chemicals. The workers' protests received unfortunate justification on March 25, 1911, when a fire spread rapidly through the downtown New York City building that housed the Triangle Shirtwaist Company in its upper stories. One hundred forty-six women died leaping from windows, their clothing in flames, or pushing against doors that had been locked to keep them inside.

Another, quieter battle was being fought in these years to end child labor. In 1904, concerned citizens formed the National Child Labor Committee (NCLC) to persuade states to regulate the employment of children. Three years later, the NCLC made the brilliant decision to hire photographer Lewis Hine to document the working lives of children in canneries, coal mines, and textile mills as well as on farms and city streets. Hine's images of child laborers with soiled, exhausted faces and ragged clothes—but a dignity seldom seen in people so young—were beautiful and heartbreaking at the same time. They did more than countless speeches by reformers could ever have done to

February 12, 1908, 2 A.M.: Lewis Hine photographed Brooklyn, New York, newsboys starting their morning round. *(Library of Congress)*

convince lawmakers that the practice of child labor had to end—or at least be controlled. Thirty-nine states passed child-labor laws between 1911 and 1913, but thousands of youthful laborers remained exempt from their provisions.

WAR CHANGES SOCIETY

McKinley had foreseen an era of peace, but by 1917 Americans were fighting a war in Europe. World War I emptied the factories and mills of the East and the slaughterhouses and meat-packing plants of the Midwest as men left their workstations to take up arms, and European immigrants stopped coming. Between 1915 and 1918, immigration averaged a little more than 250,000 annually. African Americans from the South rushed in to fill the void, seeking not only jobs but also better living conditions in the North. Historians refer to this massive exodus, which involved approximately 1.5 million people before it slowed in 1940, as the Great Migration.

The newcomers discovered that discrimination existed in the North as well—but more subtly. There were no Jim Crow laws on the books, but blacks were hired only for the least desirable jobs, denied union membership, and permitted to live only in inferior housing. When the soldiers returned home after the war, whites viewed the migrants as potential competitors in the job market and greeted them with violence. The summer of 1919 was characterized by race riots, as whites and blacks clashed in Washington, D.C., Chicago, and elsewhere.

World War I was the first of three national emergencies that the United States faced in the first half of the 20th century. The second was the Great Depression, and the third was World War II. The depression followed on the heels of the 1920s, a decade of prosperity and speculation. Americans living through the depression coped with conditions that had never existed before in the United States: unemployment on a massive scale; men in shabby shoes standing in breadlines without overcoats in winter; clouds of dust blowing across the drought-stricken Southwest—people covered their mouths and noses with cloth to keep out the flying sand. Photojournalist Margaret Bourke-White, reporting on drought conditions in Kansas in 1935, saw an entire family with masked faces and was reminded of the Ku Klux Klan. A stream of dust bowl refugees tried to survive as farm workers in California, where they were neither needed nor wanted.

President Herbert Hoover, in office just six months when the stock market crashed in October 1929, took unprecedented steps to deal with the crisis. He approved increased government spending for public works and a program of federal loans to businesses, through the Reconstruction Finance Corporation.

This "Hooverville" outside Seattle resembled many such concentrations of poverty in the United States during the Great Depression. *(Special Collections, University of Washington Libraries; 20102)*

When the economy remained flat and motionless, he directed that government funds be spent for public welfare. Hoover was in reality a caring man, but the public perceived him to be insensitive and reactionary. Americans welcomed Franklin Delano Roosevelt in 1932 as a forward-looking agent of change.

The sweeping New Deal legislation that Roosevelt sent to Congress profoundly affected working America. Some of these acts made funds available for public works projects that put millions of people on the federal payroll. Many young people finishing school discovered that the government offered their only chance of a job. Approximately 2.5 million young men worked on environmental and restoration projects with the Civilian Conservation Corps (CCC) between 1933 and 1942. After 1935, young women and students found jobs in their communities with the National Youth Administration. The Works Progress (later Work Projects) Administration (WPA), the largest and most wide-ranging of the federal employment programs, hired 8 million adults between 1935 and 1941 to do everything from recording oral histories to building courthouses to painting murals in post offices.

Other New Deal programs aided farmers and businesspeople. For example, the Agricultural Adjustment Act of 1933 sought to raise the prices that farmers received for produce by offering subsidies for fields left unplanted. The National Industrial Recovery Act of 1933 attempted to spur a business rebound by establishing voluntary codes of competition for hundreds of industries. These codes included a minimum working age for each industry, signaling the federal government's renewed commitment to regulating child labor. This act also guaranteed workers the right to join unions and bargain collectively. "The question now is," wondered William Green, president of the AFL, "will the unorganized workers of the nation exercise this legal right to unite with their fellow workers for the purpose of securing higher wages, shorter hours, and improved conditions of employment?"

The answer was *yes.* Much of the unionizing activity that occurred during these years was carried out by the Committee for Industrial Organization (CIO), a group formed within the AFL to organize unskilled workers along industrial lines. (The CIO was expelled from the AFL in 1937. In 1938, the group adopted the name Congress of Industrial Organizations.) The CIO backed the workers of General Motors Corporation when they staged a sitdown strike in 1936 and 1937 over the company's refusal to recognize the United Auto Workers as their bargaining agent. Workers occupied GM plants in Flint, Michigan, and other cities for two months and forced management to deal with the union.

The CIO was also involved in a violent strike against several of the nation's largest steel manufacturers in 1937. Ten workers lay shot to death outside the South Chicago plant of the Republic Steel Corporation before that strike was settled. It took action by the National Labor Relations Board, established in 1935, to investigate employee complaints, to force the companies to sign contracts with their workers' union, the United Steel Workers of America.

PITCHING IN TO WIN THE WAR

Between 1939 and 1943, the WPA focused on training workers to take jobs in defense plants. As war erupted in Europe and Asia and U.S. involvement became first probable and then a reality, U.S. industries shifted from the production of consumer goods to the manufacture of planes, tanks, ships, and munitions. As during World War I, industry's response created opportunities for many workers. The bustling defense plants of the West Coast hired thousands of dust bowl refugees, and throughout the nation, wartime work gave millions of women entry into traditionally male fields.

Women had come to dominate clerical work in the early 20th century, and they had increased their presence in sales and social work. Now, with so many men away fighting the war, they became "production soldiers" and learned to operate drill presses, forklifts, tractors, and other pieces of heavy equipment. "It would be easier to report on what women are not doing than on the innumerable lines in which they have replaced men," remarked the upbeat author of a Department of Commerce publication on women in wartime.

The situation was far different for the millions of black Americans who remained on relief as their white fellow citizens found jobs in the booming defense industries of 1940 and 1941. Corporations that had never hired African Americans had no intention of starting to now. The president of North American Aviation said flatly that "regardless of training, we will not employ Negroes in the North American plant. It is against company policy."

These discriminatory policies were particularly offensive to A. Philip Randolph, president of the Brotherhood of Sleeping Car Porters, the first significant African-American labor union. Randolph's long fight with the Pullman Company for union recognition had made him a nationally known figure and earned him a reputation as a spokesperson for black America. Randolph stated his belief that African Americans needed to take action against discrimination in the defense industries and that they had to do so in a big way. In January 1941 he called for 10,000 African Americans to march in Washington, D.C., to demand jobs for which they were qualified. As support for the march grew in the black community, Randolph raised his estimate of the number of marchers to 100,000. The threat of such an enormous demonstration persuaded President Roosevelt to issue an executive order ending discrimination in defense plants. In 1955, Randolph and another African-American labor leader, Willard Townsend, sat on the Executive Council of the newly formed AFL-CIO, but African Americans had yet to achieve equal representation in unions or in the workplace.

A SHAKE-UP IN ORGANIZED LABOR

It is tempting to look back on the 1950s as a time of relative stability, yet it was during this decade that the United States took part in the Korean War, Senator Joseph McCarthy cast doubt on the loyalty of numerous citizens, and the integrity of organized labor was called into question. Beginning in 1957, Senate hearings uncovered evidence of gross misuse of union funds and ties to organized crime.

The Senate committee demonstrated that Dave Beck, president of the International Brotherhood of Teamsters, Chauffeurs, Warehousemen, and Helpers of America (the IBT, or Teamsters), had used more than $4,000 of IBT money to beautify the grounds of his luxurious home—a mansion financed with $163,000 from the union treasury. Beck also had looted $85,000 to pay for hundreds of items for his own use, including golf equipment, bed linens, clothing, furniture, home appliances, and an outboard motor.

Even more damning was the evidence against Beck's successor, James Hoffa. The committee demonstrated that Hoffa had been involved in strong-arm tactics, extortion, kickbacks, and bribery and that he had associated with known criminals. Both Beck and Hoffa served time in prison for their crimes, and the AFL expelled the IBT and other corrupt unions. But organized labor had lost the prestige and public support that it had enjoyed in previous years.

In the 1960s, unions focused their energy on civil servants and white-collar workers, who constituted a growing and largely unorganized segment of the workforce. Federal employees first gained the right to unionize in 1962. State and local governments followed the federal example, and by 1979 the American Federation of State, County and Municipal Employees was one of the largest unions in the AFL.

THE ERA OF CIVIL RIGHTS

As government clerks, teachers, and postal workers were acquiring union membership cards in the early 1960s, African Americans were waging a nonviolent campaign to secure their rights as citizens. Under the guidance of the Reverend Martin Luther King, Jr., and other leaders, African Americans conducted peaceful demonstrations that gained them equal access to municipal transportation, the right to do business wherever they chose, and protection of their right to vote. The opportunity for blacks to compete with whites in the workplace was another goal of the civil rights movement, and black leaders welcomed passage of the Civil Rights Act of 1964, which outlawed discrimination in hiring. But that legislation and subsequent federal initiatives have failed to eliminate racial discrepancies in income and opportunity.

The civil rights movement reenergized the effort of women to achieve equal status with men in American society. From the time that women first worked in the factories of New England, women's rights supporters had deplored inequities in wages between women and men and the limited number of occupations open to female workers. "Doing human work is what develops human character," noted Charlotte Perkins Gilman, great-niece of Henry Ward Beecher, in the early 20th century. Women reaped no benefit from "self-sacrifice or self *anything*," she declared. Instead, they needed "to find and hold our proper place in the Work in which and by which we all live." Despite the validity of these observations, Gilman and other early female reformers failed to connect with the majority of women, who viewed themselves primarily as wives and mothers and persisted in sacrificing their own ambitions.

Wives and mothers they may have been, but they were paid workers as well. Even the post–World War II years, an era dominated by the image of mothers in the kitchen raising the children of the baby boom, saw increases in the numbers of working women. There were 167,589 women employed in skilled crafts in 1950, compared to 70,800 in 1940. In 1950, 331,140 women worked in metals and machinery crafting, compared to 175,246 in 1940. Women made gains in professional fields as well. There were 4,187 female lawyers and judges in the United States in 1940 and 6,256 in 1950; the number of female physicians and surgeons rose from 7,608 to 11,714 during the same period. Men's wages rose at twice the rate of women's, however, in the five years following World War II.

By the 1960s, when Betty Friedan and other feminists questioned the passive, nonachieving image of femininity that American society imposed on women, large numbers of women were ready to listen. Women increasingly sought entrance into male-dominated fields and used the legal system to seek redress in cases of discrimination. By the 1990s, the full-time working mother had become a highly visible and accepted member of society, although women remained underrepresented at the highest levels of corporate America and continued to earn less than men doing comparable work.

As the 21st century begins, the issues that concern American workers are both old and new. Technology continues to transform the workplace at an ever-increasing pace. The computer technology that has developed rapidly since the late 1940s has made many clerical tasks obsolete. It has made possible the storage and rapid transit of large amounts of data, enabling people to work together over long distances. Emerging scientific fields such as genetic engineering offer employment opportunities to a highly educated segment of the population. At the same time, a new wave of immigration is bringing a fresh supply of workers into the country. Many of these people are forced by circumstances to take jobs that the native-born population does not want. Others are highly trained professionals, such as physicians, or entrepreneurs who contribute to the economy by opening businesses or pioneering new industries.

The greatest obstacle for many U.S. workers today is a changing economic structure. The middle class is shrinking, as white-collar and manufacturing jobs decline and low-paying positions in the service sector proliferate. At the same time, much of the nation's wealth now belongs to a small segment of the population. The average annual income for chief executive officers of large U.S. corporations was nearly $2.9 million in 1994, if bonuses and stock options are taken into account. Salaries for CEOs rose almost 500 percent between 1980 and 1996. During a similar period, 1978 to 1995, nonsupervisory employees saw their average hourly wages fall 11 percent, from $12.85 to $11.46. Between 1975 and 1995, workers whose formal education ended with high school suffered a drop of 20 percent or more in their real income; college graduates experienced a 2 percent decline in real income over the same period. It is not surprising that many middle-class families fear slipping into poverty.

THE EYEWITNESSES

The people whose observations fill the pages of this book include well-known historical figures. They are presidents, such as Thomas Jefferson, who praised the noble farmer, and Franklin Delano Roosevelt, a man of privilege who understood the concerns of working Americans. They are also labor leaders—individuals of varied backgrounds and viewpoints who had the common goal of helping workers achieve better lives. Among these are Samuel Gompers, first president of the American Federation of Labor, a cigar maker who immigrated to the United States in the 1860s; "Big Bill" Haywood of the Industrial Workers of the World, a charismatic speaker and radical thinker who was always ready for a confrontation; and A. Philip Randolph, the son of a Florida preacher and a man of great dignity who dedicated his life to improving conditions for his race. Also heard from are John Steinbeck, one of the most famous chroniclers of depression America; Jane Addams, the social worker who founded Hull House, a settlement in a poor section of Chicago; and Andrew Carnegie and John D. Rockefeller, two great names from the history of American business. The eyewitnesses are as diverse as Malcolm X, Charles Dickens, Woody Guthrie, Cesar Chavez, and Eleanor Roosevelt.

As important as these voices are those of ordinary workers, people who might have been forgotten by history had they not left some written record of their workaday life. The only way to learn how it felt to be an American worker in different periods of our history is to hear from these workers themselves. Only a prospector could describe the physical strain of wielding a heavy sledgehammer to dig for silver in Arizona, or the skill required to strike a narrow chisel at just the right angle. No one knew better than a New England textile-mill worker how difficult it was for women in the mills to save any money or avoid sickness in winter.

Many of the eyewitness accounts come from diaries and letters written to family members and newspapers. It is from narratives such as these that we learn of a pioneer's affection for the oxen that pulled him to Minnesota and his sadness at having to sell them, a cowhand's disheartenment when his equipment and supplies are lost while crossing a river, or a Norwegian immigrant's frustration as she tries to make cheese in a land heavily populated by flies.

Eyewitness accounts come as well from the many travel books that were the equivalent of National Geographic television specials for 18th- and 19th-century America and Europe. Intrepid travelers from England, Ireland, and France who toured the young United States described their adventures for compatriots whose only view of the New World came from books. Similarly, easterners who ventured west wrote about life in distant Illinois or in the mining country of South Dakota for armchair travelers back home.

Slave narratives were popular reading material in the early and mid-19th century too. Often published by abolitionist groups to further their aims and frequently sensational in nature, these books focus on the cruelties that enslaved African Americans endured and the dangers of escape. But they also offer important glimpses into a slave's daily life, from the routine of picking cotton to the discomfort of wearing a rough flax shirt to the impossibility of pleasing an unreasonable mistress and the punishment that was inevitable.

While some eyewitness accounts were written to sway public opinion, others resulted from scholarship or the desire to entertain. Social scientists made significant contributions to the literature of work in the late 19th and early 20th centuries when they applied their investigative skills to factory populations, immigrants laboring in home sweatshops, and young women moving into clerical jobs for the first time. In contrast, the many cowboy memoirs published in the 1920s, 1930s, and 1940s fed the dreams of a reading audience that romanticized life on the western range. Yet both genres add to our understanding of what it has meant to be a working American.

Although few contemporary Americans pause to consider, as Henry Ward Beecher did, whether God is hardworking by nature, the majority would agree with Beecher that work can satisfy the spirit. As the 21st century moves forward, American workers continue to put their experiences into words in magazine and newspaper articles, interviews, investigative reports, and speeches, as well as in memoirs, an increasingly popular literary form. They speak of disappointments, frustrations, and pride; the joy of using tools and of knowing how to do a job well; and an enduring optimism. Their observations, along with those from the past, tell a story that is part of the heritage of every person working in the United States today.

Notes to the Introduction

p. xiii "The greatest of all workers . . ." Henry Ward Beecher, "Laboring Together with God." *The Christian Union,* November 10, 1875, p. 388.

p. xiii "He is the *Husbandman* . . ." Ibid.

p. xiii "God sent you not . . ." Quoted in Perry Miller, *The New England Mind: The Seventeenth Century* (Cambridge, Mass.: Harvard University Press, 1954), p. 44.

p. xiii "Whoever goes to the United States . . ." Francis J. Grund, *The Americans in Their Moral, Social, and Political Relations,* vol. 2 (London: Longman, Rees, Orme, Brown, Green and Longman, 1837), p. 3.

p. xiv ". . . the saviors of society . . ." Quoted in Daniel T. Rodgers, *The Work Ethic in Industrial America, 1850–1920* (Chicago: University of Chicago Press, 1978), p. 153.

p. xiv "The joy and moral stimulation of work . . ." Quoted in Henry Steele Commager, *Documents of American History,* 9th ed., vol.2 (Englewood Cliffs, N.J.: Prentice-Hall, 1973), p. 240.

p. xiv "America's competitive spirit . . ." Quoted in Studs Terkel, *Working* (New York: Pantheon Books, 1974), frontispiece.

p. xiv ". . . self-appointed 'inspector . . .'" Henry David Thoreau, *Walden,* in *Walden and Other Writings by Henry David Thoreau* (New York: Bantam Books, 1981), p. 118.

p. xiv "If a man walk . . ." Henry David Thoreau, "Life without Principle," in *Reform Papers.* Princeton, N.J.: Princeton University Press, 1973, p. 157.

p. xv ". . . in products, in agriculture . . ." Quoted in David S. Reynolds, *Walt Whitman's America: A Cultural Biography.* New York: Alfred A. Knopf, 1995, p. 532.

p. xv "Cultivators of the earth . . ." Quoted in Hiram L. Drache, *Legacy of the Land: Agriculture's Story to the Present* (Danville, Ill.: Interstate, 1996), p. 70.

p. xviii "Half a world behind each back." Quoted in Ray Allen Billington and Martin Ridge, *Westward Expansion: A History of the American Frontier.* 5th ed. (New York: Macmillan, 1982), p. 585.

p. xix "El Dorado on the Pacific . . ." Quoted in Howard N. Sloane and Lucille L. Sloane, *A Pictorial History of American Mining* (New York: Crown, 1970), p. 103.

p. xxi ". . . endangers the health . . ." Quoted in Lawrence L. Knutson, "Washington Yesterday." Tampa Bay Online. URL: http://www.tampabay-online.net.news/news1016.htm. Downloaded on July 5, 1999.

p. xxi ". . . a keener realization . . ." Ibid.

p. xxi "Workers of the world . . ." Joe Hill, "Workers of the World, Awaken!" In *Songs of the Workers* (Chicago: Industrial Workers of the World, 1956), p. 14.

p. xxi "I offer a resolution . . ." Quoted in Elizabeth Flexner, *Century of Struggle* (Cambridge, Mass.: Belknap Press), 1975.

p. xxiv "The question now is . . ." William Green, "Labor's Opportunity and Responsibility." *American Federationist,* June 1933, p. 693.

p. xxv "It would be easier . . ." Quoted in Eva Lapin, *Mothers in Overalls* (New York: Workers Library, 1943), p. 5.

p. xxv ". . . regardless of training . . ." Quoted in Jervis Anderson, *A. Philip Randolph: A Biographical Portrait* (New York: Harcourt Brace Jovanovich, 1973), p. 241.

p. xxvi "Doing human work . . ." Quoted in Larry Ceplair, *Charlotte Perkins Gilman: A Nonfiction Reader* (New York: Columbia University Press, 1991), p. 2.

p. xxvi ". . . self-sacrifice or self *anything* . . ." Charlotte Perkins Gilman, *Human Work* (New York: McClure, Phillips, 1904), p. 368.

1

The Yeoman Farmer
1783–1900

The United States of America, at the time of its birth, was a nation of farmers. Nine-tenths of the population tilled the soil, raised livestock, or engaged in a related occupation. By 1800, the numbers pursuing other lines of work had increased due to the growth of towns and cities, but 80 percent of the people still lived off the land. Nearly every American had grown up on a farm, and just about everyone could express an opinion on planting and harvesting.

To the nation's first citizens, no way of life was better than farming. It was widely believed that those who sustained themselves from the earth were morally pure and safe from the corruption of urban living. This agrarian tradition began with Thomas Jefferson, who wrote often about the virtues of rural life. Jefferson praised the "yeoman farmer," the small-scale, subsistence husband-man who stood for freedom and independence and who seeded the wilderness with American democracy. The Jeffersonian ideal has endured, although farming has in fact meant a hardscrabble existence in every generation. Americans still equate farm life with such values as honesty, hard work, economy, and hospitality even if the independent family farm is fast becoming a thing of the past. The concept of agrarianism is deeply rooted in the American psyche.

AGE-OLD METHODS

Thomas Jefferson, himself a farmer, experimented with agricultural methods and new crops at Monticello, his estate in central Virginia. Jefferson was one of the first American farmers to enhance or protect his soil with dung, compost, commercial fertilizers, and crop rotation. He grew hundreds of varieties of trees, shrubs, and vegetables, including more than 20 kinds of peas.

Jefferson's creative approach set him apart from his fellow farmers. Most of the yeomen whom he celebrated saw little need to change their long-held practices. They harvested grain with a sickle, as farmers had done in biblical times, or with a scythe, which was a 17th-century innovation; they threshed it—or separated the grain from the chaff—using a flail or the feet of horses or oxen. They picked ears of ripe corn by hand or cut down the cornstalks and tied them in bundles, to remove the ears later.

1

VENERATE THE PLOUGH

Early Americans revered the plow, principal tool of the noble husband-man. *(Library of Congress)*

The early American farmer pushed a plow fashioned by the local black-smith. Its moldboard (the curved plate that turns over the earth) was carved from wood, and its cutting blade, or share, was of wrought iron. Plowing was slow, hard labor. A man and a boy, aided by two or three horses or four to six oxen, could plow between one and two acres in a day.

A New Jersey inventor named Charles Newbold patented a cast-iron plow in 1797, but farmers resisted it, despite the fact that it was stronger than the plows they were using. For one thing, it was cast in a single piece, which meant that if one part broke, the entire plow had to be replaced. For another, folk wisdom held that cast iron tainted the soil and caused weeds to grow. David Peacock, also of New Jersey, patented another cast-iron plow in 1807. Peacock's plow had a separate moldboard and a steel-edged share. Its practicali-ty made it more popular than Newbold's plow, and it came on the market as the superstition about cast iron was abating.

Jethro Wood of New York did Peacock one better in 1814, when he patented a cast-iron plow with interchangeable parts. Previously, every plow had been individually crafted, with parts made to fit that implement alone. If a part broke, a new one had to be forged to match. Wood's innovation, coupled with a steel-edged share that needed little sharpening, made his plow a favorite with farmers for decades. When the community of Brighton, Massachusetts, held a plowing match in 1827, nearly every plow used in the contest was Peacock's model or of a similar design.

Early American farmers sowed seed by hand or with a broadcast seeder, a device that scattered seed over the ground, and they planted corn with a hoe or stick. In 1799, Eliakim Spooner of Vermont patented the first American grain drill, a tool that sank the seed into the soil, protecting it from heavy rains and hungry birds. But farmers were not impressed. Spooner's drill planted the seed unevenly, and it easily became clogged with cornstalks that had been plowed under prior to the sowing of winter wheat. Besides, farmers had little incentive to plant more grain: It made no sense to raise more than they could harvest. Seed drills would not become practical to use until the 1840s and the arrival of mechanical reapers.

Technological advances improved the farmer's yield, but they offered no protection from the forces of nature. Flooding or drought could wipe out crops. Western settlers saw great fires sweep across dry prairies, and plagues of insects eat up their harvests. Clouds of grasshoppers rode in on the north wind and devoured every bit of plant matter in sight: grain harvests, vegetables in the ground, the bark of young trees, cotton curtains and clothing. One of the severest grasshopper infestations struck portions of Iowa and Minnesota in 1874. Farmers covered their wells to keep the supply of drinking water clean, but they rarely had time to save anything else. Such devastation caused prolonged hunger for isolated frontier families—even starvation in some cases.

Farmers were subject as well to economic forces that were beyond their control, but they did not always accept them without protest. A significant drop in the wholesale price index in 1786 triggered an uprising in Massachusetts known as Shays's Rebellion. Farmers who could not meet contractual obligations that had been agreed to in times of high prices panicked at the thought of losing their farms and going to debtors' prison. Led by Daniel Shays, a former captain in the American Revolutionary army, the farmers attacked local courts and disrupted a session of the state supreme court in Springfield. They demanded protective legislation and a radical reduction in taxes. On January 27, 1787, they attempted to seize the federal arsenal at Springfield but were repelled by a militia force. The insurrection dragged on until June, when the movement dissolved with little gain for the farmers.

Similarly, Pennsylvania farmers became violent in 1794, when protesting a tax on whiskey, and again in 1799, when German immigrants did battle with federal tax assessors. U.S. troops quashed both rebellions, putting an end to organized violence among farmers until the 1930s.

THE INFLUENCE OF GEOGRAPHY

Farmers grew whatever their region's climate, resources, and topography would support. New Englanders dealt with a short growing season and poor, rocky soil. Those limitations, combined with the wheat rust that thrived in the Northeast, made New England unsuitable for grain production on a large scale. New England farmers raised cattle, operated dairies, and grew vegetables and fruit for themselves and for the regional markets. Sheep often succumbed to the cold winters, but New Englanders kept them anyway, for their wool. Nantucket, Martha's Vineyard, and other communities developed commercial woolen enterprises.

The typical New England farm in the late 18th and early 19th centuries covered between 100 and 200 acres. At most, about six of every 100 acres were planted in crops, and another 10 served as pasture. Cattle and hogs roamed over the remaining acreage, which was held in reserve until the fields in use became depleted.

A longer growing season and better soil made it profitable to raise wheat in the Mid-Atlantic states. Farmers there planted more acres in crops than those in the Northeast did. A representative farm in late-18th-century Pennsylvania might have 75 acres in crops and use 65 as meadows and pasture. Mid-Atlantic farmers were harvesting 10 to 20 bushels per acre at that time for markets in eastern cities and for export to the West Indies. Tobacco was an important crop in Maryland and Virginia as well.

The Deep South, with its warm climate, extended growing season, and rich, fertile earth, was ideal for farming, and a plantation system that depended on slave labor took hold there. Eighteenth-century southern planters produced tobacco, indigo, and rice, largely for export. A small number of planters raised cotton before 1793. One variety—black-seed, or long-staple cotton—was profitable, because its seeds could be removed from the cotton bolls without too much difficulty. But black-seed cotton only grew well on the Sea Islands of Georgia and South Carolina and the first 50 miles of the coastal plain. Farmers in those areas produced 3 million pounds of cotton in 1793. Short-staple cotton, another variety, flourished inland, but its seeds were so tough to remove that few farmers would plant it. Even the fastest worker could clean only a pound of short-staple cotton a day by hand.

Cotton production spread west after 1794, the year Massachusetts-born Eli Whitney patented the cotton gin. Whitney's invention used cylinders covered with wire teeth to pull cotton fibers through a screen, leaving the seeds behind. With the cotton gin, short-staple cotton became a commercially viable crop. In 1811, seven years after Whitney's invention came into use, southern fields yielded 80 million pounds of cotton. Cotton cultivation had spread west to the Mississippi River by 1814. Indigo production had ceased by that time, while sugarcane, introduced to Louisiana by French planters in 1795, remained a regional crop.

FARMING THE FRONTIER

The new nation had one seemingly inexhaustible resource: land. With the Treaty of Paris (1783), the Western world recognized the United States as an independent nation with boundaries extending north to Canada, south to Florida, and west to the Mississippi River. The federal government gained possession of all unappropriated land. Under the Land Ordinance of 1785, Congress provided for the survey and sale of this land as a way to settle the region and raise cash to pay off the federal debt. The ordinance called for the creation of townships that were six miles square and divided into 36 numbered sections, each encompassing 640 acres. Five sections in every township were reserved for schools and churches and for government purposes, such as the payment of land bounties to Revolutionary War veterans.

Eastern farmers who had depleted their soil were eager to move west, although few could come up with the $640 required for the minimum purchase of one section at a dollar per acre. They bought instead from speculators, who acquired large tracts and divided them into smaller parcels. A farmer who did not need and could not afford 640 acres might be able to buy 40 acres from a speculator and would willingly pay up to four dollars per acre. A 40-acre farm could provide adequately for a frontier family in the early 19th century while yielding a small surplus for market. Speculators thus provided a needed service, both to farmers and to the government, by bringing agriculture into the interior. Between 1795 and 1810, the population west of the Appalachians rose from 150,000 to more than 1 million. Many farmers later became speculators themselves when they improved land and then sold it—house, barns, fences, and all. They used their profit to buy new farmsteads farther west.

Additional legislation fine-tuned federal land policy. The Northwest Ordinance (1787) established the Northwest Territory on the land that constitutes modern Ohio, Indiana, Illinois, Michigan, Wisconsin, and eastern Minnesota, and it provided a system of government for settlers in that region. The Land Act of 1796 doubled the price of land in the public domain to two dollars per acre. The Frontier Land Act (1800) reduced the size of the minimum sale to a half section, or 320 acres, and allowed buyers to make two equal payments over four years. The act provided limited credit at 6 percent interest, but the new terms did little to make federal acreage more affordable for the average farmer.

In 1800, Congress dealt with the problem of squatters for the first time. The government had been employing federal troops to remove farmers who had settled illegally on public land and to destroy their crops and buildings. The squatters tended to return, however, as soon as the troops moved on. Now those settlers were demanding the right of preemption, or the opportunity to buy the property on which they were living and farming before it went on the public auction block. Legislation passed in 1800 approved the preemption of land settled before that year.

Settlement pushed farther west after 1803, when the United States paid France 60 million francs (about $15 million) for the approximately 828,000 square miles that lie between the Mississippi River and the Rocky Mountains, in the transaction known as the Louisiana Purchase. Squatters pushed farther west, too. The Preemption Act of 1830 gave squatters on surveyed public land the first right to buy their claim if they had settled on and cultivated part of it before 1829. The Preemption Act of 1841 stated that settlers had only to inhabit and cultivate the land in order to claim 160 acres. Those eligible were heads of households, widows, male citizens 21 and older, and men over 21 who had filed for citizenship. Anyone who already owned 320 acres was ineligible.

To many Americans, westward expansion seemed to be the will of God. In 1845, a New York journalist named John L. Sullivan coined the term *manifest destiny* to convey the apparent fate of the American people to occupy and govern a nation that spanned North America from east to west.

American-born and European-immigrant settlers alike saw the Homestead Act of 1862 as a symbol of American democracy. The act gave 160 acres of land in the public domain to any person who was head of a household or over 21 and who was a U.S. citizen or had applied for citizenship. Settlers could purchase the land for $1.25 an acre after six months' residence and suitable improvements, or they could reside on it for five years and gain title at no charge.

The United States was acquiring more land as a result of purchases, treaties, and annexations. The government acquired Florida in 1819 and annexed Texas as a state in 1845. Ownership of the Oregon Territory was secured from Great Britain in 1846. Two years later, in fulfillment of the treaty ending the Mexican War, Mexico turned over most of the remainder of what is now U.S. territory in the West. With the Gadsden Purchase (1853), the southernmost portion of New Mexico Territory was acquired.

The United States claimed all of this land without the consent of the Native Americans who had occupied it for centuries. In the 1830s, the U.S. government under President Andrew Jackson adopted a policy of "Indian removal" to force the native people off of desired land. Federal forces uprooted many native ethnic groups and herded them into a region set aside as "Indian Territory" (present-day Oklahoma). The government adopted a new tactic in the 1850s and began resettling Indians on reservations under direct federal supervision. The nation's Indian policy, which ostensibly promised to preserve the independence and sovereignty of the native peoples, in reality meant poverty, loss of autonomy, and quite possibly death for many American Indians.

With the native peoples on the decline, settlers moved west in large numbers. More of the continent was occupied and improved between 1870 and 1900 than between 1607 and 1870. In the years 1870 to 1900, pioneers settled on 430 million acres and placed 225 million acres under cultivation. Prior to that time, 407 million acres of U.S. territory had been occupied and 189 million improved.

Most of the people who went west after 1870 came from the Mississippi River valley. More than a million pioneers left that region between 1880 and 1890. As many as 40,000 African Americans headed for Kansas around 1879 and acquired 20,000 acres of farmland. Immigrants from Germany and the Scandinavian countries, lured by the advertising campaigns of steamship and railroad companies, relocated to Kansas, Nebraska, the Dakotas, and Minnesota. Many Irish immigrants turned to farming when their work building western railroads was done. Canadians, lured by inflated U.S. currency that doubled the buying power of their own money, also moved into the West. Nearly 850,000 people lived in Kansas in 1880, and more than 450,000 had settled in Nebraska.

The number of farms in Texas nearly tripled in the 1870s, increasing from 61,125 to 174,184. Land-hungry Americans were pressuring the federal government to open up Indian Territory for settlement, particularly 2 million acres in the middle of the territory that had not been assigned to any tribe. The U.S. cavalry played a constant game of hide-and-seek with the "Boomers," individuals intent on homesteading illegally there; the soldiers moved out any Boomers they caught.

Following instructions from Congress, President Benjamin Harrison opened the portion of the "unassigned lands" known as the Oklahoma District to settlers on April 22, 1889, at noon. When that hour arrived, 100,000 people spilled over the border of the Oklahoma District on horseback, in carriages and wagons, or on foot to lay claim to a homestead. The years ahead saw settlement encroach onto assigned lands as well. The Sac, Fox, and Potawatomi peoples lost their land in 1891, the Cheyenne and Arapaho were forced off theirs in 1892, and the Cherokee met the same fate in 1889. By 1906, the entire area of the state of Oklahoma had been opened for non-Indian settlement.

Farmers found no timber for construction on the vast central plains of North America, and nothing to burn for fuel. The first homes for many pioneer families were hillside dugouts. People lived in them until they had piled up enough bricks of prairie turf to build sod houses. A sod house was likely to have a door fashioned from wooden packing crates, with a blanket serving as a room divider. It was cool in summer and kept people and livestock warm in winter. It also offered protection from prairie fires. But it was constantly dirty, and its floor turned to mud when it rained. If there was a stream within 50 miles, the farmer hauled wood from its banks for fuel. Otherwise, the family burned buffalo and cow excrement or hay to keep warm. Farmers on the plains went without adequate fuel until railroads reached their vicinities and brought in coal.

Jethro Wood's plow, which worked so well in the East, was a hindrance on the plains of Kansas. The thick soil clung to its cast-iron parts, and the plow could barely cut through the stubborn root systems of prairie grasses. A blacksmith named John Deere was the first successful manufacturer of plows with steel shares. Steel, its highly polished surface nearly free of imperfections, slid through the prairie soil and easily turned it over. Deere carried his tools from Vermont to Illinois in 1836 and immediately began making plows, never stopping to take a day off. His diligence served him well, and by 1846 Deere and his partner, Leonard Andrus, were turning out 1,000 plows a year. Their output had jumped to 10,000 plows by 1857. By the time of the Civil War, John Deere's "singing plow"—so named because it cut cleanly through the earth—had replaced the cast-iron plow on the prairie.

Canadian farmers also moved to the western part of their nation, although the largest migrations occurred later in Canada than in the United States, because Canada is a younger country. (Independent government was proclaimed in the Dominion of Canada on July 1, 1867.) Farming was difficult in eastern and central Canada due to the massive formation of granitic and metamorphic rock, known as the Canadian Shield or Laurentian Plateau, that dominates the geography of those regions. Centuries of erosion have removed much of the topsoil from the Canadian Shield, which extends from the Great Lakes northeast to Labrador and northwest to the Arctic Ocean. Despite the hardships, the average Canadian in 1871 was a farmer. In a nation of 3.7 million people, 3.3 million inhabited rural regions. The typical farmer in Ontario or Quebec owned between 50 and 100 acres and kept some cattle and horses.

By 1880, only a small number of people had moved to the western territories of Canada. The westerly flow would begin to increase over the next 20 years and reach its peak between 1900 and 1930. Today, the prairie provinces of Alberta, Manitoba, and Saskatchewan form one of the world's most important wheat-producing regions.

A HARD, MONOTONOUS LIFE

In every region, farm women worked as hard as their husbands did. They labored in the fields with their men, weeding the rows of tobacco or corn, cutting wheat, and picking cotton. Women also did work that was strictly their own. Day after day, from morning until night, they trotted from the kitchen to the barn, from the dairy to the henhouse. They prepared meals, fed livestock, scrubbed clothes, cared for children, and churned the butter and made the cheese that would be traded to the local storekeeper for supplies. Women made soap and candles, and they collected eggs and beeswax for barter or for sale. Making clothing was women's work, too. Although factory-made cloth became increasingly available in the 19th century, many farm women harvested flax, processed the fiber, and spun the thread needed to weave linen or linsey-woolsey, the linen-and-wool blend preferred for men's pants and shirts and women's dresses. Women scoured the natural grease, or "yolk," from sheep's wool, dried the wool, and carded it, or combed it to align the fibers, before winding it into yarn.

The farm child without a heavy workload was a rarity, too. Children learned at a young age how to handle a rake, milk a cow, and bind sheaves of wheat. The typical farm family was large, with six or more children, because many hands were needed. School was an activity for the winter months, when there was nothing to plant, weed, or harvest. Children acquired a good education from their parents in the practical arts of farming and housekeeping, but illiteracy remained high in rural America.

Frontier families ate what their livestock ate: the corn that was their principal crop. White settlers in North America first learned to raise corn from the Indians. Archaeological evidence shows that Native Americans were cultivating corn, or maize, in some parts of North America as early as A.D. 1000.

For much of the year, western settlers lived on "hog and hominy," an unvarying menu of salted or smoked pork with cornbread, cornmeal mush, or boiled hominy. They enjoyed fresh meat once a year—at hog-butchering time, in late autumn, when cool weather slowed spoilage.

Farmers in all regions supplied their own milk and eggs and fresh vegetables in season. The squash, beans, pumpkins, and tomatoes that they raised were all crops adopted from the Indians. Northerners grew white potatoes, while southerners preferred sweet potatoes, both of which had been cultivated by Native Americans as well. Mid-Atlantic and New England farmers ate more wheat and rye than corn. If a store was not too far away, a family might enjoy such treats as coffee, salted fish, and sugar.

Country stores also provided something else that was highly valued by people living lonely lives on farms: social contact. The store was the community's post office and a place for trading news and gossip and for bartering the bounty of kitchen and barnyard.

Sharing work was another way to ease the loneliness. Events such as barn raisings and cornhuskings turned big jobs into social events as families pitched in to help their neighbors. Similarly, women congregated for spinning bees, to converse as they worked their spinning wheels. Sunday church services brought people together as well, and the rare visitor was warmly welcomed.

People looked forward to agricultural fairs, whether they lived in New England, in the Carolinas, or as far west as Illinois. At the fair, farm folk exhibited their finest produce, animals, and handiwork while they learned about improved agricultural methods. A lively spirit of competition prevailed as farmers pitted themselves against their neighbors in skills such as plowing and cut-

The farmers of western New York mingle with city folk at an early agricultural fair. *(Library of Congress)*

ting tobacco. In 1811, the Berkshire Agricultural Society of Massachusetts held what is thought to be the first regional fair in the United States. Approximately 100 fairs were being held throughout the country by 1819.

In 1867, agriculturists in Washington, D.C., founded the National Grange of the Patrons of Husbandry, a fraternal society that aimed to advance the social, economic, and political interests of U.S. farmers. Granges were soon formed at the state, county, and local levels, offering membership to farmers and their families as a way to ease isolation. In 1875, at the height of the movement, more than 20,000 local granges boasted a total membership of 860,000.

TECHNOLOGY AND THE FARMER: 1860–1900

More than half of the nation's 31.4 million people still lived on farms when the Civil War began. Farm products accounted for three-fourths of all exports by value, making agriculture the dominant industry in the United States.

The technology of earlier decades could no longer support most farming during and after the Civil War, for two reasons. First, the war itself robbed farms of needed manpower. Second, westward expansion demanded technological progress. The amount of acreage plowed and planted doubled between 1870 and 1900. By the end of the 19th century, nearly all of the western land that would be used for farming—in the Midwest, on the Great Plains, in California and the Pacific Northwest—was already under cultivation. Only with mechanization could farmers manage operations on this scale.

The technological innovations from this period include threshing machines, cultivators, and riding, or sulky, plows. Cyrus McCormick of Virginia is the best known of several inventors who developed reaping machines, which allowed farmers to harvest a larger crop. The grain combine, an enormous machine that did both reaping and threshing, was popular in the Far West. It was so massive that teams of 40 or more draft animals were required to pull it. This need for horsepower created a demand for the steam tractor, which

Mule teams pull combines over the hilly wheat fields of the Palouse region of eastern Washington. *(Washington State Historical Society, Tacoma; Agric/Wheat/Anim 10)*

became available in the 1890s—only to be rendered obsolete by the gasoline-powered model in the early 20th century.

The new machines reduced drudgery for farm workers and heightened their productivity. Farmers saw an opportunity to broaden their economic opportunities, thinking less about self-sufficiency and more about the commercial market. Many now specialized in a single crop and formed ties with bankers, railroad executives, and other business people. "Bonanza farms" appeared in the Red River valley of the Dakotas in the 1880s, as eastern investors bought up tracts varying in size from 5,000 to 100,000 acres. Employing gangs of workers and the newest machinery, they lowered the cost of production and increased both yield and profit. Fifty years after Thomas Jefferson's death, his ideal of the independent yeoman farmer was already a myth.

CHRONICLE OF EVENTS

1783

September 3: The Treaty of Paris is signed, officially ending the American Revolution. Great Britain recognizes the independence of its former colonies as the United States of America.

Ninety percent of the U.S. population is engaged in agriculture.

1785

May 20: Congress passes the Land Ordinance of 1785, which provides for the survey and sale of land in the public domain.

1786–87

Massachusetts farmers protest economic conditions in the uprising known as Shays's Rebellion.

1787

The Northwest Ordinance establishes the Northwest Territory and its system of government.

1793

Southern farmers produce 3 million pounds of cotton.

1794

August: Pennsylvania farmers protest violently against a tax on whiskey.

Eli Whitney patents the cotton gin.

1795

French planters introduce sugarcane to portions of Louisiana.

The population west of the Appalachians is 150,000.

1796

The Land Act of 1796 doubles the price of land in the public domain to two dollars per acre.

1797

Charles Newbold patents a cast-iron plow.

1799

German-immigrant farmers in Pennsylvania attack federal tax assessors over a misunderstood tax.

1800

The Frontier Land Act reduces the size of the minimum land sale to 320 acres and establishes credit and payment plans for buyers.

Congress approves the preemption of land settled before 1800.

Eighty percent of Americans farm the land.

1803

The United States acquires the Louisiana Purchase, doubling the area of the country.

1807

David Peacock patents a cast-iron plow with a separate moldboard and steel-edged share.

1810

The population west of the Appalachians passes 1 million.

1811

The Berkshire Agricultural Society of Massachusetts holds the nation's first regional agricultural fair.

Southern fields yield 80 million pounds of cotton.

1814

Jethro Wood patents a plow with interchangeable parts.

1819

The United States acquires Florida from Spain.

1830

The Preemption Act of 1830 gives squatters the first right to buy claims that were settled and cultivated before 1829.

1834

June: Cyrus McCormick secures a patent on the mechanical reaper.

1836

John Deere arrives in Illinois and begins manufacturing plows with steel shares.

1841

The Preemption Act of 1841 allows settlers to claim 160 acres of land by inhabiting and cultivating it.

The William Sullivan family of Custer County, Nebraska, 1888 *(Nebraska Historical Society)*

1845
Texas is annexed as a state.

1846
John Deere and his partner, Leonard Andrus, manufacture 1,000 plows.

The United States acquires the Oregon Territory from Great Britain.

1848
Mexico cedes a vast western territory to the United States.

1853
With the Gadsden Purchase, the continental United States assumes its present borders.

1857
Deere and Andrus produce 10,000 plows.

1861
April 12: Confederate guns fire on Fort Sumter in the harbor of Charleston, South Carolina, as the Civil War begins.

In the North and in the South, half the population lives on farms.

1862
The Homestead Act of 1862 gives 160 acres to any head of household or anyone over 21 who is an American citizen or who has filed for citizenship.

1865
April 9: The Civil War ends.

1867
July 1: Independent government is proclaimed in Canada.

The National Grange is established in Washington, D.C.

1874
A grasshopper infestation devastates crops in Iowa and Minnesota.

1889
April 22: The Oklahoma District of the Indian Territory is thrown open to homesteaders.

1900
Virtually all of the western land that will be used for farming is already under cultivation.

EYEWITNESS TESTIMONY

Those who labor in the earth are the chosen people of God, if ever He had a chosen people, whose breasts He has made His peculiar deposit for substantial and genuine virtue. It is the focus in which he keeps alive that sacred fire, which otherwise might escape from the face of the earth. Corruption of morals in the mass of cultivators is a phenomenon of which no age nor nation has furnished an example.

Thomas Jefferson, 1782, Notes on the State of Virginia, *in* The Life and Selected Writings of Thomas Jefferson, *p. 280.*

It is my principle that the will of the majority should prevail. If they approve the proposed constitution in all its parts, I shall concur in it cheerfully, in hopes they will amend it, whenever they shall find it works wrong. This reliance cannot deceive us, as long as we remain virtuous; and I think we shall be so, as long as agriculture is our principle object, which will be the case, while there remains vacant lands in any part of America. When we get piled upon one another in large cities, as in Europe, we shall become corrupt as in Europe, and go to eating one another as they do there.

Thomas Jefferson, letter to James Madison, December 20, 1787, in The Life and Selected Writings of Thomas Jefferson, *pp. 440–41.*

We only till our gardens with the spade; and hoe our corn only after the plough & harrow. A man can cut an acre of wheat with a sickle in a day; cradle four times as much oats or barley; and mow an acre of green grass with a naked scythe.

"James Tilton's Notes on the Agriculture of Delaware in 1788," p. 184.

Wheat, our principal crop, is generally trod out with horses, immediately after harvest. We tread out barley also, but not generally so soon as wheat. Our smaller crops, such as rye, oats, buckwheat &c. are generally threshed out, when not used for cattle in the straw. The flail is the only instrument used for threshing. This is made of two smooth tough pieces of wood, the shortest called the swingel, the longest the handle of the flail, which are connected together by a swivel made of iron, wood or the hides of animals: the two

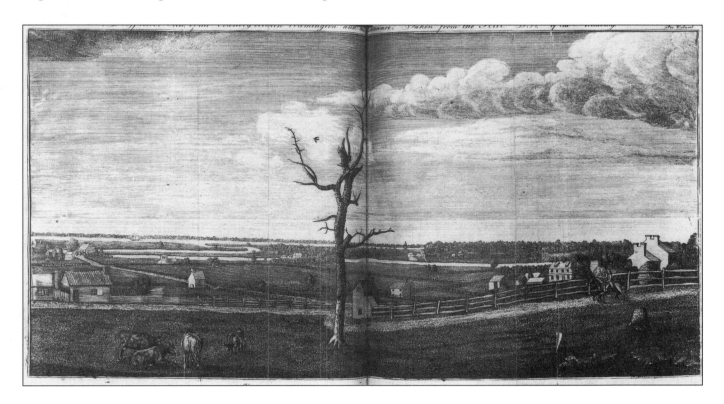

A book illustration of a farm near Wilmington, Delaware, 1787 *(Library of Congress)*

latter are esteemed the best, as it is not convenient, in striking with the flail, to have the weight preponderate at the swivel. The occasions of our farmers induce most of them to tread out their wheat & barley presently after harvest; the millers also encourage the sale at this time; and sometimes the fly renders this measure indispensable. Wealthy men, however, often keep their grain in stack or in the granary, for the best market.

"James Tilton's Notes on the Agriculture of Delaware in 1788," p. 183.

The Illinois territory produces the finest crops of corn and grain of any country in the world.

I will give you a rough estimate of produce per acre and value.

	$ Cents
Indian Corn—50 to 80 bushels	.25
	per bush.
Wheat—25 to 30	.75
Barley—say 32	.75
Oats—50	.37 ½
Tobacco—12 to 15	
hundred lbs.	4.50 per hundred lbs.
Cotton for domestic manufacture	40.00
Pork—fatted in the woods	3.50
[Ditto]—corn-fed	4.00
Beef	5.00
Hides	12.00 pr. hundd. lbs.
Maple Sugar	37.50 ———
Honey	.75 per gallon.
A day's work	.50 with board.
A labourer's board	.12 ½
A horse and man, one day	
without board.	1.00
[Ditto] with a plough	1.25
A good horse	60.00
A handsome saddle horse	100.00
A Cow	20.00
An Ox	12.00
A Sow with Pigs	6.00

Elias Pym Fordham, English traveler, Personal Narrative of Travels in Virginia, Maryland, Pennsylvania, Ohio, Indiana, Kentucky; and of a Residence in the Illinois Territory: 1817–1818, *pp. 118–19.*

In the Illinois Country, Society is yet unborn,—but it will be soon. The western parts towards St. Louis are thickest settled, and with very dissipated charac-

ters. French and Indian traders, Canadians, &c, gamblers, horsestealers, and bankrupts. Near us there are only a few farmers and hunters. Farmers, who till their own land, shear their own sheep, grow their own cotton and tobacco, the former of which their wives manufacture into clothing through every process. They tan the hides of their cattle and deer skins, and make them up into shoes and harness. They are hospitable according to their means; but, if they live near roads, expect payment for food and lodging, which is rather demanded by travellers than accepted as a favour.

Elias Pym Fordham, English traveler, Personal Narrative of Travels in Virginia, Maryland, Pennsylvania, Ohio, Indiana, Kentucky; and of a Residence in the Illinois Territory: 1817–1818, *p. 181.*

The farmers of Indiana generally arrive in the country very poor, but somehow they get a great deal of property very soon. They all work, and there are not half so many labourers for hire, as there are farmers. The former live with their employers, and are their equals, if they are men of good character; which is not always the case.

Elias Pym Fordham, English traveler, Personal Narrative of Travels in Virginia, Maryland, Pennsylvania, Ohio, Indiana, Kentucky; and of a Residence in the Illinois Territory: 1817–1818, *p. 168.*

A wealthy Kentucky farmer has 20 or 30 slaves, whom he treats rather like children than servants,—2 or 3000 acres of land, 500 acres of which are cleared and in cultivation. He lives in a bad house, keeps a plentiful table, which is covered three times a day with a great many dishes. Brandy, Whisky, and Rum are always standing at a side table. He is hospitable, but rather ostentatious, plain in his manners, and rather grave; a great politician, rather apt to censure than to praise, and a rather bigoted republican.

Elias Pym Fordham, English traveler, Personal Narrative of Travels in Virginia, Maryland, Pennsylvania, Ohio, Indiana, Kentucky; and of a Residence in the Illinois Territory: 1817–1818, *p. 180.*

[Corn] is gathered in October and November, when they only take off the ears; but as the ears are covered with a large husk, they carry them as they are to the corn-crib, and then all the neighbors collect together to help to husk it, and put it into the corn-crib. This is a high day with the Americans, and is called a Husking Frolic; plenty of whiskey is generally to be found at one of these frolics.

> *John Woods, English traveler, 1822,* Two Years' Residence in the Settlement on the English Prairie, in the Illinois Country, United States, *p. 300.*

Makee Ridge, as it was afterwards called, had among her earlier settlers a large per cent from Maine, and being shrewd, prudent, and enterprising Yankees they soon grubbed out, fenced in, broke up, and cultivated farms, built themselves frame houses which they painted white, made a turnpike road through the village one mile in length and were so far ahead of the surrounding country in style and improvements that they soon were dubbed by the settlers who came in from Hoosierdom, with the sobriquet of Nobscotters, and the ridge with the name of Penobscot, and this name like the lingering fragrance of the faded rose hangs round them still.

> *Ellery M. Hancock describing settlement in the 1830s and 1840s,* Past and Present of Allamakee County, Iowa: A Record of Settlement, Organization, Progress and Achievement, *p. 275.*

We broke twelve acres of land in 1837, and planted it in corn, wheat and potatoes. By 1838 we had three head of horses, five yoke of cattle and twenty-five hogs. Our neighbors had from a single ox to as much stock as we. The land was open to the Pacific coast. Hundreds of deer visited the salt licks, and the springs and streams of the locality. Deer would leave the finest wild pasture to ravage growing crops. So the first two or three years there was serious danger of crop destruction from the small acreage compared with the number of animals named, and from other enemies such as bears, raccoons, squirrels, blue jays and woodpeckers. From the planting to the gathering time, and even after that, the settler's crop was preyed upon day and night by a horde as hungry as himself.

> *George C. Duffield, pioneer, recalling conditions in 1837 to 1838,* "Youthtime in Frontier Iowa," *pp. 351–52.*

After we were settled in our new cabin and had our first crop planted, with my brothers, from almost the smallest to John who was grown, I was put at constructing a "defense." Not a defense against the Indians who were living all around us, it is true, but against our own stock, and that of the other settlers; from the

Indian ponies, the herds of deer, and the elk that remained. And the protection of crops, while a great problem, was not the only one. Acquiring, increasing and identifying domestic animals was an immense and important work. A few hogs, for instance, would be brought into this new country and turned out into the open with those of other settlers, where the woods, the streams and annoying enemies encouraged them to shun the settlements; to recover these animals was difficult and required a system of identification forever gone from Iowa. The difficulties increased with the population and with the numbers of live stock.

> *George C. Duffield, pioneer, recalling the years 1837 to 1842,* "Youthtime in Frontier Iowa," *p. 348.*

From 1837 to 1842, it then seemed to me, father's only thoughts were of brush, timber, fence; chop, chop, chop. Laborious, drudging, toilsome youthtime in Iowa!

> *George C. Duffield, pioneer, recalling the years 1837 to 1842,* "Youthtime in Frontier Iowa," *p. 356.*

This grain [corn] is the indigent farmer's main dependence for without it, I do not see how he could live and support his stock. It affords the means of subsistence to every living thing about his place, particularly during periods of snow, or hard frost; for not only is everything, down to the dog and cat, fond of the grain, in some shape or another, but its very stalks, leaves, and husks afford a valuable fodder for cattle and horses. Then, who but must admire the facility with which it is raised; the small amount of labour required; the trifling quantity of seed; and the most abundant return. It is not like other grain easily injured; but once ripe, there it stands, setting at defiance rain, frost, snow, and avery vicissitude of climate, often through great part of winter.

> *William Oliver, English traveler, 1843,* Eight Months in Illinois, *p. 85.*

When I commenced [seed] drilling, and for two or three years, I was ridiculed by my neighbors; some would advise me to take the implement home, break it up and cook my dinner on it.

I, however, disregarded their jeers and persevered. And now the best evidence that I can possibly bring forward in support of the drill over the broadcasting system, is the fact that all my neighbors have adopted the drill for sowing their wheat and most other small grain. . . . I think I am warranted in saying that three-fourths of all the wheat that will be grown in New Castle County the next year, will be sown with the drill.

John Jones, a New Castle County, Delaware, farmer, 1848. U.S. Patent Office, Report, *quoted in Clarence H. Danhof,* Change in Agriculture: The Northern United States, 1820–1870, *p. 207.*

. . . I have sold my farm and moved far back westward and settled entirely among the squatters and have become a squatter myself. . . . I have cleared about five hundred dollars since I have been here and my prospects at present are quite flattering. I am now building a saw mill. . . . I am also engaged pretty largely in speculating in land.

Edwin Terril of Iowa, 1848, in Allan G. Bogue, From Prairie to Corn Belt: Farming on the Illinois and Iowa Prairies in the Nineteenth Century, *p. 18.*

I see young men, my townsmen, whose misfortune it is to have inherited farms, houses, barns, cattle, and farming tools; for these are more easily acquired than got rid of. Better if they had been born in the open pasture and suckled by a wolf, that they might have seen with clearer eyes what field they were called to labor in. Who made them serfs of the soil? Why should they eat their sixty acres, when man is condemned to eat only his peck of dirt? Why should they begin digging their graves as soon as they are born? They have got to live a man's life, pushing all these things before them, and get on as well as they can. How many a poor immortal soul have I met well nigh crushed and smothered under its load, creeping down the road of life, pushing before it a barn seventy-five feet by forty, its Augean stables never cleansed, and one hundred acres of land, tillage, mowing, pasture, and wood-lot!

Henry David Thoreau, 1854, Walden, *in* Walden and Other Writings by Henry David Thoreau, *p. 108.*

The prairie is now a beautiful green interspersed with beautiful flowers in great abundance & variety. The wild rose made its appearance yesterday morning and is welcome as well as beautiful. We are introduced to some beautiful stranger almost every day in some wild and rare flower. Some of these flowers must be preserved—not that they can ever be made any more beautiful or arranged with any better taste than now.

But this great Prairie flower garden as arranged by the hand of the Creator is now exposed to the plow & the lowing herds are already making their paths and selecting their shades and watering places and it is plain that the native beauty must give way to the artificial we finished planting our corn at noon yesterday and went fishing—caught but one[.]

Mitchell Y. Jackson, June 4, 1854, "The Diary of Mitchell Y. Jackson, 1852–63," in Theodore C. Blegen, ed., Minnesota Farmers' Diaries, *p. 126.*

In 1848, I purchased a farm of 182 acres, together with a dwelling house and a good well, for $1,250; in 1853, a man from Pennsylvania offered me $4000 cash for it, and if I would sell it now, I would receive much more for it; but I do not think of it. I have now been fourteen years in America, and came soon after my arrival in this country to Illinois, when my resolution of settling here became irrevocably fixed, and I am now very glad to have executed it. I am of opinion that any man, especially however, the farmer, can acquire and obtain in Illinois, as contented and independent a living as he could anywhere else. I have travelled through many States, but was never pleased better than when settling on the exuberant soil of Illinois.

Peter Unzieker of Groveland, Illinois, November 20, 1855, in Fred Gerhard, Illinois as It Is, *p. 305.*

Let the industrious poor man know, that all he has to do, is, to become the holder of forty or eighty acres of land, build his cabin, and go to work with his team, and turn over the sod, and commence tilling the soil,—and that the laws of the land protect him against the depredations of stock—and, my word for it, we shall see, in a very short time, all our prairies brought into cultivation, and teeming with an industrious and happy population, adding millions to the wealth of the State.

James N. Brown of Island Grove, Illinois, November 28, 1855, in Fred Gerhard, Illinois as It Is, *pp. 448–49.*

My advice to farmers in the East is, to leave their rocks and hills, where they are just grubbing out a living, and come on to these splendid prairies, as they lie all ready for the plough, and where everything which the farmer plants yields such an abundant return.

John Williams of New Albany, Illinois, December 23, 1855, in Fred Gerhard, Illinois as It Is, *p. 448.*

I can raise on my farm, and have done it, 60 to 100 bushels of corn to the acre; 30 to 40 bushels of wheat per acre, and every kind of vegetables in the greatest abundance. I harvested off my farm this season 15,000 bushels of corn; two men raised for me with but little more than their own labor, about 7,000 bushels of corn and oats; this corn is now worth in the crib over 25 cents per bushel. My neighbors raised from 25 to 38 bushels of wheat per acre, and sold it on the spot at from $1 25 to $1 30 per bushel. Early in the season, Mr. Cuthbertson, a neighbor of mine, sold the crop of wheat off of 50 acres of land, as it stood, for $1500, cash.

John Williams of New Albany, Illinois, December 23, 1855, in Fred Gerhard, Illinois as It Is, *p. 304.*

Mr. Peter C. Rea, who resided twelve years in Raritan [New Jersey], near Clover Hill, and emigrated to Fulton County, Illinois, in the early part of this year, told me he had raised and sold more wheat since he had been there, than he had done in twelve years he had resided in Raritan. He simply raked and burned the cornstalks in the spring, and without ploughing the ground, sowed it with spring wheat, and harrowed it in; and in a few months he reaped a fine crop of spring wheat. He has, besides, on his farm, a good prospect for a crop of winter wheat. I ate at his house some bread made of the flour from his spring wheat, and it was as white and as good as any I ever ate in New Jersey. He also told me he should probably make as much money this year in Illinois, as he did in twelve years in New Jersey.

Letter to the Hunterdon, New Jersey, Gazette, *circa 1855, in Fred Gerhard,* Illinois as It Is, *p. 305.*

I had a nice yoke of steers which I broke and they were so well trained that when I hollered "Whoa" they would stop almost within an inch of where I wanted them to stop. Being quite an ox driver, I and another young fellow rigged up a breaking team with six yoke of oxen. We had a big grub breaker which cut twenty-four inches and we could turn over brush land which was covered with brush and small trees. We used to take contracts by the acre and did fairly well.

Later I disposed of my oxen and invested in horses and a threshing machine. It was a four-team horse power machine. We did quite a lot of threshing. Everybody in the neighborhood thought it was a big and fast thresher, as we could thresh over four hundred bushels of wheat per day, which was great in those days.

Knute Steenerson, Minnesota homesteader, describing events that occurred between 1855 and 1860, "Knute Steenerson's Recollections—The Story of a Pioneer," p. 135.

Fine sugar day as we would call it in Indiana But we have no sugarmaking here. No making of sugar troughs—spiles—furnaces camps &c My boys will know nothing of the pleasant excitement of the hurry & bustle of the "sugar making" . . . So indellably is the "sugar making" of my boyhood days fixed upon my memory that I can scarcely realize that more than thirty springs have blended with as many summers—ripened into as many mellow autumns, and been succeeded by as many frosty, blustry, ice bound, winters: since my first "sugar making" And now at this distance I can almost smell the smoke and see the blazing fire as it used to shine upon the huge forest trees through the thick black darkness of an Indiana sugar-making night[.] With equal distinctness can I see the pearly drops and hear the peculiar trickling of the sacharine fluid as it flows from the spiles upon a bright, frosty, sunshiny, morning—such as this[.]

Mitchell Y. Jackson, February 13, 1856, "The Diary of Mitchell Y. Jackson, 1852–63," in Theodore C. Blegen, ed., Minnesota Farmers' Diaries, *pp. 147–48.*

It is difficult to place a man in any situation where he feels more like an honest conqueror than he does when turning over the verdant turf of the prairies. His plough must have a keen edge, and cut from twenty-two to thirty-six inches wide. A thin sod of two or three inches thick is cut smooth and turned completely upside down. The bottom of the furrow and top of the reversed sod are as smooth as if sliced with a keen knife. Every green thing is turned out of sight, and nothing is visible but the fresh soil. When the prairie is broken, and the sod has time to decompose, the land is thoroughly subdued, and in a good condition for any crop—not a stump or a stone in the way, over a whole quarter section; free from weeds, rich, fresh, and mellow; it is the fault of the farmer if it is not kept so.

Fred Gerhard, 1857, Illinois as It Is, *p. 310.*

A pair of good horses, a wagon, one cow, a couple of pigs, several domestic fowls, two ploughs (one for breaking up the prairie, and the other for tillage), together with a few other tools and implements, are all that is necessary for a beginning. A log house can soon be erected. Thus provided for in the outset, and working with a joyful heart and honest perseverance, the confiding farmer will, surely, under the blessing of heaven, soon be enabled to replace his log hut with a cheerful dwelling-house, and to meet the payments of purchase-money as they become due, and still have a handsome surplus. In the course of a few years, therefore, one whose means in the start are rather stinted, may become an independent farmer, and enjoy his own farm and homestead free of debts.

Fred Gerhard, 1857, Illinois as It Is, *p. 446.*

I have not had a taste of fresh fish since we came out here. We talked some of going to the wapsay [Wapsipinicon River] a fishing but we did not get off and now I am so busey that I cannot go. I bought one salt codfish since we have ben out here and paid 8 3/4 cts pur lb for it and they ask 10 cts pur lb for them at the stores.

Ephraim Fairchild, settler in Wyoming Township, Iowa, July 1, 1857, in Mildred Throne, ed., "Iowa Farm Letters, 1856–1865," p. 45.

It seems like Fall it really scares me. [E]very body is prophesying that the corn will be cut down with frost. I hope not for I have promised my family that they shall have a nubbin of corn one of those days to make up for their poor fare now. My pig looks first rate considering the fare she has sour milk and pusly [purslane]. I want a Johnny cake myself too. anything but living where you dont have no meal.

Sarah Kenyon, pioneer in Oneida, Iowa, 1857, in Mildred Throne, ed., "Iowa Farm Letters, 1856–1865," p. 65.

The most intelligent and most enterprising of the farmer's daughters become school-teachers, or tenders of shops, or factory-girls. They contemn the calling of their father, and will, nine times in ten, marry a mechanic in preference to a farmer. They know that marrying a farmer is a very serious business. They remember their worn-out mothers. They thoroughly understand that the vow that binds them in marriage to a farmer seals them to a severe and homely service that will end only in death.

"Farming Life in New England," Atlantic Monthly, *August 1858, p. 341.*

Last Friday we were blessed with two little calves a *steer* and heifer. Saturday John and Ellis went to mill so I had to keep pretty busy so much I forgot to eat any dinner. Our cows did not do well but I doctered them all day. One I think is doing well but Brownie is bad yet . . . she is as poor as a snake. I cant bear to think Brownie will get so poor but I expect she will and perhaps die. We feed her with boiled wheat oats roots flaxseed &c to save her if possible.

Sarah Kenyon of Oneida, Iowa, March 18, 1860, in Mildred Throne, ed., "Iowa Farm Letters, 1856–1865," p. 77.

I have the headache about as much as ever this Winter but it seldom *floors* me nowadays. I have been making soap to day out of concentrated lye and it did not help my head any by a long chalk.

Sarah Kenyon of Oneida, Iowa, February 23, 1861, in Mildred Throne, ed., "Iowa Farm Letters, 1856–1865," p. 79.

I would say a word to those that think farming is a hard and a slow way to make money. It is so, but it is a safe way. I will tell you how I began. I was bound out at the age of 14 years until I was 21 for $100, and learn to read, write, and cipher as far as the single rule of three, and learn the trade of a farmer. At 23 I married. At that time I had added $200 more to the $100. I moved home with my father-in-law, on to a farm of 100 acres, somewhat out of repair. I then purchased a pasture, for which I paid $800, which brought me in debt $500. I carried on said farm eight years, at the halves, giving him one-half of the income of my pasture for the income of one-half of his stock. At the expiration of eight years he died. From that to the present time, I have had three-fourths of the income, paying my mother-in-law one-fourth. During that time, I have improved the farm, kept the buildings in repair, attended meeting regular, always paid the printer in advance and purchased a farm of 120 acres, for which I paid $1400. I am now out of debt, and have some money to let—besides having $400 stock in the Central Railroad, as a permanent fund.

A Vermont farmer in New England Farmer, *1861, in Clarence H. Danhof,* Change in Agriculture: The Northern United States, 1820–1870, *p. 113.*

As a farmer I have lived among farmers, without a change of residence thirty-six years; and during that period of time have had opportunity to observe the development of several generations of farmers. One generation I can trace from infancy to mature age; another which first came under my notice at manhood, are now old men; and others, according to several ages have had time more or less to exhibit what they are able to accomplish. The result of my observations, in one direction, has been that the individuals composing these several generations constantly range themselves under one of four classes. Class No. 1 is composed of those who are always poor; Class No. 2 includes those who barely make a living all their lives long; Class No. 3 numbers those who acquire a comfortable and a constantly increasing competence; and Class No. 4 is composed of those who acquire wealth. Numerically, each class diminishes as we advance in the classifications. I have said that the individuals of each generation range themselves under one or other of these heads—and I believe that I am correct in saying so, notwithstanding the constant averment of Classes Nos. 1 and 2 that their want of success is to be attributed to the circumstances surrounding them. The man himself, and what he is made of, determines to what class he will belong. It is true, surroundings are sometimes favorable and sometimes unfavorable, but the energetic and skillful will dodge the unfavorable obstacles and avail themselves with great dexterity of all that will assist their progress.

A New York farmer in Rural New Yorker, *1862, in Clarence H. Danhof,* Change in Agriculture: The Northern United States, 1820–1870, *p. 282.*

I remember I used to wonder when I heard that it would be impossible to keep the milk here as we did [in Norway]. Now I have learned that it is indeed impossible because of the heat here in the summertime. One can't make cheese out of the milk because of flies, bugs, and other insects. I don't know the names of all these insects, but this I do know: If one were to make cheese here in the summertime, the cheese itself would be alive with bugs. Toward late autumn it should be possible to keep the milk. The people who have more milk than they need simply feed it to the hogs.

It's difficult, too, to preserve the butter. One must pour brine over it or salt it; otherwise it gets full of maggots. Therefore it is best, if one is not too far from town, to sell the butter at once.

Gro Svendsen, Norwegian immigrant living in Estherville, Iowa, 1863, in Frontier Mother, *p. 39.*

My father believed in service. At seven years of age, I had regular duties. I brought firewood to the kitchen and broke nubbins for the calves and shelled corn for the chickens. I have a dim memory of helping him (and grandfather) split oak-blocks into rafting pins in the kitchen. This seems incredible to me now, and yet it must have been so.

Hamlin Garland, writer, recalling Wisconsin in 1867, A Son of the Middle Border, *p. 31.*

During the summer of my eighth year, I took part in haying and harvest, and I have a painful recollection of raking hay after the wagons, for I wore no shoes and the stubble was very sharp. I used to slip my feet along close to the ground, thus bending the stubble away from me before throwing my weight on it, otherwise walking was painful. If I were sent across the field on an errand I always sought out the path left by the broad wheels of the mowing machine and walked therein with a most delicious sense of safety.

Hamlin Garland, writer, recalling Wisconsin in 1868, A Son of the Middle Border, *p. 48.*

Johnson county [Kansas] embraces some of the best farming land in the state, and crops of all kinds are of the best quality and most abundant. Every kind of crop is said to be sure excepting wheat, which occasionally fails by being frozen out, or by the rust. A good crop averages 20 bushels per acre. Corn, such as is seldom seen in the East, is raised here, and averages about forty bushels to the acre. The yield of other grain is great; while the yield of all root crops is really marvelous. Sweet potatoes I have seen two, three, and even four feet long. Fruit of all kinds is raised with no difficulty. The growth of the trees is very rapid, the quality of the fruit is delicious and the size and yield wonderful. Grapes do well, the climate being well adapted to the growth of almost any variety.

Letter published in the Venango Spectator *(Franklin, Pennsylvania), November 26, 1869, in Paul H. Giddens, "Eastern Kansas in 1869–1870," pp. 373–74.*

The prairie grass this year was of unusual height and rankness, and since it has become dry, numerous fires have been the consequence. Almost every evening the sky may be seen lit up with one or more fires, being very destructive, burning the hay and fences of many farmers, and in some cases all the buildings. Where the precaution is taken of burning the grass for some distance around the farm while the air is still, there is no danger from it. The beauty of a prairie fire has often been described; poets have written of it; but my pen is unequal to the task, so I shall not attempt to.

Letter published in the Venango Spectator, *November 26, 1869, in Paul H. Giddens, "Eastern Kansas in 1869–1870," p. 375.*

It was well that this pioneer wife was rich in children, for she had little else. I do not suppose she ever knew what it was to have a comfortable well-aired bedroom, even in childbirth. She was practical and a good manager, and she needed to be, for her husband was as weirdly unworldly as a farmer could be. He was indeed a sad husbandman. Only the splendid abundance of the soil and the manual skills of his sons, united to the good management of his wife, kept his family fed and clothed.

Hamlin Garland, writer, describing a farm woman he knew in Wisconsin in the 1870s, A Son of the Middle Border, *pp. 20–21.*

In the fall I was to pay for my preemption claim and get a deed from the government on my holdings. It took nearly three hundred dollars and it was not an easy thing to raise so much money. I had been offered $160 for my nice young well-broken yoke of oxen, but I wanted $175. The time drew near when I had to raise the money. My neighbor was going to drive a herd to Minneapolis, so I sent my oxen with him. He came back and gave me only $80. He said that was all he got. I felt sorry for those young red and white spotted oxen, they were so gentle and well-broken. They had drawn me in a prairie schooner clear across the state. Well, I had raised some potatoes that I sold, and I managed to scratch up enough to pay the government, and I received papers on the land. It was a valuable piece of land, about one hundred acres of timber, which could be sold to prairie settlers for forty to fifty dollars per acre.

Knute Steenerson, Minnesota homesteader, recalling circumstances in 1870, "Knute Steenerson's Recollections— The Story of a Pioneer," pp. 143–44.

As we slowly crawled past the Indian territory and came into South-West-Kansas, we were astonished at the progress which even five or six months had made in the settlement of the country. When we went down in the Spring there was no farm within fifty miles of the trail; now we found that the farms had crept up to within twenty or thirty miles of the trail. What was still more interesting to us, some of these farms had taken in and reclaimed "desert land," as it was called land, that is, sparsely covered with the thick harsh buffalo grass. The farmers found that when this land was broken up it bore abundant crops, and, though it took eight and ten yoke of oxen to break it, for the matted roots of the buffalo grass went down eighteen inches or two feet, still, the cost was soon covered by the enormous crops which this virgin soil yielded.

Frank Harris describing Kansas, circa 1872, My Reminiscences as a Cowboy, *p. 182.*

We have no money nor nothing to sell to get any more clothes with as the grasshoppers destroyed all of our crops what few we had for we have not much land broke yet as we have no team of our own we have to hire one in order to get it worked what little we have to sow so you see it is rather hard on us to hire so much and get along. We managed to raise a few potatoes and some corn and a little buckwheat and that is all we have to depend on. We are very bad off for bedding not having but two quilts and two sheets in the house and have to make them serve for two beds. We have to use our clothing that we wear on the beds to keep us from suffering with the cold and then it [is] most impossible to keep warm for our house is so open.

Letter from Jennie Flint, pioneer, to Governor C. K. Davis of Minnesota, February 6, 1874, in Gilbert C. Fite, The Farmers' Frontier: 1865–1900, *p. 60.*

Reaping generally came about the 20th of July, the hottest and dryest part of the summer, and was the most pressing work of the year. It demanded early rising for the men, and it meant an all day broiling over the kitchen stove for the women. Stern, incessant toil went on inside and out from dawn till sunset, no matter how the thermometer sizzled. On many days the mercury mounted to ninety-five in the shade, but with wide fields all yellowing at the same moment, no one thought of laying off. A storm might sweep it flat, or if neglected too long, it might "crinkle."

Hamlin Garland, writer, describing life on the northern plains in 1874, A Son of the Middle Border, *p. 148.*

Our reaper in 1874 was a new model of the McCormick self-rake. . . . True the McCormick required four horses to drag it but it was effective. It was hard to believe that anything more cunning would ever come to claim the farmer's money. Weird tales of a machine on which two men rode and bound twelve acres of wheat in ten hours came to us, but we did not potently believe these reports—on the contrary we accepted the self-rake as quite the final word in harvesting machinery and cheerily bent to the binding of sheaves with their own straw in the good old time-honored way.

Hamlin Garland, writer, describing life on the northern plains in 1874, A Son of the Middle Border, *pp. 148–49.*

Although a constantly improving collection of farm machinery lightened the burdens of the husbandman, the drudgery of the housewife's dish-washing and cooking did not correspondingly lessen. I fear it increased, for with the widening of the fields came the doubling of the harvest hands, and my mother continued to do most of the housework herself—cooking, sewing, washing, churning, and nursing the sick from time to time.

Hamlin Garland, writer, describing life on the northern plains in 1874, A Son of the Middle Border, *p. 155.*

[The grasshoppers] came upon us in great numbers, in untold millions, in clouds upon clouds, until their fluttering wings looked like a sweeping snowstorm in the heavens, until their dark bodies covered everything green upon the earth. In a few hours many fields that had hung thick with long ears of golden maize were stripped of their value and left only a forest of bare yellow stalks that in their nakedness mocked the tiller of the soil.

Wichita City Eagle, *August 13, 1874, in Gilbert C. Fite,* The Farmers' Frontier: 1865–1900, *p. 61.*

Some Kansas farmers, like these depicted in *Harper's Weekly* in 1875, swept grasshoppers into a pile of hay and set the mass on fire. Others swept the insects into trenches and buried them. *(Library of Congress)*

In the year 1876 swarms of grasshoppers appeared in the country. They were flying in the air so thick sometimes that you could not see the sun on a clear day. The fences were lined with them. They devoured the grass and crops of all descriptions. The machine companies had sold many implements to the settlers, but many of the settlers left their farms never to come back, for starvation stared them in the face. So I was ordered by the agents of the machine companies to gather up the seeders, mowers, reapers, etc., and haul them into Montevideo, the county seat. I had enough machinery to cover an acre or two for sale. I had a sale now and then, but there were no bidders except the agents themselves, who bid them in for the company. In a year or two the country straightened out again, crops were raised, and the people prospered again.

Knute Steenerson, Minnesota homesteader, remembering 1876, "Knute Steenerson's Recollections— The Story of a Pioneer," p. 148.

Just after New Year's, 1877, I concluded to make an addition to our little house. I had a good load of fat hogs ready for the market. We had to have lumber and other material for the addition, so we loaded up the hogs. I got aboard and set sail. The river was running full of ice. I had to go by the way of Scandia, as they had a toll bridge across the river there. It increased the distance going and coming about fifteen miles. The weather was pretty severe, but I made the trip in good shape and got home with a big load of stuff. With it and some native lumber we did a fair piece of work.

E. D. Haney recalling events in 1877, "The Experiences of a Homesteader in Kansas," p. 319.

. . . [M]y little Sigri has gone home to her Heavenly Father. Next month, if God wills it, I shall have another child. This will be my ninth confinement. It is difficult these last days because I am always quite weak, but God, who has always been my help and comforter during my confinements, will surely help me this time, too.

Gro Svendsen, Norwegian immigrant living in Estherville, Iowa, February 11, 1877, in Frontier Mother, *p. 134.*

Wheat is king in the county of Dickinson. It covers a larger area than any other cereal. And it excites more anxious thought from the time the seed is put into the ground till it is hauled to the elevator, than any

other produce of the farm. This anxiety is not confined to the farmer alone. The mechanic, the merchant, the banker and the railroad corporations, all feel it and daily give expression to the feeling in the shape of the anxious enquiry: "Is the wheat crop a failure this year?"

A Kansas farmer in 1880, quoted in James Malin, Winter Wheat in the Golden Belt of Kansas, *p. 99.*

. . . I visited the farm of Richard Barden, Esq., about six miles to the eastward of Windom [Minnesota]. Mr. Barden, whom I had the good fortune to meet on the place, is a well-known and prominent grain dealer, residing in St. Paul. He has 2100 acres of land, 1200 of which is in wheat, with a small amount in oats and corn. The work of the farm is done by monthly labor, under the direction of a superintendent. On the place is a small, neat one-story house, the residence of the superintendent, with two large barns and a long shed. The farm is stocked with a small herd of about twenty-five very fine short-horned cows and two bulls, and a stud of about twenty high-bred mares and horses. There is but a small amount of fencing on the place; the law in Minnesota, as in most of Kansas, allowing the fence question to be decided by the various districts.

"The Bonanza Farms of the West," Atlantic Monthly, *January 1880, pp. 33–34.*

On this farm, and at other points on this road, grasshoppers were doing some damage. Earlier in the season the superintendent had made a raid upon them, and he showed me some black heaps, which he said contained fifty-six bushels of that insect plague, and which he had caught in a tar machine from the side of one quarter section.

"The Bonanza Farms of the West," Atlantic Monthly, *January 1880, p. 36.*

California is noted for its great farms of tens of thousands of acres, and the great extent of its area cultivated by tenantry. Throughout the whole region of that portion of our Western country which was not cursed by the existence of slavery there has, within the present decade, been an alarming increase in the number of great land-holders, who, with all the power of capital and cheap labor, have entered into deadly competition with the small farmer.

"The Bonanza Farms of the West," Atlantic Monthly, *January 1880, p. 42.*

In July I worked a while for my Uncle Doubleday. He set out forty thousand apple grafts, and two hundred apple trees. He had eight mules and a cow all strung out on picket ropes. We didn't have one good rain all summer, so we irrigated the whole outfit from a forty-foot well: the stock at the trough with a tow line, the trees and grafts with barrels and buckets.

Oliver Nelson remembering farming near Caldwell, Kansas,
in July 1880, The Cowman's Southwest, *p. 53.*

Our chief difficulty and trouble are the stones; they generally lie just beneath the surface, differing very much in size. Some are huge and have to be regularly trenched round and horses harnessed to a chain put round them to raise them out of the ground; when they are put on to the stone-boat and conveyed to the boundary fence. It generally falls to E——'s and my special lot to drive the stone-boat or the waggons, whilst the men with crowbars and spades go before the ploughs clearing them all away, for fear they may blunt the shares and throw them out of the furrow.

Mrs. Cecil Hall, 1884, A Lady's Life on a Farm
in Manitoba, *p. 64.*

We have had a real visitor lately—I mean one who has brought a change [of clothes], and a tooth-brush; and for the auspicious event we rigged him up a stretcher bed, the most comfortable of things, canvas stretched on to a wooden frame, with a mattress on the top. You could not wish for anything softer.

Mrs. Cecil Hall, A Lady's Life
on a Farm in Manitoba, *p. 66.*

I gathered my corn with my yoke of cattle and I got along pretty well. I planted some pumpkins with the corn and they made a little trouble on account of them. They would make a break for a pumpkin several rods away. When I came in at noon I gave them all the pumpkins they would eat, and then some. I kept it up and they bothered me but little afterward. I gathered corn in this field with cattle in 1872. The next year, 1873, I gathered in the same field with a pair of horses. My wife came out and helped me a short time. A few days ago I gathered corn in the same field in a trailer drawn by a Dodge car. This was October 6, 1926. Who can beat it?

E. D. Haney, 1926, "The Experiences
of a Homesteader in Kansas," p. 313.

2

The Role of
Enslaved Workers
1619–1865

The English founded their first permanent North American settlement at Jamestown, Virginia, in 1607. Twelve years later, the first Africans came. The captain of a Dutch ship that dropped anchor at Jamestown in late August 1619 gave a cargo of 20 Africans to the English colonists in exchange for food. The Dutch had been selling African slaves to planters in the Caribbean and in Central and South America. With that 1619 trade, they expanded their market.

Those 20 Africans and the ones who followed them to the English colonies over the next two decades were not enslaved. Like one-half to three-quarters of the whites who came to the New World before 1680, they entered indentured servitude, completing four- to seven-year terms of forced labor before being granted their freedom. The European indentured servants included prisoners who had been banished to the colonies and sold for their transportation costs as well as people who came voluntarily. Many indentured servants learned to farm during their period of servitude and later acquired their own land. There is evidence that some indentured Africans went on to join Virginia's farming community in this way.

Africans began to lose their access to liberty in 1641, when Massachusetts became the first colony to recognize slavery as a legal institution. The other colonies followed the lead of Massachusetts, and by 1750 all had established a statutory basis for slavery. Colonial laws also forbade marriage between blacks and whites, and they clarified the place of African-American children in society: black children would be enslaved or free according to the status of their mothers. By the time of the American Revolution, enslaved Africans constituted a significant portion of the North American workforce. Most were required to work in agriculture, while some carried out domestic duties or practiced skilled trades.

In 1800, the population of the United States included 893,000 enslaved persons. Most were held in the South, where planters needed a large labor supply to exploit the fertile earth, especially for cotton culture. Only about one in 24 slaves lived in the northern states, where they worked primarily as domestic servants. The Northwest Ordinance of 1787 had prohibited slavery and involuntary servitude in the Northwest Territory. By 1804, Vermont, Pennsylvania, Massachusetts, Rhode Island, Connecticut, New York, and New Jersey had passed legislation to emancipate their slaves, largely by gradual measures. Slavery, which had been a predominantly southern institution from the start, became strictly a southern one. By 1810, more than 1 million enslaved workers were raising cotton, rice, sugar, tobacco, and other crops in the South.

Certain unscrupulous whites, however, particularly in the Illinois country, coerced free blacks into entering indentured servitude for periods as long as 40 years, essentially the rest of their lives. These servants worked under conditions no different from those that existed south of the Ohio River, where slavery was permitted.

The selling price of slaves in the South increased with demand, especially after January 1, 1808, the date on which a federal ban on the importation of slaves took effect. A male field hand between the ages of 18 and 25 sold for an average price of $200 in Charleston, South Carolina, in 1790. The price had risen to $300 five years later, following the invention of the cotton gin, and to $550 in 1812. The average price for a comparable worker was between $600 and $700 in 1812 New Orleans, and it was $1,800 in the same city in 1860. Women tended to sell for about 25 percent less than men of the same age, but the women in greatest demand were those of childbearing age and proven fertility, because they were the ones most likely to increase a planter's stock. The initial cash outlay for a slave was high; yet when a farmer spread the cost over a slave's lifetime, he saw the value of his purchase.

The slave population, which totaled 4 million in 1860, represented a large capital investment for southern planters. Although most southerners still did not own slaves by 1860 and most of those who did held fewer than five, the majority of southerners supported the institution of slavery. Enslaved labor, a cornerstone of the South's economy, was a source of political power as well. According to the Constitution, each slave was counted as three-fifths of a person for purposes of representation in Congress. The enslaved people therefore increased their states' influence in the House of Representatives, but it was the whites, and not the slaves, who benefited.

A SLAVE'S WORKING LIFE

In general, enslaved African Americans received better treatment on small farms than on plantations. They worked beside the small farmer in the fields and ate what he and his family ate. A large plantation operated much like a prison camp, with men, women, and children sentenced to life at hard labor because of the quantity of melanin in their skin.

An enslaved field hand's workday began before sunrise and ended well after sundown. A horn or bell awakened plantation slaves at 4 A.M., and they were expected to be up and dressed and on their way to the fields by 4:30. In gangs of 20 or more, the people worked steadily until noon, when they were allowed 10 to 15 minutes to eat a cold meal that they had packed that morning. The tilling, planting, hoeing, weeding, or harvesting then continued until it grew too dark to see. The routine was the same, Monday through Friday, and for half a day on Saturday. The workers looked forward to Christmas, the one holiday that they were permitted to celebrate.

Opening the floodgates allowed for the submersion of rice fields. *(Library of Congress)*

Southern growers had quickly recognized that an enslaved workforce was ideal for raising cotton on a large scale. Not only did they need many laborers to plant, cultivate, and harvest the crop, but the tasks involved were easy to learn and to supervise, and they were performed throughout most of the year. In early spring, the field hands listed the soil; that is, they loosened the earth to a depth of two to three inches with a crude plow or a hoe. An adult field hand was expected to list half an acre per day. The hands then planted seeds in rows three to five feet apart. They weeded and thinned the young cotton plants with hoes during the summer growing season. When the crop was ready to harvest, every available person, including artisans and overseers, picked cotton from dawn to dusk. Sixteen-hour days were the norm during cotton cultivation and harvest.

Because cotton bolls ripen gradually, the workers picked over the fields three or four times. They transported the picked cotton to the ginning area, where they ginned it and bundled it into bales weighing approximately 500 pounds. A single bale represented the amount of cotton fiber that a planter could expect to produce from a single acre of average fertility.

Most cotton plantations also produced corn and hogs to feed their populations. Those that failed to raise enough to meet their needs had to import food from regions to the north.

The enslaved agricultural workers who raised rice on the barrier islands and riverbanks of South Carolina and Georgia saw less of their white masters than other enslaved field hands did. Rice thrived in wet conditions that were ideal for breeding mosquitoes, so the whites, fearing malaria, stayed away from the fields as much as possible.

A typical rice plantation in 1860 employed 300 enslaved African Americans, half of them men and half women. Farming began each year in December or early January, when the workers turned over and hoed the soil to ready it for the new crop. They cleaned out the canals and ditches used later in the season to flood the fields. From the middle of March through the end of April, the hands planted seed rice in shallow trenches at 12-inch intervals. Then they opened the "trunk docks," or flood gates, that let water flow through the canals and onto the fields, beginning a sequence of flooding and draining that continued throughout the growing season and mimicked the rhythm of the tides in nearby waterways.

All of the water was drained away at harvest time, when the rice plants were cut with sickles and dried. Threshing was the slaves' next task, and they accomplished it with wooden flailing sticks. They then removed the hulls from the grains of rice by grinding them with a wooden pestle inside a hollowed-out log. Finally, they passed the rice through a grating for winnowing: wind blew away the chaff as the grains of rice fell to the floor. After 1830, some growers installed steam-powered mills on their plantations to accomplish the threshing, hulling, and winnowing, but in most places these tasks were still completed by hand. The slaves finished the harvest in November, with just enough time to burn the stubble from the fields before starting the yearly cycle anew.

Because they had little direct supervision, slaves who grew rice could stop work early if they finished the day's assigned chores. Some were able to raise and sell vegetables and to acquire some property. Growing and processing sugarcane, in contrast, was a time-consuming venture that occupied most of a slave's working hours.

Raising sugarcane, one of the most taxing jobs performed by slaves
(Library of Congress)

The slaves on sugar plantations, most of whom were men, worked hardest during the harvest, because the sugar crop had to be cut and processed quickly. They labored 18 hours a day at harvest, seven days a week. First, they cut off the green growing tops of the sugarcane, which would be used as seed cane the following spring. Next, they cut down the mature cane and hauled it to the mill for processing. The typical sugar plantation had its own mill with a press to squeeze the juice from the cane, boilers to cook the juice into a syrup, and cooling vats in which the syrup crystallized. The mill operated nonstop during the harvest. In the final ritual of the growing year, the slaves and masters burned the fields. It was thought that the resulting ashes enriched the soil, although the benefit of this practice had never been demonstrated.

Digging the canals that were needed to drain excess water from the cane fields was such hard work that some Louisiana planters preferred to hire Irish immigrants to do it rather than risk the health of slaves, in whom they had a financial stake.

THE HATED SLAVE DRIVER

There was often no one the field hands hated more than the slave driver, who watched them as they toiled and prodded them to work faster, although he was an enslaved worker like themselves. There was no one they feared more, because he could single them out for punishment. Punishments usually were administered by the master himself or by his white overseer, who patrolled the plantation on horseback, armed with a knife or pistol, and often accompanied by a vicious dog. An enslaved person might receive 100 or more lashes for such an offense as breaking a household item, learning to read, being late for work, working too slowly, or "impudence," a catch-all category that included using an unpleasant tone of voice, wearing the wrong facial expression, and walking with a gait that annoyed those in charge. Even the most cautious slave never knew when he or she might inadvertently commit a punishable offense. Punishments also included branding, castration, and other forms of mutilation, as well as dog attacks.

The plantation slaves performed chores, such as chopping firewood or tending livestock, after returning from the fields at night. Only when all of the work was out of the way could the people prepare themselves an evening meal, put together a lunch for the next day, and fall into bed.

EVERYONE WORKED

On large plantations and farms, including Thomas Jefferson's Monticello, some enslaved persons worked as blacksmiths, carpenters, or coopers, or practiced other crafts. Some plantations had their own cobblers to make and repair the slaves' shoes. Artisans saw more of the outside world than most of the enslaved population did, because their owners frequently hired them out to work for others. Some of these skilled workers earned money for their services, and if they saved enough, they bought their freedom. The high level of skill attained by enslaved craftspeople is evident in the churches, mansions, and plantation houses that they built throughout the South, many of which are still standing.

Enslaved laundry workers, James Hopkinson plantation, Edisto Island, South Carolina *(New Hampshire Historical Society; Moore 510)*

Whatever his or her skill level or age, a slave was required to work as long and as hard as possible. Children carried water, hauled trash, swept, and stoked fires. Boys as young as eight went to the fields, if only to pull weeds, clear stones from the earth, or pick worms from tobacco leaves. Girls began their life in bondage with household tasks, such as kitchen work, childcare, and laundry, and they joined the field workers as teenagers. Among the women, only the domestic workers—the cooks, laundresses, and spinners—avoided field work altogether.

There was no such thing as retirement for enslaved African Americans. Work continued into old age. Aged men had light duties, such as tending livestock and kitchen gardens or sharpening and oiling tools. Older women helped with the cooking, did some sewing, and watched young children for the mothers in the field.

THE BARE NECESSITIES

Most enslaved plantation workers lived in small, windowless one-room cabins that frequently housed two families. Many cabins had dirt floors and cracks in the walls that made them drafty. A number of slave owners provided cabins with two or three rooms, windows, and fireplaces, and some plantation slaves lived in large military-style barracks. But in every case, comfort and privacy were minimal.

Enslaved people made their own furniture and utensils, and they survived on a diet that was poor and unvaried. They received regular rations of cornmeal and bacon, along with occasional rice, sweet potatoes, and molasses. They supplemented this humdrum fare by hunting, growing vegetables, and stealing the master's corn and chickens.

Clothing was rationed, too. Twice a year, the men were issued two shirts and two pairs of pants. Women were likely to receive enough cloth for two dresses, as well as a needle, thread, and buttons. Each worker was given a pair of heavy shoes in the fall, when men received a jacket. The slaves were provided with blankets every third year. Owners saw no benefit in clothing children who were too young to work. Small children were nearly naked, wearing at most a simple smock, and they always went barefoot.

House servants received hand-me-down clothing from the white family and leftovers from their kitchen. But unlike the field workers, they kept irregular hours. They could be called on to serve day or night, whenever the owners desired their assistance.

The ailments that occurred most commonly in the enslaved population were the ones that most frequently plagued all 19th-century agricultural workers. They included tetanus, contracted when wounds came in contact with contaminated soil; pneumonia; and hernia. The master's wife often doled out remedies and called in a doctor when necessary, but the workers also sought treatment from their own priest-healers, who practiced herbal medicine in the African tradition.

Remnants of African culture wove through the slaves' music, prayer, and storytelling. When permitted, the musicians among the workers played on handcrafted drums and banjos that resembled the instruments of their homelands. The people sang spirituals that had English lyrics but melodies that featured the flat-sounding notes of African songs. Similarly, many enslaved people prayed to the Christian God in the way that earlier generations had communed with the Supreme Being in Africa. Prayer—both in Africa and in the United States—involved one-on-one interaction with the creator that could inspire song, dance, and shouts of ecstasy.

Storytelling was a favorite pastime of the slaves during their infrequent periods of leisure. The peoples of Africa who lacked a written language had raised telling tales to an art form. They passed along legends and fables that explained their place in the natural world and that described the adventures of animals with human traits. Researchers who have studied African-American folktales have matched a number of their plots with those of older African tales. New World storytellers creatively adapted old stories to their new surroundings and to the foxes, crows, bears, and rabbits that they saw.

STEALING AWAY

Building and maintaining a unique culture helped enslaved African Americans withstand the cruelties that were part of their everyday lives. But it would be a mistake to assume that the slaves endured that life without protest. Some rebelled, and many more ran away. Others tried to even the score through acts of sabotage—setting fire to a field or barn, breaking equipment, or stealing from the master.

Southern whites who lived in fear of the slaves' discontent showed no mercy in their retaliation. In April 1795, when white citizens exposed a planned revolt at Pointe Coupee, Louisiana, north of New Orleans, they immediately executed 25 slaves. They wrapped 23 others in chains, loaded them onto a boat, and headed down the Mississippi River. At each landing between Pointe Coupee and New Orleans, the vigilantes hanged one prisoner and left his head on a pole as a warning to any other rebellion-minded slaves.

An enslaved blacksmith and preacher named Gabriel Prosser organized another revolt in 1801. Prosser had visions of forming and leading a new state government. On August 30, he led approximately 1,100 slaves, armed with guns and handmade weapons, toward Richmond, Virginia. Two household slaves alerted their owner about Prosser's intentions, and his army was intercepted before it could attack. Ninety-one people were captured, tried, and found guilty of playing an active role in the revolt. Prosser was hanged with his family and 24 followers on October 30. Ten conspirators were deported, and 14 others were executed between 1801 and 1803.

But the revolt that most unsettled whites was the one led by Nat Turner in Southampton County, Virginia, in 1831. Turner, like Gabriel Prosser, was an enslaved preacher who believed that God had chosen him to avenge his people. On the night of August 21, Turner and a small band of men—his "disciples"—murdered their master and his wife and children. They then headed for the town of Jerusalem, the county seat, picking up followers, stealing guns and horses, and killing about 60 whites encountered along the way.

Federal troops and state militia forces put down the insurrection, killing an unknown number of African Americans, and lynch mobs murdered many others. As many as 53 blacks were arrested for their role in the revolt and brought to trial. Twenty were hanged, 12 were transported out of Virginia, and 21 were acquitted. Nat Turner, however, escaped capture until October 30. He was quickly brought to trial in Jerusalem and hanged on November 11.

Nat Turner's rebellion led to greater restrictions on the activities of free and enslaved African Americans in the South and harsher punishments for slaves. It fueled the drive for a tough fugitive slave law, which President Millard Fillmore signed in 1850. That law ensured that captured runaways would be returned promptly to their owners, and it denied them the right to a trial by jury or to testify on their own behalf. Citizens and federal officers, in the South and in the North, were required to aid in apprehending escaped slaves. Anyone caught helping a fugitive would be fined and possibly imprisoned.

The law did little, though, to block the flow of runaway slaves to the North. Between 1825 and 1860, an estimated 100,000 people followed the North Star, stealthily fleeing slavery, although escaping meant severing ties with relatives, friends, and home. Fugitives had to make their way through unfamiliar woods and swampland. Friendless and penniless, they viewed every white as an enemy. The odds of success were slim, and recapture meant certain punishment. Escapees might be flogged, handcuffed, or sold to a plantation deeper in the South. Nevertheless, many people negotiated the network of trails and safe houses known as the Underground Railroad. Ohio became the center of Underground Railroad operations as antislavery activists conducted escapees through the state to freedom and security in Canada, beyond the jurisdiction of the fugitive slave law.

SLAVERY FALLS VICTIM TO WAR

The institution of slavery was the most significant casualty of the Civil War. On April 16, 1862, one year and one day after Confederate forces fired their first shots at Fort Sumter, Congress freed the 3,000 slaves living in the District of Columbia and compensated slave owners in the capital city $300 for every slave lost. Congress also allocated $100,000 to pay for the voluntary relocation of former slaves to Liberia or Haiti. People escaping slavery in neighboring states swarmed into Washington, swelling the city's population.

Men who had fled slavery volunteered to fight for the Union. In all, 186,000 African Americans became part of the Union's fighting force. In addition, African-American civilians built roads and bridges and performed other duties to further the war effort.

The Emancipation Proclamation freed all persons held in slavery in any region in rebellion against the United States, effective January 1, 1863. The proclamation was the tool with which President Abraham Lincoln expanded the purpose of the war. His armies had been fighting primarily to reunite the nation; after the proclamation, they were fighting to free the slaves as well.

On March 13, 1865, the government of the Confederacy, desperate for fresh fighting men, authorized the training of 300,000 slaves as soldiers. But the war was nearly over, and the training never began. The commanding general of the Confederate forces, Robert E. Lee, surrendered on April 9 of that year. Eight months later, on December 18, 1865, Congress passed the Thirteenth Amendment to the Constitution, making slavery illegal in the United States.

CHRONICLE OF EVENTS

1619

August 20: Twenty Africans who arrive at Jamestown, Virginia, are the first Africans in the English colonies in North America.

1641

Massachusetts becomes the first colony to establish a legal basis for slavery.

1750

Laws permit slavery in all 13 colonies.

1795

April: A planned slave revolt at Pointe Coupee, Louisiana, is exposed, and 48 alleged plotters are executed.

1801

August 30: Gabriel Prosser leads more than 1,000 slaves in an armed rebellion near Richmond, Virginia.

October 30: Prosser, his family, and 24 others are hanged.

1801–1803

Ten of Gabriel Prosser's followers are deported; 14 are executed.

1804

Seven northern states have passed legislation calling for the gradual emancipation of slaves.

1808

January 1: A federal ban on the importation of slaves takes effect.

An artist's depiction of Nat Turner's rebellion: 1. A mother pleading for her children's lives; 2. Slaves murdering a Mr. Travis; 3. A Mr. Barrow fending off the insurrectionists while his wife escapes; 4. Mounted dragoons pursuing the rebel slaves *(Library of Congress)*

1810
More than 1 million enslaved African Americans are doing agricultural work in the South.

1825–60
An estimated 100,000 people flee slavery and settle in the northern states or in Canada.

1831
August 21: Nat Turner leads a slave rebellion in Southampton County, Virginia, that results in the deaths of approximately 60 whites. In response, many African Americans are killed by military forces and lynch mobs. Of 53 arrested, 20 are hanged, 12 are banished from Virginia, and 21 are acquitted.

October 30: Turner is captured.

November 11: Turner is hanged in Jerusalem, Virginia.

1850
Federal law now requires all citizens to assist in the capture of runaway slaves.

1860
The population of enslaved persons totals 4 million.

1861
April 15: Confederate forces fire on Fort Sumter, near Charleston, South Carolina; the Civil War begins.

1862
April 16: Congress ends slavery in the District of Columbia.

1863
January 1: Slaves held in regions in rebellion against the United States are free, according to the Emancipation Proclamation.

1865
March 13: The Confederacy authorizes the training of 300,000 slaves as soldiers.

April 9: Robert E. Lee, commanding general of the Confederate Army of Northern Virginia, surrenders; the Civil War effectively ends.

December 18: The Thirteenth Amendment to the Constitution outlaws slavery throughout the United States.

EYEWITNESS TESTIMONY

[It is] beyond a doubt that the mental capacity of Negroes is equal to any task, and that all they need is education and freedom. The difference between those who are free and educated and those who are not can also be seen in their work. The lands of both whites and Negroes in the free states, as for example in Connecticut or Pennsylvania, are infinitely better cultivated, produce larger crops, and present in general an impression of well-being and contentment. But cross over into Maryland and Virginia, and . . . you think you are in a different world. No longer will you see well-cultivated fields, neat and even elegant farmhouses, large, well-designed barns, and big herds of fat, healthy cattle. Everything in Maryland and in Virginia bears the stamp of slavery: the parched soil, the badly managed farming, the ramshackled houses, and the few scrawny cattle that look like walking skeletons. In short, you find real poverty existing alongside a false appearance of wealth.

J. P. Brissot de Warville, French traveler, New Travels in the United States of America: 1788, *p. 237.*

Anthony was brought into Indiana by a man named Hopkins, who became Sheriff, and went with the Militia to [the 1811 battle of] Tippecanoe. He took Anthony with him as a waggoner. In that fiercely fought battle the Americans nearly yielded to the onset of the Indians. Anthony, who was safe amidst the baggage, rushed into the thickest of the fight, snatched a rifle from a dying soldier, and fought by the side of his Master. When Indiana became a state, slavery was abolished and Anthony was free. He said to his Master, "You bought me but a little while ago for a great deal of money; you will lose it, if I leave you now. I will indenture myself for 10 years." His offer was accepted by Hopkins, who afterwards *sold him as a slave for life* to some Orleans traders, who wanted to take him by force down to Louisiana, where he would have been worked, starved, and flogged into feebleness and submission. Anthony, who is as strong as an Athlete, broke from them and ran into Princeton, where his part was taken by my friend Mʳ. J——, who bought his time and treats him as a friend rather than a servant.

Elias Pym Fordham, English traveler, Personal Narrative of Travels in Virginia, Maryland, Pennsylvania, Ohio, Indiana, Kentucky; and of a Residence in the Illinois Territory: 1817–1818, *pp. 194–95.*

[Overseers must] be accustomed to early rising, and to steady, settled customs and ways. Let them learn regularity in arranging plantation business *in advance,* in order to avoid delay, confusion and loss of work; regularity in settling every one to their work betimes; in closely watching the driver or drivers, urging them on to their duty, and by a vigilant eye over every individual labourer's progress, as the day advances, ascertaining that none of these, and of course, that none of the business of the place is getting behind hand.

A Southern planter in American Farmer, *October 16, 1829, in John W. Blassingame,* The Slave Community, *p. 147.*

I may as well, here as elsewhere, record the fact that never have my slaves been a source of profit to me. That it has taken all that the profitable ones could produce to support the old, the young, and the unproductive, so that *I have supported my negroes and not they me.*

Warner L. Underwood, Kentucky slaveholder, April 17, 1833, in J. Winston Coleman, Jr., Slavery Times in Kentucky, *pp. 65–66.*

The negroes . . . are the foundation of every other species of property in the southern states: for without them real estate would be of no value; as it is physically proved that neither the climate nor the soil will ever admit of the independent labour of the whites. It is evident then, that if the negroes be emancipated, they must be *retained* to cultivate the plantations, and the proprietors obliged to hire them; which amounts to paying interest on their own capital.

Francis J. Grund, English traveler, 1837, The Americans in their Moral, Social, and Political Relations, *p. 249.*

A majority of the large plantations are on the banks of rivers, far from the public eye. A great deal of low marshy ground lies in the vicinity of most of the rivers at the south; consequently the main roads are several miles from the rivers, and generally no *public* road passes the plantations. A stranger traveling on the *ridge,* would think himself in a miserably poor country; but every two or three miles he will see a road turning off, and leading into the swamp; taking one of those roads, and traveling from two to six miles, he will come to a large gate; passing which, he will find himself in a clearing of several hundred acres of the first quality of land; passing on, he will see 30, or 40, or more slaves—men, women, boys and girls, at their task, every one with a hoe; or, if in cotton picking season, with their baskets. The overseer, with his whip, either riding or standing about among them; or if the weather is hot, sitting under a shade. At a distance, on a little rising ground, if such there be, he will see a cluster of huts, with a tolerable house in the midst, for the overseer.

The Reverend Francis Hawley, 1839, in Theodore Weld, American Slavery as It Is, *pp. 94–95.*

Males and females work together promiscuously on all the plantations. On many plantations *tasks* are given them. The best working hands can have some leisure time; but the feeble and unskilful ones, together with slender females, have indeed a hard time of it, and very often answer for non-performance of tasks at the *whipping-posts.* None who worked with me had tasks at any time. The rule was to work them from sun to sun. But when I was burning brick, they were obliged to take turns, and *sit up all night* about every other night, and work all day. On one plantation, where I spent a few weeks, the slaves were called up to work long before daylight, when business pressed, and worked until late at night; and sometimes some of them *all night.* A large portion of the slaves are owned by masters who keep them on purpose to hire out— and they usually let them to those who will give the highest wages for them, irrespective of their mode of treatment; and those who hire them, will of course try to get the greatest possible amount of work performed, with the least possible expense.

The Reverend Horace Moulton, 1839, in Theodore Weld, American Slavery as It Is, *p. 18.*

I have also known instances where seamstresses were kept in cold entries to work by the stair case lamps for one or two hours, every evening in winter—they could not see without standing up all the time, though the work was often too large and heavy for them to sew upon it in that position without great inconvenience, and yet they were expected to do their work as *well* with their cold fingers, and standing up, as if they had been sitting by a comfortable fire and provided with the necessary light. House slaves suffer a great deal also from not being allowed to leave the house without permission. If they wish to go even for a draught of water, they must *ask leave,* and if they stay longer than the mistress thinks neces-

sary, they are liable to be punished, and often are scolded or slapped, or kept from going down to the next meal.

Angelina Grimké Weld, abolitionist, 1839, in Theodore Weld, American Slavery as It Is, *p. 56.*

It was a general custom, wherever I have been, for the masters to give each of his slaves, male and female, *one peck of corn per week* for their food. This at fifty cents per bushel, which was all that it was worth when I was there, would amount to twelve and a half cents per week for board per head.

It cost me upon an average, when at the south, one dollar per day for board. The price of fourteen bushels of corn per week. This would make my board equal in amount to the board of *forty-six slaves!* This is all that good or bad masters allow their slaves round about Savannah on the plantations.

The Reverend Horace Moulton, 1839, in Theodore Weld, American Slavery as It Is, *p. 18.*

Some of the planters have no corn, others often get [run] out. The substitute for it is, the equivalent of one peck of corn either in rice or sweet potatoes; neither of which is as good for the slaves as corn. They complain more of being faint, when fed on rice or potatoes, than when fed on corn. I was with one man a few weeks who gave me his hands to do a job of work, and to save time one cooked for all the rest. The following course was taken,—Two crotched sticks were driven down at one end of the yard, and a small pole being laid on the crotches, they swung a large iron kettle on the middle of the pole; then made up a fire under the kettle and boiled the hommony; when ready, the hands were called around this kettle with their wooden plates and spoons. They dipped out and ate standing around the kettle, or sitting upon the ground, as best suited their convenience. When they had potatoes they took them out with their hands, and ate them. As soon as it was thought they had had sufficient time to swallow their food they were called to their work again. *This was the only meal they ate through the day.*

The Reverend Horace Moulton, 1839, in Theodore Weld, American Slavery as It Is, *pp. 18–19.*

When I first went upon Mr. Swan's plantation, I saw a slave in shackles or fetters, which were fastened around each ankle and firmly riveted, connected together by a chain. To the middle of this chain he had fastened a string, so as in a manner to suspend them and keep them from galling his ankles. This slave, whose name was Frank, was an intelligent, good looking man, and a very good mechanic. There was nothing vicious in his character, but he was one of those high-spirited and daring men, that whips, chains, fetters, and all the means of cruelty in the power of slavery, could not subdue. Mr. S. had employed a Mr. Beckwith to repair a boat, and told him Frank was a good mechanic, and he might have his services. Frank was sent for, his *shackles still on*. Mr. Beckwith set him to work making *trunnels* [wooden pins for joining timbers], &c. I was employed in putting up a building, and after Mr. Beckwith had done with Frank, he was sent for to assist me. Mr. Swan sent him to a blacksmith's shop and had his shackles cut off with a cold chisel. Frank was afterwards sold to a cotton planter.

Nehemiah Caulkins, 1839, in Theodore Weld,
American Slavery as It Is, *p. 13.*

To show the manner in which old and worn-out slaves are sometimes treated, I will state a fact[.] Galloway [a planter] owned a man about seventy years of age. The old man was sick and went to his hut; laid himself down on some straw with his feet to the fire, covered by a piece of an old blanket, and there lay four or five days, groaning in great distress, without any attention being paid him by his master, until death ended his miseries; he was then taken out and buried with as little ceremony and respect as would be paid to a brute.

Nehemiah Caulkins, 1839, in Theodore Weld,
American Slavery as It Is, *p. 12.*

Women are generally shown some little indulgence for three or four weeks previous to childbirth; they are at such times not often punished if they do not finish the task assigned them; it is, in some cases, passed over with a severe reprimand, and sometimes without any notice being taken of it. They are generally allowed four weeks after the birth of a child, before they are compelled to go into the field, they then take the child with them, attended sometimes by a little girl or boy, from the age of four to six, to take care of it while the mother is at work. When there is no child that can be spared, or not young enough for this service, the mother, after nursing, lays it under a

These women of Virginia, like enslaved women throughout the South, attend to their homes and families after spending the day in the fields. (*Library of Congress*)

tree, or by the side of a fence, and goes to her task, returning at stated intervals to nurse it.

Nehemiah Caulkins, 1839, in Theodore Weld,
American Slavery as It Is, *p. 12.*

She was a field hand when I came here but I soon discovered she had a great deal of intelligence and industry and she made all my pasteries, Cake and biscuits, best Candlemaker and dairy maid, she has made me many thousands of butter, she had been dairy maid for upwards of 20 years.

Martha Ogle Forman of Delaware describing her enslaved house servant Rachel Teger, 1841, in Joan M. Jensen, Loosening the Bonds: Mid-Atlantic Farm Women, 1750–1850, *p. 91.*

The field-slaves, being regarded as instruments of production, are maintained with as little cost as possible, compatible with the keeping them in good working condition; because, in proportion to the great quantity of work got out of them, and the small cost of their maintenance, will be the profit of the planter. He has every motive, therefore, to increase the one, and lessen the other, till he brings each to the point beyond which it is unsafe to carry them. In the domestic service of most private establishments here, there are often more slaves than are necessary for the labour required of them, many being kept for state, or ostentation; and as the coachman, footman, lady's maid, butler, cook, and other household servants, are continually passing before the eyes of the master and mistress, as well as their visitors and guests, they are almost sure of being well clad and kindly treated, because the sight of dirty and miserable-looking attendants would be painful to those by whom they are surrounded, as well as to themselves.

J. S. Buckingham, English traveler, 1842,
The Slave States of America, *p. 200.*

. . . [W]ithout doubting for a moment that there are many kind masters and mistresses, who do much to make the condition of their slaves easy and tolerable, it cannot but be evident to [a stranger], that the great mass of them are not treated so well as many of the brute creation; and that the dogs and horses of their masters are better fed, have less labour, less punishment, and quite as much of intellectual culture and enjoyment as the slave: for if the one has not the capacity to learn, the other is strictly forbidden to acquire the power to read. This shutting up of all the avenues to knowledge in the slaves, is, no doubt, done with a view to keep them in a state of greater dependence and subordination; but it is defended on the ground of their utter unfitness for mental improvements, and an entire deficiency of a capacity for education.

J. S. Buckingham, English traveler, 1842,
The Slave States of America, *pp. 64–65.*

And yet, so well able are the greatest number of negroes to earn their own subsistence, and conduct their own affairs, that many of them are hired out by their masters to various persons needing their labour; by which they get so much more than is necessary for their own support, that they maintain themselves out of their wages first, and then hand over the surplus, often amounting to half their earnings, to their masters, as interest or profit on the capital laid out in their purchase. One master mentioned to me his having given 1500 dollars . . . for a slave; and when I asked why he paid so large a sum for him, he answered, that the man was fully worth it, because he could earn a handsome income. But when I followed up this question by asking whether the income made by the slave's labour and skill were given to *himself,* the master replied, without being apparently conscious of the wrong, "Oh, no! his earnings belong to *me,* because I bought him; and in return for this I give him maintenance, and make a handsome profit besides."

J. S. Buckingham, English traveler, 1842,
The Slave States of America, *pp. 65–66.*

Some of the laws of Louisiana respecting slaves, are also humane and considerate. No master can sell the parents and children separately, till the latter are more than twelve years of age. A slave who is ill-treated can make a representation of his case before the local tribunal of judges; and in the event of the facts being proved on reasonable testimony—the evidence of slaves being taken in such cases—the master is compelled by law to sell the slave to another owner.

J. S. Buckingham, English traveler, 1842,
The Slave States of America, *pp. 356–57.*

Having secured seats in the mail for the north on the 22nd of January, we were standing near the stage-coach at the door of the tavern waiting for the arrival of the mail from Charleston, when it drove up with a negro male slave, about thirty years old, *chained flat on the roof,* the poor devil having been overtaken by his master after an ineffectual attempt to run away. . . .

I had seen turtles, and venison, and wild turkeys, and things of that sort, fastened to the top of a stage-coach before, but this was the first black man I ever saw arranged in this manner. Catching a glimpse of him as the stage drove up, I thought it was a bear, or some other animal on its way to the larder; but in a few minutes they handed him down from the top, holding him by the end of his chain, exactly as if he had been a baboon, and then proceeded to hoist him to the top of the stage we were to travel in, and fasten him down there just as he had been before.

G. W. Featherstonhaugh, English traveler, 1844,
Excursion Through the Slave States, *pp. 157–58.*

The home plantation of Colonel Lloyd wore the appearance of a country village. All the mechanical operations for all the farms were performed here. The shoemaking and mending, the blacksmithing, cartwrighting, coopering, weaving, and grain-grinding, were all performed by the slaves on the home plantation. The whole place wore a business-like aspect very unlike the neighboring farms. The number of houses, too, conspired to give it advantage over the neighboring farms. It was called by the slaves the *Great House Farm.* Few privileges were esteemed higher, by the slaves of the out-farms, than that of being selected to do errands at the Great House Farm.

Frederick Douglass, 1845, Narrative of the Life of
Frederick Douglass, *p. 12.*

[The carriage house] was under the care of two slaves—old Barney and young Barney—father and son. To attend to this establishment was their sole work. But it was by no means an easy employment; for in nothing was Colonel Lloyd more particular than in the management of his horses. The slightest inattention to these was unpardonable, and was visited upon those, under whose care they were placed, with the severest punishment; no excuse could shield them, if the colonel only suspected any want of attention to his horses—a supposition which he frequently indulged, and one which, of course, made the office of old and young Barney a very trying one. They never knew when they were safe from punishment. . . . If a horse did not move fast enough, or hold his head high enough, it was owing to some fault of his keepers.

Frederick Douglass, 1845, Narrative of the Life of Frederick Douglass, *p. 18.*

The men and women slaves received, as their monthly allowance of food, eight pounds of pork, or its equivalent in fish, and one bushel of corn meal. Their yearly clothing consisted of two coarse linen shirts, one pair of linen trousers, like the shirts, one jacket, one pair of trousers for winter, made of coarse negro cloth, one pair of stockings, and one pair of shoes; the whole of which could not have cost more than seven dollars. The allowance of the slave children was given to their mothers, or the old women having the care of them. The children unable to work in the field had neither shoes, stockings, jackets, nor trousers, given to them; their clothing consisted of two coarse linen shirts per year. When these failed them, they went naked until the next allowance-day. Children from seven to ten years old, of both sexes, almost naked, might be seen at all seasons of the year.

Frederick Douglass, 1845, Narrative of the Life of Frederick Douglass, *pp. 10–11.*

My mother was a field hand, and one morning was ten or fifteen minutes behind the others in getting to the field. As soon as she reached the spot where they were at work, the overseer commenced whipping her. She cried, "Oh! pray—Oh! pray—Oh! pray"—these are generally the words of slaves, when imploring mercy at the hands of their oppressors. I heard her voice, and knew it, and jumped out of my bunk, and went to the door. Though the field was some distance from the house, I could hear every crack of the whip, and every groan and cry of my poor mother.

William Wells Brown, former slave, 1847, Narrative of the Life of William W. Brown, *p. 15.*

In July, [our employer] told us, we must cultivate five hogsheads of Tobacco for our summer's work. Added to this, was the order for us to "get married," according to Slavery—or, in other words, to enrich his plantation by a family of young slaves. The alternative of this was, to be sold to a slave trader who was then in the vicinity making up a gang for a more southern market. "This information" I did not like,—more especially, as I had often been promised my freedom in a few years if I would work faithfully; and I resolved, whenever an opportunity should offer, and I could see my way clear to attempt a shorter and more certain route to freedom than to await the fulfilment of a Slaveholder's promise; for in relation to the emancipation of a slave, their promises are always forgotten before they get cold. And, if I could have any confidence in such promises, it would have inspired me with energy to almost any amount of labor, for I never desired any thing more ardently, nor was willing to make so great a sacrifice for any thing else as my liberty.

Andrew Jackson, escaped slave, 1847, Narrative and Writings of Andrew Jackson, of Kentucky, *p. 8.*

The following song I have often heard the slaves sing, when about to be carried to the far south. It is said to have been composed by a slave.

"See these poor souls from Africa
Transported to America;
We are stolen, and sold to Georgia,
Will you go along with me?
We are stolen, and sold to Georgia,
Come sound the jubilee!
See wives and husbands sold apart,
Their children's screams will break my heart;—
There's a better day a coming,
Will you go along with me?
There's a better day a coming,
Go sound the jubilee! . . ."

William Wells Brown, former slave, 1847, Narrative of the Life of William W. Brown, *p. 51.*

It was not uncommon in St. Louis to pass by an auction-stand, and behold a woman upon the auction-block, and hear the seller crying out, *"How much is offered for this woman? She is a good cook, good washer, a good obedient servant. She has got religion!"* Why should this man tell the purchasers that she has religion? I answer, because in Missouri, and as far as I have any knowledge of slavery in the other States, the religious teaching consists in teaching the slave that he must never strike a white man; that God made him for a slave; and that, when whipped, he must not find fault,—for the Bible says, "He that knoweth his master's will, and doeth it not, shall be beaten with many stripes!"

William Wells Brown, former slave, 1847,
Narrative of the Life of William W. Brown, *pp. 83–84.*

The slaveholders in that state [Maryland] often hire the children of their slaves out to non-slaveholders, not only because they save themselves the expense of taking care of them, but in this way they get among their slaves useful trades. They put a bright slave-boy with a tradesman, until he gets such a knowledge of the trade as to be able to do his own work, and then he takes him home. I remained with the stonemason until I was eleven years of age: at this time I was taken home. . . . My master owned an excellent blacksmith, who had obtained his trade in the way I have mentioned above. When I returned home at the age of eleven, I was set about assisting to do the mason-work of a new smith's shop. This being done, I was placed at the business, which I soon learned, so as to be called a "first-rate blacksmith."

James W. C. Pennington, escaped slave, 1850,
The Fugitive Blacksmith, *p. 4.*

The slaves had no butter, coffee, tea, or sugar; occasionally they were allowed milk, but not statedly; the only exception to this statement was the "harvest provisions." In harvest, when cutting the grain, which lasted from two to three weeks in the heat of summer, they were allowed some fresh meat, rice, sugar, and coffee; and also their allowance of whiskey.

James W. C. Pennington, escaped slave, 1850,
The Fugitive Blacksmith, *pp. 65–66.*

We had there [in Vicksburg, Mississippi] to pass through an examination or inspection by a city officer, whose business it was to inspect slave property that was brought to that market for sale. He examined our backs to see if we had been much scarred by the lash. He examined our limbs, to see whether we were inferior.

As it is hard to tell the ages of slaves, they look in their mouths at their teeth, and prick up the skin on the back of their hands, and if the person is very far advanced in life, when the skin is pricked up, the pucker will stand so many seconds on the back of the hand.

Henry Bibb, former slave, 1850, Narrative of the Life
and Adventures of Henry Bibb, *p. 101.*

When spectators would come in the yard, the slaves were ordered out to form a line. They were made to stand up straight, and look as sprightly as they could; and when they were asked a question, they had to answer it as promptly as they could, and try to induce the spectators to buy them. If they failed to do this, they were severely paddled after the spectators were gone. The object for using the paddle in the place of a lash was, to conceal the marks which would be made by the flogging. And the object for flogging under such circumstances, is to make the slaves anxious to be sold.

Henry Bibb, former slave, 1850, Narrative of the Life
and Adventures of Henry Bibb, *p. 103.*

The slaves are . . . all that I had imagined. . . . The women were dressed in a rough, shapeless, coarse garment, buttoned at the back, with a sort of trousers of the same material, rough shoes and stockings, the upper garment reaching nearly to the ankle; a kind of cloth, like a dirty towel, was wound round the head.

One of the women drove an ox-team; she had a large and powerful whip, with which, and a surprising strength, she belaboured and tugged the unwieldy team with great dexterity. The other women had five children, and assisted in loading the wood: the younger, about 16 years of age, had one child, and appeared to do nothing. The women, it seemed to me, worked harder than the men. . . .

Charles Casey, English traveler, 1852, Two Years
on the Farm of Uncle Sam, *pp. 136–37.*

In the slave marts, in Evans' Arcade [New Orleans], I had an opportunity of seeing . . . a sale of slaves, among which was a beautiful quadroon girl, neatly dressed, and very intelligent; her price was 2,000 dollars. The field-negroes went from 600 to 800; they were dressed up in their best clothes, and assumed their best looks. When they saw a "massa" whose appearance they liked, they chattered and laughed quite merrily, and would afford a bad text for a violent free-soiler.

Charles Casey, English traveler, 1852, Two Years on the Farm of Uncle Sam, *p. 263.*

In the latter part of August begins the cotton picking season. At this time each slave is presented with a sack. A strap is fastened to it, which goes over the neck, holding the mouth of the sack breast high, while the bottom reaches nearly to the ground. Each one is also presented with a large basket that will hold about two barrels. This is to put the cotton in when the sack is filled. The baskets are carried to the field and placed at the beginning of the rows.

When a new hand, one unaccustomed to the business, is sent for the first time into the field, he is whipped up smartly, and made for that day to pick as fast as he can possibly. At night it is weighed, so that his capability in cotton picking is known. He must bring in the same weight each night following. If it falls short, it is considered evidence that he has been laggard, and a greater or less number of lashes is the penalty.

Solomon Northup, 1853, Twelve Years a Slave, *p. 124.*

The drivers are black, who, in addition to the performance of their equal share of work, are compelled to do the whipping of their several gangs. Whips hang around their necks, and if they fail to use them thoroughly, are whipped themselves. They have a few privileges, however; for example, in cane-cutting the hands are not allowed to sit down long enough to eat their dinners. Carts filled with corn cake, cooked at the kitchen, are driven into the fields at noon. The cake is distributed by the drivers, and must be eaten with the least possible delay.

Solomon Northup, 1853, Twelve Years a Slave, *p. 171.*

The field hands, and such of them as have generally been excluded from the dwelling of their owners, look to the house servant as a pattern of politeness and gentility. And indeed, it is often the only method of obtaining any knowledge of the manners of what is called "genteel society;" hence, they are ever regarded as a privileged class; and are sometimes greatly envied, while others are bitterly hated. And too often justly, for many of them are the most despicable tale-bearers and mischief-makers, who will, for the sake of the favor of his master or mistress, frequently betray his fellow-slave, and by tattling, get him severely whipped; and for these acts of perfidy, and sometimes downright falsehood, he is often rewarded by his master, who knows it is for his interest to keep such ones about him; though he is sometimes obliged, in addition to a reward, to send him away, for fear of the vengeance of the betrayed slaves.

Austin Steward, 1857, Twenty-Two Years a Slave, and Forty Years a Freeman, *pp. 31–32.*

Even the smallest children in this enslaved family wore sacks for picking cotton. *(Collection of the New-York Historical Society)*

Slaves are never allowed to leave the plantation to which they belong, without a written pass. Should any one venture to disobey this law, he will most likely be caught by the *patrol* and given thirty-nine lashes. This patrol is always on duty every Sunday, going to each plantation under their supervision, entering the slave cabin, and examining closely the conduct of the slaves; and if they find one slave from another plantation without a pass, he is immediately punished with a severe flogging.

Austin Steward, 1857, Twenty-Two Years a Slave, and Forty Years a Freeman, *p. 27.*

I once had the misfortune to break the lock of master's shot gun, and when it came to his knowledge, he came to me in a towering passion, and charged me with what he considered the *crime* of carelessness. I denied it, and told him I knew nothing about it; but I was so terribly frightened that he saw I was guilty, and told me so, foaming with rage; and then I confessed the truth. But oh, there was no escaping the lash. Its recollection is still bitter, and ever will be. I was commanded to take off my clothes, which I did, and then master put me on the back of another slave, my arms hanging down before him and my hands clasped in his, where he was obliged to hold me with a vice-like grasp. Then master gave me the most severe flogging that I ever received, and I pray God that I may never again experience such torture.

Austin Steward, 1857, Twenty-Two Years a Slave, and Forty Years a Freeman, *p. 25.*

When I was not employed as an errand-boy, it was my duty to stand behind my master's chair, which was sometimes the whole day, never being allowed to sit in his presence. Indeed, no slave is ever allowed to sit down in the presence of their master or mistress. If a slave is addressed when sitting, he is required to spring to his feet, and instantly remove his hat, if he has one, and answer in the most humble manner, or lay the foundation for a flogging, which will not be long delayed.

Austin Steward, 1857, Twenty-Two Years a Slave, and Forty Years a Freeman, *p. 26.*

We lodged in log huts, and on the bare ground. Wooden floors were an unknown luxury. In a single room were huddled, like cattle, ten or a dozen persons, men, women and children. All ideas of refinement and decency were, of course, out of the question. There were neither bedsteads, nor furniture of any description. Our beds were collections of straw and old rags, thrown down in the corners and boxed in with boards; a single blanket the only covering. Our favorite way of sleeping, however, was on a plank, our heads raised on an old jacket and our feet toasting before the smouldering fire. The wind whistled and the rain and snow blew in through the cracks, and the damp earth soaked in the moisture till the floor was miry as a pig-sty. Such were our houses. In these wretched hovels were we penned at night,

and fed by day; here were the children born and the sick—neglected.

Josiah Henson, former slave, 1858, Father Henson's Story of His Own Life, *p. 18.*

I have no desire to represent the life of slavery as an experience of nothing but misery. God be praised, that however hedged in by circumstances, the joyful exuberance of youth will bound at times over them all. . . . In those days I had many a merry time, and would have had, had I lived with nothing but moccasins and rattle-snakes in Okafenoke swamp. Slavery did its best to make me wretched; I feel no particular obligation to it; but nature, or the blessed God of youth and joy, was mightier than slavery. Along with memories of miry cabins, frosted feet, weary toil under the blazing sun, curses and blows, there flock in others, of jolly Christmas times, dances before old massa's door for the first drink of egg-nog, extra meat at holiday times, midnight visits to apple orchards, broiling stray chickens, and first-rate tricks to dodge work. The God who makes the pup gambol, and the kitten play, and the bird sing, and the fish leap, was the author in me of many a lighthearted hour.

Josiah Henson, former slave, 1858, Father Henson's Story of His Own Life, *pp. 19–20.*

Christmas is a day of feasting, both with white and colored people. Slaves, who are lucky enough to have a few shillings, are sure to spend them for good eating; and many a turkey and pig is captured, without saying, "By your leave, sir." Those who cannot obtain these, cook a 'possum, or a raccoon, from which savory dishes can be made.

Lydia Maria Child, abolitionist, ed., 1861, Incidents in the Life of a Slave Girl, *pp. 180–81.*

We have a system which enables us to reap the fruits of the earth by a race which we save from barbarism, in returning them to their real place in the world as laborers, whilst we are enabled to cultivate the arts, the graces and accomplishments of life, to develop science, to apply ourselves to the duties of government, and to understand the affairs of the country.

A slave owner to the London Times *in 1861, in Carlton Beals,* American Earth, *p. 91.*

. . . [O]ne of the plantation slaves was brought to town, by order of his master. It was near night when he arrived, and Dr. Flint ordered him to be taken to the work house, and tied up to the joist, so that his feet would just escape the ground. In that situation he was to wait till the doctor had taken his tea. I shall never forget that night. Never before, in my life, had I heard hundreds of blows fall, in succession, on a human being. His piteous groans, and his "O, pray don't, massa," rang in my ear for months afterwards. There were many conjectures as to the cause of this terrible punishment. Some said master accused him of stealing corn; others said the slave had quarrelled with his wife, in the presence of the overseer, and had accused his master of being the father of her child. They were both black, and the child was very fair.

Lydia Maria Child, abolitionist, ed., 1861, Incidents in the Life of a Slave Girl, *p. 23.*

Slaveholders have a method, peculiar to their institution, of getting rid of *old* slaves, whose lives have been worn out in their service. I knew an old woman, who for seventy years faithfully served her master. She had become almost helpless, from hard labor and disease. Her owners moved to Alabama, and the old black woman was left to be sold to any body who would give twenty dollars for her.

Lydia Maria Child, abolitionist, ed., 1861, Incidents in the Life of a Slave Girl, *p. 27.*

On one of these sale days, I saw a mother lead seven children to the auction-block. She knew that *some* of them would be taken from her; but they took *all.* The children were sold to a slave-trader, and their mother was bought by a man in her own town. Before night her children were all far away. She begged the trader to tell her where he intended to take them; this he refused to do. How *could* he, when he knew he would sell them, one by one, wherever he could command the highest price? I met that mother in the street, and her wild, haggard face lives to-day in my mind. She wrung her hands in anguish, and exclaimed, "Gone! All gone! Why *don't* God kill me?" I had no words wherewith to comfort her. Instances of this kind are of daily, yea, of hourly occurrence.

Lydia Maria Child, abolitionist, ed., 1861, Incidents in the Life of a Slave Girl, *pp. 26–27.*

When [my master's nephew] became old enough to need a playmate to watch over him, mistress called the young slaves together, to select one for the purpose.

We were all ordered to run, jump, wrestle, turn somersets, walk on our hands, and go through the various gymnastic exercises that the imagination of our brain could invent, or the strength and activity of our limbs could endure. The selection was to be an important one, both to the mistress and the slave. Whoever should gain the place was in the future to become a house servant; . . . that unmentionable garment that buttons around the neck, which we all wore, and nothing else, was to give way to the whole suit of tow linen. Every one of us joined heartily in the contest, while old mistress sat on the piazza, watching our every movement. . . . At last the choice was made, and I was told to step aside as the "lucky boy," which order I obeyed with an alacrity seldom surpassed. . . . Mistress received me, and laid down the law which was to govern my future actions. "I give your young master over to you," said she; "and if you let him hurt himself, I'll pull your ears; if you let him cry, I'll pull your ears; if he wants any thing, and you don't give it to him, I'll pull your ears; when he goes to sleep, if you let him wake before it is time, I'll pull your ears." And right well did she keep her promise, for my ears felt the impress of her tender fingers and gold rings almost every day, and at times nearly every hour.

William Wells Brown, former slave, 1865, The Black Man, His Antecedents, His Genius, and His Achievements, *pp. 11–12.*

When I was about seven years old I witnessed, for the first time, the sale of a human being. We were living at Prince Edward, in Virginia, and master had just purchased his hogs for the winter, for which he was unable to pay in full. To escape from his embarrassment it was necessary to sell one of the slaves. Little Joe, the son of the cook, was selected as the victim. His mother was ordered to dress him up in his Sunday clothes, and send him to the house. He came in with a bright face, was placed in the scales, and was sold, like the hogs, at so much per pound. His mother was kept in ignorance of the transaction, but her suspicions were aroused. When her son started for Petersburgh in the wagon, the truth began to dawn upon her mind, and she pleaded piteously that her boy should not be taken from her; but master quieted her by telling her that he was simply going to town with the wagon, and would be back in the morning. Morning came, but little Joe did not return to his mother. Morning after morning passed, and the mother went down to the grave without ever seeing her child again. One day she was whipped for grieving for her lost boy. Colonel Burwell never liked to see one of his slaves wear a sorrowful face, and those who offended in this particular way were always punished.

Elizabeth Keckley, former slave, 1868, Behind the Scenes, *pp. 28–29.*

My first work in the morning was to dust the parlor and hall and arrange the dining room. It came awkward to me at first, but, after the madam told me how, I soon learned to do it satisfactorily. Then I had to wait on the table, sweep the large yard every morning with a brush broom and go for the mail once a week. I used to get very tired, for I was young and consequently not strong. Aside from these things which came regularly, I had to help the madam in warping the cloth. I dreaded this work, for I always got my ears boxed if I did not or could not do the work to suit her. She always made the warp herself and put it in, and I had to hand her the thread as she put it through the harness. I would get very tired at this work and, like any child, wanted to be at play, but I could not remember that the madam ever gave me that privilege.

Louis Hughes, 1897, Thirty Years a Slave, *pp. 17–18.*

During the period that I spent in slavery I was not large enough to be of much service, still I was occupied most of the time in cleaning the yards, carrying water to the men in the fields, or going to the mill, to which I used to take the corn, once a week, to be ground. The mill was about three miles from the plantation. This work I always dreaded. The heavy bag of corn would be thrown across the back of the horse, and the corn divided about evenly on each side; but in some way, almost without exception, on these trips, the corn would so shift as to become unbalanced and would fall off the horse, and often I would fall with it. As I was not strong enough to reload the corn upon the horse, I would have to wait, sometimes for many hours, till a chance passer-by came along who would help me out of my trouble. . . . [W]hen I was late in getting home I knew I would always get a severe scolding or a flogging.

Booker T. Washington, 1901, Up from Slavery, *pp. 5–6.*

In the portion of Virginia where I lived it was common to use flax as part of the clothing for the slaves. That part of the flax from which our clothing was made was largely the refuse, which of course was the cheapest and roughest part. I can scarcely imagine any torture, except, perhaps, the pulling of a tooth, that is equal to that caused by putting on a new flax shirt for the first time. It is almost equal to the feeling that one would experience if he had a dozen or more chestnut burrs, or a hundred small pin-points, in contact with his flesh. Even to this day I can recall accurately the tortures that I underwent when putting on one of these garments. The fact that my flesh was soft and tender added to the pain. But I had no choice. I had to wear the flax shirt or none; and had it been left to me to choose, I should have chosen to wear no covering.

Booker T. Washington, 1901, Up from Slavery, *p. 11.*

3

The Factory System Emerges
1733–1865

An American shoemaker, in the first decades after the Revolutionary War, would craft a single pair of shoes from start to finish, completing every step in the process himself, from measuring and cutting the leather to stitching the uppers to the soles and polishing the finished product. He had his own, often idiosyncratic, notions of proper size and fit, which he had formulated and refined during his long career. He would have entered the trade in his youth, when he was apprenticed to a master shoemaker. As an apprentice, or "greenhand," he worked in the master's shop, which might be a 10' by 10' cottage, 100 feet square. After years spent honing his skills, he graduated to the level of journeyman and became a paid employee in the shop. His status in the community was secure, well above that of the unskilled laborer or indentured worker. He purchased his own tools and perhaps a small home. With hard work and thrift, he would be master of his own shop one day.

Shoemaker, cooper, cabinetmaker, printer—the situation was the same in every trade. Workers followed a career path leading from apprentice to journeyman to independent master. Work done well bestowed honor and dignity on the craftsman, and the finished product was a source of pride, whether it was a shoe, a barrel, a chest of drawers, or a printed pamphlet.

Rapid settlement of the new nation opened up markets and increased demand. By the start of the 19th century, the manufacturing system could no longer keep up with the need for goods. Master craftsmen transformed themselves into large-scale suppliers, becoming more concerned with filling quotas and less with personal pride. Many now operated according to the "sweating system," requiring greater output from their skilled workers. They took on extra greenhands and enlarged their operations. This kind of expansion required capital, more than most journeymen could hope to amass, with the result that journeymen no longer viewed themselves as people on their way up. They were now permanent employees with little hope of owning a shop, and permanent members of the working class.

THE INDUSTRIAL REVOLUTION IN GREAT BRITAIN

Across the Atlantic Ocean, Great Britain had entered a period of profound technological change that would transform its economy from one based on

Like other early American artisans, the cooper worked in a small shop. He completed every step in barrel making. *(Science, Industry and Business Library; New York Public Library; Astor, Lenox and Tilden Foundations)*

agriculture to one based on the manufacture of goods by machinery on a large scale. The English social philosopher and economist Arnold Toynbee, who lectured to working-class audiences in the 1870s and 1880s, gave this radical economic shift the name that it bears today: the Industrial Revolution. This revolution began with a series of innovations that radically changed the British textile industry, as 18th-century inventors sought ways to streamline the processing of raw fiber into finished cloth.

The fibers of flax, wool, and cotton can be made into cloth because they cling together. Drawing and twisting the fibers (a task known as spinning) produces a long thread or yarn suitable for weaving. Spinning and weaving traditionally were home-based chores performed by hand on spinning wheels and looms. In 1733, an Englishman named John Kay invented a device, called the flying shuttle, that speeded up the process of weaving. A weaver's shuttle encases a bobbin, or spool, onto which is wound thread for the woof, or crosswise weave of the cloth. In the time-honored method of weaving on a handloom, the weaver repeatedly pushed her shuttle from one side of the warp (the lengthwise threads) to the other. In Kay's invention, a lever moved the shuttle.

By the 1750s, the flying shuttle was catching on, and spinners were having trouble keeping up with the demand for yarn. Inventors applied their scientific and practical knowledge to this problem as well, and in 1764 James Hargreaves devised the spinning jenny, a machine named for his wife (according to some accounts, his daughter). The hand-powered spinning jenny spun eight threads at once, but the thread it produced was strong enough only for the woof of the fabric, not the warp. Another inventor, Richard Arkwright, patented a spinning frame that spun multiple threads, and stronger ones, in 1769. Because the Arkwright frame was too large and heavy for home use, spinning moved to the factory setting and became an important part of the British manufacturing system. In 1769, Arkwright established a spinning mill in which horses supplied the power. He opened in 1771 a larger mill that was powered by water.

Once spinning became mechanized, the race was on for a faster loom. Edmund Cartwright developed the first power loom in 1785, but it was unreliable. Constructing such a loom was beyond the limits of 18th-century technology. Power looms would not come into use until the second decade of the 19th century.

ENERGY FROM STEAM

Dependence on water to drive machinery limited the scope of industrialization, because it meant that factories had to be built near sources of running water. The development of the steam engine made it possible to place factories at any location.

In 1705, the English blacksmith and inventor Thomas Newcomen (1663–1729) perfected a steam-powered pump that cleared water from deep coal mines. Newcomen's engine gave miners access to underground seams that had long been unreachable; despite inefficiencies in its design, it was soon used widely. In 1750, one Newcomen pump reportedly could do the work of 110 horses on treadmills or 2,520 men hauling buckets.

Newcomen had exploited the simple fact that water, when heated to the boiling point, expands into steam. In a partially closed system, the resulting pressure can be made to drive moving parts. Newcomen's engine worked by admitting steam into a cylinder, which caused a piston at the top of the cylinder to rise. The piston was attached to a mechanism that lowered a pump rod into the mine. The injection of cold water into the cylinder then condensed the steam, reduced pressure within the cylinder, and allowed the piston to fall.

But Newcomen's engine wasted a large percentage of its steam power heating and reheating the metal cylinder.

A Scottish-born maker of mathematical instruments, James Watt (1736–1819), improved the efficiency of Newcomen's steam engine. By insulating the cylinder, Watt kept it at steam temperature. He added a separate condensing chamber, linked to the cylinder by a pipe. The first commercial engine produced by James Watt and his financial backer, factory owner Matthew Boulton, was installed in a British coal mine in 1776. By 1784, Watt had perfected a rotary steam engine capable of powering factory machinery, using a design that would remain unchanged for the next 60 years. A Nottinghamshire spinning mill became the first steam-powered factory in 1785, and six years later Watt's engine had almost completely supplanted Newcomen's. In the years that followed, steam gradually replaced water as a power source in large factories, although many small operations continued to rely on water.

INDUSTRIALIZATION IN THE UNITED STATES

The Industrial Revolution occurred later in the United States than it did in Great Britain. New England merchants were just beginning to invest in cotton mills in the late 1700s, in order to compete with the cheap British goods that were flooding the market. When they sent representatives to England to recruit a skilled labor force, England saw a threat to its dominance of the market. Parliament responded by passing a law forbidding the export of textile machinery and by prohibiting textile workers from leaving the country. British factory owners, fearful of industrial spies, treated their places of business like fortresses, and British writers describing the current technology omitted key details to prevent the replication of machinery abroad. The United States responded by offering cash bounties for information about textile manufacturing.

The technology was bound to escape, and it did. The closely guarded secrets of the British textile industry came to the United States in the mind of Samuel Slater. Slater, who had been apprenticed to Arkwright at age 14, had extensive knowledge of the most advanced textile machinery. After sailing to the United States in disguise, he started building machinery according to Arkwright's specifications. In 1790 he established a mill in Pawtucket, Rhode Island, and later a second one in Massachusetts. He became one of the most successful American manufacturers of his time.

More textile mills appeared on the New England landscape as American entrepreneurs followed Slater's example. Textiles, especially cotton, became the principal factory-made goods of the 19th century. In 1814, industrialist Francis Cabot Lowell established a cotton mill at Waltham, Massachusetts, that was a technological wonder: workers in Lowell's mill completed every step in the manufacturing process, transforming raw cotton fiber into finished cloth, under a single roof. After Parliament lifted its ban on emigration for textile workers in 1825, American employers renewed their efforts to bring British workers and machinery to the United States.

Industrialization in America was not confined to textiles. The Industrial Revolution affected every kind of manufacturing. Eli Whitney, the inventor of the cotton gin, also applied his mind to the manufacture of firearms. In 1798, contracting to supply the federal government with 10,000 muskets, Whitney built a factory near New Haven, Connecticut, where he devised a way to make firearms with interchangeable parts. In so doing, he originated the assembly line, wherein each worker completes a single aspect of the overall manufacturing process. The concept of interchangeable parts was applied to the manufacture of plows, as previously described, and around 1820 to the making of timepieces. In the 1850s, workers at a factory in Waltham, Massachusetts, were using machinery to complete all the steps of watchmaking within a single factory. Thus, the key feature of the modern factory system, the mass production of standardized articles, was already in place by the mid-19th century.

Elias Howe's invention of the sewing machine, which he patented in 1846, enabled the garment industry to expand rapidly, and it turned the home into a small factory. The demand for uniforms during the Civil War led to standardized sizing, a necessity for the production of ready-made clothing. Labor now was subdivided to the degree that 17 machine operators might make a pair of trousers that previously would have been the handiwork of a single tailor. Cloth was cut to patterns in the manufacturer's shop and then pieced together by workers at home, each of whom had a single, specific task to perform.

The military's urgent need for shoes spurred the invention of shoe-stitching machinery. By the 1870s, shoemakers had moved from their cottages to factories. There were no more apprentices and journeymen among them, but binders, burnishers, cutters, bottomers, and other specialists—all of them enduring the drudgery and monotony of factory work as they performed small steps in the finely divided process of making shoes.

With machinery doing the actual work of manufacturing, skills lost their value. Some crafts, such as making cigars or felt hats, gradually disappeared from the American scene. Factory owners resorted to cheaper unskilled and semiskilled labor, and the apprentice system broke down. Many of the new factory hands had formed work habits that were at odds with the expectations of their employers. They thought nothing of taking time off to go hunting, help farmers with the harvest, or attend a celebration. They received their pay on Saturdays and immediately drank up so much of it that little work was completed on "blue Monday," which was a day of recuperation. Some employers fined their workers for drunkenness, absenteeism, and low productivity, while others rewarded steady work with gifts, such as new boots.

Because there were not enough adult males to fill all the factory jobs, due to the demands of agriculture, manufacturers increasingly hired women and children. Towns such as Lowell, Massachusetts (named for Francis Cabot Lowell), became busy manufacturing centers. Lowell, incorporated in 1836, was situated at the confluence of the Concord and Merrimack Rivers, where there was abundant water to power the machinery for carding and spinning thread as well as for weaving, dyeing, printing, and bleaching cloth. The typical New England mill was a large brick structure, five or six stories tall, employing 250 to 300 people. There were 32 such mills in Lowell in 1840, owned by 10 firms. The mills provided work to more than 8,000 people that year, or 38 percent of the city's population.

Lowell's mill owners employed young women from surrounding farms, housing them in company-run dormitories to safeguard their reputations and ease the worries of their parents. Strict rules governed dormitory life. The women were expected to be inside their boarding houses by 10 P.M., at which time the doors were locked. Some companies required their workers to attend Sunday church services. In Lowell and the other mill towns, bells rang out to summon the women to work or to meals. Bells also signaled closing time and the 10 o'clock curfew.

The workers put in 12- and 14-hour days, except on the Sabbath, and earned approximately $3.25 per week in the mid-1830s. Most of the young women spent a few years working in the mills before leaving to marry, travel west, or find employment in dressmaking or domestic work. Few wanted to return to the family farm or to marry a farmer after getting a taste of town life.

The "Lowell system" immediately sparked controversy. Newspapers reported on what they called the unhealthful nature of dormitory living and mill labor. The women were working too many hours and given too little food,

TIME TABLE OF THE LOWELL MILLS,
To take effect on and after Oct. 21st, 1851.

The Standard time being that of the meridian of Lowell, as shown by the regulator clock of JOSEPH RAYNES, 43 Central Street

	From 1st to 10th inclusive.				From 11th to 20th inclusive.				From 21st to last day of month.			
	1stBell	2dBell	3dBell	Eve.Bell	1stBell	2d Bell	3d Bell	Eve.Bell	1stBell	2dBell	3dBell	Eve.Bell
January,	5.00	6.00	6.50	*7.30	5.00	6 00	6.50	*7.30	5.00	6.00	6.50	*7.30
February,	4.30	5.30	6.40	*7.30	4.30	5.30	6.25	*7.30	4.30	5.30	6.15	*7.30
March,	5.40	6.00		*7.30	5.20	5.40		*7.30	5.05	5.25		6.35
April,	4.45	5.05		6.45	4.30	4.50		6.55	4.30	4.50		7.00
May,	4.30	4.50		7.00	4.30	4.50		7.00	4.30	4.50		7.00
June,	"	"		"	"	"		"	"	"		"
July,	"	"		"	"	"		"	"	"		"
August,	"	"		"	"	"		"	"	"		"
September,	4.40	5.00		6.45	4.50	5.10		6.30	5.00	5.20		*7.30
October,	5.10	5.30		*7.30	5.20	5.40		*7.30	5.35	5.55		*7.30
November,	4.30	5.30	6.10	*7.30	4.30	5.30	6.20	*7.30	5.00	6.00	6.35	*7.30
December,	5.00	6.00	6.45	*7.30	5.00	6.00	6.50	*7.30	5.00	6·00	6.50	*7.30

* Excepting on Saturdays from Sept. 21st to March 20th inclusive, when it is rung at 20 minutes after sunset.

YARD GATES,
Will be opened at ringing of last morning bell, of meal bells, and of evening bells; and kept open Ten minutes.

MILL GATES.
Commence hoisting Mill Gates, Two minutes before commencing work.

WORK COMMENCES,
At Ten minutes after last morning bell, and at Ten minutes after bell which "rings in" from Meals.

BREAKFAST BELLS.
During March "Ring out"........at....7.30 a. m........."Ring in" at 8.05 a. m.
April 1st to Sept. 20th inclusive.....at....7 00 " " .... " " at 7.35 " "
Sept. 21st to Oct. 31st inclusive.....at....7.30 " " .... " " at 8.05 " "
Remainder of year work commences after Breakfast.

DINNER BELLS.
"Ring out"...... ....:..... 12.30 p. m........."Ring in".... 1.05 p. m.

In all cases, the *first* stroke of the bell is considered as marking the time.

The constant ringing of bells kept mill workers on a rigid schedule.
(Baker Library, Harvard Business School)

critics stated. The crowded quarters led to illness, and independent living increased the likelihood of "debauchery." Yet investigators for the Massachusetts Legislature found the housing to be clean and safe and the workers strong and healthy. The women themselves complained of too little leisure time and no opportunity to exercise; farm life had accustomed them to hard work. With the expectation that they would leave the mills in a few years, most felt little incentive to pressure their employers for better working or living conditions.

While the Lowell system prevailed in some New England factory towns, most manufacturers operated according to the harsher "Fall River system," named for another Massachusetts town. They hired children, women, and men; paid low wages; and offered no housing.

The number of children working in U.S. factories in the early 19th century is unknown. It has been estimated that children ages seven through 12 accounted for one-third of the factory workforce in the 1820s and 1830s, and that children under 16 made up one-third to one-half of the factory labor force in New England. Wages paid to all factory workers were low, ranging from 33 cents to a few dollars per week. Men earned the most, and children the least. In southern and western Massachusetts and in Connecticut, employers frequently hired whole families and paid them one "family wage." For that reason, men with many children found themselves in greater demand than those who were single or had small families. Factory villages arose in which nearly every resident counted on employment in the mills.

THE PERCEIVED BENEFITS FOR CHILDREN

Few people at the time objected to child labor. According to popular opinion, the factories and mills performed a public service, keeping countless women and children from depending on charity and burdening society. Besides, it was believed that work built character and benefited children morally, teaching them responsibility and thrift. The descendants of the Puritans reminded one another that idleness was a sin and industry a virtue. The people who benefited most from child labor, of course, were the factory owners.

Children put in long hours that included night and overtime work. Some were laboring 84 hours a week, just like the adults. Neither the machines nor the work environment had been designed for safety, so disabling and fatal accidents were not uncommon. Under the Fall River system, children regularly worked 16-hour days and endured corporal punishment if production lagged. Employers routinely beat women and children with cowhide straps, some of which had tacks driven through their tips. An 11-year-old Rhode Island factory girl reportedly suffered a broken leg after being struck with a heavy piece of firewood. Another child survived having a board split over her head. Again, these occurrences caused little outcry: it was accepted that adults needed to beat the devil out of children from time to time.

The one aspect of child labor that rallied early reformers was illiteracy. Children who spent most of their waking hours at work had no time or energy left for school. Socially conscious individuals feared that having so many Americans grow up unable to read would have dire consequences for the nation's religious and political life. People who could not read were unable to study the Bible, and those who failed to attend school never learned the duties of citizenship. American democracy would suffer as a result.

It is no surprise, then, that the first child-labor legislation dealt with the problem of education. In 1813, Connecticut passed a law requiring manufacturers to provide the children in their employ with instruction in reading, writing, and arithmetic, but the law was not enforced. Twenty-three years later, the Massachusetts legislature prohibited the employment of any child under 15 who had attended school for less than three months during the previous year. Other states followed the lead of Massachusetts and passed compulsory education laws, while Pennsylvania set a minimum age for workers in 1848. This law stated that no one under the age of 12 was to be employed in a silk, cotton, or woolen mill in that state. All of these laws were poorly enforced, though, because legislators and citizens were unconvinced that raising healthy, safe, educated children served the national interest more than having a ready supply of cheap labor did. The issue would be debated well into the 20th century.

POISED FOR CHANGE

American industry was on the verge of explosive growth as the Civil War ended in 1865. Railroads were rapidly linking distant regions, while mining companies were exploiting the nation's vast mineral wealth. The flood of immigration that was about to occur would provide cheap, abundant labor. In 1860, the United States lagged behind Great Britain, France, and Germany in the value of its manufactured goods. By 1894, the United States would be far out in front. Its manufactures would nearly equal in value those of Britain, France, and Germany combined.

CHRONICLE OF EVENTS

1733
John Kay invents the flying shuttle.

1750s
British weavers employ the flying shuttle, creating a greater demand for thread.

1764
James Hargreaves invents the spinning jenny.

1769
Richard Arkwright patents the spinning frame and establishes his first spinning mill.

1776
The first steam engine produced by James Watt and Matthew Boulton is installed in a British coal mine.

1784
James Watt's rotary steam engine has been perfected.

New England textile workers pose with their shuttles. *(American Textile History Museum, Lowell, Massachusetts)*

1785
Edmund Cartwright builds the first power loom.

1790
Samuel Slater opens a textile mill in Pawtucket, Rhode Island, employing British technology.

1798
Eli Whitney undertakes the manufacture of firearms with standardized, interchangeable parts and makes possible the assembly line.

1813
Connecticut passes the first child-labor law, requiring employers to provide instruction to children in their hire.

1814
Francis Cabot Lowell establishes a mill at Waltham, Massachusetts, capable of turning raw cotton into finished cloth.

1825
Great Britain repeals its ban on the emigration of textile workers.

1836
The manufacturing town of Lowell, Massachusetts, is incorporated.

Massachusetts makes it illegal to employ children under 15 years of age who have had less than three months of schooling during the previous year.

1846
Elias Howe patents the sewing machine.

1848
Pennsylvania requires all textile-mill workers in the state to be at least 12 years of age.

1860
The United States trails Great Britain, France, and Germany in the value of its manufactured goods.

1861–65
Military demands lead to standardized sizing in clothing and the development of shoe-stitching machinery.

EYEWITNESS TESTIMONY

Factories which can be carried on by water-mills, wind-mills, fire, horses and machines ingeniously contrived, are not burdened with any heavy expense of boarding, lodging, clothing and paying workmen, and they supply the force of hands to a great extent without taking our people from agriculture. By wind and water machines we can make pig and bar iron, nail rods, tire, sheet-iron, sheet-copper, sheet-brass, anchors, meal of all kinds, gun-powder, writing, printing and hanging paper, snuff, linseed oil, boards, plank and scantling [timbers or iron rods used in construction]; and they assist us in finishing scythes, sickles and woolen cloths. Strange as it may appear they also card, spin and even weave, it is said, by water in the European factories. Bleaching and tanning must not be omitted, while we are speaking of the usefulness of water.

Tench Coxe, Pennsylvania statesman and writer, A View of the United States of America . . . between 1787 and 1794, *pp. 38–39.*

Extreme poverty and idleness in the citizens of a free government will ever produce vicious habits and disobedience to the laws, and must render the people fit instruments for the dangerous purposes of ambitious men. In this light the employment, in manufactures, of such of our poor, as cannot find other honest means of subsistence, is of *the utmost consequence.* A man oppressed by extreme want is prepared for all evil, and the idler is ever prone to wickedness; while the habits of industry, filling the mind with honest thoughts, and requiring the time for better purposes, do not leave leisure for meditating or executing mischief.

Tench Coxe, Pennsylvania statesman and writer, A View of the United States of America . . . between 1787 and 1794, *p. 49.*

There never was such a spirit of Industry and Zeal, to promote Manufactures in this Town and vicinity, as at present prevail. Almost every Family seems more or less engaged in this way. There are now also at work a carding-machine with a three-foot cylinder, two spinning-jennies of 60 spindles each, and one of 38 spindles, and a mill after Arkwright's construction, which carries 32 spindles by water, from which machines, as well as large quantities spun by hand, Corduroys, Jeans, Fustians [sturdy cotton and linen blends],

Denims, &c., &c., are making. There are several other Jennies erecting for the cotton as well as carding and other machines for the Wool Manufactory, among which the Wool Picker and Flying Shuttle are improvements every raiser of Sheep and Manufacturing Family should possess.

Providence Gazette and Country Journal, *August 8, 1789, in William R. Bagnall,* Samuel Slater and the Early Development of the Cotton Manufacture in the United States, *pp. 36–37.*

After passing Beverly [Massachusetts], two miles, we came to a cotton manufactory, which seems to be carrying on by the Cabots (principally). In this manufactory they have the new invented carding and spinning machines. One of the first supplies the work, and four of the latter, one of which spins eighty-four threads at a time by one person. The cotton is prepared for these machines by being first (lightly) drawn to a thread on the common wheel. There is another machine for doubling and twisting the threads for particular cloths; this also does many at a time. For winding the cotton from the spindles and preparing it for the warp, there is a reel which expedites the work greatly. A number of looms (15 or 16) were at work with spring-shuttles, which do more than double work. In short, the whole seemed perfect, and the cotton stuffs which they turn out excellent of their kind. . . .

George Washington, October 30, 1789, in William R. Bagnall, The Textile Industries of the United States, *p. 95.*

Mr. Slater came to Pawtucket early in January, 1790. . . . Mr. Slater entered into contract with William Almy and Smith Brown, and commenced building a water-frame of 24 spindles, two carding machines, and the drawing and roping frames, necessary to prepare for the spinning, and soon after added a frame of 48 spindles. He commenced sometime in the fall of 1790, or winter of 1791. I was then in my tenth year, and went to work for him, and began tending the breaker. Four children of David Arnold—Turpin, Charles, Eunice, and Ann—also Smith Wilkinson, Jabez Jenks, John and Sylvanus Jenks, and Otis Barrows, were the operatives in 1790 and 1791. These children were from seven to twelve years of age.

Smith Wilkinson, Pomfret, Connecticut, describing events of 1790 and 1791, in William R. Bagnall, The Textile Industries of the United States, *pp. 158–59.*

It is worthy of particular remark, that, in general, women and children are rendered more useful, and the latter more early useful, by manufacturing establishments, than they would otherwise be. Of the number of persons in the cotton manufactories of Great Britain, it is computed that four-sevenths, nearly, are women and children; of whom the greatest proportion are children, and many of them of a tender age.

Secretary of the Treasury Alexander Hamilton, 1791, in Grace Abbott, The Child and the State, *p. 277.*

A cotton factory is a school for the improvement of ingenuity and industry; and the improvements in machinery, combined with industrious exertion, have had a tendency to raise the conditions of the employers, and employed, in this country, and in Great-Britain they have been raised to an unparalleled degree. It must therefore follow, that factories are beneficial to mankind, and ought to be encouraged and continued, while on the scale of society, the balance is favourable to general advantage.

Samuel Ogden, 1815, Thoughts, *in Gary Kulick et al., eds.,* The New England Mill Village, *p. 313.*

Place two men to work in one room and at one sort of work, and employ one by the day and the other by the piece, and you will find that the day man is a slave to time more than at his work, and that the piece man is actively industrious at his work, and *takes no note of time,* unless it be to think it short, when work he had allotted out to do is not completed. Take the weekly amount of wages paid to each one, and the quantity of work each one has done, and you will find that the day work comes the highest, and that the piece-man by working four days in a week, will earn more than the day man's wages amount to for six days.

Samuel Ogden, 1815, Thoughts, *in Gary Kulick et al., eds.,* The New England Mill Village, *p. 314.*

I hurt my hand with a large piece of timber: this is the first day that I have been unable to work with it; but tomorrow is Sunday. I think I shall be able to work on Monday. I am learning the carpentering trade. I have 5 *s.* [shillings] per day. . . . Journeymen's wages are about 12 *s.* per day; some that take their work in lots earn 16 *s.* per day. . . . The labouring people live by the best of provisions; there is no such thing as a poor industrious man in New York: we live

more on the best of every thing here, because we have it so very cheap.

John Parks, December 8, 1827, in Benjamin Smith, ed., Twenty-Four Letters from Labourers in America to Their Friends in England, *p. 28.*

Yesterday morning Father had Notice to Quit as they are going to have all their work done by Girls. . . . Now you see the Fruits of Large Factorys. Here we are supplanted by Females that is expected to perform the same quantity of work for one half the wages the quality being out of the question. Here we are driven from one Factory to another seeking rest and finding none and when we are in work at what we may call decent wages they have so many different ways to get it all back again that it is impossible to save any thing. The very highest rents fuel Provisions wearing apparrel and every thing else at the very highest prices. The only way to remedy this is unite ourslves [*sic*] I mean our minds and bodily strength together to set about one thing at once and strive to accomplish it. I for my own part has got no money but thank God I am both able and willing to work.

Jabez Hollingworth, Woodstock, Connecticut, March 14, 1830, in Gary Kulick et al., eds., The New England Mill Village, *p. 378.*

It is a well known fact, that the principal part of the helps in cotton factories consist of boys and girls, we may safely say from six to seventeen years of age, and are confined to steady employment during the longest days in the year, from daylight until dark, allowing, at the outside, one hour and a half per day. In consequence of this close confinement, it renders it entirely impossible for the parents of such children to obtain for them any education or knowledge, save that of working that machine, which they are compelled to work, and that too with a small sum, that is hardly sufficient to support nature, while they on the other hand are rolling in wealth, off the vitals of these poor children every day. . . . [w]e are confident that not more than one-sixth of the boys and girls employed in such factories are capable of reading or writing their own name.

"Many Operatives," in the Mechanics' Free Press, *August 21, 1830, in Grace Abbott,* The Child and the State, *vol. 1, p. 279.*

In the preparatory process of picking over and assorting the sea island cotton, before it enters the machinery, there were more than 60 persons at work in one apartment, beating the flakes of cotton with sticks, in order to open them for more minute inspection. On suddenly entering this apartment, and viewing so many men and women, all simultaneously brandishing rods and beating the cotton, the loose locks of which flutter in every direction from beneath the strokes of the rods, descending with a deafening clatter, you may readily suppose that you are witnessing the disorderly scene of a mad house. The dust and small particles of cotton, floating in the air in this room, are almost suffocating, and must prove most pernicious to the health of the workmen.

> *Zachariah Allen, 1832,* The Practical Tourist, *in Gary Kulick et al., eds.,* The New England Mill Village, *p. 120.*

The proprietor of a manufactory in Manchester [New Hampshire] has many hundred persons daily entering his gates to labor, of most of whom he does not even know the names. He rarely troubles himself with investigations of their conduct whilst they are without the walls of his premises, provided they are reported to be regular at their labor whilst within them. The virtuous and vicious females are thus brought into communion without inquiry and without reproach. The contamination spreads, and the passing traveller is induced to pause at the sight, . . . to denounce the sources of present wealth, however overflowing and abundant, whilst the enriching stream is contaminating, and undermining the best interests of man.

> *Zachariah Allen, 1832,* The Practical Tourist, *in Gary Kulick et al., eds.,* The New England Mill Village, *p. 7.*

In a humid state of the atmosphere, the traveller is apprised of his approach to Manchester, when from the summit of some hill over which the road may wind, he first beholds at a distance the dark mass of smoke, which hovers like a sooty diadem over this queen of manufacturing cities. On approaching nearer, he views the numerous tall chimneys with smoky tops rising high above the roofs of the houses. A remarkable elevation is given to the vents of the furnaces, for the purpose of increasing the draught to render the combustion of the fuel more complete, and also to discharge the smoke into the air far above the windows of the houses. . . . When a slight breeze arises, this dark cloud is put in motion, and is borne away over the country in an unbroken murky vol-

ume, perceptible at the distance of twenty or thirty miles, like the long train of smoke which streams from the chimney of a steamboat, and leaves a dusky line extended far over the waters and shores.

> *Zachariah Allen, 1832,* The Practical Tourist, *in Gary Kulick et al., eds.,* The New England Mill Village, *pp. 116–17.*

From the earliest hour in the morning till late at night the streets, offices, and warehouses of the large cities are thronged by men of all trades and professions, each following his vocation like a *perpetuum mobile,* as if he never dreamt of cessation from labour, or the possibility of becoming fatigued. If a lounger should happen to be parading the street he would be sure to be justled off the side-walk, or to be pushed in every direction until he keeps time with the rest. Should he meet a friend, he will only talk to him on *business;* on change they will only hear him on *business;* and if he retire to some house of entertainment he will again be entertained with *business.* Wherever he goes the hum and bustle of *business* will follow him; and when he finally sits down to his dinner, hoping there, at least, to find an hour of rest, he will discover to his sorrow that the Americans treat that as a *business* too, and despatch it in less time than he is able to stretch his limbs under the mahogany.

> *Francis J. Grund, English traveler, 1837,* The Americans in Their Moral, Social, and Political Relations, *pp. 2–3.*

The progress of manufactures is most powerfully seconded by the inventive genius of the people. The daily improvements in machinery and the mechanic arts are equalled in no other country, and show the natural adaptation of the Americans to every thing based on the computation of numbers. In this consists the practical mathematical talent which every American possesses "by intuition," and which renders him, instinctively, a calculating merchant, and ingenious mechanic, an able navigator, and an inventive manufacturer. His mind is constantly occupied with some plan or enterprise; and being naturally inclined to mathematical investigation, he discovers daily new means of creating and increasing his capital, improving his trade, and constructing machines to diminish the amount of manual labour.

> *Francis J. Grund, English traveler, 1837,* The Americans in Their Moral, Social, and Political Relations, *p. 135.*

There are from eighty to ninety persons employed where I now am; two-thirds females; from fifteen to sixteen of the children are under twelve—and twenty between twelve and twenty-one. The youngest boy, I think, is about ten years old, and the youngest girl about nine or ten. . . . The labor of the children in the factories is very confining to them—they must be steady at it; the children are generally strapped if they do not attend to their work; it is generally done by the overseer of the room in which they are employed; I never knew severe punishment to be inflicted; they are punished for neglect of work—not for immorality. . . .

Testimony of Robert Kerr before the Pennsylvania State Senate, December 5, 1837, in Grace Abbott, The Child and the State, *vol. 1, pp. 281–82.*

Along our road, we passed villages, and often factories, the machinery whizzing, and girls looking out of the windows at the stage, with heads averted from their tasks, but still busy. These factories have two, three, or more, boarding houses near them, two stories high, and of double length—often with bean vines &c. running up round the doors; and altogether a domestic look. There are several factories in different parts of North-Adams [Massachusetts], along the banks of a stream, a wild highland rivulet, which, however, does vast work of a civilized nature. It is strange to see such a rough and untamed stream as it looks to be, so tamed down to the purposes of man, and making cottons, woollens &c—sawing boards, marbles, and giving employment to so many men and girls; and there is a sort of picturesqueness in finding these factories, supremely artificial establishments, in the midst of such wild scenery.

Nathaniel Hawthorne, "American Notebook, 1837–1838," in American Notebooks, *p. 34.*

Twelve years ago [Lowell] was a barren waste, in which the silence was interrupted only by the murmur of the little river of Concord, and the noisy dashings of the clear waters of the Merrimac, against the granite blocks that suddenly obstruct their course. At present, it is a pile of huge factories, each five, six, or seven stories high, and capped with a little white belfry, which strongly contrasts with the red masonry of the building, and is distinctly projected on the dark hills in the horizon. By the side of these larger structures rise numerous little wooden houses, painted white, with green blinds, very neat, very snug, very nicely carpeted, and with a few small trees around them, or brick houses in the English style, that is to say, simple, but tasteful without and comfortable within; on one side, fancy-goods shops and milliners' rooms without number, for the women are the majority in Lowell, and vast hotels in the American style, very much like barracks (the only barracks in Lowell); on another, canals, water-wheels, water-falls, bridges, banks, schools, and libraries, for in Lowell reading is the only recreation, and there are no less than seven journals printed here. All around are churches and meeting-houses of every sect, Episcopalian, Baptist, Congregationalist, Methodist, Universalist, Unitarian, &c., and there is also a Roman Catholic chapel. . . . [E]verywhere is heard the noise of hammers, of spindles, of bells calling the hands to their work, or dismissing them from their tasks, of coaches and six arriving or starting off, of the blowing of rocks to make a mill-race or to level a road; it is the peaceful hum of an industrious population, whose movements are regulated like clockwork; a population not native to the town, and one half of which at least will die elsewhere. . . .

Michel Chevalier, French traveler, 1839, Society, Manners and Politics in the United States, *pp. 128–29.*

Pittsburg is at present essentially pacific; if cannon and balls are seen here, it is because a trading people make it a rule to supply the market with whatever is wanted. The cannon are new, fresh from the mould, and equally at the disposition of the Sultan Mahmoud, or the Emperor of Morocco, or the government of the States, whichever will pay for them. Pittsburg is a manufacturing town, which will one day become the Birmingham [England] of America. . . . It is surrounded, like Birmingham and Manchester, with a dense, black smoke, which, bursting forth in volumes from the founderies, forges, glass-houses, and the chimneys of all the manufactories and houses, falls in flakes of soot upon the dwellings and persons of the inhabitants. . . .

Michel Chevalier, French traveler, 1839, Society, Manners and Politics in the United States, *p. 169.*

The population, which improves in its condition, as rapidly as it increases in numbers, creates an indefinite demand for the engines and machines, hollow-ware, nails, horse-shoes, glass, tools and implements, pottery, and stuffs of Pittsburg. It needs axes to fell the primitive forests, saws to convert the trees into boards, plough-shares and spades to turn up the soil once cleared. It requires steam-engines for the fleet of steamers, which throng the western waters. It must have nails, hinges, latches, and other kinds of hardware for houses; it must have white lead to paint them, glass to light them; and all these new households must have furniture and bed linen, for here every one makes himself comfortable.

Michel Chevalier, French traveler, 1839, Society, Manners and Politics in the United States, *pp. 170–71.*

The girls began to go to work in the cotton factories of Nashua and Lowell. It was an all-day ride, but that was nothing to be dreaded. It gave them a chance to behold other towns and places, and see more of the world than most of the generation had ever been able to see. They went in their plain, country-made clothes, and after working several months, would come home for a visit, or perhaps to be married, in their tasteful city dresses, and with more money in their pockets than they had ever owned before.

Augusta Worthen recalling conditions in the 1840s, The History of Sutton, New Hampshire, *p. 192.*

We know no sadder sight on earth than one of our factory villages presents, when the bell at break of day, or at the hour of breakfast, or dinner, calls out its hundreds or thousands of operatives. We stand and look at these hard working men and women hurrying in all directions, and ask ourselves, where go the proceeds of their labors? The man who employs them, and for whom they are toiling as so many slaves, is one of our city nabobs, revelling in luxury; or he is a member of our legislature, enacting laws to put money in his own pocket; or he is a member of Congress, contending for a high Tariff to tax the poor for the benefit of the rich; or in these times he is shedding crocodile tears over the deplorable condition of the poor laborer, while he docks his wages twenty-five per cent.

Orestes Brownson, 1840, "The Laboring Classes," p. 370.

The sufferings of a quiet, unassuming but useful class of females in our cities, in general sempstresses, too proud to beg or to apply to the alms-house, are not easily told. They are industrious; they do all that they can find to do; but yet the little there is for them to do, and the miserable pittance they receive for it, is hardly sufficient to keep soul and body together. And yet there is a man who employs them to make shirts, trousers, &c., and grows rich on their labors. He is one of our respectable citizens, perhaps is praised in the newspapers for his liberal donations to some charitable institution.

Orestes Brownson, 1840, "The Laboring Classes," p. 369.

It is no pleasant thing to go days without food, to lie idle for weeks, seeking work and finding none, to rise in the morning with a wife and children you love, and know not where to procure them a breakfast, and to see constantly before you no brighter prospect than the almshouse. Yet these are no unfrequent incidents in the lives of our laboring population. Even in seasons of general prosperity, when there was only the ordinary cry of "hard times," we have seen hundreds of people in a no[t] very populous village, in a wealthy portion of our common country, suffering for the want of the necessaries of life, willing to work, and yet finding no work to do.

Orestes Brownson, 1840, "The Laboring Classes," p. 368.

There are several factories in Lowell, each of which belongs to what we should term a Company of Proprietors, but what they call in America a Corporation. I went over several of these; such as a woollen factory, a carpet factory, and a cotton factory: examined them in every part; and saw them in their ordinary working aspect, with no preparation of any kind, or departure from their ordinary every-day proceedings. . . .

I happened to arrive at the first factory just as the dinner hour was over, and the girls were returning to their work; indeed, the stairs of the mill were thronged with them as I ascended. They were all well dressed, but not, to my thinking, above their condition. . . .

Charles Dickens, 1842, American Notes, *p. 65.*

They reside in various boarding-houses near at hand. The owners of the mills are particularly careful to allow no persons to enter upon the possession of these houses, whose characters have not undergone the most searching and thorough inquiry. Any complaint that is made against them by the boarders, or by any one else, is fully investigated; and if good ground of complaint be shown to exist against them, they are removed, and their occupation is handed over to some more deserving person. There are a few children employed in these factories, but not many. The laws of the State forbid their working more than nine months in the year, and require that they be educated during the other three. For this purpose there are schools in Lowell; and there are churches and chapels of various persuasions, in which the young women may observe that form of worship in which they have been educated.

Charles Dickens, 1842, American Notes, *p. 66.*

We are helping each other to get more good bread and meat (with the fixings) than we have usually had. We want plenty of good warm clothes, a plenty of nice, warm, clean beds, a plenty of coal and wood, to keep other people's houses warm, that we live in,

a plenty of good books, and time to read them; and our children to be better educated. We do not like to work all the time; we want recreation, as well as them that don't work, who go, many of them, to Saratoga, and other watering places. In a word, we are trying to get our just share of this world's blessings.

A shoemaker writing in The Awl, *August 21, 1844, in Paul G. Faler,* Mechanics and Manufacturers in the Early Industrial Revolution, *p. 182.*

Some [shoe-factory workers], I admit, will earn eight to ten dollars a week, at certain seasons; and perhaps there are some who will earn three or four hundred dollars a year; but take them as a class, it is not so. Let any manufacturer take his account book and examine it carefully, and make an average of the earnings of his workmen, and I fear not the truth of his investigation;

The Boott Cotton Mills, Lowell, Massachusetts, 1852 *(Library of Congress)*

he will find, that upon an average, as a class, they do not earn five, or even four dollars a week.

A shoemaker writing in The Awl, *September 25, 1844, in Paul G. Faler,* Mechanics and Manufacturers in the Early Industrial Revolution, *p. 92.*

There are many persons now employed in the art [of printing], who frequently, with great justice, inveigh in strong terms against the conduct of those unto whose care they were first entrusted, for suffering them to contract those ill-becoming postures which are productive of knock knees, round shoulders, and other deformities. It is deeply to be regretted, that those who undertake so important a charge, are not better qualified to fulfil that duty: instead of suffering the tender shoot to grow wild and uncultivated, when the pruning-knife, in a gentle hand, with a little admonition, would have checked its improper growth, and trained it in a right course.

What to a learner may appear fatiguing, time and habit will render easy and familiar; and though to work

with his cases on a level with his breast, may at first tire his arms, yet use will so inure him to it, that it will become afterwards equally unpleasant to work at a low frame. This method will likewise keep the body in an erect position, and prevent those effects which result from pressure on the stomach.

Thomas F. Adams, 1845, Typographia, *p. 87.*

. . . [W]e proceeded, without further delay, to one of the factories, that we might see the factory-workers as they came out to their dinners. And, to a stranger, it was an interesting sight. Several hundreds of young women, but not any children, issued from the mills immediately within view, altogether very orderly in their manner, and very respectable in their appearance. They were neatly dressed, and clean in their persons; many with their hair nicely arranged and, not a few, with it flowing in carefully curled ringlets. All wore (being the height of summer) a light calico-covered bonnet, or sort of caleche, large enough to screen the face, and with a dependent curtain shield-

Women operating power looms in 19th-century textile mills were supervised by men. *(Library of Congress)*

ing the neck and shoulders. Many wore vails and some carried silk parasols.

William Scoresby, 1845, American Factories and Their Female Operatives, *p. 14.*

Often have girls been so afraid of the "old man" they dare not ask to go out when sick, for they know he would have a great deal to say. Some girls cannot get off as much cloth as others; such ones are apt to be treated unkindly, and often reminded by the "old man" that "Sally and Dolly got off several cuts more the last four weeks; they come in long before the speed starts up and do their cleaning, and if you don't get off more next month I will send you off."

A letter in the Voice of Industry, *December 21, 1846, in Hannah Josephson,* The Golden Threads, *p. 221.*

As I grow old, and my health fails, and I find myself less able to provide for myself and live as I want to, and not be dependent on others, who have as much as they can do to provide for themselves (no doubt they would do what they could for me in an emergency, but I prefer to help myself, one way or another), I take the method you will find when it happens. I have enjoyed life as well as the most of men, but cannot bear the idea of being a helpless, dependent old man. I have paid my way so far, and owe nothing. Goodbye to all.

A shoe cutter's suicide note, circa 1848, in Paul G. Faler, Mechanics and Manufacturers in the Early Industrial Revolution, *p. 116.*

Unfitted to some extent for the purposes of commerce by the sand-bar at its mouth, see how this river [the Merrimack] was devoted from the first to the service of manufactures. Issuing from the iron region of Franconia, and flowing through still uncut forests, by inexhaustible ledges of granite, with Squam, and Winnepisiogee, and Newfound, and Massabesic lakes for its millponds, it falls over a succession of natural dams, where it has been offering its *privileges* in vain for ages, until at last the Yankee race came to *improve* them. Standing here at its mouth, look up its sparkling stream to its source,—a silver cascade which falls all the way from the White Mountains to the sea,—and behold a city on each successive plateau, a busy colony of human beaver around every fall. Not to mention Newburyport and Haverhill, see Lawrence, and Lowell, and Nashua, and Manchester, and

Concord, gleaming one above the other. When at length it has escaped from under the last of the factories it has a level and unmolested passage to the sea, a mere *waste water,* as it were, bearing little with it but its fame. . . .

Henry David Thoreau, 1849, A Week on the Concord and Merrimack Rivers, *in* Walden and Other Writings by Henry David Thoreau, *pp. 60–61.*

. . . [T]he Worker of the Nineteenth Century stands a sad and care-worn man. Once in a while a particularly flowery Fourth-of-July Oration, Political harangue, or Thanksgiving Sermon, catching him well-filled with creature-comforts and a little inclined to soar starward, will take him off his feet, and for an hour or two he will wonder if ever human lot was so blest as that of the free-born American laborer. He hurrahs, cavorts, and is ready to knock any man down who will not readily and heartily agree that this is a great country, and our industrious classes the happiest people on earth. The hallucination passes off, however, with the silvery tones of the orator, the exhilarating fumes of the liquor which inspired it. The inhaler of the bewildering gas bends his slow steps at length to his sorry domicile, or wakes therein on the morrow, in a sober and practical mood. His very exultation, now past, has rendered him more keenly susceptible to the deficiencies and impediments which hem him in: his house seems narrow; his food coarse; his furniture scanty; his prospects gloomy, and those of his children more sombre, if possible. . . .

Horace Greeley, 1850, "The Emancipation of Labor," in "Hints toward Reforms," pp. 2–3.

. . . [W]hat interested me most, was a visit to a cotton mill in the neighborhood [Augusta, Georgia],—a sample of a class of manufacturing establishments, where the poor white people of this state and of South Carolina find occupation. It is a large manufactory, and the machinery is in as perfect order as in any of the mills at the north. . . .

The girls of various ages, who are employed at the spindles, had, for the most part, a sallow, sickly complexion, and in many of their faces, I remarked that look of mingled distrust and dejection which often accompanies the condition of extreme, hopeless poverty. "These poor girls," said one of our party, "think themselves extremely fortunate to be employed here, and accept work gladly. They come from the most barren parts of Carolina and Georgia, where their families live wretchedly, often upon unwholesome food, and as idly as wretchedly, for hitherto there has been no manual occupation provided for them from which they do not shrink as disgraceful, on account of its being the occupation of slaves. In these factories negroes are not employed as operatives, and this gives the calling of the factory girl a certain dignity."

William Cullen Bryant, 1851, Letters of a Traveller, *pp. 345–46.*

At Graniteville, in South Carolina, about ten miles from the Savannah river, a neat little manufacturing village has lately been built up, where the families of the crackers, as they are called, reclaimed from their idle lives in the woods, are settled, and white labor only is employed. The enterprise is said to be in a most prosperous condition.

Only coarse cloths are made in these mills—strong, thick fabrics, suitable for negro shirting—and the demands for this kind of goods, I am told, is great.

William Cullen Bryant, 1851, Letters of a Traveller, *p. 348.*

This world is a place of business. What an infinite bustle! I am awakened almost every night by the panting of the locomotive. It interrupts my dreams. There is no sabbath. It would be glorious to see mankind at leisure for once. It is nothing but work, work, work. I cannot easily buy a blank-book to write thoughts in; they are commonly ruled for dollars and cents. An Irishman, seeing me making a minute [a note] in the fields, took it for granted that I was calculating my wages. If a man was tossed out of a window when an infant, and so made a cripple for life, or scared out of his wits by the Indians, it is regretted chiefly because he was thus incapacitated for—business! I think that there is nothing, not even crime, more opposed to poetry, to philosophy, ay, to life itself, than this incessant business.

Henry David Thoreau, 1853, "Life without Principle," in Reform Papers, *p. 156.*

Not the least interesting [about iron manufacture] is the beautiful and complete system by which every process and manipulation is so arranged that the most inexperienced person may follow the material from the heaps of coal, limestone, and ore at the upper end of the ravine, through the blast furnace, puddling fur-

naces, rolling mill, nail shops, packing room, to the canal below the plane, where the nails and other manufactured articles are shipped for market. This system is also evidenced in the fact that nothing whatever is wasted, from the coal dust, which is used to make soil, to the chips and shavings in the cooper's shop, which are used in starting fires in the puddling furnaces and throughout the mills.

"Among the Nail-Makers," Harper's New Monthly Magazine, *July 1860, pp. 154–55.*

The most favorable and interesting period for viewing the operations of the [iron] mills, as well as of the furnace, is at night, when the outside darkness brings out into strong relief the glare of the furnaces, and of the molten iron in its various stages of manufacture. When our friends, after carefully picking their way along the road from the hotel, over the plane, across rude bridges, down rickety stairways, crossing flumes and sluice-ways, and through narrow lanes between huge piles of "pigs," approached the front of the building in which the operation of puddling is carried on, they were struck with the diabolical appearance of the scene within. The furnaces and their attendants, at all times lit up with a ruddy glow, and here and there illuminated with a most intense brilliancy as they discharged their molten contents, which were run off on little trucks by men who looked more like demons in sulphurous light than like human beings; the noise and clatter of the machinery; the loud reports from the squeezer; the flying sparks from the "trains," as the iron discharged its cinder under the operation of rolling; the gloomy depths of darkness among the intricate beams above, contrasting strongly with the lurid glare below; the traversing carts and barrows; the shouting of the men; the noise of the forge as it labored to renew the tools of the workmen; altogether made up a scene of startling interest, and one not easily forgotten.

"Among the Nail-Makers," Harper's New Monthly Magazine, *July 1860, p. 158.*

. . . [T]he blast furnace . . . is a rude structure of masonry, some forty feet square on the ground by forty feet in height, having upon its top two large ovens in which the blast is heated before it enters the furnace. The chimneys of these ovens, as well as that of the furnace itself, vomit forth continually brilliant white flames, which at night time light up the hillsides with a sulphurous glare, that, taken together with the never-ceasing roar of the furnace and the mills, gives the place a weird appearance, and reminds one of the

>"Double, double, toil and trouble,
> Fire burn and cauldron bubble,"

of the Macbethian witches.

>*"Among the Nail-Makers,"* Harper's New Monthly
>Magazine, *July 1860, p. 155.*

During the last twenty-five years [1840–65], West Concord Village has undergone many changes. . . . The old tavern building is occupied as a boarding-house. One store, one carpenter's, one wheelwright's, one shoemaker's, two blacksmith's shops, a post-office, a station of the Concord and Claremont railroad, &c., are in the village, which contains sixty families, with a population of nearly three hundred. The former little pond, which was situated a short distance below the old saw-mill, and whose waters gave motion to a bark-mill, etc., has been greatly enlarged by the Holdens, who have erected just below it a brick building 130 feet long and three stories high, called "The New Factory," in which are manufactured extra white flannels. The old brick edifice below, formerly used for a grist-mill, was built by Dr. Peter Renton and John Jarvis, at a cost of about twelve thousand dollars, and converted by the Holdens into a factory for the manufacture of woollen blankets of an excellent quality. This mill was partially destroyed by fire, several months ago, but has been completely repaired with additions; both factories are warmed by steam, and the number of operatives in them is about eighty. The next mill below is called "The Mackerel Kit Factory," where twelve men are employed; they use five hundred cords of saplings in the manufacture of eighty thousand mackerel kits.

>*Levi Hutchins, 1865,* The Autobiography of Levi
>Hutchins, *pp. 139–40n.*

"Hurry up" is a phrase in the mouth of every person in the United States who requires expedition in business. This short expression fitly represents the tumbling go-ahead and spasmodic character of all classes of the people. Work, work, and work is the everlasting routine of every day life. In those trades and professions in which men are paid by the piece the application to labour by numbers of the men would almost seem to be a matter of life and death. To say that these people are extremely industrious would by no means convey a correct idea of their habits; the fact is they are selfish and savagely wild in devouring their work. If my reader can imagine a ship's crew almost famished by hunger struggling for the last biscuit it would give no bad notion of the continued craving desire manifested by the men to hurry their work and grasp all they can. In the establishment where I was myself employed there were men making from twenty to thirty dollars a week, and yet, such is the selfishness often engendered by prosperity, they were never satisfied. Many of the boys, to judge from the reckless manner in which they exhaust their physical energies, seem resolved not to be overtaken by old age.

>*James Dawson Burn, English traveler, 1865,* Three
>Years among the Working-Classes in the
>United States during the War, *p. 11.*

Q. Have you a child working in the mills?
A. Yes, I have. . . .
Q. Does he get any schooling now?
A. When he gets done the mill he is ready to go to bed. He has to be in the mill ten minutes before we start up, to wind spindles. Then he starts about his own work and keeps on till dinner time. Then he goes home, starts again at one and works till seven. When he's done he's tired enough to go to bed. Some days he has to clean and help scour during dinner hour. . . . Some days he has to clean spindles. Saturdays he's in all day.

>*Testimony of John Wild of Fall River, Massachusetts,*
>*before the Massachusetts State Legislature, 1866,*
>*in Edith Abbott, "A Study of the Early History*
>*of Child Labor in America," p. 34n.*

>With all New-Englanders an honest pride
>In the provincial energy and sense;
>But this was waste,—this woman-faculty
>Tied to machinery, part of the machine
>That wove cloth, when it might be clothing hearts
>And minds with queenly raiment. She foresaw
>The time must come when mind itself would yield
>To the machine, or leave the work to hands
>Which were hands only.

>*Lucy Larcom, 1875,* An Idyl of Work, *p. 142.*

I never cared much for machinery. The buzzing and hissing and whizzing of pulleys and rollers and spindles and flyers around me often grew tiresome. I could not see into their complications, or feel interested in them. But in a room below us we were sometimes allowed to peer in through a sort of blind door at the great water-wheel that carried the works of the whole mill. It was so huge that we could only watch a few of its spokes at a time, and part of its dripping rim, moving with a slow, measured strength through the darkness that shut it in. . . .

There were compensations for being shut in to daily toil so early. The mill itself had its lessons for us. But it was not, and could not be, the right sort of life for a child. . . .

> *Lucy Larcom, 1889,* A New England Girlhood, *pp. 154–55.*

I had been to school constantly until I was about ten years of age, when my mother, feeling obliged to have help in her work besides what I could give, and also needing the money which I could earn, allowed me, at my urgent request (for I wanted to earn *money* like the other little girls), to go to work in the mill. I worked first in the spinning-room as a "doffer." The doffers were the very youngest girls, whose work was to doff, or take off, the full bobbins, and replace them with the empty ones.

I can see myself now, racing down the alley, between the spinning-frames, carrying in front of me a bobbin-box bigger than I was. These mites had to be very swift in their movements, so as not to keep the spinning-frames stopped long, and they worked only about fifteen minutes in every hour. The rest of the time was their own, and when the overseer was kind they were allowed to read, knit, or even to go outside the mill-yard to play.

> *Harriet H. Robinson, 1898,* Loom and Spindle, *p. 30.*

4

Building a Transportation Network
1794–1900

Nineteenth-century Americans cleared forests and put in crops from the East Coast to the Mississippi River, altering forever the landscape of their nation. They turned over sod on the prairies and seeded the South with cotton clear into Texas. They built factories along eastern waterways and founded cities that overlooked the Pacific Ocean. None of these changes would have been possible without a revolution in transportation, without ways to move people and supplies to the nation's interior and get crops and manufactured goods to market.

In 1790, the year of the first U.S. census, the population of the United States totaled nearly 900,000. Just 83 years had passed since the founding of the first permanent English settlement in North America, Jamestown, Virginia, and many people still lived in communities that were unreachable by road. Towns hugged the coastline or the banks of navigable rivers, with inhabitants relying on water transport to connect them with the larger world. Whether traveling by water or by land, the first U.S. citizens employed transportation technology that had changed little in 2,000 years. On land, they journeyed by foot or relied on animal power. Human energy or wind moved their watercraft.

Few communities could spare enough workers for road building and maintenance, so the roads that existed were poor and hazardous. Wagon drivers had to remain alert for stumps that could overturn their vehicles and for fallen trees that blocked their passage. In dry weather, road dust covered travelers' hair and clothes and irritated their eyes and noses. In times of rain or thawing, roadway mud could be deep enough to stop horses and coach wheels. Sometimes logs were placed side by side over chronically wet spots to make what was called a corduroy road. This solution was hard on horses and uncomfortable for coach passengers, but it was an improvement nonetheless.

Shipping over roads such as these was an expensive undertaking. It cost $9 to move one ton of cargo 30 miles overland in 1800. For the same fee, an exporter could ship a ton of cargo across 3,000 miles of ocean. Transporting commodities on inland waterways ran into money, too. It cost $100 per ton and took three months to move goods by river from Cincinnati to New Orleans in 1814. The return trip, running against the current, was five to six times as costly. A bushel of wheat raised in the Old Northwest was worth 50 cents at a Great Lakes port, but getting it to market in New York City cost 75 cents or more. Such high shipping expenses added to the prices paid by consumers and cut into producers' profits. They caused some growers to decide that shipping their produce east was simply too costly to be worthwhile.

THE NATIONAL ROAD

In 1794, laborers finished work on the Lancaster Road, the nation's first privately built stone-paved turnpike; it connected Philadelphia and Lancaster, Pennsylvania. With the Louisiana Purchase of 1803, it was clear that further highway development was needed. The United States covered about 2 million square miles, but most of that area remained inaccessible. Few navigable rivers flowed out of the interior, and only a handful of primitive trails extended west beyond the Appalachian Mountains. In 1808, the federal government funded the National Road, which was intended to connect East Coast cities with the region west of the Appalachians and north of the Ohio River. The new road was to begin in Cumberland, Maryland, site of a mountain pass, and to end at the Mississippi River or beyond. Its eastern terminus would link with existing roads to Washington and Baltimore.

Immediately, the project captured the public's imagination. People talked with wonder about "Uncle Sam's Road," "the Great Western Road," or simply "the Road." President Thomas Jefferson foresaw a day when travelers could complete the journey from Washington to St. Louis in a mere six days.

For nearly three decades, building the road provided employment for thousands of workers. Surveyors spent two years laying out the route that the first section of road, from Cumberland to Brownsville, Pennsylvania, would follow. The actual construction began in 1811. Laborers wielding axes felled trees to cut a swath 66 feet wide through forests. They uprooted the undergrowth by hand and used horses and oxen to pull out stumps. Clearing a small strip of heavily timbered land in this way could take weeks. The work crews, which were composed almost entirely of Irish and Welsh immigrants, leveled the roadbed with picks and shovels, hauled off wagonloads of soil and rock, cut away hillsides, and filled natural depressions.

They paved the road using a method devised by a French engineer, Pierre Tresaguet, in the 1770s. Wearing metal face guards as protection against rock dust and chips, workers broke stones with long hammers from sunrise until darkness. Using standardized rings to measure the rocks, they selected stones that were seven inches in diameter to form the bottom layer of the road. They hammered these into place and topped them with a layer of three-inch rocks, which were also hammered in tightly. Constructing the road involved building stone bridges, such as the Little Crossings Bridge over the Casselman River in Maryland. With an arch that cleared 80 feet, it was the largest in the United States at that time.

By 1818, the National Road had reached the east bank of the Ohio River. It had cost $13,000 per mile to build, on average, which was more than double the projected expenditure of $6,000 per mile. In 1839, the road terminated at the capital of Illinois, Vandalia, and construction halted. People already had been using sections of the road as they were completed. In 1832, the citizens of

Richmond, Indiana, counted between 40 and 100 wagons passing through their town every day. More than 190,000 head of livestock were driven past the toll-house at Zanesville, Ohio, on their way to eastern markets. Merchants opened stores and inns along the route, and new settlements grew up around them.

STEAMBOATS AND CANALS

The steam engine not only transformed manufacturing, it improved transportation and furthered settlement as well. The first financially successful steam-powered riverboat in the United States, Robert Fulton's *North River Steamboat* (later called the *Clermont*), was launched on August 17, 1807, to carry passengers on New York's Hudson River. With two large paddlewheels turning at its sides, it completed the 150-mile trip from New York City to Albany in 24 hours. By 1820, fast, trim steamboats moved people and light cargoes along eastern rivers and up and down the Atlantic coast. The sturdy steamboats that navigated western rivers were built to handle heavy loads yet not run aground in shallow water. They transported grain and cotton to ports downriver and carried tools, cloth, traps, guns, and other supplies upstream at affordable rates. The 17 steamboats that maneuvered the Ohio-Mississippi River system in 1817 were capable of moving a combined weight of 3,290 tons. In 1855, 727 steamboats with a combined tonnage of 170,000 operated regularly along that river system.

It was not improved roads or the proliferation of steamboats that spurred the first great transportation boom of the 19th century, however, but a motion passed by the New York State Legislature in April 1817. At that time, the legislature authorized construction of a canal connecting the city of Buffalo with the state capital, Albany, 363 miles to the east. The proposed canal would link two important waterways, Lake Erie and the Hudson River, giving farmers in the Ohio River valley easier access to urban markets and seaports. With the canal, bulky freight such as grain could be shipped east by water from Cleveland, Toledo, and Chicago, which were the regional trading centers.

Construction of the Erie Canal began officially on July 4, 1817, when a judge by the name of John Richardson, the winner of the first contract to build a section of the artificial waterway, ceremoniously raised a shovel of dirt, according to an account in the *Utica Gazette*. The work continued for eight years. Some 9,000 common laborers cut down trees, dug out their roots, shoveled and piled earth, blasted away rock formations with gunpowder, moved boulders, rechanneled streams, and molded a canal bed four feet deep and 40 feet wide. To create the "deep cut" at Lockport, workers blasted a three-mile length of canal bed into a mountainside.

Working on the canal was a risky undertaking. Exploding gunpowder, collapsing canal walls, and falls from locks and aqueducts killed or injured many workers. The crew was exposed to severe weather in winter and contagious diseases in summer. An unidentified illness struck more than 1,000 men working near a 30-mile stretch of swamp in the summer of 1819. Most recovered, but several workers died. There were reports, too, of drunken workers falling into the canal's four feet of water and drowning.

Immigrants from Ireland, Great Britain, Germany, and other European countries did much of the most dangerous and difficult work. The exact ethnic makeup of the labor force is unknown, though, because contractors kept no such records. A job on the canal carried no prestige; the public perceived that canal laborers did work comparable to that of southern slaves and looked down on them for it.

People from a variety of callings found ways to contribute to the project's success. Merchants and speculators, who admittedly hoped to profit from the venture, lobbied for the canal and donated necessary land. Farmers, too, relinquished acreage, and many of them labored on the canal for part of the year. Women living along the canal route did their part by providing room and board to workers. Blacksmiths, stonemasons, and carpenters built 18 aqueducts that lifted the entire waterway over river valleys, and 83 locks to accommodate the 573-foot change in elevation between Albany and Buffalo. There were even "combined," or stacked, locks at Lockport to raise boats over a rock formation and lower them again for a total change in elevation of 60 feet. The engineers who designed those structures made up for their lack of formal training with a knack for learning by doing. Like most engineers and builders of their day, these men were more accustomed to working with wood than with the stone and iron required for much of the canal's construction. They devised machinery to pull up tree stumps, and they invented a waterproof cement when one was needed. Their innovations helped to advance building technology.

When the Erie Canal opened officially in 1825, it was already proving its worth. Teams of horses were pulling canal barges forward along finished sections at a slow but steady pace. Passengers moved at a rate of five miles per hour, heavier cargoes at two miles per hour. The canal cut travel time between Albany and Buffalo in half, to between five and seven days, and it reduced the cost of transporting goods considerably.

The success of the Erie Canal led to a flurry of canal building between 1825 and 1840, as other jurisdictions followed New York's example. Canals in eastern states connected inland regions with the seacoast. Others, like the Erie Canal, linked the Atlantic seaboard with the Ohio country. To the west, six canals provided passage between the Great Lakes and the Ohio and Mississippi River systems. The Illinois and Michigan Canal ran from the southern tip of Lake Michigan at Chicago to the Mississippi River near St. Louis. West of the Appalachians, moving goods by canal cut transportation costs by three-fourths.

By 1840, canals in the United States totaled 3,326 miles in length. Yet twenty years later, the age of canal building had ended. None of the canals constructed after 1825 had proven as profitable as the Erie Canal. In many instances, the revenue from tolls never equaled building costs. There were other problems, too. Heavy rains could wash out a canal, or its water level could drop significantly in summer and fall. Canal systems in the north froze in winter. What was more, the conditions that made canal building possible—relatively level stretches of ground and potential points of connection with natural waterways—were not to be found in every region. Large sections of the West, for example, were unreachable by water. Also, the major western rivers were notoriously tough to navigate. The Missouri River flowed over treacherous falls, and its sandbars were known to beach steamboats. Rivers such as the Columbia and the Colorado flowed through steep canyons and surprised travelers with rough, dangerous rapids. Many rivers underwent periods of flooding and drought.

The United States needed a cheap, reliable form of overland transportation and found it in the railroad. Railroads not only ended the canal era but made the steamboat all but obsolete. There were 3,566 steamboats on western rivers in 1860, but their number dwindled once the railroads arrived.

THE FIRST RAILROADS

Like the machinery in 19th-century textile mills, the railroad was a product of Britain's Industrial Revolution. In the late 18th century, the British used tramways to move heavy loads to and from mines; humans and animals pulled wheeled vehicles over cast-iron rails. Mechanics began experimenting with steam locomotives at the start of the 19th century. In 1808, an iron-mine mechanic named Richard Trevithick brought his steam locomotive, the *Catch Me Who Can,* to London, where the public eagerly paid admission to see the engine travel a circular track. But it was George Stephenson (1781–1848), an expert in coal-mining machinery, and not Trevithick who pursued steam-locomotive development. In 1814, Stephenson built his first steam locomotive for the coal-mine tramway in Killingworth, England. The locomotive, called the *Blucher,* could pull 30 tons up a slight incline at four miles per hour. Stephenson also built a locomotive for Britain's first commercial railroad, the Stockton and Darlington Railway, which opened on September 27, 1825, and transported coal, flour, and passengers on its initial run.

The first railroad in the United States, the Baltimore and Ohio, was designed to run from Baltimore to the Ohio River, following a route similar to that of the National Road. It was chartered in 1828 and had 13 miles of track in operation by 1830. The Charleston and Hamburg line, connecting the cotton plantations of Virginia and the Carolinas to the port of Charleston, South Carolina, began carrying passengers in 1831. By 1833, it had 136 miles of track in operation and the distinction of being the longest railroad in the world.

The original American railroads primarily served passengers. The technology necessary for carrying freight developed quickly, though, and by 1839 rail transport offered rates that were competitive with those of canals and Great Lakes steamboats and that were one-fifth to one-tenth that of road transport. Railroad tracks spanned 3,328 miles in 1840, almost exactly the distance covered by canals, although most of the rail miles were located east of the Appalachian Mountains. By 1850, the rail lines had crossed the mountains, spread into the Ohio and Mississippi River valleys, and entered Chicago, and they traversed 8,879 miles. Another decade brought greater changes: with about 30,000 miles of track, a comprehensive national rail network was in place. Trains carried nearly three-fourths of all goods shipped from Chicago and were largely responsible for the quadrupling of the city's population over 10 years. Some 30,000 people lived in Chicago in 1854; by 1864, the population had reached 125,000.

Canadians, too, experienced rapid growth in railroads in the 1840s and 1850s, as they sought to fulfill their own "manifest destiny." Short railways linked Canadian trading centers, connected them to forest and farming regions, and stimulated the development of factories and foundries in towns along their routes. The Great Western Railway and other lines tapped into the American market by providing direct passage between such cities as Buffalo and Detroit over Canadian rights of way. In 1861, the Grand Trunk Railway, funded largely by government investment and covering more than 1,100 miles between Sarnia, Michigan, and Montreal, with connections to Quebec and Portland, Maine, had become the longest railroad in the world.

The next great goal for American railroads was to join the East Coast and the Far West. Without a transcontinental line, it took six months to reach California from the East, whether travelers crossed the continent in wagons; sailed around Cape Horn at the tip of South America; or sailed south to Panama, journeyed overland, and then sailed north along the Pacific coast. If the western agricultural, mining, and timber industries were to supply the national market and do so profitably, they needed the railroads. But for people with capital in the mid-19th century, the question of investing in western rail lines was a tough one. There was no guaranteed profit in building railroads to undeveloped regions. Still, without the trains, development could not take place.

The first burst of western railroad construction occurred following the Civil War, and it was supported by federal subsidies. Eastern investment bankers funded a second rush in the 1880s, when they saw potential in competing with existing systems. The speed of western railway development is most striking in the cases of Kansas and Nebraska. In 1886, less than half of the track that would be laid in both states before the outbreak of World War I was in place. Three years later, Kansas had 90 percent of its 1913 total, and Nebraska had more than 80 percent.

THE FEDERAL GOVERNMENT PROVIDES ASSISTANCE

On July 1, 1862, President Lincoln signed the Pacific Railroad Act, which established a route for the first transcontinental railroad and awarded construction contracts to two railroad companies, the Central Pacific and the Union Pacific. The project would be funded through a combination of federal loans and bonuses, the sale of land granted to the railroads, and the sale of stock in the two companies to private investors. The legislation committed the government to lending the railroads $16,000 for every mile of track laid over flat ground, $48,000 per mile of track laid in mountainous regions, and $32,000 per mile of track laid anywhere else.

The Central Pacific Railroad had been formed in 1861 by a group of wealthy Californians that included Leland Stanford, who was elected governor of the state in that year. Their original goal was to build a railroad connecting the state capital, Sacramento, with the silver-mining region of Nevada and points farther east. The Central Pacific held a groundbreaking ceremony on January 8, 1863, but it did not begin laying track for 10 months, due to shortages of equipment and labor. Materials needed to build the railroad—from rails and spikes to locomotives—had to be shipped from factories in the East, and iron was in short supply due to war production.

Few men in California were willing to work for the low pay that the railroad offered. Many found it more exciting, and potentially more profitable, to prospect for gold and silver. The Central Pacific's general superintendent, Charles Crocker, suggested hiring a labor force from the population of Chinese who were coming to California in growing numbers. By 1852, the California

Chinese employees of the Central Pacific Railroad outside the entrance to the Summit Tunnel *(Library of Congress)*

Gold Rush had lured more than 20,000 Chinese to the West Coast of the United States. Some had found employment as domestic workers or farm laborers and repaid the cost of their passage to travel brokers from the $4 to $8 they earned per month, almost as if they were indentured servants.

But when it came to employing Chinese to build the Central Pacific Railroad, the company's construction superintendent, James Harvey Strobridge, would not hear of it. To his way of thinking, the Chinese were too small and delicate to do the heavy work that would be required of them. When Crocker pressed his argument, Strobridge consented to hiring 50 Chinese on a trial basis. After seeing the amount of work those 50 men performed in one 12-hour workday, though, the Central Pacific's management was ready to hire 50 more Chinese workers. As 1866 dawned, 80 percent of the Central Pacific workforce was Chinese. Nearly every fit and healthy Chinese man in California was working for the railroad. Leland Stanford was pulling strings, trying to bring 15,000 more workers into the country even though California had banned the importation of Chinese in 1858.

The white railroad workers ridiculed the "strange" habits of the Chinese, which included drinking boiled tea to avoid waterborne illness, bathing regularly, and donning clean clothes daily. Many whites dropped their tools and walked off the job rather than work beside the Chinese. To appease the whites, management assigned the Chinese to segregated units of 12 to 20 men working under white overseers. Each group had its own cook and a foreman who knew some English. The railroad also gave the white crews better pay. Typically, a Chinese worker earned between $25 and $40 a week, while a white worker received at least $40 a week.

The Union Pacific, which was going to build west and connect with the Central Pacific, held its groundbreaking in Omaha, Nebraska, in December 1863. Construction did not begin, however, until after the Civil War ended in April 1865. Once industrial production resumed in the East, steamboats carried the necessary tools, rails, and spikes up the Missouri River to Omaha.

The Union Pacific employed as many as 10,000 workers. Some had been Civil War soldiers—Union and Confederate. Approximately 1,000 were African Americans, including former slaves. Most of the rest were immigrants from Northern Europe, particularly from Ireland. Historians now estimate that Irish immigrants made up one-third of the Union Pacific workforce.

Laying track over the flat plains and deserts of the West was methodical work for the Union Pacific crews. Surveyors were followed by graders, who pounded the earth with shovels and broke up rocks with hammers and picks to make a firm, level surface for the track. Behind the graders, crews aligned the 500-pound, 28-foot rails end to end in two rows, measuring the distance between them with precision-cut bars and hammering them to the wooden crossties with sledgehammers. Locomotives then lacked the power to pull a heavily loaded train uphill, so the crews had to lay track around hills or create cuts through them.

Grenville Dodge, the Union Pacific's chief engineer, had experience in construction and surveying. As a cavalryman on the plains, he had fought the Sioux (Dakota, Lakota, Nakota) and Cheyenne. Dodge's construction bosses, the Casement brothers, Dan and Jack, speeded the progress of the Union Pacific with their invention of the supply train. This train, which followed the crew west on completed track, ensured that tools, rails, ties, and other supplies were constantly available at the point of construction. Horse-drawn wagons carried the rails from the train to the construction site. One car housed a blacksmith shop for repairing machinery and shoeing horses. Another held a dining table where, at a single sitting, 125 laborers could consume beans, bread, and meat dished out by company cooks. There were sleeping cars, too, with bunks stacked three high. But many workers preferred to camp in tents to avoid the lice that infested the sleeping cars. Towns went up slapdash along the railroad route, only to be abandoned when the construction gangs moved on.

Central Pacific crews, meanwhile, had the formidable task of laying track across the Sierra Nevada range. The laborers spent long days chipping away at rock and moving tons of earth to build embankments, one wheelbarrowful at a time. Crocker's workforce used explosives to cut 15 tunnels through solid rock, risking their lives to get the job done. The largest tunnel, cut through the 7,000-foot Summit Peak, was 1,659 feet long. Carving the Summit Tunnel took more than a year, with crews working from either end. Blasting powder was not powerful enough to break up the solid granite, so the workers used nitroglycerin, a dangerous, unstable explosive that killed some men and maimed others. (The number of people who died building the first transcontinental railroad is unknown.)

In the summer of 1865, Central Pacific crews began sculpting a roadbed into the 4,000-foot-high face of an imposing granite outcrop nicknamed Cape Horn by white workers who had made the long voyage around South America. Gaining access to the face of the cliff was the first challenge. To meet it, the Chinese wove a series of baskets, each large enough to hold a man, and lowered workers by rope from the top of the outcrop. The men in the baskets chipped holes in the rock, filled them with explosive charges, and then relied on their coworkers to haul them clear before the charges blew up. Not everyone survived, but nearly a year later there was a ledge along the side of Cape Horn wide enough for a person to stand on. From this ledge, the workers cut deeper into the outcrop, forming a flat surface that could fit train tracks.

The Union Pacific crews faced their greatest danger from the Indians of the region, who actively resisted the railroad's intrusion into the High Plains. The Sioux, Cheyenne, Arapaho, and other peoples of the region pulled up track, destroyed spikes, and ambushed trains. At Plum Creek, Nebraska, on August 6, 1867, a party of Cheyenne surprised five Union Pacific employees who were repairing a telegraph line that the Indians had torn down. The Cheyenne killed four of the men, scalped the fifth and left him for dead, and placed obstructions on a nearby track that derailed a freight train, killing the

The Cheyenne attack workers on the Kansas Pacific Railroad, in a painting by Jacob Gogolin. *(Kansas State Historical Society)*

engineer and fireman. As a result of this and similar occurrences, thousands of railroad workers took up arms or demanded protection from the cavalry.

The government applied a military solution to the problem of Indians in the West. Under leaders such as Civil War veterans Winfield Scott Hancock, George Armstrong Custer, and Philip Sheridan, U.S. forces raided and destroyed Indian villages and killed thousands of people. For more than two decades, the army would wage a war against the Native Americans of the Northern Plains, a war that saw the great majority of Indians killed or confined to reservations.

A RACE TO THE FINISH

Once the Central Pacific had cleared the mountains, the two railroads raced to cover ground, to get the most government money for miles of track laid. In 1868, the last full year of construction, the Central Pacific added 360 miles of track and the Union Pacific put down 425. So fast and furious was the competition that both railroads contracted with Brigham Young, leader of the Mormon Church, to have the Mormons grade the earth for a line of track across Utah. Railroad executives knew that only one of the tracks would be used, but they were too greedy for government dollars to care. Crews hurriedly

A crowd assembles at Promontory Summit, Utah, to witness the ceremonial driving of a spike connecting the Union Pacific and Central Pacific Railroads, as locomotives belonging to the two railways face each other on the track. Although most published accounts name Promontory Point as the site of the ceremony, writer David Haward Bain recently determined that the event occurred 30 miles to the north. Bain examined numerous original documents while researching his book *Empire Express. (Library of Congress)*

put down ties hewn from soft pine rather than oak, laid tracks that swerved precariously around hills, and built rickety wooden bridges that swayed dangerously in the wind or gave way on their weak foundations.

The two railroads repeatedly broke records for the amount of track laid in a single day. Charles Crocker of the Central Pacific bet Thomas Durant, principal stockholder of the Union Pacific, that his Chinese workers could lay 10 miles of track in one day. Crocker won his $10,000 bet on April 28, 1869, when Central Pacific crews laid a record 10 miles, 58 feet of track.

That same month, Congress established a connecting place for the two railroads near Ogden, Utah. When the two lines met at Promontory Summit, Utah, on May 10, 1869, the Union Pacific stretched 1,085 miles to Omaha, and the Central Pacific covered 690 miles from Sacramento. Leland Stanford and Thomas Durand, representing the railroads, pounded four ceremonial spikes, two of gold and two of silver, into the track connecting the two lines—although Stanford missed with the first swing of his hammer. The spikes of precious metal were purely symbolic and were later quietly removed and replaced with iron ones.

With the second burst of railroad building in the 1880s, small feeder lines connected with the larger railroads until more than 40,000 miles of track cut across the landscape west of the Mississippi. By 1900, four more transcontinental railroads had been completed. The Atchison, Topeka, and Santa Fe Railroad passed through the mining regions of Colorado before heading south to Santa Fe, New Mexico. The Southern Pacific Railroad ran close to the border with Mexico and the Gulf Coast, while the Northern Pacific connected Duluth, Minnesota, with Portland, Oregon. Canadians hammered the final spike into their first transcontinental railroad, the Canadian Pacific Railway, on November 7, 1885.

A number of speculators bought controlling interests in small western lines with the goal of creating national empires. The most notorious was Jay Gould, who had made a career of stock manipulation and fraud while managing the Erie Railroad in the East. Turning his attention westward in the 1880s, Gould bought up independent railroads in Missouri, Arkansas, Indian Territory (Oklahoma), and sections of Texas and Kansas. He put down thousands of miles of track in regions controlled by his competitors, hoping to steal their business.

Other speculators used honest tactics to build their empires. Canadian-born James J. Hill, who controlled the St. Paul, Minneapolis and Manitoba Railway in the 1880s, lured Scandinavian immigrants west by offering land at cheap prices. On one occasion, he imported a large number of purebred bulls from England and gave them to farmers throughout the Northwest. Once the newcomers had established themselves as farmers, Hill had a steady supply of grain to ship east and a guaranteed profit.

THE RAILROADS AND ECONOMIC DEVELOPMENT

The transcontinental railroads and the smaller lines that acted as tributaries to them stimulated western economic growth in two ways. First, the developing railroads were a market themselves. The railroads needed a great many wooden ties—approximately 73 million in a single year, 1890. These were increasingly supplied by the western timber industry. Western lumber also became railroad bridges, stations, and fences. Between 1870 and 1900, the railroads consumed one-fifth to one-half of the annual timber production in the United States. The fact that trains ran on coal encouraged coal mining in the West.

Second, the railroad network provided western industry with faster, cheaper access to eastern and European markets. Before the railroads reached Idaho and the West Coast, lumber had to be transported east by sea. The railroads aided the mining industry by reducing the cost of importing tools and machinery from eastern factories and by carrying ore from mines to the smelters. In 1884, the U.S. Geological Survey credited the expansion of the railroads into the Rocky Mountains with the establishment of many western mines.

CHRONICLE OF EVENTS

1794
The Lancaster Road is completed.

1807
August 17: Robert Fulton launches the *North River Steamboat,* the first commercially successful steamboat in the United States.

1808
The federal government funds the National Road.

Richard Trevithick brings his steam locomotive to London.

1811
Construction of the National Road begins.

1814
British machinist George Stephenson builds his first steam locomotive.

1817
April: The New York Legislature authorizes construction of the Erie Canal.

Workers in 1823 construct the Boonesboro Pike, a macadam road connecting Boonesboro and Hagerstown, Maryland. Stones were measured and raked into place. The surface was then compacted with a cast-iron roller. This painting is by Carl Rakeman, an employee of the U.S. Bureau of Roads from 1921 to 1952. Rakeman completed a series of oil paintings depicting the history of road transportation in the United States. *(U.S. Department of Transportation, Federal Highway Administration)*

July 4: Construction of the Erie Canal begins.

Seventeen steamboats operate on the Ohio-Mississippi River system.

1818
The National Road reaches the Ohio River.

1825
The Erie Canal opens officially.

September 25: The Stockton and Darlington Railway, Britain's first commercial railroad, opens.

1828
The Baltimore and Ohio Railroad is chartered.

1831
The Charleston and Hamburg Railroad begins carrying passengers.

1840
Canals in the United States total 3,326 miles; railroads cover 3,328 miles.

1850
Railroads service the Ohio and Mississippi River valleys and Chicago.

1860
Steamboats on western rivers number 3,566.

Union Pacific workers constructed this encampment beside the Dale Creek Bridge in Nebraska. (*Courtesy, American Antiquarian Society*)

1861

April 30: The Central Pacific Railroad Company of California is created.

Canada's Grand Trunk Railway is now the world's longest railroad.

1862

July 1: President Abraham Lincoln signs the Pacific Railroad Act.

September 2: The Union Pacific Railroad and Telegraph Company is formed.

1863

January 8: The Central Pacific Railroad holds its groundbreaking ceremony.

October: Construction of the Central Pacific Railroad begins.

December 2: The Union Pacific Railroad holds its groundbreaking ceremony in Omaha, Nebraska.

1865

May: Supplies for the Union Pacific reach Omaha; construction begins.

Summer: Central Pacific workers begin to cut the granite outcrop known as Cape Horn.

1867

August 6: In the continuing battle between the Plains peoples and the railroads, Indians attack a telegraph repair crew at Plum Creek, Nebraska, and derail a freight train.

December: Central Pacific workers complete the Summit Tunnel.

1868

Central Pacific workers lay 360 miles of track; Union Pacific crews lay 425.

The railroads employ Mormons as graders in Utah.

1869

April 28: Workers for the Central Pacific Railroad lay a record 10 miles, 58 feet of track in one day.

May 10: The Central Pacific and Union Pacific Railroads meet at Promontory Summit, Utah.

1885

November 7: The Canadian Pacific Railway is completed.

1900

Five transcontinental railroad lines have been built.

Eyewitness Testimony

So many and so important are the advantages which these States would derive from the general adoption of the proposed rail-ways, that they ought, in my humble opinion, to become an object of primary attention to the national government. The insignificant sum of two or three thousand dollars would be adequate to give the project a fair trial. On the success of this experiment a plan should be digested, "a general system of internal communication and conveyance" adopted, and the necessary surveys made for the extension of these ways in all directions, so as to embrace and unite every section of this extensive empire. It might then indeed be truly said, that these States would constitute one family, intimately connected, and held together in indissoluble bonds of union.

John Stevens, 1812, Documents Tending to Prove the Superior Advantages of Rail-Ways, *pp. 7–8.*

This work when accomplished will connect our western inland seas with the Atlantic ocean. It will diffuse the benefits of internal navigation over a surface of vast extent, blessed with a salubrious climate and luxurious soil, embracing a tract of country capable of sustaining more human beings than were ever accommodated by any work of the kind.

By this great highway, unborn millions will easily transport their surplus productions to the shores of the Atlantic, procure their supplies, and hold a useful and profitable intercourse with all the maritime nations of the earth.

The expense and labor of this great undertaking bear no proportion to its utility. Nature has kindly afforded every facility; we have all the moral and physical means within our reach and control. Let us then proceed to the work, animated by the prospect of its speedy accomplishment, and cheered with the anticipated benedictions of a grateful posterity.

Judge Joshua Hathaway, remarks at the groundbreaking of the Erie Canal, July 4, 1817, in Ronald Shaw, Erie Water West, *p. 85.*

The river, which is now rising, and open, displays a gay and busy scene. Boats and barges, some of which are schooner-rigged, are taking in or discharging cargoes. Flour is shipped here [Cincinnati], which you possibly may eat in London, and English goods block up the path along the shore. Some of these boats are

Excavating the "deep cut" at Lockport on the Erie Canal (*Library of Congress*)

manned by Sailors, and their cheerful shouts and *yo-hoing* make me forget I am 1,500 miles from the Ocean.

Elias Pym Fordham, English traveler, Personal Narrative of Travels in Virginia, Maryland, Pennsylvania, Ohio, Indiana, Kentucky; and of a Residence in the Illinois Territory: 1817–1818, *p. 192.*

Commerce is now carried on chiefly with the cities of New-Orleans, Philadelphia, New-York, and Pittsburgh. The lead is taken down the Mississippi in boats to New-Orleans, and there either sold, or shipped to Philadelphia or New-York. The dry goods with which this country is supplied are principally purchased at Philadelphia, and waggoned across the Alleghany mountains to Pittsburg, and thence taken down the Ohio and up the Mississippi in boats. The groceries are principally purchased at New-Orleans, and brought up in boats. Steam Boats have lately engrossed this business, and should they continue to multiply at the rate now indicated, will in a few years throw keel boats and barges entirely out of the question.

Henry R. Schoolcraft, 1819, A View of the Lead Mines of Missouri, *p. 44.*

Strike the Lyre! with joyous note,
Let the sound through azure float;
The task is o'er—the work complete,
And Erie's waves, with ocean meet—
Bearing afar their rich bequest,
While smiling commerce greets the west.

Buffalo Emporium and General Adviser, *October 29, 1825, in Ronald Shaw,* Erie Water West, *p. 185.*

We were situated half way between the Ohio river and the Ohio canal, when it came to be made, which was in 1825–6–7–8. That part of it nearest to us was in process of building in 1826–7, and this afforded work and money to the men who could do it during the winter, at prices they seemed glad to get and thought they were doing well to take. Hands were paid eight to ten dollars a month for chopping, digging, etc., receiving board and lodgings in addition; but every wet day was counted out, the laborer losing his time and the contractor the board. In this way, it would take all winter to make about two months time. It was hard earned money, but it was esteemed worth the labor.

William Cooper Howells, father of novelist and critic William Dean Howells, describing events occurring from 1825 through 1828, Recollections of Life in Ohio from 1813 to 1840, *pp. 138–39.*

Albany is a very elegant city, stands on a rising ground on the banks of the Hudson River; is a surprising place for trade. There commences the greatest canal I suppose that this world produces; which goes above 300 miles into the western country, and was all dug by hand. Before this was dug, great many farmers had to carry their corn and grain 2 and 300 miles to market with waggons; but now they can bring it into the canal, and then it goes to market for a trifle, by the canal-boats.

James and Harriot Parks, Greenbush, N.Y., March 16, 1828, in Benjamin Smith, ed., Twenty-Four Letters from Labourers in America to Their Friends in England, *pp. 29–30.*

The Roads are impassable—
Hardly jackassable;
I think those that travel ' em
Should turn out and gravel ' em.

Verse inscribed in an Indiana tavern register book, circa 1829, in Transportation and the Early Nation, *p. 61.*

All the dirt was moved in carts and wheelbarrows. Each teamster led two horses, one at a time, from the shovel pit to the dump, or tow path, where a dump boss directed to "haw gee and back." That was the command whether the turn to be made was haw or gee. The boss would throw his weight on the back end of the cartbed when it would tip down and shoot the dirt out backward and down the embankment, or on the level ground, or in a hole or sink according to the progress of the embankment. Then drives [sic] (or leader, more properly) would lead the horse and cart back to the shovel pit and turn and back the cart to the pit and lead the other horse and cart to the bank. While one horse was being led to the bank or tow-path, six to eight shovelers would be filling the other cart.

John T. Campbell recalling his work between 1832 and 1839 on the Wabash and Erie Canal, Indianapolis Star, July 26, 1907, in Peter Way, Common Labour, *p. 137.*

One of the greatest works now in progress here [New Orleans], is the canal planned to connect Lac Pontchartrain with the city. . . .
I only wish that the wise men at home who coolly charge the present condition of Ireland upon the inherent laziness of her population, could be transported to this spot, to look upon the hundreds of fine fellows labouring here beneath a sun that at this winter season was at times insufferably fierce, and amidst a pestilential swamp whose exhalations were foetid to a degree scarcely endurable even for a few moments; wading amongst stumps of trees, mid-deep in black mud, clearing the spaces pumped out by powerful steam-engines; wheeling, digging, hewing, or bearing burdens it made one's shoulders ache to look upon; exposed meantime to every change of temperature, in log-huts, laid down in the very swamp, on a foundation of newly-felled trees, having the water lying stagnant between the floor-logs, whose interstices, together with those of the side-walls, are open, pervious alike to sun or wind, or snow.

Tyrone Power, Irish traveler, Impressions of America during the Years 1833, 1834, and 1835, *pp. 238–39.*

The public feeling in the West, upon the subject of railroads, is excited to an extraordinary degree. The people of every town and county in the great valley, are now putting forth all their means to secure to themselves the advantages of railroads. . . . The west is now the great theatre of railroading in this country.

Editorial in the American Railroad Journal, *November 16, 1850, in* Transportation and the Early Nation, *p. 139.*

The frequent processions of barrowmen toiling their slow and weary way up the narrow plank to the sides of the cut—the high platforms erected for the cars used in moving the heavy masses of rock—the horse-drills keeping up their continual buzz as the poor, jaded animals tread to the ceaseless music, and the heated steel descends into the almost impenetrable rock—the noise of the blast which is so loud and frequent as to make one think he is going through the uproarious salute of a grand military reception, or that the 4th of July is perpetuating itself—the stampede among the men as word is passed that a fuse is fired—the scattering of the rock which follows the explosion, sometimes shooting innumerable masses of all sizes into the heavens, giving you no bad idea of Aetna and Vesuvius—the voices of the overseers and the louder utterings of the cataract, which all this scene of animation is preparing to overcome for the uses of man.

Description of construction on the St. Mary's Canal, Sault Ste. Marie, Michigan, Lake Superior Journal, *September 16, 1854, in Peter Way,* Common Labour, *p. 131.*

The men upon it are as thick as bees, there being fourteen hundred in all, and the work is going on bravely. Everything seems to be like clock work. It is quite a little spectacle to see the contrivances they have for lifting and moving the ponderous masses, which form the face stones of the locks, the cranes and the pullies, and the little bits of railroads high up in the air, upon which the stone are moved to their places, after they are raised to the requisite height.

Description of construction on the St. Mary's Canal, Sault Ste. Marie, Michigan, Lake Superior Journal, *September 16, 1854, in Peter Way,* Common Labour, *p. 235.*

Among the States of the Union, New York and Ohio have the greatest share of railroads: the former having 2795, and the latter 2725 miles. Illinois, indeed, is now but little behind them, and no doubt in a very brief time will surpass both, and possess more miles of railroad than any other State.

By means of the railroads, Illinois is in immediate communication with the East and the West, with the South and the North. The State itself is traversed by railroads in all directions—within one year's time, there will hardly be a single spot in it, from which one of the railroads cannot be reached within one day's travel.

Fred Gerhard, 1857, Illinois as It Is, *p. 427.*

Between 1 and 2 o'clock yesterday afternoon, the schooner *Artful Dodger* arrived from San Francisco and took a berth opposite the foot of I Street. She had on board the locomotive, *Gov. Stanford,* a quantity of spikes and other material for the Central Pacific Railroad. . . .

This is the first locomotive of the Central Pacific which has reached this point and numbers of people have been on the levee, looking at the engine which bears the name of the governor of the state.

Sacramento Union, *October 6, 1863, in Lynne Rhodes Mayer and Kenneth E. Vose,* Makin' Tracks, *p. 16.*

Yesterday morning the contractor laid the first rail on the western end of the Pacific Railroad, as described in the bill passed by Congress. Quite a number of persons were present to witness the work, though no notice that it was to be done had been published. Those engaged in the enterprise did not choose to have any ceremony over the affair; they made a regular business matter of an event which in the eye of the public is the first certain step taken in building the great Pacific Railroad.

Sacramento Union, *October 27, 1863, in Lynne Rhodes Mayer and Kenneth E. Vose,* Makin' Tracks, *p. 17.*

. . . [B]etween Plains and Pacific, in country and on coast, on the Columbia, on the Colorado, through all our long journey, the first question asked of us by every man and woman we have met,—whether rich or poor, high or humble,—has been, "When do you think the Pacific Railroad will be done?" or, "Why do n't or wo n't the government, now the war is over, put the soldiers to building this road?"—and their parting appeal and injunction, as well, "Do build this Pacific Road for us as soon as possible,—we wait, everything waits for that." Tender-eyed women, hard-fisted men,—pioneers, or missionaries, the martyrs and the successful,—all alike feel and speak this sentiment. It is the hunger, the prayer, the hope of all these people.

Samuel Bowles, Massachusetts publisher, 1865, Across the Continent, *p. 256.*

Men of the East! Men at Washington! You have given the toil and even the blood of a million of your brothers and fellows for four years, and spent three thousand million dollars, to rescue one section of the Republic from barbarism and from anarchy; and your triumph makes the cost cheap. Lend now a few thousand of men, and a hundred millions of money, to create a new Republic; to marry to the Nation of the Atlantic an equal if not greater Nation of the Pacific. Anticipate a new sectionalism, a new strife, by a triumph of the arts of Peace, that shall be even prouder and more reaching than the victories of your Arms. Here is payment of your great debt; here is wealth unbounded; here the commerce of the world; here the completion of a Republic that is continental; but you must come and take them with the Locomotive!

Samuel Bowles, Massachusetts publisher, 1865, Across the Continent, *p. 273.*

All hands worked from daylight to dark, the country being reconnoitered ahead of them by the chief, who indicated the streams to follow, and the controlling points in summits and river crossings. The party of location that followed the preliminary surveys had the maps and profiles of the line selected for location and devoted its energies to obtaining a line of the lowest grades and the least curvature that the country would admit.

The location party in our work on the Union Pacific was followed by the construction corps, grading generally 100 miles at a time. That distance was graded in about thirty days on the plains, as a rule, but in the mountains we sometimes had to open our grading several hundred miles ahead of our track in order to complete the grading by the time the track should reach it. All the supplies for this work had to be hauled from the end of the track, and the wagon transportation was enormous. At one time we were using at least 10,000 animals, and most of the time from 8,000 to 10,000 laborers. The bridge gangs always worked from 5 to 20 miles ahead of the track, and it was seldom that the track waited for a bridge. To supply 1 mile of track with material and supplies required about 40 cars, as on the plains everything, rails, ties, bridging, fastenings, all railway supplies, fuel for locomotives and trains, and supplies for men and animals on the entire work, had to be transported from the Missouri River. Therefore, as we moved westward, every hundred miles added vastly to our transportation. Yet the work was so systematically planned and executed that I do not remember an instance in all the construction of the line of the work being delayed a single week for want of material.

Grenville M. Dodge describing railroad construction between 1865 and 1869, How We Built the Union Pacific, *pp. 13–14.*

5,911 feet above the level of the sea—a higher altitude than is attained by any other railroad in America[—]. . . . Twelve tunnels, varying from 800 to 1650 feet in length, are in process of construction along the snow belt between the summit and Truckee River, and are being worked night and day by three shifts of men, eight hours each, every twenty-four hours—employing in these tunnels an aggregate of 8,000 laborers.

Sacramento Union, *December 31, 1866, in Dee Brown,* Hear That Lonesome Whistle Blow, *p. 77.*

Sixty years ago . . . the first steam-boat passed up the Hudson from New York to Albany. The news spread like wild-fire, although there was then no telegraph, and the banks of the entire river were almost literally lined with people, to whom the first steam-boat was a much greater wonder than the *Great Eastern* [then the world's largest ship] to the present generation.

Thurlow Weed of Catskill, New York, 1867, in William L. Stone, History of New York City, *p. 353.*

The track is making track across the trackless waste towards Green River [Wyoming] at a rapid rate. Moonlight nights and Sundays are drafted into service for extra hours whenever the material is on hand in sufficient quantities to keep the men at work. Towns along the road from Laramie west are engaged in a game of leap frog. From Big Laramie to Little Laramie; from Little Laramie to Rock Creek; from Rock Creek to Carbon; from Carbon to Benton; from Benton to Rolling Springs [Rawlins], where more shops are to be built; from there to Green River; and from Green River to Ham's Fork, Echo Canyon, Weber, Salt Lake—anywhere at all so as to be going somewhere and taking one jump farther than the town which was last in the lead.

James Chisholm reporting in the Cheyenne Daily Evening Leader, *August 10, 1868, in* South Pass, 1868, *pp. 50–51.*

The Casement Brothers are laying the track down a dry valley which is tributary to the famed Bitter creek, and they are now about twenty miles from that valley. . . . About three hundred and fifty men and sixty teams are employed in the construction force, and they average four miles of work per day.

James Chisholm reporting in the Cheyenne Daily Evening Leader, *August 19, 1868, in* South Pass, 1868, *p. 51.*

. . . [T]he Chicago and Northwestern road was forced through last fall in the most imperfect manner. It was flung down on the prairie at the rate of two miles per day, and, while the bed remained frozen, it did tolerably well. . . . The flood of the Missouri this spring was more extensive than usual, requiring, it is said, the oldest inhabitant to remember its counterpart. It put a score or more miles of the Chicago and Northwestern road completely under water, and floated it about, with its occasional rude embankments and improvised culverts, as if it was but a plaything for the Western elements. As the tide of spring travel had set in for the plains—ten times greater than ever before—the management could not afford to wait to repair the road and have trade seek a southern line to St. Joseph or St. Louis. Accordingly, it was announced officially, a week ago, that the road was repaired, while miles of the track were still frolicking with the frogs and other occupants of the ponds and lakes of the prairies.

A. K. McClure, 1869, Three Thousand Miles
through the Rocky Mountains, *p. 29.*

Whether [the Northern Pacific] shall be done or not, this great highway was an imperative necessity, and Congress, and those who have prosecuted the enterprise with such wonderful celerity, deserve the gratitude of the nation. It will make new fields to blossom where now are waste and desolation, bring fresh thousands of pioneers in the valleys and mountains along its line, and develop new sources of industry and new mines of wealth, until the bleak cliffs and the "American Desert" unite in swelling the triumphant progress of the New World.

A. K. McClure, 1869, Three Thousand
Miles through the Rocky Mountains,
p. 401.

Work is being vigorously prosecuted on the U.P.R.R. and C.P.R.R. both lines running near each other and occasionally crossing. Both companies have their pile drivers at work where the lines cross the river. From Corinne west thirty miles, the grading camps present the appearance of a mighty army. As far as the eye can reach are to be seen almost a continuous line of tents, wagons and men.

Deseret News, *Salt Lake City, March 28, 1869,*
in Lynne Rhodes Mayer and Kenneth E. Vose,
Makin' Tracks, *p. 123.*

The front of Casement's train is a truck laden with such sundries as switch stands, targets[,] . . . timbers for truck repairs, iron rods, steel bars, barrels, boxes, . . . straight-edges, wrenches[,] . . . cable, rope, cotton waste[,] . . . mattresses and an indefinable lot of dunnage . . . with a blacksmith shop in full blast in rear.

In the second car is the feed store and saddler's shop. The third is the carpenter shop and washhouse. . . . The fourth is a sleeping apartment for mule-whackers. Fifth, a general sleeping car with bunks for 144 men. Sixth, sitting and dining room for employees. Seventh, long dining room at the tables of which 200 men can be comfortably seated. Eighth, kitchen in front and counting room and telegraph office in rear. Ninth, store car. Tenth through sixteenth, all sleeping cars. Seventeenth and eighteenth, Captain Clayton's cars: the former his kitchen; the latter his parlor. . . . Nineteenth, sleeping car. Twentieth, supply car. Twenty-first and twenty-second, water cars.

Deseret News, *Salt Lake City, April 23, 1869,*
in Lynne Rhodes Mayer and Kenneth E. Vose,
Makin' Tracks, *p. 72.*

One can see all along the line of the now completed road the evidences of ingenious self protection and defense which our men learned during the war. The same curious huts and underground dwellings, which were a common sight along our army lines then, may now be seen burrowed into the sides of the hills or built up with ready adaptability in sheltered spots.

Fortnightly Review, *May 1869, in John P. Davis,*
The Union Pacific Railway, *p. 142.*

The whole organization of the force engaged in the construction of the road is . . . semi-military. The men who go ahead, locating the road, are the advance guard. Following them is the second line, cutting through the gorges, grading the road and building bridges. Then comes the main line of the army, placing the sleepers, laying the track, spiking down the rails, perfecting the alignment, ballasting the rails, and dressing up and completing the road for immediate use. . . . The advanced limit of the rail is occupied by a train of long boxcars, with hammocks swung under them, beds spread on top of them, bunks built within them, in which the sturdy, broad-shouldered pioneers of the great iron highway sleep at night and take their meals. Close behind this train come loads of ties and rails and spikes, etc., which are being thundered off upon the roadside to be ready for the track-layers. The road is graded a hundred miles in advance. The ties are laid roughly in place, then adjusted, gauged, and leveled. Then the track is laid.

Fortnightly Review, *May 1869, in John P. Davis,* The Union Pacific Railway, *p. 142.*

Track-laying on the Union Pacific is a science. . . . A light car, drawn by a single horse, gallops up to the front with its load of rails. Two men seize the end of a rail and start forward, the rest of the gang taking hold by twos, until it is clear of the car. They come forward at a run. At the word of command the rail is dropped in its place, right side up with care, while the same process goes on at the other side of the car. Less than thirty seconds to a rail for each gang, and so four rails go down to the minute! Quick work, you say, but the fellows on the Union Pacific are tremendously in earnest. The moment the car is empty it is tipped over on the side of the track to let the next loaded car pass it, and then it is tipped back again, and it is a sight to see it go flying back for another load, propelled by a horse at full gallop at the end of sixty or eighty feet of rope, ridden by a young Jehu, who drives furiously. Close behind the first gang come the gaugers, spikers, and bolters, and a lively time they make of it. It is a grand Anvil Chorus that those sturdy sledges are playing across the plains. It is in triple time, three strokes to the spike. There are ten spikes to a rail, four hundred rails to a mile, eighteen hundred miles to San Francisco.

Fortnightly Review, *May 1869, in John P. Davis,* The Union Pacific Railway, *p. 143.*

Engineering triumphs where brute force merely evades; the steam-engine has stronger lungs than mules or men; and the journey which was counted by weeks is made in hours. Such a feat as this, the Denver and Rio Grande Railroad (narrow gauge) is now performing in Colorado. A little more than a year ago I saw the plowshare cut the first furrow for its track through the cuchuras meadows at the foot of the Spanish Peaks. One day last week I looked out from

Laying Union Pacific track across the plains of Nebraska *(Library of Congress)*

car windows as we whirled past the same spot; a little town stood where then was wilderness, and on either side of our road were acres of sunflowers whose brown-centered disks of yellow looked like trembling faces still astonished at the noise. Past the Spanish Peaks; past the new town of Veta; into the Veta Pass; up, up, nine thousand feet up, across a neck of the Sangre di Cristo range itself; down the other side, and out among the foot-hills to the vast San Luis valley, the plucky little railroad has already pushed. It is a notable feat of engineering.

"A New Anvil Chorus," Scribner's Monthly,
January 1878, p. 386.

The canal and the railway have superseded the old national "pike," and it is not often now that a traveller disturbs the dust that lies upon it. The dust itself, indeed, has settled and given root to the grass and shrubbery, which in many places show how complete the decadence is. The black snakes, moccasins, and copperheads, that were always plentiful in the mountains, have become so unused to the intrusion of man that they sun themselves in the road, and a vehicle can not pass without running over them. Many of the villages which were prosperous in the coaching days have fallen asleep, and the wagon of a peddler or farmer is alone seen where once the travel was enormous.

"The Old National Pike," Harper's New Monthly
Magazine, *November 1879, p. 807.*

While the grading of the railroad bed was continuing south of Las Vegas, many camps were established along the route especially through the Glorietta Pass, and practically every camp had its saloon and gambling tent. Sometimes these necessary adjuncts belonged to the contractors, but where such was not the case the owners paid a handsome price for the privilege of having the exclusive right to conduct their business over the mileage under the control of certain contractors. Frequently, three or four soiled "doves," or camp followers, would have a tent or two at the rear of the saloon and assist the bartender in entertaining the patrons all during the night. Of course bad men and confidence men followed these camps and many an innocent wandering boy was relieved of all his belongings by running against them. Frequently, during these hold-ups the victim would become despondent over his losses, and either a killing or a suicide would ensue. In the case of killings, usually the right man got killed, and when that happened, rejoicing took the place of grief and the drinks were freely ordered.

Miguel Antonio Otero describing railroad-camp life in New Mexico in 1879, My Life on the Frontier, *p. 184.*

The train came all at once. There was no watching it approach as in a valley or prairie country. It strained and thundered triumphantly up the grade into a shouting tumult that frightened a grizzly bear in his winter quarters at Ragged Top, reverberated up and down the gulch and around the head of Terry's Peak, startled an old prospector who in his remote cabin on French Creek, did not know what was happening, and scattered out into the blue snowy valleys. . . .

The train came up beside the platform panting and heaving just as the six white stage horses had done the day before. But the train had come from Chicago in less time than it had taken the stagecoach to cross the old Sioux reservation from the Missouri River. It brought with it the speed, the luxury, and the easy contacts of the closing century.

Estelline Bennet recalling events of December 29, 1890,
Old Deadwood Days, *p. 299.*

5

The Mining Frontier
1719–1900

The desire for precious metals fueled some of the earliest exploration and colonization in North America. The Spanish, who used slave labor to mine a fortune in gold, silver, and precious stones in Central and South America in the 16th century, explored the southern regions of North America for greater riches. Francisco Vásquez de Coronado and others searched the American Southwest for the Seven Cities of Cibola, a legendary land of wealth and jewels that remained elusive.

Great Britain saw its first North American colonies as a potential source of mineral wealth. In 1606, King James I of England granted a charter to the London and Plymouth Companies specifying that one-fifth of all precious metals and one-fifteenth of all copper discovered by colonial settlers would belong to the Crown.

The native peoples of Central and South America may have fashioned statues and ornaments of gold, but the Indians of eastern North America made spear tips and arrowheads from flint, which they found on the ground or a few inches below the surface of the soil. Some peoples of the Ohio and Mississippi River valleys made tools and jewelry from copper that had been carried south from the Lake Superior region by glacial action. It comes as no surprise, therefore, that the English colonists did not find the precious metals that were so abundant far to the south.

THREE BASE MINERALS: IRON, LEAD, AND COPPER

The English colonists found some iron and lead, but they produced barely enough to meet their own needs, and certainly not enough to keep Great Britain well supplied. During the War for Independence, the Americans melted down pipes, window sashes, and even a statue of King George III on horseback to obtain lead for bullets.

After the Revolution, New Yorkers discovered iron deposits in the northern part of their state, near the St. Lawrence River valley and Lake Champlain. They built charcoal-burning furnaces for smelting and foundries for melting and molding the metal, and soon they were forging anchors, nails, and machinery for sawmills and gristmills. Iron mining and manufacture also became important in Maryland and Virginia.

Lead, the principal mineral product of the Mississippi River valley, was mined primarily by the French before 1800. In 1719, a Frenchman named Philippe Renault employed 500 enslaved Africans and 200 French miners at several sites in the region. His most productive location was the Mine la Motte, in the Ozark Hills of Missouri, which yielded an estimated 8,000 tons of lead between 1723 and 1804. In 1788, a council of the Sac and Fox (Mesquakie) Indians granted permission to mine lead on their land alongside the Mississippi River to a French Canadian, Julien Dubuque, for whom the city of Dubuque, Iowa, is named. Dubuque's workforce consisted of Indians, most of whom were women, who had learned their skills from Europeans. They used the simplest mining methods, gathering ore from near the surface or just below and collecting it in deerskin bags. They separated the lead from the ore by heating rocks and then splashing them with cold water to crack them.

In March 1807, the United States asserted its right to the minerals of the Mississippi River valley. Congress reserved all lands containing lead ore, authorizing their lease for mining. Colonel James Johnson of Kentucky secured a lease in the Fever River mining district, in present-day Illinois, in 1822. Employing experienced miners, including African-American slaves, he mined on a larger scale than anyone else in the area. An informal census taken at the Fever River site in August 1823 counted 74 men, women, and children. They lived in a crude village on a high riverbank that visitors reached by climbing a ladder from the shore. Many of the families spent the summer in tents and moved into empty mine shafts during the colder seasons. Scurvy, typhoid, and malaria continually plagued the mining families. Disease was so rampant that the inhabitants changed the name of their settlement to Galena, although the name Fever River derived from the archaic French word *forgeron,* meaning metalworker or blacksmith, not from fièvre (fever).

Word of Johnson's endeavor attracted a large number of prospectors to the region. They were soon digging everywhere, even on government and Indian land. Those who bothered to obtain leases paid their rent slowly, and the government expended little effort to collect it. In 1847, Congress voted to sell off the mineral lands.

Additional companies went into the lead-mining business and introduced improved technology. In 1864, the St. Joseph Lead Company first employed experienced Cornish miners to excavate lead at Bonne Terre, Missouri. These miners blasted ore from the earth, broke it up with hammers, and then crushed it to a powder. They heated the powder in reducing furnaces and poured the molten metal into molds.

Just as the French knew of the existence of lead in the Mississippi River valley in the 18th century, fur traders doing business near Lake Superior were aware of copper deposits in that region well before 1800. Serious copper mining did not begin in the area, however, until 1844. The Minesota Mine, which was discovered in 1847 and owed the unique spelling of its name to a clerical error, yielded the largest discrete deposit of copper ever to be found in the United States. It weighed an estimated 420 tons and measured 46 feet in length and 12.5 feet in thickness. Twenty men worked for 15 months to release it from the surrounding rock. In 1880, the mines of Michigan's Upper Peninsula provided the nation with nearly 50 million pounds of refined copper. Michigan was the major producer of copper in the United States until 1887, when the western states took the lead.

European technological advances increased production at U.S. mines beginning in the 1860s. In 1866, the Swedish inventor Alfred Nobel reduced the volatility of nitroglycerin, producing an explosive that he called dynamite. Miners quickly put it to use. The 1880s brought a French invention, the diamond drill, which was used to extract rock samples for analysis.

A Growing Demand for Coal

Coal was the chief source of Pennsylvania's mineral richness. In 1791, extensive deposits of anthracite were discovered in the eastern part of the state. Anthracite is a hard variety of coal that burns cleanly, with little flame or smoke. Most people, however, preferred to use wood, which was plentiful, as fuel. In 1839, in the town of Pottsville, Pennsylvania, Americans first used anthracite to heat furnaces for iron smelting. Coal quickly replaced charcoal as the fuel of choice in the manufacture of iron and steel. (Steel is an alloy of iron and carbon, often with an admixture of other elements.) Coal became an even more important commodity following the arrival of the steam engine, when it was used to fuel steamboats and locomotives.

Softer bituminous coal, which burns with a smoky flame, filled a great seam in the earth near the city of Pittsburgh. Pittsburgh's location, close to that deposit and at the point where the Allegheny and Monongahela Rivers join to form the Ohio River, enabled it to become one of the chief centers of iron and steel production in the United States. Coal mining began near Pittsburgh in 1784, and a manufacturer named George Anschutz constructed Pittsburgh's first blast furnace around 1792. Other business people built additional furnaces, foundries, mills, and factories in the Pittsburgh area, especially after 1850.

The annual per capita consumption of coal in the United States, which was 0.01 ton in 1800, rose to 0.1 ton by 1840 and one ton by 1880. Demand grew even more rapidly over the next 20 years as coal increasingly was used for home heating. Per capita consumption reached 2.5 tons by 1900.

The coal that kept Americans warm in winter came from three major mining regions: the Appalachian field, which encompassed parts of Pennsylvania, West Virginia, Kentucky, Tennessee, Ohio, and Alabama; a large Midwestern field that covered most of Illinois and portions of Indiana and Kentucky; and a third field that reached from Iowa through Missouri, Kansas, and Oklahoma.

At first, U.S. miners dug coal from the surface of the earth or scraped it from outcrops. Mines were open pits from which miners hauled coal by hand or with the aid of a windlass. Water seeped into the pits, and it, too, had to be removed. Underground coal mining started to gain prevalence in the 1830s, and coal miners increasingly worked deep inside drifts, tunnels, and shafts.

It took many laborers to keep the nation supplied with coal. Nearly 500,000 people worked in U.S. coal mines in 1890, including many European immigrants and children. Miners spent long days underground heaving picks, shovels, and sledgehammers. Boys age twelve and younger sat bent over on benches for 10 to 12 hours a day, separating pieces of slate from the coal that had been pulled from the mine.

Coal miners endured a life of poverty and hard work under dangerous conditions. Decades of breathing coal dust led to lung disease, which often proved fatal. A hazardous method called "room and pillar" mining took many lives in western Pennsylvania and elsewhere. Miners using this method removed coal from underground chambers or rooms, leaving pillars of coal in place to support the structure. As a final step, they removed the pillars, which contained up to half of the coal in the mine, and scrambled for safety as the ceiling collapsed.

The nation's first mining disaster occurred on March 18, 1839, when there was an explosion at the Black Heath Coal Mine near Richmond, Virginia. Of the 54 men who were in the mine at the time, only two at the shaft entrance survived. The blast was so powerful that a descending basket carrying three men was blown 100 feet into the air. On September 6, 1869, 179 miners died in Plymouth, Pennsylvania, when fire blocked the only exit from the Avondale Mine. These tragedies were just two of many. Between 2,000 and 3,000 miners died in work-related accidents each year during the 1890s.

A group of breaker boys, who had the dangerous job of separating slate from coal in the mines *(United Mine Workers of America Archives)*

Discovering victims of the disastrous
fire at the Avondale Mine,
September 1869 *(Library of Congress)*

GOLD IN CALIFORNIA

On February 2, 1848, representatives of Mexico and the United States signed
the Treaty of Guadalupe Hidalgo, ending the Mexican War. The treaty established the southern boundary of Texas at the Rio Grande and transferred
California and New Mexico to the United States. Neither the American nor
the Mexican signers knew that just two weeks earlier, on January 24, James
Marshall, an employee of merchant John Sutter, had discovered gold on Sutter's
property in the Coloma Valley of California, while building a sawmill on the
American River.

Sutter tried to keep the find secret, but his workers leaked word of it to
their families and neighbors. Many more people learned of the discovery in
May, when a local miner carried a bottle of gold dust to San Francisco. That
city nearly emptied of residents as soon as the gold went on display. The number of inhabitants dropped from approximately 1,000 to 100 as people rushed
to the Coloma Valley and the American River. Merchants hung signs in their
windows announcing, "Gone to the Diggings!" and closed their shops. Soldiers
left their posts, and sailors deserted ships in port. The desperate captain of one
ship, the *California,* kept his crew in chains until they agreed to stay on in
return for a pay increase of more than 800 percent. Within months, nearly
10,000 would-be gold miners were prospecting along a 150-mile stretch on
the western slopes of the Sierra Nevada known as the "Mother Lode."

Reports of Marshall's find traveled to Hawaii in June, to Oregon in August,
and to Mexico and South America in the fall. Easterners were hearing talk of
California gold as summer began, but few people took it seriously until
President James K. Polk confirmed the rumors in a message to Congress on

December 5. Almost immediately, people began to leave for California, journeying by ship or overland. Thousands would make the trip in 1849. Gold fever also broke out in Europe, Chile, Mexico, and China. In Australia and New Zealand, men packed themselves into every California-bound ship.

Nearly all of the prospectors—95 percent—were men, and most had little or no knowledge of mining. They engaged in placer mining, washing deposits of sand and gravel from streambeds until the heavy gold particles separated from the sand and settled to the bottom of the pan. The term *placer* is thought to derive from the Spanish *plazo de oro,* meaning place of gold. The prospectors worked with simple tools—a shovel for digging gravel and a pan for washing the pebbles. In time, some miners employed a wooden rocker to perform the same process more easily. A further innovation was the "sluice box" or "long tom," an 8-to-10-foot trough with ridges or cleats across the bottom to trap the gold.

Miners with capital used more ambitious methods. River mining involved damming a stream and diverting its flow in order to mine the dry riverbed. In hydraulic mining, miners washed the gold-bearing gravel bed with a high-velocity jet of water. A third method was quartz mining, or the underground mining of gold-bearing quartz veins; it demanded significant capital and a high level of technical skill. Prospectors learned the necessary techniques from Cornish miners and others who had come to California from mining regions in the East and Midwest.

The exact number of "forty-niners" is unknown, but California's non-Indian population, which was about 14,000 in 1848, rose to 223,856 in 1852. Towns where miners purchased supplies, such as Sacramento and Stockton, grew into cities, while rugged, sometimes violent camps with names like Skunk Gulch and Hell's Delight dotted the mining region. Sanitation was poor in the camps, and malaria, dysentery, and respiratory infections were common. The miners lived on coffee, pork, beans, flapjacks, and dried fruit. Card playing, drinking, and gambling were popular pastimes.

The prospectors inhabiting the tents and ramshackle cabins of the mining camps were often poorly equipped to survive winter in the Sierra Nevada, when heavy snows made mining impossible. Some died from exposure, and others lost fingers and toes to frostbite. Many opted to pass the winter in warmer coastal towns.

No federal law governed the sale or lease of land bearing precious minerals. Congress was too occupied with the growing crisis over slavery to take up the matter and so allowed miners to regulate their own claims. When federal legislation at last was passed in 1866, it largely conformed to the established local practices.

THE COMSTOCK LODE

In 1859, various prospectors trying their luck in the Washoe Mountains of Nevada, which extend east from the Sierra Nevada into the Great Basin, found evidence of a vein rich in metals, particularly gold and silver. The lode was named for Henry T. P. Comstock, a Canadian-born prospector with a reputation for laziness who was the first to lay claim to the land on which it was discovered. Once word of the find spread beyond the Washoe Mountains, another rush was on. Ten thousand down-on-their-luck prospectors left California for Nevada. Pioneers and drifters came from all over the country, and immigrants journeyed to Nevada from Europe, especially from Ireland and Cornwall, England. During the nearly 40 years that the lode was mined, a third of the workforce was Cornish, and another third was Irish. Only 20 percent of the miners had been born on U.S. soil.

The Comstock Lode also attracted saloon keepers and merchants who hoped to profit from any newfound wealth. The miners established settlements high on the slope of Mt. Davidson, the most notable of them Virginia City. Twenty-five saloons did a brisk business there. A miner could rent a blanket in Virginia City for a dollar a night and pay another dollar to sleep on a dirt floor.

The Comstock Lode yielded more than $300 million in gold and silver in the first 20 years that it was mined, but the majority of claims proved worthless or inaccessible. Digging the deep shafts needed to reach much of the lode required costly machinery, well beyond the budget of most miners. One successful prospector was George Hearst, who previously had failed at placer mining and storekeeping. He and his partners mined ore that earned them $91,000. Hearst's share served as seed money for the famed Hearst fortune.

In 1873, four men from Ireland made a lucky bargain when they took over the Consolidated Virginia, a mine that had been abandoned due to a lack of capital. At a depth of 1,167 feet, they cut into the richest mineral deposit ever to be found in the world. Known as the "Big Bonanza," it produced $200 million in gold and silver bullion.

Heavy timbers supported the deep underground mines of the Comstock Lode. The mining operation demanded so much wood—both for timbers and for fuel in the mining towns and processing facilities—that whole mountainsides were stripped of their forests. It has been estimated that mining the Comstock Lode consumed 600 million feet of timber.

The mines operated around the clock, with the day divided into three eight-hour shifts. Miners earned about four dollars a day and worked under terrible conditions. They risked injury and death from explosions, fires, collapsing mine walls, and machinery accidents. As the shafts and chambers reached farther into the earth, the heat within them rose. Temperatures in many of the mines topped 100 degrees Fahrenheit. At depths of 2,000 to 3,000 feet, temperatures passed 150 degrees Fahrenheit. Men stripped down to breechcloths, but they wore heavy shoes to protect their feet from the searing rock of the mine floor and the scalding water that often flowed over it. Every few minutes, the workers sought relief at ventilation shafts and cooling stations that had been provided for them. They stood under cold showers or draped themselves in towels soaked in ice water. One mining company consumed 1,000 tons of ice in its cooling stations in a single year. Nevertheless, men were known to drop dead from heat exhaustion while working.

Simply breathing presented another hazard. Levels of carbon dioxide in the mines were often high enough to cause dizziness, drowsiness, and fainting, which made accidents more likely. Carbon dioxide was also responsible for instances of suffocation. The atmosphere was rich in silver and lead compounds and in quartz, or silica, dust as well. As many as half of the miners working at the dry, higher levels of the mines developed silicosis, a lung condition that results from inhaling silica dust.

After 1873, extensive silver production in the West caused the value of silver to fall sharply on the commercial market. The U.S. Treasury was reluctant to buy silver at the official government rate (equating about 16 ounces of silver and one ounce of gold), which was inflated. For that reason, with the Coinage Act of 1873 Congress omitted the silver dollar from the list of coins authorized to be minted. Coinage of silver dollars resumed in 1878, but in 1885 President Grover Cleveland expressed concern that western silver interests had too much influence on the national economy. After the director of the U.S. Mint at Carson City, Nevada, died in March of that year, Cleveland stopped coin production there. Coinage resumed in 1886, but Carson City remained the least-used mint until it closed in 1893. By that time, the wealth of the Comstock Lode had been largely depleted. The great mines halted operation in 1898.

THE RUSH FOR GOLD CONTINUES

Rumors of gold and subsequent stampedes are a continuing theme in the history of the American West in the second half of the 19th century, although none, not even the rush to the Comstock Lode, matched the 1849 California Gold Rush in magnitude. Again and again across the West, mining towns were born, thrived briefly, and were abandoned as prospectors hurried away to stake other claims. Some mining towns endured and grew, however. Permanent settlers followed the miners to Denver City, as it was then called, in present-day Colorado; Helena in Montana Territory; and numerous other places. Along with the saloon keepers, card dealers, and prostitutes came lawyers, ministers, and journalists. Farmers moved into the fertile mountain valleys nearby.

Colorado City, a newly constructed mining town in the 1860s *(Courtesy, Colorado Historical Society; F-2782)*

In 1859, when the rush to the Washoe Mountains began, thousands of people headed for Pike's Peak in present-day Colorado. Prospectors from Georgia had seen traces of gold there in 1858, and eastern journalists had exaggerated the size of their find. By late June 1859, 100,000 hopeful miners had reached Pike's Peak. More than half headed home by August, convinced that they had been "humbugged," or defrauded. The Missouri merchants who outfitted many of them for the trip west made a fortune, but the Pike's Peak miners themselves made nothing.

Colorado did eventually prove to be a productive mining region. Eastern investors took an interest in the area around Denver and Boulder in the 1860s and excavated deep—and successful—mining shafts there. Prospectors found silver ore near Leadville in the 1870s and gold on Cripple Creek soon afterward. Colorado led the United States in mining in the 1880s and continued to dominate the U.S. mining industry for the rest of the 19th century.

Reports of gold-rich sandbars in the Fraser River drew 35,000 Californians to British Columbia in the late 1850s. But the prospectors balked at the strict regulations imposed by James Douglas, the first governor of the colony. Most irritating was the monthly tax of 21 shillings (about five dollars) that Douglas imposed on anyone wanting to mine. The meddlesome rules, coupled with frequently flooded sandbars, caused the Fraser River gold rush to be short lived.

Gold was first discovered in Idaho in 1862 and in Montana in 1864. In 1885, an Idaho prospector chasing a runaway mule happened upon rocks streaked with lead and silver. The Bunker Hill and Sullivan Mine, built on the site of his find, yielded $250 million in silver and lead.

The last great western gold stampede was the rush to the Black Hills, a mountainous area in southwestern South Dakota. For years, miners had traded stories about Indians from the region who possessed bags of gold nuggets, and about soldiers finding pay dirt in streams running through the Black Hills. The area was out of reach for most prospectors, though, because a treaty signed in 1868 guaranteed the land to the Sioux (Dakota, Lakota, Nakota) people. Federal troops guarded the reservation and turned away all intruders.

By 1874, the army was having trouble keeping trespassing prospectors out of the Black Hills. In an effort to disprove the rumors of gold once and for all, 1,200 soldiers under the command of General George A. Custer conducted an official inspection of the Black Hills. The result was not what the government had expected: the investigators found gold throughout the area. The number of people entering the Black Hills escalated sharply in 1875, and the troops could no longer keep them out. The army gave up in October of that year and opened the Black Hills to prospectors.

Immediately, 15,000 miners entered the region. They congregated near gold-rich French Creek, founded the town of Custer City, and agreed on an informal set of laws regarding mining claims. Another town, Deadwood, established in 1876, is remembered as a noisy, lawless place consisting of one saloon-lined street.

Like miners in other locales, Black Hills prospectors experienced varying degrees of luck. A miner named Moses Manuel discovered the region's most important mine, the Homestake, in April 1876 and extracted gold worth $5,000 the following winter. In 1877, Manuel sold the mine to George Hearst and two of his associates from San Francisco, who profited enormously from the venture. In one year of operation, 1888, the Homestake Company processed more than 243,000 tons of ore, earning $1.19 per ton.

By 1875, the era when an independent prospector could reasonably expect to earn a living at mining, let alone unearth a fortune, was coming to an end. As large investors came to dominate western mining between 1875 and 1900, the lone prospector could no longer compete.

CHRONICLE OF EVENTS

1719

Philippe Renault mines lead in the Mississippi River valley using the labor of enslaved Africans and French miners.

1723–1804

Renault's Mine la Motte yields approximately 8,000 tons of lead.

1788

The Sac and Fox (Mesquakie) Indians grant Julian Dubuque permission to mine lead alongside the Mississippi River.

1780s

Iron is mined in northern New York State.

1784

The mining of bituminous coal begins near Pittsburgh.

1791

Rich deposits of anthracite are discovered in eastern Pennsylvania.

1792

George Anschutz constructs the first blast furnace at Pittsburgh.

1800

The annual per capita consumption of coal in the United States is 0.01 ton.

1807

March: Congress reserves title to all lands containing lead ore and leases them for mining.

1822

James Johnson secures a lease for mining in the Fever River district of Illinois.

1839

March 18: An explosion kills 52 miners at the Black Heath Coal Mine near Richmond, Virginia.

Anthracite is first used as a fuel in iron smelting in Pennsylvania.

1840

The annual per capita consumption of coal in the United States is 0.1 ton.

1844

Copper mining begins near Lake Superior.

1847

Congress votes to sell off the mineral lands.

The Minesota Mine, site of the largest copper deposit found in the United States, is discovered.

1848

January 24: James Marshall discovers gold in California's American River.

February 2: With the signing of the Treaty of Guadalupe Hidalgo, Mexico cedes California to the United States.

May: News of Marshall's find reaches San Francisco.

December 5: President Polk, in a speech to Congress, states that gold has been discovered in California.

1849

Tens of thousands of people travel to California to prospect for gold.

1850s

Would-be miners leave California and head for the Fraser River in British Columbia.

1859

Prospectors find a rich vein of gold and silver in the Washoe Mountains of Nevada that will come to be known as the Comstock Lode.

About 100,000 miners travel to Pike's Peak in present-day Colorado; more than half become discouraged and leave.

1860s

Mining begins near Denver and Boulder in Colorado.

1862

Gold is discovered in Idaho.

1864

The St. Joseph Lead Company employs Cornish miners and improved technology at Bonne Terre, Missouri.

Gold is discovered in Montana.

1866
Alfred Nobel invents dynamite.

1868
The U.S. government and the Sioux (Dakota, Lakota, Nakota) people sign a treaty guaranteeing the Black Hills region of South Dakota to the Sioux.

1869
September 6: Fire kills 179 miners at the Avondale Mine in Plymouth, Pennsylvania.

1873
Owners of the Consolidated Virginia Mine discover the Big Bonanza, the world's richest mineral deposit.

Congress omits the silver dollar from the list of coins authorized to be minted; the price of silver falls.

1874
An army survey confirms the existence of gold in the Black Hills.

1875
The army opens the Black Hills to prospectors.

1876
Moses Manuel discovers the Homestake, the most important mine in the Black Hills.

1877
Manuel sells the Homestake Mine to George Hearst and associates.

Veteran prospectors pan for gold at Rockerville, Dakota Territory, 1889. *(Library of Congress)*

1878
Production of silver dollars resumes.

1880
The mines of Michigan's Upper Peninsula produce nearly 50 million pounds of refined copper. Michigan leads the nation in copper production.

The annual per capita consumption of coal is one ton.

1880s
French inventors develop the compressed-air drill and the diamond drill for mining.

1885
President Cleveland halts coin manufacture at the Carson City Mint.

A prospector accidentally discovers the mineral-rich site of the Bunker Hill and Sullivan Mine, the most important silver and lead deposit in Idaho.

1886
Coin production resumes at the Carson City Mint.

1887
The western states take the lead in copper production.

1888
The Homestake Mine processes more than 243,000 tons of ore.

1890
Nearly 500,000 people work in U.S. coal mines.

1890s
Between 2,000 and 3,000 coal miners die in accidents on the job each year.

1893
The Carson City Mint is closed.

1898
The mines of the Comstock Lode halt production.

1900
Annual per capita consumption of coal reaches 2.5 tons.

Eyewitness Testimony

A large proportion of those formerly engaged in mining were persons of the most abandoned character, refugees from justice in the old States; and the mines were a continued scene of riot and disorder, and many atrocities were committed. Many of those persons have fled, others have been restrained from evil practices by the influence and example of virtuous and intelligent men, and it is but justice to the inhabitants of the mines to observe, that in morals and manners they are surpassed by no other district in the Territory.

Henry R. Schoolcraft, 1819, A View of the Lead
Mines of Missouri, *p. 39.*

The *fever* and *ague* is a very rare thing at the mines. Billious complaints are the most common, but they are not fatal. During a residence of ten months at the mines, I have not witnesses a single death, or heard of any happening in the country. . . . There are, however, some losses annually sustained by the inhabitants of the mine tract, from the death of cattle, who die of the *mine sickness.* Cows and horses are frequently seen to die without any apparent cause. Cats and dogs are taken with violent fits, which never fail in a short time, to kill them. This has been accounted for, by supposing that they inhale the sulphur which is so abundantly driven off in smelting lead, and cattle are often seen licking about old furnaces.

Henry R. Schoolcraft, 1819, A View of the Lead
Mines of Missouri, *pp. 30–31.*

The lead mines at *Prairie du Chien,* are situated in the North Western Territory, and . . . are considered the richest yet found. They are still in the possession of the Sacs and Foxes, the original owners of the soil, by whom they are worked in a very imperfect manner. They were formerly wrought by M. Dubuque, under the authority of a Spanish grant, and with the consent of the Indians, but since his death they have manifested an unwillingness to allow any white man to work them, and appear to entertain a high sense of their value.

Henry R. Schoolcraft, 1819, A View of the Lead
Mines of Missouri, *p. 62.*

. . . [T]here are as yet no mines in activity in the United States; and we may consider the undertaking of mines on a regular system as a new branch in this country.

The United States would undoubtedly derive from mining the same advantages which the prosecution of it affords to other nations. It would tend to make us independent of foreign countries for the most indispensable articles of commerce; it would secure to us an abundance of metallic substances, at a cheaper rate than that for which they could be imported; and, by increasing the quantity of metals, it is evident that we improve our arts and sciences, and make new advances in civilization.

W. H. Keating, 1821, Considerations upon the
Art of Mining, *p. 75.*

. . . [W]e came upon an extensive table-land, where the trees being nearly all cut down, I supposed we were near the mine: soon after we reached some miserable log cabins on a naked plain, inhabited by the most ignorant human beings I almost ever conversed with, the mothers and wives of some of the labouring miners. A couple of miles farther on we came to the old French village of Mine la Motte, where was another set of miserable huts, in the inside of one or two of which, however, I perceived some signs of hope, such as tea things neatly arranged, bed-curtains, looking-glasses, &c., belonging to the families of some English miners, as we found upon inquiry. Speculators from all quarters seem to have resorted to this place; the French are not very numerous, and those who succeed the best are the English, who have been brought up mining in their native country; for being conversant with the throw of veins, and accustomed to follow a regular system of work, less of their labour is wasted: the Americans, however, are gradually adopting their plans, and being ingenious mechanics and persevering men, are beginning to do very well. What rather surprised me was, that even Englishmen had adopted the method of quarrying instead of sinking shafts, alleging, as the reason, that the whole vicinity was so cut up by pits made by those who followed the practice of *shallow digging,* that it was hardly practicable to do anything but quarry the ore, for which the nature of the surface offered great facilities.

G. W. Featherstonhaugh, English traveler, 1844,
Excursion through the Slave States, *p. 78.*

In the newly made raceway of the saw-mill recently erected by Captain Sutter, in the American fork, gold has been found in considerable quantities. One person brought thirty dollars worth to New Helvetia, gathered there in a short time. California, no doubt, is rich in mineral wealth; great chances here for scientific capitalists. Gold has been found in every part of the country.

Article published in the Californian, *March 15, 1848, in Hillary W. St. Clair,* Mineral Industry in Early America, *p. 17.*

The whole country, from San Francisco to Los Angeles, and from the seashore to the base of the Sierra Nevada, resounds to the sordid cry of gold! gold! gold! While the field is left half-planted, the house half-built, and everything neglected but the manufacture of picks and shovels, and the means of transportation to the spot where one man obtained $128 worth of the real stuff in one day's washing; and the average for all concerned is $20 per diem.

Article published in the Californian, *May 29, 1848, in Hillary W. St. Clair,* Mineral Industry in Early America, *p. 17.*

W. was one of the first who settled on this river [the Feather River of California], and suffered extremely from the scarcity of provisions during the last winter. By steady industry in his laborious vocation, he had accumulated about four thousand dollars. He was thinking seriously of returning to Massachusetts with what he had already gained, when in the early part of last May, a stone unexpectedly rolling from the top of Smith's Hill, on the side of which he was mining— crushed his leg in the most shocking manner. Naturally enough, the poor fellow shrank with horror, from the idea of an amputation here in the mountains; it seemed absolutely worse than death. His physician, appreciating his feelings on the subject, made every effort to save his shattered limb; but, truly, the fates seemed against him. An attack of typhoid fever reduced him to a state of great weakness, which was still further increased by erysipelas [a streptococcal infection]—a common complaint in the mountains—in its most virulent form; the latter disease settling in the fractured leg, rendered a cure utterly hopeless.

Louise A. Clappe, California, September 22, 1851, The Shirley Letters, *p. 31.*

Whether there is more profanity in the mines than elsewhere, I know not; but during the short time that I have been at Rich Bar, I have *heard* more of it than

in all my life before. Of course, the most vulgar blackguard will abstain from swearing in the *presence* of a lady; but in this rag and card-board house, one is *compelled* to hear the most sacred of names constantly profaned by the drinkers and gamblers who haunt the bar-room at all hours. And this is a custom which the gentlemanly and quiet proprietor, much as he evidently dislikes it, cannot possibly prevent.

Louise A. Clappe, California, September 30, 1851, The Shirley Letters, *pp. 42–43.*

Nick Ambrose, better known in that country as "Dutch Nick," . . . came not to mine, but to minister to the wants of the miners. He set up a large tent and ran it as a saloon and boarding-house. The boys paid him $14 per week for board and "slept themselves;" that is, they were provided with blankets of their own, and rolling up in these, they just curled down in the sagebrush, wherever and whenever they pleased.

The liquid refreshment furnished these miners by Nick was probably the first of that popular brand of whisky known as "tarantula juice" ever dispensed within the limits of Virginia City. When the boys were well charged with this whisky it made the snakes and tarantulas that bit them very sick.

William Wright relating events of 1858, History of the Big Bonanza, *p. 40.*

Now for a description of our city, it is situated on the South Platte, at the mouth of Cherry creek, about seventy miles from Pike's Peak. It has about one hundred and thirty houses, and an average of four men to the cabin. The female part is composed of four white ladies, two of whom are married, and the other two single, there are also squaws here, who are the wives of some mountain men, who have located here. When I started for this place, I expected to find but little, or no whiskey, and but few people, but I was much astonished when I found that there were about one thousand persons in the valley, and about ten barrels of whiskey.

Letter from an unknown correspondent, Auroria City, Colorado, published in the Jefferson Inquirer, *February 26, 1859, in Le Roy R. Hafen,* Colorado Gold Rush: Contemporary Letters and Reports, *p. 205.*

Where we are wintering is about twenty miles north of the mouth of Cherry creek, and in a canon at the foot of the Rocky mountains, or Black hills. We have found here the best quality of gold that has been discovered, and cannot make one dollar per day. Billy Moore, Tom, and myself are working together; we have built a good dam across the creek, and have our long tom set (the only long tom that is set and worked in the country), it works beautifully, so the old Californians say. There are six old miners in our settlement. I don't think that there is another company that came here last fall who have done more work or more extensive prospecting than we. We have prospected for some twenty miles south of the mouth of Cherry creek to the neighborhood of Long's Peak, north. Besides, we have prospected as far into the mountains as we could get on account of snow.

Letter from A. A. Brookfield, St. Vrain's Creek, Colorado, published in the Kansas City Journal of Commerce, *March 16, 1859, in Le Roy R. Hafen,* Colorado Gold Rush, *pp. 220–21.*

Dear Brother:—Since writing to you last, I have been painfully compelled to change my opinion of the prospects here, as regards gold digging. If this reaches you at the point proposed in my prior letter, heed my words, starvation must stare you in the face, no matter how well you are prepared for the trip. Robbing emigrants of their provisions will be the result of those unprepared, and more suffering will be the consequence, than ever has occurred in the history of similar adventures in the United States. That there is some gold here I do not deny, but that it will pay to dig it, by means that has ever been adopted in other mining districts I do assure you and others that it will not. I will return shortly for my old home, to once more enjoy the society of my friends.

Letter from Charles H. Nickel, Denver City, Colorado, published in the Atlanta Weekly Intelligencer, *May 11, 1859, in Le Roy R. Hafen,* Colorado Gold Rush, *pp. 228–29.*

Frame shanties pitched together as if by accident, tents of canvas, of blankets, of brush, of potato sacks and old shirts, with empty whiskey barrels for chimneys; smoking hovels of mud and stone; coyote holes in the hillsides forcibly seized by men, pits and shanties with smoke issuing from every crevice; piles of goods and rubbish on craggy points, in hollows, on rocks, in the mud, on the snow.

A newcomer describing Virginia City in 1860, in Le Roy R. Hafen et al., Western America, *p. 311.*

It was arranged that I should . . . help in any work that a boy could do. It took some little time to get out lumber for the sluice boxes, as it had to be whip-sawed from logs cut in the vicinity, there being no sawmills in that part of the country. These sluice boxes usually were from twelve to fifteen feet in length and from fourteen to eighteen inches wide, with sides six to eight inches high. In some of these boxes strips were nailed fairly close together across the bottom, making the riffles necessary to catch the gold. Six to eight lengths of these sluice boxes were then joined together on the ground to be worked, making a continuous sluice of seventy to one hundred and twenty feet in length. This was placed at a pitch sufficient to cause the water to flow through it rapidly, a ditch from the creek previously having been made to conduct water into the upper end. After all this had been done, the next work was to dig up and throw into the sluice boxes the gravel on either side, which was supposed to contain gold. The rapid flow of water would carry off the gravel and small stones, leaving the gold, which was heavier, to settle on the bottom and be caught by the riffles.

Irving Howbert writing about his experiences in June 1860, when he was 14, Memories of a Lifetime in the Pike's Peak Region, *p. 25.*

When all was ready, work was started on our claim with high hopes, but, after throwing gravel into the sluice boxes for two or three days, we concluded to turn off the water and clean up the gold from behind the riffles in order to ascertain the result of our labors. Much to our disgust the complete clean-up showed only $6.00 worth of gold for three days' work of three men and a boy. This was so disappointing that at once the party abandoned the claim and quit mining in that locality. Not all of the claims in the gulch proved as unprofitable as this one, for a number of those above our location were yielding from $100.00 to $500.00 a day per man. The owners of those claims had drawn the prizes, but apparently we had drawn a blank.

Irving Howbert writing about his experiences in 1860, when he was 14, Memories of a Lifetime in the Pike's Peak Region, *p. 26.*

At this time, gold dust was the principal medium of exchange throughout all the region now embraced in the State of Colorado. Almost every one had a small buckskin bag in which he carried his gold, and every

California prospectors divert a stream through their sluice. *(Library of Congress)*

merchant owned small scales on which was weighed the gold dust taken in payment for merchandise. The gold of the various camps differed in value according to its purity. That from some districts was worth only $16 an ounce, and from others it ran as high as $18 an ounce.

Irving Howbert commenting on the use of gold as currency in Colorado in 1860, Memories of a Lifetime in the Pike's Peak Region, *p. 27.*

I imagine it would be somewhat astonishing to a person that had never heard of the existence of gold in these mountains who might be travelling through and come suddenly into this vicinity *some dark night* where

his ears would be greeted with the whistles from a *hundred Steam Engines* and the noise of all the machinery attached. I think he would be apt to consider himself in close proximity to the *infernal regions.* I often think of it as I am riding through these mountain passes in the night on my return home from the Saw Mill, or from a trip to Denver and almost wonder at myself to think that I am here and taking an active part in making all this commotion.

George M. Pullman, September 23, 1860, in Liston E. Leyendecker, "Young Man Gone West," p. 214.

The vein [at the Gould and Curry Mine in the Washoe Mountains] is several hundred feet wide, but not all rich ore. It is distributed in great irregular masses, called chambers, because when the ore is taken out a great room or chamber is left. The miners learn by experience what ore is good and what to reject as poor. The vein runs down slanting, so that men who commenced on one side at the surface are now at work over four hundred feet under the city. It requires great skill to explore the mine and keep the sides from caving in. The timbering is unlike any I have ever seen. Stout timbers, a foot square, in short pieces from five to seven feet long, placed in a peculiar manner, run entirely across the mine in every direction, further strengthened by braces where the pressure is greatest. Yet, at times, these timbers are crushed as if they were but straws. Long tunnels run into the mine from low down the hill, and out of these the ore is taken.

William H. Brewer, professor of geology, Harvard University,
Up and Down California in 1860–1864, *p. 555.*

To know what a genuine miner is, and how he lives, you must visit the remote interior districts, and partake of his hospitality; but lest you should form an erroneous idea in regard to the accommodations, I must tell you as nearly as possible what a miner's cabin is made of and what it affords in the way of entertainment.

Usually it is constructed of the materials nearest at hand. Stone and mud answer for the walls where wood is scarce; but if wood be abundant, a kind of stockade is formed of logs placed close together and upright in the ground. The roof is made of clap-boards, or rough shingles, brush-wood covered with sod, canvas, or any thing else that may be available. I have seen roofs constructed of flour-sacks, cast-off shirts, coats, and pantaloons, all sewed together like a home-made quilt. Rawhide, with big stones on the corners, is very good in dry countries, but it is apt to become flabby and odorous in damp climates. The chimney is the most imposing part of the house. Where the location permits, the cabin is backed up against a bluff, so as to afford a chance for a substantial flue by merely cutting a hole through the bank; but where such natural facilities do not exist, the variety of material used in the construction of chimneys is wonderful. Stone, wood, scraps of sheet-iron, adobe-bricks, mud, whisky-barrels, nail-kegs, and even canvas, are the component parts. Think of a canvas chimney!

J. Ross Browne, Illustrated Mining Adventures:
California and Nevada, 1863–1865, *pp. 9–12.*

Heavy timbers support a mine in the Washoe Mountains of Nevada. *(Library of Congress)*

Those who became infected with the mining fever had one common characteristic. Every spare bit of energy was thrown into the many valuable mining claims, and there was always a kind of ticklish feeling creeping up and down our spines for fear we might have allowed some hidden treasure to escape our vigilant and wary explorations. So more claims were constantly being located, some lapping over other claims to prevent the possibility of even a fraction of the ground being lost to our company.

Miguel Antonio Otero, My Life on the Frontier,
1864–1882, *p. 226.*

Though these mining ventures proved virtually a total loss, none of us regarded ourselves as stung. We felt that we had made our contribution to the development of our section of the country [the Southwest] and argued with ourselves that if we had not invested this money in mining we would have speculated in something else. The spirit of "take a chance" was strong in the land, and along with it went the belief that he was a poor sport, indeed, who would cry over spilled milk.

Miguel Antonio Otero, My Life on the Frontier, *1864–1882, p. 229.*

The [lead] mines are lighted by means of common tallow-candles, as there is no danger from the explosive gases that prevail in coal mines. But the miner's candlestick is unique. A person about to descend into a mine is handed a candle and a lump of white clay, or "fire clay." It is about the consistence of such a lump of mud as boys use for making "mud-balls." He is expected to wrap the ball of clay around the end of his candle. The advantage of so plastic a candlestick is obvious. If a miner or visitor desires to relieve himself of his candle, all he has to do is to "stick it" up or down as the case may be, and it adheres to whatever surface it meets. This "fire-clay" of which the mining candlestick is made abounds in the lead region, and a supply is always kept for this purpose.

"Galena and Its Lead Mines," Harper's New Monthly Magazine, *May 1866, p. 690.*

After the ore is dislodged it is carried to the foot of the "shaft" by means of a wooden hand-managed railway, and then hoisted by means of tub and windlass. This, however, is a slow, laborious operation, nevertheless it is almost exclusively used. The owners of the Elevator Mine at Shullsburg have built, and now use, a machine for hoisting which is worked by horsepower. When the ore reaches the surface it is weighed and sold at a given price for 1000 pounds, and always for ready money. It is then carted off to the furnace in wagons. There it is sorted over, and the large lumps are thrown upon an open floor and broken up by hammers. The furnaces are always constructed near a water-course, and the water is conducted by a pipe into a shed. A rough wooden trough placed under the stream of water receives the mineral, and as the water falls over it the dirt is washed away, and much of the finer ore in scales or crumbs is carried along down the trough, but its specific gravity is such that it sinks upon the floor of the trench, while the water flows on and out through a drain. This fine ore is shoveled out and again subjected to the action of water outside, by being put in a wooden box open at one end, which is placed under any little fall in the watercourse. Men here stir the mineral about in the box with a common hoe, while the flow of water carries off all that remains of the dirt, the mineral again being retained by its great gravity.

"Galena and Its Lead Mines," Harper's New Monthly Magazine, *May 1866, p. 690.*

. . . [T]he mines have of late years lost something of their importance, and the quantity of lead produced has perceptibly decreased. This is accounted for by the uncertainty of the pursuits of mining, and the fact of the great agricultural wealth of the lead region. In many places one may stand in a field bearing upon its surface as large a crop of wheat, corn, or potatoes, as can be produced from an equal area in any place, and hear the miner blasting rock far beneath him. The pursuits of agriculture being so much more certain, though often slower, the mining has in a very considerable degree been abandoned for farming.

"Galena and Its Lead Mines," Harper's New Monthly Magazine, *May 1866, pp. 681–82.*

Among the Californians who may be said to have "struck it rich" here [Dakota Territory], is Major Patrick Gallagher, formerly of the California Volunteers. The Major is largely interested in the "Miners Delight" ledge, in the California District, and there is no discount on the richness of the vein. The ledge . . . has turned out some of the richest gold specimens yet obtained in this section of the country. The vein is about two feet wide, and, to use a miner's phrase, is "lousy" with gold. Major Gallagher bought into the claim, and has made arrangements to have a mill erected as soon as the weather and roads will permit. When their mill gets under way, you will be apt to hear of the Miners Delight often.

James Chisholm reporting in Sweetwater Mines, *April 1, 1868, in* South Pass, 1868, *pp. 45–46.*

Montgomery [Colorado] was the scene of a great mining excitement a few years ago. Gold and silver mines of supposed great value were discovered, a wagon road was made up the valley, a restless, mining population floated in, all the ravines and mountains were "prospected" for "leads," and a town was laid out, its streets and public square figured on paper. I know not how many houses were built, nor how large a population the place numbered; some say a thousand, others put it at two or three times that number. How many houses there were, I do not know—over seventy still remain, such as they are—some in streets, others perched against the steep hillsides. People speculated in "corner lots," and talked of a brilliant future. Four mills were built, for reducing the silver ores—one is still standing in good condition, its heavy engine, boilers, stamps and other necessary machinery all hauled by teams the weary distance across the plains and into the mountains to this place. Says one old inhabitant, who still believes in the richness of the silver leads, "Why, we had several stores, three or four hotels, more than that number of saloons—we had livery stables, gambling houses in plenty with music, *maisons de plaisir,* a theatre, and all the modern improvements." Alas for miners' hopes—the brilliant future did not come, the Great Expectations were never realized. The entire production of the mines is stated by different persons at sums of from $100,000 to $250,000—a mere bauble.

The leads were abandoned and the town deserted. Only one house is occupied by a family (Mr. Myers) and the entire population is less than a dozen in the whole region! The desolation of the mountains seems surpassed by the desolation of the deserted town.

William H. Brewer, professor of geology, Harvard University, August 8, 1869, Rocky Mountain Letters, *p. 28.*

Alder Gulch [Montana] . . . was the richest gulch of the size ever found in any of our gold regions . . . but it has gone into dilapidation, and is practically abandoned. Out of this gulch millions of gold have been taken. For ten miles it has been worked, some places as much as five hundred yards in width, and at its head are now found the richest quartz leads. Although every bushel of earth in the gulch has already been panned, still, it is lined with miners, who are now bringing the more improved systems to work it over again profitably. Ditches have been brought from lakes ten miles distant, and the hydraulic process is at present washing down the hard banks and sluicing the once-worked earth. A number of quartz-mills have already been erected on the leads at the head of this gulch, and, when brought down to proper management and legitimate enterprise, must make immense

returns to mill-owners. It is admitted, I believe, that no better-defined or richer leads are to be found on the continent than in the summit district. Imperfect machinery, worse direction, and impatient, ill-advised, and wasteful efforts at development have made failures on mines where practical men would gather fortunes.

A. K. McClure, 1869, Three Thousand Miles through the Rocky Mountains, *p. 193.*

As a rule, the successful gulch-miners are most improvident; and of the scores of men who came here without a dollar and made from ten to fifty thousand dollars of gold out of Alder Gulch, there are very few indeed who could to-day command one thousand dollars, while most of them are utterly "broke." Their necessary expenses were very heavy, but their needless expenses were usually much heavier. A newspaper would bring from one to two dollars in gold in the days of gulch-mining. . . . A letter usually cost five dollars. Flour cost from fifty cents to one dollar a pound; and everything else in proportion. A cat would sell very readily in the days of gulch-mining for one hundred dollars in gold, and the display of pets of any kind was one of the easiest means of reaching the miner's well-filled buckskin bag. Then came the gambler's claim, and the fever of speculation, and what the indulgence of the appetites left was mostly sure to be swept into the faro-bank or frittered away in some fancy purchase.

A. K. McClure, 1869, Three Thousand Miles through the Rocky Mountains, *pp. 240–41.*

The whole town [Gold Hill, Nevada] is undermined, and may be said to stand on a foundation of timbers. The ground worked out underneath the town has, however, been so thoroughly filled in with timbers and waste rock that there is no danger of it caving, though it is immediately but slowly settling. To the eastward of the town, and behind a large hill on which a portion of the town stands, a crevice has opened which is nearly a mile in length, and in places over two feet in width. This shows that the whole place, hill and all, is gradually "subsiding."

William Wright, 1876, History of the Big Bonanza, *p. 221.*

A striking feature of [Virginia City and Gold Hill], and one which at once rivets the attention of all strangers, is the immense piles of rock seen in the neighborhood of all the principal mines. In these great dump-piles are heaped the rock and earth extracted in sinking the shafts, running the drifts, and in making other underground excavations. Persons from the Atlantic States, who are in the habit of judging of the depth of a well or other excavation by the amount of rubbish seen on the surface, are greatly surprised at the size of the dumps, and their first question is: "Did all that dirt come out of one mine?" As soon as they see one of these mountains of waste rock, they begin a mental calculation as to the size of the hole left in the ground. It is no small pile of rubbish that comes out of a shaft six feet wide, twenty-two feet long, and from 1,500 to 2,500 feet deep—to say nothing of the *debris* from innumerable drifts, crosscuts and winzes [inclined shafts].

William Wright, 1876, History of
the Big Bonanza, *p. 222.*

Besides the miners there are employed a great number of timbermen, who look after the timbers and the timbering; the pump man, who takes care of the pumps; the watchmen, who go their rounds, each on his level, to look out for fire and to keep an eye on things generally; and the pick-boy, who goes about through the mine gathering up the dull picks and sending them up the shaft to be sharpened, who carries the sharp picks to the places where they are wanted, who distributes water among the men and who, in short, is general errand-boy in the mine.

William Wright, 1876, History of
the Big Bonanza, *p. 325.*

In order that the reader may obtain something like a correct idea of the appearance of the interior of a first-class mine, let him imagine it hoisted out of the ground and left standing upon the surface. He would then see before him an immense structure, four or five times as large as the greatest hotel in America, about twice or three times as wide, and over 2000 feet high. The several levels of the mine would represent the floors of the building[.] These floors would be 100 feet apart—that is, there would be in the building twenty stories, each 100 feet in height. In a grand hotel communication between these floors would be by means of an elevator; in the mine would be in use the same contrivances, but instead of an "elevator," it would be called a "cage." . . .

Upon the various floors of our mine we should see hundreds of men at work, but there would be seen between the floors, in many places, a solid mass of ore, in which the men were working their way up and rearing their scaffolding of timbers toward the floor above.

Not only would the men be seen thus at work, but there would also be seen at work on the various floors, engines and other machinery; with, high above all, the huge pump, swaying up and down its great rod, 2,000 feet in length and hung at several points with immense balance-bobs, to prevent its being pulled apart by its own weight.

Occasionally, too, we should see all of the men disappear from a floor, and soon after would be heard in rapid succession ten or a dozen stunning reports— the noise of exploding blasts.

William Wright, 1876, History of
the Big Bonanza, *pp. 322–23.*

A miner's staked-out bit of hope was his only as long as his neighbor was honest. There were no mining laws and claim-jumping was coming to be a popular pastime. A prospector held his ground by sitting on it or by digging day and night. His location notice was nothing more than a stick and a scrap of paper.

The placer mines that yielded the gold of '76 were above ground in the sunlight. It was not easy to trifle with them. But when men began running tunnels and sinking shafts and doing their mining by dim candle-light under ground, it seemed to be more difficult to distinguish their own gold from their neighbors'. Sometimes even honest men forgot or mislaid their boundaries.

Estelline Bennett recalling conditions in 1877,
Old Deadwood Days, *p. 36.*

If one possessed an ear-trumpet . . . by laying it on almost any spot of these steeply mounting hills and winding trails, one might hear the ringing of hammer and drill against the rock, the rumbling of cars through cavernous drifts, the dull thunder of blasts, even the voices of men burrowing in the heart of the mountain. One can walk, in the passages only of this underground world, for twenty-seven miles without treading the same path twice. Only those familiar with its blind ways from childhood may venture below in safety without a guide, for besides the danger of being lost, is that of wandering into some disused "labor," where the rotten timbers threaten a "cave." Within the last year, I am told, a part of "Mine Hill" has settled three inches, and everywhere above the "old workings" great cracks and holes show how the shell is constantly sinking.

"A California Mining Camp," Scribner's Monthly,
February 1878, p. 480.

[Colorado's] mines, with their prolonged subterranean workings, their stamping and crushing mills, and the smelting works which have been established near them, fill the district with noise, hubbub, and smoke by night and day; but I . . . turned altogether aside from them into a still region, where each miner in solitude was grubbing for himself, and confiding to none his finds or disappointments. Agriculture restores and beautifies, mining destroys and devastates; turning the earth inside out, making it hideous, and blighting every green thing, as it usually blights man's heart and soul. There was mining everywhere along that grand road, with all its destruction and devastation, its digging, burrowing, gulching, and sluicing; and up all along the seemingly inaccessible heights were holes with their roofs log-supported, in which solitary and patient men were selling their lives for treasure. Down by the stream, all among the icicles, men were sluicing and washing, and everywhere along the heights were the scars of hardly-passable trails, too steep even for pack-jacks, leading to the holes, and down which the miner packs the ore on his back.

Isabella L. Bird, 1879–80, A Lady's Life
in the Rocky Mountains, *p. 225.*

Weather fine. Hard, hard work. I used to think the laboring men's a hard life at the best, but their work is child's play alongside of this. Breaking stone, making mortar, shovelling dirt, etc.—fun when you come to mining. Holding the drill is something not easily acquired to do it properly. The terribly cramped and strained positions at times and strength required to manage a hole in soft ground enforces a great physical strain and much nerve when the swinger of the heavy sledge hammer has to aim over and draw in to prevent hitting you and sometimes will graze the edge of your moustache in striking a hundred pound blow upon a piece of steel 3/4 of an inch in diameter. To keep the hole straight so as not to bind it and save time and labor by finding a solid base every time is a trick requiring time and experience. The sledge

requires, of course, great care in its use. Knowing where to drill and place shots is a matter of practice too and how to prepare ground about to take the full advantage of the blast. My poor hands and arms are in a terrible state.

George Whitwell Parsons, March 31, 1880,
A Tenderfoot in Tombstone, *pp. 35–36.*

. . . Thought I'd handle my cork hat gently inside tent before putting it on and found a scorpion in that. Upon shaking blankets I killed other specimen[s] of a less dangerous type. Spiders, horse killers, etc. Quite a harvest of blood. The creeping things are getting too numerous for comfort here. The flies are simply abominable. They are worse here, it is said, than any where else. Our meals are most uncomfortable ones. Flies by the billion. The old miners never knew them so bad before anywhere.

George Whitwell Parsons, July 4, 1880,
A Tenderfoot in Tombstone, *p. 59.*

To the discovery of the precious metals, and the passion of those who search for them, we owe a knowledge and development of the Great Western wilderness which could not have been gained by a century of ordinary effort. These men have built up great states, and peopled a vast continent. Restless, pushing, bent only on gold and silver, they have had no time and less inclination to consider the rights of the original owners of the soil. Men who would demolish the house of a white friend, were gold discovered beneath it, are not likely to stickle at territorial limits, or regard the lines of Indian Reservations.

Richard Irving Dodge, 1883, Our Wild Indians, *p. 608.*

The expression of a fresh mining camp, at the height of its "boom," is something which must be seen to be comprehended. . . .

As if by magic, there grows up a sort of street, a dozen or two board shanties, with that cheapest and silliest of all shams, the battlement front, flaunting its ugly squares all along the line. Glaring signs painted on strips of cotton sheeting, bleached and unbleached, are nailed over doors. In next to no time, there will be a "mint," an "exchange," a "bank," a "Vienna bakery," a "Chinese laundry," a "hotel," and a "livery stable." Between each night and morning will blossom out crops of "real estate offices," and places where "mining properties are bought and sold," "claims located, proved, bought and sold," "surveys of mining claims made," etc.; crops also, alas, of whiskey saloons, with wicked names and lurid red curtains, danger and death signals.

"O-Be-Joyful Creek and Poverty Gulch," Atlantic Monthly, *December 1883, pp. 753–54.*

The stumps are not taken out of the pretense of a road, neither are the bowlders; nobody minds driving over them, or over anything, in fact, so he gets quick to his "claim," or to the tract in which he is feverishly "prospecting." If a brook trickles through the camp, so much the better; it can do double duty as drain and well. Luckiest they who drink highest up, but they who drink lowest down do not mind.

"O-Be-Joyful Creek and Poverty Gulch," Atlantic Monthly, *December 1883, p. 754.*

Nothing can be more certain than that, if the human race continues to advance, an age will come which will abhor and repudiate the tin can, with all its sickening contents. After a century or two of disuse and oblivion, the hideous utensil and its still more hideous foods will be relegated to their proper place as relics of a phase of barbarism; and then the exhuming of some of the huge mounds of them, now being piled up in mining camps, will be interesting to all persons curious in such matters. The miner's frying-pan also may come in for a share of analytic attention; will perhaps take a place in museums, in the long procession headed by the Indian's stone mortar and pestle. It may even come about that there will be an age catalogued in the archaeologist's lists as the tin age.

"O-Be-Joyful Creek and Poverty Gulch," Atlantic Monthly, *December 1883, p. 753.*

The most significant sight in White Cloud was a large building, evidently intended for smelting-works: every window and door boarded, and the whole place as it were barricaded by piles of rusty, battered iron machinery which would never again do duty,—piles of old iron wheels, cylinders, pipes, trays of pots, tanks, all the innumerable contrivances and devices for metal working; there they lay, in confused heaps, like the debris of a fire, or a wreck. And so they are,—debris of fire and wreck in which the hope and strength of many a heart have been lost forever.

"O-Be-Joyful Creek and Poverty Gulch," Atlantic Monthly, *December 1883, p. 757.*

Considering the heterogeneous elements of which miners' society is composed, the universal custom of carrying deadly weapons, the recklessness of men under the influence of the strongest passions, unfettered by the restraints of law, and deprived of the softening influence of reputable women, the mining communities of the present day are remarkable for the absence of crime.

Richard Irving Dodge, 1883, Our Wild Indians, *p. 608.*

One day the superintendent came in with a bunch of visitors, several of them women. As they came in the drift, I wanted to get out of their way, so stepped into this winze to let them by. I think I knew the winze was about twenty feet deep and also that there was quite a stope [an excavation to remove ore] around the top of it. But there was no work going on in the stope and no lights in it. I noticed that small pieces of white porphyry which formed the roof of the stope were dropping occasionally but I had no idea of danger. I suppose I had been standing in the winze several minutes waiting for the visitors to leave when I heard a voice somewhere near the top of the winze saying, "I wonder what is all this stuff dropping in here." At the same time I looked up the man's candle lit up the roof—and the whole top of the stope seemed to let go with a crash. I jumped the instant I saw it start and only got a few bruises on one leg. The windlass and plat at the top of the winze were brought down, and the winze itself was filled. The visitors had no trouble getting out, and they seemed more scared than I was although they had been in no danger. When we got to the surface one of the ladies in describing it said, "A fourteen year old boy came very close to getting killed." That peeved me for I was about twenty-and-a-half at that time.

Charles McClung Leonard describing events occurring in 1886, "Forty Years in Colorado Mining Camps," p. 177.

The miners I knew [in Colorado] were so different from the miner of to-day, being of American, English, Scotch, and Irish birth. Most of them came from good families and were well-educated young men, who came West for adventure. . . .

I would hang around their cabins, and they (especially the Englishmen) would lend me books, and treat me with their food sent from England. Here I first saw chocolate, orange marmalade, and Worcestershire sauce. These men always expected to strike it rich, and lived from year to year on hope. They "borned" (we always said this) the next generation of agitators and strikers, but now were satisfied with the wages received, two-fifty or three dollars per day.

Anne Ellis recalling her childhood in Colorado circa 1889,
    The Life of an Ordinary Woman, *p. 66.*

When Father returned from Excelsior Springs [Colorado] against the doctor's advice, it was because of his eagerness to see the samples from that mine tunnel that was covered with snow. . . . He reached the mine after an exhausting effort and found there a dump of very showy ore having zinc, lead, and some copper pyrites. He went into the tunnel, and found an eighteen-inch streak of the same kind of ore that was on the dump. Then he saw something that made his heart pound.

Between that streak of obvious ore and the hanging wall was a three-foot vein of quartz. There was no shining mineral in it, and most miners accustomed to silver-lead carbonates would have regarded it as worthless; but Father, with a richer experience, knew it for what it was—gold in a tellurium form. His illness was completely forgotten. For twenty years he had been searching for what he saw there; and it already belonged to him when he found it. . . .

Out on the dump Father found tons of "waste" that when assayed showed values of $3,000 a ton. . . . Why (he once said), with no better tool than an ice pick a man could have knocked off a comfortable living for a family.

*Evalyn Walsh McLean remembering events occurring in
    1896,* Father Struck It Rich, *pp. 39–40.*

Travelling to-day in foot-hill Sierras, one may see the old, rude scars of mining; trenches yawn, disordered heaps cumber the ground, yet they are no longer bare. Time, with friendly rain, and wind, and flood, slowly, surely, levels all, and a compassionate cover of innocent verdure weaves fresh and cool from mile to mile.

Clarence King, 1902, Mountaineering in
    the Sierra Nevada, *p. 378.*

6

Industry in the Gilded Age
1870–1914

For five months beginning May 10, 1876, Philadelphia hosted the Centennial Exposition, a world's fair honoring the United States of America on the occasion of its 100th birthday. In five impressive buildings, the exposition celebrated the triumphs of U.S. industry and engineering. A 19th-century writer used the word *superstructure* to describe Machinery Hall, which housed so many recent inventions: mowers and reapers, drills and lathes, Alexander Graham Bell's telephone, and George Pullman's railway sleeping car. Measuring 360 feet wide and 1,402 feet long, Machinery Hall covered 12.82 acres. Visitors stared in wonder at the 1.7-million-pound, 1,400-horsepower Corliss steam engine that stood outside the building and powered all of the exhibits inside. The massive exhibition halls and the trains arriving at the Pennsylvania Railroad's Centennial Depot—two per minute at the busiest times—exemplified the veneer of progress and prosperity that U.S. society wore in the late 19th century.

Historians refer to the years between the Civil War and the start of the 20th century as the Gilded Age, borrowing the title of an 1873 novel by Mark Twain and Charles Dudley Warner. The novel describes a society in which power and affluence form a glittering surface over a core of cheating and corruption.

The Gilded Age was an era of industrial giants, of business people who encountered no boundaries as they amassed wealth and influence, of individuals who discovered how to reap enormous benefits from an economy in transition. In 1870, agricultural production surpassed industrial output in the United States by about $500 million. Manufacturing increased four-fold over the next 30 years, so that by 1900, industrial production outstripped the farmers' yield by $8.3 billion. The Gilded Age was an era of material comfort for the middle and upper classes. But it was an era of hopelessness and hardship for millions of other Americans, the laborers who made the growth possible but failed to share in its bounty.

THE ROBBER BARONS

Kansas farmers invented the term *robber barons* to describe the ruthless railroad magnates of the late 19th century, such as Jay Gould. The name came to be

111

applied as well to industrialists and financiers who invested large sums in manufacturing, and forced competitors out of business, creating huge corporations, and seized control of entire industries.

Names from the era of the robber barons continue to be associated with corporate America. Gustavus Swift made his fortune in meatpacking, while Charles Pillsbury built an empire on grain. Frederick Weyerhaeuser's chosen business was lumber. People still link steel production with the name Andrew Carnegie, just as they think of oil when they hear the name John D. Rockefeller.

The robber barons cited a newly popular philosophy of human behavior called Social Darwinism to justify their actions. Social Darwinism, as propounded by its foremost advocate, the English journalist Herbert Spencer, was a strange extension of Charles Darwin's theory of natural selection. Darwin theorized that certain traits gave some individual animals a better chance to survive long enough to reproduce, thus allowing them to pass on those traits to their offspring. Spencer described a fiercely competitive social order driven by "the survival of the fittest." Some people were better equipped to survive in the world of work, he declared, and it was only natural for them to achieve success at the expense of "inferior" beings, such as factory workers. The rich merited wealth, just as the poor deserved destitution, and compassion was counterproductive. The steel giant Andrew Carnegie once argued that tossing a coin to a beggar violated the laws of nature. Many of the financiers who built industrial monopolies in the late 19th century had little or no contact with their employees. They viewed labor as a commodity to be purchased at the lowest possible price, worn out, and replaced.

The Rise of Standard Oil

In 1862, John Davison Rockefeller was a 23-year-old commodities trader in Cleveland, Ohio, who decided to invest $4,000 in an oil and kerosene refinery. He was gambling on success in a new industry with an uncertain future. The automobile had yet to be invented, so the demand for gasoline was small. People did use oil and kerosene, though, for lubricating machinery and for lighting. Rockefeller and his partners in the venture, three brothers named Clark, worked hard to make their business a success. On February 1, 1865, Rockefeller purchased the Clarks' interest in the refinery business, and on January 10, 1870, he and other associates, who included his brother William, reorganized the firm as Standard Oil of Ohio. To raise capital of $1 million, they sold 10,000 shares of stock in their company at $100 each.

Standard Oil was one of 250 refineries operating in the United States at that time, and it had at most 4 percent of the business. By bribing railroad executives and working out rebate schemes, and by contracting cheaper rates by agreeing to ship all his product over a particular line, Rockefeller was able to cut transportation costs and undersell the competition. By 1872, he had gained control of 21 of the 26 refineries in Cleveland, and by 1879 Standard Oil of Ohio was refining 90 percent of U.S. oil.

Secretly, and often by deceptive methods, Rockefeller acquired other companies. On January 2, 1882, he established the Standard Oil Trust. A trust is a business organization that consists of several companies united under a formal

The oil fields of Pennsylvania, 1865
(Library of Congress)

agreement to control pricing, production, or other industrial conditions, and to destroy outside competition. The companies within the trust operate as independent units, but they do not compete against one another. The Standard Oil Trust included 14 firms owned completely by the trustees and 26 owned partially. With nearly $73 million in assets, it was the largest business organization in the United States and the nation's first major monopoly. John D. Rockefeller himself was worth $18 million.

Rockefeller expanded his holdings through a process that economists call *horizontal integration*. He acquired companies with the goal of controlling one aspect of the oil industry—refining. Although his tactics gave him an unfair advantage over competitors, horizontal integration in oil and other industries helped to make the United States the world's leading manufacturing nation.

In 1880, most industries consisted of numerous small factories in competition with one another. Some factories had modern equipment and functioned efficiently, while others made do with outmoded machinery and haphazard operations. The quality of manufactured goods varied greatly; also, overproduction occurred commonly, causing prices to fall so low that profits disappeared. Horizontal integration winnowed out the least successful plants and kept the most successful in operation. It established control on the quality, supply, and price of goods.

Carnegie and Steel

Andrew Carnegie, like Rockefeller, began life humbly. Born in 1835 and an immigrant from Scotland, Carnegie started work at 13 as a bobbin boy in a Pennsylvania textile mill. By 17, he was serving as personal assistant to Thomas A. Scott, manager of the Pennsylvania Railroad. He invested his earnings and was a wealthy man by his mid-thirties.

Carnegie used his money to fund iron foundries supplying the railroads, which were replacing their wooden bridges with sturdier iron ones. He was awarded contracts to build two bridges across the Mississippi River. During the Civil War, Carnegie invested in foundries supplying the U.S. government.

In 1872, foreseeing that steel would replace iron in the construction of bridges and buildings, Carnegie built a steel plant at Braddock, Pennsylvania, at the point where the Pennsylvania Railroad, the Baltimore and Ohio Railroad, and the Ohio River meet. He concentrated his assets in the Braddock plant, and when the nation entered a depression in the mid-1870s, he was able to cut his price for steel by five dollars per ton. Carnegie's firm weathered the depression, while some of its competitors did not.

Carnegie acquired other companies, and in 1881 he consolidated his holdings as Carnegie Brothers and Company, Ltd. The new consolidation was capitalized at $5 million, and Carnegie himself owned shares worth $2.7 million. Carnegie sought to control every step in the process of producing steel, from mining the iron ore to forging the finished goods. His acquisitions included steel mills at Homestead, Pennsylvania, and majority shares of the H. C. Frick Coke Company. Coke is the hard, porous residue that remains after the volatile components in coal have been burned away. Coke emits a great deal of heat when burned (13,800 Btu/lb.) and is an efficient fuel for steel production. Carnegie invested funds of his own in the Frick Company, and by 1887 he had purchased 5,000 acres of mines and was producing 6,000 tons of coke a day. Henry Clay Frick rose to the level of second partner in the Carnegie firm, owning 11 percent of its shares.

Carnegie and Frick acquired or established steamship companies to transport iron ore from mines in the Lake Superior region to their foundries. They bought up oil fields in that region, not because they wanted to drill for oil but because owning the oil fields gave them direct access to the iron mines. Carnegie increased his annual production of steel from 322,000 tons in 1890 to 3 million tons in 1900. In 1899, when he consolidated his interests in the Carnegie Steel Company, he controlled about 25 percent of the steel production in the United States.

Carnegie sold his company to the financier J. Pierpont Morgan in January 1901 for $492 million. The deal gave Morgan, who had other steel holdings as well, an overwhelming monopoly in steel. On April 1, 1901, Morgan chartered the United States Steel Corporation in New Jersey.

LEGISLATIVE CONTROLS

Throughout the Gilded Age, the federal and state governments attempted to regulate the activities of the robber barons, who seemed to be destroying the free-market system. Smaller companies had been complaining to legislators because the lower shipping rates that big business enjoyed made it nearly impossible for them to compete. As a response, the Illinois constitution of 1870 included the first legislative attempt to control the rates charged by railroads. The constitution set a fixed maximum rate for railroad transport and established a commission to oversee the business affairs of railroads, warehouses, and grain elevators. California, Georgia, Iowa, Minnesota, and other states enacted similar legislation. The Supreme Court, however, struck down these laws in 1886, when it ruled in the case *Wabash v. Illinois.* The court determined that states could regulate only railroad shipping that occurred wholly within their boundaries. Because three-fourths of all railroad shipping crossed state lines, the laws had little impact.

American business people, meanwhile, had been calling on Congress to address the problem. The result was passage of the Interstate Commerce Act, signed by President Grover Cleveland on February 4, 1887. The act stated that shipping rates had to be "reasonable and just." It was now illegal, for example, for a railroad to charge more to transport goods a short distance than it did to haul a similar load to a more distant destination. The Interstate Commerce Act made rebates and favoritism illegal, and it set up the five-member Interstate Commerce Commission (ICC) to monitor railroad activity and report to Congress. Railroads were required to notify Congress before raising rates.

But by the 1890s, most of the nation's railroads belonged to one of six major systems, four of them owned by J. Pierpont Morgan. These railroad monopolies paid little attention to the ICC and charged whatever rates they chose.

Clearly, the government would need to curtail the power of the trusts and monopolies for the public good. In 1888, Senator John Sherman of Ohio introduced a bill to outlaw trusts and other business combinations that inhibited fair trade. Under the Sherman Antitrust Act, which became law on July 2, 1890, it was illegal to "monopolize trade" or to form any "combination or conspiracy in restraint of trade." Attempting to monopolize any aspect of interstate or international commerce was now a felony.

The act failed to be specific, though, about what it made illegal. For that reason, and because it applied only to commerce and not to production, it was largely ineffective. Twenty-five new trusts were formed in the five years following passage of the Sherman Antitrust Act. By 1904, 318 giant business combinations controlled about 40 percent of all capital invested in manufacturing in the United States.

Many of the newly created firms were holding companies. In other words, they owned a controlling share of the stock in other companies and so were able to influence their activities without becoming involved in day-to-day operations. J. Pierpont Morgan's United States Steel Corporation was a holding company. In 1896, John D. Rockefeller's organization underwent reorganization and was established as a holding company, Standard Oil of New Jersey.

The Clayton Antitrust Act of 1914 elucidated and strengthened the 1890 law. For one thing, it declared specific corporate activities to be illegal, including price-cutting to harm competitors and other forms of price discrimination. For another, it forbade one corporation from acquiring all or part of another if the result tended toward the creation of a monopoly or substantially reduced competition. The Federal Trade Commission (FTC), created in part to enforce the antitrust provisions of the Clayton Act, handled all appeals. The FTC was given the power to issue cease-and-desist orders when illegal actions had been proved.

MEAGER EARNINGS FOR MOST WORKERS

People like Rockefeller, Carnegie, and Morgan, who commanded so much attention from lawmakers and the public, represented one end of the economic spectrum. Many more Americans—the mass of ordinary workers—lived at the other end. In 1869, the *New York Times* conducted a survey and found that just one-eighth of the city's working class earned enough money to afford such extras as newspapers, family outings, beer, and tobacco. Another eighth made enough to pay for life's necessities. The remainder—three-fourths of New York's working class—lived in slums and barely got by.

As the 1880s came to a close, it took $500 to support a family of five living in a mid-sized industrial town for one year. Highly skilled workers such as glass

A Bohemian family makes cigars in a New York tenement, circa 1886, in this photograph by Jacob Riis. The Danish-born Riis documented the lives of New York's poor in the late 19th century. *(Library of Congress)*

The interior of the Triangle Shirtwaist Company following the fire of March 25, 1911 (*Franklin D. Roosevelt Library*)

blowers and iron rollers, who made up 15 percent of the working class, had yearly incomes well above $500, earning between $800 and $1,100 a year. Forty-five percent of the nation's laborers hovered just above the poverty level. Some skilled workers in this group, especially carpenters and machinists, provided their families with small houses or roomy apartments. The remaining 40 percent of the working class earned less than $500 a year. They were forced to live in crowded tenements and to count on their children's income for survival. Of that 40 percent, one-fourth were destitute. Many among them turned to begging and crime.

Some firms paid their workers in company scrip instead of money, which meant that employees were forced to shop at a company store, where prices could be set higher than at regular stores. Workers who lived in company housing had their rent and utilities deducted from their pay. Many found themselves in debt to their employer at the end of the year.

Hours were long, and job security nonexistent. The workday for bakers in New York City, for example, averaged 16.75 hours in the 1880s. A drop in market demand could mean extended unemployment for large numbers of people. In Topeka, Kansas, in 1885, a survey found that one-fifth of all skilled and unskilled workers were unemployed for at least part of the year. The fear of being replaced by a machine was very real for many laborers. As a result of improved technology, spinning and weaving mills required at most one-tenth the number of workers they had employed earlier in the century. Flour mills needed one-fourth of their previous workforce.

An increasing number of workers labored in sweatshops, which were factories housed in rundown buildings that lacked adequate sanitation. Sweatshop workers were paid by the piece, that is, for each item completed rather than by the hour or day. Wages were so inadequate that entire families could toil from sunrise until darkness and still not earn enough to meet their needs. The term *sweatshop* was also applied to piecework done in tenement homes, usually by women and children. Such work included sewing, carding snaps, and making jewelry and artificial flowers. Some home sweatshop work involved food preparation under sanitary conditions that left much to be desired. Workers who lacked knowledge about the transmission of disease often prepared food while coughing and sneezing. It was common to shell nuts with the teeth, because metal picks broke too many nut meats, and employers paid only for unbroken nuts.

Factories continued to be hazardous places, and employers offered no compensation to those injured or sickened on the job. Textile workers risked lung disease from inhaling the damp, lint-filled air in the mills. In textile mills and elsewhere, machinery still lacked safety features, and exposure to toxic substances was commonplace. It was standard procedure at many sewing shops to lock the seamstresses inside. This practice had tragic consequences on March 25, 1911, when a fire broke out at the Triangle Shirtwaist Company of New York City. One hundred forty-six women died in the fire or leaping from a window.

IMMIGRATION BUILDS A WORKFORCE

Increasingly during the Gilded Age, the workforce in manufacturing and mechanical industries was foreign-born. The U.S. population rose nearly 132 percent between 1870 and 1910, from 39,905,000 to 92,407,000, primarily because of immigration. The number of industrial laborers increased more than 300 percent over those 40 years, from 3.5 million to 14.2 million. There was a 12-fold increase in the number of iron and steelworkers, bringing that total to 326,000. The U.S. census counted 283,000 machinists in 1910, while in 1870 there had been just 55,000.

The large influx of people made the period's rapid industrialization possible, yet many U.S.-born workers resented the immigrants, whom they feared (frequently with good reason) would be willing to work for less money and thus depress wages for everyone.

Industries that needed skilled workers for specialized jobs brought immigrants to the United States as contract laborers. The workers had their transportation costs paid in exchange for a period of employment. For example, a mining company that wanted to hire an experienced miner from Ireland or Britain agreed to pay the miner's fare and a fraction of his family's fare. The miner, in turn, was obligated to work for two years at half pay, which came to about 10 dollars a month. According to the 1870 census, half of all U.S. miners were either foreign-born or the children of immigrants.

Most of the people entering the United States during this period had no jobs awaiting them, but overcrowding, lack of opportunity, and in many cases religious persecution had forced them to leave villages in their homelands. American employers, including Andrew Carnegie and the other large industrialists, were quick to hire recent immigrants. Of the 14,359 people employed at Carnegie's Pittsburgh plants between 1890 and 1910, 11,694 came from southern and eastern Europe. The accident rate among recent immigrants was high: 3,723 were killed or injured on the job between 1907 and 1910.

Many of the immigrants who sought jobs in industry were single men or married men who had left their wives and children in Europe. They planned to work for a few years and save their money before returning home to buy a farm. Despite the dangerous work environment and the low wages they received, a surprising number of these men achieved their goal. For every 100 southern and eastern Europeans who came to the United States, 44 embarked for their homelands. Most of the immigrants, however, came to stay.

Immigrant children often worked alongside their parents in factories. With the termination of slavery, southern mill owners replaced their enslaved labor force with children. By 1900, 25,000 girls and boys age 15 and younger were working in southern factories.

THE GROWTH OF CITIES

The proliferation of factories furthered the growth of cities, as workers—both foreign- and native-born—settled near their places of employment. Thirty-one percent of the population lived in cities in 1900, and that percentage would increase in the 20th century. The post–Civil War years saw the transformation of some large cities into industrial metropolises. In 1870, New York City, which then comprised only Manhattan and a few islands in the East River, already had a population approaching a million. Brooklyn, New York, was a separate industrial city, the third largest in the United States, with a population of nearly 420,000. Chicago was growing rapidly as well. To observe the landscape of Chicago was to survey 100 acres of cattle pens, 275 slaughterhouses and packinghouses, and numerous steel mills and plants.

Even small cities, such as Paterson, New Jersey, underwent great change. Paterson saw its population nearly triple between 1850 and 1875 as three large locomotive plants, 14 silk mills, and jute, linen, and mosquito-netting factories opened there.

Meeting the demand for housing, office buildings, and retail space provided work for 750,000 carpenters as well as many bricklayers, plasterers, roofers, and cabinetmakers. In such cities as New York and Chicago, it was common to see workers balancing on steel beams and cables high above the streets, building skyscrapers and bridges. The growing cities demanded more services as technology advanced. They needed wiring for electricity and telephones and tracks for trolleys.

In New York City at the start of the 20th century, construction workers were erecting the famous Flatiron Building and a second bridge across the East River, yet an estimated 70 percent of the city's population lived in 32,000 slum tenements concentrated near the Manhattan shoreline. The tenement buildings lacked adequate light, clean air, and sanitation. Streets in these neighborhoods were crowded with peddlers' carts and littered with trash. Sewer pipes frequently backed up, and they sometimes burst open. Crime thrived in the slum neighborhoods, because law enforcement was lax.

Ironworkers balance on a high girder in New York City in this 1904 charcoal drawing by Thornton Oakley. *(Library of Congress)*

Industrialization had transformed the United States into a world power and made possible the production of countless items for consumption at home and abroad. For too many years, the economy had been growing at the expense of its workforce—but American workers had not been suffering in silence. Many looked to labor unions to bring about changes that were long overdue.

CHRONICLE OF EVENTS

1870

January 10: John D. Rockefeller and associates form Standard Oil of Ohio.

3.5 million Americans are employed as industrial laborers.

The Illinois Constitution attempts to control railroad rates.

1872

Andrew Carnegie builds a steel plant at Braddock, Pennsylvania.

1873

Mark Twain and Charles Dudley Warner publish *The Gilded Age.*

1876

May 10: The Centennial Exposition opens in Philadelphia.

1879

Standard Oil of Ohio is refining 90 percent of U.S. oil.

1880

Forty percent of the working class in the United States lives below the poverty line.

1881

Carnegie consolidates his holdings to form Carnegie Brothers and Company, Ltd.

1882

January 2: Rockefeller establishes the Standard Oil Trust.

Thousands attended the opening ceremonies of the Philadelphia Centennial Exposition. *(Library of Congress)*

1886

The Supreme Court finds state laws regulating rail-road transport to be unconstitutional.

1887

February 4: President Grover Cleveland signs the Interstate Commerce Act.

1889

Forty percent of the working class earns less than $500 a year.

1890

July 2: The Sherman Antitrust Act becomes law.

1894

The United States leads the world in the value of its manufactured goods.

1896

Rockefeller establishes Standard Oil of New Jersey.

1899

Andrew Carnegie forms the Carnegie Steel Company, which controls approximately one-fourth of U.S. steel production.

1900

14.2 million Americans are employed as industrial laborers.

Andrew Carnegie speaks at the groundbreaking for the Pan American Union Building in Washington, D.C., March 11, 1908. *(Library of Congress)*

Thirty-one percent of U.S. residents live in cities.

Twenty-five thousand children work in southern factories.

1901

January: J. Pierpont Morgan buys the Carnegie Steel Company for $492 million.

April 10: Morgan charters the United States Steel Corporation.

1911

March 25: A fire at the Triangle Shirtwaist Company of New York City claims 146 lives.

1914

The Clayton Antitrust Act clarifies and strengthens the Sherman Antitrust Act.

Eyewitness Testimony

Health is the platform on which all happiness must be built. Good appetite, good digestion, and good sleep are the elements of health, and industry confers them. As use polishes metals, so labor the faculties, until the body performs its unimpeded functions with elastic cheerfulness and hearty enjoyment.

Henry Ward Beecher, 1873, "Industry and Idleness,"
in Lectures to Young Men on Various
Important Subjects, *p. 8.*

There are men who, supposing Providence to have an implacable spite against them, bemoan in the poverty of a wretched old age the misfortunes of their lives. Luck forever ran against them, and for others. One, with a good profession, lost his luck in the river, where he idled away his time a-fishing when he should have been in the office. Another, with a good trade, perpetually burnt up his luck by his hot temper, which provoked all his customers to leave him. Another, with a lucrative business, lost his luck by amazing diligence at everything but his business. Another, who steadily followed his trade, as steadily followed his bottle. . . . I never knew an early-rising, hard-working, prudent man, careful of his earnings and strictly honest, who complained of bad luck.

Henry Ward Beecher, 1873, "Industry and Idleness,"
in Lectures to Young Men on Various
Important Subjects, *p. 13.*

The ant will repair his dwelling as often as the mischievous foot crushes it; the spider will exhaust life itself, before he will live without a web; the bee can be decoyed from his labor neither by plenty nor scarcity. If summer be abundant, it toils none the less; if it be parsimonious of flowers, the tiny laborer sweeps a wider circle, and by industry repairs the frugality of the season. Man should be ashamed to be rebuked in vain by the spider, the ant, and the bee.

Henry Ward Beecher, 1873, "Industry and Idleness,"
in Lectures to Young Men on Various
Important Subjects, *p. 27.*

There are eight companies in the stone business here, only four of which are running at present; and, running or loafing, they have a store apiece. All their employees must trade in their stores; if not, "get work where you trade. We keep as good articles here as you can get elsewhere, and sell as cheap too." And that is all the satisfaction you will get for your complaint. I have had to pay $1.35 for a pair of children's shoes that I could buy outside for 50 cents, and so on with everything else, to $2 on a barrel of flour; and everybody else must do likewise. . . . And that is not all either: some of them have tenement houses, and they must be kept full; and those who live in them are in a complete state of vassalage. And that is not all: no matter how frugally you live, you never get anything ahead; and those having helpless families scarcely ever receive a dollar. They are closely watched on the books, lest they might overrun their wages; and consequently they will get nothing, only as they earn it. Such is the atrocious system here; and this is a part of free, enlightened Massachusetts!

A quarryman reporting to the Massachusetts Bureau
of Statistics and Labor, 1879, in Leon Litwack,
The American Labor Movement, *p. 17.*

Its genius for monopoly has given the Standard control of more than the product of oil and its manufacture. Wholesale merchants in all the cities of the country, except New York, have to buy and sell at the prices it makes. Merchants who buy oil of the Standard are not allowed to sell to dealers who buy of its few competitors. Some who have done so have been warned not to repeat the offense, and have been informed that, if they did so, the Standard, though under contract to supply them with oil, would cut them off, and would fight any suit they might bring through all the courts without regard to expense.

Henry D. Lloyd, 1881, "Story of a Great
Monopoly," pp. 328–29.

The time has come to face the fact that the forces of capital and industry have outgrown the forces of our government. . . . Our strong men are engaged in a headlong fight for fortune, power, precedence, success. Americans as they are, they ride over the people like Juggernaut to gain their ends. The moralists have preached to them since the world began, and have failed. The common people, the nation, must take them in hand. The people can be successful only when they are right. When monopolies succeed, the people fail; when a rich criminal escapes justice, the people are punished; when a legislature is bribed, the people are cheated.

Henry D. Lloyd, 1881, "Story of a Great Monopoly," p. 333.

A few individuals are becoming rich enough to control almost all the great markets, including the legislatures. We feel ourselves caught in the whirl of new forces, and flung forward every day a step farther into a future dim with the portents of struggle between Titans reared on steam, electricity, and credit. It is an unfortunate moment for the break-down of the science that claimed to be able to reconcile self-interest with the harmony of interests.

Henry D. Lloyd, 1882, "The Political Economy of Seventy-Three Million Dollars," p. 70.

The first clatter of machinery is heard in a room which is "all windows," where "girls," who are always girls, no matter the age, sit with eyes and hands busy at sewing-machines. No longer the "stitch, stitch, stitch" of the weary binder, but machines speeded at the rate of six hundred stitches in a minute! Their introduction came early in the "golden age" of invention, and with the advent of sole-cutting and sewing-machines, foot-power began to assert its rising importance. Now even the foot is relieved, and the machines are run almost altogether from steam shafting. In this "stitching-room" the small quarter and button piece [of a woman's high-button shoe] are "closed" on the large quarter, the seams are "rubbed down" on the inside, and a "stay" is sewed over the inside of the seam with a row of stitching on each side. The different parts of the lining are stitched together in similar manner, when outside and lining are passed along to be "closed on." A small cut on the front of the lining is the only guide by which an experienced "closer-on" knows where to begin her work, yet as with accurate eye and practiced hand the needle and "trimming knife" follow the winding outline, it seems as if she must be following a traced pattern. . . . Perhaps you may wonder at the swiftly moving machines, but if you will look at your watch you will wonder still more to find that this whole stitching has been done in fifteen minutes—scarcely more than a dressmaker would have taken in making a single hand-made button-hole in a new dress.

Howard Mudge Newhall, 1885, "A Pair of Shoes," pp. 280–82.

A gradual reduction in the number of working months of shoe operatives, caused by the ease with which labor-saving machinery can supply the market, has made the shoemaker somewhat *migratory* in his pursuit. If there is not full work at his regular place of employment he uses his spare hours in another factory, or, as is often the case in shoe-manufacturing cities, works for half the season in a factory supplying the Western market, and in a factory supplying the New England market the other half of the season. Sometimes, too, men begin a season in New York and finish in some Massachusetts shoe city. It is not uncommon for a man to "hold a job" in each of two small factories, and be returned as an employé in two factories. He would thus increase the number of employés and decrease the average wages. This migrating is done in hundreds of instances by men, women, and children operatives, and is a peculiarity whose effect it would be impossible to estimate.

Howard Mudge Newhall, 1885, "A Pair of Shoes," p. 287.

The inhabitants of typical factory villages come in contact with few people very different from themselves in ideas or education. Their employers know little of them except in the mass, and they know little of their employers save as represented to them by business officials concerned in the management. . . . While the head clerks and superintendents are still Americans, the lower overseers are now foreigners, who have acquired more skill in work, but not necessarily higher development in morals, than their fellows.

Lillie B. Chance Wyman, 1888, "Studies of Factory Life: The Village System," pp. 19–20.

If a family in the mill service, which has rented rooms from the company, withdraws its working members from the factory, it is required to leave its habitation within a reasonable time. . . .

Thus it happens that as the children grow up and leave the parents, no longer constituting a working force for them, the old man and his wife may be constrained to quit their roomy residence, and in one day all the associations of twenty or thirty years are destroyed. Since these movings are not voluntary, the sundering of old ties cannot be accompanied by the softening influence of the new hopes which are implied in the deliberate choice of a removal.

Lillie B. Chance Wyman, 1888, "Studies of Factory Life: The Village System," pp. 22–23.

Sometimes an operative arranges to pay monthly installments to a storekeeper to whom he is in debt. Then the storekeeper receives his portion directly from the factory counting-room. If the mill company owns a store, its bills against any of the help are subtracted from their wages, when the monthly accounts are made up. Rent and board are taken out in the same manner, and also the price of wood and coal furnished by the establishment. After these deductions are made, it often happens that, in the phrase of the mill-worker, very little cash "comes in" to him.

Lillie B. Chance Wyman, 1888, "Studies of Factory Life: The Village System," p. 24.

A great deal of my time has been spent among the poor girls of Lynn connected with the shoe industry, and I know that their lot is not to be envied. Often, after getting a few weeks' pay, they are thrown out on to the world, and all the winter and spring there is any amount of poverty among them. Many at these times have to live on bread and water in order to get along. There is a large class in Lynn of these homeless girls, who, for a great part of the time, undergo such hardships as I have described. . . . Some of them drift off to Boston, which is already overstocked with the unemployed of their class. I say I have had to do with these girls, and I have had them come to me a dozen times in the week for help or advice, telling me they had no money to pay for their room or to pay for food or for a nurse or for medicine. . . . I should say that one third of the girls of Lynn are homeless and subject to these changes of fortune.

A shoe stitcher quoted in the Boston Herald, *July 29, 1888, in Mary H. Blewett,* We Will Rise in Our Might, *p. 171.*

We must all have our toys; the child his rattle, the adult his hobby, the man of pleasure the fashion, the man of art his Master; and mankind in its various divisions requires a change of toys at short intervals. The same rule holds good in the business world. We have had our age of "consolidations" and "watered stocks." Not long ago everything was a "syndicate"; the word is already becoming obsolete and the fashion is for "Trusts," which will in turn no doubt give place to some new panacea, that is in turn to be displaced by another, and so on without end. The great laws of the economic world, like all laws affecting society, being the genuine outgrowth of human nature, alone remain unchanged through all these changes. Whenever consolidations, or watered stocks, or syndicates, or Trusts endeavor to circumvent these, it always has been found the result is that after the collision there is nothing left of the panaceas, while the great laws continue to grind out their irresistible consequences as before.

Andrew Carnegie, 1889, "The Bugaboo of Trusts," p. 141.

It is well, nay, essential for the progress of the race, that the houses of some should be homes for all that is highest and best in literature and the arts, and for all the refinements of civilization, rather than that none should be so. Much better this great irregularity than universal squalor. . . . The "good old times" were not good old times. Neither master nor servant was as well situated then as to-day. A relapse to old conditions would be disastrous to both—not the least so to him who serves—and would sweep away civilization with it. But whether the change be for good or ill, it is upon us, beyond our power to alter, and therefore to be accepted and made the best of. It is a waste of time to criticise the inevitable.

Andrew Carnegie, 1889, "Wealth," pp. 653–54.

In one large and long-established manufactory in one of the Eastern States the proprietors testify that it would require five hundred persons, working by hand processes and in the old way in the shops by the roadside, to make as many women's boots and shoes as one hundred persons now make with the aid of machinery and by congregated labor, a contraction of eighty per cent in this particular case. In another division of the same industry the number of men required to produce a given quantity of boots and shoes has been reduced one half, while, in still another locality, and on another quality of boots, being entirely for women's wear, where formerly a first-class workman could turn out six pairs in one week, he will now turn out eighteen pairs. A well-known firm in the West engaged in the manufacture of boots and shoes finds that it would take one hundred and twenty persons, working by hand, to produce the amount of work done in its factory by sixty employees, and that the handwork would not compare in workmanship and appearance by fifty per cent.

Carroll D. Wright, 1895, The Industrial Evolution of the United States, *p. 327.*

We are living at the beginning of the age of mind, as illustrated by the results of inventive genius. It is the age of intellect, of brain—for brain is king, and machinery is the king's prime minister. Wealth of mind and wealth of purse may struggle for mastery, but the former usually wins. . . . It is natural and logical that under such a sovereignty inventions should not only typify the progress of the race, but that they should also have a clearly marked influence upon the morals of peoples, a mixed influence, to be sure, as men are what we call good or evil, but on the whole with the good vastly predominant.

Carrol D. Wright, 1895, The Industrial Evolution of the United States, *p. 345.*

. . . I think that the opportunity for rising from the ranks of labor to the ranks of the employers has largely gone by. I do not mean to say wiped out entirely, but I mean to say largely eliminated. The man who set up a small printing office with a little job press and a few cases of type, and would go out and solicit work and make a little money out of it—that class of men is being rapidly eliminated. I was independent to the extent that as long as I had my trade I could earn my living, but today that is not true; and that character of men is wiped out almost entirely. The large printing office with its improved machinery makes it impossible for me to compete with them.

From the testimony of Jacob G. Schonfarber, a printer, before the U.S. House of Representatives, December 5, 1899, in Leon Litwack, The American Labor Movement, *p. 9.*

We were tired out when we reached the stockyards [of Chicago], so we stopped on the bridge and looked into the river out there. It was so full of grease and dirt and sticks and boxes that it looked like a big, wide, dirty street, except in some places, where it boiled up. It made me sick to look at it. When I looked away I could see on one side some big fields full of holes, and these were the city dumps. On the other side were the stockyards, with twenty tall slaughter house chimneys. The wind blew a big smell from them to us. Then we walked on between the yards and the dumps and all the houses looked bad and poor. In our house my room was in the basement. I lay down on the floor with three other men and the air was rotten. I did not go to sleep for a long time. I knew then that money was everything I needed. My money was almost gone and I thought that I would soon die unless I got a job, for this was not like home. Here money was everything and a man without money must die.

Antanas Kaztauskis, 1904, "From Lithuania to the Chicago Stockyards," p. 245.

We went to the doors of one big slaughter house. There was a crowd of about 200 men waiting there for a job. They looked hungry and kept watching the door. At last a special policeman came out and began pointing to men, one by one. Each one jumped forward. Twenty-three were taken. Then they all went inside, and all the others turned their faces away and looked tired. I remember one boy sat down and cried, just next to me, on a pile of boards.

Antanas Kaztauskis, 1904, "From Lithuania to the Chicago Stockyards," p. 246.

I have heard some big talk . . . about my American freedom of contract, but I do not think I had much freedom in bargaining for this job with the Meat Trust. My job was in the cattle killing room. I pushed the blood along the gutter. Some people think these jobs make men bad. I do not think so. The men who do the killing are not as bad as the ladies with fine clothes who come every day to look at it, because they have to do it. The cattle do not suffer. They are knocked senseless with a big hammer and are dead before they wake up. This is done not to spare them pain, but because if they got hot and sweating with fear and pain the meat would not be so good. I soon saw that every job in the room was done like this—so as to save everything and make money. One Lithuanian, who worked with me, said, "They get all the blood out of cattle and all the work out of us men." This was true, for we worked that first day from six in the morning till seven at night. The next day we worked from six in the morning till eight at night. The next day we had no work. So we had no good, regular hours. It was hot in the room that summer, and the hot blood made it worse.

Antanas Kaztauskis, 1904, "From Lithuania to the Chicago Stockyards," p. 246.

[The Standard Oil Company] has been conscienceless and brazen in utter disregard of public and private rights. Ultimately there can be but one result if the methods and ambitions of this great corporation are not checked and made to observe the limits of the public welfare. It will become greater than the State, will dictate terms to the State and force its non-competitive, socialistic, destructive methods into every line of business. It has forgotten and now denies the great American principle of a "square deal" for every man. In many localities the startling condition prevails that the majority of people accept this denial of equality of opportunity as the best condition available. Such a state of mind in the average citizen is the danger point in public affairs. As yet perhaps this state of mind is limited to sections, but it is the seed of a dangerous growth. More than all the questions of big profits or little profits, monopoly or no monopoly, is the importance of assuring all the people all the time that all men are equal before the law and equal in opportunity before the law.

Edward Wallace Hoch, governor of Kansas, 1905,
"Kansas and the Standard Oil Company," pp. 461–62.

. . . [I]t was Saturday night, and life was running at flood-tide all over the great city. . . . At the stroke of bell, at the clang of deep-mouthed gong, at the scream of siren whistle, the sluice-gates were lifted from the great human reservoirs of factory and shop and office, and their myriad toilers burst forth with the cumulative violence of six days' restraint.

It was a shabby carnival of nations that jostled one another at this windy corner—Italian, Spanish, German, Slav, Jew, Greek, with a preponderance of Irish and "free-born" Americans. The general air was one of unwonted happiness and freedom. The atmosphere of holiday liberty was vibrant with the expectation of Saturday-night abandon to fun and frolic or wild carousal.

Dorothy Richardson, 1905, The Long Day, *pp. 109–10.*

We saved some, but somethin' always comes. Sickness is the worst. When you drive on eight looms all the time in busy season you get sort of "spent," and you catch cold easy. In winter they don't shovel off the paths half the time 'round them mills, and you got to go right out of the mill to your knees in snow. Then like as not you have to wait a long time in the snow for the freight trains to pass. Some of the girls take sick awful sudden and never get back for their pay envelopes—they go that quick sometimes. It was like that when you got so tired "drivin'" at eight looms, and when they gave us twelve looms I didn't see that we could make out to live

at all. . . . But that don't make no matter—there's plenty waitin' at the gates for our jobs, I guess.

"Mary," a textile-mill worker, 1905, in Gertrude Barnum,
"The Story of a Fall River Mill Girl," pp. 242–43.

Probably the greatest single obstacle to the progress and happiness of the American people lies in the willingness of so many men to invest their time and money in multiplying competitive industries instead of opening up new fields, and putting their money into lines of industry and development that are needed. It requires a better type of mind to seek out and to support or to create the new than to follow the worn paths of accepted success; but here is the great chance in our still rapidly developing country. The penalty of a selfish attempt to make the world confer a living without contributing to the progress or happiness of mankind is generally a failure to the individual.

John D. Rockefeller, 1909, Random Reminiscences
of Men and Events, *pp. 144–45.*

A jaunty John D. Rockefeller is dressed for golf in 1908. *(Library of Congress)*

The profits of the Standard Oil Company did not come from the advantages given by railroads. The railroads, rather, were the ones who profited by the traffic of the Standard Oil Company, and whatever advantage it received in its constant efforts to reduce rates of freight was only one of the many elements of lessening cost to the consumer which enabled us to increase our volume of business the world over because we could reduce the selling price.

John D. Rockefeller, 1909, Random Reminiscences of Men and Events, *p. 111.*

We devoted ourselves exclusively to the oil business and its products. The company never went into outside ventures, but kept to the enormous task of perfecting its own organization. We educated our own men; we trained many of them from boyhood; we strove to keep them loyal by providing them full scope for their ability; they were given opportunities to buy stock, and the company itself helped them to finance their purchases. Not only here in America, but all over the world, our young men were given chances to advance themselves, and the sons of the old partners were welcomed to the councils and responsibilities of the administration. I may say that the company has been in all its history, and I am sure it is at present, a most happy association of busy people.

John D. Rockefeller, 1909, Random Reminiscences of Men and Events, *pp. 88–89.*

The conditions under which the work is carried on [in a Carnegie Steel plant] seem to an outsider fairly intolerable. The din in the great vaulted sheds makes speech hard. Men who have worked near the engines, though their organs of hearing remain in physically good condition, sometimes become almost oblivious to ordinary sound. Some work where the heat is intense; and before the open doors of furnaces full of white-hot metal they must wear smoked glasses to temper the glare. This heat, exhausting in summer, makes a man in winter doubly susceptible to the cold without. While for the men directing the processes the physical exertion is often not great, most of the laborers perform heavy manual toil. And everywhere is the danger of accident from constantly moving machinery, from bars of glowing steel, from engines moving along the tracks in the yard. The men, of course, grow used to these dangers, but a new peril lies in the carelessness that results from such familiari-ty, for human nature cannot be eternally on guard; men would be unable to do their work if they became too cautious.

The nature of the work, with the heat and its inherent hazard, makes much of it exhausting. Yet these men for the most part keep it up twelve hours a day.

Margaret Byington, 1910, Homestead, *pp. 35–36.*

I have seen a girl in the desquamating stage of scarlet fever (when her throat was so bad that she could not speak above a whisper) tying ostrich feathers in the Italian district [of New York City]. These feathers were being made for one the biggest feather factories in the lower part of the city. She told me herself she had been sick with scarlet fever for ten days, but had been upstairs in a neighbor's room working for over a week. . . .

Men, women, and children suffering from tuberculosis and attending tuberculosis clinics were found picking nuts and working on feathers and dolls' clothes. In one family three members were attending the dispensary for treatment, all suffering from tuberculosis. All were working at picking nuts.

Miss Watson of the National Child Labor Committee, 1912, in Grace Abbott, The Child and the State, *pp. 362–63.*

The stories told by some of the flower makers show more vividly than statistics what their home responsibilities are. One girl, eighteen years old, had worked four years in paper box factories but after an injury to her finger from an unguarded machine she applied at a flower shop as learner at $4.00 a week. After six months this sum was increased to $4.50. In May, when interviewed, the dull season had begun and until September she expected to work only three days a week, earning $2.25. "That isn't enough to pay for what I eat," she said. She was hoping for a second increase of 50 cents a week in September, and she figured that if the family could hold out until autumn she could work overtime four nights a week, beginning in November, and in addition could bring work home at night, from which she and her mother, her sister, and a brother twelve years old could earn together $3.00 a week. But she feared that she would be obliged to look immediately for work in another trade and miss that 50 cents raise and that opportunity to work overtime in the shop, and later make flowers at night. Her father had deserted the family. Her brother, who had been a driver for a woolen goods house, had been out of work three months, having lost his job because of a strike. A younger sister was a learner in an ostrich feather shop, earning $3.50. That sum plus the flower maker's $2.25 was at the moment the family income to support the mother, two sons, and two daughters.

Mary Van Kleeck, 1913, Artificial Flower Makers, *pp. 80–81.*

In a tenement on Macdougal Street lives a family of seven—grandmother, father, mother, and four children aged four years, three years, two years, and one month respectively. All excepting the father and the two babies make violets. The three-year-old girl picks apart the petals; her sister, aged four years, separates the stems, dipping an end of each into paste spread on a piece of board on the kitchen table; and the mother and grandmother slip the petals up the stems.

"We all must work if we want to earn anything," said the mother. They are paid 10 cents for a gross, 144 flowers, and if they work steadily from 8 or 9 o'clock in the morning until 7 or 8 at night, they may make 12 gross, $1.20. In the busy season their combined earnings are usually $7.00 a week. During five months, from April to October, they have no work. They live in three rooms for which they pay $10 a month. The kitchen, which is used as a workroom, is lighted only by a window into an adjoining room. The father is a porter. Both he and his wife were born in Italy but came to New York when they were children. The wife when a child, before she was able to work in a factory, made flowers at home. Later she worked in a candy factory.

Mary Van Kleeck, 1913, Artificial Flower Makers, *pp. 94–95.*

Twenty years ago, when we went from house to house caring for the sick, manufacturing was carried on in the tenements on a scale that does not exist today. With no little consternation we saw toys and infants' clothing, and sometimes food itself, made under conditions that would not have been tolerated in factories, even at that time. And the connection of remote communities and individuals with the East Side of New York was impressed upon us when we saw a roomful of children's clothing shipped to the Southern trade from a tenement where there were sixteen cases of measles. One of our patients, in an advanced stage of tuberculosis, until our appearance on the scene sat coughing in her bed, making cigarettes and moistening the paper with her lips. In another tenement in a nearby street we found children ill with scarlet fever. The parents worked as finishers of women's cloaks of good quality, evidently meant to be worn by the well-to-do. The garments covered the little patients, and the bed on which they lay was practically used as a work-table.

Lillian D. Wald, 1915, "The House on Henry Street," p. 812.

The New York Department of Labor, during the two years ending August, 1913, had 284 cases of industrial diseases reported to it. Of this number 239, or nearly 85 per cent., were caused by lead poisoning; 8, or about 3 per cent., were caused by brass, mercury, phosphorus, and wood alcohol poisoning; 5, or about 2 per cent., contracted anthrax; 30, or about 10 per cent., were subject to caisson disease [nitrogen narcosis] when working in shafts and tunnels. Of the lead poisonings about one-fourth occurred among workers in the manufacture of electric batteries and in the painting of vehicles, and nearly a half in house painting.

W. Jett Lauck and Edgar Sydenstrecker, 1917, Conditions of Labor in American Industries, *pp. 213–14.*

In the glass bottle factories investigated, the glass dust comes partly from the glass on the floor [according to a government report], but far more from what is known as "blow-over," the name given to those gossamer-like flakes of filmy glass that are usually found floating in the air of a bottle house. When a bottle has been blown into form in a mold it is necessary to detach the blowpipe without injuring the neck of the bottle. To do this the glass between the top of the mold and the butt of the blowpipe is blown into a thin bubble which can be easily broken. This can be done so as to cause practically no blow-over, but it is "quicker and easier to blow hard enough to inflate and burst this portion of the glass by internal air pressure. When this is done the bubble explodes with a popping noise and its walls fly into the air, often into the mold-boy's face, and the light particles of glass float in the air currents of the room." . . .

The report says:

"In some factories at times the air is so full of this floating glass that the hair is whitened by merely passing through the room. It sticks to the perspiration on the faces and arms of the boys and men, and becomes

a source of considerable irritation. Getting into the eyes, it becomes especially troublesome."
W. Jett Lauck and Edgar Sydenstrecker, 1917, Conditions of Labor in American Industries, *pp. 215–26.*

The tuberculosis rate has been found to be considerably higher than the average for all occupations among glass and stone workers and among grinders and polishers in metal working plants, and suggests the harmful effect of working in certain substances. In brass foundries, for example, the dense clouds of deflagrated zinc arising from the molten metal have injurious effects.
W. Jett Lauck and Edgar Sydenstrecker, 1917, Conditions of Labor in American Industries, *p. 215.*

The Federal report on woman and child wage-earners stated that in cotton mills . . . the light in the weaving-rooms only was good. Ventilation was apt to be poor. The temperature of the mills was often found to be high, and in certain rooms the humidity was excessive. In the Southern mills over 80 per cent., of the toilets were unclean, and in over 50 per cent., in both sections, there was no reasonable privacy of approach. Wash rooms and dressing rooms were rare.
W. Jett Lauck and Edgar Sydenstrecker, 1917, Conditions of Labor in American Industries, *p. 218.*

Why, today, while over the civilized world there is so much distress, so much want, what is the cry that goes up? What is the current explanation of the hard times? Over-production! There are so many clothes that men must go ragged; so much coal in the bitter winters people have to shiver; such over-filled granaries that people actually die by starvation! Want due to over-production! Was a greater absurdity ever uttered?
Henry George, 1918, "The Crime of Poverty," p. 35.

I was first conscious of the blaring mouths of furnaces. There were five of them, and men with shovels in line, marching within a yard, hurling a white gravel down red throats. Two of the men were stripped, and their backs were shiny in the red flare.
Charles Rumford Walker, who worked in a steel mill in 1919, Steel, *p. 8.*

The pit was an area of perhaps half an acre, with open sides and a roof. Two cranes traversed its entire extent, and a railway passed through its outer edge, bearing mammoth moulds, seven feet high above their flat cars.

Every furnace protruded a spout, and, when the molten steel inside was "cooked," tilted backward slightly and poured into a ladle. A bunch of things happened before that pouring. Men appeared on a narrow platform with a very twisted railing, near the spout, and worked for a time with rods. They prodded up inside, till a tiny stream of fire broke through. Then you could see them start back in the nick of time to escape the deluge of molten steel. The stream in the spout would swell to the circumference of a man's body, and fall into the ladle, that oversized bucket thing. . . . A dizzying tide of sparks accompanied the stream, and shot out quite far into the pit, at times causing men to slap themselves to keep their clothing from breaking out into a blaze. There were always staccato human voices against the mechanical noise, and you distinguished by inflection, whether you heard command, or assent, or warning, or simply the lubrications of profanity.
Charles Rumford Walker, who worked in a steel mill in 1919, Steel, *pp. 19–20.*

Inside a Pittsburgh steel mill *(Library of Congress)*

The heat was bad at times (from 120 to 130 degrees when you're right in it, I should guess). It was like constantly sticking your head into the fireplace. When you had a cake or two of newly turned slag, glowing on both sides, you worked like hell to get your pick work done and come out. I found a given amount of work in heat fatigued at three times the rate of the same work in a cooler atmosphere. But it was exciting, at all events, and preferable to monotony.

Charles Rumford Walker, who worked in a steel mill in 1919, Steel, *p. 22.*

If you approach the [Italian] district from the south, by way of Canal or Broome streets, you will notice the odor of chocolate from some candy factory, or the strong smell of glue from a paper-box plant. On the west side, along Hudson and Greenwich streets, alluring signs advertise the homes of famous salad dressings, spices, groceries, or pickles. Approach from Broadway and you pass crowded workrooms where men's clothing is made by the wholesale, hats turned out by the gross, and flowers and feathers pasted, branched, and packed for shipment to the farthest corners of the country. You pick your way through the narrow, crowded streets of Mercer, Greene, or West Broadway, where heavily loaded trucks are delivering huge rolls of cloth or carrying away the finished products in the form of underwear, neckwear, shirtwaists, or mattresses and burial supplies. To the north of the neighborhood lies the center of the industry of women's and children's clothing, not only for New York City but for the whole United States as well. Here cloaks and suits are stitched and finished for wearers from Maine to Oregon, dresses of silk, wool, or cotton for the women of Dakota or Texas, and clothing for the children of San Francisco or Atlanta. Gray buildings of 15 or 20 stories tower high to the heavens, each floor vibrating with the motion of heavy-power sewing machines. In the height of the season every nook of each loft is filled with men and women straining every nerve to satisfy the frantic demands of jobber and retailer.

Louise C. Odencrantz, 1919, Italian Women in Industry, *pp. 31–32.*

In a long, narrow room, down on Cherry Street, lighted only by a skylight, two Italian women were found standing and bending while they sorted bales of dusty waste paper. Neither could speak a word of English and neither knew that they were violating any law because they worked ten and a half hours every day, from seven in the morning until six at night. They only knew that at the end of a week's work the Italian owner, who was a friend, handed them each a five-dollar bill.

Louise C. Odencrantz, 1919, Italian Women in Industry, *p. 80.*

The family . . . had an income of $907.34 with which to support a family of twelve. The father, a peddler of cheese, whose earnings were casual and spasmodic, preferred bullying every cent of their wages from his two young daughters, who were the chief support of the family, to going out himself in disagreeable weather to sell his wares. . . . The two girls, sixteen and eighteen years old, worked in a factory where negligees were made, and their piece-rate wages were subject to decided seasonal fluctuations. . . . Toward the end of the year the oldest boy became fourteen and went to work, but he, too, shifted from one job to another and was sick in addition, so that his contribution was negligible. The mother, a woman of only thirty-six, who had 15 children, 10 of whom were living and three of whom were babies two years old or less, was too worn with childbirths and the care of her family to undertake even home work.

Louise C. Odencrantz, 1919, Italian Women in Industry, *pp. 212–14.*

Many of the cheaper garments, such as overalls and workingmen's blouses, are now made almost exclusively in the factory, while some of the most expensive garments, requiring hand finishing, are sent to the sweat shops for completion. Not infrequently expensive suitings, overcoats, women's and children's clothing of the finest quality were found being finished in such quarters, and in direct contact with various diseases. . . . Not infrequently such a disease as smallpox has broken out in communities, and the local authorities have been quite unable to determine its source. Such diseases may have come directly through the wearing of clothing which had been finished in the sweat shop.

Ezra Thayer Towne, 1924, Social Problems, *p. 104.*

7

Labor Organizes
1788–1918

Hours before daylight on July 6, 1892, a steamboat tugged two barges up the Monongahela River toward Homestead, Pennsylvania, a community of 12,000 located seven miles east of Pittsburgh. The barges carried 300 men armed with Winchester rifles, all employees of the Pinkerton National Detective Agency. The men had been hired by the Carnegie Steel Company to protect its property from the 3,800 people who made steel boiler plates and girders in Carnegie's Homestead plant, members of the Amalgamated Association of Iron, Steel and Tin Workers, who had gone on strike and taken over the town. The striking workers had hanged in effigy Carnegie's operating manager, Henry Clay Frick, and a mill superintendent, and Frick was determined to regain control. (Andrew Carnegie was in Europe at the time.)

As the barges approached the Homestead plant, a mob of striking workers and sympathetic townspeople broke through the 12-foot, barbed-wire-topped fence that management had erected around the mill. Voices in the crowd warned the Pinkertons to leave, but a plank went down, and the armed men marched ashore.

The first shots came from the Homestead side. The Pinkertons fired back, and cries went out that someone was wounded. Women grabbed their children and ran as the men of Homestead hunkered down behind piles of scrap metal in preparation for a long battle. The Pinkertons turned and sought safety on the barge farther from shore, but they found themselves stranded. The steamboat that had pulled them to Homestead was well on its way downstream.

From 4 A.M. until 5 P.M., the strikers traded gunfire with the Pinkertons. At one point, they hauled out a small cannon and attempted to sink the barge. When that tactic failed, they emptied barrels of oil onto the water and set the river on fire. Soon, a white flag could be seen flying from the barge. The Pinkertons, having already lost three of their number, were surrendering their rifles and bullets in exchange for safe passage out of town. The people of Homestead agreed to those terms, but they were too enraged at the sight of seven workers lying dead to let the Pinkertons go peacefully. They stoned and taunted the hired guards as the men headed toward the train that would carry them back to Pittsburgh.

Strikers occupy the railroad station at Homestead, Pennsylvania, as part of their effort to control access to the town. *(Carnegie Library of Pittsburgh)*

The issue that had precipitated the Homestead strike was wages. In accordance with an existing agreement between labor and management, common laborers had been earning about 14 cents an hour. While some skilled laborers had been taking home $280 per month, most had earned considerably less. The agreement had expired on June 30, 1892, and management had announced a pay cut of 18 percent to 26 percent.

Suspecting that Frick would bring in "scabs," or nonunion strikebreakers, to fill their places in the plants, the striking steelworkers had formed an advisory committee and taken control of Homestead. Committee members watched every entrance to town, allowing no one to enter without their consent. Management had asked the sheriff of Allegheny County for 100 deputies, but public sentiment was with the strikers; the sheriff failed to find enough people willing to be sworn in.

The strikers defeated the Pinkerton force, but their chances of a victory over management rapidly dwindled in the days that followed. On July 12, Governor Robert E. Pattison of Pennsylvania ordered state militia forces into Homestead. The plant reopened on July 27 with 1,000 scabs working under military protection. Steelworkers throughout the state demonstrated their support for the Homestead workers by striking in sympathy with their cause. But then the powerful Carnegie Steel Company, with assets worth $25 million, took legal action. Its lawyers secured three indictments against the strike's leaders for murder, two for aggravated riot, and one for conspiracy. In addition, 27 strikers were indicted for treason against the state of Pennsylvania.

Just as no citizen of Homestead was willing to protect the interests of Carnegie Steel as a deputy sheriff, no jury wanted to convict the strike leaders.

They were cleared of all charges in court. But the union remained defeated, its treasury emptied by legal expenses. Forty years would pass before another union exercised power within the U.S. steel industry.

The strike at Homestead was not the first confrontation between workers and their employers to occur in the United States, but it was one of the largest such incidents witnessed in 19th-century America. Nor was the Amalgamated Association of Iron, Steel and Tin Workers the nation's only labor organization—although it was the largest union in the United States when the strike began. American laborers traditionally have found strength in numbers. The feeling of brotherhood that exists among U.S. workers was evident as early as July 23, 1788, when more than 4,000 mechanics, carpenters, blacksmiths, tailors, and other artisans paraded in New York City to celebrate the ratification of the Constitution.

The American labor movement has embraced men and women in manufacturing, transportation, and mining—in virtually every important industry. Its story is one of strife, suspicion, and sacrifice. It is a story of countless working people risking what little security they had in the hope of better pay, improved working conditions, and a brighter future for themselves, their families, and the generations of laborers who would follow them. Many of their efforts ended in failure, as the Homestead strike did. But their persistence gradually brought success in the form of better treatment and dignity on the job.

THE FIRST LABOR UNIONS

Eighteenth-century journeymen often banded together informally before confronting their employers about long hours, low pay, and other grievances. Benevolent societies, in which journeymen pooled their resources to provide death benefits to widows and aid to members who were ill or unemployed, were common as well.

In 1794, the cordwainers (shoemakers) of Philadelphia organized the nation's first lasting labor union, the Federal Society of Journeymen Cordwainers. Any cordwainer in the city could join for an initiation fee of 50 cents and monthly dues of about five cents. Members had to agree not to work alongside nonunion cordwainers and to accept nothing less than the union wage. Printers organized in New York City at the same time, and other craft unions appeared. The most powerful weapon these unions could wield was the strike—withholding their most marketable asset, their skill—and they used it repeatedly to further their interests. Journeymen printers struck in Philadelphia in 1786 to protest a drop in wages. Bakers in Charleston, South Carolina, struck in the same year after the city council passed an ordinance controlling the price of bread. Early strikes tended to be disorganized and to last from a few hours to several days.

Two factors eventually caused the early unions to fail. First, the courts mistrusted unions and refused to accord them legal status. U.S. judges followed the example of the British courts, which looked upon labor unions as illegal conspiracies that acted to restrain fair trade. Labor organizers could expect to be prosecuted and convicted in early 19th-century America. Second, economic downturns made workers unwilling to unite against their employers and put their jobs at risk.

Working people retained their desire to have a public voice, however. That wish gave rise to the Working Man's Party, formed in Philadelphia in 1828 as the first political party in the world to represent the interests of laborers. Sixty more workers' parties soon sprang up throughout the nation and flourished briefly. These parties promoted a 10-hour workday, equal educational opportunities for all children, and an end to imprisonment for debt. In 1829, the Workingmen's Party of New York nominated 11 artisans, including machinists, carpenters, a cooper, a painter, and a whitesmith, or tinsmith, as candidates for the state assembly.

Internal disagreements over ideology splintered and ultimately caused the collapse of the workers' parties, but labor unions soon reappeared. Even a small labor federation, the National Trades Union Council, was established in 1834. Having observed the failure of the workers' parties, these organizations shunned any political affiliation. Strikes occurred again, too. Journeymen carpenters struck in Boston in 1825 to protest a workday that lasted from sunrise to sundown. The master carpenters who employed the journeymen defended the practice as customary, and they prevailed. An 1835 strike in Philadelphia was more successful and resulted in the establishment of a 10-hour workday.

During the same period, laborers were beginning to organize in Canada. French-speaking artisans in Quebec City and Montreal were holding meetings, aiding the infirm, and sponsoring lectures and programs of entertainment.

Throughout the early years of its history, the strength and stamina of the labor movement would depend on the health of the economy. An economic depression in the United States known as the Panic of 1837, for example, destroyed half of the jobs in industry and dealt a serious blow to organized labor. The labor movement gained legitimacy when the Massachusetts Supreme Court rejected the notion of conspiracy in a case involving a Boston boot makers' union in 1842, but that decision had little immediate impact. The depression had prompted many workers to abandon industry and the unions and, possibly, move west.

Some artisans, inspired by the thinking of European socialists, formed cooperatives in the 1830s and 1840s. Cooperatives were manufacturing enterprises in which the workers themselves owned the means of production, turned out goods for sale, and shared the earnings. Some of these artisans had been influenced by Charles Fourier, a French philosopher and socialist who advocated the reorganization of society. Fourier taught that industrialization was fragmenting communities, causing insecurity, and possibly paving the way for anarchy. He envisioned a social system in which large numbers of people lived in enormous communal buildings, sharing work and wealth. Karl Marx was influential as well, especially after 1848, the year *The Communist Manifesto,* by Marx and Friedrich Engels, was published. Marx predicted that the dissatisfied working masses would rise up to defeat the capitalist elite, creating a classless society. European immigrants imported Marxist thinking into the U.S. workplace.

The best-known U.S. cooperative was the Journeymen's Moulders' Union Foundry, organized in Cincinnati in 1848 with an investment of approximately $2,100 contributed by the workers. Other cooperatives included the Boston Tailors' Cooperative Union and the Shirt Sewers' Cooperative Union Depot of New York City. Many cooperatives were short-lived. The Cincinnati iron molders' group, for example, was unable to weather economic depression in 1849. Interest in unions quickly revived as the economy rebounded, and so did the impetus to strike. Approximately 400 strikes occurred in 1853 and 1854, mostly to demand higher wages. By 1860, some 100 unions were active in New York, Boston, Philadelphia, and other large cities. Most restricted their membership to skilled artisans. The hundreds of thousands of unskilled workers laboring in textile mills and factories usually did not form unions or strike.

Many employers were openly hostile to union organization among their workers, while others had no quarrel with unions as long as they confined their activities to providing social benefits to members. When it came to setting wages and work hours and deciding whether to hire or fire, employers insisted that they knew best.

BRINGING DISTANT AND DIVERSE WORKERS TOGETHER

Once manufacturers were able to distribute their goods throughout the nation, union leaders saw a need to coordinate the efforts of workers in diverse regions. A number of international unions—so-called because they had local chapters in both the United States and Canada—were starting to take shape. The printers' union of Quebec City, for example, merged into the National Typographical Union at Cincinnati in 1852. Other international groups included the Cigarmakers' International Union, several coal-mining unions, and the Knights of St. Crispin, which represented workers in the shoe industry. One of the most noteworthy of these organizations was the Iron Molders' International Union, which was organized in 1859 and headed by William Sylvis, the first U.S. labor leader to achieve national significance.

The son of a Pennsylvania wagon maker, Sylvis built his union into a strong international organization through tireless effort. He visited foundries and shops throughout the United States and Canada, often against the wishes of employers, in order to listen to workers' concerns and incorporate them into the union's goals. Sylvis cared nothing for money unless it could further the union cause. He chose a life of poverty, wearing clothing that was threadbare and burned by the splashing of molten iron in foundries.

Laborers in every union shared a desire to improve their working and living conditions. The next logical step in the pursuit of that goal was to organize on a large scale. The nation's first major labor organization, the Noble and Holy Order of the Knights of Labor, was founded in Philadelphia on December 28, 1869, by a garment worker named Uriah Stephens. It was a small, secret society, complete with rituals and handshakes; it enlisted all kinds of workers—with lawyers, bankers, professional gamblers, and liquor dealers among the few exceptions. In 1881, the Knights of Labor abandoned its veil of secrecy, and in 1883 leadership passed to Grand Master Workman Terence V. Powderly, a machinist.

Farmers, skilled craftspeople, and others joined the 15,000 "mixed assemblies" of the Knights of Labor that were established in U.S. cities between 1869 and 1895. The first Canadian assembly was organized in Hamilton, Ontario, in 1881. The Knights of Labor was unusual among labor organizations in its willingness to admit women and African Americans. The social activists Susan B. Anthony, Elizabeth Cady Stanton, and Frances Willard were among its members.

The aims of the Knights of Labor were both lofty and pragmatic: to embrace all American workers and to replace the capitalist system, as well as to secure an eight-hour workday, end child labor, and gain wages for women that equaled those paid to men. The Knights of Labor preferred to work toward its goals by educating the public and using established channels to change laws. Its leaders sanctioned strikes only as a last resort, if employers refused to negotiate or workers were victimized.

THE MOLLY MAGUIRES

Many laborers were less reluctant to express their dissatisfaction by striking. Among them were the anthracite coal miners of eastern Pennsylvania, who had engaged in a series of strikes beginning in 1870 to protest cuts in wages. About 85 percent of the miners belonged to the Workingmen's Benevolent Association, a union established in 1868. Some also were part of a secret society that had its roots in Ireland, the Ancient Order of Hibernians. These men were known popularly in Pennsylvania as the Molly Maguires, having adopted the name of a widow who in the 1840s had led assaults on English landlords in Ulster. The Molly Maguires were alleged to have terrorized mine foremen and superintendents during a strike in 1871 and during the "Long Strike of 1875," which began in January of that year over wage cuts. They were blamed for destroying mine property, threatening and assaulting mine personnel, and carrying out 16 assassinations. During the 1875 strike, the Molly Maguires allegedly derailed railroad coal cars, chased strikebreakers from the coal fields, and sniped at mine officials.

Franklin Benjamin Gowen, owner of the Pennsylvania and Reading Railroad, which controlled many of the mines, hired Pinkerton detective James McParlan to infiltrate the Molly Maguires and acquire proof of their criminal activities. McParlan, himself an Ulster native, posed as a man wanted on murder charges in Buffalo, New York. He easily won the confidence of the Molly Maguires and attained a position of responsibility within the organization.

The coal miners were able to maintain their 1875 strike for several months in part because sympathetic shopkeepers provided food for them on credit. By May, though, the merchants were unwilling to extend further credit to the strikers, so many miners, hungry and without resources, returned to work. At this point, union leaders offered to end the strike if the mine operators would agree to a weekly wage of $15 for six eight-hour shifts. But with Italian-immigrant strikebreakers working in the mines, the operators had no incentive to bargain.

Fall arrived, and McParlan had gathered the evidence that would lead to a series of arrests among the Molly Maguires. His testimony at their trial, though sometimes questionable, helped to secure 24 convictions. Ten Molly Maguires were hanged for murder, and the others served jail terms ranging from two to seven years. The striking miners went back to work on their employers' terms; they were to wait until 1890 and the formation of the United Mine Workers before they had an effective union.

Public opinion was strongly antiunion following the violence on the coal fields, and for several decades politicians and historians praised James McParlan for ridding the nation of a dangerous element. Scholars now acknowledge that the mine operators staged some of the crimes attributed to the Molly Maguires in order to justify the destruction of their society. How much responsibility for the bloodshed and property damage actually rests with the Molly Maguires may never be known. The members left no records of their meetings or evidence of their actions.

STRIKES OCCUR NATIONWIDE

The railroad strike of 1877 also did little to help the union cause. Forty brakemen and firemen employed by the Baltimore and Ohio Railroad walked off the job in July 1877 to protest pay cuts during an economic depression. The use of state militia forces to end the walkout enraged the citizens of Baltimore, who clashed with the soldiers. The Baltimore and Ohio train crews had no union; nevertheless, the strike spread to eight other railroad lines, halting rail traffic nationwide. Workers from other industries joined the strike, which degenerated into riots in some cities. In Pittsburgh, thousands of iron workers and other laborers defeated federal troops that had been dispatched from Philadelphia to stop disturbances in their city, and they burned the property of the Pennsylvania Railroad. Worker committees seized control of several towns in Ohio and Indiana and halted industrial production until employers agreed to their demands. When striking workers shut down industry in St. Louis, frightened city officials got out of town. In San Francisco, angry mobs destroyed railroad property and rioted in the city's Chinese neighborhood. More than 100 U.S. workers died that summer in street brawls. By August 1, however, the strike had been brutally crushed, and labor's concerns had been rejected with scorn.

Such violence was repeated as workers staged bitter strikes in coal fields, silver mines, steel mills, and textile mills. Most ended in defeat for the striking workers. The Knights of Labor first became involved in a strike in 1883, when telegraphers struck against Jay Gould and Western Union. Although this strike failed as well, it drew dissatisfied workers to the organization. Membership grew to more than 74,000 in 1884 and to 100,000 in 1885. In that year, the Knights of Labor staged a successful strike against Jay Gould's southwestern rail lines. On March 7 of that year, mechanics of the Missouri Pacific Railroad in Missouri, Kansas, and Texas struck to have their wages restored following a pay cut. The strikers soon numbered 9,000, which prompted the governors of Kansas and Missouri to intervene. The governors secured an agreement that ended the strike, reinstated wages, and assured the striking workers that they would be rehired.

Membership in the Knights of Labor reached 729,677 in 1886, when another strike against the Gould system occurred. This strike was called when a foreman on the Texas and Pacific Railroad who was prominent in the local Knights of Labor assembly was fired for incompetence. The Knights asserted that the foreman's termination violated the agreement ending the strike of 1885. Almost 10,000 workers joined the walkout and succeeded in stopping freight traffic along the lines on which they worked. Leaders ended the strike in less than a month with the expectation that railroad officials and the workers would agree to a solution, but the railroads refused to meet with a worker committee. The company hired new laborers to replace the strikers, and the freight trains began moving under police protection.

Its defeat in the strike of 1886 heralded the decline of the Knights of Labor. Conflicts among the leadership and disputes with national trade unions weakened the organization and caused many skilled laborers to leave its ranks. The Knights of Labor continued its activities through 1894, but in 1917 it was formally dissolved.

HAYMARKET

In 1886, a call went out across the United States for a general strike in favor of an eight-hour workday. The eight-hour movement had instant appeal for political radicals, such as the Black International, a group of anarchists based in Chicago who had been seeking an issue that would enable them to promote their philosophy of revolutionary violence. (It is interesting to note that an eight-hour workday was not then unheard of in the United States. As a result of an act of Congress, federal workers on special projects had worked an eight-hour day since 1868. In 1872, Congress extended the eight-hour day to all federal employees.)

About 40,000 Chicago workers stayed off the job on May 1, 1886, the date set for the general strike. Some employers, especially packinghouse owners, headed off a strike in the plants by granting a shorter workday to their staffs. But two days later, an encounter between striking workers and strikebreakers at the McCormick Harvester plant in Chicago led to police intervention and four deaths. The anarchists used this situation to their advantage, passing out flyers that called for a mass meeting of workers to be held on the evening of May 4 in Haymarket Square, an open space surrounded by lumberyards and packinghouses.

Approximately 3,000 people showed up for the meeting and listened to speeches by August Spies and Albert Parsons, two prominent anarchists. As the third speaker, Samuel Fielden, rose to the podium, rain began to fall, and most of the audience left. Mayor Carter H. Harrison, who was on hand to observe the proceedings, went home as well.

Soon after the mayor departed, Police Inspector John Bonfeld led 180 officers into the square and ordered the assembly to disperse. Suddenly, a bomb exploded within the police ranks. One officer died on the scene, and 66 were injured; seven of the wounded would die later. The police retaliated by firing into the crowd, killing four people. Estimates of those wounded range from 50 to 100 and more.

The identity of the bomb thrower was unknown and remains so to this day. The public blamed the anarchists for the slaughter, however, and demanded that the guilty be caught. The police arrested eight well-known anarchists, although only three—Spies, Parsons, and Fielden—had attended the meeting in Haymarket Square. The prosecutors at their trial presented no evidence linking the defendants to the bombing, but the jury found all eight anarchists guilty anyway. Seven received death sentences, while one, Oscar Neebe, was sentenced to 15 years in prison.

Four men went to the gallows on November 11, 1887. Samuel Fielden and another condemned man had successfully petitioned for executive clemency and had their sentences commuted to life in prison. Another, 21-year-old Louis Lingg, had committed suicide in prison.

The Haymarket incident and the trial that followed it captured the attention of people throughout the world. In 1889, an amnesty organization began to work for the release of the three men remaining in prison. They achieved success in 1893, when Illinois governor John P. Altgeld pardoned the three anarchists. Altgeld faulted the judge, jury, and prosecution in the case for serving public opinion rather than justice. As for the eight-hour movement, it was largely forgotten. Most of the packinghouse workers who had gained a shorter day before the May 1 strike now saw it taken away.

THE AMERICAN FEDERATION OF LABOR

In December 1886, the craft unions that had belonged to the Knights of Labor formed a new coalition, the American Federation of Labor (AFL), which would dominate the American labor movement for half a century. Its first president was Samuel Gompers, who had presided over the Cigar Makers Union. Gompers had come to the United States from England at age 13 as an apprentice cigar maker. He would lead the AFL until his death in 1924, with the exception of a one-year period in 1894 and 1895, when he was defeated in the organizational election.

The AFL was a loose alliance of independent unions, with little actual power over those unions. Its leaders worked tirelessly to raise wages, shorten the workweek, and improve job conditions for the skilled artisans who were its members. But it was criticized for ignoring the needs of the many thousands of semiskilled and unskilled workers who labored in factories or in plants owned by the great trusts. As a concession, the AFL admitted two unions with many unskilled workers among their members, the large and powerful United Mine Workers and the Garment Workers. By 1900, the AFL included 48 national unions, claimed 500,000 members, and was growing rapidly. Membership had reached 2.5 million when the United States entered World War I in 1917, and five million at the war's end.

Employers often resisted union activity among their workers, viewing it as a threat to their companies' continued growth. Management responded to labor organization and demonstrations with a variety of tactics. They paid armed guards to protect their property and spies to report on union activity. Many union organizers found themselves branded as troublemakers, fired, and possibly blacklisted. Some employers required workers to sign "yellow dog" contracts, in which they agreed not to join a union. The bad feelings that existed between management and labor led to a series of acrimonious strikes in the 1890s, including the Homestead Steel Strike of 1892, and the famous Pullman Strike of 1894.

THE PULLMAN STRIKE

On May 11, 1894, 3,000 employees of the Pullman Palace Car Company, which manufactured railroad sleeping cars near Chicago, walked off the job. The workers were members of the American Railway Union (ARU); management had just cut wages for the fifth time. The company had produced an unusually large number of sleeping cars in 1892 and 1893 to accommodate visitors traveling to the World's Columbian Exposition in Chicago. Many cars had sat idle once the fair closed, and the production of new ones had dropped significantly. The strikers were also angry because management had discharged workers who had acted on a bargaining committee even though company president George M. Pullman had assured the committee that none of its members would be fired or discriminated against. Pullman now was refusing to sit down with an arbitrator.

Another purpose of the strike was to protest the high fees charged for rent and utilities in Pullman's company town, fees that remained constant while wages went down. One worker received a check for two cents after rent and other expenses were deducted from his pay. He kept the check instead of cashing it and reportedly had it framed.

The ARU had been founded in 1893 to represent white railway workers. Although it was a young organization, its membership already totaled 150,000 in 1894. Union members throughout the railroad industry honored the strike by refusing to handle Pullman cars. By June 28, 125,000 workers were involved in the boycott, and 20 railroads had been affected.

Fearful of what such a boycott could do to the nation's transport system, railroad management took strong steps to end it. The General Managers Association, a group representing the leadership of 25 railroads serving Chicago, hired strikebreakers to couple Pullman cars to as many trains as possible, including mail trains. Chains and padlocks were sometimes added. Management then warned that any worker unwilling to handle those cars would be fired and that interfering with the mails was a federal offense. On July 2, the general managers secured a court injunction ordering the ARU to stop pressuring railroad workers not to work, and forbidding anyone from interfering with the mails or disrupting interstate rail commerce. ARU presi-

Federal troops summoned to Chicago to protect rail traffic during the Pullman strike of 1894 camp beside Lake Michigan. *(Chicago Historical Society; ICHi-04906)*

dent Eugene V. Debs offered to end the strike if Pullman would reinstate the striking workers, but to Pullman and the railroad executives, negotiating with Debs would be condoning anarchy. The strike would continue.

On Independence Day, President Cleveland sent four infantry companies to Chicago to enforce the injunction. Martial law was declared in the city, but the military presence brought carnage rather than order. Thirty people died in one confrontation when soldiers fired into a crowd protesting the movement of a train by troops.

On July 7, Debs and other strike leaders were arrested on conspiracy charges but were released on bond. They were arrested again on July 17 and were sent to jail when the circuit court ruled that they had violated the Sherman Anti-Trust Act by engaging in a conspiracy to restrain interstate commerce. By that time, the Pullman strike had affected rail transportation in 27 states and territories and had halted nearly all transcontinental service. The ARU called off the boycott on August 2, but the Pullman workers continued their strike into the fall, ending it only when they could no longer afford to stay off the job.

Debs, who had first gone to work in the railroad yards at age 14, converted to socialism during his six months in jail, convinced by his experiences that workers could never achieve their goals under capitalism. He was to be the Socialist Party candidate in five presidential elections.

Samuel Gompers and his associates, meanwhile, began to seek a way for organized labor to gain acceptance within the industrial community. AFL leaders sought the cooperation of business; they barred member unions from engaging in sympathy strikes, in which workers not directly involved walk off the job in support of strikers.

THE INDUSTRIAL WORKERS OF THE WORLD

In 1905, an organization was formed to unite the unskilled workers in whom the AFL and its unions had no interest. This group, the Industrial Workers of the World (IWW), or "Wobblies," shared the Knights of Labor's aspiration of putting an end to capitalism. Its leadership dreamed of achieving immediate results, of creating a single massive union and leading the nation's workers in "one big strike" in which they would seize the means of production. Speaking to crowds on street corners and in community meeting halls, IWW leaders such as loud, charismatic "Big Bill" Haywood recruited 10,000 members—migrant workers, mill hands, lumberjacks, and stevedores among them. In contrast with the Knights of Labor, the Wobblies rejected collective bargaining, or negotiating with employers, relying instead on direct action, including strikes, boycotts, and sabotage. Its members readily responded to the prospect of violence.

The IWW staged many dramatic strikes and refined the strike process, introducing such tactics as mass picketing and the sit-down strike, in which workers refused to leave their plant or factory until management met their demands. The IWW achieved its greatest victory leading the textile workers of Lawrence, Massachusetts, in a strike in 1912.

The 85,000 people who lived in Lawrence included approximately 30,000 mill hands. Most mill workers were immigrants from Italy, Russia, Poland, and other European countries, earning less than nine dollars a week on average—when the mills operated at full capacity. During slack periods, which were not infrequent in the textile industry, earnings might drop as low as $2.30 per week. Families augmented these wages by sending their children to work, but life remained a struggle, and infant mortality was high. Because every penny counted, a pay cut of about 3.5 percent, effective January 1, 1912, was significant. People began to walk off the job on January 12, the first payday after the cut in wages.

Barely one-tenth of the Lawrence textile workers belonged to unions, yet the strike soon involved 20,000 men and women. It succeeded because two IWW leaders, Joseph J. Ettor and Arturo Giovannitti, went to Lawrence and assumed control. Ettor, who was in his twenties, was the son of a man severely wounded in Haymarket Square. The Italian-born Giovannitti was a poet and the editor of a radical newspaper. Ettor and Giovannitti held mass rallies to keep the workers united, organized picket lines, and saw to it that needy people received relief. Their appeal for funds brought contributions from labor unions, social-welfare agencies, and private citizens. The donations made $1,000 available each day of the strike for food and living expenses. In a move that increased public sympathy for the workers, the two leaders arranged for 400 children of strikers to be placed in foster homes outside the community.

The strike spread to the mill towns of Fall River and Haverhill, and the governor of Massachusetts declared martial law. Riots occurred when the mill owners tried to reopen their plants, and one striker was killed. Police arrested Ettor and Giovannitti as accessories to murder; Big Bill Haywood came to Lawrence to lead the strike.

The mill owners hired a man to plant dynamite in shops and businesses around the city in the hope that any explosions would be blamed on the IWW. When the plot was uncovered, authorities arrested the head of the American Woolen Company, the largest employer in Lawrence.

For once, public opinion sided with the strikers in a major labor dispute and not with management. People throughout the United States spoke out against the police attacks that they read about in their newspapers, especially the clubbing of women and children that occurred when officers tried to stop 40 children from leaving Lawrence.

On March 12, with the strikers showing no weakening of their resolve, the American Woolen Company ended the strike by agreeing to most of the workers' demands. Wages increased 5 percent to 25 percent, employees received time-and-a-quarter for working overtime, and strikers were assured that they would experience no discrimination in being rehired. Some 200,000 textile workers throughout Massachusetts also saw their working conditions improve.

In the final chapter of the story of the Lawrence strike, Ettor and Giovannitti stood trial for murder. The fact that no evidence linked them to the crime might not have won them an acquittal, but the IWW financed a skillful defense, and the mill workers of Lawrence threatened to strike again if the two men were not set free. Ettor and Giovannitti made speeches to the jury in which they rededicated themselves to the revolutionary philosophy and aims of the IWW, including violence and the destruction of capitalism. Both men were acquitted.

Soon after U.S. entry into World War I, the government cracked down on radicals, including the Wobblies. The Socialist Party had invited suspicion by criticizing U.S. involvement in the war and claiming that soldiers were being

sent to their deaths to protect the interests of capitalists. Also, the victory of communism in the Russian Revolution of 1917 had cast suspicion on the motives of leftists in the United States. Federal agents closed IWW union halls and confiscated their records and publications. Between 1905 and 1917, the Wobblies had led about 150 strikes and recruited 100,000 members but had built few lasting unions. The organization continued to exist for several years following 1917, but it never regained its former strength.

If some labor organizations had strong political leanings, the AFL traditionally had avoided lending its support to any political party or candidate for office. That policy changed in March 1906, when a "bill of grievances" submitted to President Theodore Roosevelt and the Congress by the AFL Executive Committee was not acted upon. From then on, the AFL worked to influence election results, primarily by supporting Democratic candidates, who seemed more receptive than Republicans to the organization's legislative agenda. In 1912, the AFL backed Woodrow Wilson's candidacy for president. It was rewarded for that support in 1914 with passage of the Clayton Act, which limited management's ability to obtain court injunctions.

The year 1913 saw the creation of the U.S. Department of Labor, charged with promoting the interests of laborers, improving working conditions, and fostering opportunities for gainful employment. As an executive department of the federal government, it was to be administered by a secretary, who was a

Police block strikers from entering the Lawrence, Massachusetts, mills during the 1912 strike. *(Library of Congress)*

member of the president's cabinet. In 1916, Congress passed the Adamson Act, which established an eight-hour day for the rail industry. Enacted under the threat of a national rail strike, the Adamson Act was the first federal law limiting the workday to eight hours in private industry. By the end of World War I, the eight-hour day and the 48-hour week were the norm in most industries, but they were secured primarily through collective bargaining between unions and employers rather than through legislation.

A century earlier, labor unions had been looked upon as subversive. By 1918, after demonstrating the ability to influence elections and federal legislation, organized labor had become an acknowledged force in American society.

CHRONICLE OF EVENTS

1786
Journeymen printers strike in Philadelphia.
     Bakers strike in Charleston, South Carolina.

1788
July 23: More than 4,000 artisans march in New York City to celebrate ratification of the Constitution.

1794
The first enduring labor union in the United States, the Federal Society of Journeymen Cordwainers, is formed in Philadelphia.

1825
Journeymen carpenters strike unsuccessfully in Boston for a shorter workday.

1828
The Working Man's Party is founded in Philadelphia.

1834
The National Trades Union Council is established.

1835
Striking workers in Philadelphia gain a 10-hour workday.

1837
An economic depression destroys many unions and half of all industrial jobs.

1842
The Massachusetts Supreme Court grants legal status to labor unions.

1848
The Journeymen's Moulders' Union Foundry, the best-known cooperative of the 1830s and 1840s, is established in Cincinnati.

1859
The Iron Molders' International Union is organized.

1860
Approximately 100 labor unions are active in major U.S. cities.

1868
Following an act of Congress, federal workers on special projects now work an eight-hour day.

1869
December 28: The Knights of Labor is formed as a secret society in Philadelphia.

1872
All federal workers work eight-hour days.

1875
January: Pennsylvania coal miners strike over wage cuts; violence and destruction of mine property are attributed to the Molly Maguires.

1877
July: Employees of the Baltimore and Ohio Railroad walk off the job; the strike spreads to eight other rail lines.

1881
The Knights of Labor abandons secrecy.

1883
Terence Powderly assumes leadership of the Knights of Labor.

1885
March: The Knights of Labor leads a successful strike against Jay Gould's southwestern rail system.

1886
March: A second strike against the Gould system fails.
     May 1: Some 40,000 Chicago workers strike for an eight-hour day.
     May 3: Striking workers confront strike-breakers outside the McCormick Harvester plant in Chicago.
     May 4: Anarchists organize a rally in Chicago's Haymarket Square; a bomb kills seven police officers; police gunfire kills four people.
     December: The American Federation of Labor is formed.

1887
November 11: Four men are hanged for the bombing in Haymarket Square.

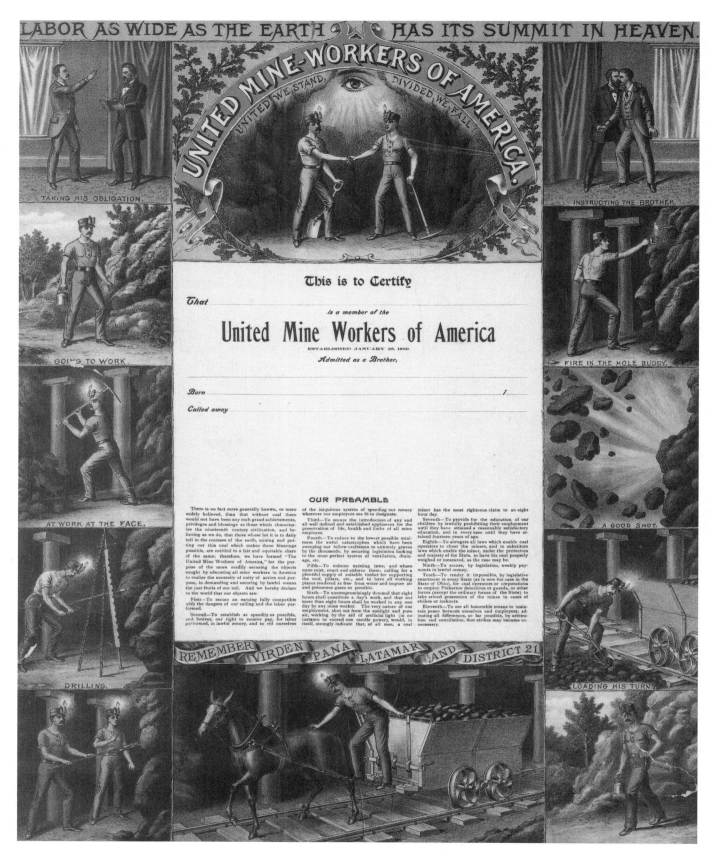

A United Mine Workers membership certificate, decorated with idealized scenes of a miner's life. *(Library of Congress)*

Membership in the Knights of Labor reaches 729,677.

1890

The United Mine Workers is established.

1892

June 30: Employees of the Carnegie Steel Company in Homestead, Pennsylvania, strike following announcement of a pay cut.

July 6: Strikers in Homestead defeat 300 armed Pinkerton guards.

July 12: Governor Robert E. Pettison orders state militia forces into Homestead.

July 27: The Homestead plant reopens under military protection.

1893

Illinois governor John P. Altgeld pardons three men imprisoned for the Haymarket bombing.

1894

May 11: Three thousand employees of the Pullman Palace Car Company go on strike.

June 28: About 125,000 members of the American Railway Union refuse to handle Pullman cars; the strike now affects 20 railroads.

July 2: The General Managers Association obtains an injunction in the hope of ending the strike.

July 4: President Grover Cleveland orders troops to Chicago.

July 7: Eugene V. Debs and other strike leaders are arrested for the first time.

July 17: Debs and other strike leaders are arrested again; the strike affects rail service in 27 states and territories.

August 2: The ARU calls off the boycott of Pullman cars.

Fall: The Pullman workers end their strike.

1900

The AFL includes 48 national unions, with approximately 500,000 members.

1905

The Industrial Workers of the World is founded.

1906

Theodore Roosevelt's Republican government fails to act on a bill of grievances submitted by the AFL; organized labor supports Democratic candidates.

1912

January 12: Textile-mill workers in Lawrence, Massachusetts, strike to protest a cut in pay.

March 12: Lawrence's mill owners agree to the striking workers' demands.

The AFL backs Woodrow Wilson's candidacy for president.

1913

The U.S. Department of Labor is created.

1914

The Clayton Act limits management's ability to obtain court injunctions.

1916

The Adamson Act establishes an eight-hour day in the rail industry.

1917

The Knights of Labor is formally dissolved.

The government closes the meeting places of the IWW and confiscates its records.

1918

AFL membership reaches five million.

Most industrial laborers work eight-hour days and 48-hour weeks.

EYEWITNESS TESTIMONY

This federal ship will our commerce revive
　　And merchants and shipwrights and joiners shall thrive.

Banner carried in the parade of artisans celebrating ratification of the Constitution, New York City, July 23, 1788, in Sean Wilentz, Chants Democratic, *p. 87.*

The real object . . . of [the Mechanics' Union of Trade Associations] is to avert, if possible, the desolating evils which must inevitably arise from a depreciation of the intrinsic value of human labour; to raise the mechanical and productive classes to that condition of true independence and equality which their practical skill and ingenuity, their immense utility to the nation and their growing intelligence are beginning imperiously to demand; to promote, equally, the happiness, prosperity and welfare of the whole community—to aid in conferring a due and full proportion of that invaluable promoter of happiness, leisure, upon all its useful members; and to assist, in conjunction with such other institutions of this nature as shall hereafter be formed throughout the union, in establishing a just balance of power, both mental, moral, political and scientific, between all the various classes and individuals which constitute society at large.

Mechanics' Union of Trade Association of Philadelphia, October 25, 1828, Mechanic's Free Press, *in William A. Sullivan,* The Industrial Worker in Pennsylvania: 1800–1840, *p. 100.*

We shall oppose the establishment of all exclusive privileges, all monopolies, and all exemptions of one class more than another from an equal share of the burdens of society; all of which, to whatever class or order of men they are extended, we consider highly anti-republican, oppressive and unjust. We consider it an exclusive privilege for one portion of the community to have the means of education in colleges, while another is restricted to common schools, or, perhaps, by extreme poverty, even deprived of the limited education to be acquired in those establishments. Our voice, therefore, shall be raised in favor of a system of education which shall be open to all, as in a real republic it should be.

George H. Evans, mechanic and editor, October 31, 1829, Working Man's Advocate, *in Frank T. Carlton, "The Workingmen's Party of New York City: 1829–1831," p. 404.*

He who does any thing whereby any part of his species is made wiser, better, healthier, or happier, belongs to our party and we will welcome him as a brother. It is not a community of name only, it is one of interest and feeling. All these have a common interest that honest industry should be respected and rewarded—that services rendered to society should be *duly* estimated and *adequately* compensated: and, my friends, I believe in my soul that all our party who understand their own interests, act upon these principles.

Robert Rantoul, Jr., 1833–34, "An Address to the Workingmen of the United States," p. 55.

In no time since the creation, in no nation under the sun, have workingmen beheld that path open before them, in which we are invited to walk. There are no obstacles in the way to deter us from entering it, but only such as operate as incentives to the resolute. Advancement in life courts us to accept it, and nothing can snatch it from our grasp but some unpardonable vice inherent in our own character.

　　The fault, dear Brutus, is not in our stars,
　　　　But in ourselves, if we are underlings.

　　On, then, brethren of the honorable fraternity of the workingmen of these United States of America. Let us speed our course in the strait way. Let no man deceive us. Let no man control us. Let us pursue steadfastly our best interests, and hold, with an iron gripe, these our invaluable rights.

Robert Rantoul, Jr., 1833–34, "An Address to the Workingmen of the United States," p. 103.

One of the first strikes of cotton-factory operatives that ever took place in this country was that in Lowell, in October, 1836. When it was announced that the wages were to be cut down, great indignation was felt, and it was decided to strike, *en masse*. This was done. The mills were shut down, and the girls went in procession from their several corporations to the "grove" on Chapel Hill, and listened to "incendiary" speeches from early labor reformers. . . .

　　Cutting down the wages was not their only grievance, nor the only cause of this strike. Hitherto the corporations had paid twenty-five cents a week towards the board of each operative, and now it was their purpose to have the girls pay the sum; and this, in addition to the cut in the wages, would make a difference of at least one dollar a week. It was estimated that as many as twelve or fifteen hundred girls turned out, and walked in procession through the streets. . . .

When the day came on which the girls were to turn out, those in the upper rooms started first, and so many of them left that our mill was at once shut down. Then, when the girls in my room stood irresolute, uncertain what to do, asking each other, "Would you?" or "Shall we turn out" and not one of them having the courage to lead off, I, who began to think they would not go out, after all their talk, became impatient, and started on ahead, saying, with childish bravado, "I don't care what you do, *I* am going to turn out, whether anyone else does or not;" and I marched out, and was followed by the others. . . .

It is hardly necessary to say that so far as results were concerned this strike did no good.

Harriet H. Robinson describing a strike in Lowell, Massachusetts, in October 1836, Loom and Spindle, *pp. 83–85.*

. . . [T]he young ladies employed in the Spinning Room of Mill No. 2, Dwight Corporation, made a very quiet and successful "strike" on Monday. The Spinning machinery was set in motion in the morning, but there was no girls to tend it. They had heard the rumor that their wages were to be cut down, upon which they determined to quit. They silently kept their resolve, and remained out until Tuesday afternoon, when they were requested to return to their employment, with an addition to their previous wages of fifty cents per week. The Ladies connected with the other mills ought certainly to present them with a banner, as a tribute of esteem.

Voice of Industry, *November 21, 1845, in Hannah Josephson,* The Golden Threads, *p. 268.*

The recent Strikes for Wages in different parts of the country, but especially those of the Iron-Puddlers of Pittsburgh, suggest grave and yet hopeful thoughts. In reading the proceedings of the Strikers, an observer's attention will be arrested by their emphatic though unconscious condemnation of our entire Social framework as defective and unjust. Probably half of these men never harbored the idea of a Social reconstruction—never even heard of it. Ask them one by one if such an idea could be made to work, and they would shake their heads and say, "It is all well in theory, but it will never do in practice." But when they come to differ with their employers, they at once assume the defectiveness of our present Social polity, and argue from it as a point by nobody disputed: "We *ought* to be paid so much, [thus runs their logic] because we *need* and they can *afford* it." "*Ought*," do you say, friends? Do n't you realize that the whole world around is based upon *must* instead of *ought?* Which one of you, though earning fifteen dollars per week, ever paid five cents more than the market price for a bushel of potatoes, or a basket of eggs, or a quarter of mutton, because the seller *ought* to be fairly paid for his labor, and could n't really *afford* to sell at the market rate?

Horace Greeley, 1850, "Strikes and Their Remedy," in Hints toward Reforms, *pp. 364–65.*

What position are we, the mechanics of America, to hold in society? Are we to receive an equivalent for our labor sufficient to maintain us in comparative independence and respectability, to procure the means with which to educate our children and qualify them to play their part in the world's drama? or must we be forced to bow the suppliant knee to wealth, and earn by unprofitable toil a life too void of solace to confirm the very chains that bind us to our doom?

In union there is strength, and in the formation of a national organization, embracing every moulder in the country, a union founded upon a basis broad as the land in which we live, lies our only hope. Single-handed we can accomplish nothing, but united there is no power of wrong we may not openly defy. Let the moulders of such places as have not already moved in this matter organize as quickly as possible and connect themselves with the national organization. Do not be humbugged into the idea that this thing cannot succeed.

William Sylvis addressing the Iron Moulders' Convention, Philadelphia, July 5, 1859, in Terence V. Powderly, Thirty Years of Labor, *p. 27.*

One of two things is always present when an advance of wages is given—either a demand on the part of the men, or a fear that such a demand will be made. Had no union ever been formed, and employers felt perfectly sure that no demand for increased pay would be made, would they ever have given it?

Workingmen throughout the States are now working for considerable less wages than they received four and five years ago; and how, let me ask, have we got the small advance thus far secured? By fighting for

William Sylvis, seated, with an unidentified man. *(Tamiment Institute Library, New York University)*

it—by making demands, and backing them up by whatever power we could command. So persistent and bitter has been the opposition to an increase of wages, that what little we have secured, has cost us very nearly as much as the amount received. It is no difficult matter to see what would now be our condition, had we no unions.

William Sylvis, "Address Delivered at Buffalo, New York, January, 1864," in James C. Sylvis, The Life, Speeches, Labors and Essays of William H. Sylvis, *p. 166.*

One of the most beautiful and beneficial results flowing from our organization is the universal and widespread acquaintance that has sprung up among the members: a feeling of brotherhood everywhere exists; an interest in each other's welfare has broken down, to a vast extent, that old feeling of selfishness that

used to exist among us; a feeling of manly independence has taken the place of that cringing and crawling spirit that used to make us the scorn of honest men.

William Sylvis, "Address delivered at Buffalo, New York, January, 1864," in James C. Sylvis, The Life, Speeches, Labors and Essays of William H. Sylvis, *pp. 166–67.*

The "Molly Maguire" is an Irishman, or the son of an Irishman, professing the Roman Catholic faith. That he is a blot and disgrace to the land of his fathers, as well as to the land of his adoption, is felt more strongly by the great body of the Irish people than by any other class of the community.

He must profess the Catholic faith, and yet, to be a member of the order, he must remain outside of the pale of the Church and be denied Christian burial.

By those ignorant of the true facts of the case, the knowledge that a "Molly Maguire" must be an Irishman and a Catholic is used as an argument against the Church. But the charge rests upon no foundation whatever. It may be possible that more than one Catholic priest has sympathized with the order, but if so it has been in violation not only of his religion but also of his Church government. A priest, like any other mortal, may be tempted and fall. The "Molly" has had money, influence, power, to disorganize the congregation and inflict personal injury. In very many instances he is an open and avowed infidel, intensely wicked and beyond control.

F. P. Dewees, 1877, The Molly Maguires: The Origin, Growth, and Character of the Organization, *pp. 346–47.*

The railroad rebellion [of 1877] was spontaneous. In those days before the establishment of collective bargaining as an orderly system for presenting grievances to employers as the preliminary to securing an adjustment based on mutuality, the only way the workers could secure the attention of employers was through some demonstration of protest in the form of a strike. The strike grew steadily until it surpassed in numbers and importance all previous industrial movements. Strikers and sympathetic workmen crowded into the streets. The New York papers said at the time that so far as the arguments were concerned, the workers had the best of the situation, but that they could not win because of the weakness of the unions. The authorities grew apprehensive and asked for military protection. Then the fight was on. Long pent-up resentment found vent in destruction. The primitive weapons, fire and violence, were labor's response to arbitrary force.

In New York we were stirred deeply. While we had put our faith in constructive methods, yet the sky of Pittsburgh reddened by fires started by company agents and desperate men denied all other recourse, brought us the message that human aspiration had not been killed or cowed.

Samuel Gompers remembering the rail strike of 1877,
Seventy Years of Life and Labor, *pp. 140–41.*

Like lightning the clubs descended and ascended. Every stroke hit a new head whose owner went solid to the ground or bowled in continued sommersaults. The officers seemed to put their whole souls into this commendable work. . . . Those who did not get hit fled as fast as legs could carry them, and . . . a howling chorus of pain could be heard at the high trestle more than a mile away. The rout was complete and final.

A clash between police and strikers in Buffalo, New York, described in the Buffalo Weekly Courier, *July 25, 1877, in Robert V. Bruce,* 1877: Year of Violence, *p. 201.*

They were blackguarding us in the most scandalous manner. Men, women and half-grown boys. It was the most outrageous language I ever heard in my life. When we would go up and attempt to drive them away, they would just stand and spit at us, and call us all sorts of names. But my men stood it, and walked up and down, and paid no attention to them.

Captain John Ryan of the Pennsylvania State Fencibles reporting on the behavior of striking workers in 1877, in Robert V. Bruce, 1877: Year of Violence, *p. 153.*

The great strike of 1877 in Pennsylvania made victims of hundreds of Knights of Labor, who left the state and went in all directions carrying with them no murderous lance. . . . Perhaps we did not always give the public to understand that love of neighbor was our aim for we had to strike, boycott, and do other things not supposed to be in accord with the Ten Commandments. But remember that for the first time in human history labor, in the last quarter of the nineteenth century, stood at least partially solidified, partially organized, and partially united in opposition to a power that had its origin in the first lockout, on the day that Adam and Eve were locked out of that

rather exclusive garden in which fruit was grown with apples a specialty.

Terence V. Powderly reflecting on the rail strike of 1877,
The Path I Trod, *p. 60.*

The Cigar Manufacturers' Association had declared that under no circumstances would any leaders of the strike be employed for at least six months. As a consequence, for nearly four months I was out of employment. I had parted with everything of any value in the house, and my wife and I were every day expecting a newcomer in addition to the five children we already had.

My family helped in every way possible. Part of the time they were hungry and without the necessaries of life. Never once did my wife falter. Blacklisted, I desperately sought employment, going home at night where my brave wife prepared soup out of water, salt, pepper, and flour. One night when there was no food in the house and our little girl was very ill I returned home to find a fellow-worker, Jack Polak, had called and offered my wife $30 a week for three months if she would persuade me to give up the union and return to work. I turned to my wife and said, "Well, what did you tell him?" My wife, indignant at the question answered: "What do you suppose I said to him with one child dying and another coming? Of course I took the money." Stunned by the blow I fell in a chair. My wife, all tenderness and sympathy, seeing I didn't understand exclaimed: "Good God, Sam, how could you ask such a question? Don't you know I resented the insult?"

Samuel Gompers writing about his life in the aftermath of a strike in 1877 and 1878, Seventy Years of Life and Labor, *pp. 155–56.*

To the Knights of Labor, all who toiled might find entrance and a welcome. The scavenger doing his work on the street was admitted on exactly the same terms of equality as the highest priced or most skilled artisan. The name of the Order was never printed and seldom spoken. Only in the assembly was it mentioned and then only that the newly initiated might know the name of the Order he had joined. . . .

When a candidate was presented for initiation, he was asked three questions. First: "Do you believe in God, the Creator and Universal Father of all?" Second: "Do you obey the Universal Ordinance of God, in gaining your bread by the sweat of your brow?" Third: "Are you willing to take a solemn vow binding you to secrecy, obedience, and mutual assistance?" On receiving affirmative answers to these questions the applicant would be admitted and initiated. If he declined, he would be pledged to secrecy as to all he had seen and heard and respectfully dismissed.

Terence V. Powderly describing initiation in the Knights of Labor in 1878, The Path I Trod, *p. 49.*

In 1878, of forty thousand cigarmakers in the entire country at least ten thousand were Chinamen employed in the cigar industry on the Pacific Coast. . . . As their standards of living were far lower than those of white men, they were willing to work for wages that would not support white men. Unless protective measures were taken, it was evident that the whole industry would soon be "Chinaized." The Pacific Coast white cigarmakers at that time organized independently, were using a white label to distinguish white men's work done under white men's standards. But local organization was an inadequate protection against the strong tide of Chinese immigration that threatened to flood the West.

California did not have authority to exclude Chinese workmen and Federal law was needed. Our International recognized that though competition with Chinese cigarmakers was then confined to the coast, the cigar industry of the East had to compete with the industry of the West in all markets, but alone it was not strong enough to secure protective legislation. During several strikes in the East, we had to meet the threats of employers to import Chinese strike breakers. This was an element in deciding the cigarmakers to give early and hearty endorsement to the movement for a national organization of labor unions, for the help of all wage-earners was needed in support of Chinese exclusion.

Samuel Gompers discussing Chinese cigar makers in 1878, Seventy Years of Life and Labor, *pp. 216–17.*

Civilization, at the lifting of the finger of some Knight of Labor, is to be disintegrated. Chicago, which now sends its messages to Wall Street in forty-five seconds, is to be thrown back into the wilderness. A new organization of workingmen, the Knights of Labor, has sprung into existence within a year or two, and already numbers two hundred thousand members. Its principle is the unification of labor. Its motto, finer than the formulas of the economists, is, Injustice to one is injustice to all. Its purpose is to settle the differences between employers and employed, without strikes, if possible, but if a strike must be made, to back it up with the strength of the whole body. Twenty-five years' experience has taught these men that individual trades-unions can be crushed out. They are going to "pool," like the railroads.

Henry D. Lloyd, July 1882, "The Political Economy of Seventy-Three Million Dollars," p. 75.

My own belief, based upon careful examination of all the conditions surrounding this Haymarket affair, is that the bomb was thrown by a man in the employ of certain monopolists, who was sent from New York city to Chicago for that purpose, to break up the eight-hour movement, thrust the active men into prison, and scare and terrify the workingmen into submission. Such a course was advocated by all the leading mouth-pieces (newspapers) of monopoly America just prior to May 1. They carried out their programme and obtained the results they desired.

Is it lawful and constitutional to put innocent men to death? Is it lawful and constitutional to punish us for the deed of a man acting in furtherance of a conspiracy of the monopolists to crush out the eight-hour movement? Every "law and order" tyrant from Chicago to St. Petersburg cries, "Yes!"

Albert R. Parsons reflecting on the events of May 4, 1886, "Autobiography of Albert R. Parsons," in Philip S. Foner, ed., The Autobiographies of the Haymarket Martyrs, *p. 51.*

Revolutions are no more made than earthquakes and cyclones. Revolutions are the effect of certain causes and conditions. . . . I do believe . . . that the revolution is near at hand—in fact, that it is upon us. But is the physician responsible for the death of the patient because he foretold that death? If any one is to be blamed for the coming revolution it is the ruling class who steadily refuses to make concessions as reforms become necessary; who maintain that they can call a halt to progress, and dictate a standstill to the eternal forces of which they themselves are but the whimsical creation.

August Spies, October 1886, "Address of August Spies," in The Famous Speeches of the Eight Chicago Anarchists in Court, *p. 15.*

Our large factories and mines, and the machinery of exchange and transportation, apart from every other consideration, have become too vast for private control. Individuals can no longer monopolize them.

Everywhere, wherever we cast our eyes, we find forced upon our attention the unnatural and injurious effects of unregulated private production. We see how one man, or a number of men, have not only brought into the embrace of their private ownership a few inventions in technical lines, but have also confiscated for their exclusive advantage all natural powers, such as water, steam, and electricity. Every fresh invention, every discovery belongs to them. The world exists for them only. That they destroy their fellow beings right and left they little care. That, by their machinery, they even work the bodies of little children into gold pieces, they hold to be an especially good work and a genuine Christian act. They murder, as we have said, little children and women by hard labor, while they let strong men go hungry for lack of work.

August Spies, October 1886, "Address of August Spies," in The Famous Speeches of the Eight Chicago Anarchists in Court, *p. 20.*

It is not unusual to hear strikes condemned as foolish efforts resulting simply in waste of money, and scorn and indignation are expressed at the stupidity which the strikers show in thus jeopardizing their bread and butter. It is easy to see that men sometimes strike as they might catch the measles, because such is the prevalent epidemic, or as they might drink because they have formed the habit. Still all such action cannot be relegated to this category of irresponsible movement, for though some strikes may be unwise, or some leaders unprincipled, the average workman strikes because he believes that by so doing he may help his fellows and in the far future benefit his children. There is an element of the pathetic and the heroic in the most foolish strike that has ever been inaugurated. There is an element of loyalty in it; moreover, there is the deliberate preference of a future and an ideal good to the enjoyment of present comfort.

Lillie B. Chance Wyman, November 1888, "Studies of Factory Life: Black-Listing at Fall River," pp. 611–12.

It has somewhere been said that the Order of the Knights of Labor grew out of a failure, but the details were not given, and they were not necessary; but the failure hinted at, and the failure which really led to the organization of the Knights of Labor, was the failure of the trade union to grapple and satisfactorily deal with the labor question on its broad, far-reaching basic principle: the right of all to have a say in the affairs of one. It was because the trade union failed to recognize the rights of man, and looked only to the rights of the tradesman, that the Knights of Labor became a possibility.

Terence V. Powderly, 1889, Thirty Years of Labor, *p. 83.*

. . [R]emember that it was by the application of Chinese "cheap labor" to the building of railroads, the reclamation of swamp-lands, to mining, fruit-culture, and manufacturing, that an immense vista of employment was opened up for Caucasians, and that millions are now enabled to live in comfort and luxury where formerly adventurers and desperadoes disputed with wild beasts and wilder men for the possession of the land. Even when the Chinaman's work is menial (and he does it because he must live, and is too honest to steal and too proud to go to the almshouse), he is employed because of the scarcity of such laborers. It is proved that his work enables many to turn their whole attention to something else, so that even the hoodlum may don a clean shirt at least once a month. You may as well run down machinery as to sneer at Chinese cheap labor. Machines live on nothing at all; they have displaced millions of laborers; why not do away with machines?

Yan Phou Lee, April 1889, "The Chinese Must Stay," p. 479.

When I got to Homestead I gathered together a number of the leaders of the workmen, the Advisory Committee having been disbanded, and asked them to go with me to where the crowd was assembled, and try to persuade the men to consent to the safe departure of the Pinkertons. The crowd was so large and the excitement so great that it was impossible to get any definite expression of the wishes of the men, but I must say there was a strong feeling manifested to permit the guards to depart without disturbance or further bloodshed.

William Weihe, July 1892, president of the Amalgamated Association of Iron, Steel and Tin Workers, in Myron R. Stowell, "Fort Frick," pp. 67–68.

The crowd at the surrender [of the Pinkertons] reminded me of some enormous picnic or outdoor gathering on a holiday. The hills on all sides were black with people massed together. When the cannon was masked in front of the barge, the Pinkertons knew it was all up with them, and tried to make the best terms possible with the determined crowd on the shore. The latter took them from the boat in double file and for a moment did not know what to do with them. Cries of "To the woods! To the woods! Lynch the dogs!" were heard on all sides. . . .

The poor guards . . . were forced to march through the town to the rink. On both sides stood lines of enraged laborers and their friends, hooting and yelling as they passed. As the guards proceeded up the gauntlet they were kicked, cuffed and beaten from all sides. . . . Women and girls ran out of the lines and with sticks and clubs beat the poor wretches. One woman had a stocking filled with iron, and with it she struck one of the Pinkerton men over the head. . . .

While the men were being formed in line for the march to the rink, part of the strikers boarded the boats. They ransacked everything and secured 360 rifles. There was no wrecking. The men just took from the boats what they considered of value, and then burned them.

John Martin, railroad ticket agent, describing the surrender of the Pinkertons at Homestead, Pennsylvania, July 6, 1892, in Myron R. Stowell, "Fort Frick," pp. 69–72.

I am not a lawyer, but I don't think it necessary to be one to know what constitutes treason and what patriotism. Shall patriotism be measured by the yard-stick of the Carnegie firm or be weighed as their pig iron? Is it because these men in those latter days like those in Boston harbor, declared they had some rights and dared maintain them that they shall be declared traitors? . . . Now some of your men are in prison, others out on bail, but you are now out three and one-half months on strike with your ranks practically unbroken. I would not ask you to stand out one moment longer than your rights demanded, but are there not some acts of the Carnegie firm that show you that you are working in a winning cause? Because you are here in Homestead you don't know the great victory you have won. In all great lockouts there are certain inconveniences to suffer and these must be endured, but if you were to end the struggle to-day you have won a victory. There are employers fair and unfair, and when they think of offering a reduction of wages to their employees in the future

the fight you have waged will have some effect in the carrying out of this resolve. Don't you think your stand will have its effect on the workmen of this country? Not only here, but throughout the civilized globe, this fight will have its effect. The fraternity of the wage-workers of the civilized world is at hand.

Samuel Gompers speaking in Homestead, Pennsylvania, October 21, 1892, in Arthur G. Burgoyne, Homestead, *pp. 217–18.*

In Clinton Place, New York, a few doors west of Broadway, . . . one finds on the lintel of an old house, once a residence but now an office building, a modest sign that reads: "The American Federation of Labour, Samuel Gompers, President." The halls are rather dark and dingy, and one climbs two flights to find the rooms of the Federation. But the journey will be worth while if the caller is fortunate enough to find Mr. Gompers at his desk. He is not prone to careless absence from his place of work, but the manifold duties of his position frequently take him to distant parts of the country. The quarters of the American Federation are unadorned enough to allay any suspicion that the chief officers of this great combination of the trades unions of the country are disposed to revel in luxurious appointments. Everything is as severely plain as it can be; and the stiff common chairs invite no loiterers. . . .

Mr. Samuel Gompers has been heard by many audiences besides those composed of working men and members of the constituent orders of the Federation. He is a short but massively framed man of perhaps forty-five years, with a strong and handsome face and suave manner, a business-like yet not too abrupt deportment, and a diction as discriminating and clear as one is taught to expect from a college professor.

W. T. Stead, 1894, Chicago To-Day, *pp. 138–39.*

At the time we laid down our tools, we were building a car for $19.50 that we should have got $36 for. After the second cut in our wages the stores refused to give us credit, as they knew we could not pay in full from one pay day to another. More trouble began. The Company would not give us our checks at the shops as usual, but sent us to the Company's bank, where they would have a better chance to squeeze us for the rent it was impossible to pay. I have seen myself and fellow workmen pleading with the rent agent to leave us enough to buy some member of the family a pair of shoes or some other necessity. Then when our last cut came, that was the straw that broke the camel's back; we could not stand it any longer; I, like a good many others, had to stop carrying my dinner, as what I had to carry would have run through the basket. I have seen one of my companions on the next car to mine, so weak from the lack of proper food, that he would have to rest on the way going home.

A Pullman Company employee, July 21, 1894, in William H. Carwardine, The Pullman Strike, *pp. 104–5.*

Up to the beginning of the strike, I had run in debt about one hundred dollars; one half of this for rent, the rest for groceries and meat. I have reported for work every day that the shops were open for work, up till the strike began, and never missed even one hour. . . . I have a wife and four children, and it was for them that I struck, as I think that when a man is sober and steady, and has a saving wife, one who is willing to help along, and after working two and a half years for a company he finds himself in debt for a common living, something must be wrong.

A Pullman Company employee, July 22, 1894, in William H. Carwardine, The Pullman Strike, *p. 79.*

The American Railway Union is like unto a tree; taking into its membership every class of men working on a railroad, each class of men representing a branch of the tree, and when properly organized each class will be kept to itself in all technical matters, but in all matters of general concern the whole organization operates as one, which is unlike the old organizations, where each class has a constitution unto itself. This is a compact organization of all classes, having one constitution for all.

Testimony of George W. Howard, railway worker and vice president of the American Railway Union, before the U.S. Strike Commission, August 15, 1894, in Report of the Chicago Strike of June–July, 1894, *p. 11.*

I am from Cleveland and I've been a railroader eight years. When business got slack last winter I was pulled off with several others, and I haven't worked five weeks altogether since the first of the year. I have a wife and three children depending on me, and for six months we have been living from hand to mouth. When the agent who hired me to come to Chicago asked me if I would go, I told him I would see my

wife first. I went home and found her in tears in the dreary outlook. My children were actually in want of bread, and it didn't take me long to make up my mind about coming to Chicago. I am a Union man at heart, but when wife and children are in danger of starving I feel it my duty to work for them, even should I be killed in the endeavour.

A strikebreaker hired during the Pullman boycott, 1894, in W. T. Stead, Chicago To-Day, *p. 245.*

The effect of the Pullman boycott and strike will be to teach capitalists, syndicates and trusts that it will be to their interest to make concessions to the working people that they have not made heretofore. Capitalists and corporations should be conciliatory, not arrogant. The isolation of employers and employees is not possible—the two should be on friendly terms. The movement brought on foot by the American Railway Union shows the rising tide of the labour movement. It inaugurates the era of mutual concessions. It is a protest against the frightful conditions existing. It must act as a check to the arrogance of the moneyed classes.

Samuel Gompers, speaking prior to the defeat of the Pullman strike, 1894, in W. T. Stead, Chicago To-Day, *p. 262.*

A general acceptance of the doctrine proclaimed by the American Railway Union would mean a plunge from the highest civilization into the most degraded barbarism, for even semi-barbarians impose limitations upon the individual right of reprisal. In a word the expedient to which the leaders of the American Railway Union had recourse, set at defiance the fundamental principles of civilization and went in the face of all law, and all right, and all justice, and all decency.

Joseph Nimmo, Jr., The Insurrection of June and July 1894 Growing Out of the Pullman Strike at Chicago, Ill., *p. 25.*

Certain anarchistic defenders of the recent insurrection have seen fit to characterize the action taken by the government as an assault upon the interests of labor. This is absurd. It is the plaint of baffled lawlessness. In this whole matter the government has proved itself to be both the friend and the protector of labor. It protected the laborers at Pullman, and on all the railroads interrupted by the insurrection against themselves. For what could have been more suicidal than the attempts of those employes to destroy the very industrial establishments which were affording to them and their families the means of living. Besides the interruption of railroad transportation, if long continued would have prevented an hundred times as many laborers engaged in agriculture, in manufactures, in mining and in other employments from pursuing their gainful occupations, for transportation is to-day the life of all trade and of all industry. The Army can be used for no other purpose than to protect the people of this country in the pursuit of their businesses in life and to prevent their government from becoming the foot-ball of domestic violence.

Joseph Nimmo, Jr., The Insurrection of June and July 1894 Growing Out of the Pullman Strike at Chicago, Ill., *pp. 28–29.*

To hew and dig, to build and repair, to toil and starve, is not conquering in any proper sense of the term. Conquerors are not clothed in rags. Conquerors do not starve. The homes of conquerors are not huts, dark and dismal, where wives and children moan like the night winds and sob like the rain. Conquerors are not clubbed as if they were thieves, shot down as if they were vagabond dogs, nor imprisoned as if they were felons, by the decrees of despots. No! Conquerors rule—their word is law. Labor is not in the condition of a conqueror in the United States. . . .

Why is it that labor does not conquer anything? Why does it not assert its mighty power? Why does it not rule in congress, in legislatures and in courts? I answer because it is factionalized, because it will not unify, because, for some inscrutable reason, it prefers division, weakness and slavery, rather than unity, strength and victory.

Eugene V. Debs, "Labor Omnia Vincit," September 1895, in Writings and Speeches of Eugene V. Debs, *pp. 5–6.*

The American Railway Union was born with a sympathetic soul. Its ears were attuned to the melodies of mercy, to catch the whispered wailings of the oppressed. It had eyes to scan the fields of labor, a tongue to denounce the wrong, hands to grasp the oppressed and a will to lift them out of the sloughs of despondency to highlands of security and prosperity.

. . . [I]f in all the land the American Railway Union has an enemy, one or a million, I challenge them all to stand up before the labor world and give a reason why they have maligned and persecuted the order. I am not here to assert the infallibility of the organization or its officials, or to claim exemption from error. But I am here to declare to every friend of American toilers, regardless of banner, name or craft, that if the American Railway Union has erred, it has been on the side of sympathy, mercy and humanity. . . .

Eugene V. Debs, "Liberty," November 22, 1895, in Writings and Speeches of Eugene V. Debs, *p. 12.*

Before 1899 the coal fields of Pennsylvania were not organized. Immigrants poured into the country and they worked cheap. There was always a surplus of immigrant labor, solicited in Europe by the coal companies, so as to keep wages down to the barest living. Hours of work down under ground were cruelly long. Fourteen hours a day was not uncommon, thirteen, twelve. The life or limb of the miner was unprotected by any laws. Families lived in company owned shacks that were not fit for their pigs. Children died by the hundreds due to the ignorance and poverty of their parents. . . .

The United Mine Workers decided to organize these fields and work for human conditions for human beings. Organizers were put to work. Whenever the spirit of the men in the mines grew strong enough a strike was called.

Mary Harris Jones describing conditions in Arnot, Pennsylvania, in 1899, Autobiography of Mother Jones, *p. 30.*

This is the Continental Congress of the working-class. We are here to confederate the workers of this country into a working-class movement that shall have for its purpose the emancipation of the working-class from the slave bondage of capitalism. There is no organization, or there seems to be no labor organization, that has for its purpose the same object as that for which you are called together to-day. The aims and objects of this organization shall be to put the working-class in possession of the economic power, the means of life, in control of the machinery of production and distribution, without regard to capitalist masters.

Big Bill Haywood, speech at the First Convention of the Industrial Workers of the World, June 27, 1905, in William D. Haywood, Bill Haywood's Book, *p. 181.*

In capitalist society the working man is not, in fact, a man at all; as a wage worker, he is simply merchandise; he is bought in the open market the same as hair, hides, salt, or any other form of merchandise. The very terminology of the capitalist system proves that he is not a man in any sense of that term.

When the capitalist needs you as a workingman to operate his machine, he does not advertise, he does not call for men, but for "hands" and when you see a placard posted, "Fifty hands wanted," you stop on the instant; you know that that means *you,* and you take a beeline for the bureau of employment to offer yourself in evidence of the fact that you are a "hand." When the capitalist advertises for hands, that is what he wants.

He would be insulted if you were to call him a "hand."

Eugene V. Debs, speech at Grand Central Palace, New York City, December 10, 1905, in Jean Y. Tussey, ed., Eugene V. Debs Speaks, *p. 122.*

The Industrial Workers is organized, not to conciliate, but to fight the capitalist class. We have no object in concealing any part of our mission; we would have it perfectly understood. We deny that there is anything in common between workingmen and capitalists. We insist that workingmen must organize to get rid of capitalists and make themselves the masters of the tools with which they work, freely employ themselves, secure to themselves all they produce, and enjoy to the full the fruit of their labors.

Eugene V. Debs, speech at Grand Central Palace, New York City, December 10, 1905, in Jean Y. Tussey, ed., Eugene V. Debs Speaks, *p. 125.*

Homestead gives at the first a sense of the stress of industry rather than of the old time household cheer which its name suggests. The banks of the brown Monongahela are preempted on one side by the railroad, on the other by unsightly stretches of mill yards. Gray plumes of smoke hang heavily from the stacks of the long, low mill buildings, and noise and effort dominate what once were quiet pasture lands.

On the slope which rises steeply behind the mill are the Carnegie Library and the "mansion" of the mill superintendent, with the larger and more attractive dwellings of the town grouped about two small parks. Here and there the towers of a church rise in relief. The green of the parks modifies the first impression of dreariness by one of prosperity such as is not infrequent in American industrial towns. Turn up a side street, however, and you pass uniform frame houses, closely built and dulled by the smoke; and below, on the flats behind the mill, are cluttered alleys, unsightly and unsanitary, the dwelling place of the Slavic laborers. The trees are dwarfed and the foliage withered by the fumes; the air is gray, and only from the top of the hill above the smoke is the sky clear blue.

Margaret Byington, 1910, Homestead, *p. 3.*

And who is Joe Ettor? And what is he like? And what is he fighting for? In appearance he is a short, stocky Italian with a well-shaped head, crowned with a thick shock of hair upon which a small hat sets rather jauntily. He wears a flannel shirt and a large bow for a tie. . . . He has a kindly, boyish face, which lights up with humor and then sobers with scorn. He has an apparently unlimited supply of physical vitality, and a voice that is strong and resonant, which seems to grow stronger the more he uses it. For over a week he has been speaking incessantly in the largest halls of the city and on the open common, and Monday evening, when he addressed a crowd that filled every seat and every available bit of standing room of the large city hall of the adjoining city of Haverhill, his voice was just as clear and strong as when he took command of the situation a week and a half before. On Thursday last, when he addressed a crowd of nearly 20,000 workers from the bandstand on Lawrence Common, he asked all who were out on strike willingly, to raise their hands, and the carrying quality of his rather remarkable voice was manifested by raised hands on the very outskirts of that great crowd.

The Reverend Nicholas Vanderpuyl of Haverhill, Massachusetts, January 24, 1912, in Justus Ebert, The Trial of a New Society, *p. 40.*

[The strike at Lawrence, Massachusetts] was a wonderful strike, the most significant strike, the greatest that has ever been carried on in this country or any other country. Not because it was so large numerically, but because we were able to bring together so many different nationalities. And the most significant part of that strike was that it was a democracy. The strikers handled their own affairs. There was no president of the organization who looked in and said, "Howdydo." There were no members of an executive board. There was no one the boss could see except the strikers. The strikers had a committee of 56, representing 27 different languages. The boss would have to see all the committee to do any business with them. And immediately behind that committee was a substitute committee of another 56 prepared in the event of the original committee's being arrested. Every official in touch with affairs at Lawrence had a substitute selected to take his place in the event of being thrown in jail.

William D. Haywood commenting on the Lawrence, Massachusetts, textile strike of 1912, Bill Haywood's Book, *p. 255.*

. . . [T]he first strike that breaks again in this Commonwealth or any other place in America where the work and the help and the intelligence of Joseph J. Ettor and Arturo Giovannitti will be needed and necessary, there we shall go again, regardless of any fear and of any threat. We shall return again to our humble efforts, obscure, unknown, misunderstood soldiers of this mighty army of the working class of the world, which, out of the shadows and the darkness of the past, is striving towards the destined goal, which is the emancipation of human kind, which is the establishment of love and brotherhood and justice for every man and every woman on this earth.

Arturo Giovannitti addressing the jury at his murder trial, 1912, in Justus Ebert, The Trial of a New Society, *p. 148.*

It was in the fine art of agitation that the I.W.W. excelled. Back of our efforts to stir up industrial discontent was the class-war wisdom born of experience. . . . This knowledge was part of the training and education of all I.W.W. members. So thoroughly was the rank and file indoctrinated with this creed that we could boast, "There are no leaders among us—we are all leaders." Every member, regardless of rank and station in the organization, considered himself as capable as anyone else of developing a potential strike situation into a victory for labor. The procedure, perfected over a period of years, was simple: First came appraisal of the job to determine immediate complaints; then, the trick of magnifying all minor complaints into

The Industrial Workers of the World demonstrate in New York City in 1914. *(Library of Congress)*

major grievances. That was called "sowing the seeds of discontent." Once the seeds took root, the rest was easy. First, the distribution of propaganda or strike leaflets and posters; then, meetings at the factory gates, followed as soon as possible by a mass meeting to draw up demands, appoint organization and publicity committees, and prepare to picket the plant and line up new members. The organization committee, being at all times in control, was the backbone of any strike.

Ralph Chaplin describing his work with the Industrial Workers of the World in 1916, Wobbly, *pp. 176–77.*

With the I.W.W. there were only two kinds of people in the world—those who were with us and those who were against us. There was no middle ground when it came to the sacrosanct dogma of eternal enmity between the "haves" and the "have-nots."

Ralph Chaplin summing up the outlook of IWW members in 1916, Wobbly, *p. 147.*

. . . [I]n a dingy I.W.W. reading-room . . . I found pamphlets in which sabotage was discussed from the ethical point of view. A wobbly writer described it as a "war measure" in the conflict between the capitalist class and the working class, and in war everything was fair and moral. The wobblies admitted that sabotage on the part of the workers was no goody-goody method, but defended it on the ground that it certainly was no worse than the methods to which the capitalists were resorting in the economic warfare. If the workers, in their efforts to gain economic advantages, damaged property and destroyed materials, did not the bosses, in the interest of profits, destroy property with a ruthless and careless hand? Have they not laid waste the country's national resources with utter lack of consideration for their human values—forests, mines, land, and waterways? Did they not dump cargoes of coffee and other goods into the sea, burn fields of cotton, wheat, and corn, throw trainloads of potatoes to waste—all in the interest of higher incomes? . . .

All of this, the wobblies insisted, was sabotage, just as their doings were sabotage; the ethical difference between the worker and the capitalist with their respective forms of sabotage was that the former was open and honest about it, and the latter dishonest, practicing destruction secretly, under the guise of business, the while condemning proletarian *saboteurs* as criminals.

Louis Adamic describing his experiences in 1920, Dynamite, *pp. 374–75.*

Organized labor has often been criticized for not jeopardizing its whole organization to rescue the unorganized or the "unskilled" workers as our critical friends diplomatically term them. That which labor's adverse critics define as "unskilled labor" is really unorganized labor. There are now a large number of workers who formerly were regarded as unskilled but who have been organized. Standards of work, wages, and hours have been so far improved that these critics no longer refer to them as "unskilled."

As I look back over the years I have spent in the service of the labor movement and review the various groups of workers that have been designated as unorganizable because unskilled, lack of organization stands out clearly as due wholly to lack of courage, lack of persistence, lack of vision. Every occupation calls for skill. There may be a difference in degree, but that is largely individual. The more knowledge a man has, the more efficient he becomes as a workman—whether his occupation be that of ditch-digger or engineer. The so-called skilled trades had to go through the same struggle to secure organization as any other group. In truth, those of us who helped to build pioneer organizations fought a fight of intensity and desperation little dreamed of in this modern period when labor organizations have achieved standing and power.

Samuel Gompers, circa 1924, Seventy Years of Life and Labor, *pp. 147–48.*

Economic betterment—today, tomorrow, in home and shop, was the foundation upon which trade unions have been builded. Economic power is the basis upon which may be developed power in other fields. It is the foundation of all organized society. Whoever or whatever controls economic power directs and shapes development for the group or the nation. Because I early grasped this fundamental truth, I was never deluded or led astray by rosy theory or fascinating plan that did not square with my fundamental. . . . This is the reason it was often hard to have patience with well-meaning, enthusiastic but misinformed persons who have wanted the trade union movement to forsake this simple truth.

Samuel Gompers, circa 1924, Seventy Years of Life and Labor, *pp. 286–87.*

8

The Cowboy
1840–1886

At the close of the Civil War, as manufacturing was about to undergo rapid growth and railroads were stretching across the west, the cattle industry was being born in southern Texas. The cradle of land between the Rio Grande and the Nueces River offered adequate water and grass to support herds of Texas longhorn as well as a mild climate and shrubs and mesquite for shelter. The lean, leggy longhorns were descended from *criollo* cattle brought to the New World on Spanish ships in the 16th century and from such varieties as the English longhorn.

The growing eastern population was hungry for meat, even the tough, stringy beef of the longhorn, and the developing railroad network made it possible to bring Texas cattle east. The railroads did not yet connect Texas with eastern markets, but they did reach into Kansas. Because the depletion of the great buffalo herds had opened up countless acres of grazing land on the Great Plains, cattle ranchers could drive their herds north to meet the railroads. Bringing the cattle safely north was the cowboy's principal task.

The American cowboy has achieved the status of mythic hero in popular culture. He is presented in novels and films as independent and fearless, riding hard and fast, relying on his wits and his six-shooter to survive. In reality, he was an agricultural worker who put in many hours of hard labor under rigorous and often hazardous conditions and was poorly paid for his efforts.

TEXAS CATTLE

As early as the 1840s, some Texas cattle ranchers were driving their herds to the heavily populated markets of New Orleans, Los Angeles, and San Francisco. The potential profits were high: a steer valued at five dollars in Texas might fetch $160 in California.

The longhorn required little water and could fend off many predators with its horns, which measured five to six feet from tip to tip, but the California trail was arduous nonetheless for cattle, drivers, and horses. Traveling herds often encountered no water for very long stretches, and the water they did find was likely to be alkaline and therefore poisonous. The basalt that covered parts of the terrain as a result of ancient lava flows cut through horses' hoofs. Also, the cattle's horns offered no protection from armed Apache and outlaws who frequented the trail.

Some ranchers had begun to drive their cattle north to Kansas City and St. Louis, where they could sell beef to residents and work animals to California-bound pioneers. But they faced a serious obstacle: the Texas longhorn carried a tick that transmitted splenic fever (also called Texas or Spanish fever). Following many years of exposure, the longhorn had become resistant to this disease, but it was often fatal to other breeds of cattle. For that reason Missouri and Kansas farmers did not want longhorns anywhere near their livestock. They were known to shoot at Texas herds or drive them off course. By 1861, Texas cattle had been banned from all parts of Missouri. The establishment of a quarantine line in 1867 kept longhorns from venturing near the most heavily settled portions of Kansas. Some drovers paid farmers off in order to be able to move their cattle forward, while others guided their animals into Indian Territory (Oklahoma) to wait for winter, when freezing temperatures killed the ticks. Meanwhile, they kept a constant watch for fast-moving prairie fires, which could ruin the grazing for miles.

Even if ranchers succeeded in getting their cattle to market, the people of Kansas City and St. Louis could consume only so much meat. Therefore, although Texas ranchers wanted to get their herds north without impediments, what they really needed to do was to get them east. In 1867, a tall, gregarious livestock trader named Joseph G. McCoy devised a way for them to do just that. Foreseeing that he could make a fortune in Texas cattle, McCoy scouted for a town adjacent to a railroad line where he could set himself up in business buying herds and shipping them out. Abilene, Kansas, was 1,000 miles from the Nueces River of Texas, but it offered access to the Kansas Pacific and Hannibal and St. Joseph Railroads, which would allow McCoy to ship cattle to Chicago and then east. He immediately went to work transforming Abilene into the nation's first cow town. After building an office, cattle barn, and shipping yard, he sent an assistant on a tour of Indian Territory to track down drovers who were grazing their herds there and lure them to Abilene.

The fact that Abilene was located within a section of Kansas where longhorns were prohibited stopped some drovers from going there, but others went anyway. On September 5, 1867, McCoy sent his first shipment, 20 carloads of cattle, to Chicago. By the end of their year, he had shipped out 25,000 head.

McCoy's business venture proved so successful that the cattle industry expanded west into Colorado, New Mexico, and Arizona. Ranchers introduced other varieties of cattle to the western range and bred them with longhorns to produce stock that reached maturity more quickly and provided more and better meat. McCoy's enterprise ushered in the era of the cowboy.

ON THE TRAIL

Cowboys were hired hands who tended cattle as they grazed on the open range, rounded up the herds twice a year, and drove them from the ranch to market. On the trail, they kept the herd organized and moving forward during the day, bedded the animals down at dusk, and took turns watching over them at night. A cowboy on a cattle drive slept beneath blankets and quilts spread under the open sky. A canvas tarpaulin offered protection at night if mosquitoes were plentiful, but it was of little help in keeping out the rain.

A cowboy spent much of the workday on horseback and depended on his mount for survival. His horse carried him over long stretches of desert to springs as surely as it helped him escape from wild animals, human foes, and the occasional charging longhorn. Cowboys rode the strong, sturdy Spanish mustangs that ran wild over the prairie. A wild horse, or bronco, had to be captured and "broken" before it could be taught the skills needed to herd cattle. A cowboy broke a wild mustang by saddling it, mounting it, and holding on while the horse bucked and tried to throw him. In time, the horse grew accustomed to the feel of a saddle and rider on its back. Cowboys known as bronco busters specialized in taming wild mustangs and often earned their living traveling from ranch to ranch.

The typical cowboy was a single man in his teens or twenties. Data on the racial and ethnic composition of the cowboy population is inconclusive. Some scholars have determined that of the 35,000 cowboys who rode the cattle trails between 1866 and 1895, approximately 25 percent were African American and 12 percent were Mexican. They base their findings on surviving trail-herd crew lists that identify members by race or nationality, on the knowledge that there were some outfits whose members were all or nearly all African American, and on the fact that many former slaves lived in Texas following the Civil War and were available for work. Other researchers think that 25 percent is too high an estimate for the number of African-American cowboys. They accept the photographic record, which presents a cowboy population that is almost exclusively white, as reliable evidence for a smaller percentage of African Americans.

A number of African-American cowboys achieved notoriety. Nat Love, who was known as "Deadwood Dick" to readers of adventure stories, was born into slavery in Tennessee in 1854. He became a trail herder at age 15 and later a rodeo performer. Bill Pickett, the African-American rodeo star, is credited with inventing the technique of "bulldogging," or leaping from a galloping horse onto a steer's horns and wrestling the animal to the ground. (Today, bulldogging is considered cruel and dangerous.)

About 12 hands would travel with a herd of 3,000 longhorns. The trail boss, the most experienced crew member, rode 10 to 12 miles ahead of the rest to look for pastureland, water, and a suitable campsite, while the cowhands rode with the herd. Six cowboys rode in pairs on opposite sides of the herd. Those in the "point position" took the lead, followed by the "swing" riders, who helped when necessary to turn the herd to a new direction. The two "flank" riders kept a watchful eye for strays. Additional cowboys, "riding drag" (usually those with the least experience) rode in the dusty, undesirable position behind the herd.

A day on the trail began before sunrise. After a quick breakfast and strong coffee, the cowboys got the herd moving. The distance covered averaged 10 miles a day but was dependent on the availability of grass and water.

The wrangler, who tended the saddle horses not in use, held the lowliest job on a cattle drive. The cook, in contrast, enjoyed a measure of prestige. The cook drove the chuck wagon, drawn by oxen or mules over gentle or rough terrain. He prepared meals from staples that could be transported without

Riding drag, the least desirable position, behind the herd *(Western History
Collections, University of Oklahoma)*

spoilage: cornmeal, bacon, beans, molasses, and salt. At times, fresh meat supplemented the everyday fare.

It took 90 days to travel the famous Chisholm Trail, from Texas to Abilene,
Kansas, with a herd of cattle. Several wide rivers crossed the trail, including the
Colorado, the Brazos, the Red, and the Canadian Rivers, and it was the cowboys' job to guide the cattle across each one. So many cattle journeyed along
the Chisholm Trail—more than a million between 1867 and 1872—that it
came to resemble an actual road. The animals' hoofs trampled through the veg-
etation a path that was 400 yards wide in some places. Rain and wind then
eroded the trail so that its level was below that of the surrounding plains. The
Western and Cimmaron Trails, which wended north to Dodge City, Kansas,
another cow town, were also well traveled.

In the 1870s, southwestern ranchers began driving their cattle to the
northern plains to fatten them on the region's fertile grasslands, because fattened cattle were fetching high prices from Chicago meatpackers. Herds following the Goodnight-Loving Trail (named for Charles Goodnight and Oliver
Loving, the cattlemen who pioneered it) went west from Texas to New
Mexico, in order to avoid the territory of the Comanche, before heading north
through Colorado to Wyoming. The trip from Texas to the High Plains took
six months. In 1879, herds of longhorn were taken to Montana to establish a
cattle industry there. Soon, settlements such as Sydney in Nebraska and Pine
Bluffs and Cheyenne in Wyoming developed into cattle towns. As the industry
grew, the market for beef increased. By 1880, the federal government was buying 50,000 head of cattle every year to feed the residents of western Indian
reservations.

Cowboys on the trail often sang to the cattle, especially after sundown,
because the human voice raised in song seemed to calm the herd and make
stampedes less likely. A loud clap of thunder, the sudden sprinting of a wild animal, or even the clattering of cooking pots could cause panic in a herd of cattle
and cause them to run, en masse, for three or four miles. A cowhand on

Cattle cross a river in southern Alberta, Canada. The Canadian cattle industry developed after 1880 in southern Saskatchewan and Alberta (then part of the Northwest Territories). *(Glenbow Archives, Calgary, Canada; NB[H]-16-492)*

horseback caught off guard in the midst of a stampeding herd risked being injured or even crushed to death, but usually it was only cattle that suffered. Cowboys scouring the range for strays after a stampede frequently came upon animals that had been trampled or left with broken bones or horns.

The cowboy faced danger on the trail from predators both animal and human. Swimming a herd across a swift, swollen river in springtime also presented risks to cattle and cowhands alike. Frightened cattle might mill, or swim in circles, and exhaust themselves. They might drift downstream and face a steep cliff on the opposite bank rather than a low rise or level ground. More than one cowboy drowned while attempting to redirect cattle in midstream.

For all of his hard work, and for the isolation and hazards that his job entailed, the cowboy received low wages. While a trail boss might earn $125 per month, an ordinary hand could expect to receive from $20 to $30 per month from the 1860s through the 1880s, although an experienced hand might receive $5 to $10 more. A cook's monthly wages varied from about $5 more than what the average cowhand received to twice as much. Many cowboys had no income during the slow winter months.

In the 1880s, Eleanor Marx Aveling and Edward Aveling, the daughter and son-in-law of Karl Marx, toured the United States for the purpose of observing working conditions. Cowboys were among the most overworked and poorly paid laborers they encountered. Not only were wages low, but cowboys had to purchase their own equipment as well. A saddle, boots, spurs, a revolver, and chaps (leather britches worn over woolen or denim pants for added protection) could cost as much as $150—more than most cowboys earned for an entire three-month cattle drive.

Because their work kept them widely dispersed, cowboys found it nearly impossible to form a union. Their employers, many of whom belonged to powerful regional ranchers' associations, quashed all attempts at organization. In 1886, cowboys working near the Powder River in Montana struck in the hope of a guaranteed monthly wage of $40. The local Stock Growers' Association brought in scabs and put down the strike. Jack Flagg, the leader of the striking cowboys, found himself fired and blacklisted. Western journalists shied away from reporting on the cowboys' situation, because they feared retaliation from the ranchers.

The cowboys received their pay at trail's end after delivering the herd to Abilene, Dodge City, or another cow town. Much of their money soon went for a room and bath, new clothes, a hearty meal, whiskey, and women. Many residents kept to their houses when cowboys were in town, because the young men had a reputation for getting drunk, riding wildly through the unpaved streets, and shooting recklessly in all directions. Sometimes they shot one another to death—either in brawls or purely by accident. Local authorities usually dismissed charges in such cases, because the town valued the money that the cowboys brought in. Cattle thieves, in contrast, experienced another kind of justice altogether, one that was swift and severe. Western ranchers had no tolerance for such thievery, and many lynchings occurred.

After a few days of revelry in town, it was time for the cowboys to head south. Most traveled by train, possibly going to New Orleans before drifting back along the Gulf Coast to Texas.

THE ROUNDUP

Before 1880, when barbed-wire fencing was introduced, western ranchers permitted their cattle to roam freely on the range. Animals from neighboring ranches could mingle in the open country, because their brands identified their owners. Twice a year, in the spring and fall, ranchers rounded up and counted their cattle. The spring roundup in the Southwest was a method for harvesting the animals that were to be sold. It was also a way to collect the calves for branding and, if they were male, castration. The smaller fall roundup allowed for the branding of any calves that had been missed in the spring. Neighboring ranches usually worked together at roundup time to make a big job easier. A roundup was also a social occasion, similar to the farmers' barn raising or cornhusking, when cowboys from different ranches enjoyed singing, card playing, joking, and conversation.

When the roundup began, cowboys from eight to ten ranches met at a central location. Small groups moved out in every direction for a distance of 15 to 20 miles, forming an enormous circle, before making camp. The next morning, the hands began riding over a section of range, bringing the cattle together and gradually contracting the great circle.

Once the cattle were all in one place, branding could begin. Cowhands determined the ownership of a calf by the brand that its mother wore. They roped the bellowing calf as its alarmed mother tried to protect it, and dragged it to the branding fire. Two cowboys called flankers grabbed the calf, flipped it onto its side, and held it to the ground as the ironman pressed the hot branding iron to its skin.

AN OVERSTOCKED RANGE

The western cattle industry was booming in the early 1880s, and investors from as far away as London and Edinburgh wanted to share in the profits to be earned from supplying Americans with beef. British speculators invested $45

The Hay Creek Ranch in Alberta, Canada, resembled many western cattle ranches of the 1880s. *(Glenbow Archives, Calgary, Canada; NA-2278-1)*

million in U.S. cattle ranches in the 1880s. In 1885, an English syndicate, the Espuela Land and Cattle Company, Ltd., of London, bought the 500,000-acre Spur Ranch, which reached into four Texas counties. Throughout the West, the cattle population exploded.

There were 250,000 head of cattle in one territory, Montana, in 1880. In 1883, there were 600,000. In Montana and elsewhere, in fact, more cattle grazed on the range than the land could support. The most nourishing grasses, buffalo and grama grass, were disappearing from the plains by 1885, and inedible plants were replacing them. Where it had taken five acres of grazing land to support one steer in 1870, it required 50 acres in 1880.

Ranchers jealously fenced in their land in the 1880s to prevent their herds from mixing with those of competitors. Not only did they fear losing cattle to a rival, but they had grown careful about breeding and did not want to contaminate the bloodlines of their herds. More and more ranchers now preferred to raise varieties of cattle, such as the white-faced Hereford, that fattened quickly and produced high-quality meat. The Texas longhorn started to disappear from the range.

The combination of a declining food supply and fenced-in ranches led to disaster in the cattle industry when the cold winter of 1885–86 was followed by even more severe weather in 1886–87. The blizzards that swept onto the plains were worse than any storms that the settlers or ranchers could recall. The herds, already malnourished, were unable to feed in the deep snow. With visibility reduced, cattle ran into fences, fell on top of one another and froze to death. Some ranchers lost 85 percent of their cattle. Many animals survived with frozen ears, feet, and tails.

The industry recovered slowly from these losses as ranchers changed some of their practices. Many, for example, began to raise hay for feed. But the numbers of western cattle never returned to the levels of the early 1880s.

THE ERA OF THE COWBOY ENDS

As railroads penetrated the Southwest and shipping points were established closer to the ranches, the long cattle drive became a thing of the past. Ranchers needed fewer workers to handle cattle kept in enclosed pastures, and they referred to them now not as cowboys but as ranch hands. The monthly wage paid to hands decreased steadily between 1885 and the early 20th century. For example, the average monthly wage paid to a hand at the Spur Ranch was $38.72 in 1885; by 1904, it had dropped to $29.66.

Cowboys who had managed to put away some money established herds of their own and became small ranchers. Many cowboys left the range and took up other kinds of work. Bones Hooks, an African-American bronco buster from the Texas panhandle, became a Pullman porter, but he never forgot how to rope and ride. Witnesses have recalled that on one occasion, while his train waited in a station, Hooks put down the brushes he used to clean passengers' clothes, took off his porter's jacket and cap, and broke a wild horse that no one else had been able to ride.

CHRONICLE OF EVENTS

1500s
Spanish ships transport criollo cattle, ancestors of the Texas longhorns, to the New World.

1840s
Texas cattle ranchers begin driving their herds to New Orleans, California, and Missouri.

1854
Nat Love, who gained fame as the cowboy hero Deadwood Dick, is born in slavery in Tennessee.

1861
Texas longhorns are banned from Missouri.

1866–95
Thirty-five thousand cowboys ride the western cattle trails.

1867
The longhorn is banned from eastern Kansas.

Joseph G. McCoy establishes a cattle market at Abilene, Kansas.

September 5: McCoy sends his first shipment of cattle to Chicago.

McCoy ships 25,000 cattle by year's end.

1867–72
More than a million head of cattle travel the Chisholm Trail.

1870s
Ranchers begin fattening herds on the northern plains.

1870
Five acres of grazing land are needed to support one steer.

1879
Herds of longhorn arrive in Montana; a cattle industry is established there.

1880s
Eleanor Marx Aveling and Edward Aveling observe the poor working conditions that American cowboys endure.

British speculators invest in the western cattle industry.

1880
The U.S. government is buying 50,000 head of cattle per year to feed the population on Indian reservations.

Cattle ranchers start to enclose their ranches with barbed-wire fencing.

Fifty acres of grazing land are needed to support one steer.

There are 250,000 head of cattle in Montana alone.

1883
Western cattle country is becoming seriously overcrowded.

There are now 600,000 head of cattle in Montana.

1885
The wages paid to western cowboys begin a steady decline.

The Espuela Land and Cattle Company, Ltd. of London buys the Spur Ranch in Texas.

1885–87
Severe winter weather kills hundreds of thousands of cattle.

1886
Cowboys working near the Powder River in Montana strike for higher wages; the Stock Growers' Association puts down the strike.

EYEWITNESS TESTIMONY

[May] *13th* Big Thunder Storm last night Stampede lost 100 Beeves hunted all day found 50 all tired. Every thing discouraging

14th Concluded to cross Brazos swam our cattle & Horses & built Raft & Rafted our provisions & blankets &c over Swam River with rope & then hauled wagon over lost Most of our Kitchen furniture such as camp Kittles Coffee Pots Cups Plates Canteens &c &c

15 back at River bringing up wagon Hunting Oxen & other *lost* property. Rain poured down for one Hour. It does nothing but rain got all our *traps* together that was not lost & thought we were ready for off dark rainy night cattle all left us & in morning not one Beef to be seen

16th Hunt Beeves is the word—all Hands discouraged. & are determined to go 200 Beeves out & nothing to eat

17th No breakfast pack & off is the order. all Hands gave the Brazos one good harty dam & started for Buchanan travelled 10 miles & camped found 50 beeves (nothing to eat

From the diary of George C. Duffield, in "Driving Cattle from Texas to Iowa, 1866," W. W. Baldwin, ed., Annals of Iowa, *April 1924, p. 251.*

Another regular job we had was keeping the wolves away from the cattle, as the big Lobo wolves did much damage to unprotected herds. They would travel in packs of fifty or seventy-five, and stealthily creep up to where the cattle were grazing, when they would divide into several packs, each pack singling out a nice fat steer or heifer. Most of them would rush at the unfortunate animals' head, while one would come up from the rear and hamstring it, rendering it entirely helpless and an easy victim to their prey. Whenever we would sight a pack of Lobo wolves, we lost no time in

Western photographer William Henry Jackson's portrait of a group of Texas cowboys *(Library of Congress)*

heading them away from the cattle. They never attacked a man, but it took many cattle to satisfy their appetites.

Jim McIntire, who first worked as a cowboy in 1869, Early Days in Texas: A Trip to Hell and Heaven, pp. 31–32.

The original cow-boy of this country was essentially a creature of circumstance, and mainly a product of western and southwestern Texas. Armed to the teeth, booted and spurred, long-haired, and covered with the broad-brimmed sombrero—the distinctive badge of his calling—his personal appearance proclaimed the sort of man he was.

Joseph Nimmo, Jr., describing cowboys prior to 1870, "The American Cow-Boy," p. 880.

It was difficult to secure sufficient experienced cowboys for these round-ups and we often had to fill in with what were termed "tenderfeet."

For these the older experienced cowmen would usually have something in cold storage that would, as a rule, take the conceit out of them. Should he make the remark that he could ride anything, he would be given the chance to ride the worst bucking outlaw horse in the bunch. If he stayed in his saddle his fellow cowboys would show him more respect but should he "pull leather" or get thrown, the cowmen and cowboys would joke and ridicule him unmercifully. When these practical jokes would be carried too far I would interfere and protect him. With sympathy and encouragement I have seen some of these timid tenderfeet turn out to be some of the best riders, ropers and expert cattlemen in the outfit.

John Bratt remembering roundups occurring in Texas, 1870–74, Trails of Yesterday, pp. 198–99.

The life of the cowboy, especially on these round-ups, was a hard one and full of perils. The percentage of deaths and disability on the range at this time was said to be greater than in a military campaign. He had to conquer the "outlaw" and vicious broncho; the pitfalls of the plains—prairie dog, wolf and badger holes—were often in his track; he swam swollen rivers, crossed wash-outs and quicksand, stopped the mad rush of stampeding herds, faced pelting rains accompanied by terrible thunderstorms, the bolts of lightning often killing cattle in the bunches he was herding. No wonder he suffered the pangs of rheumatism brought on by excessive rough-riding

and too much sleeping on round-ups (generally about four hours out of the twenty-four), under the stars in all kinds of weather with sometimes nothing but his slicker and saddle blanket to cover him.

John Bratt remembering roundups occurring in Texas, 1870–74, Trails of Yesterday, p. 199.

The cowboy's bed was a sort of one man affair and he nearly always slept alone. As one old cowhand expressed it: "I'd just as soon sleep with a wet dog as to sleep with a man." His bed was made up of blankets, comforters, called by the boys "suggans" or "soogans". The bed was packed, rolled in a "tarpaulin". It was shortened to "tarp" and consisted of a piece of canvas about 7 feet wide and 14 to 18 feet long and of extra heavy duck. This tarp was layed out flat and the bed made up on one end and the other end pulled up over the bedding. The boy crawls into this bed and no matter how hard it rains he sleeps as dry as if he was under a roof.

Frank M. King writing about cowboy life in the 1870s and 1880s, Longhorn Trail Drivers, pp. 133–34.

At a roundup, from out the great herd an animal might break for liberty. One single cowboy reins his pony and makes the charge to return that animal to the roundup. He had no orders to do so. Any cowhand on the works could have done it, but one waddy [cowboy] knew it was up to him and he acted. No confusion, no questions, no hesitation. For the moment he is boss and if, in his judgment, it is necessary to rope and tie this critter—that is the result. No time to ask for orders, no time to give them, no humiliation by asking for help and no insult by having help offered—simply time to do the job. Once done there is no criticism, neither is there commendation. He was expected to do it.

Frank M. King writing about cowboy life in the 1870s and 1880s, Longhorn Trail Drivers, pp. 16–17.

Sometimes on a clear night the cattle would be bedded down, when the air would suddenly become warm and still. Then distant thunder could be heard and phosphorus would shine on the long horns of the cattle and on the horses' ears. Then we knew a storm was brewing. Suddenly like a streak of lightning every steer jumped to its feet and was away on the run. The entire herd seemed to move like one huge animal.

In such instances the cowboys tried to keep in the lead so that the steers could eventually be turned in a circle. If the lightning and thunder and rain continued, the frightened animals would keep running for several miles.

Finally when they were herded there was water standing everywhere, and it was difficult or impossible to bed them again. Then the cowboys, cold and miserable, and often wet to the skin, stood guard the remainder of the night. Maybe one or two broke into song, but it took a brave lad to sing under such conditions.

Frank Collinson recalling a cattle drive of 1873,
Life in the Saddle, *pp. 35–36.*

Some folks pity the bull in the ring at Spanish and Mexican bullfights. I pitied the old Texas longhorns that came to such a sad end, after weathering the trail so nobly. In my mind they were the real sports. They were among the wildest known cattle and made good beef. They also made good work animals and helped to haul heavy loads across the Plains. They could get along without water longer than any other cattle. They had harder and better hoofs. I'm sorry that they are gone from the range.

Frank Collinson recalling a trail drive of 1873,
Life in the Saddle, *p. 42.*

It would cost but little effort or expense to add a hundred comforts, not to say luxuries, to the life of a drover and his cow-boys. They sleep on the ground, with a pair of blankets for bed and cover. No tent is used, scarcely any cooking utensils, and such a thing as a camp cook-stove is unknown. The warm water of the branch or the standing pool is drank; often it is yellow with alkali and other poisons. No wonder the cow-boy gets sallow and unhealthy, and deteriorates in manhood until often he becomes capable of any contemptible thing. . . .

Joseph G. McCoy, 1874, Historic Sketches of the
Cattle Trade of the West and Southwest, *pp. 137–38.*

When North with their herds, a Texan drover always prefers the prairie to any inclosure to handle his stock, for there, mounted on his pony, he feels at home and knows just how to manage; besides he has a fixed, constitutional prejudice against doing anything on foot that can possibly be done on horseback, not to speak of the almost universal fear they entertain of being among their stock on foot. They are jus-

tified, to some extent at least, in indulging this wholesome fear; for but few Texan bullocks will hesitate, when inclosed alone in a strong corral, to show decided belligerent proclivities, or to furiously charge the venturesome wight who dares to show himself on foot within the inclosure.

Joseph G. McCoy, 1874, Historic Sketches of the
Cattle Trade of the West and Southwest, *pp. 81–82.*

On the trail we were each allowed to take a pair of bed blankets and a sack containing a little extra clothing. No more load than was considered actually necessary was to be allowed on the wagon, for there would be no wagon road over most of the country which we were to traverse, and there was plenty of rough country, with creeks and steep-banked rivers to be crossed. We had no tents or shelter of any sort other than our blankets. Our food and cooking utensils were the same as those used in cow camps of the brush country. No provision was made for the care of men in case of accident. Should anyone become injured, wounded, or sick, he would be strictly "out of luck." A quick recovery and a sudden death were the only desirable alternatives in such cases, for much of the time the outfit would be far from the settlements and from medical or surgical aid.

*J. H. Cook remembering his first cattle drive
from Texas to Kansas in 1874,* Fifty Years
on the Old Frontier, *p. 40.*

Drovers consider that the cattle do themselves great injury by running round in a circle, which is termed in cow-boy parlance, "milling," and it can only be stayed by standing at a distance and hallooing or singing to them. The writer has many times sat upon the fence of a shipping yard and sang to an enclosed herd whilst a train would be rushing by. And it is surprising how quiet the herd will be so long as they can hear the human voice; but if they fail to hear it above the din of the train, a rush is made, and the yards bursted asunder, unless very strong. Singing hymns to Texan steers is the peculiar forte of a genuine cowboy, but the spirit of true piety does not abound in the sentiment.

Joseph G. McCoy, 1874, Historic Sketches of the
Cattle Trade of the West and Southwest, *p. 101.*

Whilst the herd is being held upon the same grazing grounds, often one or more of the cow-boys, not on duty, will mount their ponies and go to the village nearest camp and spend a few hours; learn all the items of news or gossip concerning other herds and the cow-boys belonging thereto. Besides seeing the sights, he gets such little articles as may be wanted by himself and comrades at camp; of these a supply of tobacco, both chewing and smoking forms one of the principle, and often recurring wants. The cow-boy almost invariably smokes or chews tobacco—generally both; for the time drags dull at camp or herd ground. Their is nothing new or exciting occurring to break the monotony of daily routine events.

Joseph G. McCoy, 1874, Historic Sketches of the Cattle Trade of the West and Southwest, *p. 134.*

One remarkable feature is observable as being worthy of note, and that is how completely the herd becomes broken to follow the trail. Certain cattle will take the lead, and others will select certain places in the line, and certain ones bring up the rear, and the same cattle can be seen at their post, marching along like a column of soldiers, every day during the entire journey, unless they become lame, when they will fall back to the rear. A herd of one thousand cattle will stretch out from one to two miles whilst traveling on the trail, and is a very beautiful sight, inspiring the drover with enthusiasm akin to that enkindled in the breast of the military hero by the sight of marching columns of men.

Joseph G. McCoy, 1874, Historic Sketches of the Cattle Trade of the West and Southwest, *pp. 93–95.*

Cowboys of the Oklahoma panhandle enjoy a bath, circa 1880. *(Kansas State Historical Society)*

Too much praise or credit cannot be given to those old-time trail cooks who were numbered among the *good* ones. A camp cook could do more toward making life pleasant for those about him than any other man in an outfit, especially on those trail trips. A good-natured, hustling cook meant a lot to a trail boss. A cheery voice ringing out about daybreak, shouting, "Roll out there, fellers, and hear the little birdies sing their praises to God!" or "Arise and shine and give God the glory!" would make the most crusty waddie grin as he crawled out to partake of his morning meal even when he was extremely short of sleep.

J. H. Cook remembering his first cattle drive from Texas to Kansas in 1874, Fifty Years on the Old Frontier, *p. 39.*

I could read, identify, and place every brand or mark placed on a horse or steer between the Gulf of Mexico and the borders of Canada, to the North and from Missouri to California.

Nat Love, who worked as a cowboy between 1874 and 1890, quoted in Philip Durham and Everett L. Jones, The Negro Cowboys, *p. 192.*

Sometimes cattle would drift before a storm for many miles. This was about the hardest job a cowboy had to do in locating a herd on the free open range before the days of the wire fence. He couldn't and didn't carry much, if any, supplies with him, and there were times he would have to go for days with nothing but fresh meat to eat. There was plenty wild game then, and always being armed, he could kill meat for his needs, but it was not what one would term "high livin'". I know, 'cause I've tried it.

Frank M. King describing cowboy life in Clay County, Texas, in 1877, Wranglin' the Past, *p. 49.*

Every bright star in the sky were named by the early cowboys on the cattle trails, and every one of them could tell you the time within ten minutes of their rising or disappearing down the horizon. Some of them names were never found in any book, but we knew which ones was meant when the boys spoke of The Diamond, the Ellenrods, Job's Coffin, the Seven Stars, Midnight Triangle, the Big Dipper. The Big Dipper were really our clock, as we could tell by the position of the stars in it just what time it were, within ten–fifteen minutes maybe.

Jesse James Benton recalling his first cattle drive in 1877, Cow by the Tail, *p. 45.*

The camp was in a draw near Crooked creek: a nice grassy plot, some elm and cottonwood in sight south, blackjacks six miles west, no fencing. They burned surface coal (cow chips). There was the general run of cow camp furniture: a cook stove setting out on the ground and a covered wagon filled with grub and plunder. We had two large ticks [mattress sacks] made of feather ticking, which I filled with buffalo grass; we put them on the ground, and all crawled up on them that could. Some bedded down on the grass and covered with saddle blankets that smelled too much like a tired horse.

Oliver Nelson relating his experiences as a cowboy between 1878 and 1893, The Cowman's Southwest, *p. 61.*

Since very few cattle owners brand on the right side, this calf must be turned over in order that the men handling the irons can brand it properly. Now for the flop of the calf. Each man must act quickly and together. The one having the tail catches the under hind leg and the one at the head takes hold on the under front leg and the flop is accomplished. Now the man at the rear must remove the rope but both must sit tight in their positions thus holding the calf firmly while the brand is applied and the ears marked. This being done, the calf is released. If both men sit tight, each holding his hold and making flop simultaneously, it is seldom a calf gets up while being branded.

W. P. Ricketts describing the method of branding employed in 1879, 50 Years in the Saddle, *pp. 19–20.*

Branding calves: Two men hold each animal down while a third applies the hot iron. (*Western History Collections, University of Oklahoma*)

A man marking the calves should be handy and careful with the knife as there are many earmarks, and if not put on right they are ugly and useless. It is a good idea to avoid leaving sharp points anywhere on the ears as these freeze off, the ear becomes disfigured and there is no guide as to ownership.

W. P. Ricketts, who learned to mark calves' ears in Wyoming in 1879, 50 Years in the Saddle, *p. 21.*

Beside the carcass of a dead horse was a newly made grave. An examination showed that the animal had been killed by lightning. Evidently the thunderbolt had carried instant death to both horse and rider. There was no one to explain, but no explanation was needed. Some Texas cowboy on duty had cashed in—had been killed by lightning and was buried beside the body of his faithful horse. Wolves had nearly devoured the animal's carcass but had not molested the cowboy's grave. There on the wild plains of western Kansas he had been buried, without a woman's tears, without a single tribute of flowers, and doubtless without a coffin. Perhaps a slicker was his only winding sheet. We never learned anything of his history, but here was a solemn admonition to the cowboy that death lurked in the storms that swept over the plains with vivid flashes of lightning.

Baylis John Fletcher, who worked on a cattle drive in 1879, Up the Trail in '79, *p. 49.*

The more you ride your horse after cattle, if you take care of him, the better horse he makes. A horse with small ears, bug eyes, small throatlatch and short-coupled, will as a rule make the best horse, but you have to be an expert rider to set in your saddle when you ride that kind into a herd of cattle. I've seen the best riders dumped off, as the only man that can ride such a one with ease is the man that trained him.

Jesse James Benton remembering his work on a Texas cattle ranch, 1879–80, Cow by the Tail, *p. 66.*

No one who never worked on western cattle ranges during a droughty season can visualize the heartbreaking task. It is not pleasant to ride hosses with their ribs showing after cattle that can hardly walk, trying to move them to some favorable spot; to have to knock little calves in the head in order to save their poor mothers; or, as in many instances, to see little sunken-eyed calves bawling for mothers that had had to give up the struggle.

Frank M. King describing the suffering of cattle from drought prior to 1880, Wranglin' the Past, *p. 57.*

Life slid along amazin'. The weather was dry, but turning cool. The grass was fine, cattle doing good. There were bunches—five hundred to two thousand head—scattered along the creeks three or four miles apart. About half were native, not so wild as Texas cattle. The boys would herd them during day time, bed them on high ground, spend the night in camp, and look them up early in the morning.

Oliver Nelson writing about a cattle drive between Texas and Kansas in 1880, The Cowman's Southwest, *p. 61.*

Ed Willson and Chuck Pierson were typical cowboys of the '80 type and knew their animals from horn to heel.

Chuck, on any of the string of eight horses furnished him, was the best in the pen or on the open prairie with the lariat of any cow-hand I ever saw; and it kept "rasslers," hot iron men, earmarker, dewlaper, and wattler busy to relieve his rope as he brought the calves or older stock close to the fire by the hind feet. . . .

Willson knew brands and marks and could read them where others failed. On a beef gather he would seldom take off his spurs, chaps or boots, from the time the roundup started until the beeves were safely corralled in the loading pens. . . .

Charles A. Guernsey describing two cowboys of his acquaintance, circa 1880, Wyoming Cowboy Days, *pp. 53–54.*

There are various ways to determine the age of cattle; a calf up to two years old has what is called calf's teeth or small teeth. At the age of two years two of these small teeth in the center shed, and two large teeth come in their place, and so on each year, until the animal has a full mouth of large teeth. Also at the age of three the horn becomes more or less smooth and the first wrinkle begins to show on the horn just next to the hair on the head. Then each year another wrinkle comes at four and so on each year, so that when a steer is fully three years old he has one wrinkle; at four he has two wrinkles; at five he has three wrinkles, and so on until his horn is rough again. God fixed it that way for the convenience of buying and selling.

H. H. Halsell, who worked as a cowboy in New Mexico in 1880 and staked out a ranch in Indian Territory in 1881, Cowboys and Cattleland, *pp. 221–22.*

Although a cow is a stupid creature, when a cowboy says, "That man has good cow sense," he means it as a compliment. Washing your face is "bathing out your countenance or washing your profile." "Eyeing" is a person who pokes himself into other people's business. Going courting is "going galing." If a cowboy has a sweetheart, he will not confess it to the hands or anyone else. And if anyone hints anything about it, he simply closes up as silent as the Sphinx. Cutting a rusty is "doing your best." A two-gun man is one who "shoots with a gun in each hand." A goofy means a "nervous man." To throw a calf he bawls out "hot iron." The other answers, "Here with the goods."

H. H. Halsell, who worked as a cowboy in New Mexico in 1880 and staked out a ranch in Indian Territory in 1881, Cowboys and Cattleland, *p. 220.*

The boys had very little chance or time for amusement, and while there are thousands of cowboy songs, mighty few cow hands could carry a tune in a hand basket. When a boy came along who could really sing or play the "mouth organ" (harmonica) he could have a job in any camp, and if he wasn't a top hand his short-comings were overlooked so long as he would sing or play.

Frank M. King recalling cowboy entertainment in the 1880s, Wranglin' the Past, *p. 93.*

Our food was sour-dough biscuits, bacon, corn, tomatoes, beans, and beef. The beef was cut into small pieces and flour pounded into it, together with salt and pepper. Then it was dropped into a Dutch oven with some four or five inches of melted tallow, smoking hot. When the meat was brown we added a thin batter of brown flour and water to make a gravy. The boys would open a can of tomatoes, put on some sugar, salt, and pepper, and eat. They filled up on coffee as black as tar, rolled a cigarette, pulled up the cinches on their horses, and were ready for a hard ride.

Evan G. Barnard describing cowboy life between 1882 and 1885, A Rider of the Cherokee Strip, *p. 57.*

We always rode something like seventy-five feet away from the cattle, and sang a song or made some kind of noise. That was done so that the cattle would not be frightened if we happened to have to ride near them suddenly. If they heard us singing or humming a tune, they knew what was coming. Also the noise we made

kept the coyotes away from the herd. They often prowled around and scared the cows that had calves.

Evan G. Barnard describing cowboy life between 1882 and 1885, A Rider of the Cherokee Strip, *p. 37.*

A large herd of cattle will be guarded by a number of men, who have a common place for eating and sleeping, but they are never there together. Day and night, in good weather and bad weather, some of them must be with the herd. The men are divided up into reliefs, each relief being on duty in the saddle not less than eight hours of the twenty-four, and each individual having a specified beat sometimes eight or ten miles long. Each relief must go around the whole herd, see that all are quiet and unmolested. The outside limits are carefully watched, and if any animals have strayed beyond them, their trail must be followed up, and the fugitives driven back to their proper grazing ground. Under ordinary circumstances, and when the herd is simply being held on certain good grazing ground, with abundance of water, these duties are comparatively easy; but when the grass is poor, and water scarce, the animals stray continually, and great watchfulness and labor are required for their care.

Richard Irving Dodge, 1883, Our Wild Indians: Thirty-three Years" Personal Experience among the Red Men of the Great West, *pp. 609–10.*

The cow-boy, . . . is usually the most reckless of all the reckless desperadoes developed on the frontier. Disregarding equally the rights and lives of others, and utterly reckless of his own life; always ready with his weapons and spoiling for a fight, he is the terror of all who come near him, his visits to the frontier towns of Kansas and Nebraska being regarded as a calamity second only to a western tornado. His idea of enjoyment is to fill himself full of bad whiskey, mount his mustang, tear through the streets, whooping, yelling, flourishing and firing his pistols until the streets are deserted and every house closed, then with a grim smile of happiness he dashes off to his comrades to excite their envy by graphic pictures of his own exploits and the terror of the timid townspeople.

Richard Irving Dodge, 1883, Our Wild Indians: Thirty-three Years' Personal Experience among the Red Men of the Great West, *p. 611.*

The boys had been out for some weeks and run out of bread, the man they sent for it was delayed on account of rain and swollen streams, having to go sixty miles. We were camped on a little spring branch and had been living on beef straight for several days, when, our man came driving in with plenty of grub, the little hollow was ever afterward called Happy Hollow.

Will S. James, a missionary who preached to the cowboys between 1884 and 1893, recounting his experiences, 27 Years a Mavrick, *p. 87.*

The cowboy rides into the herd, cuts out a cow with an unbranded calf, throws his well-directed lasso, catches and jerks the calf to the ground, which another herder quickly brands and releases from the lasso; and then they seek out another victim. Some of the herd-owners collect all their cows and calves in a bunch, drive them to their home ranches, and do the branding there after the general round-up is over.

Walter Baron von Richthofen, 1885, Cattle-Raising on the Plains of North America, *p. 21.*

After you have mastered the cow business thoroughly—that is, learned how not to dread getting into mud up to your ears, jumping your horse into a swollen stream when the water is freezing, nor running your horse at full speed, trying to stop a stampeded herd, on a dark night, when your course has to be guided by the sound of the frightened steer's hoofs—you command *good* wages, which will be from $25.00 to $60.00 per month. . . .

Charles A. Siringo, 1885, A Texas Cow Boy or, Fifteen Years on the Hurricane Deck of a Spanish Pony, *in William W. Savage, Jr.,* Cowboy Life, *p. 75.*

A cowboys outfit is something like a Boston dudes' rig, it can be bought for a small or large amount of money according to the purchasers' means and inclinations.

If you wish to put on style and at the same time have a serviceable outfit, you can invest $500.00 very handy; that is by going or sending to Texas or Old Mexico the only place where such costly outfits are kept.

Your saddle would cost $100. although the Mexicans have them as high as $300.00. An other $50.00 for a gold mounted Mexican sombraro (hat). And $100.00 for a silver mounted bridle and spurs to match. Now a $50.00 saddle-blanket to match your saddle and another $25.00 for a squirt and "Re-etta" (raw-hide rope). Your Colts "45" pearl-handled gold

mounted pistol would cost $50.00, a Winchester to match, $75.00 and $25.00 for a pair of Angora goat leggings, making a total of $475.00 leaving $25.00 out of the $500.00 to buy a Spanish buggy with.

Charles A. Siringo, 1885, A Texas Cow Boy or, Fifteen Years on the Hurricane Deck of a Spanish Pony, *in William W. Savage, Jr.,* Cowboy Life, *pp. 57–58.*

From 1885 and for about ten years thereafter it was just cattle, nothing more—only a fight to hold your own. The roundups started with the first green grass, usually in April, and continued until November and it was ride and ride hard all the time. We would send men out on the outside work and they would often be away for six months. They would work with the outside wagons and throw the cattle back towards the headquarters ranch. Often they would work as far south as Pecos town on the Pecos, and sometimes below that, and as far north as old Fort Sumner, a distance up and down the river of two hundred and fifty miles.

James F. Hinkle describing working conditions from 1885 through 1895, Early Days of a Cowboy on the Pecos, *p. 6.*

Most all the cowboys we only knew as and called "punchers." They were young and active and willing. There was a great fellowship feeling, a common union, among them. But it was work and hard work. There were no union hours. It was from daylight until dark, except the three winter months.

James F. Hinkle recalling cowboy life between 1885 and 1895, Early Days of a Cowboy on the Pecos, *p. 14.*

One very noticeable characteristic of the cowpunchers of those days was that they did not talk very much. Whether this was on account of life on the open range or being alone so much, no one seems to know, but it was a fact. It was a common expression on the plains to say: "One could see farther and see less; more cows and less milk; ride farther and talk less."

James F. Hinkle describing cowboys of the period 1885–95, Early Days of a Cowboy on the Pecos, *p. 18.*

During the last fifteen years the American cow-boy has occupied a place sufficiently important to entitle him to a considerable share of public attention. His occupation is unique. In the exercise of his function he is always a man on horseback. His duty as a worker in the cattle business is at times to ride over the range in order to see that straying cattle do not rove too far from the assigned limits of the herd of which he has charge; at times to drive the herd from one locality to another; and at times to "round up" the dispersed cattle, by which is meant to collect them together for the purpose of branding calves, or of selecting beef cattle, which latter are driven to railroad stations for shipment to market. The chief qualifications of efficiency in this calling are courage, physical alertness, ability to endure exposure and fatigue, horsemanship, and skill in the use of the lariat.

Joseph Nimmo, Jr., November 1886,
"The American Cow-Boy," p. 880.

For several years the entire region from Kansas and Colorado at the south to Montana and Dakota at the north was infested by cattle-thieves. The country afforded apparently illimitable scope for this nefarious traffic. It seemed at one time somewhat a matter of doubt as to which should prosper most, the herdsmen or the cattle-thieves. . . . When the latter were arrested within the limits of the efficient administration of the law, they were handed over to the civil authorities. But when caught beyond the limits of organized counties, administrative justice was extemporized. The cattle-men and the cow-boys themselves supplied judges, jurymen, witnesses, attorneys, constables, and executioners. Sometimes a level-headed cow-boy was placed upon the judicial bench. The cattle-men assert that the extreme and only penalty was never inflicted except upon the clearest evidence of guilt.

When the verdict of guilty was pronounced, a short shrift, and a stout rope, and a grave without a coffin or a winding-sheet, ended the proceedings.

Joseph Nimmo, Jr., November 1886,
"The American Cow-Boy," p. 882.

Of course eggs were scarce those days and very high in price, and an egg was a great prize for the cowboy. When we would go to town and eat in a restaurant if they had any eggs each boy would order a half a dozen and eat his eggs straight.

Con Price remembering life in 1886, when he worked on a
ranch near the Saskatchewan River, Trails I Rode, p. 58.

. . . I kept warm enough. But not any too warm. For that was the celebrated winter of '86–'87 that broke the back of the range cattle business. . . .

Think of riding all day in a blinding snowstorm, the temperature fifty and sixty below zero, and no dinner. You'd get one bunch of cattle up the hill and another one would be coming down behind you, and it was all so slow, plunging after them through the deep snow that way; you'd have to fight every step of the road. The horses' feet were cut and bleeding from the heavy crust, and the cattle had the hair and hide wore off their legs to the knees and hocks. It was surely hell to see big four-year-old steers just able to stagger along.

E. C. Abbott remembering the brutal winter of 1886–87,
We Pointed Them North: Recollections of a
Cowpuncher, *pp. 206–7.*

It was a great sight when all those twenty-five hundred cattle got in the water at once—they strung out like a real trail herd. When they hit the main current it took them down stream about a quarter of a mile. When the leaders got out of that current they had their eyes on those cattle on the far side and they tried to swim up stream, so that it made a beautiful half circle with the lead cattle swimming up stream out of the current and the tail end of the herd going down stream on the near side of the river.

Con Price describing cattle crossing the Yellowstone River
in 1887, Trails I Rode, *p. 37.*

Billie Demick was an expert at making rawhide lariats. He spent his spare time making them, and it required a month or more to make a good one. He killed big jaw steers, cut out his plaits, braided a thirty- or forty-foot lariat, and made his own hondo [honda, or open knot]. After he got one made, some cowpuncher would ride into camp and say, "Demick, I would sure like to have this lariat."

Demick would say, "Well, it is yours," and start making another one.

Evan G. Barnard describing the lariat-making skill
of a cowboy in the Indian Territory in 1887, A Rider of
the Cherokee Strip, *p. 111.*

The calf throwers work always two together. A man on a horse goes in the roundup, ropes a calf around the neck, drags it out to the fire where they are heating the branding irons. One man catches the rope up close to the man on the horse and goes down the line to the calf, which is bucking and bawling, trying to get away; he holds the rope up at its neck with one hand, reaches over its back with the other and catches it in the flank, and as the calf jumps in the air, it is laid on its side. Then the other man, his partner, is there. He grabs it by the top hind leg and sits on the ground and puts his feet against the bottom hind leg up close to its body, pulls back on the leg he holds and pushes forward on the other leg, while the man who has thrown the calf sits on the calf and holds the top front foot with his knees on the calf's shoulder. In this way 'tis quick and easy to brand calves.

J. E. McCauley describing a fall roundup in 1890 Texas,
A Stove-up Cowboy's Story, pp. 11–12.

As to the actual work and wages of the cowboy. The work is necessarily extremely arduous and dangerous. For some six to eight months in the year—*i.e.,* the working time on the plains—he has not only to be in the saddle from morn to night, but often the whole night through as well. To look after these huge Western herds of cattle, to keep a cool head during stampedes and "milling" is no small matter. "I have been with a party," says John Sullivan [a cowboy interviewed by the authors], "when we were obliged to ride 200 miles before we got the cattle under, ... in all that time not one of us took a moment's rest or a bit to eat." In getting the cattle across streams milling often occurs, *i.e.,* the beasts take fright and swim round and round and in every direction but that of the shore. As a consequence "many a good cowboy has been drowned," and it is not "uncommon for a party to spent three weeks or a month in getting a herd of 4,000 cattle across a stream." Further, there are innumerable dangers from bands of marauders, Indians, and prairie fires to face; and, into the bargain, the herd must not only be delivered safe and all told, but they must have increased in weight since leaving the ranch. "The rule is, the cowboy must fatten the cattle on the trail, *no matter how thin he may grow himself.*"

Edward Aveling and Eleanor Marx Aveling, 1891, The
Working-Class Movement in America, pp. 159–61.

With all his faults, and he has his share, [the cowboy] has a heart in him as big in its willingness as the Texas Capitol, is a friend in need and a friend indeed, and his soul is as precious in the sight of Him who says "Whosever [*sic*] will may come" as the wealthiest nabob who walks the streets of New York. My personal observation and experience have taught me that no man living has a greater regard for the feelings of others than has the cow-boy.

Will S. James, 1893, 27 Years a Mavrick, p. 49.

Many people go to Texas, or did so in the early days, expecting to sit down and grow rich; in fact they come out there to grow up with the country, and many of them go up before the country does.

Of all countries in my knowledge, I do not know of one that has so little use for a lazy man, while a man with a small capital can start easier and live better there than anywhere I can mention, provided he has energy and pluck. Still, a poor man who is lazy and thriftless might just as well be in Hades with his back broke as in Texas, especially in the western part. The easiest place in the State for him is down in the piney woods of eastern Texas, where he can chew pine rosin and dry up, making it easy for the wind to blow him away.

Will S. James, 1893, 27 Years a Mavrick, pp. 179–80.

... [W]hat we dreaded most were the quicksands. You can only tell them when your horse begins to shift his feet uneasily, or you feel a kind of tremor beneath you. They were the worst things for the cattle, too. You know, when a cow sinks in one of them and stays there all night, the sand gradually settles around her till she might as well be in a bed of concrete. You have to dig her out—if she's alive—and then you find the circulation clean gone out of her legs.

John H. Culley, range manager for the Bull Ranch, San
Miguel County, New Mexico, from 1893 until 1897,
Cattle, Horses and Men, p. 19.

9

The Movement to End Child Labor
1875–1924

At the dawn of the 20th century, Edgar Gardner Murphy was a 31-year-old Episcopalian priest who had channeled his abundant energy into improving life for the residents of Montgomery, Alabama. He had founded a church for the city's African-American Episcopalians, helped to build and furnish a YMCA, and persuaded steel magnate Andrew Carnegie to give Montgomery its first public library. In 1900, Murphy organized a conference in Montgomery at which speakers, black and white, representing all parts of the nation, lectured on the social problems facing the South.

One of these problems was child labor. Shellfish canneries along the Gulf Coast were employing children as young as four and five years of age to shuck oysters and peel shrimp. Many of the small workers were the children of Polish immigrants who had been lured to the canneries by assurances of a healthful

Manuel, a five-year-old shrimp picker in Mississippi, standing before a pile of oyster shells. Photographed by Lewis Hine in 1911 *(Library of Congress)*

work environment close to the sea. Instead, the children—and their parents, who often worked in the canneries as well—found long hours, hard work, poverty, and dismal living conditions in the vermin-infested shacks that the canneries provided for them.

Cannery workers were paid by the pot of seafood shelled, rather than by the hour. In an attempt to earn a decent wage, they started work as early as 4 A.M. The illiteracy rate among children in the canneries of Texas, Louisiana, and Mississippi was extremely high. More than one in 10 never attended school at all, and many who were enrolled in school attended only intermittently. Also, the Gulf Coast canneries posed a unique health risk. Shrimp secrete a corrosive acid that causes the skin of handlers to peel and crack. In order to stop the bleeding and toughen their skin, workers dipped their hands in alum, a harsh mineral salt.

Conditions were deplorable, too, in the cotton mills of Georgia and the Carolinas, where small children stood on boxes to reach the machines that they operated. The thousands of children who worked in textile mills, in the South and in New England, were on their feet for 10 to 12 hours a day, darting their fingers into fast-moving machinery as they tended bobbins, spun thread, and made buttonholes. Some children inspected cloth or swept dusty floors.

Reverend Murphy was incensed to discover that although Alabama had enacted child-labor legislation, northern capitalists with financial interests in southern mills had exerted their influence to get the new laws repealed. All this inspired Murphy to adopt a new cause, the plight of the South's working children. In 1901, together with citizens from North and South Carolina, Georgia, and his own state, he founded the Alabama Child Labor Committee to work for lasting change.

MORE THAN ONE-FIFTH OF CHILDREN WORKED

In 1900, child labor was a national problem that had become impossible to ignore. Working children were no longer confined to factories and home sweatshops. They were a constant presence on city streets, hawking newspapers or peddling fruit, flowers, nuts, candy, and ribbon. Children shined shoes, ran errands, made deliveries, and hauled firewood. According to the U.S. census of 1900, 1,750,000 children between the ages of 10 and 15—nearly 20 percent in that age group—were part of the paid workforce. The census total excluded laborers under age 10 and those working "off the books" or on the streets, so the actual number of working children was much higher. Many of the young workers were the children of recent immigrants.

Children employed in the street trades who stood on hard pavement all day sustained permanent damage to their growing legs and feet. Juvenile street workers commonly suffered from chronic respiratory infections, tuberculosis, and exposure to cold. Some delivery boys and newsboys froze to death in the wagons where they slept. Also, their work brought many children into contact with criminals and prostitutes and so contributed to delinquency.

Children on the streets worked many hours each week in all kinds of weather. Newsboys reported to work by 5 A.M., and those who sold evening editions were out until well past midnight. The average newsboy at the start of the 20th century was 12 years old, but many were as young as five. Because

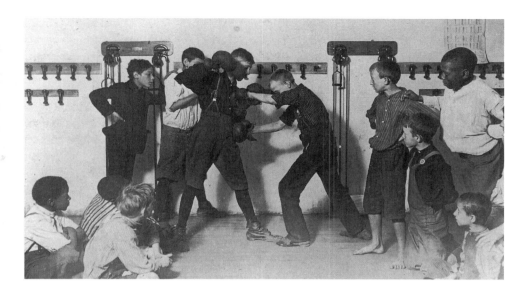

A boxing lesson at the Newsboys' Protective Association, Cincinnati, Ohio, August 1908. Photographed by Lewis Hine *(Library of Congress)*

small children struggling to earn money evoked pity in the newspaper-buying public, the youngest newsboys often made the most sales. Newsboys—and the small number of newsgirls—received no salary or commission. They paid cash for their papers, and any unsold copies represented a loss. Most came from impoverished backgrounds, and many were homeless, living on the streets or in lodging houses such as the ones operated by the Children's Aid Society in New York City.

Newsboys were not the only children who worked into the night. Night work was common in some industries, especially in glass factories, where furnaces were kept running around the clock. When the night shift ended at 3 A.M., many children dropped to the glass-factory floor or curled up in a packing crate to sleep until the morning streetcars started to run. The alternative was to walk a long distance home in the dark.

Most of the girls employed in glass factories decorated glassware or packed finished goods for shipment. Nearly all of the boys worked in the furnace room, where the temperature remained at 100 to 130 degrees Fahrenheit. They were required to stand for long periods or to squat near the blazing furnaces, where they were exposed to intense heat and bright light. (Glass becomes molten at 3,133 degrees Fahrenheit.) Children in glass factories suffered stiff necks, rheumatism, headaches, and rashes, as well as colds, pneumonia, and tuberculosis. Molten glass burned the skin, and shards of broken glass caused deep cuts.

There was no doubt that work of all kinds interfered with learning. New Jersey's labor commissioners calculated in 1885 that of an estimated 343,897 children of school age residing in their state, 89,254 did not attend school. Most in the latter group worked in factories or mines. The numbers in New York were even more alarming. New York had 1,685,000 residents between the ages of five and 21, but an average daily school attendance of only 583,142.

ORGANIZED EFFORTS AT REFORM

As early as 1875, philanthropists and social reformers in the United States were expressing for the welfare of children concern that went beyond solicitude regarding their education. Reformers now targeted children's health, safety, and quality of life as well. In 1875, Elbridge Gerry, a New York attorney who served as counsel for the Society for the Prevention of Cruelty to Animals, founded the New York Society for the Prevention of Cruelty to Children (SPCC), the first organization of its kind in the world. The society's objective at the outset was to remove children from homes where they suffered abuse or neglect. In 1884, the SPCC drafted a regulatory factory bill and submitted it to the New York state legislature. If passed into law, the bill would have prohibited children under 14 from factory work and provided for a 60-hour workweek for anyone under 21.

The proposal died, due to opposition from manufacturers, who argued that New York would lose business to other states if the bill were passed, and from the public, including parents who relied on their children's income. In 1886, however, New York did pass a factory act that barred children under 13 from working in factories in rural areas. This law, passed purely for political reasons, was as ineffective as it was unenforceable. Only a few of New York's many factories were in rural locations, which meant that most were exempt from the law. The only proof of a child's age required was the word of a parent, so a child could remain on the payroll if a parent was willing to lie. Finally, the law provided for only one inspector to monitor factories throughout the state and required that person to report to the legislature just once a year.

As the SPCC continued to press for stronger legislation in New York, Reverend Murphy's organization took shape in the South. Murphy went into textile mills and photographed children at work. He published articles and pamphlets in which he compared child labor to slavery. Manufacturers denied that child laborers were being exploited and defended their business practices by stating that the South's economy depended on child labor as it had once depended on slavery. They accused reformers of advocating socialism and of caving in to northern interference in southern affairs.

Murphy and his supporters made enough noise, however, to get the attention of state lawmakers. In 1903, the Alabama legislature passed a law banning children under 14 from factory work. The law exempted orphaned children 10 to 14 years old and other children under 14 who could prove that work was a financial necessity. This law was an important first step for Alabama, but the state still had a long way to go. The legislature had provided no means for enforcing the new law or for inspecting factories for compliance. Also, Alabama still lacked a compulsory education law. The South lagged behind other regions in this regard, because many southern whites objected to spending tax dollars to educate African-American children. Yet throughout the South, blacks took advantage of educational opportunities at higher rates than whites did. Many in the African-American community viewed schooling as a means to a better standard of living. In 1918, Mississippi would become the last state to enact a compulsory education law, albeit an anemic one that left it up to communities to decide how many weeks of schooling should be compulsory.

In 1904, a number of prominent men and women from across the United States founded the National Child Labor Committee (NCLC), which was to gather and disseminate information on child labor and lobby for legislation. In addition to Edgar Gardner Murphy, the members included Adolph S. Ochs, publisher of the *New York Times;* Charles Eliot, president of Harvard University;

Jane Addams, the distinguished social worker; James H. Kirkland, chancellor of Vanderbilt University; Owen R. Lovejoy, a minister from Michigan; and Ben B. Lindsey, a juvenile court judge from Denver.

In 1907, the NCLC hired Lewis Hine, a teacher at New York's Ethical Culture School who had been photographing the immigrants arriving at Ellis Island, to investigate child labor and photograph working children.

THE PATIENT CRUSADER

Lewis Hine quit his teaching job in 1908 to devote all of his time to his work on child labor. For 11 years, he traveled in the United States, creating a now-famous collection of photographs documenting children at work. The NCLC would use Hine's photographs to influence public opinion and persuade state legislatures to pass child-labor laws.

Hine began his work in the anthracite-mining region of Pennsylvania, where he photographed boys hauling wagonloads of coal like mules and children maimed for life in mining accidents. Gently but persistently, he coaxed children into describing the tedium of working in the mines 12 to 14 hours a day, six days a week. The children admitted to Hine that they feared being injured or crushed in a mining accident, or smothered by falling coal. They complained about the foul air that they breathed day after day.

Hine learned that children were at risk in other parts of the rural United States as well. In the sugar-beet fields of Colorado, Nebraska, and Wisconsin, Hine discovered young children doing the hazardous job of topping beets: holding a beet against one knee and lopping of the leafy top with a 16-inch, pronged knife. A moment's carelessness could result in hooking oneself in the leg. Seven-year-old toppers worked 12-hour shifts, taking a single break at noon, and their young backs ached from long days of bending. These children were not helping out on their families' farms but were hired hands like their parents. They were migrant workers who traveled the countryside, following the crops.

The NCLC published Hine's photographs and data in newspapers, magazines, pamphlets, and newsletters, which they distributed throughout the United States at town meetings, state fairs, and other public gatherings. People were shocked at what they read; they filled the auditoriums where Lewis Hine lectured and displayed his pictures.

Like the Alabama Child Labor Committee and the SPCC, the NCLC pressed state legislatures to pass child-labor laws. In 1910, the group's members developed a model piece of legislation called the Uniform Child Labor Law, which they made available to state governments to show them the kind of law that was needed. The model law set a minimum age of 14 for factory work and 16 for mining, and made documentary proof of age a requirement for employment. It limited the workday to eight hours for laborers between 14 and 16 years of age and prohibited night work for anyone under 16. Finally, it barred children from working in dangerous or unhealthy settings.

Between 1911 and 1913, as the public viewed Lewis Hine's pictures and the NCLC pressured legislators, 39 states passed child-labor laws. Most fell short of the NCLC guidelines, and in most cases compliance was voluntary. The state laws lacked uniformity: some banned night work for children; others did not.

Where night work was permitted, the minimum age varied from 14 to 21. The laws allowed exceptions, such as instances of family poverty. Also, as was the case with the New York Factory Act of 1886, states made no provisions for enforcing the new laws. Nonetheless, the reformers continued to work for comprehensive legislation, and by 1916 37 states had outlawed night work for minors.

Manufacturers, of course, protested vehemently against the child-labor laws, even dredging up the old argument that idleness posed a greater threat to children than hard work did. The strongest opposition came from the glass manufacturers of Pennsylvania and West Virginia, who were against any regulation of night work. They insisted that their furnaces had to be kept running 24 hours a day, because it took a long time to get cold furnaces up to temperature. They argued too that night was the coolest time to work in a glass factory. The glass industry had so much influence in Pennsylvania that when the state banned night work for children in 1909, glass factories were exempted. They enjoyed that exemption for another six years. West Virginia delayed prohibiting children from night work until 1919.

THE PUSH FOR A FEDERAL LAW

In 1906, Senator Albert J. Beveridge of Indiana called on the federal government to tackle the problem of child labor. Beveridge introduced a bill in the

Glass-factory workers, Morgantown, West West Virginia, October 1908. Photographed by Lewis Hine *(Library of Congress)*

Senate that would outlaw the employment of children in factories and mines. At the same time, Representative Herbert Parsons of New York introduced similar legislation in the House of Representatives. Neither man was able to stir up much support for his bill, even from the NCLC. Many Americans thought that by regulating child labor, the federal government would be assuming power not granted to it by the Constitution. They held the opinion that the question of child labor was one appropriately left to the states to resolve. States' rights was a sensitive issue for much of the population at the start of the 20th century, one that brought to mind the bitter disputes over the right of states to permit slavery that had preceded the Civil War. Edgar Gardner Murphy felt so strongly that federal regulation of child labor was undesirable and unconstitutional that he resigned from the Alabama Child Labor Committee when in 1907 it endorsed the Beveridge Bill.

In 1916, President Woodrow Wilson called on Congress to pass a child-labor law. The lawmakers responded, and on September 1, 1916, the first federal child labor law was adopted. It set a national minimum age of 14 in industries producing nonagricultural goods for interstate commerce or export, to take effect September 1, 1917. The law limited children to working six days a week and not after 7 P.M.

The Constitution gave Congress the power to regulate interstate and foreign commerce, but on June 3, 1918, the U.S. Supreme Court decided that Congress could not extend that power to restrict child labor and accordingly declared the new law unconstitutional. Nevertheless, the law had worked: during the nine months in which it was in effect, the number of children working in industry had been substantially, albeit temporarily, reduced.

Congress took action again in 1919, attaching a child-labor bill to a revenue act. The Child Labor Tax Law, which became operative on April 25, 1919, assessed a 10 percent tax on the net profits of mines and factories employing children. It established a minimum age of 14 for workers in most jobs, and of 16 for night work and mining. The 1919 law required documentary proof of age, and like the earlier federal legislation, it limited working hours for minors. It remained the law of the land until May 15, 1922, when the Supreme Court declared it unconstitutional. The court held that the Child Labor Tax Law was an invalid exercise of the congressional power to tax.

The number of working children had decreased 50 percent between 1919 and 1922; however, one million children between the ages of 10 and 15—one of every 12 in that age group—still worked long hours under hazardous conditions. Their ranks swelled again after 1922.

A movement now grew to end child labor by amending the Constitution to give Congress the power that it needed. The NCLC, which had reversed its position and come out in favor of federal intervention, endorsed a proposed amendment. A number of major political organizations, including the Democratic and Republican National Committees, the National League of Women Voters, the National Education Association, the AFL, and several national women's groups, supported the amendment as well. These organizations waged a tough campaign to influence the opinion of legislators and the general public.

Many former opponents of federal legislation had been persuaded, for a variety of reasons, that government controls were necessary. For one thing, a

As late as 1937, children were still doing the dangerous job of digging and topping sugar beets. This photograph was taken in Montana. *(Library of Congress)*

lack of uniformity in state laws meant that people who were morally opposed to purchasing goods made by children had no assurances that items offered for sale had been manufactured by adults. For another, children and employers could easily cross boundaries from states where child labor was illegal to those where it was permitted. Children could enter a neighboring state—even walking across the border in some cases—to find a job. Also, employers of home sweatshop labor could distribute work in another state.

Manufacturers, who opposed the amendment, also tried to influence public opinion. Members of business groups such as the National Association of Manufacturers and the American Farm Bureau Federation distributed leaflets, wrote editorials, and made speeches denouncing the proposed amendment. The manufacturers' message deliberately conveyed false information, stating that communists had backed the amendment, and that the amendment would give Congress the power to pass a child-labor law so extreme as to make it illegal for children to perform chores in their own homes.

How much influence the reformers or the manufacturers actually had is difficult to determine. In 1924, both the Senate and the House of Representatives passed an amendment empowering Congress to limit, regulate, and prohibit the labor of persons under the age of 18 by a two-thirds vote. The amendment was then submitted to the states for ratification. Only 28 state legislatures ratified the amendment, eight fewer than the 36 required. Americans would wait until the 1930s, when economic catastrophe forced them to tackle a variety of difficult social issues, to adopt federal standards for the employment of youth.

CHRONICLE OF EVENTS

1875

Elbridge Gerry establishes the New York Society for the Prevention of Cruelty to Children (SPCC).

1884

The SPCC submits a regulatory factory bill to the New York Legislature.

1886

New York passes a weaker factory act.

1900

The U.S. Census Bureau reports that 1,750,000 children aged 10 to 15 are gainfully employed.

1901

The Reverend Edgar Gardner Murphy forms the Alabama Child Labor Committee.

1903

The Alabama Legislature bars children under 14 from factory work.

1904

The National Child Labor Committee (NCLC) is founded.

1906

Senator Albert J. Beveridge of Indiana and Representative Herbert Parsons of New York introduce child-labor bills in Congress.

Exhausted from working a full day, pupils at a New York City night school in the 1890s struggle to stay awake. Photographed by Jacob Riis *(Library of Congress)*

1907

Edgar Gardner Murphy resigns from the Alabama Child Labor Committee.

1907–18

Lewis Hine documents child labor in the United States for the NCLC.

1910

The NCLC develops a model child-labor law for the states.

1911–13

Thirty-nine states pass child-labor laws.

1916

September 1: The first national child-labor law is enacted.

Night work is illegal for minors in 37 states.

1918

June 3: The U.S. Supreme Court declares the 1916 child-labor law unconstitutional.

Mississippi becomes the last state to enact a compulsory education law.

1919

April 25: The Child Labor Tax Law becomes operative.

1919–22

The number of working children in the United States declines by 50 percent.

1922

May 15: The Supreme Court declares the Child Labor Tax Law unconstitutional.

1924

Congress passes an amendment to the Constitution giving itself the power to regulate child labor; the number of states ratifying the amendment falls short of the 36 required.

EYEWITNESS TESTIMONY

Two little newsboys slept one winter in the iron tube of the bridge at Harlem; two others made their bed in a burned-out safe in Wall Street. Sometimes they ensconced themselves in the cabin of a ferry-boat, and thus spent the night. Old boilers, barges, steps, and, above all, steam-gratings, were their favorite beds.

In those days the writer would frequently see ten or a dozen of them, piled together to keep one another warm, under the stairs of the printing-offices.

Charles Loring Brace remembering conditions prior to 1854, when the first lodging house for street boys opened in New York City, The Dangerous Classes of New York, *p. 100.*

In the course of a year the population of a town passes through the Lodging-house [of the Children's Aid Society]—in 1869 and '70, *eight thousand eight hundred and thirty-five* different boys. Many are put in good homes; some find places for themselves; others drift away—no one knows whither. They are an army of orphans—regiments of children who have not a home or a friend—a multitude of little street-rovers who have no place where to lay their heads. They are being educated in the streets rapidly to be thieves and burglars and criminals.

Charles Loring Brace describing conditions circa 1870, The Dangerous Classes of New York, *p. 106.*

I remember asking one little lad his age, in Pittston, Pennsylvania, during the anthracite coal strike of 1902. He certainly did not look more than ten years old, but he answered boldly, "I'm thirteen, sir." When I asked him how long he had been at work, he replied, "More'n a year gone, sir." Afterward I met his father at one of the strikers' meetings, and he told me that the lad was only a few days over eleven years of age, and that he went to work as a "breaker boy" before he was ten. "We'm a big fam'ly," he said in excuse. "There's six kids an' th' missis an' me. Wi' me pay so small, I was glad to give a quarter to have the papers (certificate) filled out so's he could bring in a trifle like other boys." Afterward I came across several similar cases.

John Spargo recalling events of 1902, The Bitter Cry of the Children, *pp. 143–44.*

From November until May a breaker boy always wears a cap and tippet, and overcoat if he possesses one, but because he has to rely largely upon the sense of touch, he cannot cover his finger-tips with mittens or gloves; from the chafing of the coal his fingers sometimes bleed, and his nails are worn down to the quick. The hours of toil for slate-pickers are supposed to be from seven in the morning until noon, and from one to six in the afternoon; but when the colliery is running on "full capacity orders," the noon recess is reduced to half an hour, and the goodnight whistle does not blow until half-past six. For his eleven hours' work the breaker boy gets no more pay than for ten.

Francis H. Nichols, February 1903, "Children of the Coal Shadow," in Edna D. Bullock, comp., Selected Articles on Child Labor, *pp. 134–35.*

The coal so closely resembles slate that it can be detected only by the closest scrutiny, and the childish faces are compelled to bend so low over the chutes that prematurely round shoulders and narrow chests are the inevitable result. In front of the chutes is an open space reserved for the "breaker boss," who watches the boys as intently as they watch the coal.

The boss is armed with a stick, with which he occasionally raps on the head and shoulders a boy who betrays lack of zeal.

Francis H. Nichols, February 1903, "Children of the Coal Shadow," in Edna D. Bullock, comp., Selected Articles on Child Labor, *p. 134.*

In the spring of 1903 I went to Kensington, Pennsylvania, where seventy-five thousand textile workers were on strike. Of this number at least ten thousand were little children. . . . Every day little children came into Union Headquarters, some with their hands off, some with the thumb missing, some with their fingers off at the knuckle. They were stooped little things, round shouldered and skinny. Many of them were not over ten years of age, although the state law prohibited their working before they were twelve years of age.

The law was poorly enforced and the mothers of these children often swore falsely as to their children's age. In a single block in Kensington, fourteen women, mothers of twenty-two children all under twelve, explained it was a question of starvation or perjury. That the fathers had been killed or maimed at the mines.

I asked the newspaper men why they didn't publish the facts about child labor in Pennsylvania. They said they couldn't because the mill owners had stock in the papers.

Mary Harris Jones describing her actions in spring 1903, Autobiography of Mother Jones, *p. 71.*

We marched to Twentieth Street [in New York City]. I told an immense crowd of the horrors of child labor in the mills around the anthracite region and I showed them some of the children. I showed them Eddie Dunphy, a little fellow of twelve, whose job it was to sit all day on a high stool, handing in the right thread to another worker. Eleven hours a day he sat on the high stool with dangerous machinery all about him. All day long, winter and summer, spring and fall, for three dollars a week.

And then I showed them Gussie Rangnew, a little girl from whom all childhood had gone. Her face was like an old woman's. Gussie packed stockings in a factory, eleven hours a day for a few cents a day.

Mary Harris Jones describing a demonstration in New York City in 1903, Autobiography of Mother Jones, *p. 79.*

We want President [Theodore] Roosevelt to hear the wail of the children who never have a chance to go to school but work eleven and twelve hours a day in the textile mills of Pennsylvania; who weave the carpets that he and you walk upon; and the lace curtains in your windows, and the clothes of the people. Fifty years ago there was a cry against slavery and men gave up their lives to stop the selling of black children on the block. Today the white child is sold for two dollars a week to the manufacturers. . . .

In Georgia where children work day and night in the cotton mills they have just passed a bill to protect song birds. What about the little children from whom all song is gone?

Mary Harris Jones speaking at a demonstration in New York City in 1903, Autobiography of Mother Jones, *p. 80.*

The movement of a population from industrial dependence to industrial competence, from distress and poverty to comfort and property, is not a process of ease for any of its elements. Above all, the industrial readjustment of a population, moving from the conditions of agriculture to the conditions of manufacture, must bear with severity upon every form and aspect of the family life. But this process, however painful, must be adjusted with the maximum of compassion to the lives of the helpless and defenceless. The chief burden of this readjustment should not be laid upon the child. The life of the child should be, not the point of the severest pressure and the acutest suffering, but the point of chief protection.

Edgar Gardner Murphy, 1904, Problems of the Present South, *p. 114.*

It is true that the work of the factory—especially for the younger children—is often lighter than the work brought to the child upon the farm. But the benumbing power of factory labor lies not so much in its hardness as in its monotony. Picking up toothpicks from a pile, one by one, and depositing them in another, may be light work, but when continued for twelve hours a day it is a work to break the will and nerve of a strong man. The work of the factory means usually doing the same small task over and over again—moment in and moment out, hour after hour, day after day. Its reactive effect upon the mind is dulness, apathy, a mechanical and stolid spirit, without vivacity or hope.

Edgar Gardner Murphy, 1904, Problems of the Present South, *p. 108.*

One of the most serious phases of the Southern factory system, especially as that system touches the life and fate of the child, lies in the habit of "long hours." I have known mills in which for ten and twelve days at a time the factory hands—children and all—were called to work before sunrise and were dismissed from work only after sunset, laboring from dark to dark. I have repeatedly seen them at labor for twelve, thirteen, even fourteen hours per day. In the period of the holidays or at other "rush times" I have seen children of eight and nine years of age leaving the factory as late as 9.30 o'clock at night, and finding their way with their own little lanterns, through the unlighted streets of the mill village, to their squalid homes.

Edgar Gardner Murphy, 1904, Problems of the Present South, *pp. 118–19.*

It is true that the outward lot of the child of the mill family is sometimes better than that of the poor white child of the country. But where this is true, it is true not because of child labor, but in spite of it. There are men at the East who claim that the condition of the child in the sweat-shop is a "vast improvement" on the condition of the child in the crowded foreign city where it once lived. Does that prove that the sweat-shop labor of its tiny hands is responsible for the change? No. Is child labor responsible for the better condition of the factory child? Its life may share in the general improvement of conditions, but the child, instead of receiving, as childhood should, the maximum of immunity from distress, and the largest freedom which the new environment affords, is bearing in its tender strength the greatest burden and the heaviest curse of the new prosperity. Let us not be guilty of mental confusion. Let us not credit the good fortune of the family to the misfortune of the child.

Edgar Gardner Murphy, 1904, Problems of the Present South, *pp. 139–40.*

I saw little girls going to and fro before scores of revolving spindles, having their short dresses tied with a cord to keep them from being entangled in the machinery as they stretched on tiptoe to catch the broken thread. And these little girls in short dresses, standing before these whirlers—some of them making twenty-five thousand revolutions a minute—from 6 P.M. to 6 A.M., get drowsy. It means more waste—the waste of nerve and tissue of future mothers in the commonwealth of Pennsylvania.

Peter Roberts, December 17, 1904, "Child Labor in Eastern Pennsylvania," in Edna D. Bullock, comp., Selected Articles on Child Labor, *p. 157.*

The higher the type of living being the finer the organism, the longer the period of time required for its maturing. The young of birds and of the lower animals are full grown after a few days or a few weeks. They acquire with incredible rapidity the use of inherited instincts, and after the shortest infancy are ready to take up the struggle for existence after the fashion of their species. The human being requires a period of preparation extending over years before he is ready to take up the struggle for existence after the human fashion. First infancy, then childhood, then early youth; and during all that period he must remain dependent on the protection and the nurture of adult kinsfolk. If that period is curtailed the end of Nature in this highest type of living being—man—is thwarted. It is for this reason that premature toil is such a curse. The child must develop physically, and to do so it must play; the child must develop mentally, and to do so it must be sent to school; the child must

develop morally, and to do so it must be kept within the guarded precincts of the home.

Felix Adler, May 19, 1905, "Child Labor in the United States and Its Great Attendant Evils," in Edna D. Bullock, comp., Selected Articles on Child Labor, *p. 23.*

I shall never forget my first visit to a glass factory at night. It was a big wooden structure, so loosely built that it afforded little protection from draughts, surrounded by a high fence with several rows of barbed wire stretched across the top. I went with the foreman of the factory and he explained to me the reason for the stockade-like fence. "It keeps the young imps inside once we've got 'em for the night shift," he said. The "young imps" were, of course, the boys employed, about forty in number, at least ten of whom were less than twelve years of age.

John Spargo, 1906, The Bitter Cry of the Children, *pp. 155–56.*

By the side of each mould sat a "take-out boy," who, with tongs, took the half-finished bottles—not yet provided with necks—out of the moulds. Then other boys, called "snapper-ups," took these bodies of bottles in their tongs and put the small ends into gas-heated moulds till they were red-hot. Then the boys took them out with almost incredible quickness and passed them to other men, "finishers," who shaped the necks of the bottles into their final form. Then the "carrying-in boys," sometimes called "carrier pigeons," took the red-hot bottles from the benches, three or four at a time, upon big asbestos shovels to the annealing oven, where they are gradually cooled off to insure even contraction and to prevent breaking in consequence of too rapid cooling. The work of these "carrying-in boys," several of whom were less than twelve years old, was by far the hardest of all. They were kept on a slow run all the time from the benches to the annealing oven and back again. I can readily believe what many manufacturers assert, that it is difficult to get men to do this work, because men cannot stand the pace and get tired too quickly.

John Spargo, 1906, The Bitter Cry of the Children, *pp. 157–58.*

I once stood in a breaker for half an hour and tried to do the work a twelve-year-old boy was doing day after day, for ten hours at a stretch, for sixty cents a day. The gloom of the breaker appalled me. Outside the sun shone brightly, the air was pellucid, and the birds sang in chorus with the trees and the rivers. Within the breaker there was blackness, clouds of deadly dust enfolded everything, the harsh, grinding roar of the machinery and the ceaseless rushing of coal through the chutes filled the ears. I tried to pick out the pieces of slate from the hurrying stream of coal, often missing them; my hands were bruised and cut in a few minutes; I was covered from head to foot with coal dust, and for many hours afterwards I was expectorating some of the small particles of anthracite I had swallowed.

I could not do that work and live, but there were boys of ten and twelve years of age doing it for fifty and sixty cents a day. Some of them had never been inside of a school; few of them could read a child's primer.

John Spargo, 1906, The Bitter Cry
of the Children, *pp. 164–65.*

In the manufacture of felt hats, little girls are often employed at the machines which tear the fur from the skins of rabbits and other animals. Recently, I stood and watched a young girl working at such a machine; she wore a newspaper pinned over her head and a handkerchief tied over her mouth. She was white with dust from head to feet, and when she stooped to pick anything from the floor the dust would fall from her paper head-covering in little heaps. About seven feet from the mouth of the machine was a window through which poured thick volumes of dust as it was belched out from the machine. I placed a sheet of paper on the inner sill of the window and in twenty minutes it was covered with a layer of fine dust, half an inch deep. Yet that girl works midway between the window and the machine, in the very centre of the volume of dust, sixty hours a week.

John Spargo, 1906, The Bitter Cry
of the Children, *p. 176.*

Children employed as varnishers in cheap furniture factories inhale poisonous fumes all day long and suffer from a variety of intestinal troubles in consequence. The gilding of picture frames produces a stiffening of the fingers. The children who are employed in the manufacture of wall papers and poisonous paints suffer from slow poisoning. . . . Children employed in morocco leather works are often nauseated and fall easy victims to consumption. The little boys who make matches, and the little girls who pack them in boxes, suffer from phosphorous necrosis, or "phossy-jaw," a gangrene of the lower jaw due to phosphor poisoning. Boys employed in type foundries and stereotyping establishments are employed on the most dangerous part of the work, namely, rubbing the type and the plates, and lead poisoning is excessively prevalent among them as a result.

John Spargo, 1906, The Bitter Cry
of the Children, *pp. 178–79.*

[Four-year-olds] are pulling basting threads so that you and I may wear cheap garments; they are arranging the petals of artificial flowers; they are sorting beads; they are pasting boxes. They do more than that. I know of a room where a dozen or more little children are seated on the floor, surrounded by barrels, and in those barrels is found human hair, matted, tangled, and blood-stained—you can imagine the condition, for it is not my hair or yours that is cut off in the hour of death.

John Spargo, 1906, The Bitter Cry
of the Children, *pp. 172–73.*

Let us glance into the weaving-rooms of the cotton mills and behold in the hot, damp, decaying atmosphere the little wan figures flying in hideous cotillion among looms and wheels—children choked and blinded by clouds of lint forever molting from the webs, children deafened by the jar and uproar of an eternal Niagara of machines, children silenced utterly in the desert desolation in the heart of the never-ceasing clamor, children that seem like specter-shapes, doomed to silence and done with life, beckoning to one another across some thunder-shaken Inferno. . . .

In the southern cotton mills, where the doors shut out the odor of the magnolia and shut in the reeking damps and clouds of lint, and where the mocking bird outside keeps obbligato to the whirring wheels within, we find a gaunt goblin army of children keeping their forced march on the factory-floors—an army that outwatches the sun by day and the stars by night.

*Edwin Markham, September 1906, "Child
at the Loom," in Julia E. Johnsen, comp.,* Selected
Articles on Child Labor, *pp. 76–77.*

If we have the power to *prohibit* the transportation in interstate commerce of cattle *without a certificate, well or ill;* if we have the power to *prohibit* the transportation

A spinner employed at the Globe Cotton Mill, Augusta, Georgia, January 1909. Photographed by Lewis Hine *(Library of Congress)*

of certain *insects;* if we have the power to *prohibit* the transportation of loose *hay* in vessels; if we have the power to *prohibit* the transportation of gold and silver goods merely because they have two words on them, and all *under the interstate-commerce clause;* if we have the power to prohibit convict-made goods, why have we not the power to prohibit the transportation in interstate commerce of child-labor-made goods?

Senator Albert J. Beveridge, December 6, 1906, in Grace Abbott, The Child and the State, *p. 475.*

A visitor of the relief society found Rosina aged thirteen years, helping her mother and father in the work of finishing trousers. Since the arrival of the family in the United States seven years before, neither Rosina nor Vincenza had attended school, and neither could read or write. With the father ill of tuberculosis, Vincenza no longer able to work, and four younger children, aged

eleven, seven, five and two years, to be cared for, Rosina, who had helped to support the family since she was six years old, was now the chief wage earner. Her brother, Giuseppe, aged eleven years helped in the sewing after school hours. But at the price of four cents a pair, for "felling" seams, finishing linings, and sewing buttons on trousers, all the workers in the family,—father, mother and two children, by united effort, could not earn more than four or five dollars a week. . . .

All that the law could do for Rosina was to add school work to the ceaseless toil in which she had spent her days since early childhood.

Mary Van Kleeck, March 1910, "Child Labor in New York City Tenements," in Edna D. Bullock, Selected Articles on Child Labor, *pp. 128–29.*

From statements made by themselves, I have record of thirteen children employed in the Gulf Coast canneries from three to five years of age, twenty-five from six to eight years of age, and fifteen from nine to eleven years of age. The mother of three-year-old Alma told me proudly, "Yes, I'm learnin' her the trade." The little one's sisters, Grace and Maud, three and five years old, helped, but Alma was "the fastest."

It is not rare to see children four and five years old struggling with the rough and heavy oyster shells, and in one day earning about five cents. The earnings of the very little ones are usually not over five cents a day. Bill, a lad of five, said he made fifteen cents; and his mother added, "He kin when he wants to work, but he won't keep at it." Several children of seven to eight years earn from ten cents to "two bits."

I wish I could take you into one of the long, dingy shucking sheds at three o'clock some cold damp morning. You would find several hundred women and children lined up on both sides of the low cars of oysters which have just been steamed in order that they may be more easily opened. The shucking is a simple process, and, as the bodies of the workers sway back and forth with rhythm, one is reminded forcibly of sweatshop scenes in the large cities.

> *Lewis Hine in Rene Banche, January 1912,*
> *"Shrimps and Babies," in Julia E. Johnsen, comp.,*
> Selected Articles on Child Labor, *p. 97.*

I recall a boy who had worked steadily for two years as a helper in a smelting establishment, and had conscientiously brought home all his wages, one night suddenly announcing to his family that he "was too tired and too hot to go on." As no amount of persuasion could make him alter his decision, the family finally threatened to bring him into the Juvenile Court on a charge of incorrigibility, whereupon the boy disappeared and such efforts as the family have been able to make in the two years since, have failed to find him. They are convinced that "he is trying a spell of tramping" and wish that they "had let him have a vacation the first summer when he wanted it so bad."

> *Jane Addams, 1912,* The Spirit of Youth
> and the City Streets, *pp. 112–13.*

I remember a little colored girl in [a] New York school who was drawing for the pattern she was about to embroider, a carefully elaborated acanthus leaf. Upon my inquiry as to the design, she replied: "It is what the Egyptians used to put on everything, because they saw it so much growing in the Nile; and then the Greeks copied it, and sometimes you can find it now on the buildings downtown." She added, shyly: "Of course, I like it awfully well because it was first used by people living in Africa where the colored folks come from." Such a reasonable interest in work not only reacts upon the worker, but is, of course, registered in the product itself. Such genuine pleasure is in pitiful contrast to the usual manifestation of the play spirit as it is found in the factories, where, at the best, its expression is illicit and often is attended with great danger.

> *Jane Addams, 1912,* The Spirit of Youth
> and the City Streets, *pp. 122–23.*

The child of the working class represents the human rubbish-pile, the waste material of the industrial world. In our age of efficiency, the horns and the hoofs of cattle, the bristles of the pig, the tar from coal, scraps of iron, of meat and paper, all the waste products of industry are being utilized.

The working people have for a long time possessed an unsuspected mine of wealth. They have, through ignorance, large families of children beyond their earning power to rear; and now the economic waste material these children represent is being utilized. All that is needed to make an iron and steel machine perfect in its money-making power is the addition of a human cog. A child will do as well for this human cog as a man, and so a use has been found for the children of the working people. As commercial waste products they are the source of some of our largest fortunes.

> *Helen M. Todd, April 1913, "Why Children Work: The*
> *Children's Answer," in Edna D. Bullock, comp.,* Selected
> Articles on Child Labor, *p. 211.*

Ask any twenty children in a factory the question: "Why are you working?" The answers will show you that a great part of child labor comes from the premature death or disability of the father through industrial accident or disease, or the unemployment of the father through being engaged in an industry which occupies its people only a portion of the year, at low wages.

Over and over again, in answer to the question, "What does your father do?" the reply is, "He's sick"; and the same story unfolds in every factory from most of the children you question: "He's got the brass chills"; "He's got consumption"; "He's got blood-poisoning"; "He's paralyzed"; "He can't use his hands"; "He works in a foundry, and the cupola burst, and he got burned"; "A rail fell on his foot, and it's smashed"; "He's dead—he got killed." He worked in the steel mills, or the stockyards, or on the railroad, and the engine ran over him; he was burned with molten metal, or crushed by falling beams, or maimed by an explosion.

Helen M. Todd, April 1913, "Why Children Work: The Children's Answer," in Edna D. Bullock, comp., Selected Articles on Child Labor, *p. 209.*

In the office the child stood before me, stooped and passive, covered with dust, looking at nothing, apparently thinking of nothing.

All my stock of little jokes and playful remarks died within me as I looked at him. I could not imagine him smiling or his eyes lighting up. He seemed the very gray breath of weariness. "Sit down," I said. "What is your name?" "Adolph Jenson." "How old are you, Adolph?" "'Bout fifteen." "When did you begin to work?" "I don' know." "How old were you when you started to work?" "'Bout thirteen, I guess." "When do you come to work in the morning?" No answer. "Listen, Adolph. What time must you start to work?" "'Bout six-thirty." "Six-thirty! Where do you live?" "1430 Larrabee Street." "Why, that's 'way out north. What time do you get up?" No answer. "Adolph, what time do you get up, dear?" "'Bout five." "When do you stop work?" "Six o'clock." "Do you have an hour for lunch?" "Yes'm." "Do you ever play?" "No'm." "What do you do at night?" He seemed not to hear. His loose, dusty clothes hung about him in shapeless lines, and he sat with his eyes fixed on the floor. "What do you do evenings, Adolph?" I insisted. He raised his dull eyes. "I go to night school," he said, and dropped them again. "Do you like to work?" He shook his head. "Do you like school?" I put my hand on his arm to rouse him. He shook his head again. "Do you ever play with the other boys—ball or anything?" "No." "How long have you had that cough?" "I don't know."

Helen M. Todd, April 1913, "Why Children Work: The Children's Answer," pp. 212–13.

Each year the tenements of Philadelphia pour their hundreds into the cranberry bogs [of New Jersey]. A padrone herds them and drives them, and not even Legree, in his day of glory, ever exercised more autocratic power over human beings. He charges his victims double railroad fare; operates a commissary at which his herd must buy bad food at exorbitant prices; and, as a final gouge, exacts money "presents" at the end of the season.

The cranberry vine is only a few inches high, and the workers must double up on their knees and progress by a series of jerks. It is a crop that requires occasional flooding, so that the ground is always soggy with occasional pools here and there. Foreign vines scratch the hands; swarms of mosquitoes inflame the lacerations; and there are storms now and then from which there is no shelter. Children as young as five are in the army that the padrone herds across the bogs from dawn to dusk, for there is the fear of frost; and what is human health in comparison with a perishable crop?

Edwin Markham et al., 1914, Children in Bondage, *pp. 34–35.*

Many children, both white and colored, work on the tobacco plantations of the South, weeding and "worming" and hoeing, driven on not infrequently by the oaths of heartless overseers. In North Carolina, one-fourth of the tobacco workers are children. In one factory there are four hundred colored children. Some are over ten years of age, but many children of six and seven are working beside their mothers. A child of only three years can straighten out leaves for wrappers, and a little worker of four is good help at stripping. A ten-year-old is often an expert "roller."

Edwin Markham et al., 1914, Children in Bondage, *p. 139.*

No wonder that the factory master is looking for "small girls." Little girls are "good": they ask for nothing, they object to nothing. They are timid; so they do not cry out against hard conditions, nor resent the flood of vulgarity washing over their souls. They do not complain when their fingers are caught and crushed in the machines. They know "you ought to keep wide awake and not take your eyes off your work." And these "good" little girls are quick to go to the hospital with their bleeding fingers, anxious not to offend the overseer with bloodstains on the boxes.

Edwin Markham et al., 1914, Children in Bondage, *pp. 130–31.*

When I first went to work at night . . . the long standing up hurt my feet, and my back pained all the time. Mother cried when I told her how I felt, and that made me feel so bad that I didn't tell her any more. My eyes hurt always from watching the threads at night. Sometimes I see threads everywhere. When I look at other things, I see threads, running across them. Sometimes the threads seem to be cutting into my eyes.

A girl quoted in Edwin Markham et al.,
Children in Bondage, *p. 160.*

Besides working at machine or with needle, there is still another industry for the little daughters of the tenements. The mother is always busy or else is away, packing her bundles to or from the contractor's shop. The older girl, therefore, must assume the work and care of the family. She becomes the "little mother," washing, scrubbing, cooking, caring for the other children; carrying coal and ashes, water; doing the errands and shopping for the young ones below her and the elders above. While other children are playing with dolls and mud pies, these "little mothers" are cooking, and tending baby. "My baby's teething; I had to walk with my baby all night, so's't mamma could sleep," said a heavy-eyed nine-year-old. "I had to walk, cause I'd go to sleep if I stopped walking."

Edwin Markham et al., 1914,
Children in Bondage, *p. 92.*

The burden of caring for younger siblings often fell to girls in poor urban families of the Gilded Age. Photographed by Jacob Riis *(Library of Congress)*

One face follows me still, the gaunt face of a boy crouched like a caryatid, pasting tiny labels on the margins of cigarette-boxes. All day long he stuck little oblongs of paper marked with runic words: "Cork tips," "Cork tips," "Cork tips." That was his one message to the universe. His pay was twenty-five cents a thousand; and he sat there, growing bent and haggard, and spending all his energies to promulgate to humanity this news about cork tips. Other boys of his age were away climbing mountains, swimming rivers, and reading Walter Scott. But this deadly drudgery, this death-in-life, is what a "high stage of civilization" provides for *him.* If perchance he should rebel, this is the fate provided for the *next* child waiting in the long line of little lads pushed into these prisons by poverty.

> *Edwin Markham et al., 1914,* Children in Bondage, *pp. 131–32.*

Into each of [the] distributing rooms came nightly . . . from 40 to 80 men and boys. They began to arrive at about 6 P.M.; and while they waited for the 9.45 edition they gambled, fought, drank, boasted, and swore the time away.

On receiving the night edition it was the custom of the men and boys who gathered here to go out peddling their papers, and to return between midnight and 3 in the morning to "check in" for their stock and go home, or more frequently, to sleep in these rooms on the iron tables, or the floor, until the issuance of the morning edition.

> *Elsa Wertheim, 1917, "Chicago Children in the Street Trades," in Nettie P. McGill,* Children in Street Work, *p. 16.*

A dozen different roads radiate from Scottsbluff [Nebraska]. It is along these roads, in the early dawn and even while it is still quite dark, that the children of the beet fields go forth for their day's work. I saw them in November when the frost lay thick on the prairies and when the harvest was at its height. But the work had been going on since April, steadily and monotonously.

The harvest is probably the most bitter time of all. It is then that the children must pull the heavy beets from the ground, stooping until their backs ache and pulling until their wrists are weary. After the beets have been pulled the tops are sliced off with a sharp knife. Then the beets are piled into carts and hauled to a nearby factory. Sugar beets are heavy. A child of eleven or twelve years often lifts a total of several tons a day!

> *Henry F. Pringle, April 9, 1924, "Set the Children Free," in Julia E. Johnsen, comp.,* Selected Articles on Child Labor, *p. 318.*

The public encourages child labor by its willful patronage of the small boy. The newsboy seated on the doorstep of the public building gets the major portion of the business without exertion on his part, while the adult worker strives in vain to secure his share of the sales. The same principle obtains with the child working elsewhere; sympathy for the child blinds reason and foresight, and thus the child is allowed to continue his work. The public must learn that it is not efficient kindness to purchase the goods that are made by child labor under bad conditions, nor to purchase the small child's wares even when he begs piteously.

> *George B. Mangold, 1924,* Problems of Child Welfare, *p. 334.*

The radiation from the glass was intense enough at some places of work to burn seriously. Radiation from the red hot bottles handled in taking-out sometimes burned the knuckles of the worker's hands through the canvas gloves worn. Girls in one factory overcame this difficulty in part by wrapping their fingers with strips of cloth before putting on their gloves. The hands of the skilled glass workers became callous to the heat, but the hands of young workers in glass factories are very tender. Wristlets or long sleeves were usually worn to protect the arms from radiation.

The faces of some girls working in constant heat were red and irritated from the radiation from hot glass.

> *Pennsylvania Department of Labor and Industry, 1927, "Opportunities and Conditions of Work for Minors under 18 in the Glassware Industry," in Grace Abbott,* The Child and the State, *p. 397.*

Minors under 18 were in some danger of lead poisoning in one plant which made lead lamp bases. Two boys aged 16 and 17 were casting the forms from molten metal, a composition 90 per cent lead and 10 per cent antimony. The four inch exhaust pipe leading from the hoods over the pots of molten metal had no exhaust fans to force ventilation. The chief lead hazard was from dust due to the bad housekeeping in the casting room for lead was splashed anywhere.

Pennsylvania Department of Labor and Industry, 1927, "Opportunities and Conditions of Work for Minors under 18 in the Glassware Industry," in Grace Abbott, The Child and the State, *p. 396.*

. . . [M]any newsboys have irregular meals and even more have meals at improper hours. The peak of newspaper sales comes at the hours most newsboys' families are having their suppers. A hot evening meal, the principal one of the day, was out of the question, therefore, for large numbers of the boys. Even those who sold papers only until 6.30 or 7 usually went home to leftovers from the family supper, not always kept hot. Many had no supper until 8 P.M. or later or got a "hot dog" sandwich, a cup of coffee, or some stale cakes in the intervals of their work. Some boys ate a cheap meal at down-town restaurants. On Saturdays, when many sold all day, they often had nothing to eat but an unsubstantial bite snatched here or there until they reached home late at night. Boys selling morning papers sometimes breakfasted at 5 or earlier, sold until 8 or 8.30, and then rushed to school; others, obliged to be out too early for the family meal, ate no breakfast or sold two or three hours before having anything to eat.

Nettie P. McGill, 1928, Children in Street Work, *pp. 20–21.*

It may be that for healthy, well-clad boys the dangers of exposure to very cold or inclement weather are at a minimum, though anyone who has waited even 15 minutes for a street car in a soaking rain or a cold wind will realize that several hours of standing on a corner under such conditions is not a comfortable experience. Certainly the younger newsboys standing outside hotels and at the entrances to restaurants on snowy or bitter cold winter nights often look as if they were suffering.

Nettie P. McGill, 1928, Children in Street Work, *p. 21.*

10

The Great Depression
1929–1941

For much of the nation's history, the amount of work needing to be done seemed abundant. One's place in society was certain. That position might be dictated by circumstance rather than by choice, and the conditions of work might leave much to be desired. Still, it was an article of faith that whether you were a child or an adult, educated or illiterate, immigrant or native born, America could find a job for you.

The Great Depression of the 1930s robbed thousands of their work and part of their identity. The realization that a job might not be there, no matter how hard they were willing to work, amounted to a loss of innocence for many people. It became customary to blame the depression on the stock market crash of October 1929. Historians and economists who study that era agree, however, that there was no single triggering event. Instead, a variety of factors, including an unstable world economy in the aftermath of World War I and the financial policies of U.S. and foreign leaders, led to international economic collapse.

THE EXUBERANT DECADE

Americans were optimistic in the 1920s. If reflecting on the recent past meant recalling that 115,000 of their fellow citizens had died in the Great War, they preferred to face forward. U.S. factories were producing consumer goods at an unprecedented rate, turning out hundreds of thousands of radios, gramophones, toasters, and vacuum cleaners. The automobile was changing the way people lived, allowing city workers to settle in grassy suburbs and giving rural youth a way to get into town. Working people, who put in 49 hours a week on average in 1926 and who took home a little more than $26 per week, might not have been able to afford every convenience of modern life, but they were confident that someday they would.

The prevailing optimism fueled speculation among those who could afford it—and among some who could not. People invested in land, buying up building lots in Southern California in the hope of selling them at a profit. Approximately 1.3 million people did relocate to California in the 1920s, but by 1924 there were many more lots on the market than there were potential buyers, and quite a few investors went bankrupt. Speculators also set their sights on Florida; by late 1925 2,000 real-estate firms were doing business in Miami alone. The Florida boom went bust in August 1926, when a strong hurricane struck the state, killing 400 people and damaging many acres of beachfront property.

Hundreds of people who had never touched a plow took up farming in the years following World War I, when the Wartime Food Control Act set a minimum price for wheat of $2 per bushel. (In 1910, the average price of wheat had been 91 cents a bushel.) Even experienced farmers refinanced their land in order to increase their holdings and enjoy a greater share of the profits that were waiting to be made. The money to finance much of this speculation came from bank loans. The number of state and national banks in the United States more than doubled between 1900 and 1920, rising from 14,054 to 30,909. Many of these banks were poorly managed and all too eager to make large, unsecured loans.

But land was not the only avenue for speculation, and bankers were not the only ones lending money. Americans were investing in the stock market in record numbers and frequently making their stock purchases on margin. In other words, brokers would extend credit to customers wanting to buy stock and receive payment later, when the stock earned a profit. People were making fortunes on paper. Wall Street newcomers mortgaged their homes, took out loans, and sold government securities in order to share in the stock-market boom. In 1927, 577 million shares were traded on the New York Stock Exchange, which was a remarkably large number for that time. In 1928, 920 million shares were traded, and in 1929 the total reached 1.1 billion. As that year dawned, much of the available capital in the United States was tied up in the stock market, and the value of stocks was inflated to an alarming degree.

THE ECONOMY DECLINES

By August 1929, consumers were buying fewer manufactured goods. Wages had failed to keep up with the rate of production, and now production started to decline, along with personal income and wholesale prices for manufactured goods and farm products. Stock prices started to fall at midyear, which prompted some people to sell their holdings and salvage a profit. The result was a further drop in prices.

A wave of selling began in October 1929, and prices on Wall Street fell dramatically. On Wednesday, October 23, investors lost an estimated $5 billion. Small players and those who had purchased stocks on margin saw their holdings wiped out. "Black Thursday," October 24, was a day of panic, with a record 12,894,650 shares being traded on the New York Stock Exchange. In desperation, a group of New York's leading financiers injected $340 million into the market, but even they could not reverse the downslide. On the following Tuesday, October 29, the market succumbed to chaos. More than 16 million shares of stock were traded, with investors losing as much as $74 billion. Stock prices continued to drop in the days that followed, reaching their lowest levels on November 13.

Economists have pointed out that the crisis on Wall Street was not enough by itself to plunge the United States and much of the world into depression. Most Americans, after all, had not put money into the stock market. In tracing the roots of the Great Depression, it is necessary to look to Europe as well. The United States had loaned its World War I allies $11 billion between 1914 and 1918 and had invested $15.7 billion overseas following the war. In theory, that money would enable foreign nations to buy U.S. goods, but in reality it was not enough. A larger investment in Europe by both the government and private sources was needed, but the money was unavailable, because it was in the stock market. A tariff act passed in 1930 worsened the situation in Europe, because it kept foreign goods out of the United States.

The economists of the 1920s and 1930s had observed that business in the United States operated in cycles: periods of expansion preceded crisis, recession, and recovery. No one knew why this happened, but depressions, or "panics," had punctuated the economic history of the United States since the start of the Industrial Revolution. Yet as months passed and they watched banks fail, factories close, and workers lose their jobs, some economists wondered whether the business cycle as they understood it was a thing of the past.

Today, to look back on the Great Depression is to consider a block of time that lasted from 1929 roughly until the start of World War II. People living through that period, however, did not know that the hard times would ever end; that is what made the depression so frightening.

President Herbert Hoover, a Republican, and his advisers were at a loss as to what to do. The conservative approach was to do nothing, to let the economy correct itself. According to this line of thinking, a depression was a purification process, one that rid the system of inefficient businesses and poorly made products. A stronger, leaner economy would emerge from the ordeal, given time.

Hoover had avoided placing controls on business in the past; faced with the depression, however, he rejected advice to do nothing and pondered steps to take. He persuaded Congress to pass a small tax cut to stimulate spending and investing, and on January 22, 1932, he signed a bill establishing the Reconstruction Finance Corporation (RFC), a government agency with the authority to lend money to banks and other businesses. Hoover stopped short of requesting emergency relief funds, though, because he considered it the province of municipalities and private charities to look after the poor and hungry. Meanwhile, neighborhood soup kitchens were being quickly overburdened.

FRANKLIN D. ROOSEVELT AND THE NEW DEAL

By 1932, the worst year of the depression, 5,000 banks had failed, factory production had been cut in half, construction had ceased, and about 12 million workers were unemployed. More than 60,000 evictions took place in New York City alone in the first three weeks of January. Over the course of the year, 273,000 families nationwide lost their homes to foreclosure.

Americans witnessed things that they never expected to see in their communities, such as hungry children ringing doorbells to beg for food, and empty stores lining Main Street. Customers jammed the lobbies of banks, demanding their money. Couples postponed their weddings, and families fell apart.

A man out of work, a common sight in depression America *(Franklin D. Roosevelt Library)*

Desperate parents brought small children to orphanages or gave them to relatives who were better off. People filled their stomachs with hot water and fried flour, and even that at times only on alternate days.

As the year progressed, it became plain that the public had lost confidence in the economy and in the government. Agricultural prices were so low that farmers saw no point in harvesting their crops and bringing them to market. The United States was the only industrialized nation with no unemployment insurance program or system of social security, yet Hoover remained opposed to instituting any kind of federal relief program. His Reconstruction Finance Corporation had come under fire for aiding the "big boys" at the expense of small business owners, as the public perceived that too many RFC loans went to large corporations or to firms owing money to the major banks. Hoover insisted—and would still be insisting 20 years later—that the bulk of the money went to small businesses. Still, he reversed his thinking and ordered government funds to be made available for public welfare programs, but it was too late; the president appeared hopelessly out of touch with the crisis that had interrupted so many lives. He denied that anyone was starving in the United States and allowed himself to be photographed feeding his dog on the White House lawn.

It was against this backdrop in November 1932 that U.S. voters elected as their president Franklin Delano Roosevelt, a Democrat who promised relief, recovery, and reform. Roosevelt recited the oath of office on March 4, 1933, and promptly declared a bank holiday lasting from Monday, March 6, through Thursday, March 9. His goals were to stop the runs on banks that were occurring, calm depositors' fears, and give bankers time to get their affairs in order. This approach met with some success: when the banks reopened, people deposited $10 million more than they withdrew. The Emergency Banking Act, which Congress passed on March 9, authorized the Treasury to print more paper currency, so that there would be money available for depositors to withdraw when they needed it.

Roosevelt initiated a series of laws, known as the New Deal, that permanently enlarged the government's role in regulating economic activity and developing resources. New Deal legislation increased federal control over the money supply and the policies of the Federal Reserve. Observing the impact of this legislation on the economy gave policymakers insight into the effects of taxation and government borrowing and spending. The lessons learned enabled subsequent administrations to limit the severity of future recessions. The New Deal failed to stimulate full economic recovery, but it got millions of people working again, saved thousands of farms and homes from foreclosure, increased factory production, and lifted corporate profits to their highest levels since the stock-market crash. New Deal legislation established the Federal Deposit Insurance Corporation (FDIC) to insure bank deposits, the Securities and Exchange Commission to regulate the stock market, and Social Security.

JOBS FOR YOUTH

The first New Deal agency to be created was the Civilian Conservation Corps (CCC), which addressed the problem of unemployment among young men; Roosevelt signed it into law on April 5. The CCC was intended to employ 250,000 men between the ages of 18 and 25 on public-works ventures, primarily in parks and forests and on range land. (The ages of eligibility were later expanded to 17 and 28.)

CCC crews completed conservation and restoration projects throughout the nation. They built nearly 47,000 bridges and 3,000 lookout towers and completed 33,000 miles of terracing. They restored Revolutionary and Civil War battlefields and such historic sites as Colonial Williamsburg. They also planted trees and fought forest fires and insect pests. The amphitheater at Mt. Tamalpais State Park in California was a CCC project, built with 5,000 blocks of stone weighing more than 600 pounds each.

The program admitted only those who were unemployed and members of families on relief. African Americans accounted for 10 percent of enrollment, a percentage that was in keeping with their numbers in the U.S. population, if not with their suffering as a result of the depression—a larger proportion of blacks than whites was unemployed. By June 30, 1933, 275,000 young men of all races had enrolled, a fraction of the 2.5 million that the CCC would employ between 1933 and 1942, when the corps disbanded. Most young men served for six to nine months.

The "boys," as CCC workers were called, earned $30 a month but received only $5 of each paycheck as pocket money. The bulk of their earnings went directly to their families. There was little that a CCC boy needed to buy, though. The government provided his meals, transportation, clothing, and medical care, and it quartered him in a tent or barracks.

Regular army and reserve officers supervised the camps, with military efficiency. At a typical camp employing 150 to 200, reveille sounded at 6 A.M., Monday through Friday, and the boys sat down to breakfast at 6:30. They worked between 8 A.M. and 4 P.M.; they had their evenings free. Lights went out at 10 P.M. sharp. Teachers on the government payroll gave instruction in reading and writing to the 2.5 percent who entered the camps illiterate. CCC enrollees learned employable trades and earned high school diplomas, and more than 40,000 received college degrees.

Roosevelt's critics—of whom there were many—used the word *Hitlerism* to describe the CCC, complaining that the corps had too much in common with the forced labor initiatives being instituted by Adolf Hitler in Germany. Roosevelt had considered starting a similar project while governor of New York in the 1920s, however, and he now dismissed any suggestion that he was following Hitler's example. By executive order on June 26, 1935, he established a second work program for young adults, the National Youth Administration (NYA). The NYA offered employment to women between the ages of 16 and 25, to young men unable to perform hard physical labor, and to students needing funds to finish their education. The NYA made it possible for many high school and college students to remain in school.

HELP FOR FARMERS

On March 16, 1933, Roosevelt presented Congress with a wide-reaching farm bill, which became law as the Agricultural Adjustment Act (AAA) on May 12. The AAA was designed to adjust farm production to bring it into line with national consumption and to raise produce prices to pre–World War I levels. In September 1927, wheat had been selling for only slightly more than it had before the war. Farmers had watched the price of wheat and other crops decline over the years that followed. The AAA targeted six farm products— cotton, wheat, hogs, rice, tobacco, and milk—because changes in their prices were most likely to benefit the economy overall.

For example, though in 1933 the nation already had enough surplus cotton to last three years, that spring farmers had planted more than 40 million acres in cotton, which amounted to 12 percent more acreage than had been devoted to cotton the previous year. If they had harvested all of that cotton, farmers could have expected to sell it for five cents a pound, a price too low to yield a profit. (Cotton had sold for 16 cents a pound in 1929.) The intent of the AAA was to reduce the acres harvested by one-fourth, so that farmers, selling less cotton, would receive a higher price.

The goal sounded simple enough, but achieving it required enormous effort. There were 1.8 million cotton growers in 16 states, and government agents had to explain the program to each one. Participation was voluntary. Farmers who agreed to take part signed a contract renting a portion of their land to the Department of Agriculture. They then plowed under part of their crop in exchange for either a lump sum or a smaller check and the option to buy cotton, in the amount that had been destroyed, for six cents a pound later in the season. More than a million cotton farmers accepted the government's offer, but the program had limited success. Cotton sold for nine cents a pound in September, somewhat less than what had been hoped for. Ironically, the program hurt many tenant farmers and sharecroppers, who lost their homes and their livelihoods when landlords elected to take part in the AAA plan.

Another initiative intended to help rural Americans was the Tennessee Valley Authority, which gained legal status on May 18, 1933. The agency was created to oversee the construction of a series of dams in the Tennessee River valley basin. The dam system was intended to control flooding and erosion in the region, provide affordable electric power to rural communities, and improve conditions for navigation on the Tennessee River. By the late 1930s, TVA dams were furnishing power to 83 municipal electric companies and 45 rural electric cooperatives. Commercial traffic on the Tennessee River more than quadrupled between 1933 and 1941.

THE NATIONAL INDUSTRIAL RECOVERY ACT

The National Industrial Recovery Act, which Roosevelt signed on June 16, 1933, was intended to reduce unemployment and to aid business recovery by setting standards for fair competition. The act and the agency to which it gave rise, the National Recovery Administration, became collectively known as the NRA. The act authorized the largest public-works program ever to be undertaken by the U.S. government. Headed by Secretary of Commerce Harold L. Ickes, the Public Works Administration (PWA) spent a total of six billion dollars and employed 500,000 people a year to complete more than 34,000 projects throughout the United States. The PWA built schools, courthouses, and post offices. Its workers modernized railroads and installed municipal water systems. The PWA completed Boulder Dam (now Hoover Dam) on the Colorado River in Arizona, which had been begun during Hoover's presidency but was nearly out of funds. Other significant PWA undertakings include the Bonneville Dam in the Columbia River Gorge between Oregon and Washington, the Grand Coulee Dam on the Columbia River in Washington, and its most expensive project, the $42 million Triborough Bridge, connecting the boroughs of Queens, Brooklyn, and Manhattan in New York City. More PWA money—$252 million—went to New York City than to any other municipality.

The National Industrial Recovery Act also affected business directly, by establishing codes of competition for 500 industries. Initially, the act targeted the 10 industries employing the most people: textiles, coal, petroleum, steel, automobiles, clothing manufactures, lumber, construction, wholesale trade, and retail trade. The president chose Hugh S. Johnson, who had helped draft the legislation, to oversee the implementation of the industrial codes. Johnson was an assistant to the financier Bernard Baruch, one of Roosevelt's advisers.

Not only did the National Industrial Recovery Act establish a minimum wage and maximum working hours for each industry, but Section 7(a) of the law contained the first federal guarantee of workers' rights to union membership and collective bargaining. Roosevelt appointed Senator Robert F. Wagner of New York to head the National Labor Board, the body that was to deal with disputes between labor and management.

As with the AAA, participation in NRA programs was voluntary. To encourage cooperation, the government issued signs bearing the NRA symbol (a blue eagle) and its slogan ("We Do Our Part") to businesses complying with NRA guidelines, so that customers could choose to patronize them.

The National Industrial Recovery Act also set a minimum age of 16 for employment in most industries and of 18 in mining and logging. Immediately, the number of working children dropped 72 percent, and the mining and logging industries lost 150,000 juvenile workers. Roosevelt confidently declared that child labor had been abolished in the United States.

The president had spoken too soon. The Supreme Court struck down nine key pieces of New Deal legislation in 1935 and 1936. On May 27, 1935, a day referred to as "Black Monday" within the Roosevelt administration, the chief justice, Charles Evans Hughes, read the Court's opinion in a case of a poultry firm that had violated provisions of the National Industrial Recovery Act. The justices unanimously agreed that in passing this legislation, Congress had overstepped its authority. The Court found the Agricultural Adjustment Act to be unconstitutional as well.

Roosevelt soon feared that much of his work to combat the depression was being undone. Within a year of the Court's decision on the NRA, for example, the number of working children rose 150 percent. Roosevelt sought a way to alter the membership of the Supreme Court, which he viewed as too conservative and too inflexible in its interpretation of the Constitution.

Six of the nine justices of the Supreme Court were more than 70 years old when Roosevelt took office, and four of these six were rigidly conservative men who tended to vote as a bloc. None retired during Roosevelt's first term as president, giving him no opportunity to appoint someone to the court who was more sympathetic to his ideas. Determined to overcome the obstacle that the Supreme Court presented, Roosevelt drafted the Judiciary Reorganization Bill of 1937, in which he proposed adding one justice to the Court for every member over age 70 who declined to retire within six months. (Justices over 70 with 10 years of service could retire at full pay.) The reason for the bill, Roosevelt argued, was to help the Court handle a backlog of cases. The plan was not without precedent; the number of Supreme Court justices had fluctuated under previous administrations, beginning with that of John Adams. But there had been nine Supreme Court justices since 1869.

The proposal to "pack" the Court inspired criticism from the president's friends and enemies alike, and the bill was defeated in Congress. As things turned out, Roosevelt appointed five justices to the Supreme Court during his second term, following the retirements of four sitting justices and the unexpected death of a fifth.

A SECOND NEW DEAL

Meanwhile, the administration was producing another wave of legislation, which many historians call the Second New Deal. May 6, 1935, marked the establishment of the Works Progress Administration (later called the Work Projects Administration), or WPA, a program designed to get adults working and off public assistance. The WPA gave work to 8 million people between 1935 and the start of World War II, more than any other New Deal agency. The WPA employed men and women with a broad mix of skills, including biologists, engineers, construction workers, librarians, dietitians, plumbers, physicians, and librarians, to name just a few.

People on the WPA payroll paved 650,000 miles of roadway and built or repaired 124,000 bridges. They cleared slums, created parks and playgrounds, and constructed public buildings and airports. Some WPA employees taught job-training and literacy classes, while others operated medical and dental clinics, translated books into braille, and recorded talking books for the blind. Monthly salaries ranged from $19 for an unskilled laborer to $94 for someone with a high level of technical skill. The average WPA worker received $41.57 per month at the close of 1935.

The WPA also gave employment to people in the creative and performing arts, people who were enduring privation like the rest of the nation. Writers worked on a variety of projects, including the American Guide book series, a collection of 378 publications describing the 48 states, major cities, important waterways, and historic sites. The novelist Richard Wright wrote a chapter on Harlem for the WPA book *New York Panorama*. Meanwhile, other writers completed oral history projects or helped to compile the Historical Records Survey by inventorying public documents, summarizing court records, and indexing old files in newspaper offices.

The WPA founded 155 orchestras in cities throughout the United States, as well as bands, chamber-music ensembles, and choral groups. The agency

WPA workers clean the streets of Louisville, Kentucky. *(Franklin D. Roosevelt Library)*

employed as many as 15,000 musicians at one time to perform, teach, and research American folk music.

Ben Shahn and Jacob Lawrence were among the 5,000 artists hired to paint murals and posters, photograph historic houses, staff community art centers, and teach classes in drawing, painting, and sculpture. In addition, WPA artists compiled the *Index of American Design,* a catalog of folk art containing 7,000 illustrations. The WPA also employed actors, playwrights, and stagehands to bring a variety of entertainment into communities—everything from serious drama to circus performances and puppet shows.

The Second New Deal also included the National Labor Relations Act, which became law on July 5, 1935, a little more than a month after the Supreme Court struck down the NRA. The National Labor Relations Act, which is often called the Wagner Act after its author, Senator Wagner, went beyond Section 7(a) of the National Industrial Recovery Act in addressing the concerns of organized labor. It guaranteed the right to form unions and granted federal protection to the collective bargaining process. It also barred employers from interfering with union organizing activities and from firing any worker for joining a union. In addition, the Wagner Act established the National Labor Relations Board (NLRB), to hear worker complaints and conduct elections for workers who wanted a union. The board was granted the right to subpoena witnesses and records as it investigated disputes. The NLRB continues today to perform these tasks.

The Fair Labor Standards Act (FLSA) of 1938 set a minimum wage and maximum hours for most workers. Under the FLSA, children age 14 and 15 could hold a job only if work did not interfere with their schooling or their health. No one under 18 was permitted to work in mining, logging, or other dangerous occupations. The minimum wage would increase from 25 cents an hour to 40 cents an hour over two years, and because it applied to workers of all ages, employers no longer found it profitable to hire children in place of adults—in many instances. The law applied, however, to only 25 percent of working children. It failed to protect children whose employers did business within one state and those who sold newspapers or worked on farms. Still, the 1940 census revealed a 41 percent decline in workers age 14 and 15, and a 30 percent decline in workers age 16 and 17. Working children between the ages of 10 and 13 and those employed on farms were omitted from the count.

THE DUST BOWL EXODUS

For thousands living in the middle of the nation, a severe drought compounded the hardship of the Great Depression. The drought of the mid-1930s punished a vast stretch of the country, from Texas to South Dakota. It most profoundly affected portions of Oklahoma, Texas, Kansas, Colorado, and New Mexico, which collectively became known as the dust bowl. In a region where poor conservation practices and overgrazing had left the earth vulnerable to erosion, winds swept dry topsoil into the air to create vast dust storms. The dark clouds traveled as swiftly as 50 miles per hour and were visible from a distance of 30 miles. Soil particles fell to earth like fine snow, forming drifts along fences and piling up in roads. One of the worst storms began on May 9, 1934, and raged for three days as the jet stream carried silt across the Mississippi River and dropped it over the East. The sky grew so dark in New York,

Boston, and other eastern cities that streetlights shone at noon. The winds left many farmers with fields of red-clay hardpan that was inhospitable to crops and nearly impossible to plow.

Dust bowl farmers were already coping with falling prices, depleted soil, and foreclosures. Tenants worked more than 60 percent of the farmland in Oklahoma, Texas, and Arkansas, and many were facing eviction. Unemployment was higher in the towns and cities of the dust bowl than in any other agricultural region. As state and local relief funds became exhausted, the homeless and hungry crowded into squatters' camps on the outskirts of towns. About 2,000 people lived in one such camp outside Oklahoma City.

In 1932, 1,000 farmers who could not make their mortgage payments were losing their land every week. After the drought came, hundreds of thousands packed up and left. Oklahoma lost 440,000 people in the 1930s, and Kansas lost 227,000. Most of the African Americans who fled the dust bowl traveled to northern cities. Some whites went north as well, but the majority streamed west. Many looked for jobs building dams or logging in the Northwest, while many more headed for California, the state with the greatest agricultural wealth. California's valleys abounded in oranges, peaches, grapes, cherries, nuts, apples, lettuce, cotton, avocados, and more.

Migrants who had relatives or friends among the 310,000 southwesterners who had settled in California between 1910 and 1930 gravitated toward Los Angeles, San Diego, and other populous communities. The rest looked for work on farms. If a family's car held up, the journey along U.S. Route 66 could be completed in three days. More than 1 million people left the dust bowl for California between 1935 and 1940.

Most farms in California were corporate enterprises, covering thousands of acres and controlled by absentee businessmen. Growers had depended on a migrant labor force since the 1880s, when they had hired Chinese workers to tend fields and harvest crops. When immigration restrictions limited the number of Chinese entering the United States, growers turned to Japanese and Filipino immigrants and then to Mexicans.

Instead of jobs in farming, most dust bowl refugees found hostility and want. California already had too many migrant workers, and communities resented demands made on their resources by "Okies" and "Arkies," people they viewed as outsiders. In 1938, the California legislature passed a law—later ruled unconstitutional by the U.S. Supreme Court—making it illegal for indigent people to enter the state, and many migrants reached the California border after a long trip only to be turned away. Those lucky enough to cross the state border and find work earned barely enough to feed their families during the growing season; in winter, when the work disappeared, they discovered themselves to be in the same straits as everyone else. The provisions of the National Labor Relations Act, including the minimum wage, did not apply to farm workers.

Distrustful of unions, some of the newcomers took work as scabs when the longtime, largely Mexican migrant labor force struck for higher wages. Between 1930 and 1939, more than 125,000 agricultural workers in California took part in 140 strikes that were orchestrated by the communist leaders of the Cannery and Agricultural Workers' Industrial Union. Some of the work stoppages, such as the San Joaquin valley cotton strike that began on October 4, 1933, turned violent. That incident, which involved between 18,000 and 20,000 laborers, was the largest agricultural strike in U.S. history and affected cotton production throughout the state. Before the strike ended on October 28, three protesters had been killed and hundreds of people injured. The union had secured a 25 percent pay increase for the cotton harvesters and claimed a victory—only to see its headquarters destroyed and its leadership arrested.

It was nearly impossible for dust bowl refugees to find a decent place to live, whether they had work or not. The housing that growers provided for their workers lacked running water and adequate sanitation. The unemployed congregated in makeshift roadside camps, where they built shelters from cardboard, scrap lumber, carpeting, branches, and tin cans—whatever they could find. Water for drinking and washing in these wretched places came from filthy drainage ditches. Some children died of starvation and disease, while most survived malnourished. Hookworm, deficiency diseases, and respiratory infections thrived, and townspeople living nearby feared epidemics of serious illness. Dust bowl migrants living in the shantytowns that grew up outside agricultural centers such as Bakersfield sent their children to the local schools and, if they met the state's residency requirement, applied for emergency relief.

By 1936, the federal government had established several camps in California to house some of the people who failed to qualify for state assistance. The government camps were clean and well managed, with adequate showers and rest rooms. A family could have a cabin or a tent platform in exchange for 10 cents or two hours of work a day. However, the government camps—the only New Deal measure directed toward California's migrant-labor population—eased only a fraction of the suffering experienced by that group.

OUT OF THE DEPRESSION AND INTO WAR

The New Deal alleviated much of the misery that prevailed in the early 1930s, but it failed to bring the United States out of the depression. It would take another war to do that. In March 1939, as Adolf Hitler's army seized Czechoslovakia, 6 million Americans—half of them minorities—remained unemployed. The nation's leaders recognized European fascism as a threat to world peace, and they were also keeping a wary eye on Japan, which had taken over Manchuria in 1932 and had occupied key Chinese ports in 1937 and 1938. Great Britain and France declared war on Germany on September 3, 1939, two days after Hitler's invasion of Poland. On June 17, 1940, French premier Henri Philippe Pétain, perceiving the impossibility of protecting Paris from invasion, signed an armistice that gave Germany control of northern France and the Atlantic coast. Pétain established the capital of unoccupied France at Vichy in the southeast, leaving Britain to fight the war alone.

"Lend Lease" legislation, which Roosevelt signed on January 10, 1941, gave the president authority to provide the British with whatever supplies they might need to carry on the war, from planes, tanks, and guns to food. The government built up U.S. arsenals as well, because it seemed increasingly likely that the United States would have to enter the conflict.

Preparing for the eventuality of war necessitated government defense spending and an industrial commitment on a scale that had never been seen

Workers at the Boeing Aircraft Corporation, many long unemployed during the depression, pose before the wings of a B-17 "Flying Fortress," circa 1942. *(National Archives)*

before. Congress authorized more than $12 billion in defense spending in June and July 1940, an amount far greater than had been spent on social programs in any previous year. U.S. factories geared up to produce 100,000 machine guns and 50,000 war planes annually; U.S. shipbuilders outfitted the navy with 257 ships, including 27 aircraft carriers, in rapid order. Unemployment plummeted as men and women found jobs in defense plants.

Approximately 16 million Americans served in the armed forces during World War II. On the home front and overseas, there were plenty of jobs needing to be done. American workers had reclaimed their identity.

CHRONICLE OF EVENTS

1927

Five hundred seventy-seven million shares of stock are traded on the New York Stock Exchange.

1928

Nine hundred twenty million shares are traded on the New York Stock Exchange.

1929

August: The economy shows signs of trouble, including a drop in consumer spending and declines in production, wholesale prices, and personal income.

October: The stock market experiences a wave of selling and dropping prices.

October 23: American stock-market investors lose approximately $5 billion.

October 24: Stock prices continue their decline, with nearly 13 million shares being traded.

October 29: More than 16 million shares are traded on the New York Stock Exchange; investors lose an estimated $74 billion.

November 13: Stock prices reach their lowest level.

In all, 1.1 billion shares of stock are traded this year on the New York Stock Exchange.

1932

Considered the worst year of the depression, with 12 million unemployed.

January 22: Herbert Hoover signs legislation creating the Reconstruction Finance Corporation to lend money to business.

Japan takes over Manchuria.

1933

March 4: Franklin D. Roosevelt is sworn in as the 32d president of the United States.

March 6–9: A bank holiday, declared by Roosevelt, is in effect.

April 5: The Civilian Conservation Corps (CCC), which employs young men on public works projects, is established.

May 12: The Agricultural Adjustment Act (AAA) becomes law. The AAA is designed to limit farm production and raise agricultural prices.

May 18: Roosevelt signs legislation creating the Tennessee Valley Authority.

June 16: Roosevelt signs the National Industrial Recovery Act, which sets standards for fair competition in industry.

October 4: Cotton harvesters strike in Pixley, California; three people die, and hundreds are injured, as the strikers clash with growers and law enforcement.

1935–40

More than 1 million people migrate from the Southwest to California.

1935

May 6: The Works Progress Administration is established to employ adults on a variety of government-sponsored projects.

May 27: The Supreme Court strikes down the National Industrial Recovery Act, one of nine pieces of New Deal legislation that the court will declare unconstitutional.

June 26: Roosevelt creates the National Youth Administration by executive order.

July 5: The National Labor Relations Act, protecting the right of workers to unionize, becomes law.

1937–38

Japan occupies important Chinese ports.

1938

June 25: Roosevelt signs the Fair Labor Standards Act, which establishes a minimum wage and maximum working hours, and regulates child labor.

1939

March: German military forces occupy Czechoslovakia.

September 1: Hitler's armies invade Poland.

September 3: Great Britain and France declare war on Germany.

1940

June 17: French premier Henri Philippe Pétain signs an armistice giving Germany control of northern France and the Atlantic coast; Pétain establishes the capital of unoccupied France at Vichy.

June and July: Congress authorizes more than $12 billion in defense spending.

A farmer's son plays on a soil drift created by drought and wind near Liberal, Kansas, May 1936. (*Library of Congress*)

1941

January 10: Legislation signed on this date gives Roosevelt authority to provide Great Britain with supplies needed to carry on the war.

December 7: Japanese forces attack the U.S. naval base at Pearl Harbor, Hawaii.

December 8: The United States declares war on Japan, an event that marks U.S. entry into World War II.

EYEWITNESS TESTIMONY

No Congress of the United States ever assembled, on surveying the state of the Union, has met with a more pleasing prospect than that which appears at the present time. In the domestic field there is tranquillity and contentment, harmonious relations between management and wage earner, freedom from industrial strife, and the highest record of years of prosperity. . . . The great wealth created by our enterprise and industry, and saved by our economy, has had the widest distribution among our own people, and has gone out in a steady stream to serve the charity and the business of the world. The requirements of existence have passed beyond the standard of necessity into the region of luxury. Enlarging production is consumed by an increasing demand at home and an expanding commerce abroad. The country can regard the present with satisfaction and anticipate the future with optimism.

Calvin Coolidge, message to Congress, December 4, 1928, in Donald R. McCoy, Calvin Coolidge, *p. 392.*

Fair weather cannot always continue. The economic cycle is in progress today, as it was in the past. The Federal Reserve System has put the banks in a strong position, but it has not changed human nature. More people are borrowing and speculating today than ever in our history. Sooner or later a crash is coming and it may be terrific. Wise are those investors who now get out of debt and reef their sails. . . .

Sooner or later the stock market boom will collapse like the Florida boom. Some day the time is coming when the market will begin to slide off, sellers will exceed buyers, and paper profits will begin to disappear. Then there will immediately be a stampede to save what paper profits then exist. . . . As soon as word gets abroad that the large American investment trusts are selling, the European houses will begin to sell out their customers who are now buying in the American market. The general public will then follow with a desire to cash in, then margin accounts will be closed out, and then there may be a stampede for selling which will exceed anything that the Stock Exchange has ever witnessed.

Roger Babson, economist, September 1929, in William K. Klingaman, 1929: The Year of the Great Crash, *pp. 232–33.*

It is difficult to recapture the tone of the first half-year after the crash. I think that under the strain of three years of worry, we have forgotten that we ourselves lived in December, 1929, and March, 1930; we have created another population for those days, so that we can say to ourselves that if "they" had been resourceful, energetic, and courageous, they could have prevented the miseries which later fell upon us. That "they" should have gone on living, more or less calmly, more or less comfortably, when the obvious duty before them was to confront the facts of the situation and prevent the downfall of the social and industrial system, mystifies us and makes us vaguely resentful; vaguely, because in the backs of our minds float the images of ourselves in that time. For ourselves we make excuses; we were not told, we were ordered to do business as usual. So "they" turn into our leaders and we have a scapegoat at last.

Gilbert Seldes, The Years of the Locust (America, 1929–1932), *pp. 43–44.*

It was an over-long winter [1929–30], a terrible time. The bottom had dropped out of the country, it seemed. With the passing of each week the Depression deepened. More factories were closing down, and at night I began to see in the streets men and women pawing over the contents of restaurant garbage cans set out for the sanitation department trucks. Pride was being eaten away, and in the eyes of many people I passed in the street I saw a cornered, hunted look. The national disaster had become so huge, and the answers to its solution so elusive, that men and women slowly began to accept their fate as a new way of life, as inmates thrown into prison gradually reconcile themselves to an existence behind stone walls.

Albert Halper, writer, remembering the winter of 1929–30 in New York City, Good-bye, Union Square, *p. 50.*

[1930] was a year of suicides, not only among stockbrokers but also among wealthy dilettantes. It was a year when faces looked white and nervous; a year of insomnia and sleeping tablets. It was a year when classmates and former friends became involved in speakeasy brawls, divorces, defalcations and even murders; the underworld and the upper world were close to each other. Most of all it was a year when a new mood became perceptible, a mood of doubt and even defeat. People began to wonder whether it wasn't possible that not only their ideas but their whole lives had been set in the wrong direction.

Malcolm Cowley recalling 1930, in William K. Klingaman, 1929: The Year of the Great Crash, p. 335.

Every newspaper and magazine I read showed photographs of men queued up at breadlines and employment halls seeking food and work. And this poverty attacked my family wherever it caught us. Yet hunger, I learned, was less frightening in the summer. I could walk slower and give more freely of what energy I had. And it was easier when the moon shone and the stars twinkled over the warm evenings, and love was close at hand.

Gordon Parks recalling what it was like to be young in the summer of 1930, A Choice of Weapons, *p. 81.*

In Lowell [Massachusetts] I saw shabby men leaning against walls and lamp-posts, and standing on street corners singly or in twos or threes; pathetic, silent, middle-aged men in torn, frayed overcoats or even without overcoats, broken shoes on their feet (in a town manufacturing shoes!), slumped in postures of hopeless discontent, their faces sunken and their eyes shifty and bewildered—men who winced and jerked queerly when they noticed me looking at them, and shuffled off uncertainly, wringing their hands in a mingling of vague desperation and of resentment at my gaze.

Louis Adamic, who traveled to Lowell, Massachusetts, in the autumn of 1930, My America, *p. 268.*

This country is not in good condition.

Calvin Coolidge, January 20, 1931, in Louis Adamic, My America, *p. 262.*

Mules, through government-aid loans, fare better than human beings through Red Cross relief. The mule is allowed $8 per month for feed; a family of six in Bolivar County [Mississippi], a typical illustration, receives $11.67 worth of groceries for one month. These prices are based upon local retail quotations. The human ration is fixed locally, Red Cross national representatives declare.

John B. Hudson reporting on conditions in Mississippi, February 25, 1931, in "Drought: Field Reports from Five of the States Most Seriously Affected," p. 38.

A system—call it what you will—under which it is possible for five or six millions of willing and able-bodied men to be out of work and unable to secure work for months at a time, and with no other source of income, cannot be said to be perfect or even satisfactory; on the contrary, it can be said to have failed in at least one very important detail. I can think of nothing more deplorable than the condition of a man, able and anxious to work, but unable to secure work, with no resources but his labor and, perhaps, with others even more helpless, dependent upon him. Unless he is willing to starve and see those who justly look to him for support also starve, his only alternative is to seek charity and, failing in that, to steal. While I do not like to say so, I would be less than candid if I did not say that in such circumstances I would steal before I would starve.

Daniel Willard, president of the Baltimore and Ohio Railroad Company, March 27, 1931, in Charles A. Beard, America Faces the Future, *p. 31.*

What happened to John Bentley, 29, house painter, born in Kansas of American parents, union member? Well, there was this depression in the building trades, and he heard of a job farther east. He had a job for a short time. Now here he is in the line. His face is clear-cut, English, with a long upper lip. The type of man who should be upstanding and brisk. His shoulders sag, his shoes are broken. Defeat and bitterness are in his expression. The slight defiance in his answers is of the man who dares you to ask him how he happened to come [to be] on a breadline.

Mary Heaton Vorse, April 29, 1931, "School for Bums," p. 292.

Usually when times are hard and people are out of work, Fifth Avenue and Broadway know nothing about it. This is the first time these streets have lost their glittering shine. The shabby, shifting, ebbing men out of work have taken it from them.

On a street corner near Fiftieth Street was a store which had been turned into a free restaurant for the unemployed. Well dressed young ladies were cutting sandwiches for all who wanted to come in and get one. In the middle of each table stood a pot of mustard. There were men with well brushed clothes, men who looked like old bums, young white-collar men, all engulfing enormous sandwiches, cheese spread with mustard—three sandwiches to a person and coffee.

Mary Heaton Vorse, April 29, 1931, "School for Bums," p. 293.

Of the number of people losing their all, because they cannot raise a few dollars, there is no record as yet. Maybe there will never be. One can only generalize and say that the white-collar class is suffering today with the mechanic. The man who has spent thousands upon his education is no more secure than a laborer. The misery, doubt and defeat piles up, an incalculable mountain.

Mary Heaton Vorse, April 29, 1931,
"School for Bums," p. 294.

Depressions are not new experiences, though none has hitherto been so widespread. We have passed through no less than fifteen major depressions in the last century. We have learned something as the result of each of these experiences. From this one we shall gain stiffening and economic discipline, a greater knowledge upon which we must build a better safeguarded system. We have come out of each previous depression into a period of prosperity greater than ever before. We shall do so this time.

Herbert Hoover, June 15, 1931, in Charles A. Beard,
America Faces the Future, *pp. 386–87.*

The Reconstruction Finance Corporation is made up of fine men, honest, and mean well [*sic*] and if it was water they were distributing it would help the people the plan was meant to help. For water goes down hill and moistens everything in its way, but gold or money goes uphill. The Reconstruction loaned the railroads money, medium and small banks money, and all they did with it was pay off what they owed to New York banks. So the money went uphill instead of down. You can drop a bag of gold in Death Valley, which is below sea level, and before Saturday it will be home to papa J. P. [Morgan].

Will Rogers, 1931, in Edward Robb Ellis,
A Nation in Torment, *p. 194.*

. . . Mr. Hoover, running for re-election with a weary momentum . . . said grass would grow in the streets if Roosevelt were elected. He should have looked. Grass was already growing in the streets. Farmers dumped milk, burned crops to keep prices from collapsing. Armed neighbors guarded homes against mortgage-foreclosing sheriffs. Grass was growing not only in the streets but between the rusting tracks of factory railroad sidings.

John Steinbeck remembering conditions in 1932,
"A Primer on the 30's," p. 85.

Every man has a right to life; and this means that he has also a right to make a comfortable living. He may by sloth or crime decline to exercise that right; but it may not be denied him. We have no actual famine or dearth; our industrial and agricultural mechanism can produce enough and to spare. Our government formal and informal, political and economic, owes to every one an avenue to possess himself of a portion of that plenty sufficient for his needs, through his own work.

Every man has a right to his own property; which means a right to be assured, to the fullest extent attainable, in the safety of his savings. By no other means can men carry the burdens of those parts of life which, in the nature of things, afford no chance of labor; childhood, sickness, old age. In all thought of property, this right is paramount; all other property rights must yield to it. If, in accord with this principle, we must restrict the operations of the speculator, the manipulator, even the financier, I believe we must accept the restriction as needful, not to hamper individualism but to protect it.

Franklin Delano Roosevelt, "Every Man Has a Right to Life," campaign speech delivered September 23, 1932, in Howard Zinn, ed., New Deal Thought, *pp. 50–51.*

The crowd of visitors who watched the President-elect approach the Capitol were not sure how they would get home again, how they would pay their hotel bills. Everywhere it was the same. The normal flow of money had stopped. The nation's economic life was in a state of suspended animation.

The people were waiting—the ragged farmers listening at the squeaky radios of busted cross-roads stores—the unemployed, 15,000,000 of them now—the nomads on the roads and the citizens of Hooverville—the small businessmen who hadn't cleared expenses for two years—the workingmen whose wages were half what they used to be—the white-collar workers whose savings and investments had vanished—the professional men whose practices had shrunk to nothing—even many of the biggest businessmen themselves who were disgusted with the havoc which their reckless fellows had brought about. Everyone felt the solemnity of the moment. Everybody was a little frightened, a little bewildered, but the overwhelming emotion was hope. The country had hit the absolute bottom. There was nowhere to go but up.

Jonathan Norton Leonard recalling Inauguration Day, March 4, 1933, Three Years Down, *pp. 315–16.*

. . . [O]ur common difficulties . . . concern, Thank God, only material things. Values have shrunken to fantastic levels; taxes have risen; our ability to pay has fallen, government of all kinds is faced by serious curtailment of income; the means of exchange are frozen in the currents of trade; the withered leaves of industrial enterprise lie on every side; farmers find no markets for their produce; the savings of many years in thousands of families are gone.

More important, a host of unemployed citizens face the grim problem of existence, and an equally great number toil with little return. Only a foolish optimist can deny the dark realities of the moment.

Yet our distress comes from no failure of substance. We are striken by no plague of locusts. Compared with the perils which our forefathers conquered because they believed and were not afraid, we have still much to be thankful for. Nature still offers her bounty and human efforts have multiplied it. Plenty is at our doorstep, but a generous use of it languishes in the very sight of the supply.

Franklin Delano Roosevelt, March 4, 1933, First Inaugural Address.

In the old days we could send people from the cities to the country. If they went out today they would meet another army of unemployed coming back from the country to the city; that outlet is closed. What can these people do? They have been driven from our parks; they have been driven from our streets; they have been driven from our buildings, and in this city [Ottawa] they actually took refuge on the garbage heaps.

J. S. Woodsworth in the Canadian House of Commons, 1933, describing depression conditions in Canada, in Kenneth McNaught, The Pelican History of Canada, *p. 247.*

[The National Industrial Recovery Act] is also a challenge to labor. Workers too, are here given a new charter of rights long sought and hitherto denied. But they know that the first move expected by the Nation is a great cooperation of all employers by one single mass action, to improve the case of workers on a scale never attempted in any nation. Industries can do this only if they have the support of the whole public and especially of their own workers. *This is not a law to foment discord and it will not be executed as such. This is a time for mutual confidence and help and we can safely rely on the sense of fair play among all Americans to assure every indus-try which now moves forward promptly in this united drive against depression that its workers will be with it to a man.*

Franklin Delano Roosevelt laying out the policy of the National Industrial Recovery Act, 1933, in Hugh S. Johnson, The Blue Eagle from Egg to Earth, *p. 344.*

The basic principles of the National Recovery Act are sound and simple.

On the one hand they permit and encourage each great industry to organize and act as one under direct governmental supervision. This right had been denied by statute before the passage of this law.

On the other hand they permit and encourage the workers in each industry to organize and act as one. This right has been at least hampered and impaired by court decisions based on the Common Law before the passage of the National Recovery Act.

In other words this act asks for cooperation between industry, labor and government as one great team, to preserve the economic health of the nation and it permits the organization of both industry and labor without which such cooperation would be wholly impossible.

This is a profound change in economic policy of a great nation. It is something new under the sun. It is the President's own concept. No exponent of economic theory suggested this plan to him.

Hugh S. Johnson, 1933, in E. David Cronon, ed., Labor and the New Deal, *p. 6.*

In a company house I visited [in West Virginia], where the people had evidently seen better days, the man showed me his weekly pay slips. A small amount had been deducted toward his bill at the company store and for his rent and for oil for his mine lamp. These deductions left him less than a dollar in cash each week. There were six children in the family, and they acted as though they were afraid of strangers. I noticed a bowl on the table filled with scraps, the kind that you or I might give to a dog, and I saw children, evidently looking for their noon-day meal, take a handful out of that bowl and go out munching. That was all they had to eat.

As I went out, two of the children had gathered enough courage to stand by the door, the little boy holding a white rabbit in his arms. It was evident it was a most cherished pet. The little girl was thin and scrawny, and had a gleam in her eyes as she looked at her brother. Turning to me she said: "He thinks we

The Great Depression 221

are not going to eat it, but we are," and at that the small boy fled down the [road] clutching the rabbit closer than ever.

Eleanor Roosevelt describing a visit to a West Virginia coal-mining family in 1933, This I Remember, *pp. 126–27.*

The power of organization is immense. A fully organized and unchecked industry could exploit and dominate a whole nation. A fully organized and unchecked labor could do exactly the same. There must be responsibility in each such organization. There must be a check on these great powers. Our government is government of the whole people. Its principal excuse for existence is protection of the whole people. These vast organizations of industry and of labor must each be responsible to government and each must admit governmental participation and control. No industrial combination must be permitted to practice monopolistic oppression and exploitation. No labor combination must be permitted to paralyze a whole industry by the unchecked use of power. These three principles, then—organization—cooperation—government participation—are of the very essence of the National Recovery Act.

Hugh S. Johnson, 1933, in Cletus E. Daniel, Bitter Harvest, *p. 170.*

Over two million of us eventually joined the Corps. We planted millions of trees, fought the Dutch elm disease, built fishponds, fed wildlife, cleared tremendous areas of beach and camping ground; and forty-seven recruits lost their lives fighting forest fires. We were earning our keep. But when July came the depression still choked the country, and I knew that it would still be around when our time was up in October. There would probably be even less for us to go back to by then. . . . [T]he employment offices, park benches and hobo villages would still be full.

Gordon Parks, who joined the Civilian Conservation Corps in 1933, A Choice of Weapons, *p. 156.*

One observer who visited the [Tennessee River] Valley just before TVA began operations thought there was then a stir of hope mixed with apprehension. People were waiting, they hardly knew what for. They had waited a long time. At the Wilson Dam two generators out of eight installed, out of at least sixteen for which there was room and power, were running. Not all the time, either. A single power com-

pany was buying the output. It didn't need it all the time. The Valley in early 1933 was like that.

R. L. Duffus describing the Wilson Dam, a Tennessee Valley Authority project, as it was in early 1933, The Valley and Its People, *pp. 54–55.*

He who sees a great many dams in process will still wonder at this miracle.

He will remember driving through the mud to get to the Guntersville site when the first cofferdam was beginning to take shape. How could form come out of that chaos?

Norrisville Dam, near Knoxville, Tennessee, a TVA project completed in 1936 *(National Archives)*

He will remember the shovels wrestling with the earth down in the cofferdam at Pickwick. What would happen if the rising river topped the dam? We'd have warning, says the engineer; we'd take them out in time. If the coffer washed out—we'd build it again.

He will remember the littered landscape at Chickamauga, and how his guide seemed to see as plainly as though it were there each form and angle of the completed structure; and how he came back, and they were there.

He will remember the man cutting hay in what was soon to be the bottom of the Cherokee reservoir, and how the little farm and the house among the trees seemed as though they were to be there forever—but they weren't.

He will remember the awesome tunnels and scraped cliffs at Fontana, and how impossible it was that a river in this setting could ever be controlled—but it was destined to be, and the engineers never had the least doubt about it.

It was never just one dam that was being built, any more than it is ever just one battle that is being fought in a war. It was all the dams, each related to the others. It was a whole river system that was being brought under control. As the engineers liked to say, it was an assembly line of dams.

R. L. Duffus reflecting on the building of Tennessee Valley Authority dams, 1933–44, The Valley and Its People, *pp. 79–81.*

. . . [W]e lived on coffee and talk. Talking was the great Depression pastime. Unlike the movies, talk was free, and a great river of talk flowed through the house, rising at suppertime, and cresting as my bedtime approached before subsiding into a murmur that trickled along past midnight. . . .

Russell Baker writing about family life in Belleville, New Jersey, 1933–36, Growing Up, *pp. 115–16.*

President Roosevelt has staked his political future and that of his party upon the success of a recovery program which was to bring order out of chaos and place the economic activities of the nation on new and solid foundations. The aim, now that the program has been unfolded, is seen to be the reorganization of American society on collectivist lines, with the Federal government as the central source of authority and Federal power the directing and compelling force. The fruits of the program have been some artificial stimulation of business and industry, some artificial relief for the farmers, and some artificial mitigation of unemployment and personal suffering, but in their pursuit the Administration has become a dictatorship, the public debt has been swollen to unprecedented peace-time proportions, the gold standard has been abandoned, and the dollar has been left to find its level in the shifting sands of commodity prices. There is no dictionary that defines "recovery" in such terms.

William MacDonald, 1934, The Menace of Recovery, *p. 373.*

. . . [B]y 1934, we really began to suffer. . . . Our mother knew, I guess, dozens of ways to cook things with bread and out of bread. Stewed tomatoes with bread, maybe that would be a meal. Something like French toast, if we had any eggs. Bread pudding, sometimes with raisins in it. If we got hold of some hamburger, it came to the table more bread than meat. . . .

But there were times when there wasn't even a nickel and we would be so hungry we were dizzy. My mother would boil a big pot of dandelion greens, and we would eat that. I remember that some small-minded neighbor put it out, and children would tease us, that we ate "fried grass." Sometimes, if we were lucky, we would have oatmeal or cornmeal mush three times a day. Or mush in the morning and cornbread at night.

Malcolm X remembering hard times in 1934, The Autobiography of Malcolm X, *p. 13.*

. . . [T]he real victims of the New Deal are obsolete ideas and irrelevant ideals. Ideas and ideals can die—can even be brutally murdered—with less suffering than the Old Order casually inflicted on a million undernourished children. Let them die and let them pass in the inextinguishable laughter of the gods.

John Franklin Carter, 1934, The New Dealers, *p. 404.*

This spring after a terrible winter there was no rain. The [midwestern] village where I live has not exchanged money for two years. They have bartered and exchanged their produce. Last year some had nothing to exchange. We cut down trees in the front yard for fuel and tried to live off the miserable crop of potatoes of last year.

Since April there has been hope of rain and even up until the day after Decoration day, until that bitter afternoon when the hot winds came and made any hope after that impossible. During April the farmers said that the winter wheat would be all right if it would rain even next week. The peas went in. They raise a lot of peas for the canneries both in Wisconsin and Minnesota. The peas came up a little ways and then fell down as if they had been mowed down. We waited to put in the corn day after day.

Then came a terrifying wind from the Dakotas, blew tens of thousands of dollars worth of onion seed away and half of North Dakota blew into Ohio with the spring sowing. That wind was a terror and blew dust and seed so high you couldn't drive through it in mid-day.

A kind of terror grew in the folk. It was too much, added up with the low prices they got, the drought, heat and high wind. . . . They all shut themselves up as if some terrific crisis, some horrible massacre, were about to occur. . . . The winter wheat and rye began to whiten. A thin stand. You could sit in your house and look about and see the fields whiten and the wheat seemed to go back into the ground. You could see it stand still and then creep back into the ground.

Meridel Le Sueur, September 1934, "Cows and Horses Are Hungry," in Jack Salzman, ed., Years of Protest, *pp. 61–62.*

Vitamin K they call it—the dust which sifts under the door sills, and stings in the eyes, and seasons every spoonful of food. The dust storms have distinct personalities, rising in formation like rolling clouds, creeping up silently like formless fog, approaching violently like a tornado. Where has it come from? It provides topics of endless speculation. Red, it is the topsoil from Oklahoma; brown, it is the fertile earth of western Kansas; the good grazing land of Texas and New Mexico sweeps by as a murky yellow haze. Or, tracing it locally, "My uncle will be along pretty soon," they say; "I just saw his farm go by."

The town dwellers stack their linen in trunks, stuff wet cloths along the window sills, estimate the tons of sand in the darkened air above them, paste cloth masks on their faces with adhesive tape, and try

to joke about Vitamin K. But on the farms and ranches there is an attitude of despair.

Margaret Bourke-White, May 22, 1935, "Dust Changes America," p. 597.

[The National Industrial Recovery Act] abolished child labor. It ran out the sweatshops. It established the principle of regulated hours, wages, and working conditions. It went far toward removing wages from the area of predatory competition. It added to the rights and the freedom of human labor.

Now it is simple to say "created nearly 3,000,000 jobs"—"ran out the sweatshops"—"abolished child labor"—et cet., but it is *not* easy to measure, it is impossible to exaggerate, the human value of these things—to temper despair, to restore hope, to awaken the conscience of a country, to help give back to twelve million people the pride and decency of independent living—words cannot define nor even thought appraise the meaning of these benefits. It is for this reason that I regard NRA as a holy thing.

Hugh S. Johnson, 1935, The Blue Eagle from Egg to Earth, *p. x.*

Anyone who wants to understand the ways of the Civilian Conservation Corps should begin by invoking this vast, untamed America and letting it, in his imagination, settle about him. It is mostly on such earth that the 1,700 odd camps, for two years the centers of life for 370,000 young Americans . . . have been planted. From the camps these men have gone forth daily to labor in forest or on prairie or desert. There they have experienced the simple discipline of ordered living and association with two hundred others of their own age. . . .

This untamed America as the camps know it is chiefly forest land. More than 75 per cent of the 1,648 companies which were operating this April were in timbered regions in National Forests, National Parks, State Parks, or Indian reservations. Most of the others lay on desert floors, on slopes of sagebrush, greasewood, or chapparal, or on the "lone prairie." Only a few touched the edges of towns or cities, and even for the men in them the town was an experience of perhaps a day and half a week as against five in the open. These little villages show on no map that can be purchased in a city shop. Sometimes no reliable map exists at all to show their location. I have ridden behind an Army chauffeur, with a Corps Area

A CCC enrollee assigned to a conservation project scales a rock in a quarry. *(Library of Congress)*

map as his guide, and seen him hunt his camp for an hour. Only by questioning at country filling stations, by nosing up dirt roads, by guessing hazardously at rude forks can one stumble at last upon the more elusive of them.

Frank Ernest Hill writing about the Civilian Conservation Corps, 1935, The School in the Camps, *p. 1.*

When W.P.A. came, we were delighted because it offered work. There were even writers' projects. I couldn't get on one, but a lot of very fine people did. I was given the project of taking a census of all the dogs on the Monterey Peninsula, their breeds, weight and characters. I did it very thoroughly and, since I knew my reports were not likely to get to the hands of the mighty, I wrote some pretty searching character studies of poodles and beagles and hounds.

John Steinbeck recalling the impact of the Works Progress Administration in 1935, "A Primer on the 30's," *p. 89.*

Now I can look my children straight in the eyes. I've regained my self-respect. Relief is all right to keep one from starving, but well—it takes something from you. Sitting around and waiting for your case worker to bring you a check and the kids in the house find you contribute nothing toward their support, very soon they begin to lose respect for you. It's different now. I'm the breadwinner of the house and everybody respects me.

A clerical worker after three weeks of employment with the WPA, circa 1935, in Barbara Blumberg, The New Deal and the Unemployed, *p. 75.*

When many of our sturdy schools and bridges and public buildings have passed with the weight of years, some of the music brought to public performance by governmental intervention in a relief emergency may still be played and sung by generations of Americans. The dawn of a music culture identifiably America's own . . . is already discernible on the horizon.

Ferde Grofé evaluating the impact of music written by composers on the WPA payroll between 1935 and 1943, in Barbara Blumberg, The New Deal and the Unemployed, *p. 205.*

. . . [N]o other state has ever cared whether its artists as a group lived or died; other governments have hired certain individual artists to glorify their operations and have even granted a small pension from time to time to some artist with fame or influence, but to consider, in a time of general distress, starving artists as artists and not simply as paupers is unique to the Roosevelt Administration.

W. H. Auden weighing the importance of the WPA between 1935 and 1943, in Barbara Blumberg, The New Deal and the Unemployed, *p. 294.*

Morning, noon, and night the men go through the process of lining up for their meals, slowly moving into the dining room, picking up a tray and being handed a knife, fork, and spoon, passing by a counter where food is thrown on their plates, being directed by waiters to a seat at a long board table, sitting on a backless bench at a common table where all men shovel in their food, and on their way out of the dining room depositing the dirty dishes in certain receptacles. . . .

Today's dinner consisted of soup, stew, no meat, cornstarch pudding, bread, and "coffee." Many of the men left their hats and coats on. Everybody shoveled in their food. Across from me today sat a bum. He mixed all his food in one bowl and gulped it down; then he grabbed for some extra bread and broke that up, poured some coffee on it and lifted the bowl to his lips and drank the bread and coffee. Most of the men make a noise when they eat. I tried not to watch but it can't be helped.

A homeless man describing his trip to a Chicago soup kitchen, 1936, in Edwin H. Sutherland and Harvey J. Locke, Twenty Thousand Homeless Men, *pp. 3–5.*

I'm a boy of 12 years. . . . My father hasn't worked for 5 months. He went plenty times to relief, he filled out application. They won't give us anything. I don't know why. . . . We haven't paid 4 months rent, Everyday the landlord rings the door bell, we don't open the door for him. We are afraid that will be put out, been put out before, and don't want to happen again. We haven't paid the gas bill, and the electric bill, haven't paid grocery bill for 3 months. My brother goes to Lane Tech. High School. he's eighteen years old, hasn't gone to school for 2 weeks because he got no carfare. I have a sister she's twenty years, she can't find work. My father he staying home. All the time he's crying because he can't find work. I told him why are you crying daddy, and daddy said why shouldn't I cry when there is nothing in the house. I feel sorry for him. That night I couldn't sleep. . . . Were American citizens and were born in Chicago, Ill. and I don't know why they don't help us. . . .

Anonymous letter to Franklin Delano Roosevelt, February 1936, in Robert S. McElvaine, ed., Down and Out in the Great Depression, *p. 117.*

There were 30 boys from my county in Arkansas who went into the CCC the same day in 1936. We took a train west from Little Rock, and they called our names when we stopped at Clarksville. It was about midnight. They put us on a truck and hauled us to a camp in the woods at the end of a dead-end road, in rugged country. It just worried me. I was 17 and scared of most everything.

The boys in camp came out in their skivvies hollerin' "Fresh meat!" They meant us. We were all poor, hardly anybody had been away from home before. Three of the 30 ran off that night and never came back. They issued us two dress uniforms and two work uniforms and two pairs of Army shoes, and that scared me too because it was more clothes than I'd seen before. And they said that if we lost any clothes

our parents would have to pay, and I knew mine couldn't.

Wayman Wells describing his arrival at a Civilian Conservation Corps camp in 1936, in Donald Dale Jackson, "They Were Poor, Hungry, and Built to Last," pp. 66–67.

Frequently during my service with the Securities and Exchange Commission I encountered issuers, underwriters, promoters, brokers, dealers, stock exchange officials and persons of all types involved in the securities business who firmly believed that the legislation of Congress in 1933 and 1934 represented devices of the devil himself. The investment business was doomed; the stock market had met up with a fatal paralysis as a result of these reforms!

Well, what happened? Instead of getting worse, business got better. I pleaded, I argued, I entreated that the thing to do was to be natural, not hysterical. Later, the more intelligent of the investment community realized that the legislation was sound, that its objectives were worthwhile, and that in the long run there would result from these reform activities great benefit to the decent people in business. To their amazement there was an immediate gain in securities sales and trading which fair-minded men had to attribute to the Commission's inspiring restoration of the public confidence.

Joseph P. Kennedy, 1936, I'm for Roosevelt, *p. 9.*

At this season of the year, when California's great crops are coming into harvest, the heavy grapes, the prunes, the apples and lettuce and the rapidly maturing cotton, our highways swarm with the migrant workers, that shifting group of nomadic, poverty-stricken harvesters driven by hunger and the threat of hunger from crop to crop, from harvest to harvest, up and down the state and into Oregon to some extent, and into Washington a little. But it is California which has and needs the majority of these new gypsies. . . .

To the casual traveler on the great highways the movements of the migrants are mysterious if they are seen at all, for suddenly the roads will be filled with open rattletrap cars loaded with children and with dirty bedding, with fire-blackened cooking utensils. The boxcars and gondolas on the railroad lines will be filled with men. And then, just as suddenly, they will have disappeared from the main routes. On side roads and near rivers where there is little travel the squalid, filthy squatters' camp will have been set up, and the orchards will be filled with pickers and cutters and driers. . . .

They arrive in California usually having used up every resource to get here, even to the selling of the poor blankets and utensils and tools on the way to buy gasoline. They arrive bewildered and beaten and usually in a state of semi-starvation, with only one necessity to face immediately, and that is to find work at any wage in order that the family may eat.

And there is only one field in California that can receive them. Ineligible for relief, they must become migratory field workers.

> *John Steinbeck, 1936,* The Harvest Gypsies,
> *pp. 19–21.*

We got a nickel a bushel for citrus fruits. On the grapefruits you had to ring them. You hold a ring in your hand . . . and it has a little thing that slips down over your thumb. You climb the tree and you put that ring around the grapefruit. If the grapefruit slips through, you can't pick it. And any grapefruit that's in your box—you can work real hard, especially if you want to make enough to buy food that day—you'll pick some that aren't big enough. Then when you carry your box up and they check it, they throw out all the ones that go through the ring.

> *Peggy Terry, who migrated from Kentucky*
> *to the Rio Grande Valley in 1937,*
> *in Studs Terkel,* Hard Times, *p. 49.*

Every Californian must be concerned over a situation which creates an army of migrant laborers who are left without employment. A humane government cannot permit them to lack for food. Unquestionably they are at a less advantageous position than they were in the states from which they came, and obviously the situation as it now exists will become even more complex in the course of years. Thoughtful people will wonder, then, if it is advisable to continue an industry which attracts so many thousands of wage earners for this state—for what necessarily must be temporary employment. In the absence of some means of earning a livelihood later public authority must rescue them from starvation through taxation levied upon the public as a whole, and the amount needed even now is in excess of any profit that comes to the state through the growing of cotton. So it would appear that if the grower is directly advan-

taged, indirectly he and all the other permanent residents of the state are disadvantaged.

> Bakersfield Californian, *February 10, 1938, in Walter J.*
> *Stein,* California and the Dust Bowl Migration, *p. 78.*

> Rather drink muddy water
> An sleep in a hollow log
>
> Than to be in California
> Treated like a dirty dog.
> *"California Blues," song recorded in a migrant camp,*
> *date uncertain, in Walter J. Stein,* California
> and the Dust Bowl Migration, *p. 64.*

Government has a final responsibility for the well-being of its citizenship. If private cooperative endeavor fails to provide work for willing hands and relief for the unfortunate, those suffering hardship from no fault of their own have a right to call upon the government for aid; and a government worthy of its name must make a fitting response.

> *Franklin Delano Roosevelt, 1938, in Frank Kingdon,*
> As FDR Said, *p. 97.*

At four-forty-five A.M. streets around the Skidway in Stockton [California] are jammed with men—Mexicans, Filipinos, Italians, and other immigrants, Americans from Oklahoma and Arkansas and probably every other state in the Union. Last night some of them looked like bums. They drank. Some drank on the curb pints of wine charged with "dynamite." Their life is generally low. Bums. Some slept in fifteen-cent flop houses or in the open, or spent the night in two-bit brothels. "Why not? What else is there to this life?" But now, quarter to five, with the rich California sun well up in the blue sky, none look like bums. They are sober. Workers. Thousands of them waiting to be bought off the curb for a day.

Huge trucks with trailers pull in. They are after men for beets. Two bits an hour. No, no more! Smaller trucks for cherry-pickers. Two bits a bucket. No, no more! One truck offers twenty-seven and a half cents a bucket. There is a rush. Fifty men climb aboard. The contractor needs only twenty. He picks his crew. The others climb down.

> *Louis Adamic, 1938,* My America, *p. 382.*

The camp was bigger than the town itself. People had dragged old car fenders up from the dumps, wired them from the limbs of oak trees a few feet off of the ground and this was a roof for some of them. Others had taken old canvas sacks or wagon sheets, stretched the canvas over little limbs cut so the forks braced each other, and that was a house for those folks. I heard two brothers standing back looking at their house saying, "I ain't lost my hand as a carpenter, yet." "My old eyes can still see to hit a nail." They'd carried buckets and tin cans out of the heap, flattened them on the ground, then nailed the tin onto crooked boards, and that was a mansion for them. Lots of people, families mostly, had some bedclothes with them, and I could see the old, stinky, gummy quilts and blankets hung up like tents, and two or three kids of all ages playing around underneath. There was scatterings of cardboard shacks, where the people had lugged cartons, cases, packing boxes out from town and tacked them into a house. They was easy to build, but the first rain that hit them, they was goners. . . .

Gunny sacks, old clothes, hay and straw, fermenting bedclothes, are usually piled full of kids playing, or grown-ups resting and waiting for the word "work" to come.

Woody Guthrie describing a "Hooverville"
outside Sacramento, California, summer 1938,
Bound for Glory, *pp. 328–30.*

When they arrive in the fertile valleys of the West, the migrants are the most ragged, half-starved, forgotten element in our population, needy, the butt of the jibes of those who look down on "fruit tramps," but with a surprising morale in the midst of misery, and a will to work. These people are not hand-picked failures. They are the human materials cruelly dislocated by the process of human erosion. They have been scattered like the shavings from a clean-cutting plane, or like the dust of their farms, literally blown out. And they trek west, these American whites, at the end of a long immigrant line of Chinese, Japanese, Koreans, Negroes, Hindustanis, Mexicans, Filipinos, to serve the crops and farmers.

Far western agricultural communities depend upon prompt arrival of adequate supplies of mobile labor. But the development of normal relationships between citizen and community and between employer and employee, is not favored by constant movement. The laborer who comes to aid finds little welcome beyond the work he performs and the money he spends. "This rancher has us for two or three weeks, and then he's through with me. He knows me till he's through with me." "Residenters" look askance at nomads, and treat them as "outlanders." Children are stigmatized at school as "pea pickers." "Okies" and "Arkies" become terms of opprobrium, and citizens can imagine a lettuce strike as "a war between California and Oklahoma."

Dorothea Lange and Paul Schuster Taylor, 1939,
An American Exodus, *p. 148.*

Roosevelt! You're my man!
When the time come
I ain't got a cent
You buy my groceries
and pay my rent.
Mr. Roosevelt, you're my man!

A song heard by writer Richard Wright on
the streets of Harlem, circa 1940, in Barbara Blumberg,
The New Deal and the Unemployed, *pp. 291–92.*

11

The Labor Movement in Growth and Decline
1917–1999

Membership in the American Federation of Labor had reached 2.5 million by the start of World War I. That number doubled by the end of the war, in part because the federal government promoted peace between labor and management during the war years, to prevent strikes and keep production high. Woodrow Wilson rewarded Samuel Gompers's support of the war effort with a position on the Advisory Committee to the Council of National Defense. Gompers also attended the Peace Conference of 1919, as chairman of the Commission on International Labor Legislation.

When the war was over, American business leaders felt free once more to combat organization among their employees. Many companies now refused to deal with unions that had been formed during the war with the government's help. Management again employed armed guards and labor spies and brought in scabs when strikes took place. Active union members were blacklisted, as in the past. Some employers discouraged unions by offering benefits such as life insurance and pension plans. Some also formed "company unions," which were worker organizations whose membership was limited to the employees of one firm. Workers in company unions had no real voice and very little power, because management controlled their agenda.

Labor tested its muscle with a series of strikes in 1919 and 1920. Sixty thousand members of the Amalgamated Clothing Workers struck for three months in 1919 and gained a 44-hour week and a 15 percent raise. Strikes occurred with varying success among sewing-machine operators, cigar makers, and actors in New York, and among transportation workers in Chicago. A widespread mining strike shut down every bituminous coal mine in the country. Boston's police force struck, while in Seattle a general walkout in support of striking shipyard workers brought commerce to a halt. Strikes occurring in 1919 alone involved 8.5 million workers.

The American Federation of Labor had never abandoned its hope of organizing steelworkers following the strike at Homestead in 1892, and 1919 seemed like a good time to try again. The pay that steelworkers received in exchange for their 12-hour days left 38 percent of them living below subsistence level at the same time that owners were enjoying high profits due to price increases. The AFL, which had recently organized Chicago's packing-house workers, felt confident of success.

The federation's Chicago branch, headed by John Fitzpatrick, formed a new steelworkers' union, which in September 1919 approached United States Steel, the world's largest steel manufacturer, with a list of demands. The union insisted on recognition as bargaining agent for the workers in order to provide a system for handling grievances. Fitzpatrick and his associates also called for a raise in wages and an end to the 12-hour workday. Elbert H. Gary, chief executive officer of United States Steel, refused to deal with the union leaders, believing that his employees were fairly compensated for their work. Gary also doubted the motives of Fitzpatrick's associate William Z. Foster, a former member of the IWW who was known as a political radical. The Russian Revolution of 1917 had inspired many left-leaning activists to involve themselves in union activities, in what they viewed as a struggle between the proletariat and the capitalist class. Gary and other industrialists distrusted both the communists within the labor movement and their own foreign-born employees, whom they suspected of having imported subversive ideas from Europe.

On September 10, the mill workers employed by United States Steel voted in favor of a general strike that was set to begin September 22. President Wilson called on the union leaders to postpone the walkout, but his request was ignored. The industrywide strike went ahead as scheduled.

The actual number of workers who stayed off the job on the first day, either voluntarily or as a result of intimidation, is unknown. The union claimed that 279,000 of the nation's 350,000 steel-mill workers struck, while management's estimate was much lower, about 20 percent. Most workers remained on the job in Pittsburgh, the center of world steel production, and most walked out in Chicago. Operations in Youngstown, Ohio, where United States Steel and several smaller companies had plants, were practically shut down. Management pointed out that many workers had received letters threatening their safety or that of their families if they reported to work.

Violence erupted in several cities. Two strikers died and 50 were injured in confrontations with company guards in Buffalo, New York, and two workers were killed in Farrell, Pennsylvania. On September 29, Bethlehem Steel rejected the union's demands, and one-fourth of its workforce walked out. But the strike quickly lost momentum. Workers gradually returned to their jobs, and by November most steel mills had resumed full operations. The strike limped along until early January 1920, when the AFL admitted defeat.

The success of business's antiunion campaign is evident not just in the failure of the Steel Strike of 1919 but also in the fact that union membership declined to 3.5 million by 1929, to include just 6 percent of the workforce. The Great Depression dealt another serious blow to organized labor, and membership dropped to 2.5 million in 1933. Unions of construction and railroad workers were especially hard hit, losing a third of their members.

LABOR'S RESPONSE TO THE NRA

Convinced that strong labor unions could stimulate economic recovery, Franklin D. Roosevelt included protection for unions in his New Deal legislation, beginning with Section 7(a) of the National Industrial Recovery Act, which guaranteed workers' right to organize. Immediately, the decline in union membership was reversed, and hundreds of thousands of workers enrolled. The United Mine Workers (UMW), an organization nearly wiped out by the depression, welcomed 300,000 new members in a few months. Under the leadership of John L. Lewis, the UMW became the nation's largest union, one that admitted all mine workers regardless of skill level. Lewis declared that the National Industrial Recovery Act was labor's Emancipation Proclamation. William Green, who had replaced Samuel Gompers as president of the AFL in 1924, reached farther back in history to find a document for comparison: he called the new legislation the Magna Charta of labor. Green announced at the AFL's annual convention in October 1933 that the affiliated unions had gained more than 1.5 million members in the months since the NRA was passed, enough to cancel out the losses of the previous decade.

Participating companies, however, quickly took advantage of the federal government's failure to provide a mechanism for enforcing Section 7(a). In some places, such as towns where the major employers enjoyed strong public support, companies brazenly fired union activists. Meanwhile, many workers grew disillusioned when union membership brought them few immediate benefits. Although nearly 1,900 strikes occurred in 1934, most came to nothing or won only small concessions from management. The majority of people who had recently joined the unions now departed.

The Wagner Act banned the tactics that companies had used to interfere with the establishment and growth of unions, and it created the National Labor Relations Board to enforce its provisions. Many employers expected that the Supreme Court would declare the act unconstitutional; nevertheless, they adopted a war mentality in their dealings with workers, stocking up on guns, ammunition, and tear gas, and hiring and arming guards. The Pinkerton National Detective Agency provided spies to 309 corporate clients during this period, including such industrial giants as the Pennsylvania Railroad and General Motors Corporation. General Motors spent nearly $1 million to hire labor spies in the 19 months between January 1934 and July 1936, using the services of 14 different agencies. GM's outlay was just a fraction of the $80 million that businesses were spending each year to combat union growth, according to a congressional report.

THE CIO AND THE WORKING MASSES

Most unions in the AFL were organized by craft, but there were voices in the federation echoing the sentiments of the Knights of Labor and calling for the unionization of all workers, skilled and unskilled. In 1935, a number of union leaders within the AFL formed a committee for the purpose of organizing the many unskilled and semiskilled laborers who worked in heavy industry. Under the leadership of John L. Lewis, they formed the Committee for Industrial Organization (CIO) to recruit members from the factory floor and assign them to new or existing unions. (The objections of most craft unions to the CIO's organizing methods would result in the expulsion of the 32 international unions constituting the CIO from the AFL in 1937. These unions would regroup as the Congress of Industrial Organizations, also known as the CIO, in 1938.)

In 1936, the CIO targeted the General Motors Corporation, the world's largest producer of automobiles and the third largest corporation in the United States; GM was resisting the efforts of the United Auto Workers to organize its employees. Despite the depression, GM would earn a profit of $227,940,000 in 1936. Company president Alfred P. Sloan would receive a salary of $374,505, while GM's 250,000 workers would earn far less—$1,150 for the year, on average. Wages were not the only grievance. Many automotive workers were unhappy about a belt-line production system that was geared to speed. They felt that they were being driven to work at an unrealistically rapid pace and treated as pieces of equipment rather than as human beings.

On November 13, 1936, a group of workers at GM's Fisher Body Plant 1, in Flint, Michigan, staged a brief sit-down strike, occupying their workplace and demanding—and receiving—concessions from management. This was not the first sit-down strike to occur in the United States. In 1906, the IWW had led a "stay-in" strike at a General Electric plant in Schenectady, New York. More recently, sit-down strikes at the rubber plants of Akron, Ohio, had evolved, with help from the CIO, into a conventional strike that had shut down the Goodyear Tire and Rubber Company in February and March 1936.

When the strike at Fisher Body Plant 1 achieved some success, General Motors workers rushed to join the UAW. Sit-down strikes and conventional strikes soon disrupted factory output throughout GM's manufacturing empire, in Atlanta, Kansas City, Cleveland, and Detroit. In the assembly-line system that prevailed in the automobile industry, a strike or slowdown in one plant could significantly affect production throughout the company. Employers could not bring in strikebreakers to counteract a sit-down because the workers had possession of the facilities, and they hesitated to launch an assault on the strikers and risk damaging valuable equipment.

On December 30, UAW vice president Bob Travis ordered a sit-down strike at Fisher Body Plants 1 and 2 in Flint, where most of GM's manufacturing took place. Production at GM came to a halt in what would be the longest and most famous sit-down strike in the history of the American labor movement. The strike would last 44 days and directly involve 140,000 workers.

In January 1937, as the CIO handled publicity and public relations, volunteers from the Cooks and Chefs' Union prepared three meals a day for the 5,000 striking workers now living in the plants, and women's groups picketed outside. To relieve boredom in the occupied facilities and keep morale high, the strike leaders scheduled calisthenics, musical performances, and other diversions for the men. (No women had been allowed to remain in the plants.)

The strikers were willing to end their sit-down if management would agree to a list of demands. They wanted recognition of the UAW as sole bargaining agent for GM employees, fixed rates of pay with time-and-a-half for overtime, a 30-hour week and six-hour day, reinstatement of workers fired for union activity, a seniority system, and regulation of the belt line by worker committees cooperating with management.

On January 11, an encounter known as the "Battle of the Running Bulls" took place when police officers using clubs and buckshot tried to enter the occupied buildings. The strikers responded with a barrage of automobile parts, nuts and bolts, pipes, and soft-drink bottles—whatever could be thrown from the plant windows served as a weapon. They used a fire hose to shoot a stream of ice-cold water at their assailants. The police employed guns and tear gas but ultimately withdrew. Fourteen strikers were treated at a hospital for bullet wounds, but the workers retained control of the plant. Michigan governor Frank Murphy then ordered 1,500 National Guardsmen to Flint to prevent further hostilities.

Twice General Motors cut off heat and electricity to the occupied plants in the hope of forcing the workers out but later restored power. Such moves reflected management's ambivalence about how to respond to the strike. William Knudsen, GM's vice president in charge of operations, was willing to accommodate workers in their demands, but financial vice president Donaldson Brown remained wary of a continued union presence. Such vacillation prevented General Motors from mounting an effective response and allowed the union to direct the course of events. The strike ended in February 1937, when Murphy and Roosevelt pressured General Motors into recognizing the union. The auto manufacturer actually conceded very little, agreeing to negotiate exclusively with the UAW for six months in the 17 plants that had been closed by the strike. But the UAW and all unions saw the victory as a new beginning. Labor leaders announced that the years of failure and employer retaliation were over: unions had gained a new legitimacy.

At the same time that the UAW was negotiating with General Motors in Michigan, the CIO was organizing GM's Canadian employees. The CIO gave many Canadian workers their first opportunity to join a labor union, and membership increased nearly 37 percent in Canada between 1937 and 1938.

In the United States, sit-down strikes now closed plants owned by the Chrysler Corporation, the Ford Motor Company, and other industrial firms. In a single month, March 1937, there were 170 sit-down strikes in the United States, involving more than 167,000 workers. If their position was strong enough, union negotiators held out for closed-shop contracts, in which employers agreed to hire only union members.

In 1939, the Supreme Court upheld a lower-court determination that sit-down strikes were illegal, and American labor stopped employing this tactic.

THE LITTLE STEEL STRIKE

The CIO had had its eye on the steel industry from the start. In 1937 it established the Steel Workers Organizing Committee (SWOC), headed by Lewis's assistant, Philip Murray, to unionize the nation's steel workers.

Murray first approached United States Steel, which now employed 220,000 people, produced about 40 percent of the nation's steel, and was known popularly as "Big Steel." On March 2, 1937, United States Steel announced that it had agreed to recognize the SWOC as the bargaining agent for its employees and to sign a contract giving workers higher wages and greater benefits. All of this had been accomplished without any overt pressure from Murray's committee. United States Steel's leaders had foreseen that a costly strike would result if they resisted unionization and that it probably would end in victory for the CIO. Also, any steel manufacturer hoping to obtain government contracts for naval armor plate was required to operate on a 40-hour schedule. With war in Europe a real possibility and its eye on a lucrative government contract, United States Steel was ready to grant what labor demanded. By May 1, 58 small steel companies had followed its lead and signed contracts with the SWOC. Jones and Laughlin, the fourth largest steel producer, signed with the SWOC on May 20.

Not every large steel manufacturer welcomed the union. Republic Steel, Bethlehem Steel, Youngstown Sheet and Tube, National Steel, and Inland Steel—a group known collectively as "Little Steel"—dug in their heels. Tom M. Girdler of Republic Steel spoke for all of them when he promised to resist any effort to organize his employees. Girdler's company prepared for trouble, arming a 370-member private police force with guns, gas grenades, and billy clubs.

The refusal of Girdler and his associates to allow union organization resulted in the Little Steel Strike, one of the bitterest confrontations between labor and management to occur in the United States. The strike began in May 1937 and lasted for six weeks. Eighteen picketers died as a result of unprovoked attacks by police and company guards, and hundreds were injured. The bloodiest incident took place on May 30, 1937, when police shot at striking steelworkers and their families outside Republic Steel's South Chicago plant. The demonstrators defended themselves with rocks and steel bolts fired from slingshots, but police bullets proved far more lethal. Ten workers died in the skirmish, which is remembered as the Memorial Day Massacre; 29 demonstrators and 26 police officers were hospitalized. Most of the dead and wounded steelworkers had been shot in the back. The strikers put one wounded man, a worker named Earl Handley, in a police car for transport to a hospital, but the officers dragged him out. He subsequently died. Another striker, Kenneth Reed, bled to death in a patrol wagon. A Senate investigation later determined that the demonstrators could have been dispersed without violence.

Police count the casualties following the Memorial Day massacre of 1937. *(Walter P. Reuther Library, Wayne State University)*

The strike ended in success for Little Steel, but the SWOC filed charges with the National Labor Relations Board, accusing the steel companies of unfair labor practices. The board conducted an investigation in 1937 and 1938 and concluded that Republic Steel had violated the provisions of the Wagner Act. Republic appealed the ruling in court, but it was upheld. The company was required to reinstate 7,000 strikers and issue back pay totaling $2 million. In 1945, Republic paid $350,000 to settle lawsuits filed in behalf of workers killed or injured in the strike.

The union was the ultimate winner. In 1941, the NLRB compared the names of SWOC members with the payrolls of several steel manufacturers, including Republic Steel, and determined that the majority of the companies' workers were union members. The union therefore was entitled by law to be the bargaining agent for all of the employees. The companies of Little Steel had no choice at that time but to sign contracts with the union that was now named the United Steel Workers of America.

PEACEFUL RELATIONS DURING WORLD WAR II

By 1941, nine million American workers belonged to labor unions, and large segments of the workforce in most industries had been organized. The government kept tight control over labor-management relations during World War II, as it had done throughout the First World War. The War Labor Board, created in 1942, established a mechanism known as maintenance-of-membership to promote cooperation between unions and employers. It gave new employees in plants with union contracts the freedom to join a union if they chose to do so, but once they joined, they were required to remain union members as long as they held their jobs. Unions could organize the workers in nonunion plants, but they could not hold strikes. Also, the federal government was empowered to take over any defense-industry operation threatened by a strike. Union membership made great gains during the war years, with the UAW experiencing the most significant growth, doubling its membership to 1 million by 1944. By 1945, nearly 15 million workers in the United States were union members.

Once the war ended, unions no longer had to suppress their demands and were free to hold strikes again. Ten thousand strikes took place in 1945 and 1946, more than occurred in the United States in any other two-year period. This "strike wave" affected the railroad, coal, oil, steel, telephone, electrical, and maritime industries and involved 4.5 million workers. While union members benefited from the strikes, the unions themselves lost much of their public support. There was an enormous demand for automobiles, home appliances, and other goods that had been unavailable during the war, and the public feared that union demands for better wages might lead to higher price tags on those items. To many people, the unions appeared greedy and irresponsible, willing to jeopardize postwar prosperity for their own aggrandizement.

In June 1947, Congress curbed labor's freedom to organize new unions and to strike, by passing the Labor-Management Relations Act, better known as the Taft-Hartley Act. This law strengthened the rights of employers who were opposed to unionization, and it attempted to balance power between labor and management. Employers could now argue against the formation of a union by their workers and stop strikes and picketing more easily. The president could now ask permission of Congress to issue an 80-day injunction against any strike that threatened national safety. Now unions too were held accountable for unfair practices.

The closed shop was deemed illegal by the Taft-Hartley Act. The best arrangement that organized labor could hope for was a union shop, one in which workers were required to join the union within a month or two of being hired. In an agency shop, workers were not required to join a union, but they did have to pay for any services that the union provided for them. Workers in an open shop were not obligated to join a union or pay a fee. In all instances, at least half of a plant's employees had to be union members if the union was to represent all of them as a bargaining unit.

One controversial provision of the Taft-Hartley Act was its requirement that union officials sign an affidavit denying any communist affiliation in order for their unions to use the services of the NLRB. Most union officers were staunch anticommunists in the early years of the cold war and signed without hesitation, although two unions with no communists among their leadership, the United Mine Workers and the International Typographical Union, refused to sign, on principle. The affidavit presented a dilemma, however, for many in the CIO, where one-fourth of the membership belonged to communist-led unions.

Samuel Gompers had expelled thousands of communists from the AFL in 1923, but the CIO traditionally had welcomed people of all political persuasions as long as they were dedicated to the union cause. During World War II, when the Soviet Union was allied with the United States, the communists within the American labor movement shared the short-term political goals of other union leaders. But following the war, the communists seemed more interested in furthering the aims of the Soviet Union than in improving labor's lot.

Philip Murray, who had succeeded John L. Lewis as president of the CIO in 1940, believed that it was in labor's best interest to support Democratic candidates for public office, while the communists in his organization were working on behalf of the Progressive Party. The communists were attacking the foreign policy of President Harry S. Truman, and Murray suspected that they were holding strikes to weaken the United States rather than to advance the aims of labor.

The situation came to a head at the 1949 CIO convention, when the leadership expelled the United Electrical, Radio, and Machine Workers, a large communist-dominated union, and the smaller Farm Equipment Workers Union. Additional procommunist unions were driven from the CIO in 1950. In all, the CIO expelled 11 unions with almost 1 million members. The organization amended its constitution to ban communists, fascists, and members of totalitarian groups from serving as CIO officers or executive board members.

Philip Murray died of a heart attack on November 9, 1952, after leading the CIO for 12 years. Less than two weeks later, William Green, longtime president of the AFL, died as well. The two new presidents, George Meany of the AFL and Walter Reuther of the CIO, viewed a merger of their organizations as an effective way to advance labor's cause. The principal issue that had divided

George Meany and Walter Reuther join hands to celebrate the formation of the AFL-CIO. *(The George Meany Memorial Archives)*

them—the formation of unions according to craft or industry—was no longer a matter of controversy. During the first week of December 1955, America's labor leaders gathered in New York City to attend the first annual convention of the combined AFL-CIO. With Meany as its president, the organization represented 15 million workers, or more than 85 percent of union membership in the United States.

THE SENATE INVESTIGATES CORRUPT LEADERSHIP

In January 1957, a Senate select committee was formed to investigate allegations of corruption in organized labor. John McClellan, a Democrat from Arkansas, headed the committee. The unions held as much as $30 billion in their pension and welfare funds, and union members and the public had a right to know if that money was being mishandled. The investigation, one of the longest ever conducted by the U.S. Congress, continued for two and one-half years and included testimony from 1,526 witnesses. The activities described in that testimony went beyond the misuse of funds. Union officials and business-people testified on the Senate floor about bribery, extortion, strong-arm tactics, and the abuse of power. The hearings shocked the American people and damaged public opinion of organized labor.

Organized crime had infiltrated a few AFL unions in the 1920s and 1930s, primarily unions of construction workers, truckers, stevedores, and garment workers. Only the garment trades had managed to expel the criminal influence. In 1951, members of the International Longshoremen's Association (ILA), a powerful union along the Atlantic and Gulf Coasts, staged a wildcat strike—a sudden, unsanctioned work stoppage—to call attention to their dissatisfaction with corruption at high levels within their union.

The New York State Crime Commission looked into the situation on the docks and in 1953 made public its findings. The investigation revealed that the union had implemented a system of organized theft in which cargo was routinely taken from steamship lines. The union had also extorted fees from truckers loading and unloading freight at the dockside, including those who did the actual lifting themselves. Rank-and-file union members had hesitated to speak out, because they depended on union representatives for their daily work assignments. A stevedore knew that in order to be selected for a job, he had to demonstrate loyalty to the union.

George Meany expelled the ILA at the 1953 AFL convention and chartered a new longshoremen's union, but intense rivalry between the two organizations led to a series of wildcat strikes that frequently tied up the Port of New York over the next few years.

In early 1957, Meany learned from Robert F. Kennedy, counsel to the McClellan Committee, that Senate investigators had uncovered evidence that Dave Beck, president of the International Brotherhood of Teamsters, Chauffeurs, Warehousemen, and Helpers of America (IBT), had been systematically looting his union's treasury. Meany brought the issue before the AFL-CIO executive council, which voted to cooperate fully with a congressional probe.

The IBT was the largest and wealthiest union in the United States in the 1950s. Its membership totaled 1.3 million, and it controlled nearly $250 million in welfare and pension assets. Testimony during the televised hearings revealed that in 1946 Beck had used $36,000 in IBT funds to pay off a personal loan. Between 1949 and 1953, he had taken more than $85,000 to pay his bills and support a lavish lifestyle, and he had diverted nearly $200,000 from the union treasury to finance the building of a mansion and subsequent improvements on it. The nation also learned that politicians, judges, and police chiefs had regularly received bribes from the Teamsters.

The evidence showed that Beck and James Hoffa, an IBT international vice president, had dominated and intimidated union officials, IBT membership, and employers with whom the union had contracts. They had hired thugs to alter the viewpoints of adversaries with beatings and bombings, and they had replaced independent-minded union officers with "trustees," or underlings who were willing to follow orders. At one time, these trustees supervised more than 100 local unions. Beck invoked the Fifth Amendment 50 times in the course of his testimony, refusing to respond to committee questions on the grounds that his answers might be self-incriminating. But even without his responses, there was enough evidence against Beck to lead to his conviction and imprisonment for larceny and federal tax evasion. In December 1957, the AFL-CIO expelled the Teamsters.

On May 26, 1957, Beck announced that he would not seek reelection as IBT president. He was succeeded by Hoffa, who was a target of the committee's investigation as well. Most union members cared more about Hoffa's skill at procuring lucrative contracts than about his alleged ties to organized crime. In hearings that began in July 1958, the McClellan Committee proved that Hoffa had sanctioned the use of physical force against union opponents. The committee also presented evidence linking him to several murders. Hoffa was shown to have misappropriated $9.5 million in union funds, employed the services of known criminals, and tampered with the judicial process to avoid imprisonment. He held the IBT presidency until 1971, although he began serving a 13-year prison term in 1964.

The McClellan Committee hearings led Congress to pass the Labor-Management Disclosure Act, better known as the Landrum-Griffin Act, in 1959. This law provides for regulation of union elections and supervision of union finances. It also protects union members from unethical labor leaders and employers.

ORGANIZATION IN THE PUBLIC SECTOR

America's unions were born among people who worked with their hands, and their membership traditionally had been blue collar. By 1960, the nation's labor leaders recognized the need to focus their organizing activity on white-collar workers and civil servants. They knew that automation was eliminating thousands of jobs in manufacturing and that with training, many displaced laborers would find employment as salespeople or clerical workers, for whom there was a rising demand. In fact, public-sector employment reached 10.5 million in 1966. With the economy strong and jobs plentiful, civil servants and teachers were willing to take the risks that unionization entailed in order to improve their working conditions.

In 1959, Mayor Robert F. Wagner of New York City recognized the right of public employees to engage in collective bargaining; in so doing, he set an example for other municipalities to follow. In 1962, President John F. Kennedy issued Executive Order 10988, giving employees of the executive branch of the federal government the right to join unions and bargain collectively. By 1977, 20 states had passed legislation extending those rights to their employees. Nearly 40 percent of public workers belonged to unions in 1979. The American Federation of State, County and Municipal Employees claimed nearly 1 million members and was one of the largest unions affiliated with the AFL.

In the 1970s, communities throughout the nation dealt with strikes by firefighters, police, and teachers. Postal workers held a two-week work stoppage in 1970 that ended only when President Richard Nixon declared the situation a national emergency. In 1975, 2.2 percent of public employees took part in 428 strikes. The largest such incident occurred in Pennsylvania, where more than 80,000 state, county, and city workers staged a walkout.

Striking California grape pickers entreat vineyard workers to join them. *(The George Meany Memorial Archives)*

Another group to be organized in the 1960s was the population of migrant farm workers, many of whom were Mexican Americans. Most of these laborers worked 12-hour days for very low wages and lived in poverty. The protections of federal labor laws still excluded them, due to opposition from wealthy and powerful growers. In 1962, a community activist named Cesar Chavez formed the National Farm Workers Association (NFWA), with the immediate goal of creating a union for California's grape pickers, and the long-term plan of organizing farm laborers nationwide. Chavez viewed his union activities as part of a larger effort to gain dignity and equal opportunities for Mexican Americans, a struggle he referred to as *la causa*.

In 1965, the 2,000 members of the NFWA voted to join with an AFL-CIO group that recently had been established, to form the United Farm Workers Organizing Committee. The combined union struck first against California vineyards and then against the growers of table grapes. Interest in the strike spread beyond the state, leading to a nationwide boycott of California grapes. Sales of grapes were cut in half as millions of people showed their support of the strikers at the produce counter. In 1970, after more than four years of the strike and boycott, 26 growers reached an agreement with the United Farm Workers. Organization has not solved all of the problems faced by migrant laborers, however, and many continue to live in poverty.

THE INFLUENCE OF UNIONS WANES

When the AFL-CIO was formed in 1955, its leaders expected to double their numbers over the next decade. They viewed the coming together of two giant labor federations as an opportunity to bring the benefits of union membership to millions of people. Yet the gains failed to materialize. AFL-CIO membership in

1964 was about equal to that of 1955. The workforce was growing, but the number of workers in unions was stagnant.

Companies interested in cutting costs began to find ways to avoid providing the salaries and benefits demanded in union contracts. Beginning in the mid-1960s, a number of manufacturers relocated some of their operations to rural areas of the West and South, where a nonunion labor force was willing to work for lower wages. Employees in unions increasingly found themselves left behind in aging plants that received little attention or investment. More recently, the search for cheaper labor has prompted many U.S. firms to move their manufacturing operations overseas.

The energy crises of the 1970s brought on severe recessions and high inflation. The federal government responded to public pressure for lower prices by deregulating the airline and trucking industries between 1977 and 1980, relying on the free-market system to drive rates down. A number of airlines and trucking firms merged or went out of business as a result.

The economy revived following the recessions, and employment increased rapidly as technology advanced at an unprecedented rate. But union membership declined in most industries. New companies were less willing to listen to union demands than their predecessors had been. Many preferred to address workers' concerns through their human resources departments rather than through collective bargaining. Corporations such as MCI and Sprint, which arose following the break-up of AT&T in 1983, remain strongly antiunion.

Does organized labor have a future in the United States? In 1999, membership in the AFL-CIO was slightly more than 13 million, and unions represented less than 10 percent of private-sector employees. John Sweeney, who was elected president of the AFL-CIO in 1995, has warned that organized labor risks becoming irrelevant unless it can aggressively recruit new members. In recent years, union organizers have targeted the growing health-care industry, in the belief that doctors, nurses, and other health professionals have concerns that need to be addressed. The Service Employees International Union, an organization of 300,000 public service workers, was the third-largest union in the AFL-CIO by membership in 1999, occupying the position held by the United Brotherhood of Carpenters in 1955. These workers are largely women of color, and many are immigrants, while the typical union member of earlier decades was a white male. But like the steelworkers of 1919 and the GM employees occupying Fisher Body Plant 1 in 1936, they want dignity in the workplace, and they want to be heard.

CHRONICLE OF EVENTS

1917

Membership in the American Federation of Labor totals 2.5 million.

1918

AFL membership reaches five million.

1919

Samuel Gompers attends the International Peace Conference as chairman of the Commission on International Labor Legislation.

Strikes occurring in the United States involve 8.5 million workers.

September 22: Between 70,000 and 279,000 steelworkers go on strike. Four strikers die in violent confrontations with management.

September 29: One-fourth of the workforce at Bethlehem Steel joins the strike.

November: Most striking steelworkers have returned to their jobs.

1920

January: The AFL acknowledges defeat in the Steel Strike of 1919.

1923

Samuel Gompers expels thousands of communists from the AFL.

1924

William Green replaces Samuel Gompers as president of the AFL.

1929

Union membership has declined to 3.5 million workers, or 6 percent of the workforce.

1933

Union membership reaches a low of 2.5 million.

June 16: Franklin D. Roosevelt signs the National Industrial Recovery Act. Section 7(a) protects the right of workers to organize. The decline in union membership reverses.

October: At the annual convention of the AFL, federation president William Green announces a gain of more than 1.5 million members for affiliated unions.

1934

Nearly 1,900 strikes occur in the United States.

1935

July 5: The National Labor Relations Act goes into effect, protecting workers' rights and establishing the National Labor Relations Board to investigate complaints against management and conduct elections for workers wanting to unionize.

The Committee for Industrial Organization (CIO) is formed within the AFL.

1936

February and March: A strike conducted with assistance from the CIO shuts down the Goodyear Tire and Rubber Company.

November 13: Workers at GM's Fisher Body Plant 1 in Flint, Michigan, stage a brief sit-down strike and gain some concessions from management. Strikes erupt at GM plants in other cities.

December 30: Bob Travis, president of the United Automobile Workers, orders a sit-down strike at Fisher Body Plants 1 and 2.

1937

January: The General Motors strike continues.

January 11: The Battle of the Running Bulls takes place, as strikers successfully defend occupied GM plants against an attempt by police officers to take possession of them. Fourteen strikers require medical treatment for bullet wounds.

February: President Franklin D. Roosevelt and Michigan governor Frank Murphy pressure General Motors into recognizing the UAW, and the strike ends.

March: More than 167,000 U.S. workers take part in 170 sit-down strikes.

March 2: United States Steel announces its decision to recognize the Steel Workers Organizing Committee (SWOC) as bargaining agent for its employees and to give workers better wages and benefits.

May: The employees of the companies known collectively as Little Steel begin a strike that will last six weeks and end in a victory for management.

May 1: Fifty-eight small steel companies have signed contracts with the SWOC.

May 20: Jones and Laughlin signs a contract with the SWOC.

May 30: Police attack picketers outside Republic Steel's South Chicago plant, killing 10.

Citing a difference in organizing philosophy, the AFL expels the unions of the CIO.

1937–38

Union membership reaches 37 percent among Canadian workers.

The NLRB investigates charges that Republic Steel engaged in unfair labor practices during the strike. The board concludes that Republic had violated recent provisions of the Wagner Act.

1938

The unions of the CIO form a new organization, the Congress of Industrial Organizations, which now is known by the initials CIO.

1939

The Supreme Court decides that sit-down strikes are illegal.

1940

Philip Murray becomes president of the CIO.

1941

The NLRB determines that the majority of workers at Republic Steel and other firms are SWOC members. The companies sign contracts with the union that is now named the United Steel Workers.

Nine million U.S. workers belong to labor unions.

1942

The federal government creates the War Labor Board to oversee relations between unions and management during World War II.

1944

Membership in the UAW reaches one million.

1945

Republic Steel pays $350,000 to settle lawsuits resulting from the Little Steel strike.

Nearly 15 million U.S. workers belong to unions.

1945–46

Ten thousand strikes occur in the United States, involving 4.5 million workers.

1947

June: the Labor-Management Relations Act, or Taft-Hartley Act, attempts to balance power between labor and management.

1949

The CIO expels two communist-dominated unions, the United Electrical, Radio, and Machine Workers and the Farm Equipment Workers Union.

1950

Additional unions with communist leadership are expelled from the CIO. Communists, fascists, and members of totalitarian groups are forbidden from serving as CIO officers or executive board members.

1951

Members of the International Longshoremen's Association (ILA) stage a wildcat strike to express dissatisfaction with corrupt leadership.

1952

November: Both Philip Murray and William Green die. George Meany becomes AFL president; Walter Reuther now heads the CIO.

1953

An investigation by the New York State Crime Commission reveals that ILA leadership has engaged in systematic theft and extortion. The AFL expels the ILA and establishes a new longshoremen's union.

1955

December: The AFL and CIO unite to form a single federation, the AFL-CIO, with Meany as president. Membership totals 15 million.

1957

January: The Senate forms a select committee to investigate corruption in organized labor, headed by John McClellan of Arkansas. Committee counsel Robert F. Kennedy informs Meany that investigators have evidence implicating Dave Beck, president of the International Brotherhood of Teamsters, Chauffeurs, Warehousemen, and Helpers of America (IBT) in illegal activity. The AFL-CIO executive council votes to cooperate with the congressional inquiry.

May 26: Beck announces that he will not seek reelection as IBT president. James Hoffa, another target of the Senate investigation who has ties to organized crime, succeeds him.

December: The AFL expels the IBT after revelations in the McClellan Committee hearings result in the conviction and sentencing of Beck.

1959

The Landrum-Griffin Act is passed, providing for regulation of union elections and supervision of union finances.

Mayor Robert F. Wagner of New York City recognizes the right of public employees to engage in collective bargaining.

1962

President John F. Kennedy issues an executive order giving employees of the executive branch of the federal government the right to join unions.

Cesar Chavez forms the National Farm Workers Association.

1964

James Hoffa begins serving a 13-year prison term.

Membership in the AFL-CIO is nearly equal to what it was in 1955.

1965

The United Farm Workers is formed and begins striking against California vineyards and growers of table grapes. A nationwide boycott of California grapes begins.

1970

U.S. postal workers hold a two-week work stoppage.

Twenty-six growers sign contracts with the United Farm Workers.

1971

Hoffa resigns as IBT president.

1975

More than 2 percent of public employees participate in 428 strikes.

Members of Local 231 of the Michigan Federation of Teachers walk a picket line in downtown Detroit in September 1967. *(Walter P. Reuther Library, Wayne State University)*

1977

The employees of 20 states may now join unions and bargain collectively.

1977–80

The federal government deregulates the airline and trucking industries.

1979

Nearly 40 percent of public-sector workers belong to unions.

1983

The break-up of AT&T gives rise to smaller telephone corporations such as MCI and Sprint, which are antiunion in philosophy.

1995

John Sweeney is elected president of the AFL-CIO.

1999

Membership in the AFL-CIO totals slightly more than 13 million.

Unions represent less than 10 percent of workers in the private sector.

EYEWITNESS TESTIMONY

When an employer contracts with the union labor leaders he immediately drives all of his employees into the unions. Otherwise, they can not get employment. That is a part of the reason for trying to organize the men, and that is why we have been such an obstruction. I am not antagonizing unions, I am not saying that they have not a perfect right to form unions, of course they have; but we are not obliged to contract with them if we do not choose to do so; and we think, because of many things that have happened—and some of them are happening today—that unionism is not a good thing for the employer or employee today, either one. . . .

Elbert H. Gary testifying before the Senate Committee on Education and Labor, 1919, in Colston E. Warne, ed., The Steel Strike of 1919, *p. 35.*

Was the steel strike . . . worth the great suffering and expenditure of effort that it cost the steel workers? I say yes; even though it failed to accomplish the immediate objects it had in view. No strike is ever wholly lost. Even the least effective of them serve the most useful purpose of checking the employers' exploitation. They are a protection to the workers' standards of life. Better by far a losing fight than none at all. An unresisting working class would soon find itself on a rice diet. But the steel strike has done more than serve merely as a warning that the limit of exploitation has been reached; it has given the steel workers a confidence in their ability to organize and to fight effectively, which will eventually inspire them on to victory. This precious result alone is well worth all the hardships the strike cost them.

William Z. Foster, 1920, The Great Steel Strike and Its Lessons, *p. 233.*

If a workman desires to join a labor union he is, of course, at liberty to do so, and in that case he should not be discriminated against by an "open shop" so long as he respects the rights of his employer and his co-employes and in every way conforms to the laws of the land. The "open shop," as heretofore publicly defined is what we believe in and stand for.

But still, our opinion is that the existence and conduct of labor unions, in this country at least, are inimical to the best interests of the employes, the employers and the general public. It has been claimed

that a large number of the leaders, including the most influential, are foreign born.

Elbert H. Gary speaking at the annual meeting of stockholders, United States Steel, April 18, 1921, in Colston E. Warne, ed., The Steel Strike of 1919, *p. 28.*

The hour has arrived when Labor can be free, free to organize. Congress has established your legal right to organize. Workers everywhere should avail themselves of the opportunity thus presented.

The National Industrial Recovery Act will mean much to you and your families if you organize into bona fide trade unions. It will mean little if you fail to do so.

In the name of Organized Labor I appeal to all classes of workers to act quickly, to organize immediately, to realize all the benefits and rights to which you are entitled through organization under the provisions of the National Industrial Recovery Act.

William Green, June 1933, "Labor's Opportunity and Responsibility," p. 694.

The automobile manufacturers' labor policy is this: The industry must not be unionized, and to keep the unions from gaining a foothold, we must take every precaution and spare no expense. Among the experienced automotive workers living in Detroit and the vicinity, only those have been and are being rehired whom the plant employment managers know to be "safe," or who can secure personal O.K.'s from prominent citizens in Detroit, such as well-known judges and commanders of American Legion posts. Workers known to be inclined, however slightly, toward unionism or radicalism are almost generally taboo in the production department, whether on relief or not. Those hired are watched by stool pigeons, who in some plants go so far as to search the men's overcoat pockets for possible radical literature. . . .

In recent months, with production increasing, it has been necessary for the companies to bring in tens of thousands of people from outside, principally from the South, and put them to work in the busy plants. . . . The majority of them are young fellows. They have had no close contact with modern industry or with labor unionism—this, of course, is their best qualification. Their number in Detroit is variously estimated at between fifteen and thirty thousand, with more of them coming weekly. . . . They are employed at simple, standardized tasks in production departments, for which very little or no training is necessary, at 45 or 50 cents an hour, except in Ford's, where the wages are slightly higher. These workers are happy to receive this pay and are much "safer"—for the next few months, anyhow, while big production is on—than local labor, poisoned by ideas of unionism and perhaps even more dangerous notions.

Louis Adamic, February 13, 1935, "The Hill-Billies Come to Detroit," p. 177.

Let him who will, be he economic tyrant or sordid mercenary, pit his strength against this mighty upsurge of human sentiment now being crystallized in the hearts of thirty millions of workers who clamor for the establishment of industrial democracy and for participation in its tangible fruits. He is a madman or a fool who believes that this river of human sentiment, flowing as it does from the hearts of these thirty millions, who with their dependents constitute two-thirds of the population of the United States of America, can be dammed or impounded by the erection of arbitrary barriers of restraint.

John L. Lewis, July 6, 1936, in Mary Heaton Vorse, Labor's New Millions, p. 285.

The wages paid its common unskilled workers is a good test of the liberality of an industry's wage policy. Put to this test the steel industry makes an extremely bad showing. This is made clear by the fact that the steel industry, with hourly earnings of 47.9 cents in March, 1936, ranks no higher than fourteenth, and in the matter of weekly earnings, with $16.77 occupies twentieth place out of the possible list of 21 industries for which returns are given by the National Industrial Conference Board. . . .

On the other hand, the profits of the industry have been relatively as enormous as its wage payments have been small. Greater payments have not been made to wage and salary workers because the large monopoly earnings realized have been used to pay dividends on fictitious capital stock, to add physical values in the way of plant extensions, and to multiply the machines that displace human labor.

John L. Lewis, July 6, 1936, "Industrial Democracy in Steel," in Howard Zinn, ed., New Deal Thought, *p. 208.*

Organized labor in America accepts the challenge of the omnipresent overlords of steel to fight for the prize of economic freedom and industrial democracy. The issue involves the security of every man or woman who works for a living by hand or by brain. The issue cuts across every major economic, social and political problem now pressing with incalculable weight upon the 130 millions of people of this nation. It is an issue of whether the working population of this country shall have a voice in determining their destiny or whether they shall serve as indentured servants for a financial and economic dictatorship which would shamelessly exploit our natural resources and debase the soul and destroy the pride of a free people. On such an issue there can be no compromise for labor or for a thoughtful citizenship.

John L. Lewis, July 6, 1936, "Industrial Democracy in Steel," in Howard Zinn, ed., New Deal Thought, *p. 210.*

The Flint sit-down strikes became the focus. Those were splendid boys in those plants. Nothing would have gotten them out except troops. They were all set to lick any army of vigilantes and police that Flint could muster. They were set to lick anybody except cannons and bayonets. They developed their own defensive measures and invented weapons of protection. Not only did they have fire hose laid out at all the windows. But they had worked out means for using steam in some of them.

Not only that. They found in the paint room a large quantity of drums of some kind of an inflammable oil used in painting cars. They rolled these drums around to windows at all sides of the plant strategically chosen to command all spaces in front and at the sides where vigilante gangs could be mustered. They attached hose to these steel drums and hand pumps. By experimentation they found they could spray this oil out the window to cover an area of some 150 feet. They were all set to spray that area with oil and then they had wads of waste ready to light and throw down until they could have ringed the factory with a wall of fire, which they could have kept feeding by pumping out oil.

John L. Lewis recalling events of 1936 and 1937, in Sidney Fine, ed., "John L. Lewis Discusses the General Motors Sit-Down Strike," p. 567.

The sitdown is the most effective form of strike. It permits the strikers to remain in comfort, even if somewhat bored, instead of trampling about on the

Sit-down strikers occupy Fisher Body Plant 3, Flint, Michigan, 1937. *(Library of Congress)*

picket line in heat, cold, wind, and wet. It obviates the most unpleasant and demoralizing feature of a strike, the use of strike-breakers. It eliminates violence, or at least places responsibility for it squarely on the police. It promotes the morale of the strikers. Above all it is a forcible reminder to workers, to management, to shareholders, and to the public that legal title is not the final answer to the question of possession. Who has the better human and natural right to call the Fisher plant his—I, whose connection with General Motors is determined by the price recorded on the New York Stock Exchange, or the worker whose life and livelihood are bound up in the operation of making cars? I bought my shares at long odds and probably have already collected the purchase price in dividends. When I place a winning bet in a horse race I do not claim a share in ownership of the horse. I know from my political economy that my position is the result of labor and sacrifice. Whose? Not mine. Obviously the enormous mass of wealth represented by the capitalization of General Motors, repeatedly enlarged by split-ups and stock dividends, is the surplus resulting from the toil of millions of workers over many years. Obviously they have not shared fairly in the wealth they have produced.

> *Robert Morss Lovett, January 30, 1937,*
> *"A G.M. Stockholder Visits Flint," in Howard Zinn, ed.,*
> New Deal Thought, *p. 216.*

I know of but one method to insure safety for the future—labor must become articulate. The millions of workers must express themselves through the medium of organization of their industries or callings. The workers must be made economically free, in order to assure them the maximum of opportunity to champion and defend the elemental principles of human liberty. It was for this purpose that the Committee for Industrial Organization was formed and it is toward this end that we are struggling.

> *John L. Lewis, circa 1937, in Mary Heaton Vorse,*
> Labor's New Millions, *p. 284.*

To see and hear ten thousand union men and women on guard and picket duty—to be a part and feel the spirit of many thousands, all battling together for a better life, is an exciting, overwhelming feeling that probably comes to each person but once.

I thought, "Let General Motors come out to Fisher 1 and look at this picket line—500 women and thousands of men—and dare deny the strength and numbers of the union."

> *Eleanor Gustafson, striking General Motors worker, 1937,*
> *in Mary Heaton Vorse,* Labor's New Millions, *p. 85.*

Inside Fisher 2 Bob Travis stood on a chair and told the terms of peace to the Fisher 2 boys. Here were the boys who had been on the front of the battle line. They were young but they had the tempered and matured faces which a long fight gives. Here they had sat for 44 days and nights. Suspense had been heavy and long drawn out in Fisher No. 2. Here they had created a disciplined world of their own. Here they had risked their lives as the bullet holes through the windows on the second floor still tell. They had won their first battle, for everyone of these shock troops of unionism knew that the battle for the union was only the beginning.

> *Mary Heaton Vorse reporting in the* United Automobile
> Worker, *February 13, 1937, in Albert Fried, ed.,*
> Except to Walk Free, *p. 242.*

I went to the meeting, and they decided to make a picket line at the front of the company. . . . I went out with the rest of them and started to walk over to the plant. I was about one hundred yards behind the head of the line when the uproar began. They were like trapped rats, panic-stricken, terrified.

I saw a woman fall as she was being clubbed by the policemen. She was bleeding and looked like she was dying. I ran over to help her and leaned down to pick her up, when the police hit me over the head. I was out after that.

Joseph Hickey, a striker injured outside Republic Steel's South Chicago Plant, quoted in the New York Times, *June 1, 1937, in Louis B. Snyder and Richard B. Morris, eds.,* A Treasury of Great Reporting, *p. 519.*

Women, children, men, were running and falling and screaming like madmen. I turned and ran, too, but when I went just a few feet a bullet hit me in the arm. Some motorist picked me up and took me to the hospital.

Peter Mrkonjich, a striker injured outside Republic Steel's South Chicago Plant, quoted in the Chicago Daily News, *June 1, 1937, in Louis B. Snyder and Richard B. Morris, eds.,* A Treasury of Great Reporting, *p. 519.*

[The National Guard] drug me out of my car by the feet and injured my back. One of the National Guards told the other to take my glasses off of me and he will smash my face. When he tried to take my glasses off, I bit his fingers. Then he let me have my glasses.

They stole my watch off my wrist and hid it in their pocket, the wrist-band was broken and fell on the ground. I reached in his pocket and got my watch. . . .

Is this Fascist Italy or Germany, or is it America, where we are supposed to have Democracy?

Mrs. Fred King, CIO typist, describing her experience in Canton, Ohio, after martial law was declared in the Little Steel Strike, July 7, 1937, in Mary Heaton Vorse, Labor's New Millions, *pp. 150–51.*

This movement of labor will go on until the purchasing power of the American people is restored; until we have the means to buy and consume the products of American industry.

This movement of labor will go on until there is a more equitable and just distribution of our national wealth.

This movement will go on until the social order is reconstructed on a basis that will be fair, decent, and honest.

This movement will go on until the guarantees of the Declaration of Independence and of the Constitution are enjoyed by all the people, and not by a privileged few.

Let us hail then, the coming of this new day in the life of labor. Let us resolve in the spirit of our forefathers to do our part in building the foundation upon which we can erect a real superstructure of industrial democracy and social security.

To this end we can all dedicate ourselves to unselfish service in the cause of progress and humanity.

John L. Lewis, Labor Day, 1937, in Mary Heaton Vorse, Labor's New Millions, *p. 295.*

The Republic Steel Corporation deliberately and with open defiance violated practically every provision of the National Labor Relations Act. Their employees who joined with the Steel Workers Organizing Committee—merely becoming members of a labor organization—were summarily discharged. Charges have been filed with several regional directors of the Labor Relations Board for hundreds of such employees—left without any means of livelihood because Tom Girdler didn't believe that the acts of Congress could possibly include him or his organization.

Philip Murray testifying before the U.S. Senate, 1937, in E. David Cronon, ed., Labor and the New Deal, *p. 46.*

. . . [D]o not let anyone tell you that we went in there to steal anyone's union at . . . any of those plants, because there were no unions there. We were invited in there by the employees of those corporations. Do you think it would be possible for my organization to go into the city of Youngstown if there was a strong, independent union there functioning well, and influence those men to come over in large numbers into my union if they were satisfied with their own situation and had a good union there? I could not do that. No union could do it. You have got to give these men working in these mills the kind of a union they want, and I cannot give them any other kind of a union, and nobody else can push any other kind of a union down their throats. And we have given them that kind of union.

Philip Murray testifying before the U.S. Senate, 1937, in E. David Cronon, ed., Labor and the New Deal, *p. 48.*

. . . [T]he fundamental issue in this strike is not one involving wages, hours, or working conditions in Republic plants. This is not a strike in the sense that a large body of our employees quit work because of grievances against the company. What has happened is that an invading army descended upon our plants and forced many of our employees from their jobs.

Fully 23,000 of our employees have remained at work throughout the strike despite threats and violence and many additional thousands have been kept from work against their will.

The basic issue of this strike is the right of American citizens to work free from molestation, violence, coercion, and intimidation by a labor organization whose apparent policy is either to rule or to ruin American industry.

Tom Girdler testifying before the U.S. Senate, 1937, in
E. David Cronon, ed., Labor and the New Deal, *p. 49.*

We are interested in industrial stability, and have striven to advance it whenever the opportunity offered. It is to the interest of the legitimate hat manufacturers not to encourage competition based upon substandard labor conditions or starvation wages or long hours. They must realize, as we have long since discovered, that where the meanest employer is permitted to set the pace, a pace which the others, under our system of competition, must either follow or retire from the race, they themselves will sooner or later find that they cannot remain in the industry and produce hats at a profit.

General Executive Board of the United Hatters,
Cap and Millinery Workers, 1939, in Charles H. Green,
The Headwear Workers, *pp. 244–45.*

A trade union is a voluntary association of free men held together by common loyalties, common objectives, common hopes, common aspirations and common ideals. How does a voluntary association of free men function? It draws its strength from the basic loyalty of the people who make up its membership, and its strength grows out of the fact that because of that basic loyalty they also have the kind of discipline that free men must exercise on a voluntary basis if they are going to exist and work together as free men. . . .

The Communist minority in our organization [the CIO], like the disciplined Communist majority throughout the world, wants the rights and privileges without the obligations and responsibilities, and we are saying here and now that those people who claim the rights and privileges must also be prepared to accept the responsibilities and the obligations.

There is room in our movement for an honest difference of opinion. Sincere opposition is a healthy thing in the labor movement. But there is a fundamental difference between honest opposition and sincere difference of opinion and the kind of obstructionism and sabotage carried on by the Communist minority, because the Communist minority is a trade union opposition group who disagree with C.I.O. policies, because they believe that there are other policies that ought to take the place of our current policies. They are not a trade union group.

Walter Reuther, 1949, in Albert Fried, ed.,
Except to Walk Free, *pp. 282–83.*

During the three and one-half years since the enactment of the Taft-Hartley Act I have talked to many labor audiences and discussed their problems with hundreds of union members. I have yet to find anyone who can point to a specific case in which the law has resulted in any unfair treatment of a labor union. In spite of the difficulties which any comprehensive statute of this kind develops in practice, I think it can be said that it has worked well and introduced a new tone of justice and fair dealing which did not previously exist.

Robert A. Taft, March 1951, "The Taft-Hartley Act:
A Favorable View," p. 195.

The Taft-Hartley Act expressly recognizes not merely the right of employees to join labor unions and participate in group activities, but also a corresponding right to refrain from doing so if they choose. To protect this right the law forbids a labor organization to coerce individual employees into signing up with a union or joining a strike being conducted by a union. Such coercion frequently takes the form of mass picketing by large numbers of union members who, by abusive language, threats, and frequently actual violence, compel employees to stay out of a plant, although by trying to continue work they have indicated their desire to have no part in the strike. If our national labor laws are to assure genuine freedom of employees to choose whether they will join an organization and what form they will join, then laws obviously should prohibit all coercion, and not merely coercion from one source—employers.

Robert A. Taft, March 1951, "The Taft-Hartley Act:
A Favorable View," pp. 195–96.

While professing to "balance the scales" between unions and employers, the authors of the [Taft-Hartley Act] added the weight of the government to the advantage already enjoyed by the antiunion employer and gave him new power, without responsibility. While claiming an intent to make unions more "responsible," they stripped unions of their necessary powers, without which responsibility is meaningless. Under the guise of protecting the rights of the individual worker, they exalted the strikebreaker into a position of special privilege, and deprived union members of their basic rights. Under the pretense of correcting its "abuses," they frustrated collective bargaining, substituted governmental fiat, and withheld union recognition from millions of workers who suffer for the lack of it.

Such pious hypocrisy is the chief attribute of the Taft-Hartley Act itself, and of the apologetics of its proponents. This may be good politics, but no sincere person could mistake it for good government.

William Green, March 1951, "The Taft-Hartley Act:
A Critical View," p. 201.

There is need today for more organization and more collective bargaining—not less. In many areas of the country labor unions still operate in an intensely hostile environment. The proportion of the labor force that belongs to trade unions is still smaller in the United States than in most other industrial countries. Far from being too powerful, labor organization in America is not yet strong enough to perform the task that is required of it.

The Taft-Hartley Act does violence to all of the sound and tested principles which have in the past provided the basis for harmonious relations between labor and management. Labor fervently hopes that this act will be repealed before it can do further injury to the legitimate interests of either party.

William Green, March 1951, "The Taft-Hartley Act:
A Critical View," p. 205.

Under the Taft-Hartley Act—but not under the Wagner Act—the employer is placed in a position to covertly threaten and coerce his employees not to join the union.

Under the Taft-Hartley Act—but not under the Wagner Act—a limit has been placed on how frequently representation elections may be held....

Under the Taft-Hartley Act—but not under the Wagner Act—every legal certification as the collective-bargaining agent requires a long drawn-out formal election.

Under the Taft-Hartley Act—but not under the Wagner Act—full legal protection of collective-bargaining rights is available to a union only when the Federal Government—through its National Labor Relations Board—grants a license or certificate to a union.

George Meany, November 6, 1953,
in "What Labor Wants," p. 62.

It's not my idea to build a great big union just for the sake of having a great big union. That doesn't mean a thing to me.

I want labor peace, and I feel that the best way to get labor peace is to get the people who would normally belong in one federation—and, after all, they all came from one federation originally—to get them back into the one federation. Because with all its faults the federation idea has worked.

We've made a lot of mistakes, and we will make a lot more, but taking the over-all picture we have brought to the American worker a greater share of that which he produces than any other worker on earth gets. We don't think that came about because some captains of industry sat down in a board room and decided it would be good for that to happen.

George Meany on the possible joining of the AFL and
CIO, November 6, 1953, in "What Labor Wants," p. 56.

We thought we knew a few things about trade union corruption, but we didn't know the half of it, one-tenth of it, or the one-hundredth part of it. We didn't know, for instance, that we had unions where a criminal record was almost a prerequisite to holding office under the national union. We didn't know that we had top trade union leaders who made it a practice to secretly borrow the funds of their union. We didn't know that there were top trade union leaders who used the funds for phony real estate deals in which the victims of the fraud were their own members. And we didn't know that there were trade union leaders who charged to the union treasury such items as speed boats, perfume, silk stockings, brassieres, color TV, refrigerators, and every thing else under the sun. We didn't know about those things.

George Meany, 1957, in Joseph C. Goulden,
Meany, p. 261.

Never before in the history of the Congress . . . has any investigation drawn the cascades of mail that descended upon the members of the Select Committee and upon the staff. . . .

These were the subjects that cropped up day after day in thousands upon thousands of letters: fear, threats, undemocratic procedures, rigged elections, disappearances of union funds, assessments for political purposes without consultation of the rank and file, discrimination by reason of race, creed, or color, "sweetheart" contracts that callously sold the membership down the river, kickbacks, Communism, domination by known racketeers, locals placed in trusteeship (often unjustly and for the sole purpose of protecting the national leaders' positions of power) for periods of one to twenty years. In one instance an Operating Engineers local was in trusteeship for thirty years! The letters cried out about violence and intimidation, bombings, graft paid to public officials, withholding of union books and membership cards, featherbedding, coercion upon small businessmen to join unions under threat of violence, failure to audit union books for periods ranging from one year to a quarter-century, no meeting notices, no meetings, boycotts, goon tactics, self-perpetuating dictatorships, shakedowns, paper locals, vandalism.

Finally, there were hundreds of communications which charged to union officials the crimes of murder, arson, dynamiting, larceny, embezzlement, fraud, assault, and extortion, as well as almost every other felony contained in the statute books.

John L. McClellan remembering the Senate investigation of corruption in organized labor in 1957 and 1958, Crime without Punishment, *pp. 71–72.*

At birth, it is a Teamster who drives the ambulance to the hospital. At death, a Teamster who drives the

James R. Hoffa (center table, right) testifies before the Senate committee investigating corruption in organized labor, August 1957. *(Library of Congress)*

hearse to the grave. Between birth and death, it is the Teamsters who drive the trucks that bring you your meat, milk, clothing and drugs, pick up your garbage and perform many other essential services.

The individual truck driver is honest, and so are the vast majority of local Teamster officials—but they are completely under the control and domination of certain corrupt officials at the top. Picture this power, then, and the chaos that could result if these officials were to gain control also over sea and other transportation outlets. Such a force could conceivably cause anyone—management and labor alike—to capitulate to its every whim. . . .

With Hoffa at the controls of the union that will dominate the transportation alliance, *this power would certainly be in the wrong hands.*

> *Robert F. Kennedy, 1958, in C. David Heymann,*
> RFK, *pp. 133–34.*

We are the transportation of America, and we control because raw materials must be transported in and finished products must be transported out.

> *James Hoffa, circa 1958, in C. David Heymann,*
> RFK, *p. 134.*

For more that 10 years I worked for the CSO [Community Service Organization]. As the organization grew, we found ourselves meeting in fancier and fancier motels and holding expensive conventions. Doctors, lawyers and politicians began joining. They would get elected to some office in the organization and then, for all practical purposes, leave. . . . When I became general director I began to press for a program to organize farm workers into a union, an idea most of the leadership opposed. So I started a revolt within the CSO. I refused to sit at the head table at meetings, refused to wear a suit and tie, and finally I even refused to shave and cut my hair. It used to embarrass some of the professionals. At every meeting

I got up and gave my standard speech: we shouldn't meet in fancy motels, we were getting away from the people, farm workers had to be organized. But nothing happened. In March of '62 I resigned and came to Delano [California] to begin organizing the Valley on my own.

> *Cesar Chavez recalling his work with the Community*
> *Service Organization in the 1950s and 1960s,*
> *"The Organizer's Tale," in Staughton Lynd,*
> *ed.,* American Labor Radicalism, *p. 141.*

There are vivid memories from my childhood—what we had to go through because of low wages and the conditions, basically because there was no union. I suppose if I wanted to be fair I could say that I'm trying to settle a personal score. I could dramatize it by saying that I want to bring social justice to the farm workers. But the truth is that I went through a lot of hell, and a lot of people did. If we can even the score a little for the workers then we are doing something. Besides, I don't know any other work I like to do better than this. I really don't, you know.

> *Cesar Chavez, July 1966, "The Organizer's Tale,"*
> *in Staughton Lynd, ed.,* American Labor
> Radicalism, *pp. 146–47.*

The clear demarcation between private and public sectors is gone. With some exception, it has vanished beneath a maze of overlapping functions, parallel efforts, incredibly complex relationships. Traditional distinctions between labor-management relations in the private and public sectors have become irrelevant. One cannot argue logically about the uniqueness of public service when confronted with public bus drivers in New York City and private bus drivers in Washington, D.C., performing identical services.

> *Jerry Wurf, president of the American Federation of State,*
> *County and Municipal Employees (AFSCME), 1969,*
> *in Joseph A. Beirne,* A Challenge to Labor, *p. 149.*

12 African Americans Seek Equality in the Workplace
1865–1996

Organized labor's long battle with the leaders of industry improved job conditions for millions of U.S. workers, but not for all. Throughout most of the history of the American labor movement, unions excluded African Americans from their ranks, forcing them to engage in a separate struggle, to overcome formidable obstacles on their own. Like their white counterparts, black laborers have fought for decent wages, a shorter workweek, and other benefits. But they have also combatted the racism that so often kept them out of occupations for which they were qualified. They have campaigned long and hard for union representation.

THE SITUATION AFTER THE CIVIL WAR

When enslaved African Americans gained their freedom following the Civil War, southern growers sought to preserve the plantation system to the extent possible, with former slaves supplying cheap labor and remaining in a subordinate social position. State legislatures throughout the South passed Black Codes, which were laws restricting the activities of African Americans. The laws determined where African Americans could buy or rent property and when they could be on the streets. They imposed strong penalties for vagrancy, to force blacks into accepting low wages. Black workers could face arrest and stiff fines if they quit their jobs.

Wages for African Americans in the South ranged from $9 to $15 per month for a man and from $5 to $10 per month for a woman. But even if they received food, shelter, and fuel from their employers as well, most African Americans in the Reconstruction South earned less than the amount that had been paid for the hiring-out of an enslaved worker. Former slaves who had been trained as artisans in the antebellum period also dealt with opposition and occasional violence from white craftspeople who feared competition.

Most of the newly free people had been agricultural workers before the war, and with opportunities severely limited, they continued to do the work that they knew best. In 1880, 75 percent of African Americans lived in the

African-American women picking cotton in the 1920s, much as their forebears did under slavery *(National Archives)*

former Confederate states. Few managed to put together enough capital to buy land, so most were sharecroppers.

Despite the hardship, many people managed to hold onto a dream of a better existence. In 1879, when the visionary Benjamin "Pap" Singleton of Tennessee talked of building self-sufficient black towns in Kansas, thousands followed him there. Hoping to turn their backs on squalor and a dead-end existence, African Americans founded settlements in Kansas, California, Oklahoma, and other places, but most of these utopias failed.

BOOKER T. WASHINGTON AND VOCATIONAL TRAINING

In 1881, a teacher and former slave named Booker T. Washington organized a school in Tuskegee, Alabama, to train members of his race in trades that would make them useful to society. Students at Tuskegee received instruction in carpentry, domestic work, machinery repair, mattress making, and other lines of work. In 1892, Washington held the first in a series of farmers' conferences at the institute, to instruct African-American farmers in financial management and modern agricultural practices. Washington believed that racial discrimination could only be eliminated gradually, that the establishment of a skilled African-American working class would lead in time to complete integration and acceptance.

Many African Americans viewed Washington's approach as a viable route to financial security. His thinking appealed to whites, too, because he advocated social separation and a lower economic status for blacks. With white approval, Washington became the spokesperson for millions of African Americans.

His ideas did not go unchallenged, though. The noted intellectual W. E. B. Du Bois resented Washington's capitulation to white interests and saw in his

The Creamery Division, Tuskegee Institute *(Library of Congress)*

training method a formula for permanent lower-class status. Pointing out that even vocational schools needed well-trained teachers, Du Bois called for the education of the "Talented Tenth"—the brightest segment of the African-American population—to become the leaders of the black community and examples for others to emulate.

Critics such as the poet Paul Laurence Dunbar found fault with Washington for failing to take the needs and aspirations of individuals into account. Recalling his own school years, Dunbar said that as a young man with literary ambitions he would have been miserable if condemned to training in manual labor. It must be kept in mind, however, that at a time when factory-made goods were replacing the wares of skilled artisans, Washington's strategy was applicable at best only to a fraction of the African-American community.

Labor Unions Discriminate against Blacks

A few 19th-century labor unions welcomed African Americans, but most barred them from membership. Many whites refused to work alongside blacks or insisted that blacks were incapable of mastering skills, although there was plenty of evidence to the contrary. Lewis H. Douglass, a son of Frederick Douglass, is a notable example of someone who ran up against the discriminatory policy of a labor union. He was denied membership in the Columbia Typographical Union of Washington, D.C., although he had mastered the printing trade as a child in his father's newspaper office.

Exclusion from labor unions meant being denied the benefits gained for workers through the efforts of organized labor. It also meant exclusion from apprenticeship programs in many cases, and African Americans who were unable to get training could not work at skilled trades even outside the framework of the labor movement.

In 1867, a committee within the National Labor Union (NLU), a Baltimore-based coalition representing 60,000 workers, issued a report calling for unity between black and white laborers. When the report brought no noticeable change in the policies of member unions, a group of African-American delegates pressured the organization at its 1869 convention to adopt a resolution in favor of the formation of separate unions for blacks, to be affiliated with the NLU. But again no action was taken, and NLU leadership remained silent on the issue of including African Americans.

The Colored National Labor Union (CNLU) was formed in 1869 in Washington, D.C., to protest the exclusion of African Americans from the mainstream labor movement. This organization of independent state and local unions elected prominent African Americans, including Frederick Douglass and Henry Highland Garnet, to positions of leadership. Although the CNLU existed only until 1874, it encouraged African-American workers to form their own labor federations at the state level.

The Knights of Labor was unique among 19th-century labor organizations in its willingness to admit African Americans, and by 1886 60,000 African Americans belonged to its assemblies. (The order consistently excluded Chinese workers, however.) In Virginia, half of the order's 10,000 to 15,000 members were black, and black female laundry, domestic, and tobacco workers made up several local assemblies.

But African Americans became disenchanted with the Knights of Labor in November 1886, when the national organization failed to aid striking sugar workers. The Louisiana sugar workers, most of whom were black and members of the Knights of Labor, were earning about 40 cents a day when they struck for higher wages. The local sugar growers' association responded to the strike swiftly and violently. Workers were routed from their cabins and clubbed, and two lynchings occurred. Militia forces fired on the strikers, killing four. When the leaders of the Knights of Labor refused to get involved, the strike lost its

The Chesapeake Marine Rail Way and Dry Dock Company of Maryland was one of the most prosperous businesses owned by African Americans in the 19th century. *(Maryland Historical Society, Baltimore, Maryland)*

momentum, and the defeated workers returned to the sugar fields. In 1894, the Knights of Labor announced that the only solution to the race problem in the United States would be to transport the African-American population to Africa, using federal funds.

Many African Americans were admitted to the United Mine Workers when that union was established in 1890. The UMW inherited much of its early membership from the Knights of Labor, and African Americans had been mining coal in the South since before the Civil War. They accounted for half of the miners working near Birmingham, Alabama, in the late 19th century. The UMW constitution prohibited discrimination based on race, creed, or nationality, and by 1902 it claimed more than 20,000 black members.

African Americans were also included in unionization efforts in industries where they formed a large percentage of the workforce. Because whites found dock work undesirable, most of the longshoremen in southern coastal ports were black. The longshoremen's union therefore counted a significant number of African Americans among its members. Similarly, blacks accounted for approximately half of all workers in the yellow-pine industry of Louisiana and Texas. In 1912 their union, the Brotherhood of Timber Workers, had a membership of 20,000, half of whom had been organized into separate "colored lodges."

Samuel Gompers urged the unions in the American Federation of Labor to create separate locals for African Americans in the 1880s and 1890s. The AFL barred from membership any union that excluded blacks completely, and in 1890, the National Association of Machinists was denied affiliation with the AFL because its membership was restricted to whites. By 1900, however, the AFL was no longer enforcing the rule against restrictions.

THE GREAT MIGRATION

In the first decades of the 20th century, nearly 1.5 million African Americans left the rural South to seek a better life in northern cities. In this massive relocation of people, known as the Great Migration, the African-American population almost doubled in the Northeast and increased by 60 percent in the North Central states.

People had good reasons to leave the South. Tenant farming, always a difficult way to scrape out a living, became even harder when an infestation of boll weevils destroyed the cotton crop in 1915 and 1916. Flooding in the summer of 1915 added to the hardship as well.

In the 1890s, southern states had succeeded in disenfranchising African Americans. Legislatures passed laws requiring the paying of poll taxes, the ownership of property, and the passing of biased literacy tests for individuals registering to vote, which put poor and poorly educated African Americans at a disadvantage. In 1898, Louisiana lawmakers added a "grandfather clause" to the state constitution. This provision limited eligible voters to men whose fathers and grandfathers had been qualified to vote in 1867. Of course, no African Americans had been qualified to vote in that year.

Eliminating black voters cleared the way for southern whites to enact the infamous "Jim Crow laws," which essentially created a distinct social structure for African Americans within the larger community. These laws required blacks to use separate public facilities, such as schools, restaurants, waiting rooms, and railroad cars. The U.S. Supreme Court sanctioned this practice in 1896 in the case of *Plessy v. Ferguson*. The court ruled that maintaining "separate" facilities was legal as long as those facilities were "equal." Jim Crowism prevailed, and in fact the services provided for blacks were decidedly inferior.

The North promised jobs in industry and greater freedom. At the same time that northern factories were operating at full capacity to supply the forces of World War I with weaponry, tanks, uniforms, and other equipment, their principal source of labor, immigration from Europe, had stopped. Crossing the ocean in wartime was simply too dangerous. Also, many white male laborers had left their jobs to join the fight overseas. (More than 20,000 African Americans also served in Europe during World War I.)

People vacated the fields and small towns of the Southeast, the Mississippi Delta, Texas, and Arkansas. Some were persuaded to leave by recruiters who offered free transportation and promised high wages. Others paid their own train fare. African-American professionals left the South as well, following the population that they served. The impact in the North of the Great Migration was enormous. Chicago's African-American population increased 148.2 percent between 1910 and 1920; the number of African Americans in New York City rose 63 percent during the same period. Philadelphia, St. Louis, Indianapolis, and other cities also experienced significant increases in their African-American populations. African Americans stepping off trains in Northern cities hoped to fill vacant jobs. They also sought an escape from lynchings and biased courts and to have the opportunity to vote and to live and trade wherever they pleased.

Equality eluded African Americans in the North much as it had in the South. They were hired to work in ammunition factories, meat packinghouses, and iron and steel mills, but most often at low-level jobs. In Illinois and other places, factory employees were assigned to work areas, lunchrooms, and restrooms according to race. The housing available to blacks in northern cities was expensive and substandard, and businesses that depended on white patronage denied them service. The only opportunity that many blacks had to work in industries that excluded them was as strikebreakers, or scabs. Some employers transported African-American strikebreakers to northern cities from the South.

The rapidly changing racial balance precipitated violence in some places. One of the worst race riots of the 20th century took place in East St. Louis, Illinois, in 1917. At least 40 people were killed, including a two-year-old child, who was shot to death. Hundreds more were injured in the confrontation, which had its roots in a labor dispute that had occurred the year before. At that time, a packinghouse owner had hired black strikebreakers as permanent replacements for 2,500 white workers who had staged a walkout.

Competition for jobs was a motivating factor for some of the riots that erupted in Washington, D.C., Chicago, and other U.S. cities and towns during the "Red Summer" of 1919. In Chicago, the July 27 drowning of a black boy who had been stoned by whites while swimming in Lake Michigan touched off several days of fighting. Thirty-eight people died, 537 were injured, and 1,000 were left homeless. In Chicago, as in East St. Louis, anger over earlier labor actions had been simmering. For example, in 1894, blacks hired to replace striking white workers at a Chicago slaughterhouse had been kept on the payroll and admitted to a new union that was formed. In 1904, striking white meatpackers saw themselves swiftly replaced by 10,000 impoverished black scabs.

A massacre took place in the rural community of Elaine, Arkansas, after African-American sharecroppers formed a union to protect their rights. The farmers had waited until July 1919 to receive payment for their 1918 crop, only to get half of what they were due. A courageous few banded together to form the Progressive Farmers and Household Union of America, which soon had lodges in seven counties. The union organized an effort to withhold the cotton harvest from landlords until farmers received adequate and timely compensation. But the growers used violence to snuff out the union and silence its demands. At least 100 blacks, as well as several whites, were killed in Elaine, and several sharecroppers served long prison sentences for their role in the protest.

In May 1920, A. Philip Randolph and Chandler Owen, two Harlem socialists who published a radical weekly called *The Messenger,* formed the Friends of Negro Freedom to educate working blacks about political and labor issues. The organization sponsored lectures in Harlem by such persons as Walter White of the NAACP and Norman Thomas, the outspoken socialist, but by 1924 it was defunct. The American Negro Labor Congress (ANLC), a group with communist leanings, held its first meeting in Chicago in October 1925. The ANLC sought to unite all African-American and interracial labor organizations and to promote integration in the larger labor movement. It too did not last.

The most important black labor organization to emerge in the 1920s was the Brotherhood of Sleeping Car Porters (BSCP), founded in 1925 and headed by A. Philip Randolph. The African-American porters employed by the Pullman Company to serve rail passengers earned $67.50 per month in 1925, on average, for 300 to 400 hours of work—significantly less than whites with comparable jobs. The porters, who were frequently away from home due to the nature of their work, were required to pay for their own meals and hotel rooms while traveling. It was impossible for a porter to find a better job with a competing firm, because the Pullman Company had a monopoly on railway sleeping cars.

Randolph, who had never been a Pullman porter, accepted the presidency of the BSCP because he saw helping the porters as a way to improve opportunities for all African Americans. He carried on a 12-year struggle to force the Pullman Company to recognize the union and to agree to a contract guaranteeing better pay and working conditions for the porters. The BSCP was admitted to the AFL in 1929, although it was denied full membership status because it lacked adequate funds. The BSCP and the Pullman Company signed a contract on August 25, 1937—for the first time, a major U.S. company had entered into an agreement with a union of black workers.

AFRICAN-AMERICANS WEATHER THE DEPRESSION

The Great Depression began sooner and was more severe for blacks than for the larger white population. By the stock market crash of October 1929, 20 percent of African-American factory workers had already lost their jobs. The National Urban League determined in 1931 that the proportion of unemployed was 30 percent to 60 percent higher among blacks in many cities than among whites. Nationwide, the percentage of unemployed African Americans was four to six times as high as the percentage of African Americans in the overall population. Black workers were often the first to be fired when a business suffered a reverse, and many were let go so that needy whites could have their jobs. In 1935, Atlanta officials reported that 65 percent of all able-bodied African-American adults in their city needed public assistance. In St. Louis, where African Americans made up 9 percent of the population, they accounted for 60 percent of relief cases. Relief was distributed unequally as well: charity soup kitchens in the North and South commonly denied service to blacks.

Some New Deal programs benefited African Americans. For example, although the Civilian Conservation Corps was strictly segregated, 200,000 blacks worked in CCC camps between 1933 and 1942. Ten percent of participants in the National Youth Administration's student program were black, as were 13 percent in NYA out-of-school programs. One million African Americans gained employment on WPA projects, although the program's racial policy varied from one region to another. The artist Jacob Lawrence was employed by the WPA, as were the writers Claude McKay, Zora Neale Hurston, Richard Wright, and Ralph Ellison. In addition, the Public Works Administration Housing Division required that specific percentages of skilled craft workers on PWA construction projects be African American.

Other New Deal measures were more beneficial to whites than to blacks. The National Industrial Recovery Act set a lower minimum wage in industries employing large numbers of African Americans, such as tobacco and steel, than in other industries, causing blacks in Memphis, Tennessee, to call the legislation the "Negro Removal Act." In addition, the provisions of the Agricultural Adjustment Act, which in theory applied equally to all farmers, permitted southern white landlords to keep money that was intended for their black tenants. The Fair Labor Standards Act of 1938 excluded agricultural and domestic workers, a group that included several million African Americans.

Many labor unions became more exclusionary during the depression in order to protect the jobs of white workers. A. Philip Randolph and his associate Milton Webster repeatedly introduced resolutions at the annual convention of the AFL to have the word "white" removed from union constitutions and to require member unions to admit blacks, but the motions were dismissed. It was this discrimination on the part of organized labor that prevented most African-American workers from enjoying the benefits of Section 7(a) of the National Industrial Recovery Act.

The CIO, however, actively organized all workers, regardless of race. CIO leaders, including John L. Lewis, recognized that if their efforts in steel and other heavy industries were to be successful, African Americans had to be included. (Approximately 85,000 steel workers were black in 1936.) The CIO also placed some African Americans in leadership positions. For these reasons, the CIO secured the endorsement of the National Negro Congress (NNC), which was founded in 1936 to address the problems of African Americans. The NNC, and Randolph as its first president, viewed the unionization of black workers as one of its most pressing concerns. Randolph resigned from the presidency of the NNC in 1940, because communists were contributing substantially to its financial support and had come to dominate its agenda. Many members followed Randolph's lead and withdrew, and the NNC fell apart.

The NNC was not the only organization formed by African Americans to help themselves financially during the depression. Others included the Colored Merchants Association, which opened stores in New York and gave blacks the opportunity to buy merchandise collectively at reduced prices; the St. Louis–based Jobs-for-Negroes movement, which encouraged people to boycott stores in black neighborhoods that employed only whites; and the Citizens League for Fair Play, which pressured white-owned businesses in New York to hire blacks with the slogan, "Don't Buy Where You Can't Work." The effort in New York resulted in hundreds of jobs for African Americans in stores and with public utilities.

Tenant farmers hoping to improve their situation had nowhere to turn for help. In the summer of 1934, 18 sharecroppers, blacks and whites, met in a one-room school in Arkansas to form the Southern Tenant Farmers' Union (STFU). The organization grew rapidly, gaining 10,000 members in one year. The STFU endeavored to bring the plight of tenant farmers to the nation's attention. In January 1939, the union gathered 1,700 homeless sharecroppers and their families in a camp along Highway 61 in Missouri. For nearly a week, the families congregated around roadside campfires for warmth and showed passing motorists and visiting reporters how they were obliged to live. They were forced to evacuate their camps after the governor of Missouri declared the site a health hazard, but they had drawn attention to their desperate circumstances. Infighting weakened and finally destroyed the STFU, as its leaders argued over whether to join the CIO and ignored the sharecroppers they had pledged to represent.

GAINS DURING WORLD WAR II

As U.S. industries geared up for war production in the late 1930s, African Americans were among the many thousands seeking jobs in defense plants. Industry needed a large workforce in order to supply Great Britain with armaments to use against Germany. Companies such as North American Aviation, Inc., were building new plants, while others, including General Motors, were converting existing facilities to wartime production. Black workers soon discovered, though, that defense plants were unwilling to hire them, and unions remained opposed to granting them membership on an equal basis with whites. Some corporations brought in white workers from distant rural areas rather than hire blacks already living nearby.

A. Philip Randolph was of the opinion that only by putting pressure on the federal government could African Americans secure for themselves the same opportunities that were open to white workers. He therefore issued a statement to the press on January 15, 1941, announcing plans for a march of 10,000 African Americans in Washington, D.C., to demand jobs in the defense industries and an end to segregation in the U.S. armed forces. He formed a March on Washington Committee, which included such prominent people as Walter White, Dr. Rayford Logan of Howard University, and the Reverend Adam Clayton Powell of the Abyssinian Baptist Church in New York City. The movement was popular with the black population, and by spring Randolph was boasting that 100,000 marchers would arrive in Washington for the July 1 demonstration.

Franklin D. Roosevelt and his advisers were alarmed at the thought of so many African Americans needing food and shelter in the segregated capital and asked Randolph to call off the protest. Even First Lady Eleanor Roosevelt, who normally supported efforts to achieve racial equality, thought the march would be a mistake. She feared that if violence broke out in Washington, the cause of civil rights would be set back rather than advanced.

On June 25, 1941, six days before the scheduled march, Roosevelt issued Executive Order 8802, requiring the defense industries to hire workers without regard for race, creed, color, or national origin. He also formed the Fair Employment Practices Committee (FEPC) to investigate complaints of discrimination and to redress grievances. The president had not integrated the armed forces, but Randolph was satisfied enough to call off the march.

By March 1942, African Americans accounted for nearly 3 percent of war-production workers. By late 1944, they accounted for 8.3 percent. In January 1945, 25 percent of the labor force in foundries, 11.7 percent in shipyards, and 11.8 percent in blast furnaces and steel mills was black. But discrimination continued. Companies still failed to make use of the skills black workers brought to the workplace, hiring them for the lowest-level jobs regardless of ability. Employers argued that their objective was production, not social reform. Craft unions such as the International Brotherhood of Boilermakers continued to admit African Americans only to segregated auxiliaries. In 1942, the National Urban League reported that 19 international unions—10 of them affiliated with the AFL—practiced overt racial discrimination. The volume of complaints was too great for the FEPC to handle.

White employees who objected to working beside blacks responded to government-mandated integration with "hate strikes" in some cities. One such incident occurred in Philadelphia in 1944, after the FEPC ordered the city's transport system to hire African-American operators. The strike that took place when the blacks showed up for work was so disruptive that the governor requested army intervention. There were incidents of violence in such places as Beaufort, Texas, where white shipyard employees dropped hot rivets on newly hired black coworkers.

THE POSTWAR YEARS

Most of the gains achieved by African-American workers between 1942 and 1945 were lost when industry reconverted to peacetime production. Because blacks had been among the last workers to be hired by defense plants, many were among the first fired. Also, blacks represented a large percentage of the unskilled workforce, which was the group most affected by postwar layoffs. A 1946 FEPC report stated that the rate of unemployment was higher among blacks than among whites in six of seven war-production centers surveyed.

African Americans from the South continued to relocate to northern cities after the war as the mechanical cotton picker and other new equipment reduced the need for agricultural laborers. They joined a population of northern blacks who were struggling to keep their jobs at a time when the demand for unskilled labor in industry was declining. Also, as manufacturers followed the fleeing white population to outlying suburbs, the expense of transportation became an additional barrier against employment for black city residents. Many people living in inner-city ghettoes found themselves trapped in poverty and unemployment.

Domestic service was the principal occupation of African-American women, giving employment to 782,520, or 40 percent of the black female workforce, in 1950. The number of black women working in clothing factories increased 350 percent in the 1940s, making the garment industry the third-largest industrial employer of African-American women in the United States, outranked only by laundries and dry-cleaning establishments.

African Americans enlarged their opportunities in military and government service during this period. In 1948, responding to pressure from A. Philip Randolph, President Harry S. Truman issued two executive orders that created opportunities for African Americans. The first called for an end to segregation in the U.S. military, and the second mandated fair employment in the federal government.

Equal representation in organized labor remained elusive, however. The AFL, at its 1946 convention, voted to abolish segregated local chapters. Two African Americans, Randolph and Willard Townsend of the United Transport Service Employees, were elected in 1955 to the AFL-CIO's 29-member Executive Council. All member unions but three had deleted the exclusionary clauses from their constitutions by this time, but racial discrimination persisted in organized labor and in industry. Beginning in 1959, Randolph introduced a resolution at the yearly AFL-CIO conventions calling for the organization's Civil Rights Department to investigate the extent of discrimination in member unions and to institute strong punitive measures against any union refusing to alter its practices. The resolution repeatedly failed to pass, and Randolph's recurrent introduction of it led to his censure in 1961.

Herbert Hill, labor secretary of the NAACP, reported in 1960 that many AFL-CIO unions continued to restrict African Americans to segregated locals and that black workers in the steel and auto industries were largely confined to unskilled jobs. Estimates of the percentage of African-American wage earners categorized as unskilled in 1960 range from 50 percent to 84 percent. Approximately 30 percent of African Americans lived below the poverty line, and black unemployment was rising, although the nation as a whole enjoyed prosperity.

Because economic advancement was viewed as a way to gain social equality, the need for jobs and improved working conditions for African Americans was a force that drove the civil rights movement of the 1960s. In 1962, the Southern Christian leadership Conference (SCLC), under the direction of its president, the Reverend Martin Luther King, Jr., launched Operation Breadbasket to promote the employment of black workers and the establishment of black-owned businesses. The hiring of black salespeople by downtown department stores was one of the demands made by the SCLC in Birmingham, Alabama, in 1963.

The Negro American Labor Council, which was founded in 1960 with Randolph as president, organized the historic March on Washington of August 28, 1963, to draw attention to unemployment and low wages in the black community. At the time the march was held, the unemployment rate for blacks was 114 percent higher than it was for whites. The average black family earned

$3,500 a year in 1963, while the average white family earned $6,500. More than 40,000 representatives of organized labor took part in the march, and two nationally known labor leaders, Randolph and Walter Reuther, were on the leadership committee. The efforts of Randolph, King, and their followers helped to secure passage of the 1964 Civil Rights Act, of which Title VII outlawed discrimination in hiring. The act also established the Equal Employment Opportunity Commission (EEOC) to enforce its provisions.

More needed to be done, though. In the months prior to his death in April 1968, King was helping striking garbage collectors in Memphis to secure a living wage and recognition for their union. The Reverend Ralph Abernathy, who assumed the SCLC presidency following King's death, continued the campaign to aid black workers by leading demonstrations of striking hospital employees in Charleston, South Carolina, in 1969. He succeeded in bringing together the workers and representatives of the municipal government, which employed them. The two groups reached a settlement that included a raise in pay and recognition of the union as the workers' bargaining agent.

In 1971, the Reverend Jesse Jackson, who had headed Operation Breadbasket in Chicago, founded Operation PUSH (People United to Serve Humanity) to effect economic change. Jackson secured commitments from the Coca-Cola Company, Kentucky Fried Chicken, Anheuser-Busch, Burger King, and other large corporations to hire more African Americans and to conduct a larger percentage of their business in minority communities.

AFFIRMATIVE-ACTION PLANS

The federal government had begun to take a more active approach to integrating the workplace in 1969, when the U.S. Department of Labor issued guidelines for the employment of minority workers on federally assisted construction projects. Under these provisions, contractors on projects exceeding $500,000 in cost were required to hire specific numbers or percentages of minority workers. Similar "affirmative action" policies soon governed hiring, promotions, and school admissions in the public and private sectors, as well as the awarding of government contracts. The objectives of affirmative action generally were threefold: to overcome bias in hiring and promotion, to open career opportunities to minority applicants who might have been denied the economic and educational advantages that had benefited white applicants, and to remedy past discrimination.

From the 1970s through the present, the American people and the judicial system have worked to define fair and legal affirmative action. Blacks and whites alike have questioned not only whether it is in a worker's best interest to receive preferential treatment but also whether success on one's own merit is possible for most minority men and women in the United States.

The impact of affirmative action on white workers has been controversial as well. In 1978, in deciding the case *Regents of the University of California v. Bakke,* the U.S. Supreme Court upheld a decision of the California Supreme Court that Allan Bakke be admitted to the medical school at the University of California at Davis. Bakke, who had twice been denied admission to the school while minority applicants with lower test scores were accepted, had charged that the school's admission policy was unconstitutional.

The court's decision in the Bakke case offered no guidance for schools, government agencies, or corporations regarding admissions and hiring, but later decisions have provided clarification. In 1984, the court ruled that a valid, established seniority system supercedes the need to maintain racial quotas in times of workforce cutbacks. In three separate decisions in 1986 and 1987, the court stated that affirmative-action plans could be used to remedy past discrimination even if the people hired were not the best-qualified candidates.

Many people have concluded that affirmative action has accomplished its aims and is no longer necessary. A 1995 survey conducted by the *Washington Post,* the Kaiser Family Foundation, and Harvard University found that approximately half of whites in the United States thought that most blacks held jobs comparable to those held by whites, and that 12 percent considered blacks to be better off financially than whites. In 1996, such misperceptions helped persuade California voters to approve a civil rights initiative known popularly as Proposition 209, which outlawed public policies that considered race or gender in education, hiring, and the awarding of contracts.

More African Americans are employed as physicians, lawyers, architects, and engineers than in the past, but in every field, black professionals earn less than whites do. The inequity extends to workers in all categories, and the economic situation for African Americans is deteriorating. A study by the Ford Foundation and the Rural Economic Policy Program of the Aspen Institute has found that 40 percent of black workers were earning poverty-level wages in 1987, compared to 33 percent of black workers in 1979. (A family of four with an annual income of $12,000 was classified as poor in 1987.) In addition, the number of employed black men living below the poverty line was up 161 percent. Also, although 407,000 college-educated black women entered the labor pool between 1979 and 1987, the number earning $36,000 or more declined by 10,000. The researchers attributed these changes to declines in the manufacturing sector in the early 1980s and cutbacks in government jobs that had affected blacks to a greater degree than whites. The battle for racial equality in the workplace therefore continues.

CHRONICLE OF EVENTS

1865
November 24: Mississippi enacts the first Black Codes in the South, forbidding African Americans to serve on juries, testify against whites, bear arms, or hold meetings. Unemployed blacks can be arrested.

1867
A committee of the National Labor Union (NLU) calls for unity between black and white workers.

1869
December 12: The Colored National Labor Union (CNLU) is formed in Washington, D.C., to improve working conditions for African Americans; the NLU adopts a resolution in favor of separate unions for blacks.

1874
The CNLU ceases to function.

1879
Benjamin "Pap" Singleton brings African-American settlers to Kansas.

1880
Three-fourths of African Americans live in the former Confederate states; most are sharecroppers.

1881
Booker T. Washington founds the Tuskegee Institute in Alabama to provide vocational training to blacks.

1886
Sixty thousand African Americans belong to the Knights of Labor.

November: Sugar workers strike in Louisiana; Knights of Labor leadership refuses to assist them.

1890
The United Mine Workers (UMW) is established and extends membership to African Americans.

Mississippi is the first southern state to place restrictions on voting, including a poll tax and literacy test.

1892
Booker T. Washington holds the first of several farmers' conferences at the Tuskegee Institute.

1894
The Knights of Labor calls for the deportation of American blacks to Africa.

African-American strikebreakers are kept on the payroll at a Chicago slaughterhouse and admitted to a union.

1896
May 18: In deciding the case *Plessy v. Ferguson,* the U.S. Supreme Court upholds the constitutionality of "separate but equal" public facilities.

1898
Louisiana limits voting to those men whose fathers and grandfathers were qualified to vote in 1867.

1902
More than 20,000 African Americans belong to the UMW.

1904
Ten thousand African Americans are hired to replace strikers at a Chicago meatpacking plant.

1915
Flooding and an infestation of boll weevils create hardship for southern farmers.

1916–40
Nearly 1.5 million African Americans migrate from the South to urban communities in the North. History remembers this mass movement of people as the Great Migration.

1917
July 1–3: At least 40 people die in rioting in East St. Louis, Illinois.

1919
July 27: The drowning death of a boy who is stoned from the shore of Lake Michigan touches off a race riot that leaves 38 people dead and 537 injured.

Racial violence also occurs in Washington, D.C.; Elaine, Arkansas; and other cities and towns.

1920
May: A. Philip Randolph and Chandler Owen form the Friends of Negro Freedom to educate African Americans about socialism and labor issues; the organization is active until 1924.

1925

August 25: The Brotherhood of Sleeping Car Porters (BSCP) is formed in Harlem with A. Philip Randolph as president.

October: The short-lived American Negro Labor Congress holds its first meeting in Chicago.

1929

Twenty percent of African-American factory workers are unemployed prior to the stock-market crash.

The BSCP is admitted to the American Federation of Labor (AFL).

1931

The proportion of unemployed workers is 30 percent to 60 percent higher among blacks than among whites, according to the National Urban League.

1933–42

Approximately 200,000 African Americans work in Civilian Conservation Corps (CCC) camps.

1934

Arkansas sharecroppers form the Southern Tenant Farmers' Union (STFU).

1935

Sixty-five percent of able-bodied African-American adults in Atlanta require public assistance; African Americans account for 60 percent of relief cases in St. Louis.

1936

About 85,000 steel workers are black.

February 14: The National Negro Congress (NNC) holds its first meeting; A. Philip Randolph presides.

1937

August 25: The Pullman Company becomes the first major U.S. corporation to sign a contract with a union of black workers when it reaches an agreement with the BSCP.

1939

January: The STFU organizes a week-long protest against poverty conditions by sharecroppers along Highway 61 in Missouri.

1940

Randolph resigns from the NNC because of communist infiltration of the group.

1941

January 15: Randolph threatens to lead a march of 10,000 African Americans in Washington, D.C., unless President Roosevelt issues an executive order halting discriminatory hiring in defense plants; by spring, Randolph estimates that 100,000 marchers will come to Washington on July 1.

June 25: Roosevelt issues Executive Order 8802, requiring defense industries to hire workers without regard for race, creed, color, or national origin. He forms the Fair Employment Practices Committee (FEPC) to handle grievances.

1942

March: African Americans account for nearly 3 percent of war-production workers.

Nineteen international unions practice overt discrimination, according to the National Urban League.

A hate strike erupts in Philadelphia when the FEPC orders the hiring of African-American transport operators.

1944

By late in the year, 8.3 percent of defense workers are black.

1945

January: Black workers make up 25 percent of the workforce in foundries, 11.7 percent in shipbuilding, and 11.8 percent in blast furnaces.

1946

The FEPC reports that unemployment is higher among blacks than among whites in six of seven war-production centers surveyed.

The AFL votes to abolish segregated auxiliary unions.

1948

July 26: President Harry S. Truman signs Executive Order 9981, calling for an end to military segregation.

1950

Domestic work is the principal occupation of African-American women.

1955

A. Philip Randolph and Willard Townsend are elected to the AFL-CIO executive council.

1959

Randolph introduces a resolution at the AFL-CIO convention calling for an investigation of discrimination in member unions.

1960

Herbert Hill of the NAACP reports that many AFL-CIO unions as well as the steel and auto industries continue to practice discrimination.

Randolph founds the Negro American Labor Council.

1961

Randolph is censored at the AFL-CIO convention for his continued outspokenness on discriminatory practices.

1962

The Reverend Martin Luther King, Jr., and his organization, the Southern Christian Leadership Conference (SCLC), launch Operation Breadbasket to promote black employment and black business ownership.

1963

April–May: The SCLC leads civil rights demonstrations in Birmingham, Alabama, in part to demand the hiring of black salespeople in downtown stores.

August 28: Approximately 250,000 people attend the March on Washington to publicize the need for jobs and opportunities for African Americans. The average black family earns $3,500 a year; the average white family earns $6,500 a year.

1964

President Lyndon B. Johnson signs civil rights legislation that outlaws discrimination in hiring.

Organized labor was a highly visible presence at the 1963 March on Washington for Jobs and Freedom. *(Walter P. Reuther Library, Wayne State University)*

1968

March 28: The Reverend Martin Luther King, Jr., marches with striking sanitation workers in Memphis, Tennessee.

April 4: King is assassinated outside his Memphis motel room.

1969

April: The Reverend Ralph Abernathy leads demonstrations of striking hospital workers in Charleston, South Carolina.

The U.S. Department of Labor issues guidelines for the hiring of minorities on federally assisted construction projects.

1971

The Reverend Jesse Jackson founds Operation PUSH to improve economic conditions for African Americans.

1978

June 28: In the case *Regents of the University of California v. Bakke,* the U.S. Supreme Court rules that schools cannot apply rigid admissions quotas that ignore academic qualifications, although they may consider race in granting admission.

1986

March and July: The Supreme Court decides in two cases that employment preferences based on race, color, or gender may be used to rectify past discrimination.

1987

In deciding the case *Johnson v. Transportation Agency, Santa Clara County, California,* the Supreme Court rules that women and minorities may be hired even if they are not the best-qualified candidates.

1996

November 4: California voters approve Proposition 209, outlawing public policies that consider race or gender in hiring, promotion, school admissions, and the awarding of contracts.

EYEWITNESS TESTIMONY

I do not inveigh against higher education; I simply maintain that the sort of education the colored people of the South stand most in need of is *elementary and industrial*. They should be instructed for the work to be done. . . . Men may be spoiled by education, even as they are spoiled by illiteracy. Education is the preparation for a future work; hence men should be educated with special reference to that work.

If left to themselves men usually select intuitively the course of preparation best suited to their tastes and capacities. But the colored youth of the South have been allured and seduced from their natural inclination by the premiums placed upon theological, classical and professional training for the purpose of sustaining the reputation and continuance of "colleges" and their professorships.

I do not hesitate to say that if the vast sums of money already expended and now being spent in the equipment and maintenance of colleges and universities for the so called "higher education" of colored youth had been expended in the establishment and maintenance of primary schools and schools of applied science, the race would have profited vastly more than it has, both mentally and materially, while the results would have operated far more advantageously to the State, and satisfactorily to the munificent benefactors.

T. Thomas Fortune, 1884, Black and White, *pp. 81–82.*

. . . [A]ny work looking towards the permanent improvement of the Negro South must have for one of its aims the fitting of him to live friendly and peaceably with his white neighbors both socially and politically. In spite of all talks of exodus, the Negro's home is permanently in the South: for coming to the bread-and-meat side of the question, the white man needs the Negro, and the Negro needs the white man. His home being permanently in the South, it is our duty to help him prepare himself to live there an independent, educated citizen.

Booker T. Washington, "The Educational Outlook in the South," July 16, 1884, in The Booker T. Washington Papers, *vol. 2, pp. 257–58.*

Many southerners are losing considerable sleep just at this time, worrying over the organization of Knights of Labor assemblies among their colored employees. They know such action means a fight for decent wages and treatment, in which the organized blacks of the South will be supported by thousands of Knights of Labor Assemblies in the North and the enormous amount of money at their command.

Cleveland Gazette, December 25, 1886, in Sidney H. Kessler, "The Organization of Negroes in the Knights of Labor," p. 266.

It is high time that the negro race in America was asserting itself, and not looking for legislation through any party that now exists. The noble Order of the Knights of Labor teaches equal privileges to all, special favors to none, as in our local assemblies women are on equality with men; there is no discrimination on account of race or sex. I believe the Knights of Labor have a mission here on earth, and monopoly will not be able to down the Order until that mission has been fulfilled. Just as the abolitionists agitated against human slavery, so the Knights of Labor will agitate against wage-slavery. We as men and women come in competition with white men and women. We must do our share as we receive some of the benefits of their labor. We hear a great deal about the race problem. . . . Let all colored men and women join the Order of the Knights of Labor where as men and women we will get some semblance of justice and recognition.

W. E. Turner, member of the Knights of Labor from Chicago, March 5, 1891, in Sidney H. Kessler, "The Organization of Negroes in the Knights of Labor," pp. 274–75.

While we admit that our labor organizations are our best friends, it would be well to teach some of our white brothers that a man is a man no matter what the color of his skin may be. We have nothing but the best of words to say for labor organizations, and hope they may continue in the same line of actions, and we are confident that they will not only better the conditions of the working class, but will also wipe out all class and race distinctions, and in the meantime the Negro will be found as loyal to labor organizations as his white brother. It has been said that the Negro as a union man was a failure, but we are inclined to think that those words were uttered more from a prejudiced mind than as a truthful statement. Let us hope for better days for organized labor with the Negro in the ranks doing his share in the way of emancipating labor.

R. L. Davis, United Mine Workers' Journal, *May 25, 1893, in Philip S. Foner and Ronald L. Lewis, eds.,* Black Workers, *pp. 268–69.*

Does the A.F. of L. compel its affiliated organizations to accept colored workmen? I answer no! Decidedly not. No more than it compels organizations to accept Americans, Frenchmen, Englishmen, Irishmen, or even Hottentots.

What the American Federation of Labor declares by its policy, [is] that organization should not declare *against* accepting the colored man *because he is colored.* . . .

If a man or set of men array themselves for any cause against the interests of the workers their organizations have the right to say that their membership is barred. It should be at the wrong-doer against labor, it should not be a nationality or a race against whom the doors are barred.

Samuel Gompers in Locomotive Firemen's Magazine, *July 1896, in Bernard Mandel, "Samuel Gompers and the Negro Workers," p. 39.*

It may well be asked by one who has not carefully considered the matter: "What has become of all those skilled farm-hands that used to be on the old plantations? Where are those wonderful cooks we hear about, where those exquisitely trained house servants, those cabinet makers, and the jacks-of-all-trades that were the pride of the South?" This is easily answered,—they are mostly dead. The survivors are too old to work. "But did they not train their children?" is the natural question. Alas! the answer is "no." Their skill was so commonplace to them, and to their former masters, that neither thought of it as being a hard-earned or desirable accomplishment: it was natural, like breathing. Their children would have it as a matter of course. What their children needed was education. So they went out into the world, the ambitious ones, and got education, and forgot the necessity of the ordinary training to live.

Booker T. Washington, 1899, The Future of the American Negro, *pp. 52–53.*

The practical exclusion of the Negro from the trades and industries of a great city like Philadelphia is a situation by no means easy to explain. It is often said simply: the foreigners and trades unions have crowded Negroes out on account of race prejudice and left employers and philanthropists helpless in the matter. This is not strictly true. What the trades unions and white workmen have done is to seize an economic advantage plainly offered them. This opportunity arose from three causes: Here was a mass of black workmen of whom very few were by previous training fitted to become the mechanics and artisans of a new industrial development; here, too, were an increasing mass of foreigners and native Americans who were unusually well fitted to take part in the new industries; finally, most people were willing and many eager that Negroes should be kept as menial servants rather than develop into industrial factors. This was the situation, and here was the opportunity for the white workmen; they were by previous training better workmen on the average than Negroes; they were stronger numerically and the result was that every new industrial enterprise started in the city took white workmen. Soon the white workmen were strong enough to go a step further than this and practically prohibit Negroes from entering trades under any circumstances; this affected not only new enterprises, but also old trades like carpentering, masonry, plastering and the like. The supply of Negroes for such trades could not keep pace with the extraordinary growth of the city and a large number of white workmen entered the field. They immediately combined against Negroes primarily to raise wages; the standard of living of the Negroes lets them accept low wages, and, conversely, long necessity of accepting the meagre wages offered have made a low standard of living. Thus partially by taking advantage of race prejudice, partially by greater economic efficiency and partially by the endeavor to maintain and raise wages, white workmen have not only monopolized the new industrial opportunities of an age which has transformed Philadelphia from a colonial town to a world-city, but have also been enabled to take from the Negro workman the opportunities he already enjoyed in certain lines of work.

W. E. B. Du Bois, 1899, The Philadelphia Negro, *pp. 126–27.*

As bad as slavery was, almost every large plantation in the South during that time was, in a measure, an industrial school. It had its farming department, its blacksmith, wheelwright, brickmaking, carpentry, and sewing departments. Thus at the close of the war our people were in possession of all the common and skilled labor in the South. For nearly twenty years after the war we overlooked the value of the antebellum training, and no one was trained to replace these skilled men and women who were soon to pass away; and now, as skilled laborers from foreign countries, with not only educated hands but trained brains, begin to come into the South and take these positions once held by us, we are gradually waking up to the fact that we must compete with the white man in the industrial world if we would hold our own.

Booker T. Washington, 1900, "Signs of Progress among the Negroes," in Philip S. Foner and Ronald L. Lewis, eds., Black Workers, *p. 278.*

The black men of America have a duty to perform, a duty stern and delicate,—a forward movement to oppose a part of the work of their greatest leader. So far as Mr. Washington preaches Thrift, Patience, and Industrial Training for the masses, we must hold up his hands and strive with him, rejoicing in his honors and glorying in the strength of this Joshua called of God and of man to lead the headless host. But so far as Mr. Washington apologizes for injustice, North or South, does not rightly value the privilege and duty of voting, belittles the emasculating effects of caste distinctions, and opposes the higher training and ambition of our brighter minds,—so far as he, the South, or the Nation, does this,—we must unceasingly and firmly oppose them.

W. E. B. Du Bois, 1903, The Souls of Black Folk, *in* W. E. B. Du Bois: Writings, *p. 404.*

A certain proportion of the white people of the United States are determined that a man with a black skin must be ever and always a hewer of wood or drawer of water. His brain may have the genius of a Dumas or a Frederick Douglass, but if in its veins flows a trace of black blood he is condemned to occupations that stunt and dwarf his mentality.

North and south alike this condition exists. If the problem seems more acute in the old slave states it is only because its proportions are more commanding. The spirit which condemns the black man to his own restricted sphere, industrially as well as socially, exists quite as much among the whites north as south of Mason and Dixon's line.

Florida Labor Journal, *July 24, 1903, in Julius Jacobson, ed.,* The Negro and the American Labor Movement, *pp. 122–23.*

I was born March 15, 1909. My father was a roofer. In those days they put slates on the roofs and he was a slater. It was a very skilled job. You had to nail the slate. They used to make a fancy diamond with different colors. Every time the white guys got ready to do this they sent him for the bucket of beer so that he wouldn't learn it. But when they got ready to send him for the beer, he would find something wrong. He didn't know where his hammer was or he had to get something before he went, and in the meantime he would be watching. He learned it and he could do it beautifully. He'd say, "I'm the best. I stole it from those bastards but I'm the best." He became so good he didn't have to work with contractors any more. He could go out on his own.

And he was a union man. There was a dual union—one for whites and one for blacks. He said we should have one big union but a white and a black is better than none. He was making big money—eight dollars a day. I used to brag that "My father makes eight dollars a day." But he taught me that "You got to belong to the union, even if it's a black union. If I wasn't in the union I wouldn't make eight dollars a day."

Sylvia Woods, social activist, describing her father's experiences as a roofer and union member, circa 1909, in Alice Lynd and Staughton Lynd, eds., Rank and File, *p. 105.*

One of the first and most surprising things the country boy learns in the city is that work is not always to be had; that it is something a man has to go out and look for. Another thing he very soon learns is that there is a great deal of difference between skilled and unskilled labor, and that the man who has learned to do some one thing well, no matter how small it may be, is looked upon with a certain respect, whether he has a white skin or a black skin; while the man who has never learned to do anything well simply does not count in the industrial world.

Booker T. Washington, June 1913, "The Negro and the Labor Unions," p. 756.

If a thousand whites work at a place,
Each one there is my "boss."

An African-American plantation worker at the time of the Great Migration, in Negro Migration in 1916–1917, *p. 105.*

The Negro exodus is the most serious economic matter that confronts the people of Mississippi today. . . . We may as well face the facts, even when the facts are very ugly and very much against us. The plain truth of the matter is the white people of Mississippi are not giving the Negro a square deal. And this applies not merely to Mississippi, but to all the other States in the South. How can we expect to hold our Negro labor when we are not paying decent living wages? Have we any right to abuse the Negro for moving to the northern States, where he is tempted by high wages, when we are not paying him his worth at home? If you, Mr. White Man, believed that you could greatly benefit your financial condition by moving to some other section of the country, would you lose any time in doing so? * * * And that is just what the Negro is doing.

Editorial in the Daily News, *Jackson, Mississippi, in* Negro Migration in 1916–1917, *pp. 111–12.*

Everybody seems to be asleep about what is going on right under our noses—that is, everybody but those farmers who waked up on mornings recently to find every Negro over 21 on their places gone—to Cleveland, to Pittsburgh, to Chicago, to Indianapolis. Better jobs, better treatment, higher pay—the bait held out is being swallowed by thousands of them about us. And while our very solvency is being sucked from underneath us we go about our affairs as usual—our police raid pool rooms for "loafing Negroes," bring in 12, keep them in the barracks all night, and next morning find that 10 of them have steady jobs and were there merely to spend an hour in the only indoor recreation they have; our county officers hear of a disturbance at a Negro resort and bring in fifty-odd men, women, boys, and girls to spend the night in jail, to make a bond at 10 per cent, to hire lawyers, to mortgage half of two months' wages to get back their jobs Monday morning, although but a half-dozen could have been guilty of the disorderly conduct. It was a week following that several Macon employers found good Negroes, men trained in their work, secure and respected in their jobs, valuable assets to their white employers, had suddenly gone and left for Cleveland. . . .

Editorial in the Macon Telegraph, *in* Negro Migration in 1916–1917, *p. 106.*

At Uniontown, Ala., the president of the Planters' and Merchants' Bank told of a 2,000-acre plantation near by that had only two or three Negro families left on

it. Other plantations in this section were in more or less the same condition. The whole southwestern portion of Alabama has been hard hit by the exodus; and particularly have suffered the large plantations that are owned by absentee landlords, whose agents usually had no authority to care for the suffering tenants after the destruction caused by the boll weevil and the floods. Similar conditions are to be seen in northern and eastern Mississippi. For the region about Meridian, the chamber of commerce reported that the acreage cultivated had been reduced. At Oklona an officer of the First National Bank said many thousands of acres formerly cultivated thereabout were now lying idle. The editor of the Oklona Messenger, many colored business men, farmers, and tenants confirmed the banker's report. Some farms hereabout are turning to dairying; but, as the editor pointed out, they will need many laborers even for that work. He felt, too, that there was little likelihood that cotton growing would be materially lessened for any great length of time. So the loss of labor was keenly felt in any event. He did not blame the Negroes for leaving. Many whites, he reported, had gone for the same reasons—boll weevils and floods, with the chance to better their condition.

W. T. B. Williams, "The Negro Exodus from the South," in Negro Migration in 1916–1917, *p. 99.*

The exodus is carrying off in considerable numbers not only the common laborers from the farms and industries of the South but also many of the skilled Negro mechanics from the larger cities, like New Orleans, Montgomery, Birmingham, Savannah, and Charleston; many of the trained workers with less skill; and even Negro business men, ministers, and physicians. For example, in several sections I found cotton-oil-mill men in doubt as to whether they would be able to find enough of their trained hands to operate the mills to advantage when they planned to begin work. A certain Negro medical college publishes a striking list of its graduates who have recently moved from the South to the North. Five out of one class are reported to have gone to Chicago. I know personally of several colored physicians with fine practices and good standing in southern cities who have pulled up within the last 18 months and gone North.

W. T. B. Williams, "The Negro Exodus from the South," in Negro Migration in 1916–1917, *p. 95.*

[African Americans] are being engaged in many lines of industry, especially in the steel and allied industries, where large numbers from the southern iron districts are finding work in which they are already skilled. The demand is so great that notices of jobs for wages ranging from $3.00 to $6.00 a day are frequently read in the colored churches of northern cities. The opinion regarding Negro labor is constantly rising, and many employers are testifying that it is as good as any they ever had. And so the Negro has this chance, the first in his history, to get his hand upon the thing by which men live, to become for the first time a real factor in the world of labor. He has at last come into what is rightfully his own, the opportunity that has heretofore been denied him and given to the stranger.

But the Negro comes up against a problem he has never had to face before, and that is union labor. In the North, in almost every field the unions shut him out, and he finds himself in the position of an independent or a scab. Many colored men skilled in their trades have had to turn to common labor because they were not allowed to join the unions.

James Weldon Johnson, 1918, in Philip S. Foner and Ronald L. Lewis, eds., Black Workers, *p. 353.*

It is practically impossible for any colored man or woman to become a boiler maker or book binder, an electrical worker or glass maker, a worker in jewelry or leather, a machinist or metal polisher, a paper maker or piano builder, a plumber or a potter, a printer or a pressman, a telegrapher or a railway trackman, an electrotyper or stove mounter, a textile worker or tile layer, a trunk maker, upholsterer, carpenter, locomotive engineer, switchman, stone cutter, baker, blacksmith, boot and shoemaker, tailor, or any of a dozen other important well-paid employments, without encountering the open determination and unscrupulous opposition of the whole united labor movement of America. That further than this, if he should want to become a painter, mason, carpenter, plasterer, brickmaker or fireman he would be subject to humiliating discriminations by his fellow Union workers and be deprived of work at every possible opportunity, even in defiance of their own Union laws. If, braving this outrageous attitude of the Unions, he succeeds in some small establishment or at some exceptional time at gaining employment, he must be labeled as a "scab" throughout the length and breadth of the land and written down as one who, for

his selfish advantage, seeks to overthrow the labor uplift of a century.

The recent convention of the American Federation of Labor, at Buffalo, is no proof of change of heart. Grudgingly, unwillingly, almost insultingly, this Federation yields to us inch by inch the status of half-a-man, denying and withholding every privilege it dares at all times.

W. E. B. Du Bois, March 1918, "The Black Man and the Unions," p. 217.

I have always said that my family came down the agricultural ladder. My father was a tenant farmer who owned his team and farming tools. My grandfather owned his own farm and lived near Halls, Tennessee. He was also a Baptist preacher. From the time I was 8 years old I worked for wages on the farm. I worked for 50 cents per day upwards. I made my first sharecrop about 1919.

H. L. Mitchell, cofounder of the Southern Tenant Farmers' Union (STFU), recounting his family's employment history through 1919, in Marc S. Miller, ed., Working Lives, *p. 126.*

We arrived at Lambert, Mississippi, at 9:15 p.m. While the engine was being supplied with water, the flagman, Mr. Shields, and I were looking the train over, beginning at the caboose and proceeding toward the engine. When I reached a point of about 40 car lengths, I was suddenly stopped by three white men, who had passed the flagman, Mr. Shields, and did not interfere with him, but halted me demanding that I throw up my hands at the point of pistols.

They snatched my lantern and threw it away, and had me to march across the field about a mile. They asked me didn't I know that they didn't want any Negroes braking on the head end of those trains. One of them wanted to beat me up, but the other two insisted he not do it, "because he is a good old Negro, I know him," is what one of them said. They warned me not to come through there. After being closely questioned and threatened with violence, they finally turned me loose.

Bob Grant, African-American railroad brakeman, describing an incident of February 15, 1921, in Sterling D. Spero and Abram L. Harris, The Black Worker, *p. 298.*

When the black man was introduced into the industrial equation it was deemed the privilege of any white man to exploit him for his economic advantage. This traditional conceit still survives. The Negro is yet regarded as an industrial tool, the surplus fruitage of whose labor should inure to the advantage of some white overlord. Just as capital feels that God ordained its prerogative to exploit labor as an agency to swell its own profit, so the white man, rich or poor, regards the Negro as the appointed instrument for his own aggrandizement. If there were no surplus productivity, capital would have no use for labor, white or black. The Negro thus becomes the victim of double exploitation. He shares the inferior estimate which capital places upon labor as subsidiary to its higher prerogative, and at the same time is the victim of the age old conceit of the divine right of the white race to exploit the lesser breeds of men.

Kelly Miller, November 1925, "The Negro as a Workingman," p. 310.

In all of the leading lines of industry the white workmen organize either to shut out the Negro competitor or to shunt him aside into separate lines of work, with a lower level of dignity and a lesser rate of compensation. The bricklayer must be white, the hod-carrier may be black. The Negro may indeed bring the brick to the scaffold, but should he attempt to adjust it in its place in the wall the white bricklayer would throw down his trowel in indignant protest. The Negro fireman may shovel coal and make steam for the engine, but must never put his hand on the throttle.

Kelly Miller, November 1925, "The Negro as a Workingman," pp. 311–12.

Probably the most burning question before Black America today is "Should the Pullman porters be organized into the American Federation of Labor?"

The history of the colored worker in his efforts to affiliate himself with the organized unions in this country is one vast tragedy of cracked skulls, broken necks and prison stripes, resulting from the organized colored worker having been used as a cat's paw during the period of strikes, which are always called as soon as the colored brother gets organized.

It would appear that the more practical thing to do, would be to seek to win the Pullman Company officials to the point where he will be promoted to branches of the service where the work will change the status of the man, but to make a serving porter a directing executive, it cannot be done.

This organization business is probably going to be annoying for quite a time but the men who appreciate their positions had better listen, for none know better than they that it does not require the knowledge of a college professor to do a Pullman bed and they are waiting for the opportunity to try their hand.

Melville Chisum, African-American politician, in the Louisville News, *December 26, 1925, in Sterling D. Spero and Abram L. Harris,* The Black Worker, *pp. 438–39.*

I worked for the Pullman Company from 1928 to 1964. It was a hard job. We had a rest period: 10 P.M. to 2, for one porter, and 2 to 6, for the other. During that time, one man guarded two cars. From 6 in the morning to 10 at night, he was plenty busy with his one car: touch it up all the time, clean up, call a man at a certain time. You get that man off, you run back and tidy up the place, you run back and bring a new man in. By that time, they holler, "All aboard!" you got to get that step up. You have to touch up the men's room, the ladies' room, the vestibule. . . .

Maximum sleep was four hours a night. And some trips were Chicago to Los Angeles, Chicago to Miami. Before the Brotherhood, we had to cover 11,000 miles a month. No established time. Sometimes it took four-hundred hours to make it.

E. D. Nixon describing the Pullman porter's job between 1928, when he first worked as a porter, and 1937, when the Brotherhood of Sleeping Car Porters negotiated its first contract with the Pullman Company, in Studs Terkel, Hard Times, *pp. 117–18.*

Back when I was growing up [in the 1930s], the "successful" Lansing Negroes were such as waiters and bootblacks. To be a janitor at some downtown store was to be highly respected. The real "elite," the "big shots," the "voices of the race," were the waiters at the Lansing Country Club and the shoeshine boys at the state capitol. The only Negroes who really had any money were the ones in the numbers racket, or who ran the gambling houses, or who in some other way lived parasitically off the poorest ones, who were the masses. No Negroes were hired then by Lansing's big Oldsmobile plant, or the Reo plant. . . . The bulk of the Negroes were either on Welfare, or W.P.A., or they starved.

Malcolm X describing work opportunities for African Americans in Lansing, Michigan, in the 1930s, The Autobiography of Malcolm X, *p. 5.*

During the Depression I had a [cotton] crop of my own. . . .

I usually made forty and forty-five bales, more sometimes, and I had enough money to run me through the winter, to buy new children's clothes for school and to buy groceries to last till the next time they start to furnish over in the spring. They didn't never give us nothing until the first of April. But I was wise. I'd buy enough of what I couldn't raise to last till April or May. I was raising hogs, had cows, and made my own garden and put up dry food, beans and peas and all that. I done worked myself to death.

Naomi Williams, STFU member from Gould, Arkansas, explaining how she survived economically in the 1930s, in Marc S. Miller, ed., Working Lives, *p. 125.*

Thirty-two bullet holes were found in the walls of the shack belonging to A. B. Brookins, sixty-five-year-old Negro preacher, song leader of the [Southern Tenant Farmers' Union]. The attack on his home was made at 2 o'clock in the morning by carloads of planters' deputies. Mr. Brookins led his people in song in a tightly packed union hall at Marked Tree . . . two weeks ago. Men, women, and children were crushed together, so that the walls of the hall seemed too frail to stand the strain. Kerosene lamps gave an insufficient, smelly light, while Brookins's hands were weaving shadows against the wall as he led their song: "Though we are evicted we shall not be moved, Just like a tree planted by the water, We shall not be moved." Brookins was jailed along with [STFU President W. H.] Stultz last November on the same charge—interfering with labor.

John Herling, March 29, 1935, "Field Notes from Arkansas," p. 419.

In our laundry they had only white girls first. Then later they started taking on colored girls but this is the way they did it: a colored girl would come in and the boss said, "We can't take you on. The white girls don't want to work with you." The colored girl would start to go and he'd say, "I'll take you, but you got to work

Sharecroppers evicted for belonging to the Southern Tenant Farmers' Union, Arkansas, 1936 *(Library of Congress)*

for less money than the white girls." They incited one against the other and later they cut the white girls, saying they could get colored girls cheaper.

An African-American laundry worker, 1937, in Cheryl Lynn Greenberg, "Or Does It Explode?," p. 80.

Our company policy is to NOT discriminate against Negroes and we have in past years employed them. However, we have found sharp discrimination by white employees who object to working alongside of Negroes. We would have resisted this outrageous attitude, and insisted upon at least a token representation of Negro workers in our plant, except that unsettled labor conditions during the past year made it inadvisable to antagonize white workers.

A firm comments to the Massachusetts Legislature on the hiring of African Americans in 1942, in Report of the Massachusetts Commission on the Employment Problems of Negroes, p. 16.

The [AFL] cannot continue to exist with a part of its members who are white as first-class union men and another part who are colored as second-class union men. This division of the house of labor is fatal to its existence and future. . . . Even though these international unions are autonomous [the AFL] ought to have the courage to say to them, "Your policy is wrong and it is up to you to bring your policy in harmony and in conformity with the basic principle of the American Federation of Labor, as expressed in the constitution." . . . If the AFL claims that it is the house of labor then it cannot escape criticism for the wrongs committed in that house. If the AFL is justified in claiming credit for numerical increase in general membership, it must bear the guilt for the lack of increase in Negro union membership because of a narrow racial policy.

A. Philip Randolph at the 1943 AFL Convention, in Jervis Anderson, A. Philip Randolph: A Biographical Portrait, p. 289.

More than one-third of the jobs in Washington are with the federal government. Therefore, discriminatory practices of government agencies . . . are important to District [of Columbia] Negroes. The District government itself has only a small proportion of Negro employees, and most of these are confined to unskilled and menial jobs. Partial exceptions to this are the Metropolitan Police, the segregated Fire Service, and the school system with its segregated staff. A ranking District official during the [Second World War] told an interviewer: "Negroes in the District of Columbia have no right to ask for jobs on the basis of merit," the rationalization being that whites own most of the property and pay the bulk of municipal taxes.

Negroes are confined to the lowest paid and least skilled jobs in private employment. In 1940, three-fourths of all Negro workers in Washington were domestics, service workers or laborers, while only one-eighth of the white workers held jobs of that type. At the other end of the scale, only one-eighth of all Negro workers were clerks, salesmen, managers, proprietors or professionals, while two-thirds of the white workers were in jobs of this kind. There are similar striking racial differences in average income and length of workweek.

President's Committee on Civil Rights, 1947, To Secure These Rights, pp. 92–93.

Things have improved somewhat since the day when Booker T. Washington commented that "in the North the Negro can spend a dollar but cannot earn it, while in the South he can earn a dollar but cannot spend it." But the employment situation is still bad in the North. A survey of 55 cities showed that in only 19 of them were Negroes employed as clerks or store salesmen. (The prejudice in this connection was least in New York City, but even here the number of such Negro employees was usually held carefully to a token half dozen or so.) The rise of closed labor unions has aggravated the problem considerably. The same survey showed that only 10 of the 55 cities were without discriminatory unions. The worst offenders are the unions of skilled workers, but inconsistencies, evasions and run-arounds are practiced by all types.

George S. Schuyler, June 1949, "Jim Crow in the North," p. 667.

Columbus, Ohio: "Negroes are excluded from membership [in the plumbers union]. The transfer cards of Negroes coming into the Columbus area are not honored. Apprenticeship programs not open to Negroes."

Tampa, Florida: "Strongly anti-Negro throughout the South. No Negro membership likely unless change in policy."

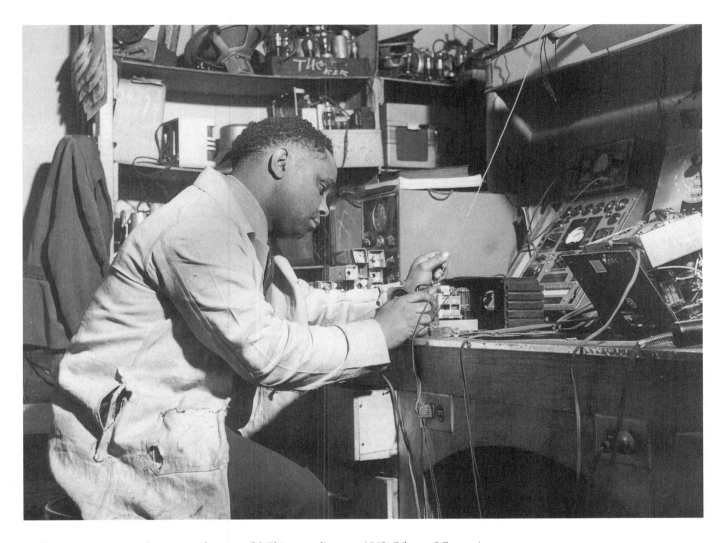

William Green, owner and operator of a successful Chicago radio store, 1942 *(Library of Congress)*

San Francisco, California: "Outstanding resistance by some unions have made it virtually impossible to place Negroes in certain categories of craft union skill. The Plumbers Union is one of the worst offenders."

Excerpts from a National Urban League survey of local plumbers unions, 1958, in Ray Marshall, The Negro Worker, *pp. 76–77.*

Labor unions can play a tremendous role in making economic justice a reality for the Negro. Trade unions are engaged in a struggle to advance the economic welfare of those American citizens whose wages are their livelihood. Since the American Negro is virtually nonexistent as the owner and manager of mass production industry, he must depend on the payment of wages for his economic survival.

There are in the United States 16.5 million members of approximately 150 bona fide trade unions. Of this number 142 are national and international affiliated organizations of the AFL-CIO. The unions forming the AFL-CIO include 1.3 million Negroes among their 13.5 million members. Only the combined religious institutions serving the Negro community can claim a greater membership of Negroes. The Negro then has the right to expect the resources of the American trade union movement to be used in assuring him—like all the rest of its members—of a proper place in American society. He has gained this right along with all the other workers whose mutual efforts have built this country's free and democratic trade unions.

Martin Luther King, Jr., 1958, Stride toward Freedom, *pp. 202–3.*

The Negro today is not struggling for some abstract, vague rights, but for concrete and prompt improvement in his way of life. What will it profit him to be able to send his children to an integrated school if the family income is insufficient to buy them school clothes? What will he gain by being permitted to move to an integrated neighborhood if he cannot afford to do so because he is unemployed or has a low-paying job with no future? . . . Of what advantage is it to the Negro to establish that he can be served in integrated restaurants, or accommodated in integrated hotels, if he is bound to the kind of financial servitude which will not allow him to take a vacation or even to take his wife out to dine? Negroes must not only have the right to go into any establishment open to the public, but they must also be absorbed into our economic system in such a manner that they can afford to exercise that right.

Martin Luther King, Jr., 1964, Why We Can't Wait, *pp. 135–36.*

Down there our regular salary is 30 cents an hour in Mississippi. You know, it seems incredible to believe that people are working for that but that is what it was when I left Mississippi just yesterday. Those people are chopping cotton for 30 cents an hour and tractor drivers are driving tractors for 60 cents an hour. Those tractor drivers and those cotton pickers work from 12 to 14 hours a day, and I hear you talk about an eight hour day. That word in Mississippi doesn't exist. And we are attempting to organize to combat these conditions where we can raise the standard of living.

An African-American agricultural laborer, 1965, in Organized Labor and the Black Worker, *p. 22.*

No American working man in the 1930's suffered the poverty and the lack of dignity that twenty million Negroes are suffering today in this country, and the only way that those brothers and sisters of ours can get any justice in America is by doing what they are doing today. And this country of ours has got to see to it that those people who fight and die for our country have equal dignity with every other citizen in this country.

Albert J. Fitzgerald, general president, United Electrical, Radio and Machine Workers of America, 1967, in Organized Labor and the Black Worker, *p. 8.*

. . . Memphis can take deep pride in the prompt and efficient way its law enforcement officers handled the volatile situation. Police were on the job as the strikers and their leaders boiled out of the meeting and started a march on Main Street.

They had guns, but they didn't shoot.

They had Mace, the new irritant gas which incapacitates but does not permanently injure—and they used it. They went into action as soon as fired-up marchers attacked a police car. . . .

How much better to do it this way than to be late and soft . . . letting disturbances grow into full-scale rioting.

Memphis Press-Scimitar reporting on the sanitation workers' strike, February 24, 1968, in Philip S. Foner and Ronald L. Lewis, eds., Black Workers, *p. 591.*

We were 500 black men and women committed to the well-being of the sick men, women, and children of Charleston. As a reward, we only asked to be paid decently so that we could invest in a better way of life for ourselves and our families; we only asked for the justified right to unite and organize ourselves into a stronger body of hard working people who could walk down the hospital corridors, as well as our community with dignity and self-respect and with the assurance of representation in a time of grievance.

The strike was also symbolic of the fact that the hospital workers at the Medical University Hospital and the Charleston County Hospital would no longer accept part-time wages for a full-time job and that they would no longer stand quietly in a life of poverty, exploitation and discrimination. Yes, this was the time to stand up and yell loudly for an end to these conditions, this was a time to stand up and be counted for what we know in our heart was right.

Donna M. Whack, ward clerk, Charleston County Hospital, remembering the hospital workers' strike of 1969, in Philip S. Foner and Ronald L. Lewis, eds., Black Workers, *p. 613.*

It wasn't all exciting. . . . There was some hard work involved. The walking, walking and more walking. The hours and efforts spent trying to get programs together for mass meetings. The sacrifice to my husband and children. . . . There were times my children didn't see me all day and sometimes not even at night because of the time I had to spend away from home. . . .

There were days I wanted to cry, I was so depressed, because it seemed that inspite of all the hard work and sweat, that we weren't accomplishing anything, but I knew within myself that I had to keep on working even harder because [the union] didn't lie to us, they laid it on the line and let us know just how hard it was going to be. . . .

I had to go to jail a couple of times, for anything else, I know if I could help it, I would never permit myself to be jailed, looking back I know if I had it to do again I would do the same thing.

Claire G. Brown, obstetrical technician, recalling the Charleston, South Carolina, hospital workers' strike of 1969, in Philip S. Foner and Ronald L. Lewis, eds., Black Workers, *p. 612.*

We have the right to go to almost any school in America, but we can't pay the tuition. We have the right to move into almost any neighborhood in America, but we can't pay the house note. We have the right to buy almost any car in America and we do buy them, *for about two months,* but we can't keep up the notes. So now we find ourselves in an era where we have the right to swim in a pool where there is no water; the right to go on a vacation without the money to take that vacation.

Jesse L. Jackson, 1972, "Three Challenges to Organized Labor," p. 310.

You will show me an Abraham Lincoln that did something for Black folk, I'll show a Frederick Douglass helping to write his speeches. You'll show me a Franklin D. Roosevelt, making progress with Black people, I'll show an A. Philip Randolph, threatening to march on Washington. You'll show me a John Kennedy, coming out a decent man, I'll show you a Martin Luther King, the prophet putting pressure on him to make him do it.

Jesse L. Jackson, 1972, "Three Challenges to Organized Labor," p. 315.

The latest statistics show that a white high school dropout, without giving him a name, has more job options than a black high school graduate, without giving him a name. As late as 1950, when I was growing up in the South, and they were telling me how qualified we had to be, 65 to 70 percent of the labor force in this country, skilled and semiskilled, were white males without a high school diploma. At that time, a black with a college degree couldn't be a policeman. As late as 1960, 46 percent of the skilled and semiskilled labor force in high-paying union jobs were white males without a high school diploma. . . .

There is substantial evidence that many blacks are still categorically rejected because of race, whereas our character and intelligence are not even tested. There is no evidence that there are no black coaches in the National Football League because we can't figure out X's and O's. There is no evidence that there are no black baseball managers because we don't understand baseball. The real evidence is something very different from that.

Jesse L. Jackson, 1978, A Conversation with the Reverend Jesse Jackson, *p. 25.*

13

The Changing Role of Women
1776–1999

For as long as the United States has existed, most of its women have worked. Eighteenth-century families depended on the toil of women for daily existence, for the making of farm products, and for the manufacture of cloth, candles, soap, and other household goods. Once the Industrial Revolution was under way, manufacturers exploited skills that female workers long had practiced at home, such as spinning, weaving, and sewing. They brought young, single women from farms into their factories by offering good wages and a protected living environment. The first generation of women working in the New England mills viewed their jobs as temporary. They earned enough to send a portion of their wages home and to keep some for spending and for their dowries.

Women also found employment as domestic servants. As large numbers of Germans and Irish entered the United States in the 1840s and 1850s, many young immigrant women were hired as maids and kitchen help, receiving meals and board in their employers' homes as partial compensation. They tended to work for a native-born family for a few years, and then marry.

Following the Civil War, class differences among women became more apparent in the social roles that they played. A women's rights movement emerged as activists pushed for the right to vote and to give all women access to birth control and education. The women calling for reform were largely affluent white northerners who employed other women to clean their houses, cook their meals, and care for their children.

The activists lobbied for change as factories proliferated, the population increased, and economic need forced more women into the labor market. The number of female wage earners tripled between 1865 and 1890. In 1870, women accounted for 14 percent of the entire labor force and one-fourth of nonagricultural workers. There were 323,370 women factory workers in 1870, according to the U.S. Census, nearly 100,000 more than in 1850. Eighty percent of female factory workers were employed in the garment industry, and as the number who were foreign born rose, the Lowell system of dormitory housing disappeared. By 1890, clothing manufacture alone employed nearly 390,000 women, and laundries and cleaning establishments gave work to 100,000 more.

Women in factories were paid less than half what their male coworkers received. In 1890, on average, a woman earned 46 cents for every dollar earned by a man. Many female workers were poorly fed and clothed, and they lived in substandard housing. They were less interested in gaining the vote than in securing wages equal to those of men, a safe work environment, and hours that allowed them to get home before they were exhausted. These workers received little real help from the women's movement.

Only two 19th-century craft unions, the printers and the cigar makers, admitted women as members. Women at times attempted to organize themselves, but usually with little success. The most notable women's union of the 19th century was the Laundry Workers Union of Troy, New York, whose members made and laundered detachable collars for men's shirts. These collars had been invented in Troy, and their manufacture and care had become an important industry in the city. Unhappy with low pay and temperatures that reached 100 degrees Fahrenheit in the laundry rooms, the women called a strike in 1863 and gained a raise in wages. They struck again for better pay in 1869, and

Milking the cows, traditionally a woman's job on early American farms *(Princeton University Library)*

they received public endorsements from men prominent in the labor movement, including William Sylvis. The women held a picnic on July 19 and raised $1,200; they talked of starting their own cooperative laundry to draw business away from the established firms. On July 31, however, the members voted to dissolve their union and end the strike. The sudden death of William Sylvis had discouraged them and diverted the attention of other labor leaders who had been lending support.

Women again became visibly active in the labor movement in the 1880s, with the rise of the Knights of Labor. Women were organized in the same assemblies as men or in separate assemblies of their own. The first women's assembly was chartered in 1881; 113 were chartered in 1886. Organized sometimes by craft and sometimes by geography, the assemblies welcomed textile workers, servants, clerks, seamstresses, laundry workers, printers, teachers, and others as members. There was an assembly of shirt-collar workers in Troy, New York, and an assembly of stocking knitters in St. Louis. The American Federation of Labor took little interest in organizing women during this period, because most female laborers were in poorly paid, unskilled lines of work. The AFL did appoint a woman organizer, Mary E. Kenney, in 1892, but her efforts received little backing from the federation's men, and they were soon discontinued.

THE WORKING WOMAN ENTERS THE 20TH CENTURY

In 1900, one-fifth of women in the United States worked for wages. Nearly all belonged to the lower classes. Although, middle-class women rarely worked, employment outside the home had become the norm for single, working-class women. The workforce also included significant numbers of widows, divorced women, and married women whose husbands were ill, disabled, or unemployed. Most married women of the working class preferred the role of housewife to the "double day" of housecleaning and outside work, and therefore they stayed home if they could afford to do so. Also, having a working wife reflected negatively on a man's ability as a breadwinner. Black married women were more likely to work outside the home than white wives were, because discrimination made it difficult for their husbands to find jobs that paid a decent wage.

According to the U.S. Census of 1900, most of the nation's 5 million working women pursued traditionally "female" occupations, including domestic service, sewing, teaching, jobs in laundry establishments, nursing, and textile manufacturing. The census ignored women who earned money at home by taking in laundry, caring for the children of others, or giving lodging to boarders. Such ways of augmenting the family income were common. For example, a 1918 survey of working-class households in Philadelphia found that one-fourth included boarders. Lodgers most often lived in households headed by women, and they tended to be unmarried female relatives who not only paid board but also helped with housework and childcare.

The paying jobs available to women were often extensions of housework and were always poorly compensated. But many women were now doing clerical work, making inroads in a field that had been dominated by men. In 1870, nearly all bookkeepers, clerks, stenographers, and copyists were male. By 1900,

The first telephone operators were men, but by 1890, when this picture was taken, women dominated the profession. *(Property of AT&T Archives. Reprinted with permission of AT&T)*

women made up one-third of the clerical workforce. By 1920, half of all clerical workers were female. Working women preferred the clean, quiet, safe environment of the office to the dirt, noise, and hazards of the factory. Salaries for clerical workers declined, however, as the percentage of women in the field rose.

Technological innovations such as the manual typewriter were responsible for bringing many of those women into American offices. Christopher Latham Sholes, a Milwaukee printer, invented the typewriter in 1867, but it was unavailable until 1874, when gun manufacturer Philo Remington produced 1,000 machines. The typewriter caught on—unhappily for Sholes, who had sold the rights to his invention prematurely and failed to profit from it. In 1888, the YWCA offered the first typing classes in New York City, and by 1899 all departmental records in the U.S. Treasury were being typed rather than handwritten. Thirty firms were manufacturing typewriters at the turn of the 20th century. The proliferation of telephones and adding machines also increased the need for clerical workers, as did increased record keeping on the part of many businesses.

The hiring of women depended in large part on race and ethnicity. Most female office workers were white and native born, as were most teachers and most women in another formerly all-male field, sales. Foreign-born women made up the majority of domestic workers and cotton-mill operatives, while half of the women employed in commercial laundries were African American.

Not only were working women moving into new occupations, they were also moving out of the family home. Although many married women and widows were in the labor force, the typical working woman in both the late 19th and early 20th centuries was young and single. In the 1890s she lived with her parents, but in the early 1900s she was more likely to live on her own in an urban setting. Increasingly, young women from outlying towns and rural regions sought clerical work in U.S. cities. These women lived frugally, often helping to support their families. Immigrant women sent part of their earnings to relatives who had remained in their homelands, while recent African-American and Hispanic migrants to northern cities mailed money to family members in the South and Southwest. Many unmarried working women lived in shared apartments, boardinghouses, or YWCA facilities. With the exception of the Phillis Wheatley branches operating in several cities, the YWCA rejected African-American and Hispanic residents.

An estimated 76,700 women were union members in 1910; the actual number is unknown, because only some unions kept records of their membership by sex. The Women's Trade Union League (WTUL), an alliance of women from all social classes, worked to assist women in unions and to increase their numbers. The WTUL had branches in Boston, New York, and Chicago when it was formed in 1903. By 1911, branches were active in 11 cities. The WTUL helped women organize unions and improve working conditions. The latter goal often required members to aid striking workers.

The WTUL provided administrative help, bail, and other financial assistance during the shirtwaist workers' strike of 1909, the first large strike of female workers in the United States. The strike began on November 9, following an impassioned speech by Clara Lemlich, a young immigrant, at a meeting of Local 25 of the International Ladies' Garment Workers' Union. After detailing the hardships she had experienced as a garment worker, Lemlich incited her audience to stand and take an old Jewish oath: "If I turn traitor to the cause I now pledge, may this hand wither from the arm I now raise!"

For 13 weeks, the garment workers picketed on the icy sidewalks outside their workplaces—including the Triangle Shirtwaist Company. The strike spread to Philadelphia when the union learned that manufacturers were sending work to that city for completion. Estimates of the number of strike participants range from 10,000 to 30,000. The U.S. Department of Labor has estimated that 15,000 people took part. The picketers were frequently ill and often lacked money for rent, winter clothing, and medical care. The strike ended gradually, as individual shops reached agreements with their workers. Although the strike cannot be called a failure, the gains made were less than what was hoped for. Most firms agreed to a union shop, a raise in wages, a 52-hour workweek, and paid legal holidays. Some of the largest manufacturers, however, refused to recognize the union at all.

During a strike involving 45,000 Chicago garment workers in 1911, the WTUL prepared thousands of meals, housed homeless workers, and persuaded landlords to accept late rent payments from participants in the 14-week-long walkout.

Increasing numbers of women learned the value of organization in the first years of the 20th century. In 1912 and 1913, unionized saleswomen struck for shorter hours and better wages in Lafayette, Indiana; Buffalo, New York; and New York City. In the same period, laundry workers in San Francisco used their union's clout to gain a pay increase of 30 percent and protection from constant exposure to harsh washing soda and ammonia.

U.S. entry into World War I divided the leaders of the WTUL. Some went to work for government agencies, while others objected to the nation's participation in the war and joined the peace movement. Approximately 10 million women entered the paid workforce at this time, filling in for men who were fighting the war. Women made steel, cut lumber, operated printing presses, and repaired railroad tracks. They could be seen delivering mail and collecting fares on streetcars. The gains were temporary, though; following the armistice, men reclaimed their jobs, and the number of working women returned to its previous level.

GAINING THE FULL RIGHTS OF CITIZENSHIP

Women gained the vote with the ratification of the 19th Amendment in 1920. As they began to assert their rights as citizens, they participated more actively in politics and public service than ever before. Holding down a job became a way for young middle-class women to assert their independence and adult status. Because they were more likely than working-class women to have completed high school and possibly to have had some post-secondary education, they received preference in hiring for clerical jobs. Also, growing numbers of middle-class women entered professional fields such as health care, education, and social work. Female graduates of newly established schools of social work at Columbia University, the University of Chicago, and other colleges and universities tackled such issues as maternal and child health, workplace safety, and consumer protection.

The decline in immigration resulting from World War I drew both middle-class and working-class women into the labor force, while a lower birth rate made it easier for many women to work outside the home. Reductions in child labor meant that children no longer contributed financially to poor households, and so were less desirable. Also, the teachings of Sigmund Freud and other students of human development were affecting the way middle- and upper-class parents approached child rearing. Many now had fewer children, in order to devote more time and energy to nurturing each child.

Technology, too, was altering homemakers' lives, by offering a variety of labor-saving devices that consumers couldn't wait to snap up. In 1928, with two-thirds of U.S. homes wired for electricity, Americans bought 6,828,000 vacuum cleaners, 15.2 million electric irons, and 5 million washing machines. These appliances did reduce the time women spent on housework, but not as much as might be imagined. Standards of cleanliness rose during the 1920s, and many middle-class women took on work that once had been sent out or delegated to servants, such as laundry.

A paying job promised upward mobility to increasing numbers of women, and by 1930 one in four women worked outside the home. With the onset of the Great Depression, America's working women encountered circumstances different from those faced by men. Working wives, for example, came under fire. Many employers and members of the public expressed the opinion that in a time when jobs were scarce, only one person in a family should be employed. Married women who worked, it seemed, took jobs away from men with families to support. Eighty-two percent of persons questioned in a 1936 Gallup poll stated that women should not work if their husbands had jobs, and many supported legal restrictions on working wives. The proper role for a wife and mother, most people agreed, was caring for her home and family.

It is difficult now to imagine that laws have denied women employment based on their marital status in the 20th century, but the Federal Economy Act of 1932 prohibited the employment by the federal government of both parties in a marriage. Although the law targeted neither men nor women overtly, it was the wives in such couples who usually left government service. States and municipalities followed the example of the federal government and enacted similar laws, while corporations established varying policies regarding the employment of married women. Companies and agencies without formal restriction rules discriminated against women with husbands as well. Many teachers, social workers, librarians, and other qualified professionals were forced into clerical work, because any available jobs in their fields went to men.

Despite societal pressures and discriminatory laws, married and unmarried women entered the labor force in record numbers during the depression. Employment of women increased 4 percent in the 1930s, as the number of men employed decreased 11 percent. One reason for this shifting balance was the growth of clerical jobs. The great volume of record keeping and information reporting necessary to operate public and private assistance programs created an enormous demand for office workers in Washington, D.C., and elsewhere. Federal employment nearly doubled between 1929 and 1939. With clerical work increasingly a woman's occupation, many women found jobs while their husbands could not. The husbands of one-third of working wives earned less than $600 a year in the late 1930s—about half the median income; middle-class families came to rely on women's paychecks.

The gap in earnings between men and women narrowed during the 1930s, principally because men's earnings fell. In 1930, women earned 58 cents for every dollar earned by men. By 1935, women were earning 65 cents for every dollar that men received.

More women joined labor unions in the 1930s than in previous decades, largely because of the CIO's effort to recruit them. Female union membership rose from 300,000 to 800,000 between 1933 and 1938. The number of women belonging to unions would rise to a much higher level in the decade to come—reaching 3 million in 1943—as women stepped into the work arena to replace men who were fighting overseas in World War II and to take jobs in the burgeoning defense industries. Many of those women were granted union membership only for the duration of the war.

The labor shortage created by the war caused Americans to reverse their attitudes about working wives. The federal government now called on the public and private sectors to alter their policies regarding the hiring of married women and to help women with children overcome barriers to outside employment.

The unique needs created by World War II gave many women entry into lines of work that traditionally had been dominated by men. The Women's Land Army, organized by the Department of Agriculture, hired women to work in the fields, to fill in for the many farmers who had entered military service. Between 1942 and 1945, the Women's Land Army employed an estimated 1.5 million women who had never farmed before. An equal number of women found agricultural work on their own. Women also became precision toolmakers and drill-press operators. They learned to handle overhead cranes and blowtorches as they constructed battleships and aircraft engines. Manufacturers were skeptical about hiring women at first, but they had no choice.

Many women viewed working in defense plants as a way of fulfilling their duty as citizens during wartime. "Rosie the Riveter," with sleeves rolled up and curls tied in a scarf, became a popular image of the American woman doing her part on the home front. Women were also drawn to factories by the good pay that was offered. Labor unions insisted that employers pay women in skilled manufacturing jobs the same wages that men had earned, in order to protect the incomes of veterans returning to civilian life after the war. Thousands of women quit their jobs as waitresses, laundry workers, and even teachers to take more lucrative positions in defense plants. Large numbers of housewives entered the workforce, many for the first time.

More women—and especially married women—now worked for wages than ever before. The number of working women in the United States reached 20.6 million at the height of the war. This number included approximately 1.5 million African-American women who found jobs in manufacturing. Government

Women make generators for wartime use at the General Motors plant in Rochester, New York, 1942. *(Library of Congress)*

propaganda and advertising repeatedly told working women that their jobs were temporary, that they would one day surrender them to returning veterans and go back to their traditional roles. But a survey conducted by the U.S. Women's Bureau in 1944 and 1945 found that women liked the autonomy and money that employment provided. Seventy-five percent of those questioned planned to continue working in peacetime.

Women also participated more directly in the war effort by enlisting in the military to fill noncombat roles as cooks, mechanics, clerks, and especially nurses. One-third of all trained nurses working during World War II served in the armed forces. Although women in military service were barred from flying planes, the War Department established two civilian units of female pilots, the Women's Auxiliary Ferrying Squadron (WAFS) and the Women Airforce Service Pilots (WASP), to move military planes and transport cargo within the United States. Civilian women served as well with the American Red Cross and the United Service Organization at home and overseas.

A RETURN TO OLD VALUES?

Americans had waited a long time for the prosperity of the postwar years; many couples had delayed marriage and children until after the war. The society that had voiced disapproval of working wives during the depression had not changed its attitude very much, and most people expected women to surrender their jobs in industry to men and focus on their homes and families. In fact, many women were glad to devote all of their energy to their husbands and children; the U.S. marriage rate of 16.4 per 1,000 people in 1946 was the highest on record for any country in the 20th century. But large numbers of women resented their dismissal from high-paying industrial jobs after the war, and 1946 also saw twice as many women as men apply to the U.S. Employment Service for skilled and semiskilled jobs in manufacturing.

The conflict that women experienced between societal expectations and the need to fulfill personal goals intensified in the 1950s. Married women felt pressure to devote their full time to home and children from such sources as television, which presented an idealized image of the stay-at-home suburban mother, and Benjamin Spock, M.D., who stressed the importance of maternal attention to young children's development in his best-selling *Baby and Child Care*. Yet not every family could afford the suburban home and modern appliances without a second income, and many women felt frustrated when confined to the housewife's role. The number of mothers in the workforce therefore increased during the 1950s, although working brought women worries that they were shortchanging their husbands and children. Most likely to work were women whose children were high school age or older. They were followed by mothers of school-age children and those with toddlers and infants. Part-time employment allowed many women to work outside the home yet devote sufficient time to their housework and children. The number of women working fewer than 50 weeks a year or 35 hours a week climbed through the 1950s and 1960s.

Curiously, despite the widespread glorification of home and motherhood, the United States needed its working women. The economy was growing, and there were too few male laborers to fill available jobs, due to low birthrates in the decades of the depression and World War II. Two million clerical jobs were created between 1950 and 1960, along with 1 million jobs in the service sector, and most of these went to women. Women also entered traditionally male fields, such as engineering and drafting. It became more common to see women bus drivers, welders, and printers.

African-American women in particular made gains during this decade. The number of black women in clerical jobs increased 150 percent during the 1950s, while the number of white clerical workers increased by less than 50 percent. Higher percentages of black women also found jobs in teaching and nursing. Few African-American women had the luxury of choosing whether or not to work. Due to high unemployment among black men and the low wages they tended to receive, most black women grew up with the expectation that outside employment would be a necessary condition of their adult lives.

A New Consciousness

The civil rights movement, which began in the 1950s and gained energy in the early 1960s, caused some women to examine their position in society and to push for opportunities equal to those available to men. In 1963, the U.S. Commission on the Status of Women, which had been established in 1961 by John F. Kennedy at the urging of Eleanor Roosevelt, formally stated its positions. The commission came out against discrimination based on sex in government employment and in favor of equal pay for comparable work.

Also in 1963, Betty Friedan published *The Feminine Mystique,* a book that spoke for a large number of American women. Friedan described a myth of femininity, created by society and perpetuated by industry and the media, in which a woman most wanted marriage and a family and understood that her own ambitions were less important than those of her husband. Friedan wrote about legions of women who had accepted the myth and as a result felt trapped, frustrated, and bored. To a reader at the start of the 21st century, *The Feminine Mystique* seems naive in its narrow focus on educated white women of the middle class, but in the 1960s it caused many people to think anew about the role of women in society and in relation to men. Such issues as the division of housework and child care between men and women became topics of serious debate. Some feminists even proposed that women be paid for doing housework.

In 1966, Friedan and other feminists founded the National Organization for Women (NOW), a political-action group. The united call for change that would become known as the women's liberation movement was rapidly taking shape. The predominantly middle-class members of NOW cooperated with female unionists and other women in the labor force to lobby for salaries equal to those men received, federally funded child care for working mothers, flexible work hours to permit women to tend to family needs, paid maternity leave, and equitable distribution of Social Security. Feminists worked for passage of the Equal Rights Amendment (ERA), drafted in 1921 by suffragist Alice Paul, which would make the protection of women's rights a provision of the Constitution.

Of the 7.8 million women who entered the workforce in the 1960s, 5.2 million took clerical jobs. Nevertheless, women increasingly entered male-dominated fields and sought the higher education that would give them entry into largely male professions. With passage of the Civil Rights Act of 1964, federal law banned for the first time discrimination based on sex in employment. By October 1965, women had submitted 152 complaints to the Equal Employment Opportunity Commission concerning employer violations of Title VII of the act. With passage of the Equal Employment Opportunity Act of 1972, women and minorities could pursue such complaints through the court system.

Gaining access to high-paying, traditionally male jobs became essential for many women in the 1970s, for two principal reasons. First, the high inflation that characterized much of the decade made many more families dependent on two incomes simply to meet expenses. Second, more women were the sole breadwinners for their families or for themselves. Women were living longer—and for longer periods as widows—than in years past. Also, the age of women at first marriage was rising, which meant that women were supporting themselves for longer periods than in previous decades. A rising divorce rate left many women with the expense of maintaining a household and all or part of the burden of raising children. By 1980, half of all marriages would end in divorce.

As the full-time working mother gained social acceptance, Congress renewed debate on the Equal Rights Amendment, which a House subcommittee had last considered in 1948. By 1972, the amendment had been passed by both houses of Congress and sent to the states for ratification within seven years. Congress later extended the deadline for ratification to June 30, 1982, but the amendment was ratified by only 35 states, three short of the 38 that were required. The amendment was controversial even among feminists. Some feared that if ratified it would nullify state laws that protected women workers from heavy lifting, excessive hours, and night work, laws that early reformers had striven hard to gain. Supporters have reintroduced the Equal Rights Amendment into every subsequent Congress, but to date it has not advanced to another ratification vote.

Women's participation in labor unions in the 1970s failed to reflect their presence in the workforce. According to U.S. Department of Labor statistics, 45 unions with a combined membership of 2.2 million had no female members in 1970. Also, unions with high percentages of women among their members were led almost exclusively by men. The International Ladies' Garment Workers Union, with a female membership of 80 percent in 1976, had one woman among its 20 vice presidents. Similarly, only one of 28 vice presidents of the predominantly female Amalgamated Clothing Workers was a woman. The inequity extended to the AFL-CIO, which had no women on its 35-member executive council.

In March 1974, more than 3,000 women from 58 unions met in Chicago to form the Coalition of Labor Union Women (CLUW), a group dedicated to organizing women and increasing their participation in union policy making. The CLUW also addressed issues of concern to all working women, including discrimination in hiring, promotion, and pay; the need for adequate child care and maternity benefits; and the election of more women to political office. In 1999, the CLUW would have more than 75 chapters nationwide.

The number of women belonging to labor unions and employee associations rose from 5.4 million in 1975 to 6.9 million in 1985. The fastest-growing unions were those in occupations that employed many women, including health care, civil service, and teaching. Concerned about their image as well as the women they represented, labor unions began to let women play a more active role at conferences and conventions and to include them on executive boards.

Many women benefited significantly from union membership, gaining pension plans, medical coverage, maternity and sick leave, and paid vacations. Unions offered counseling services, legal aid, and credit-union membership, and they handled grievances related to sex and race discrimination and also sexual harassment, an issue of increasing concern in the 1980s.

The feminization of poverty was another social and political issue in the 1980s. At a time when women constituted 42 percent of the workforce and more women were moving into high-level positions, 40 percent of female-headed households subsisted below the poverty line. Three-quarters of the poor in the United States were female. A high rate of teen pregnancy contributed to this situation, as did fathers who were unable or unwilling to pay child support, a shortage of job-training programs, and the high cost of day care. At the same time, the economic distance between the poor and the middle and upper classes was increasing: the rich were getting richer, and the poor, poorer.

In 1990, three-fifths of American women worked for wages, which meant that 56 million women were in the workforce. More than half of wives worked, with the majority holding full-time jobs. Paid labor had become an anticipated part of life for women of every economic level and racial or ethnic group.

THE MORE THINGS CHANGE . . .

Women had taken giant steps toward achieving equality in the workplace by 1990, but the "gender gap"—the discrepancy between wages paid to women and men for comparable work—persisted. A woman earned 70 cents for every dollar earned by a man, on average. Also, although female executives could now be found in virtually every field, many women climbing the corporate ladder encountered an invisible barrier, or "glass ceiling," a level within their organization above which they could not rise, regardless of their qualifications. They discovered that discrimination, sexual harassment, and a lack of concern for the needs of women as mothers persisted even at the highest levels of U.S. business.

Affirmative-action programs have allowed many women to prove their competence in executive positions. The benefits of affirmative action for women at the University of Minnesota mirror those achieved at other organizations. That university instituted its affirmative-action program in 1980. By 1989, the presence of women in administrative posts had increased from 26 percent to 54 percent. The number of women who were tenure-track faculty members rose from 20 percent to 30 percent, and the number who were tenured faculty members increased from 14 percent to 17 percent.

In the 19th century, only the poor put in a "double day," working a full shift and then doing the bulk of the chores necessary to maintain the home. Today, the double day is a way of life for the majority of working mothers. Juggling the responsibilities of home and the job has remained a challenge for women. Many have met it in part by postponing marriage and childbearing until they have established their careers, by having fewer children, and by relying on commercial child care, often of poor quality.

Women did most of the nation's unpaid household work in the 19th century, and they still do. They were overrepresented in the lowest-paying, least-desirable jobs, and they still are. Women, whatever their educational and economic status, continue to perform traditionally female duties, caring for the young and the old, nursing the sick, and volunteering in their schools and communities.

CHRONICLE OF EVENTS

1776
The work of women in homes and on farms permits families to maintain day-to-day existence.

1790
The first textile mills begin production in the United States; women will provide a significant portion of the labor in these and other factories.

1840s
German and Irish immigrant women are hired as servants by native-born families.

1863
The Laundry Workers Union of Troy, New York, strikes successfully for higher wages.

1867
Christopher Latham Sholes invents the typewriter.

1869
Spring: The Laundry Workers Union stages a second strike.

July 31: The laundry workers give up the strike and vote to disband their union.

1870
Women make up 14 percent of the workforce; 323,370 women are employed in factories.

Clerical workers are predominantly male.

1874
Gun manufacturer Philo Remington produces 1,000 typewriters.

1881
The first women's assembly of the Knights of Labor is chartered.

1886
One hundred thirteen women's assemblies of the Knights of Labor are chartered.

1888
The YWCA offers typing classes in New York City.

1890
Approximately 390,000 women are employed in clothing manufacture.

For every dollar a man earns, a woman earns 46 cents.

1892
The American Federation of Labor appoints a woman organizer, Mary E. Kenney.

1899
All departmental records in the U.S. Treasury are typed.

1900s
Increasingly, single working women live independently in U.S. cities.

1900
Twenty percent of U.S. women, 5 million in all, are gainfully employed.

One-third of clerical workers are female.

1903
The Women's Trade Union League (WTUL) is founded, with branches in New York, Boston, and Chicago.

1909
November 9: An emotional speech by garment worker Clara Lemlich precipitates a 13-week strike by shirtwaist workers in New York and Philadelphia.

1910
About 76,700 women belong to labor unions.

1911
Branches of the WTUL are active in 11 U.S. cities.

The WTUL aids striking garment workers in Chicago.

1912–13
Sales clerks strike in Lafayette, Indiana; Buffalo, New York; and New York City. Laundry workers strike in San Francisco.

1918
One-fourth of working-class households in Philadelphia include boarders.

Jewish women sold produce, fish, clothing, and household items from pushcarts on the Lower East Side of Manhattan at the turn of the 20th century. Women also operated grocery stores, candy stores, and butcher shops in the Jewish community. *(Library of Congress)*

1920

August 26: The Nineteenth Amendment is ratified, giving women the right to vote.

Half of clerical workers in the United States are women.

1921

Suffragist Alice Paul drafts the Equal Rights Amendment.

1930

One-fourth of women work outside the home.

A woman earns 58 cents for every dollar earned by a man.

1932

The Federal Economy Act prohibits the employment of both partners in a marriage by the federal government.

1933

Three hundred thousand women belong to labor unions.

1935

A woman earns 65 cents for every dollar earned by a man.

1936

Most Americans in a nationwide poll state that a woman should not work if her husband is employed.

1938

Labor-union membership includes 800,000 women.

1942–45

The Women's Land Army employs 1.5 million women; the same number find agricultural work independently.

1943

Three million women belong to labor unions.

1944–45

Seventy-five percent of working women polled plan to hold a job in peacetime.

1946

The marriage rate in the U.S. reaches 16.4 per 1,000 people.

1950–60

Two million clerical jobs and 1 million service jobs are created.

The number of African-American women in clerical jobs increases 150 percent.

1960–69

Some 7.8 million women enter the workforce; of that number, 5.2 million are in clerical jobs.

1961

President John F. Kennedy establishes the U.S. Commission on the Status of Women.

1963

The Commission on the Status of Women announces that it opposes discrimination based on sex in government employment and favors equal pay for men and women doing comparable work.

Betty Friedan publishes *The Feminine Mystique.*

1964

July 2: A civil rights act is passed that bans discrimination based on sex for the first time in the United States.

1965

October: Women have submitted 152 complaints of discrimination to the Equal Employment Opportunity Commission.

1966

The National Organization for Women is founded.

1970

Forty-five unions with a combined membership of 2.2 million have no women members; women are underrepresented in the leadership of unions with large female constituencies.

1972

The Equal Employment Opportunity Act gives women and minorities the right to pursue complaints of discrimination in the court system.

The Senate and the House of Representatives pass the Equal Rights Amendment and send it to the states for ratification.

1974

March: The Coalition of Labor Union Women (CLUW) is founded.

1975

Approximately 5.4 million women belong to labor unions.

1980

Half of all marriages end in divorce.

1982

June 30: The Equal Rights Amendment is withdrawn after it fails to gain the 38 votes needed for ratification.

1985

About 6.9 million women belong to labor unions.

1990

Sixty percent of American women are wage earners; more than 50 percent of married women work.

A woman earns 70 cents for every dollar earned by a man.

1999

The CLUW maintains 75 chapters nationwide.

EYEWITNESS TESTIMONY

. . . [S]eeing no other opening for herself, [my mother] sold her small estate, and moved to Lowell, with the intention of taking a corporation-house for mill-girl boarders. Some of the family objected, for the Old World traditions about factory life were anything but attractive; and they were current in New England until the experiment at Lowell had shown that independent and intelligent workers invariably give their own character to their occupation. My mother had visited Lowell, and she was willing and glad, knowing all about the place, to make it our home.

The change involved a great deal of work. "Boarders" signified a large house, many beds, and an indefinite number of people. Such piles of sewing accumulated before us! A sewing-bee, volunteered by the neighbors, reduced the quantity a little, and our child-fingers had to take their part. But the seams of those sheets did look to me as if they were miles long!

Lucy Larcom describing the opening and operation of a boardinghouse in 1830, A New England Girlhood, *p. 146.*

My mother kept forty boarders, most of them men, mill-hands, and she did all her housework, with what help her children could give her between schools; for we all, even the baby three years old, were kept at school. My part in the housework was to wash the dishes, and I was obliged to stand on a cricket [stool] in order to reach the sink!

Harriet H. Robinson listing the responsibilities of family members operating a Lowell, Massachusetts, boardinghouse, circa 1835, Loom and Spindle, *p. 29.*

. . . [W]e find in PERSONAL SERVICE, that the restaurant employees generally complain of long hours, no dinner hour to speak of, and the great strain upon them from being busy all day on their feet. They all complain of a low state of health, and are pretty much tired out on reaching home. Of those giving testimony on their work and its effect on the health, two were found working noons only (about three hours), not being able to stand the strain of long hours, and being obliged to adopt this plan in order to get a little rest. Others report themselves troubled with rheumatism, tired and careworn, or not in good health, but obliged to work, although in one case

particularly, in great distress from some lung or throat trouble.

In TRADE, a bookkeeper was found who had ruined her eyes, by bringing her books home nights and working until twelve and one o'clock. Among the saleswomen, "standing all day" is generally reported as being very trying on their health and strength. In one store, no stools are provided, the girls being obliged to go to one end of the store to sit down. The employer does not countenance help sitting down while customers are in the store, and as they are generally busy all day, there is little or no time when the store is vacant, the result being, practically, that the girls stand all day.

Carroll D. Wright, 1889, The Working Girls of Boston, *p. 70.*

In the *Clothing* business, the general testimony is that the work is very hard, and is the cause of a great deal of sickness among the working girls so employed. The tax on the strength is very great, and it would seem that unless a girl is strong and robust, the work soon proves too severe for her, and if followed thereafter results disastrously. The running of heavy sewing machines by foot power soon breaks down a girl's health, as several girls have testified. One girl says that steam was introduced six months ago to her great satisfaction, and she thinks foot power machines too severe for female operators. The girls think all the machines should be run by steam.

Other girls object to standing so much, and say that being on their feet all day and then walking to their homes makes them very tired at night.

Carroll D. Wright, 1889, The Working Girls of Boston, *p. 72.*

About sixty girls board and lodge at the Young Women's Christian Association building, Warrenton Street; they pay from $3.00 to $5.00 per week, including washing; they have religious services night and morning and are expected to attend church at least once on Sunday; also, they are obliged to be in the house before 10 o'clock at night at which time the doors are locked. All these girls are struggling hard to secure an honest livelihood and are surrounded by good moral influences and are living virtuous lives; this is the testimony of those in charge.

Carroll D. Wright, 1889, The Working Girls of Boston, *p. 122.*

Girls living away from home, in boarding and lodging houses, the latter especially, are oftentimes obliged to practise very close economy in living, one girl being reported as taking her meals at restaurants, and often going without her supper as well as other meals, because she did not have the money to pay for them; another, as going without meat for weeks, eating bread only without butter, and seldom able to buy a baker's pie, while in the case of three sisters living in one room, with all meals at restaurants where employed, they are only able to get a bare living without any of life's comforts; they economize in every way possible, buy food and cook it themslevs Sundays, and when invited out to dinner (which is only rarely), they make a "field-day" of it.

In the same way, girls speak of their dress, say that it is almost impossible in many cases to buy new clothes, they depending largely upon what is given them in the way of old dresses and other garments by relatives or friends; others spend little or nothing for clothes each year, or have a new suit once in two or three years. One girl says "it costs every cent she earns for board and other expenses," and that she was obliged to take ten dollars that she had saved for a new dress and pay a doctor's bill, and that she is in consequence nearly destitute of clothing suitable for street or store wear. This matter of dress, she says, has a great deal to do with one's success in seeking employment, a poorly dressed woman being refused on the score generally of "just hired" [someone else], while a shabbily dressed girl is entirely ignored.

> *Carroll D. Wright, 1889,* The Working Girls of Boston, *p. 114.*

If the domestic employee were taken from the home of the employer and encouraged to find for herself avenues of improvement and entertainment, her social condition would be greatly improved. She must be made to see that the reason why she does not rise to the social position to which she aspires, is not because her work is degrading, but because her conversation is often ungrammatical and lacking in interest, her dress sometimes untidy and devoid of taste, and her manner not always agreeable. She must do her part towards improving her social condition. It is true, that probably at first comparatively few domestics would avail themselves of such privileges, *but just as long as social and intellectual advantages do not exist anywhere for this class, just so long will the intelligent and capable young woman most needed in this occupation shun it for others where such opportunities do exist.*

> *Lucy Maynard Salmon, 1897,* Domestic Service, *p. 207.*

Ladies wonder how their girls can complain of loneliness in a house full of people, but oh! it is the worst kind of loneliness—their share is but the work of the house, they do not share in the pleasures and delights of a home. One must remember that there is a difference between a *house,* a place of shelter, and a *home,* a place where all your affections are centred. Real love exists between my employer and myself, yet at times I grow almost desperate from the sense of being cut off from those pleasures to which I had always been accustomed. I belong to the same church as my employer, yet have no share in the social life of the church.

> *A servant, 1897, in Lucy Maynard Salmon,* Domestic Service, *p. 151.*

To the young man confronting life the world lies wide. Such powers as he may use, must use. If he chooses wrong at first, he may choose again, and yet again. Not effective or successful in one channel, he may do better in another. The growing, varied needs of all mankind call on him for the varied service in which he finds his growth. What he wants to be, he may strive to be. What he wants to get, he may strive to get. Wealth, power, social distinction, fame,—what he wants he can try for.

To the young woman confronting life there is the same world beyond, there are the same human energies and human desires and ambition within. But all that she may wish to have, all that she may wish to do, must come through a single channel and a single choice. Wealth, power, social distinction, fame,—not only these, but home and happiness, reputation, ease and pleasure, her bread and butter,—all, must come to her through a small gold ring. This is a heavy pressure. It has accumulated behind her through heredity, and continued about her through environment. It has been subtly trained into her through education, till she herself has come to think it a right condition, and pours its influence upon her daughter with increasing impetus.

> *Charlotte Perkins Gilman, 1900,* Women and Economics, *pp. 71–72.*

In a confidential feminine way we will consider the interests of the woman who is about to determine the extent of her money value to the world. First of all, she must realize that it is not enough that from her proud estate she is willing to enter business. That attitude is in itself a handicap. The truth, a hard one, too, is that the world is already full of workers, and there really is no place for untried hands. Then you must *make* a place, and to do this the woman that works must be of the right sort or her work is desultory and ineffectual. Failure is not always the fault of the occupation chosen, nor of the woman's talents, but comes because she lacks those traits of character that force success.

Helen Churchill Candee, 1900, How Women May Earn a Living, *p. 3.*

When a girl or woman comes to the knowledge that she must earn her living, she seems afraid to take the initiative. "So many avenues are now open to women," is the stock argument of those who idly fancy that this makes things easier. As a matter of fact it makes a choice far harder. Years ago when there were but half a dozen occupations that society sanctioned, the talented followed art, the practical took boarders, and the well-educated taught school. It was easy to know which of these things suited the case. But now, with a long list unfolded, there is a feeling of confusion which brings indecision and indirection.

Helen Churchill Candee, 1900, How Women May Earn a Living, *pp. 3–4.*

"Typewriting is not what it used to be," say the women who have followed the industry since it began, and even admitting that it is a far more remunerative occupation than many others at which self-supporting women are engaged, the pay is far from high.

Typewriters [typists] used to be employed only by large and prosperous firms, and few were to be had. Naturally those few commanded high prices for their labor, and naturally, too, this led others into the field in search of like remuneration. Then inventors and manufacturers produced cheaper typewriting machines, and the unavoidable result was a market too well supplied with operators for wages to continue high. But the fact nevertheless stands, that the efficient typewriter draws high pay even to-day, and that "there is room higher up," in this calling as well as in more ambitious ones.

With this thought in view, no one need be deterred from taking up an occupation that seems from the outside to be overcrowded. Indeed, it is hard in these days to find a clear field, and it is only by superiority of industry or ability that one can hope to win.

Helen Churchill Candee, 1900, How Women May Earn a Living, *pp. 47–48.*

I came to New York in the winter of 1902 to face the question of breadwinning. My capital consisted of forty dollars, a few serviceable clothes, and good health. My previous training was more or less social, but practical enough to give me the courage to do what I was told. Therefore, when a girl, facing the same facts as myself, told me to apply for a vacancy in the publishing-house in which she worked I did so, stating that my experience was limited, references obtainable, and need of work instant and actual.

My interview with the manager was satisfactory to him and stimulating to me. I was engaged at six dollars a week, agreeing to learn the details of each department of magazine manufacture at this sum, until I was an asset and not a liability. I also agreed to work at night when required. . . .

At the end of three months I was promoted to eight dollars a week. During this time I had spent my capital. I could not draw from any source except my pay-envelope each Friday—unless I worked at night, when I made fifty cents.

"The Girl Who Comes to the City," Part 1, Harper's Bazar, *February 1908, p. 170.*

In my new position there were but three girls employed—the stenographer, the general office assistant, and myself. . . .

I looked with interested awe on the stenographer and the other office assistant, and especially at their typewriters, which they used with so much skill. The assistant asked me if I would not like to learn typewriting. I explained that I had no money to pay for tuition; whereupon she laughed, rolled a clean sheet of paper into her machine, motioned me to take her seat, and said, "Then do it without learning."

I was wild with delight as she stood over me, showing me the first few essentials, and my joy at finding I could actually write words, and in a few minutes even sentences, knew no bounds.

When she saw my eagerness the assistant promised to let me help her in various ways, if the employer were willing, as she was much overworked. Fortunately he consented, and decided to pay me a salary of $6 a week instead of a piece rate, so that I could do general work.

"The Girl Who Comes to the City," Part 1, Harper's
Bazar, *February 1908, p. 172.*

I left my native town in the Mohawk Valley one cold, blistering day in March for New York. The fear and trembling which filled my heart on that eventful day would be impossible to describe. When I arrived at the Grand Central Station I was met by some school acquaintances, who assured me that I would have no trouble in getting a position in a week or two at the longest. Their buoyant hopes helped to revive my spirits, and I felt quite like a new being as they took me to their boarding-place on West Twenty-fourth Street.

After a night's rest, I felt more like doing something. There is something about the noise, the teeming life, of New York which always puts new life into me, something of the fighting spirit; a feeling, as it were, that the fittest will survive.

"The Girl Who Comes to the City," Part 2, Harper's
Bazar, *March 1908, p. 277.*

Never before in civilization have such numbers of young girls been suddenly released from the protection of the home and permitted to walk unattended upon city streets and to work under alien roofs; for the first time they are being prized more for their labor power than for their innocence, their tender beauty, their ephemeral gaiety. Society cares more for the products they manufacture than for their immemorial ability to reaffirm the charm of existence.

Jane Addams, 1909, The Spirit of Youth and the
City Streets, *p. 5.*

Apparently the modern city sees in . . . girls only two possibilities, both of them commercial: first, a chance to utilize by day their new and tender labor power in its factories and shops, and then another chance in the evening to extract from them their petty wages by pandering to their love of pleasure.

As these overworked girls stream along the street, the rest of us see only the self-conscious walk, the giggling speech, the preposterous clothing. And yet through the huge hat, with its wilderness of bedrag-

gled feathers, the girl announces to the world that she is here. She demands attention to the fact of her existence, she states that she is ready to live, to take her place in the world.

Jane Addams, 1909, The Spirit of Youth and the
City Streets, *p. 8.*

. . . [T]hree things are notable about [the shirtwaist workers'] strike: In every shop there are always a few girls in the lead. Some of these have been agitating for a long time, some are new and are having their first experience as leaders. But these leaders are invariably the best paid, the ones who get the most wages, in each shop. They are the ones who have less reason to complain. They have carried their sisters along with them by very force of their own determination and the spirit of resistance to the general conditions prevailing. One has but to associate with these fine, high-strung, intelligent and courageous girls to appreciate their moral caliber and their capacity for self-sacrifice and devotion.

Secondly, while the majority of the shirtwaist makers are Jews, and the union business is usually conducted in Jewish [Yiddish], yet they have succeeded in getting 3,000 Italians to strike with them. It has been difficult to reach the Italians heretofore and get them into the union. Now the start has been made and a separate Italian headquarters established, with special Italian literature and Italian speakers; it is believed the workers of this nationality are permanently enlisted in the union cause.

Lastly, the comparatively minor role played by men, both in numbers and in direction, is something new in the history of labor strikes in this country. The principal union officials are men, it is true, but the strike has been inspired by women; it is mainly women who have done the picketing, been arrested, fined, run the risk of assault, received ill-treatment from police and police courts alike, and shown themselves eager to sacrifice without stint to bring about better conditions in the shops and factories.

William Mailly, December 23, 1909,
"The Working Girls' Strike," p. 1419.

So far as industrial employments are concerned, they were considered especially suited to women at a time when men did not regard such work as profitable enough for themselves. By prior right of occupation, and by the invitation of early philanthropists and statesmen, the workingwoman holds a place of her own in this field. In the days when the earliest factories were calling for operatives the public moralist denounced her for "eating the bread of idleness," if she refused to obey the call. Now that there is some fear lest profuse immigration may give us an oversupply of labor, and that there may not be work enough for the men, it is the public moralist again who finds that her proper place is at home and that the world of industry was created for men. . . . The efforts of the professional woman to realize a new ideal of pecuniary independence, which have taken her out of the home and into new and varied occupations, belong to recent, if not contemporary history. But this history, for her, covers a social revolution, and the world she faces is a new one. The woman of the working classes finds it, so far as her measure of opportunity goes, very much as her great grandmother left it.

Edith Abbott, 1910, Women in Industry, *p. 323.*

We were poor people, and ever since I was old enough to understand the talk it was always about jobs—losing jobs, getting a new job, somebody having a better job than you, somebody taking your job away from you. Having a job seemed to be what life was for. Not having it was failure and death. Never an intimation of any purpose or reason in life beyond the job. It was nicer, of course, if one got a job one liked, but always the best job for a person was the job that paid the most money. . . .

When it was time to graduate from grammar school my teacher called each of us separately to her desk and asked us, little children of thirteen and fourteen, what we were going to do. Everybody was going to do something—study stenography or be an errand girl or an office boy or a tailor's apprentice. A few were going on to high school. I wanted to go to high school. But that whole school term there had been talk at home of how soon I should earn money, and how much so-and-so earned already, and she only two years older than I. Nothing was urged on me at home; my father and mother were too gentle and too hopeless of [i.e., about] us all. But under their despair, and under the prompting of my schooling, I too told my teacher I would get a job. And I did, wrapping bundles in a department store at three dollars a week.

Anonymous, November 1925, "The Fetish of the Job,"
p. 731.

If a keen student of society of the eighteenth century, like Adam Smith, came back to live among us for a while, two things, I believe, would impress him more than anything else. The first would obviously be the great wealth of our mechanical equipment, the ten thousand external aids of our daily life. . . . The second thing he would observe would be the remarkable change in the status of women. . . .

The whole aspect of woman's life has been changed, and community life has been correspondingly transformed. A hundred years ago women had only one career to look forward to, and that was home-making; to-day the average American girl thinks of many other fields for her activities. Home-making as a career is being relegated, for the most part, in the minds of young people to a secondary place. Even if most educated women still look forward to marriage as an ultimate goal, their first and immediate choice is very often along other lines.

Louis I. Dublin, September 1926, "Home-Making
and Careers," pp. 335–36.

All women, whatever their training, whatever their ultimate ambition, should receive instruction in the art of home-making as a matter of course. It should be assumed by our educators that every woman will marry and have a family. But it should be equally understood that many will wish to earn their living in productive work outside the home. Provision must therefore be made for the training of these women who have special aptitudes in the professions. Lest I appear too practical, I must emphasize the great importance of providing cultural opportunities in the curricula which are not particularly associated with home-making or practical affairs, but which are dedicated to the enlightenment and refinement of the personality.

Louis I. Dublin, September 1926, "Home-Making
and Careers," p. 340.

In spite of all the success stories with which the public is regaled, comparatively few [women], even of the officer class, receive more than five thousand a year. I was one of the many who made even less—who, again and again, took over "men's work" only to find that by some strange and elusive alchemy it had become "women's work" and was rated accordingly. Yet, in spite of my low financial status, I was considered a successful woman. Colleges, chambers of commerce, clubs, asked me to talk about my work, while magazines and newspapers "told how I did it" and syndicated my words of advice. Of the young men who started with me, and who were of the same intellectual and social status, not one is getting less than fifteen or twenty thousand a year at the lowest, not one but is considered in his prime at fifty.

A businesswoman, November 1926, "Unfinished Jobs,"
p. 641.

. . . [F]or the women of Morrisonville [Virginia] life had few rewards. Both my mother and my grandmother kept house very much as women did before the Civil War. . . . Their lives were hard, endless, dirty labor. They had no electricity, gas, plumbing, or central heating. No refrigerator, no radio, no telephone, no automatic laundry, no vacuum cleaner. Lacking indoor toilets, they had to empty, scour, and fumigate each morning the noisome slop jars which sat in bedrooms during the night. . . .

They scrubbed floors on hands and knees, thrashed rugs with carpet beaters, killed and plucked their own chickens, baked bread and pastries, grew and canned their own vegetables, patched the family's clothing on treadle-operated sewing machines, deloused the chicken coops, preserved fruits, picked potato bugs and tomato worms to protect their garden crop, darned stockings, made jelly and relishes, rose before the men to start the stove for breakfast and pack lunch pails, polished the chimneys of kerosene lamps, and even found time to tend the geraniums, hollyhocks, nasturtiums, dahlias, and peonies that grew around every house. By the end of a summer day a Morrisonville woman had toiled like a serf.

Russell Baker detailing a woman's work in Morrisonville,
Virginia, 1928–30, Growing Up, *p. 43.*

It is a warm summer morning; the employment department of the store . . . is crowded with "girls"— for in a department store every woman is a girl—girls of every type and of every age: girls who are under seventeen, with and without working certificates; girls who are graduates of the high schools or grammar schools of Manhattan and its environs; girls who have never held any kind of job; girls who have tried out every occupation offered in the want-ad columns of the city newspapers; girls who are brides seeking employment so that their wages may help out until husbands are given promotions or to provide a reserve

fund for the time when the first baby will arrive; girls who are mothers with children whom they wish to keep in school well dressed and with money in their pockets to pay for school entertainments, to buy the school annual, or to meet the expenses of the graduation outfit; girls who are grandmothers left without means of support; girls who are widows by grass or by sod whose husbands have died without leaving insurance or from whom alimony cannot be collected; but girls, all girls who if they are successful applicants will become Miss Moore, Miss Smith, Miss Kuntz, Miss Levinsky, Miss Du Costa, or Miss O'Brien in the departments to which they will be assigned.

Frances R. Donovan, 1929, The Saleslady, *p. 4.*

I had to be there at eight every morning to make breakfast before the man went to work. The only lunch I made would be for the nurse, the child, and myself, because the woman was out somewhere playing bridge. Then they'd come home about five-thirty, but it'd be six-thirty when I put the dinner on the table cause they'd be getting ready to go out. Then I'd serve the dinner, wash the dishes, and go home to my child around eight-thirty. It was nine o'clock before I got home to see my child. But it wasn't just me, it was everybody. That's the way it was and it isn't much better than that today. They get a little more money, but the same thing is going on.

Josephine Hunter, who was a domestic worker in Tennessee
in the 1930s, in Fran Leeper Buss, comp., Dignity, *p. 33.*

Some girls think that as long as mother takes in washing, keeps ten or twelve boarders or takes in sewing she isn't working. But I say that either one of the three is as hard work as women can do. So if they do this at home and don't get any wages for it, why would it not be all right for them to go to a factory and receive pay for what they do?

A worker in a rayon mill, circa 1931, in Grace Hutchins,
Women Who Work, *p. 183.*

A woman doing factory work and home work, both, has far too great a burden and shouldn't be allowed to carry it. That women should not be permitted to work at night is the consensus of opinion of experts in all the greatest countries and has been accepted by governments of those countries.

Authorities on industrial hygiene all agree that night work for women is bad. Nearly all women who

These women took over railroad jobs vacated by men fighting in World War II. *(National Archives)*

are subject to night work are women with families and children and have housework to do. They don't get enough sleep; they are burning the candle at both ends.

Governor Ely of Massachusetts, January 1933, in Grace Hutchins, Women Who Work, *pp. 114–15.*

Most of the two hundred women in the cigar-rolling department, where I worked, had home responsibilities before and after the day's work. It was supposedly a 9-hour day, but really longer, since we came into the plant at 7:15 a.m., and seldom got out before 5:45 p.m., with three quarters of an hour out for lunch eaten right there at our benches. It was winter, barely light when we went into the factory in the morning and dark when we came out at night. The sun might as well never have shone for all we saw of it through the small dirty windows of the plant.

Yet many a woman worker there had already done at least an hour's work, usually more, preparing the breakfast, getting the children up and ready for school or day nursery and the beds made before she came to the factory. When she washed up, ready to leave the plant at night, each one was planning what she would buy on the way home to cook for supper, and it would be at least 7 p.m. before she could have the food ready. She would compare notes with neighboring workers as to what the husband liked to have cooked for supper.

Grace Hutchins, 1934, Women Who Work, *pp. 43–44.*

The wife is inescapably the builder of the home and the guardian of its children. These duties are necessarily neglected by working wives. Probably no laws could or should be enacted to bar married women from jobs. But business and industry, by agreement, could establish rules under which married women would be employed in exceptional cases, the first of which would be that the husband was not able to provide a living for the family. We want no dictators telling women what to do; but the country cannot ignore the deterioration of the home, due to the pressure of married women in industry.

William B. Arnold, editor, San Antonio Weekly Dispatch, *July 14, 1939, in Julia Kirk Blackwelder,* Women of the Depression, *p. 126.*

We have come a long ways from the days when the War Manpower Commission had its job analysts figure out that there were 1,800 key processes in war jobs which women could perform[,] in an effort to persuade employers to hire women. The concept of "suitability" of women for jobs has gone by the board. Women can now do any job that men can do. But there are undoubtedly some jobs which are not as desirable—like coal mining—as long as there are sufficient men around. It all depends on how severe the manpower situation is in determining what jobs women will be assigned to. If necessary, they can mine coal, as they do in the Soviet Union.

After all, who ever thought of women in this country working near blast furnaces or messing around with ladles of hot molten iron? Yet it has come to pass. There are over 5,000 women employed in the Carnegie-Illinois steel mill in Gary, Ind.

Eva Lapin, 1943, Mothers in Overalls, *p. 5.*

We have on our rolls at the present time approximately 2,000 Negro women, the majority of whom have been added in the last six to nine months. They are engaged on forty-five separate and distinct occupational classifications covering a rather wide range of skills. Included among their assignments are bench hands on various kinds of partial and final assemblies, cable formers, clerks, inspectors, many kind of machine operators, solderers, stock selectors, electrical testers and wiremen.

Personnel director of an electrical manufacturing company, 1943, in Eva Lapin, Mothers in Overalls, *p. 9.*

I, who hate heights, climbed stair after stair after stair till I thought I must be close to the sun. I stopped on the top deck. I, who hate confined spaces, went through narrow corridors, stumbling my way over rubber-coated leads [lead castings used as ballast on naval vessels]—dozens of them, scores of them, even hundreds of them. I went into a room about four feet by ten where two shipfitters, a shipfitter's helper, a chipper, and I all worked. I welded in the poop deck lying on the floor while another welder spattered sparks from the ceiling and chippers like giant woodpeckers shattered our eardrums. I, who've taken welding, and have sat at a bench welding flat and vertical plates, was told to weld braces along a baseboard below a door opening. On these a heavy steel door was braced while it was hung to a fine degree of accuracy. I welded more braces along the side, and along the top. I did overhead welding, horizontal, flat, vertical. I welded around curved hinges which were placed so close to the side wall that I had to bend my rod in a curve to get it in. I made some good welds and some frightful ones. But now a door in the poop deck of an oil tanker is hanging, four feet by six of solid steel, by *my* welds. Pretty exciting!

Augusta H. Clawson, 1944, Shipyard Diary of a Woman Welder, *p. 58.*

I'm learning to weld with one hand. It's often necessary because the other hand has to hang on to a support in a precarious spot. I learned it several days ago when I saw a woman on her knees welding with only one hand. I expressed surprise, and she said, "It's the only way to do it." She was right.

Augusta H. Clawson, 1944, Shipyard Diary of a Woman Welder, *p. 78.*

HELP WANTED: DOMESTIC: FEMALE. All cooking, cleaning, laundering, sewing, meal planning, shopping, weekday chauffering, social secretarial service, and complete care of three children. Salary at employer's option. Time off if possible.

No one in her right senses would apply for such a job. No one in his right senses, even a desperate widower, would place such an advertisement. Yet it correctly describes the average wife and mother's situation, in which most women remain for love, but many because they have no way out.

Edith M. Stern, January 1949, "Women Are Household Slaves," p. 71.

The practice of housewifery gives the lie to the theory of almost every objective of higher education. The educated individual should have a community, a national, a world viewpoint; but that is pretty difficult to get and hold when you are continually involved with cleaning toilets, ironing shirts, peeling potatoes, darning socks and minding children. The educated should read widely; but reading requires time and concentration and besides, the conscientious housewife has her own five-foot shelf of recipes and books on child psychology to occupy her. Most frustrating of all, education leads one to believe that a project attempted should be systematically carried through to completion. In housewifery there is inevitable hopping from one unrelated, unfinished task to another; start the dinner—get at the mending—collect the baby—take down the laundry—finish the dinner is about the maximum height of efficiency. This innate incoherence of housewifery is like a mental patient's flight of ideas; nothing leads quite logically from one thing to another; and the woman schooled like her husband to think generally and in sequence, has a bad time of it intellectually and emotionally as a result.

Edith M. Stern, January 1949, "Women Are Household Slaves," p. 75.

Since the American woman has expressed the opinion that she can do anything as well as men, and has invaded all the masculine fields without proving it, her grip has begun to slip. She still dominates the browbeaten male in this country but there are signs that he is getting ready to revolt. It has not become clear that, with only one exception, men can do everything better than women. Nature has neglected to supply the men with facilities for parturition. I suggest to the ladies that, before it is too late, they begin again to practice childbearing, the one activity in which they can be certain of demonstrating superiority over the male.

Waverly Root, April 1949, "Women Have Nothing to Kick About," pp. 404–5.

Women constitute not only an essential, but also a distinctive part of our manpower resources. They are

essential because without their presence in the labor force we could neither produce and distribute the goods nor provide the educational, health, and other social services which characterize American society. They constitute a distinctive manpower resource because the structure and the substance of the lives of most women are fundamentally determined by their functions as wives, mothers, and homemakers.

National Manpower Council, 1957, Womanpower, p. 9.

I felt trapped. I *was* trapped. Trapped by the endless merry-go-round of chores for a growing family, trapped by the inexperience of toddlers who would fall into the cellar if I didn't grab them, whose skin would redden if I didn't keep diapers whirling on and off them, who would starve if I didn't prepare endless formulas and rush endless supplies of food into their gaping little mouths. . . .

With entrapment came resentment. What was a person of my intelligence doing dealing with these subhuman creatures? The skills of my hands and brain were going to waste. The most intricate maneuvers I now performed were tying muddy shoelaces and pushing a pin through two layers of cloth. The most complicated problem my brain handled was how to get the day's dishes done before paterfamilias walked into the house. Housework was an affront to common sense. . . .

Marguerite Kurth Frey, April 1961, "I'm Proud to Be a Housewife," in Robert Stein, ed., Why Young Mothers Feel Trapped, pp. 140–41.

I . . . began to think and read seriously about the problems and uncertainties of the so-called "educated women" in the modern world. In my confusion I had scarcely been aware of the fact that I was not alone, that many other wives and mothers, like myself, were grappling with the problem of their own identities.

Barbara O'Neill, November 1963, "I Went Back to College," in Robert Stein, ed., Why Young Mothers Feel Trapped, p. 40.

The only way for a woman, as for a man, to find herself, to know herself as a person, is by creative work of her own. There is no other way. But a job, any job, is not the answer—in fact, it can be part of the trap. Women who do not look for jobs equal to their actual capacity, who do not let themselves develop the lifetime interests and goals which require serious education and training, who take a job at twenty or forty to "help out at home" or just to kill extra time, are walking, almost as surely as the ones who stay inside the housewife trap, to a nonexistent future.

Betty Friedan, 1963, The Feminine Mystique, *p. 344.*

Who knows what women can be when they are finally free to become themselves? Who knows what women's intelligence will contribute when it can be nourished without denying love? Who knows of the possibilities of love when men and women share not only children, home, and garden, not only the fulfillment of their biological roles, but the responsibilities and passions of the work that creates the human future and the full human knowledge of who they are? It has barely begun, the search of women for themselves. But the time is at hand when the voices of the feminine mystique can no longer drown out the inner voice that is driving women on to become complete.

Betty Friedan, 1963, The Feminine Mystique,
p. 378.

The workplace will never be woman-ized merely by virtue of women working there. It has to be actively woman-ized by the women entering the trades who can say: "I'm here, I'm going to do my job as myself, not as one of the boys, I am valid without your acceptance, get out of the way—I'm trying to get my job done." I remember after one particularly bad day in the lunch room when the woman-bashing ("jokes") had reached a particularly hateful pitch and I started to cry. One of the guys said they were just trying to toughen me up, that I needed a thick skin to make it in a man's trade. I reminded them that it was not a man's trade, merely a male-dominated trade. I told them that I didn't need a thick skin to solve a mechanical problem, I didn't need to be tough to take a pump apart and rebuild it, I didn't need their macho initiation rites to turn a wrench.

Jessica Hopkins, stationary engineer, 1988, in Molly Martin, Hard-Hatted Women, *p. 43.*

I loved carpentry immediately and still love it. I love the feel and smell of wood, love having something come out just the way I planned it, love knowing that my work helps to make people's lives better. I remember being on housing jobs that were being framed in wood; getting my tools and walking to my position on the site in the half-dark of daybreak when all was quiet, smelling the distinctive odor of wood and feeling joy in the brief moments before the noise of our work lacerated the peace. The work itself is always something I enjoy. It doesn't matter if it's digging ditches or doing a fine piece of cabinetry—it's honest work that I can be proud of.

Pat Cull, carpenter, 1988, in Molly Martin, Hard-Hatted Women, *pp. 51–52.*

Patrick empties the garbage occasionally and sweeps. That's all. He does no cooking, no washing, no anything else. How do I feel? Furious. If our marriage ends, it will be on this issue. And it just might.

A 26-year-old legal secretary, 1989, in Arlie Hochschild, The Second Shift, *p. 212.*

Many young men and women grew up inside busy, strained two-job families. When I ask them about the advantages of having grown up in a two-job family, they mention the education, the family vacations, the financial needs their parents' wages met. And they generally agree with the student who said: "It's sure made me self-reliant. I can cook by myself, do my homework without prodding. I wouldn't be so independent if my mom had been home all the time." When I ask them about the disadvantages, they sometimes recall a bad memory, like this one: "When I was ten, I had to come home and empty the ashtrays and make the salad for dinner and start my homework in the house alone. I survived, but I hated it." . . . When asked to put the advantages and disadvantages together, both men and women felt the advantages won; they want to have two-job families, too, but somehow not in the same way.

Arlie Hochschild, 1989, The Second Shift, *p. 264.*

14
The American Worker Faces the Future
1946–1999

The story of America's workers is one of optimism, of people seeing potential in their environment or within themselves and making it a reality. Of course, it was the potential for profit that fueled the growth of factories, the proliferation of mines, and the rise of the western cattle industry. But Americans have also acted on other well-grounded hopes. Generations of early settlers envisioned farms where there was wilderness, and a nation stretching across the continent, from one ocean to another. Industrial laborers who formed unions and stood up to powerful corporations believed that a better life was possible for themselves and their families. African Americans who boarded northbound trains in the early 20th century or who gathered with a quarter-million others in Washington, D.C., in August 1963 understood that greater opportunities would one day be theirs.

As American workers enter the 21st century, they face challenges similar to those encountered by earlier generations. The technological advances of recent decades have had an impact on the workplace that rivals that of the Industrial Revolution. Once again, immigrants are entering the United States in large numbers and finding a place for themselves in the workforce. At the same time, sweatshops and child labor persist.

But the greatest challenge facing working America at the start of the 21st century is a new one. The economy is becoming polarized, with job growth occurring in high-paid technical fields and in the low-paying service sector. Fewer people have cause to be optimistic, as raising their standard of living becomes less an achievable goal and more a dream.

A TECHNOLOGICAL REVOLUTION

Technological advances in the second half of the 20th century have made the computer an essential element of the workplace for millions of people, allowing them to store and process information and to communicate in ways that were impossible a generation ago. With a personal computer linked via telephone to the office, many workers no longer need to commute.

Although mathematicians were developing machines to perform calculations with some success in the 19th century, the world's first digital computer was developed by American engineers during World War II to predict the trajectories of bombs and shells. The Electrical Numerical Integrator and Calculator (ENIAC), built by J. Presper Eckert, Jr., and John W. Mauchly of the University of Pennsylvania, took up 1,800 feet of floor space, weighed 30 tons, and required 18,000 vacuum tubes. It was capable of performing 5,000 addition calculations per minute, but it had to be reset manually for each series of computations.

Mathematician John von Neumann contributed the "von Neumann architecture" to computer design. This is a method for dividing the logical functions of a computer among its physical components, a method that is still used. Von Newmann also found a way to store complex instructions in a computer's memory, thereby eliminating the need for continual human programming. In addition, he developed an operation known as conditional control transfer, which permitted a sequence of computer calculations to be stopped and restarted at any point. Von Neumann's innovations made possible the first high-speed computers, which were built in 1947. These computers were still large by modern standards, but they took up less space than the ENIAC. They included the EDVAC and the UNIVAC, the first computers to be sold commercially.

Developments made in the 1950s significantly improved the capability and reliability of computers. One such development was the magnetic-core memory. Bits of information could now be stored on small magnetic rings instead of on the large drums that had been used previously. Another was the transistor, a semiconductor that was smaller than the old electron tubes, used less power, and had a longer life. Integrated circuits—in which many transistors are fabricated on an underlying layer of silicon—reduced both the size and cost of computers. Around 1960, the photo printing of conductive circuit boards eliminated the need for wiring. By the 1970s, complex assemblies had become available on tiny chips.

In the 1970s, several young computer enthusiasts who lacked college degrees perceived that there would be a large demand in the general population for small, user-friendly computers, and they possessed the technical knowledge needed to create them. Steven Jobs and Stephen Wozniak formed Apple Computers, Inc., and introduced their first personal computer, the Apple I, in 1976. The Apple I appealed primarily to hobbyists, but later models, including the Apple II, Apple IIe, and Macintosh, introduced between 1977 and 1983, found an enthusiastic market in offices, hospitals, laboratories, and homes. Some personal computers available in the late 1980s could process four million instructions per second.

While Jobs and Wozniak were putting computers on the nation's desktops, Bill Gates's Microsoft Corporation was creating software for some of the early personal computers, or PCs. The Microsoft Disk Operating System (MS-DOS), developed for the International Business Machines PC and compatible machines in 1980, gave IBM computers a competitive advantage. In 1985, Microsoft made available the first mouse-operated Windows system for IBM compatible computers. Advances such as electronic mail, computer networking, and electronic publishing capabilities have broadened the computer's use as a workplace tool. The development of software with applications for scientific and medical research, information processing, and telecommunications has resulted in employment of a large number of highly paid workers.

Millions of people are responding to the changing needs of the workplace by furthering their education in computer applications and other fields so as to make themselves more employable. The National Center for Education Statistics reported that 40 million adults in the United States received job-related training in 1999. Some took courses in a traditional college setting. Of the 15.2 million students enrolled in U.S. colleges and universities in 1999, more than 6 million were age 25 or older, and 1.6 million were 40 or older. Many were taking advantage of tuition-reimbursement programs offered by their employers, and some engaged in "cyberlearning"—completing college courses on line. Meanwhile, "corporate universities" grew in popularity. These are institutions run by corporations to provide work-related training to their employees. Most offer no degrees. There were 1,600 such schools operating in the United States in 1999, up from 400 in 1988. With the average worker now expected to change jobs seven times over the course of his or her career, continuing education is often essential rather than optional.

MAKING DISCOVERIES—AND PROFITS

Genetic engineering is an example of a high-growth, highly profitable field that did not exist 30 years ago. The ability to manipulate genes to create organisms with desired characteristics promises crops that are more resistant to disease or frost and richer in nutrients; livestock that produces more meat and milk; and adequate supplies of substances for medical use, including insulin and the clotting factor in human blood. This emerging field also offers the possibility of diagnosing, treating, and preventing diseases that have a genetic component. Advances in genetic engineering have resulted in a strong bond between the scientific laboratory and the corporate boardroom.

Understanding of the functions of individual genes and their locations along the chromosome has increased substantially since James Watson and Francis Crick determined the structure of the DNA molecule in 1953. In 1982, two U.S. scientists, Richard Palmiter and Ralph Brinser, working with teams at the University of Washington and the University of Pennsylvania, transferred the gene responsible for producing a growth hormone in rats into the cells of a mouse. The mouse grew to twice the normal size. Researchers in other laboratories subsequently created additional "transgenic" organisms, animals and plants containing genetic material from more than one species. Companies and universities began acquiring patents on techniques that were developed in their laboratories. One research group, for example, patented a genetically engineered mouse in 1991. Known as an oncomouse, this animal inherits a tendency to develop human cancers and is therefore valuable in medical research. Owners of such patents are paid a royalty whenever another researcher employs the techniques that they perfected.

Genetic engineering has led to controversy. People throughout the world are concerned that the effects of altered species on the environment and on human health are unknown. Ethical questions, such as whether humans have the right to manipulate genetic material or use animals in this way, have yet to be decided as well. Nevertheless, genetic engineering is a growing branch of scientific research that promises high salaries to individuals with the necessary education to enter it.

IMMIGRANTS: WORKING HARD FOR LOW WAGES

In the 1990s, approximately 1 million people entered the United States each year, legally or illegally. They came primarily from Central America, Asia, the Middle East, eastern Europe, and Africa. Although some native-born workers have expressed worries that immigrants are taking jobs that might otherwise have gone to them, most of the newcomers are filling jobs that other workers do not want.

Many immigrants, lacking the English skills, the training, and possibly the documentation needed to get a better job, have no choice but to perform some of the dirtiest, most dangerous, lowest-paying work available. These jobs include ditch digging, heavy lifting, and construction work. Some perform the same work as union laborers—painting, window washing, carpentry, and the like—but for lower wages, a fact that has angered union members and officials. They are often hired by the day and have no health insurance or other benefits. Immigrants also work in agriculture, the garment industry, and nurseries. According to the U.S. census of 1990, the three most common occupations for female immigrants were production samplers and weighers, household servants, and tailors. Foreign-born women accounted for nearly half of the people employed in these fields. More than 50 percent of men working as tailors, restaurant help, and cooks were immigrants as well.

The past two decades have witnessed a new proliferation of sweatshops in the United States. In an estimated 2,000 locations in New York and other cities, immigrant women endure conditions reminiscent of the 19th century: 10- and 11-hour workdays, six days a week; no overtime or paid holidays; and filthy, unsafe conditions. U.S. Department of Labor inspectors have described as commonplace malfunctioning toilets and workers eating on dirty floors in sweatshops.

Modern-day sweatshops have been known to employ children as young as 12, and child labor continues illegally in agriculture as well. In 1989, the Department of Labor reported that 20,000 children were injured in farm accidents each year, and 300 killed.

Nationwide, immigrants earn 15 percent less, on average, than U.S.-born workers do. Some, however, are highly trained professionals who command good salaries. Currently, 160,000 of the 650,000 physicians practicing medicine in the United States were born and educated overseas. Twenty-six thousand come from India alone. These doctors, like unskilled immigrant workers, also fill a niche: many practice in inner-city hospitals and rural clinics, places where native-born physicians prefer not to work. Immigrants also have contributed to the economy by opening businesses. In at least one instance, they have developed an entire industry: the flourishing nail-salon industry was created largely by Asian immigrants. One million women in the United States now visit a nail salon weekly.

A NATION OF CONTRASTS

The U.S. economy at the start of the 21st century has been described as having an hourglass shape. Opportunities for advancement are plentiful in occupations requiring the highest levels of technical skill, and salaries in these positions are rising rapidly. There has been growth as well in the number of jobs at the lowest level of the economy, but workers in these positions find it hard to survive on the wages they are paid. People in midlevel jobs paying average salaries, however, have watched their options disappear as corporations have trimmed payrolls to cut costs and moved manufacturing operations out of the country, to such places as China, Indonesia, and Guatemala, where labor is cheap.

Although the steel and textile industries have been losing jobs since the late 1970s, the trend to relocate plants overseas has spread to other industries in recent years. In 1979, manufacturing employed 22 percent of American workers. In 1999, it employed 15 percent. The United States lost 330,000 manufacturing jobs between January 1998 and April 1999, a period in which 2.8 million jobs were created. The growth occurred in the low-paying service sector. Workers employed in manufacturing earned $565 a week, on average, in 1998, while service workers earned an average $430. Salaries in retail sales were lower still: $253 per week, on average.

The U.S. Census Bureau estimated the median income in the United States to be somewhere between $46,500 and $50,000 in 1999. This means that half of all families earned more than this amount, and half earned less. To maintain a midlevel income in the late 1990s required a greater effort than in years past. Middle-class couples with one or two children worked an average 3,860 hours in 1997, compared to 3,236 hours in 1979. They showed a greater increase in hours worked during that period than low-income or high-income families. Only 28 percent of middle-income families had one wage earner in 1999, according to the Census Bureau, and most of those households were headed by a single adult. As economists watch the middle class decline in numbers, they express concern that the United States is evolving into a two-tier society of wealthy and poor.

Between 1980 and 1989, the incomes of the richest 1 percent of Americans grew nearly 63 percent. These families enjoyed more than half of all income growth occurring during this period. They acquired their wealth not just from salaries but from profits on stocks and bonds. The wealthiest 0.5 percent of Americans owned 64 percent of all bonds and 37.4 percent of all corporate stocks in 1989.

Many other families, meanwhile, worked longer hours for less money and did without adequate housing or health care. The average worker's wages fell 4.9 percent between 1979 and 1989, as more and more people were forced to take jobs that did not pay enough to keep a family of four out of poverty. Twenty-eight percent of workers earned poverty-level wages in 1989, up from 25.1 percent in 1979. A study conducted by the RAND Corporation found that in 1999, wages for the lowest-paid workers, when adjusted for inflation, were about one-third lower than they had been in the 1970s. Minorities and the young have been disproportionately affected. The poverty rate among African Americans reached 32.7 percent in 1991; among Hispanics it reached 28.7 percent. One-fifth of all children were poor in 1991.

CAN OPTIMISM ENDURE?

Clearly, it requires optimism to come to the United States from another country and start a new life—as much now as 100 years ago. Even in the unfortunate case of immigrants laboring in 21st-century sweatshops, many people find better working and living conditions in the United States than in the lands they left behind. People continuing their training have expectations of a higher-paying or more challenging job. Even couples toiling long hours to keep their families afloat nurture hopes of financially secure futures. It remains to be seen, however, whether the optimism that inspired earlier generations of American workers will be shared by the majority of workers or by only a few.

CHRONICLE OF EVENTS

1946
J. Presper Eckert, Jr., and John W. Mauchly build the ENIAC, the first digital computer.

1947
The first high-speed computers, including the EDVAC and UNIVAC, become available.

1950s
Advances in computer technology from this decade include the magnetic core memory and the transistor.

1953
James Watson and Francis Crick determine the structure of the DNA molecule.

1960
The photo printing of conductive circuit boards is now possible.

1976
Apple Computers, Inc., introduces the Apple I personal computer.

1977–83
Apple Computers introduces the Apple II, Apple IIe, Macintosh, and other models.

1979
Manufacturing employs 22 percent of American workers.

Middle-class couples with one or two children work 3,236 hours, on average.

1980
Bill Gates develops the MS-DOS operating system for IBM-compatible computers.

1980s
Twenty thousand children are injured in farm accidents each year, and 300 are killed.

The incomes of the richest 1 percent of the population grow 63 percent, while the average worker's wages fall 4.9 percent.

1982
Scientists at the University of Washington and the University of Pennsylvania transfer a gene from a rat into the cells of a mouse.

1985
Microsoft Corporation introduces its first Windows operating system for personal computers.

1988
Businesses operate 400 corporate universities for their employees.

1989
The wealthiest 0.5 percent of Americans own 64 percent of bonds and 37.4 percent of corporate stocks.

1990s
About 1 million immigrants enter the United States each year.

1991
The genetically engineered oncomouse is patented.

Poverty affects 32.7 percent of African Americans and 28.7 percent of Hispanics.

One-fifth of all children are poor.

1997
Middle-class couples with one or two children work 3,860 hours, on average.

1999
Forty million adults take part in work-related continuing education.

More than six million people age 25 or older are enrolled in colleges and universities.

Approximately 1,600 corporate universities offer job-related training.

Manufacturing employs 15 percent of workers in the United States.

The median income is between $46,500 and $50,000.

Seventy-two percent of middle-class families have two wage earners.

The wages of the lowest-paid workers, when adjusted for inflation, are one-third lower than they were in the 1970s.

EYEWITNESS TESTIMONY

My great concern now is that we have an economic policy that allows us to lose steel jobs to Japan, textile jobs to the Pacific, and electronics jobs to Mexico. We lose jobs paying $8 and $10 an hour. . . . I'm concerned about the quality of jobs, and our economic policy right now is terrible for the American worker. American workers can compete with foreign workers in terms of production, but they cannot compete with the slave labor forces of totalitarian regimes. I see it as a fundamental weakness in our foreign policy.

Jesse L. Jackson, 1978, A Conversation with the Reverend Jesse Jackson, *p. 12.*

If you go back and look at the development of transportation, we had trolley cars which were fastened to the tracks. We also had tremendously expensive automobiles. They were individually built. Then along came the Model T. It cost between $300 and $600, and you could have any color you wanted as long as it was black. And people started to own them. Now, I can remember sitting on Riverside Drive (in New York City) on a Sunday afternoon and watching all the beautiful horses and carriages go by. It was a dirt road. After we began to get Model Ts, we blacktopped the roads, we built concrete roads, people moved to the suburbs. It was the beginning of a whole new world. I think you can say that the microcomputers are the model Ts—people can own them. . . .

Goodness only knows what'll happen afterwards because when we got the Model T, you couldn't have dreamed of a 747.

Grace Murray Hopper, computer pioneer, December 1983, in Corey Sandler, "Keeping Up with Grace," p. 204.

Companies are downsizing. There's a large workforce, and they're capable of taking anyone's job at any time. So companies have no incentive to give anybody any more. Basically, the feeling is, if you don't like it, there's the door, there's others out there. And they're right. So I don't see the average worker gaining anything in the foreseeable future.

A 48-year-old systems analyst, 1996, in John J. Sweeney with David Kusnet, America Needs a Raise, *p. 38.*

Today, middle and lower-income workers are being compressed into a vast new working class, and when it comes to concerns over the future, I now get the same questions from janitors making $15,000 a year as I get from computer operators making $40,000 a year:

"How can I have a family without holding down three jobs to do it?"

"What can I do to make sure my children get a good education?"

"What happens to my family if someone gets sick?" . . .

How we answer them will determine whether or not we live in a permanent two-tier society, with the American Dream being enjoyed by a precious few at the top, and the rest of us, all of us together, at the bottom.

John J. Sweeney, August 13, 1998, Remarks at the Rainbow/PUSH Labor Breakfast, *p. 2.*

I called those non-union painters a scab or a rat or worse. But I did a 180-degree turnaround. These immigrants, as you call them, they're good men. Most of them work hard, though they might not know what they're doing. But we're all workers. I don't have a problem with them anymore.

Ray Cook, union painter, 1998, in William Booth, "By the Sweat of Their Brows, a New Economy," p. A10.

I believe "deindustrialization" is the single biggest challenge facing us in the 21st century.

In our new deregulated global economy, too many giant corporations are competing not through ingenuity or innovation or technology, but by shopping indiscriminately from underdeveloped nation to underdeveloped nation for the cheapest source of labor. . . .

What does "deindustrialization" mean for working families?

Indeed, what does it mean for soon-to-be college graduates who aren't likely to be depending on manufacturing jobs for their future?

For working families, the implacations are devastating. . . . There's a cartoon about job growth that's been passed around Washington for the past couple of years—it shows a harried worker with the caption, "I know we're creating more and more new jobs because I've got three of them myself."

John J. Sweeney, April 13, 1999, 10th Annual Philip Murray Memorial Labor Lecture, *p. 3.*

Change is the constant in the new world of work, and managing that change is the most important skill that any worker can acquire. Continuing education and lifelong learning are the critical "future work" tools for any worker, at any age, in any job.

Alexis M. Herman, U.S. secretary of labor, 1999, in Tom Callahan, "Go to School. AGAIN," p. 6.

America justified its declaration of independence with the starling principle that all people are self-evidently equal. Nonetheless, in the more than two centeries since this declaration, income inequality has grown, except for the period that began with the mid-1930's and ended with the late 1960's . . .

There is little support for the cynical view that Americans don't really take their egalitarian ideal seriously. They do, and what's more, nearly half consider present economic inequalities morally wrong. . . .

I would contend that the willingness of many Americans to accept the widening income gap, despite their moral reservations about it, grows out of a deep and abiding national conviction: whatever differences fortune may have dictated between people, where it really matters all of us are of truly equal worth.

Orlando Patterson, May 7, 2000, "Everything Changes Money," New York Times Magazine, *p. 91*

APPENDIX A
Documents

1. Extracts from the Land Ordinance of 1785
2. Advertisement in a Portsmouth, New Hampshire, newspaper, March 1802
3. A deed of indenture recorded in Pope County, Illinois, 1815
4. Notice to mechanics and farmers, *Illinois Intelligencer,* March 8, 1818
5. An Act Authorizing an Examination into the Practicability of Connecting Lake Erie with the Ohio River by a Canal, January 31, 1822
6. Twelve propositions of the North Carolina slave code, 1830
7. Extract from the account book of Robert C. Holland, M.D., of Lexington, Kentucky, 1834
8. Advertisement for John Deere's plow, *Rock River Register,* March 10, 1843
9. Regulations for the boardinghouses of the Middlesex Company, Lowell, Massachusetts, ca. 1846
10. The Massachusetts Compulsory School Law of 1850
11. Entry in the memorandum book of a Massachusetts manufacturer, January 27, 1858
12. Rules and regulations adopted at Gold Hill, Utah Territory, June 11, 1859
13. Extracts from the Pacific Railway Act of July 1, 1862
14. The Emancipation Proclamation, January 1, 1863
15. Preamble to the constitution of the Cigar Makers' International Union of America, 1864
16. Extract from a brochure for eastern emigrants issued by the Northern Pacific Railroad Company, ca. 1870
17. West Virginia requests federal assistance in handling the railroad strike of 1877
18. Preamble to the constitution of the Knights of Labor, 1878
19. Extracts from a Children's Aid Society report on visits to New York City night schools, ca. 1880
20. Yellow-dog contract, Western Union Telegraph Company, 1883
21. Extract from the Sherman Anti-Trust Act, July 2, 1890
22. The sheriff of Allegheny County requests that state militia forces be sent to Homestead, Pennsylvania, July 10, 1892
23. Appeal issued to the people of Chicago, May 28, 1894
24. Extract from a statement from the Pullman strikers, June 15, 1894
25. President Grover Cleveland declares martial law in Chicago, July 8, 1894
26. Handbill calling for African-American strikebreakers, distributed in Birmingham, Alabama, 1896
27. Preamble to the constitution of the Industrial Workers of the World, 1908
28. Average Annual Income of Workingmen's Families in the United States, Summary from Recent Investigations (1901–1910)

1. EXTRACTS FROM THE LAND ORDINANCE OF 1785

An Ordinance for ascertaining the mode of disposing of Lands in the Western territory. . . .

The Surveyors as they are respectively qualified shall proceed to divide the said territory into townships of six miles square, by lines running due north and south and others crossing these at right angles as near as may be, unless where the boundaries of the late Indian purchases may render the same impracticable, and then they shall depart from this rule no farther than such particular circumstances may require; and each surveyor shall be allowed and paid at the rate of two dollars for every mile in length he shall run, including the wages of chain carriers, markers and every other expence attending the same.

The first line running north and south as aforesaid shall begin on the river Ohio at a point that shall be found to be due north from the western termination of a line which has been run as the southern boundary of the state of Pennsylvania and the first line running east and west shall begin at the same point and shall extend throughout the whole territory. Provided that nothing herein shall be construed as fixing the western boundary of the State of Pennsylvania. The geographer shall designate the townships or fractional parts of townships by numbers progressively from south to North, always beginning each range with number one; and the ranges shall be distinguished by their progressive numbers to the westward. The first range extending from the Ohio to the lake Erie being marked number one. The Geographer shall personally attend to the running of the first east and west line and shall take the latitude of the extremes of the first north and south line and of the mouths of the principal rivers.

The lines shall be measured with a chain; shall be plainly marked by chaps on the trees and exactly described on a plat, whereon shall be noted by the Surveyor, at their proper distances, all mines, salt springs, salt licks and mill seats, that shall come to his knowledge, and all water courses mountains and other remarkable and permanent things over or near which such lines shall pass and also the quality of the lands.

The plats of the townships respectively shall be marked by subdivisions into lots of one mile square or 640 acres, in the same direction as the external lines and numbered from 1 to 36, always beginning the succeeding range of the lots with the number next to that with which the preceding one concluded. And where, from the causes before mentioned, only a fractional part of a township shall be surveyed, the lots protracted thereon shall bear the same numbers as if the township had been entire. And the surveyors in running the external lines of the townships shall at the interval of every mile mark corners for the lots which are adjacent, always designating the same in a different manner from those of the townships . . .

There shall be reserved for the United States out of every township the four lots being numbered, 8. 11. 26. 29 and out of every fractional part of a township so many lots of the same numbers as shall be found thereon for future sale: There shall be reserved the lot N 16 of every township for the maintenance of public schools within the said township; also one third part of all gold, silver, lead and copper mines, to be sold or otherwise disposed of as Congress shall hereafter direct.

2. ADVERTISEMENT IN A PORTSMOUTH, NEW HAMPSHIRE, NEWSPAPER, MARCH 1802

COTTON YARN

ALMY & BROWN, Providence, State of Rhode Island, being principally concerned in the most extensive COTTON MILLS on the Continent, have for sale a large assortment of Cotton Yarn suitable for Warp or Filling, and also of Two and Three Threaded Yarn, suitable for knitting or weaving Stockings, of equal quality to any in America; they are enabled to supply their customers, and others who may want, on as low terms as any person in the United States, and on short notice.

Orders from every part of the country will be duly attended to by addressing by post, or otherwise, to the subscribers.

3. A DEED OF INDENTURE RECORDED IN POPE COUNTY, ILLINOIS, 1815

This indenture made this twenty second day of June in the year of our Lord, one thousand Eight hundred and fifteen, between Silvey a Negroe Woman about the age of twenty four years, last out of the State of Kaintuck and Livingston County, of the one part, and John Morris of the Illinois Territory and Gallaton County of the other part, WITNESSETH, that the said Silvey for and in consideration of the sum of four hundred Dollars, to me paid in hand courant Money of the United States, at or before the signing and delivery of these presents, the Receipt whereof She doth hereby acknoledge, and in conformity to a law of the said Teritory respecting the Introduction of Negroes and Melattoes into the saim, hath put placed and bind himself to the said Morris, to serve him from the date hereof, during the Term and in full of forty years next enshuing, or in other words from the date heroff untill the twenty second day of June, in the year of our Lord one thousand eight hundred and fifty five, during all which term, the said Silvey, the said John Morris shall well and truly serve, and all his lawfull commands every whair obey, and that She shall not embezzel or waiste her said Masters Goods nor lend them to any person without her said Masters consent, or leave. Nor shall She at any time absent herself from her said Masters Service, or leave, but as a good and faithfull servant, shall and will at all times demean herself towards her said Master, during the Term aforesaid. And the said John Morrice covenants and agrees too and with the said Silvey, that he will furnish her with good and suficient Meat, Drink, lodging and apparell, together with all other needful conveniences fit for such a Servant, during the said Term. And for the true performance of each of the above and aforementioned, Covenants, and Agreements, each of the above and aforementioned parties, bind themselves each to the other, firmly by these presents.

4. NOTICE TO MECHANICS AND FARMERS, *ILLINOIS INTELLIGENCER,* MARCH 8, 1818

MECHANICS of every description are much wanted at Edwardsville: more particularly the following, *a Taylor, Shoemaker, Waggon Maker, Hatter, Saddler, Tanner and Currier.* From *four* to *six Carpenters* and *Joiners,* and from *four* to *six ax-men,* and from *six* to *eight farming labourers,* will find immediate employment and good wages; for further particulars enquire of col. Benjamin Stephenson and Doctor Jos. Bowers, at Edwardsville, or James Mason at St. Louis.

Edwardsville is the seat of justice for Madison county, Illinois territory, and has the land-office established there for the district of Edwardsville; and is surrounded on three sides by the Goshen settlement, which is one of the best settlements in the territory; besides the adjacent country in every direction, is equal in point of fertility of soil, to any other in the western region.

5. AN ACT AUTHORIZING AN EXAMINATION INTO THE PRACTICABILITY OF CONNECTING LAKE ERIE WITH THE OHIO RIVER BY A CANAL, JANUARY 31, 1822

Whereas, a navigable communication between Lake Erie and the Ohio river would greatly promote the agricultural, manufacturing and commercial interests of the good people of the state of Ohio; and would unite, by the cementing influence of interest and commercial intercourse, the most remote parts of the United States, thereby strengthening the bonds of their political Union: And whereas, the practicability of making such navigable communication, has not been satisfactorily ascertained by an experienced and skilful engineer: Therefore, with a view to obtain accurate information touching this highly interesting subject,

Sec. 1. *Be it enacted by the General Assembly of the state of Ohio,* That the Governor be, and he is hereby authorized to employ an approved practical engineer, whose duty it shall be to make such surveys and examinations of the country between Lake Erie and the Ohio river, with a view to ascertain the practicability of uniting those waters by a navigable canal, as is directed in this act.

Sec. 2. *Be it further enacted,* That Benjamin Tappan, Alfred Kelly, Thomas Worthington, Ethan A. Brown, Jeremiah Morrow, Isaac Minor and Ebenezer Buckingham, jr. be, and they are hereby appointed commissioners, whose duty it shall be to cause such examinations, surveys and estimates to be made by the engineer as aforesaid, as may be necessary to ascertain the practicability of connecting Lake Erie with the Ohio river by a canal through the following routes, viz: from Sandusky bay to the Ohio river; from the Maumee river to the Ohio river; from the Lake to the river aforesaid by the sources of the Cuyahoga and Black river and the Muskingum rivers; and from the lake by the sources of the Grand and Mahoning rivers to the Ohio river: And it shall be their duty to make, or cause estimates to be made, as near as can be, of the probable cost of cutting a canal on each of said routes, if found practicable; and to make an estimate of their comparative advantages for a canal, which estimates it shall be their duty to report, so far as may be completed, to the next General Assembly, accompanied with their views generally, and such information touching the contemplated improvements as they may deem important.

Sec. 3. *Be it further enacted,* That it shall be the duty of the commissioners aforesaid, to meet at Columbus at as early a day as an engineer can be obtained, on the notification of the Governor, who shall name the time, and at such other times and places as they may deem necessary for the promotion of the objects hereby intended. And it shall be their duty, when convened as aforesaid, to make the necessary arrangements and preparations for the commencement of the proposed surveys and examinations—to employ the necessary assistants to enable the engineer to discharge the duties required of him—to take the necessary measures to obtain such information generally, as will promote the objects of the surveys and estimates hereby authorized; and to make report of the same as required by the second section of this act. And it shall be their further duty, or a majority of them to report to the next General Assembly, such views and information as they may be enabled to obtain as to the ways and means of making such canal, should it be found practicable.

Sec. 4. *And be it further enacted,* That a sum not exceeding six thousand dollars, be and the same is hereby appropriated, for the payment of the charges and expences which may be incurred in making the surveys and estimates hereby authorized, to be paid out of any money in the treasury not otherwise appropriated, on the certificate of the commissioners accompanied by proper vouchers.

JOHN BIGGER,
Speaker of the House of Representatives.
ALLEN TRIMBLE,
Speaker of the Senate.

6. TWELVE PROPOSITIONS OF THE NORTH CAROLINA SLAVE CODE, 1830

I. The master may determine the kind, and degree, and time of labour to which the slave shall be subjected.

II. The master may supply the slave with such food and clothing only, but as to quantity and quality, as he may think proper or find convenient.

III. The master may, at his discretion, inflict any punishment upon the person of his slave.

IV. All the power of the master over his slave may be exercised not by himself only in person, but by any one whom he may assign as his agent.

V. Slaves have no legal rights of property in things, real or personal; but whatever they may acquire belongs, in point of law, to their master.

VI. The slave, being a personal chattel, is at all times liable to be sold absolutely, or mortgaged or leased, at the will of his master.

VII. He may also be sold by processes of law for the satisfaction of the debts of a living or the debts and bequests of a deceased master, at the suit of creditors or legatees.

VIII. A slave cannot be a party before a judicial tribunal, in any species of action against his master, no matter how atrocious may have been the injury received from him.

IX. Slaves cannot redeem themselves, nor obtain a change of masters, though cruel treatment may have rendered such change necessary for their personal safety.

X. Slaves being objects of property, if injured by third persons, their owners may bring suit, and recover damages, for the injury.

XI. Slaves can make no contract.

XII. Slavery is hereditary and perpetual.

7. EXTRACT FROM THE ACCOUNT BOOK OF ROBERT C. HOLLAND, M.D., OF LEXINGTON, KENTUCKY, 1834

July 1,	To visit Self & Lady & 2 children	$3.00
July 6,	To visit Lady & Consultation	5.00
July 14,	To visit negro child & 3 doses Med[icine]	2.00
Aug 3,	To extract tooth, negro girl	.50
Aug 17,	To vaccinating 7 persons till they took virus	5.00
Sept 4,	To services negro woman (Charlotte) during spell of sickness, about 2 weeks & med[icine]	7.00
Oct 10,	To obstetrical services for Amy (black)	8.00
Oct 19,	To visit negro child, pres[cription], 2 cathartics & worm oil	1.75

Oct 23,   To 2 visits Self & two
           negroes & pres[cription]   2.50

8. ADVERTISEMENT FOR JOHN DEERE'S PLOW, *ROCK RIVER REGISTER,* MARCH 10, 1843

John Deere respectfully informs his friends and customers, the agricultural community, of this and adjoining counties, and dealers in Ploughs, that he is now prepared to fill orders for the same on presentation.

The Moldboard of this well, and so favorably known PLOUGH, is made of wrought iron, and the share of steel, $5/_{16th}$ of an inch thick, which carries a fine sharp edge. The whole face of the mold board and share is ground smooth, so that it scours perfectly bright in any soil, and will not choke in the foulest of ground. It will do more work in a day, and do it much better and with less labor, to both team and holder, than the ordinary ploughs that do not scour, and in consequence of the ground being better prepared, the agriculturist obtains a much heavier crop.

The price of Ploughs, in consequence of hard times, will be reduced from last year's prices. Grand detour, Feb. 3, 1843.

9. REGULATIONS FOR THE BOARDING-HOUSES OF THE MIDDLESEX COMPANY, LOWELL, MASSACHUSETTS, CA. 1846

The tenants of the Boarding Houses are not to board, or permit any part of their houses to be occupied by any person except those in the employ of the Company.

They will be considered answerable for any improper conduct in their houses, and are not to permit their boarders to have company at unseasonable hours.

The doors must be closed at ten o'clock in the evening, and no one admitted after that time without some reasonable excuse.

The keepers of the Boarding Houses must give an account of the number, names, and employment of their boarders, when required; and report the names of such as are guilty of any improper conduct, or are not in the regular habit of attending public worship.

The buildings and yards about them must be kept clean and in good order, and if they are injured otherwise than from ordinary use, all necessary repairs will be made, and charged to the occupant.

It is indispensable that all persons in the employ of the Middlesex Company should be vaccinated who have not been, as also the families with whom they board; which will be done at the expense of the Company.

SAMUEL LAWRENCE, Agent

10. THE MASSACHUSETTS COMPULSORY SCHOOL LAW OF 1850

Section 1. Each of the several cities and towns in this Commonwealth is hereby authorized and empowered to make all needful provisions and arrangements concerning habitual truants, and children not attending school, without any regular and lawful occupation, growing up in ignorance, between the ages of six and fifteen years; and also all such ordinances and by-laws, respecting such children, as shall be deemed most conducive to their welfare, and the good order of such city or town; and there shall be annexed to such ordinances, suitable penalties, not exceeding, for any one breach, a fine of twenty dollars: *provided,* that said ordinances and by-laws shall be approved by the court of common pleas for the county, and shall not be repugnant to laws of the Commonwealth.

Sec. 2. The several cities and towns, availing themselves of the provisions of this act, shall appoint, at the annual meetings of said towns, or annually by the mayor and aldermen of said cities, three or more persons, who alone shall be authorized to make the complaints, in every case of violation of said ordinances or by-laws, to the justice of the peace, or other judicial officer, who, by said ordinances, shall have jurisdiction in the matter, which persons, thus appointed, shall alone have authority to carry into execution the judgments of said justices of the peace or other judicial officer.

Sec. 3. The said justices of the peace, or other judicial officers, shall in all cases, at their discretion, in place of the fine aforesaid, be authorized to order children, proved before them to be growing up in truancy, and without the benefit of education provided for them by law, to be placed, for such periods of time as they may judge expedient, in such institution of instruction or house of reformation, or other suitable situation, as may be assigned or provided for the purpose, under the authority conveyed by the first section of this act, in each city or town availing itself of the powers herein granted.

11. ENTRY IN THE MEMORANDUM BOOK OF A MASSACHUSETTS MANUFACTURER, JANUARY 27, 1858

Dennis Rier of Newbury Port has this day engaged to come with his family to work in our factory on the following conditions. He is to be here about the 20th of next month and is to have the following wages per week

Himself	$5.00
His son Robert Rier, 10 years of age	0.83
Daughter Mary, 12 years of age	1.25
Son William, 13 years of age	1.50
Son Michael, 16 years of age	2.00
	10.58
His sister, Abigail Smith	2.33
Her daughter Sally, 8 years of age	0.75
Son Samuel, 13 years of age	1.50
	4.58

12. RULES AND REGULATIONS ADOPTED AT GOLD HILL, UTAH TERRITORY, JUNE 11, 1859

Sec. 1. Any person who shall willfully and with malice aforethought take the life of any person, shall, upon being duly convicted thereof, suffer the penalty of death by hanging.

Sec. 2. Any person who shall wilfully wound another, shall upon conviction thereof, suffer such penalty as the jury may determine.

Sec. 3. Any person found guilty of robbery or theft, shall, upon conviction, be punished with stripes or banishment, as the jury may determine.

Sec. 4. Any person found guilty of assault and battery, or exhibiting deadly weapons, shall, upon conviction, be fined or banished, as the jury may determine.

Sec. 5. No banking games, under any consideration, shall be allowed in this district, under the penalty of final banishment from the district.

13. EXTRACTS FROM THE PACIFIC RAILWAY ACT OF JULY 1, 1862

An Act to aid in the Construction of a Railroad and Telegraph Line from the Missouri River to the Pacific Ocean, and to secure to the Government the Use of the same for Postal, Military, and Other Purposes. . . .

. . . [T]he Union Pacific Railroad Company . . . is hereby authorized and empowered to lay out, locate, construct, furnish, maintain, and enjoy a continuous railroad and telegraph, with the appurtenances, from a point on the one hundredth meridian of longitude west from Greenwich, between the south margin of the valley of the Republican River and the north margin of the valley of the Platte River, in the Territory of Nebraska, to the western boundary of Nevada Territory, upon the route and terms hereinafter provided, and is hereby vested with all the powers, privileges, and immunities necessary to carry into effect the purposes of this act as herein set forth. . . .

Sec. 2. *And be it further enacted,* That the right of way through the public lands be, and the same is hereby, granted to said company for the construction of said railroad and telegraph line; and the right, power, and authority is hereby given to said company to take from the public lands adjacent to the line of said road, earth, stone, timber, and other materials for the construction thereof; said right of way is granted to said railroad to the extent of two hundred feet in width on each side of said railroad where it may pass over the public lands, including all necessary grounds for stations, buildings, workshops, and depots, machine shops, switches, side tracks, turntables, and water stations. The United States shall extinguish as rapidly as may be the Indian titles to all lands falling under the operation of this act and required for the said right of way and grants hereinafter made. . . .

Sec. 8. *And be it further enacted,* That the line of said railroad and telegraph shall commence at a point on the one hundredth meridian of longitude west from Greenwich, between the south margin of the valley of the Republican River and the north margin of the valley of the Platte River, in the Territory of Nebraska, at a point to be fixed by the President of the United States, after actual surveys; thence running westerly upon the most direct, central, and practicable route, through the territories of the United States, to the western boundary of the Territory of Nevada, there to meet and connect with the line of the Central Pacific Railroad Company of California.

Sec. 9. *And be it further enacted,* That . . . [t]he Central Pacific Railroad Company of California, a corporation existing under the laws of the State of California, are hereby authorized to construct a railroad and telegraph line from the Pacific coast, at or near San Francisco, or the navigable waters of the Sacramento River, to the eastern boundary of California, upon the same terms and conditions, in all respects, as are contained in this act for the construction of said railroad and telegraph line first mentioned, and to meet and connect with the first mentioned railroad and telegraph line on the eastern boundary of California. . . .

Sec. 10. *And be it further enacted,* That . . . in case said first-named company shall complete their line to the eastern boundary of California before it is completed across said State by the Central Pacific Railroad Company of California, said first-named company is hereby authorized to continue in constructing the same through California, with the consent of said State, upon the terms mentioned in this act, until said roads shall meet and connect, and the whole line of said railroad and telegraph is completed; and the Central Pacific Railroad Company of California, after completing its road across said State, is authorized to continue the construction of said railroad and telegraph through the Territories of the United States to the Missouri River, including the branch roads specified in this act, upon the routes hereinbefore and hereinafter indicated, on the terms and conditions provided in this act in relation to the said Union Pacific Railroad Company, until said roads shall meet and connect, and the whole line of said railroad and branches and telegraph is completed.

14. THE EMANCIPATION PROCLAMATION, JANUARY 1, 1863

By the President of the United States of America: A Proclamation.

Whereas on the 22d day of September, A.D. 1862, a proclamation was issued by the President of the United States, containing, among other things, the following, to wit:

"That on the 1st day of January, A.D. 1863, all persons held as slaves within any State or designated part of a State the people whereof shall then be in rebellion against the United States shall be then, thenceforward, and forever free; and the executive government of the United States, including the military and naval authority thereof, will recognize and maintain the freedom of such persons and will do no act or acts to repress such persons, or any of them, in any efforts they may make for their actual freedom.

"That the executive will on the 1st day of January aforesaid, by proclamation, designate the States and parts of States, if any, in which the people thereof, respectively, shall then be in rebellion against the United States; and the fact that any State or the people thereof shall on that day be in good faith represented in the Congress of the United States by members chosen thereto at elections wherein a majority of the qualified voters of such States shall have participated shall, in the absence of strong countervailing testimony, be deemed conclusive evidence that such State and the people thereof are not then in rebellion against the United States."

Now, therefore, I, Abraham Lincoln, President of the United States, by virtue of the power in me vested as Commander-in-Chief of the Army and Navy of the United States in time of actual armed rebellion against the authority and government of the United States, and as a fit and necessary war measure for suppressing said rebellion, do, on this 1st day of January, A.D. 1863, and in accordance with my purpose so to do, publicly proclaimed for the full period of one hundred days from the first day above mentioned, order and designate as the States and parts of States wherein the people thereof, respectively, are this day in rebellion against the United States the following, to wit:

Arkansas, Texas, Louisiana (except the parishes of St. Bernard, Plaquemines, Jefferson, St. John, St. Charles, St. James, Ascension, Assumption, Terrebonne, Lafourche, St. Mary, St. Martin, and Orleans, including the city of New Orleans), Mississippi, Alabama, Florida, Georgia, South Carolina, North Carolina, and Virginia (except the forty-eight counties designated as West Virginia, and also the counties of Berkeley, Accomac, Northhampton, Elizabeth City, York, Princess Anne, and Norfolk, including the cities of Norfolk and Portsmouth), and which excepted parts are for the present left precisely as if this proclamation were not issued.

And by virtue of the power and for the purpose aforesaid, I do order and declare that all persons held as slaves within said designated States and parts of States are, and henceforward shall be, free; and that the Executive Government of the United States, including the military and naval authorities thereof, will recognize and maintain the freedom of said persons.

And I hereby enjoin upon the people so declared to be free to abstain from all violence, unless in necessary self-defense; and I recommend to them that, in all cases when allowed, they labor faithfully for reasonable wages.

And I further declare and make known that such persons of suitable condition will be received into the armed service of the United States to garrison forts, positions, stations, and other places, and to man vessels of all sorts in said service.

And upon this act, sincerely believed to be an act of justice, warranted by the Constitution upon military necessity, I invoke the considerate judgment of mankind and the gracious favor of Almighty God.

15. PREAMBLE TO THE CONSTITUTION OF THE CIGAR MAKERS' INTERNATIONAL UNION OF AMERICA, 1864

Labor has no protection—the weak are devoured by the strong. All wealth and power center in the hands of the few, and the many are their victims and bondsmen. In all countries and at all times capital has been used to monopolize particular branches of business, until the vast and various industrial pursuits of the world are rapidly coming under the immediate control of a comparatively small portion of mankind, tending, if not checked by the toiling millions, to enslave and impoverish them.

Labor is the creator of all wealth, and as such the laborer is at least entitled to a remuneration sufficient to enable himself and family to enjoy more of the leisure that rightfully belongs to him, more social advantages, more of the benefits, privileges and emoluments of the world; in a word, all those rights and privileges necessary to make him capable of enjoying, appreciating, defending and perpetuating the blessings of modern civilization. Past experience teaches us that labor has so far been unable to arrest the encroachments of capital, neither has it been able to obtain justice from lawmaking power. This is due to a lack of practical organization and unity of action. "In union there is strength." Organization and united action are the only means by which the laboring classes can gain any advantage for themselves. Good and strong labor organizations are enabled to defend and preserve the interests of the working people. By organization we are able to assist each other in cases of strikes and lock-outs, sickness and death. And through organization only the workers, as a class, are able to gain legislative advantages.

No one will dispute the beneficial results attendant upon harmonious and intelligent action, and it is imperatively the duty of man to do all in his power to secure thorough organization and unity of action. In the performance of that duty we have formed the Cigar Makers' International Union of America, with a view to securing the organization of every cigar maker, for the purpose of elevating the material, moral and intellectual welfare of the craft by the following means:

1. By gratuitously furnishing employment.

2. By mutual pecuniary aid in case of strikes and lock-outs, sickness and death.

3. By advancing money for traveling.

4. By defending members involved in legal difficulties consequent upon the discharge of their official duties to the union.

5. By the issuing of a trade journal defending the interests of the union of the trade.

6. By using all honorable means to effect a national federation of trade unions.

7. By prevailing upon the Legislature to secure, first the prohibition of child labor under fourteen years of age; the establishment of a normal day's labor to consist of not more than eight hours per day for all classes; the abolition of the truck system, tenement house cigar manufacture, and the system of letting out by contract the convict labor in prisons and reformatory institutions; the legalization of trade unions and the establishment of bureaus of labor statistics.

16. EXTRACT FROM A BROCHURE FOR EASTERN EMIGRANTS ISSUED BY THE NORTHERN PACIFIC RAILROAD COMPANY, CA. 1870

Pages of incontestable evidence could be introduced here to prove that nowhere in the world can such large crops of wheat, barley, rye, oats, potatoes and other roots be raised as on and about the Land Grant of the Northern Pacific Railroad; that nowhere in the world are there such apples, pears, plums, and cherries as those grown on and about all the Grant west of the Rocky Mountains; that fruit-trees there invariably bear generally in two, at most in three years, from the graft; that the curculio and other insects destructive to fruit here are wholly unknown there; that nowhere do shade, fuel, and fruit-trees grow so rapidly, vigorously, and beautifully, as there; that nowhere in the world is there a grass to be compared to that combination of timothy and oats, the "bunch grass," which covers most of this Land Grant, and which on the ground is perfect hay in July and in January; that nowhere is such possibility of grazing cattle in vast herds without shelter, prepared fodder, or care, as exists all over the regions to be traversed by the Road on both sides of the Rocky Mountains, whose universally diffused "bunch grass" has justly given to it the name of "the graziers' paradise."

The materials for the greatest lumber trade the world has seen exist on and near the Western end of this Land Grant, and maintain with a single interruption to the eastern foot of the Rocky Mountains. Forests of fir of three varieties, of cedar of two varieties, of pine, spruce, hemlock, cypress, ash, curled maple, and black and white oak envelop Puget Sound, and cover the larger part of Washington Territory, surpassing the woods of all the rest of the globe in the size, quality and quantity of the timber. The firs in innumerable localities will cut 120,000 feet to the acre. Trees are common whose circumferences range from 20 to 50 feet, and whose heights vary from 200 to upward of 300 feet. The paradox of firs too large to be profitably cut into lumber, is to be seen all over Western Washington. These are rejected by the choppers, and trees having diameters ranging only from 30 to 50 inches are selected, and these yield from 70 to 200 feet of solid trunk free from limbs and knots. The cedars of Washington are as thick, through, as the firs, but not as tall. So prodigal is Nature in this region, and so wastefully fastidious is man, that lands yielding only 30,000 feet of lumber to the acre are considered to be hardly worth cutting over. Forests yielding 100,000 feet and upward are common all around Puget Sound. The wood of the firs and cedars, unequaled for lightness, straightness of cleavage, and resistance of moisture, and stronger than oak and more retentive of spikes and tree-nails, will supplant all other material for ship-building on both shores of the Pacific Ocean. This product of the as yet scarcely scarred forests of Washington Territory, was sold in California, South America, Australia, Japan, China, the East Indies and Europe.

From the eastern foothills of the Rocky Mountains to Puget Sound, this Land Grant belts the richest mineral deposits on this continent, consisting of gold, silver, platinum, lead, copper, iron and rock-salt. The banks and bars of every stream running from the Rocky range into the Columbia, Yellowstone, Missouri, and Puget Sound will pan out gold. At the eastern end of the Grant, and on or near the line of the road, are inexhaustible deposits of copper and of the famed Lake Superior magnetic iron ores.

This Land Grant has an abundance of fuel—coal, lignite, and wood. Bituminous coal of the best quality outcrops for thirty miles on the eastern rim of Puget Sound. Three veins have been opened which can be cheaply worked, the lowest being sixteen feet thick. West of the Cascade range of mountains coal is found and mined at different points all the way from Willamette Valley to Bellingham Bay. It has been found near the Cowlitz and Snoqualmie Pass of the Cascades. It outcrops on the Yellowstone and the headwaters of the Missouri. It is extensively mined for Government and public use at the great bend of the Missouri.

The way-traffic and way-travel on the Northern Pacific Railroad will be that which will inevitably spring from a wide belt of this continent whose soil will yield immense crops of grain, fruit, and vegetables, whose pasturage is the marvel of travelers, the mildness of whose climate is seemingly a paradox, but is superabundantly testified to by man and beast. The domestic cattle of Montana, Idaho, Washington, and Dakota, range out all winter and are fat in March. The Mexican horses, stolen by the Sioux, Cheyennes, and Assiniboines, are turned out to shift for themselves on the fall of snow, from latitude 45 up to 53, and come in in the spring fat, sleek, and strong. Unsheltered, unfed, they thrive in the open air on grass reached by pawing off with their hoofs the occasional covers of snow. Much of the line of the Northern Pacific road passes through the winter homes of countless herds of buffaloes, elk, deer, and antelopes.

17. WEST VIRGINIA REQUESTS FEDERAL ASSISTANCE IN HANDLING THE RAILROAD STRIKE OF 1877

Wheeling, July 18, 1877

To His Excellency, R. B. Hayes,
President of the U.S.
Washington, D.C.:

Owing to unlawful combinations and domestic violence now existing at Martinsburg and at other points along the line of the Baltimore and Ohio railroad, it is impossible with any force at my command to execute the laws of the State. I therefore call upon your Excellency for the assistance of the United States military to protect the law abiding people of the State against domestic violence, and to maintain supremacy of the law.

The Legislature is not now in session and could not assemble in time to take any action in the emergency. A force of from two to three hundred troops should be sent without delay to Martinsburg, where my aid, Col. Delaplain, will meet and confer with the officer in command.

H. M. Mathews
Governor of West Va.

18. Preamble to the Constitution of the Knights of Labor, 1878

The recent alarming development and aggression of aggregated wealth, which, unless checked, will inevitably lead to the pauperization and hopeless degradation of the toiling masses, render it imperative, if we desire to enjoy the blessings of life, that a check should be placed upon its power and upon unjust accumulation, and a system adopted which will secure to the laborer the fruits of his toil; and as this much-desired object can only be accomplished by the thorough unification of labor, and the united efforts of those who obey the divine injunction that "in the sweat of thy brow shalt thou eat bread," we have formed the [*name of local assembly*] with a view to securing the organization and direction, by co-operative effort, of the power of the industrial classes; and we submit to the world the objects sought to be accomplished by our organization, calling upon all who believe in securing "the greatest good to the greatest number" to aid and assist us.

Objectives

I. To bring within the folds of organization every department of productive industry, making knowledge a standpoint for action, and industrial, moral worth, not wealth, the true standard of individual and national greatness.

II. To secure to the toilers a proper share of the wealth that they create; more of the leisure that rightfully belongs to them; more [social] advantages; more of the benefits, privileges, and emoluments of the world; in a word, all those rights and privileges necessary to make them capable of enjoying, appreciating, defending, and perpetuating the blessings of good government.

III. To arrive at the true condition of the producing masses in their educational, moral, and financial condition, by demanding from the various governments the establishment of bureaus of Labor Statistics.

IV. The establishment of co-operative institutions, productive and distributive.

V. The reserving of the public lands—the heritage of the people—for the actual settler. Not another acre [is to be allocated] for railroads or speculators.

VI. The abrogation of all laws that do not bear equally upon capital and labor, the removal of unjust technicalities, delays, and discriminations in the administration of justice, and the adopting of measures providing for the health and safety of those engaged in mining, manufacturing, or building pursuits.

VII. The enactment of laws to compel chartered corporations to pay their employees weekly, in full, for labor performed during the preceding week, in the lawful money of the country.

VIII. The enactment of laws giving mechanics and laborers a first lien on their work for their full wages.

IX. The abolishment of the contract system on national, state, and municipal work.

X. The substitution of arbitration for strikes, whenever and wherever employers and employes are willing to meet on equitable grounds.

XI. The prohibition of the employment of children in workshops, mines and factories before attaining their fourteenth year.

XII. To abolish the system of letting out by contract the labor of convicts in our prisons and reformatory institutions.

XIII. To secure for both sexes equal pay for equal work.

XIV. The reduction of the hours of labor to eight per day, so that the laborers may have more time for social enjoyment and intellectual improvement, and be enabled to reap the advantages conferred by the labor-saving machinery which their brains have created.

XV. To prevail upon governments to establish a purely national circulating medium, based upon the faith and resources of the nation, and issued directly to the people, without the intervention of any system of banking corporations, which money shall be a legal tender in payment of all debts, public or private.

19. EXTRACTS FROM A CHILDREN'S AID SOCIETY REPORT ON VISITS TO NEW YORK CITY NIGHT SCHOOLS, CA. 1880

There were some hundred children [at the Crosby Street School]; their occupations were as follows: They put up insect-powder drive wagons, tend oyster-saloons; are tinsmiths, engravers, office-boys, in type-founderies, at screws, in blacksmith-shops; make cigars, polish, work at packing tobacco, in barber-shops, at paper-stands; are cash-boys, light porters, make artificial flowers, work at hair; are errand boys, make ink, are in Singer's sewing-machine factory, and printing-offices; some post bills, some are paint-scrapers, some peddlers; they pack snuff, attend poultry-stands at market, in shoe-stores and hat-stores, tend stands, and help painters and carpenters.

At the Fifth-ward School (No. 141 Hudson Street), were fifty boys and girls. One of them, speaking of her occupation, said: "I work at feathers, cutting the feathers from cock's tails. It is a very busy time now. They took in forty new hands today. I get three dollars and fifty cents a week: next week I'll get more. I go to work at eight o'clock and leave off at six. The feathers are cut from the stem, then steamed, and curled, and packed. They are sent then to Paris, but more South and West." One boy said he worked at twisting twine; another drove a "hoisting-horse," another blacked boots, etc.

At the Eleventh-ward School, foot of East Eleventh Street, there was an interesting class of boys and girls under thirteen years of age. One boy said he was employed during the day in making chains of beads, and says that a number of the boys and girls present are in the same business. Another said he worked at coloring maps. Another blows an organ for a music-teacher.

20. YELLOW-DOG CONTRACT, WESTERN UNION TELEGRAPH COMPANY, 1883

I, ... of . . . . in consideration of my present reemployment by the Western Union Telegraph Co. hereby promise and agree to and with the said company that I will forthwith abandon any and all membership, connection or affiliation with any organization or society, whether secret or open, which in any wise attempts to regulate the conditions of my services or the payment thereof while in the employment now undertaken. I hereby further agree that I will, while in the employ of said company, render good and faithful service to the best of my ability, and will not in anywise renew or re-enter upon any relations or membership whatsoever in or with any such organizations or society. Dated . . . . 1883. Signed . . . . Address . . . . (Seal) Accepted for the Western Union Telegraph Co. . . . ., Superintendent

21. EXTRACT FROM THE SHERMAN ANTI-TRUST ACT, JULY 2, 1890

An ACT to protect trade and commerce against unlawful restraints and monopolies. . . .

Be it enacted

Sec. 1. Every contract, combination in the form of trust or otherwise, or conspiracy, in restraint of trade or commerce among the several States, or with foreign nations, is hereby declared to be illegal. Every person who shall make any such contract or engage in any such combination or conspiracy, shall be deemed guilty of a misdemeanor, and, on conviction thereof, shall be punished by fine not exceeding five thousand dollars, or by imprisonment not exceeding one year, or by both said punishments, in the discretion of the court.

Sec. 2. Every person who shall monopolize, or attempt to monopolize, or combine or conspire with any other person or persons, to monopolize any part of the trade or commerce among the several States, or with foreign nations, shall be deemed guilty of a misdemeanor, and, on conviction thereof, shall be punished by fine not exceeding five thousand dollars, or by imprisonment not exceeding one year, or by both said punishments, in the discretion of the court.

Sec. 3. Every contract, combination in form of trust or otherwise, or conspiracy, in restraint of trade or commerce in any Territory of the United States or of the District of Columbia, or in restraint of trade or commerce between any such Territory and another, or between any such Territory or Territories and any State or States or the District of Columbia, or with foreign nations, or between the District of Columbia and any State or States or foreign nations, is hereby declared illegal. Every person who shall make any such contract or engage in any such combination or conspiracy, shall be deemed guilty of a misdemeanor, and, on conviction thereof, shall be punished by fine not exceeding five thousand dollars, or by imprisonment not exceeding one year, or by both said punishments, in the discretion of the court.

Sec. 4. The several circuit courts of the United States are hereby invested with jurisdiction to prevent and restrain violations of this act; and it shall be the duty of the several district attorneys of the United States, in their respective districts, under the direction of the Attorney-General, to institute proceedings in equity to prevent and restrain such violations. Such proceedings may be by way of petition setting forth the case and praying that such violation shall be enjoined or otherwise prohibited. When the parties complained of shall have been duly notified of such petition the courts shall proceed, as soon as may be, to the hearing and determination of the case; and pending such petition and before final decrees, the court may at any time make such temporary restraining order or prohibition as shall be deemed just in the premises.

Sec. 5. Whenever it shall appear to the court before which any proceeding under Section four of this act may be pending, that the ends of justice require that other parties should be brought before the court, the court may cause them to be summoned, whether they reside in the district in which the court is held or not; and subpoenas to that end may be served in any district by the marshal thereof.

Sec. 6. Any property owned under any contract or by any combination, or pursuant to any conspiracy (and being the subject thereof) mentioned in section one of this act, and being in the course of transportation from one State to another, or to a foreign country, shall be forfeited to the United States, and may be seized and condemned by like proceedings as those provided by law for the forfeiture, seizure, and condemnation of property imported into the United States contrary to law.

Sec. 7. Any person who shall be injured in his business or property by any other person or corporation by reason of anything forbidden or declared to be unlawful by this act, may sue therefor in any circuit court of the United States in the district in which the defendant resides or is found, without respect to the amount in controversy, and shall recover threefold the damages by him sustained, and the costs of suit, including a reasonable attorney's fee.

Sec. 8. That the word "person," or "persons," wherever used in this act shall be deemed to include corporations and associations existing under or authorized by the laws of either the United States, the laws of any of the Territories, the laws of any State, or the laws of any foreign country.

22. The Sheriff of Allegheny County Requests That State Militia Forces Be Sent to Homestead, Pennsylvania, July 10, 1892

Robert E. Pattison, Governor,
    Harrisburg, Pa.:

The situation at Homestead has not improved. While all is quiet there, the strikers are in control, and openly express to me and the public their determination that the works shall not be operated unless by themselves. After making all efforts in my power, I have failed to secure a posse respectable enough in numbers to accomplish anything, and I am satisfied that no posse raised by civil authorities can do anything to change the condition of affairs, and that any attempt by an inadequate force to restore the right of law will only result in further armed resistance and consequent loss of life. Only a large military force will enable me to control matters. I believe if such a force is sent the disorderly element will be overawed and order will be restored. I therefore call upon you for assistance.

William H. McCleary, Sheriff

23. Appeal Issued to the People of Chicago, May 28, 1894

TO THE PUBLIC OF CHICAGO:—The people of Pullman are destitute and starving. Over 5000 human beings are in dire necessity and appeal to the liberal-minded people of Chicago for help. Their unfortunate condition is not due to any fault of theirs. They have been noted for their thrift, sobriety, and industry. The fault lies in the hard times and a hard taskmaster. Forced for years to work on starvation wages, so that dividends could be paid on watered stock, they have at last struck against the soulless corporation which sought to fatten on the very marrow of their bones.

They struck against a slavery worse than that of the negroes of the south. These, at least, were well fed and well cared for, while the white slaves of Pullman, worked they ever so willingly, could not earn enough to clothe and feed themselves decently—hardly enough to keep body and soul together.

Now that they have struck for living wages, for a fair day's pay for a fair day's work, they find themselves penniless, with gaunt famine and despair staring them in the face.

Big-hearted, open-handed citizens of this big-hearted City of Chicago, these unfortunates turn to you appealing for aid. Help them as you would wish to be helped in the hour of affliction. Their cause is the cause of humanity. Their struggle is the struggle of honest industry against corporate greed.

24. Extract from a Statement from the Pullman Strikers, June 15, 1894

To the Convention of the American Railway Union, assembled in Uhlich Hall, Chicago. . . .

Mr. President and Brothers of the American Railway Union: We struck at Pullman because we were without hope. We joined the American Railway Union because it gave us a glimmer of hope. Twenty thousand souls, men, women, and little ones, have their eyes turned toward this convention to-day, straining eagerly through dark despondency for a glimmer of the heaven-sent message you alone can give us on this earth.

In stating to this body our grievances it is hard to tell where to begin. You all must know that the proximate cause of our strike was the discharge of two members of our grievance committee the day after George M. Pullman, himself, and Thomas H. Wickes, his second vice-president, had guaranteed them absolute immunity. The more remote causes are still imminent. Five reductions in wages, in work, and in conditions of employment swept through the shops at Pullman between May and December, 1893. The last was the most severe, amounting to nearly 30 per cent, and our rents had not fallen. We owed Pullman $70,000 when we struck May 11. We owe him twice as much to-day. He does not evict us for two reasons: One, the force of popular sentiment and public opinion; the other because he hopes to starve us out, to break through in the back of the American Railway Union, and to deduct from our miserable wages when we are forced to return to him the last dollar we owe him for the occupancy of his houses.

Rents all over the city in every quarter of its vast extent have fallen, in some cases to one-half.

Residences, compared with which ours are hovels, can be had a few miles away at the prices we have been contributing to make a millionaire a billionaire. What we pay $15 for in Pullman is leased for $8 in Roseland; and remember that just as no man or woman of our 4,000 toilers has ever felt the friendly pressure of George M. Pullman's hand, so no man or woman of us all has ever owned or can ever hope to own one inch of George M. Pullman's land. Why, even the very streets are his. His ground has never been platted of record, and to-day he may debar any man who has acquiring rights as his tenant from walking in his highways. And those streets; do you know what he has named them? He says after the four great inventors in methods of transportation. And do you know what their names are? Why, Fulton, Stephenson, Watt, and Pullman.

Water which Pullman buys from the city at 8 cents a thousand gallons he retails to us at 500 per cent advance and claims he is losing $400 a month on it. Gas which sells at 75 cents per thousand feet in Hyde Park, just north of us, he sells for $2.25. When we went to tell him our grievances he said we were all his "children."

Pullman, both the man and the town, is an ulcer on the body politic. He owns the houses, the school-houses, and churches of God in the town he gave his once humble name. The revenue he derives from these, the wages he pays out with one hand—the Pullman Palace Car Company, he takes back with the other—the Pullman Land Association. He is able by this to bid under any contract car shop in this country. His competitors in business, to meet this, must reduce the wages of their men. This gives him the excuse to reduce ours to conform to the market. His business rivals must in turn scale down; so must he. And thus the merry war—the dance of skeletons bathed in human tears—goes on, and it will go on, brothers, forever, unless you, the American Railway Union, stop it; end it; crush it out.

Our town is beautiful. In all these thirteen years no word of scandal has arisen against one of our women, young or old. What city of 20,000 persons can show the like? Since our strike, the arrests, which used to average four or five a day, has dwindled down to less than one a week. We are peaceable; we are orderly, and but for the kindly beneficence of kindly-hearted people in and about Chicago we would be starving. We are not desperate to-day, because we are not hungry, and our wives and children are not begging for bread. But George M. Pullman, who ran away from the public opinion that has arisen against him, like the genii from the battle in the Arabian Nights, is not feeding us. He is patiently seated beside his millions waiting for what? To see us starve. . . .

George M. Pullman, you know, has cut our wages from 30 to 70 per cent. George M. Pullman has caused to be paid in the last year the regular quarterly dividend of 2 per cent on his stock and an extra slice of 1½ per cent, making 9½ per cent on $30,000,000 of capital. George M. Pullman, you know, took three contracts on which he lost less than $5,000. Because he loved us? No. Because it was cheaper to lose a little money in his freight car and his coach shops than to let his workingmen go, but that petty loss, more than made up by us from money we needed to clothe our wives and little ones, was his excuse for effecting a gigantic reduction of wages in every department of his great works, of cutting men and boys and girls with equal zeal, including everyone in the repair shops of the Pullman Palace cars on which such preposterous profits have been made.

George M. Pullman will tell you, if you could go to him to-day, that he was paying better wages than any other car shops in the land. George M. Pullman might better save his breath. We have worked too often beside graduates from other establishments not to know that work for work and skill for skill, no one can compete with us at wages paid for work well done. If his wage list showed a trifle higher, our efficiency still left us heavily the loser. He does not figure on our brain and muscle. He makes his paltry computation in dollars and cents. We will make you proud of us, brothers, if you will give us the hand we need. Help us make our country better and more wholesome. Pull us out of our slough of despond. Teach arrogant grinders of the faces of the poor that there is still a God in Israel, and if need be a Jehovah—a God of battles. Do this, and on that last great day you will stand, as we hope to stand, before the great white throne "like gentlemen unafraid."

25. PRESIDENT GROVER CLEVELAND DECLARES MARTIAL LAW IN CHICAGO, JULY 8, 1894

Whereas by reason of the unlawful obstructions, combinations, and assemblages of persons, it has become impracticable, in the judgment of the President, to enforce by the ordinary course of judicial procedure by the laws of the United States with the State of Illinois, and especially the city of Chicago, and, whereas for the purpose of enforcing the faithful execution of the laws of the States, protecting property and removing obstructions to United States mails in the State and city aforesaid, the President has employed part of the military forces of the United States.

Now, therefore, I, Grover Cleveland, President of the United States, do hereby admonish all good citizens, and all persons who may be or may become within the city and State aforesaid against aiding, countenancing, encouraging, or taking part in such unlawful obstructions, combinations, or assemblages. I hereby warn all persons engaged in or in any way connected with the unlawful obstructions, combinations, or assemblages to disperse and retire peaceably to their respective abodes on or before 12 o'clock noon on the 9th day of July. Those who disregard this warning and persist in taking part with the riotous mob in forcibly resisting or obstructing the execution of the laws of the United States, or interfering with the functions of Government, or destroying or attempting to destroy property belonging to the United States, or under its protection, cannot be regarded otherwise than public enemies. The troops employed against such riotous mob will act with all moderation and forbearance consistent with the accomplishment of the desired end; but stern necessities confront them, and will not with certainty permit a discrimination between the guilty participants and those who may be mingled with them through curiosity and without criminal intent. The only safe course, therefore, for those not actually unlawfully participating is to abide in their own homes, or not to be found in the neighbourhood of riotous assemblages. While there will be no hesitation or vacillation in the decisive treatment of the guilty, the warning is especially intended to protect the innocent. Whereof, I hereunto set my hand, and have caused the Seal of the United States to be hereto affixed.

Done at the city of Washington, the 8th day of July, in the year of Our Lord one thousand eight hundred and ninety-four, and in the year of the Independence of the United States of America one hundred and eighteenth.

(Signed) Grover Cleveland, President.

W. Q. Gresham, Secretary of State

26. HANDBILL CALLING FOR AFRICAN-AMERICAN STRIKEBREAKERS, DISTRIBUTED IN BIRMINGHAM, ALABAMA, 1896

WANTED! COLORED coal-miners for Weir City, Kan., district, the paradise for colored people. Ninety-seven cents per ton, September 1 to March 1; 87 ½ cents per ton March 1 to September 1, for screened coal over seven-eighths opening. Special train will leave Birmingham the 13th. Transportation advanced. Get ready and go to the land of promise.

27. PREAMBLE TO THE CONSTITUTION OF THE INDUSTRIAL WORKERS OF THE WORLD, 1908

The working class and the employing class have nothing in common. There can be no peace so long as hunger and want are found among millions of working people and the few, who make up the employing class, have all the good things of life.

Between these two classes a struggle must go on until the workers of the world organize as a class, take possession of the earth and the machinery of production, and abolish the wage system.

We find that the centering of the management of industries into fewer and fewer hands makes the trade unions unable to cope with the ever growing power of the employing class. The trade unions foster a state of affairs which allows one set of workers to be pitted against another set of workers in the same industry, thereby helping defeat one another in wage wars. Moreover, the trade unions aid the employing class to mislead the workers into the belief that the working class have interests in common with their employers.

These conditions can be changed and the interest of the working class upheld only by an organization formed in such a way that all its members in any one industry, or in all industries if necessary, cease work whenever a strike or lockout is on in any department thereof, thus making an injury to one an injury to all.

Instead of the conservative motto, "A fair day's wage for a fair day's work," we must inscribe on our banner the revolutionary watchword, "Abolition of the wage system."

It is the historic mission of the working class to do away with capitalism. The army of production must be organized, not only for the everyday struggle with capitalists, but also to carry on production when capitalism shall have been overthrown. By organizing industrially we are forming the structure of the new society within the shell of the old.

28. AVERAGE ANNUAL INCOME OF WORKINGMEN'S FAMILIES IN THE UNITED STATES, SUMMARY FROM RECENT INVESTIGATIONS (1901–1910)

Year	Source of Data	Number of Families Included in Data	Average Annual Income
1901	Bureau of Labor's Cost of Living study, all sections of U.S., industries and races of workers	25,440	$749
1903–4	Mrs. L. B. More: budgetary study of families in Greenwich Village, New York City	200	851
1907	R. C. Chapin: budgetary study of families of varied races and occupations in New York City	391	838
1907	New York State Conference of Charities and Corrections: studies of families of varied races and occupations in Rochester, New York	100	600
1908	M. F. Byington (Russell Sage Foundation): families of steel workers in Homestead, Pa.	90	349
1908–9	Bureau of Labor: studies of silk, cotton, men's clothing, and glass workers' families in various localities in which mothers and children were wage-earners	8,741	883
1908–9	Immigration Commission: data for families in 38 principal industries in all		

| 1909–10 | eastern and southern sections, of all races | 15,726 | 721 |
| | University of Chicago Settlement: families of Chicago stock-yards workers, principally of races of recent immigration | 184 | 442 |

Source: W. Jett Lauck and Edgar Sydenstrecker, *Conditions of Labor in American Industries,* p. 248.

29. RULES FOR PICKETS DISTRIBUTED DURING THE GARMENT WORKERS' STRIKE OF 1909

Don't walk in groups of more than two or three[.]

Don't stand in front of the shop; Walk up and down the block.

Don't stop the person you wish to talk to; Walk alongside of him.

Don't get excited and shout when you are talking[.]

Don't put your hand on the person you are speaking to. Don't touch his sleeve or button. This may be construed as a "technical assault[.]"

Don't call any one "scab" or use abusive language of any kind.

Plead, persuade, appeal, but do not threaten.

If a policeman arrest you and you are sure that you have committed no offence, take down his number and give it to your union officers.

30. NOTICE POSTED IN LAWRENCE, MASSACHUSETTS, 1912

STRIKE

Quash The Indictment

Against Ettor & Giovannitti

FELLOW WORKERS—CITIZENS—COMRADES: Do not let the Capitalist Editors befog the present situation for you. In the present disclosures revealing the Dynamite Planting by the Contemptible WOOD and his Gang of Hirelings, do not forget the real motive of the PLANT. Capitalist Editors say it was to discredit the strikers—that was only part of it—the bigger motive was TO GET EXCUSE to ARREST ETTOR AND GIOVANNITTI. The Dynamite Planter was sent to plant the dynamite in Ettor's headquarters—only his unfamiliarity with the building caused it to be left on the other side of the partition in the cobbler's shop.

This was a week before Ettor and Giovannitti were arrested for murder. When one PLANT failed the dastardly crew put up another. They started the disturbances that led to the killing of Anna LaPizzo. The whole thing is now exposed.

Innocent men have spent eight months in jail. Demand an IMMEDIATE special session of the court and the quashing of the indictment against Ettor and Giovannitti.

And furthermore demand of Governor Foss and your state government a thorough investigation of the conduct of Judge Mahoney, Judge Brown and District Attorney Atwill, who are accused of "white-washing" and shielding these criminals of wealth. Demand these things—and DEMAND THEM NOW.

If Ettor and Giovannitti are not released from jail by September 30, all the workers, whether organized or unorganized, ARE URGED TO STRIKE until these innocent men are released.

ETTOR-GIOVANNITTI DEFENSE COMMITTEE

Central Bldg., Lawrence, Mass.

31. LETTER FROM THE ITALIAN GIRLS' INDUSTRIAL LEAGUE OF NEW YORK CITY TO THE NEW YORK STATE LEGISLATURE, MARCH 7, 1912

To Whom it May Concern:

We, the members of the Italian Girls' Industrial League, have come to the conclusion that the girls of this state are working too many hours a week and we think that the 54 hour bill ought to be passed and not only passed but inforced. Now in our club we represent all different lines of industry. We have the flower trade, we have the hair trade, the embroiderers, the book binders, the cloak makers, childrens' dresses, shirt waist makers, dress makers, sales ladies, candy makers & a good many other trades & also a brush maker. We also know of girls that work in candy factories that go to work at 7 in the morning and work through until seven in the evening, with only ½ hour for lunch & only get 7 cents for the extra hour & in the flowers the girls have to work so hard & when they are busy they have to work overtime & also take work home. They do not care whether a girl is sick or not, she has to work, but when they are slack they do not care whether a girl needs work or not, she is laid off. We could tell you so much of other trades but it would take up too much space. We think it would be a very good idea if some of you gentlemen would go & visit some of the different factories and see for their selves, & I do not think they would be very long in passing that bill. We do also want to speak about the canneries up state. We think it an outrage that those people have to work such long hours not only for the girls and women but for those innocent little children who have to work so hard when they ought to be at play.

from   Mrs. Maria Gonzaga, President.

32. Extracts from the *Manual of the New York Society for the Prevention of Cruelty to Children*, 1913

Sec. 120. *Certificate of Incorporation.*—Five or more persons may become a corporation for the prevention of cruelty to children, or the prevention of cruelty to animals, by making, acknowledging and filing a certificate, stating the particular objects for which the corporation is to be formed; the name of the proposed corporation; the county in which its operations are to be conducted; the town, village or city in which its principal office is to be located; the number of its directors not less than five nor more than thirty; the names and places of residence of the persons to be its directors until its first annual meeting; and the time for holding such annual meeting. . . .

Sec. 122. *Special Powers.*—A corporation formed for the purpose of preventing cruelty to children may prefer a complaint before any court, tribunal or magistrate having jurisdiction, for the violation of any law relating to or affecting children, and may aid in presenting the law and facts to such court, tribunal or magistrate in any proceeding therein.

* * * * * *

A corporation for the prevention of cruelty to children may be appointed guardian of the person of a minor child during its minority by a court of record, or a judge thereof, and may receive and retain any child at its own expense on commitment by a court or magistrate.

All magistrates and peace officers shall aid such a corporation, its officers, agents and members in the enforcement of laws relating to or affecting children, and for the prevention of cruelty to animals.

33. Notice to the Delegates to the Central Trades and Labor Union Meeting in East St. Louis, Illinois, May 28, 1917

GREETING: The immigration of the southern Negro into our city for the past eight months has reached the point where drastic action must be taken if we intend to work and live peaceably in this community.

Since this influx of undesirable Negroes has started, no less than 10,000 have come into this locality.

These men are being used to the detriment of our white citizens by some of the capitalists and a few of the real estate owners.

On next Monday evening the entire body of delegates to the Central Trades and Labor Union will call upon the mayor and city council and demand that they take some action to retard this growing menace and also devise a way to get rid of a certion portion of those who are already here.

This is not a protest against the Negro who has been a long resident of East St. Louis and is a law-abiding citizen.

We earnestly request that you be in attendance on next Monday evening at 8 o'clock, at 137 Collinsville Avenue, where we will meet and then go to the city hall.

This is more important than any local meeting, so be sure you are there.

Fraternally,
        CENTRAL TRADES AND LABOR UNION

34. U.S. Department of Labor Estimates of Negro Migration in the North, September 1917

Minimum estimate of number of Negro migrants in Pennsylvania, 1916–17, based on number of Negroes employed in 1917 in excess of number employed in 1915.

Pennsylvania:	
Pittsburgh	18,500
Philadelphia	32,000

Steelton	3,000
Harrisburg	2,000
Coatesville	6,000
Chester	3,000
Johnstown	3,000
Altoona	1,000
Pennsylvania Railroad (outside large cities)	1,000
Northwestern Pennsylvania:	
Erie, Oil City, Franklin, and Stoneboro	6,000
Northeastern Pennsylvania:	
Scranton, Wilkes-Barre, Easton, and Reading	7,000
Total for Pennsylvania	84,000

Estimate of extent of Philadelphia migration, based on number of Negroes employed in Philadelphia August, 1917.

Pennsylvania Railroad camps:	
Girard	170
Mantau Junction	300
Frankford Junction	60
Eastern Pennsylvania camps	150
Baltimore and Ohio camps	120
Reading camps	300
	1,100
Midvale Steel Co	4,000
Atlantic Refining Co	1,000
Franklin Sugar Refining Co	700
Keystone Paving & Construction Co. (Chester)	1,100
Westinghouse-Church-Kerr (Essington)	600
Eddystone Munition Corporation	600
Disston Saw Co	400
Total estimated number in plants visited	8,400
Estimated number in plants in contracting work not visited	7,750
Estimated number women and children	16,250
Total for Philadelphia	33,500

Estimate of Pittsburgh migration, based on number employed in Allegheny County, August, 1917.

	Number of Negroes employed
Carnegie Steel Co. (four plants)	4,000
Jones & Laughlin Steel Co	1,400
Westinghouse Co	900
Edgewater Steel Co	400
Union Switch & Signal Co	200
Harbison & Walker	250
National Tube Co. (all plants)	250
Pressed Steel Car Co	25

Pittsburgh Forge & Iron Co	75
Moorehead Bros	200
American Steel & Wire Co	25
Clinton Iron & Steel Co	25
Oliver Iron & Steel Co	40
Carbon Steel Co	200
Crucible Steel Co	400
A. M. Byers Co	200
Lockhart Steel Co	160
Mesta Machine Co	50
Marshall Foundry Co	25
Pennsylvania Railroad camps	300
Baltimore & Ohio Railroad camps	100
Total employed	9,225

Minimum number of migrants in Ohio (estimate based on visits and reports).

Cleveland	10,000
Cincinnati	6,000
Columbus	3,000
Dayton	3,000
Toledo	3,000
Canton	3,000
Akron	3,000
Middletown	1,000
Camp Sherman, Chillicothe	2,000
Portsmouth	300
Baltimore & Ohio camps	400
Pennsylvania Railroad camps	800
Contractors	1,000
Traction companies	1,000
Total for Ohio	37,500

Reported number of Negro migrants in New Jersey, September, 1917.

New York Central camp, Weehawken	500
Erie camps:	
Weehawken	300
Jersey City	100
Philadelphia & Reading, Pennsylvania Railroad, etc., camps	1,300
Jersey City	3,000
Newark	7,000
Carneys Point	800
Trenton	3,000
Camden	2,000
Bayonne, Paterson, and Perth Amboy	4,000
Wrightstown and South Jersey	3,000
Total for New Jersey	25,000

35. LETTER TO ELBERT H. GARY OF UNITED STATES STEEL FROM THE COMMITTEE FOR ORGANIZING IRON AND STEEL WORKERS, AUGUST 26, 1919

Hon. Elbert H. Gary,
Chairman Finance Committee
United States Steel Corporation
71 Broadway, New York City
Dear Sir:

During a general campaign of organization and education conducted under the auspices of the American Federation of Labor, many thousands of men employed in the iron and steel industry made application and were enrolled as members of the various organizations to which they were assigned.

This work has been carried on to a point where we feel justified in stating to you that we represent the sentiment of the vast majority of the employees in this industry, and acting on behalf of them, we solicit of you that a hearing be given to the undersigned Committee, who have been selected by the duly accredited representatives of the employees, to place before you matters that are of vital concern to them, and concerning hours of labor, wages, working conditions and the right of collective bargaining.

The Committee called at your office at 3 P.M., Tuesday, August 26, and requested a conference. We were advised by your messenger that you wished to be excused from a personal interview at this time and requested us to have our business in writing and whatever matters we wished to submit would be taken up by yourself and your colleagues and given consideration.

Therefore we are submitting in brief the principal subjects that we desired to have a conference on. The committee has an important meeting in another city on Thursday next and will leave New York at 5 o'clock on August 27, 1919. May we respectfully request that your answer be sent before that time to Mr. John Fitzpatrick, Continental Hotel, Broadway and Forty-first Street, New York City.

Very truly yours,
JOHN FITZPATRICK
D. J. DAVIS
WM. HANNON
EDW. J. EVANS
WM. Z. FOSTER
Committee

36. ELBERT H. GARY'S REPLY TO THE COMMITTEE, AUGUST 27, 1919

Messrs. John Fitzpatrick, David J. Davis, William Hannon, Wm. Z. Foster, Edw. J. Evans, Committee
Gentlemen:

Receipt of your communication of August 26 instant is acknowledged. We do not think you are authorized to represent the sentiment of a majority of the employees of the United States Steel Corporation and its subsidiaries. We express no opinion concerning any other members of the iron and steel industry.

As heretofore publicly stated and repeated, our Corporation and subsidiaries, although they do not combat labor unions as such, decline to discuss business with them. The Corporation and subsidiaries are opposed to the "closed shop." They stand for the "open shop," which permits one to engage in any line of employment whether one does or does not belong to a labor union. This best promotes the welfare of both employees and employers. In view of the well-known attitude as above expressed, the officers of the Corporation respectfully decline to discuss with you, as representatives of a labor union, any matter relating to employees. In doing so no personal discourtesy is intended.

In all decisions and acts of the Corporation and subsidiaries pertaining to employees and employment their interests are of highest importance. In wage rates, living and working conditions, conservation of life and health, care and comfort in times of sickness or old age, and providing facilities for the general welfare and happiness of employees and their families, the Corporation and subsidiaries have endeavored to occupy a leading and advanced position among employers.

It will be the object of the Corporation and subsidiaries to give such consideration to employees as to show them their loyal and efficient service in the past is appreciated, and that they may expect in the future fair treatment.

Respectfully yours,
E. H. Gary, Chairman

37. THE COMMITTEE FOR ORGANIZING IRON AND STEEL WORKERS NOTIFIES ELBERT H. GARY OF THE VOTE TO STRIKE, AUGUST 27, 1919

Hon. Elbert H. Gary, Chairman

Finance Committee,
United States Steel Corporation
71 Broadway, New York, N.Y.
Dear Sir:

We have received your answer to our request for a conference on behalf of the employees of your Corporation, and we understand the first paragraph of your answer to be an absolute refusal on the part of your corporation to concede to your employees the right of collective bargaining.

You question the authority of our committee to represent the majority of your employees. The only way by which we can prove our authority is to put the strike vote into effect and we sincerely hope that you will not force a strike to prove this point.

We asked for a conference for the purpose of arranging a meeting where the questions of wages, hours, conditions of employment, and collective bargaining might be discussed. Your answer is a flat refusal for such conference, which raises the question, if the accredited representatives of your employees and the international unions affiliated with the American Federation of Labor and the Federation itself are denied a conference, what chance have the employees as such to secure any consideration of the views they entertain or the complaints they are justified in making.

We noted particularly your definition of the attitude of your Corporation on the question of the open and closed shop, and the positive declaration in refusing to meet representatives of union labor. These subjects are matters that might well be discussed in conference. There has not anything arisen between your Corporation and the employees whom we represent in which the question of "the closed shop" has been even mooted.

We read with great care your statement as to the interest the Corporation takes in the lives and welfare of the employees and their families, and if that were true even in a minor degree, we would not be pressing consideration, through a conference, of the terrible conditions that exist. The conditions of employment, the home life, the misery in the hovels of the steel workers is beyond description. You may not be aware that the standard of life of the average steel worker is below the pauper line, which means that charitable institutions furnish to the pauper a better home, more food, clothing, light and heat than many steel workers can bring into their lives

upon the compensation received for putting forth their very best efforts in the steel industry. Surely this is a matter which might well be discussed in conference.

You also made reference to the attitude of your Corporation in not opposing or preventing your employees from joining labor organizations. It is a matter of common knowledge that the tactics employed by your Corporation and subsidiaries have for years most effectively prevented any attempt at organization by your employees. We feel that a conference would be valuable to your Corporation for the purpose of getting facts of which, judging from your letter, you seem to be misinformed.

Some few days are still at the disposal of our committee before the time limit will have expired when there will be no discretion left to the committee but to enforce the decree of your employees whom we have the honor to represent.

We submit that reason and fairness should obtain rather than that the alternative shall be compulsory upon us.

Surely reasonable men can find a common ground upon which we can all stand and prosper.

If you will communicate with us further upon this entire matter, please address your communication to the National Hotel, Washington, D.C., where we will be Thursday and Friday, August 28 and 29.

Very truly yours,
JOHN FITZPATRICK
D. J. DAVIS
WM. HANNON
EDW. J. EVANS
WM. Z. FOSTER
Committee

38. EXTRACT FROM *PRESENT SITUATION IN CHILD LABOR,* HOUSE REPORT 395, 68TH CONGRESS, 1ST SESSION, 1924

Number of Working Children in 1920

The decennial census is our only source of information as to the total number of working children in the United States as a whole. In 1920 over one million (1,060,858) children ten to fifteen years of age, inclusive, were reported by census enumerators as "engaged in gainful occupations." This number was approximately one-twelfth of the total number (12,052,582) of children of that age in the entire country, as the following table shows:

Per cent of children engaged in gainful occupations, by sex: 1920

Children 10 to 15 years of age, inclusive
Engaged in gainful occupations

Sex	Total	Number	Per cent
Both Sexes	12,502,582	1,060,858	8.5
Male	6,294,085	714,248	11.3
Female	6,207,597	346,610	5.6

The number of child workers ten to thirteen years of age, inclusive, was 378,063. The census does not report the number of working children under ten years of age.

Geographical Distribution of Child Labor

Child labor is confined to no one section of the country. According to the 1920 census the proportion of the total child population ten to fifteen years of age, inclusive, "employed in gainful occupations" ranged from 3 per cent in the three Pacific coast states to 17 per cent in the east south central states, comprising Kentucky, Tennessee, Alabama, and Mississippi. In Mississippi more than one-fourth of all the children ten to fifteen years of age were at work; in Alabama and in South Carolina, 24 per cent; in Georgia, 21 per cent; and in Arkansas, 19 per cent. Of the New England states, Rhode Island had the largest proportion of children from ten to fifteen years of age, 13 per cent, "employed in gainful occupations." Except in the south, no other state has so large a percentage of employed children as this.

The Occupations of the Working Children

Of the 1,060,858 children ten to fifteen years of age, inclusive, who were reported by the census to be "gainfully employed" in 1920, 647,309, or 61 per cent, were in agricultural pursuits and 413,549 were in non-agricultural pursuits. Since the employment of children in agriculture is usually on the home farm,[1] is seasonal instead of continuous, and is out of doors, it is with reference to the more than four hundred thousand children in non-agricultural pursuits that the advocates of the Federal child labor amendment have been principally concerned. The occupations of these working children were as follows in 1920:

Number and per cent distribution, by occupation, of children 10 to 15 years of age, inclusive, engaged in selected non-agricultural pursuits, for the United States, 1920.[2]

Occupation	Number	Per cent distribution
All non-agricultural pursuits	413,549	100.0
Messenger, bundle, and office boys and girls[3]	48,028	11.6
Servants and waiters	41,586	10.1
Salesmen and saleswomen (stores)[4]	30,370	7.3
Clerks (except clerks in stores)	22,521	5.4
Cotton-mill operatives	21,875	5.3
Newsboys	20,706	5.0
Iron and steel industry operatives	12,904	3.1
Clothing-industry operatives	11,757	2.8
Lumber and furniture industry operatives	10,585	2.6
Silk-mill operatives	10,023	2.4
Shoe-factory operatives	7,545	1.8
Woolen and worsted mill operatives	7,077	1.7
Coal-mine operatives	5,850	1.4
All other occupations	162,722	39.3

[1]Eighty-eight per cent of the children engaged in agricultural pursuits in 1920 were employed on the home farm.

[2]Fourteenth Census of the United States, 1920: Children in Gainful Occupations.

[3]Except telegraph messengers.

[4]Includes clerks in stores.

39. Cases Representative of the Heat in Glassware Furnace Rooms, Pennsylvania Department of Labor, 1927

Mould boy at blow shop, 100°F., 27 per cent relative humidity:

Girl of 16, constant exposure; 8 hour day, 48 hour week. (Outdoor temperature 71°F., 56 per cent relative humidity.)

Taking-out at bottle machine, 112°F.:[1]

Boy of 16, constant exposure under blast of artificial wind; 7½ hour day, 45 hour week. (Outdoor temperature 70°F.)[1]

Warming-in at glory hole, 103°F., 33 per cent relative humidity:

Boy of 17, exposure 30 seconds out of one minute, artificial wind used; 8½ hour day, 46¾ hour week. (Outdoor temperature 79°F., 53 per cent relative humidity.)

Carrying-in 110°F., 16 per cent relative humidity:

Boy of 16, exposure by peanut roaster 5 out of 30 seconds, little artificial wind; 86°F., 39 per cent relative humidity at lehr [oven used to anneal glass], exposure 3 out of 30 seconds; 8 hour day, 48 hour week. (Outdoor temperature 71°F., 56 per cent relative humidity.)

Examples of the highest temperature recorded and those most trying on account of humidity are as follows:

119°F., 17 per cent relative humidity:

Girl of 17 taking ware out of automatic machine, constant exposure under strong blast of artificial wind except for a 15 minute rest period every hour; 8 hour day, 48 hour week. (Outdoor temperature 79°F., 53 per cent relative humidity.)

130°F.:[1]

Girl of 16 putting ware into lehr, exposure of about 5 out of 30 seconds; 84°F. for 15 seconds at shop; intermediate temperatures for other 10 seconds of 30 second period; no artificial wind directly on girl; 8 hour day, 44 hour week. (Outdoor temperature 68°F.)[1]

107°F., 47 per cent relative humidity:

Boy of 15 putting ware into lehr, exposure 5 seconds out of 2 minutes; 99°F. at shop for 30 seconds; 95°F., 55 per cent relative humidity, general room temperature for other 85 seconds of 2 minute period; no artificial wind; 8 hour day, 44 hour week. (Outdoor temperature 89°F., 63 per cent relative humidity.)

[1]No humidity reading obtained.

40. RESOLUTION ADOPTED BY THE ILLINOIS BRANCH OF THE RAILWAY MAIL ASSOCIATION PROTESTING THE APPOINTMENT OF AN AFRICAN-AMERICAN CLERK-IN-CHARGE AT THE TERMINAL RAILWAY POST OFFICE, CHICAGO, 1929

WHEREAS, a colored clerk has been appointed in the Chicago, Illinois, Terminal R.P.O., and

WHEREAS, said clerk-in-charge has direct supervision over thirty-three clerks of Caucasian birth; and

WHEREAS, this does not create harmonious relations between clerks and clerks-in-charge, nor would it in any other case similar in character, nor can the best interests of the service be obtained under such condition; and

WHEREAS, we believe that no colored clerk-in-charge can supervise the work of clerks of Caucasian birth to the best advantage, nor to the best welfare of the employees, therefore be it

Resolved, That the Illinois Branch Sixth Division R.M.A., in regular session assembled vigorously protest this assignment or any future assignment of a [black] clerk-in-charge who will have direct supervision over a crew any of whom are of Caucasian birth.

41. EXTRACTS FROM EMERGENCY CONSERVATION WORK: AN ACT, MARCH 31, 1933

For the relief of unemployment through the performance of useful public work, and for other purposes.

Be it enacted by the Senate and the House of Representatives of the United States of America in Congress assembled, That for the purpose of relieving the acute condition of widespread distress and unemployment now existing in the United States, and in order to provide for the restoration of the country's depleted natural resources and the advancement of an orderly program of useful public works, the President is authorized, under such rules and regulations as he may prescribe and by utilizing such existing departments or agencies as he may designate, to provide for employing citizens of the United States who are unemployed, in the construction, maintenance, and carrying on of works of a public nature in connection with the forestation of lands belonging to the United States or to the several states which are suitable for timber production, the prevention of forest fires, floods and soil erosion, plant pest and disease control, the construction, maintenance or repair of paths, trails, and fire lanes in the national parks and national forests, and such other work on the public domain, national and state, and government reservations incidental to or necessary in connection with any projects of the character enumerated, as the President may determine to be desirable: Provided, That the President may in his discretion extend the provisions of this act to lands owned by counties and municipalities and lands in private ownership, but only for the purpose of doing thereon such kinds of cooperative work as are now provided for by acts of Congress in preventing and controlling forest fires and the attacks of forest tree pests and diseases and such work as is necessary in the public interest to control floods.

The President is further authorized by regulation, to provide for housing the persons so employed and for furnishing them with such subsistence, clothing, medical attention and hospitalization and cash allowance, as may be necessary, during the period they are so employed, and, in his discretion, to provide for the transportation of such persons to and from the places of employment.

That in employing citizens for the purposes of this act no discrimination shall be made on account of race, color, or creed; and no person under conviction for crime and serving sentence therefore shall be employed under the provisions of this act. The President is further authorized to allocate funds available for the purposes of this act, for forest research, including forest products investigations by the Forest Products Laboratory.

Sec. 2. For the purpose of carrying out the provisions of this act the President is authorized to enter into such contracts or agreements with states as may be necessary, including provisions for utilization of existing State administrative agencies, and the President, or the head of any department or agency authorized by him to construct any project or to carry on any such public works, shall be authorized to acquire real property by purchase, donation, condemnation, or otherwise ...

Sec. 4. For the purpose of carrying out the provisions of this act, there is hereby authorized to be expended, under the direction of the President, out of any unobligated moneys heretofore appropriated for public works, except for projects on which actual construction has been commenced or may be commenced within 90 days, and except maintenance funds for river and harbor improvements already allocated, such sums as may be necessary; and an amount equal to the amount so expended is hereby authorized to be appropriated for the same purposes for which such moneys were originally appropriated.

42. Section 7(a) of the National Industrial Recovery Act, June 16, 1933

Every code of fair competition, agreement, and license approved, prescribed, or issued under this title shall contain the following conditions: (1) That employees shall have the right to organize and bargain collectively through representatives of their own choosing, and shall be free from the interference, restraint, or coercion of employers of labor, or their agents, in the designation of such representatives or in self-organization or in other concerted activities for the purpose of collective bargaining or other mutual aid or protection; (2) that no employee and no one seeking employment shall be required as a condition of employment to join any company union or to refrain from joining, organizing, or assisting a labor organization of his own choosing; and (3) that employers shall comply with the maximum hours of labor, minimum rates of pay, and other conditions of employment, approved or prescribed by the President.

43. Code Adopted by the Cannery and Agricultural Workers Industrial Union, August 5, 1933

1. A minimum wage of 50 cents per hour for unskilled, and 75 cents per hour for skilled field, shed, packing house, and cannery workers.

2. A maximum eight-hour day, with time-and-a-half for overtime; and when a worker is called on the job and does not work a full day he is to be paid for not less than 6 hours.

3. Corresponding wage increases with rising cost of commodities.

4. Equal pay for equal work for men, women and young workers.

5. Abolition of child labor to the age of sixteen (16).

6. Abolition of all forms of contract system.

7. Recognition of the Cannery & Agricultural Workers Industrial Union as representatives of the agricultural workers in the State of California.

8. All negotiations between Union and growers or mediators to be finally decided upon by the workers.

9. Free sanitary housing, wood, light and water, and transportation to and from jobs at great distance; schools and nurseries for children of migratory parents.

10. Immediate cash relief for unemployed agricultural workers and Federal unemployment insurance.

11. The right of the workers to organize into the union of their choice, to strike, and to picket.

12. No discrimination on the job or in relief because of race, color or creed.

44. Extract from the National Labor Relations Act, July 5, 1935

Rights of Employees

Sec. 7. Employees shall have the right of self-organization, to form, join, or assist labor organizations, to bargain collectively through representatives of their own choosing, and to engage in concerted activities, for the purpose of collective bargaining or other mutual aid or protection.

Sec. 8. It shall be an unfair labor practice for an employer—

(1) To interfere with, restrain, or coerce employees in the exercise of the rights guaranteed in section 7.

(2) To dominate or interfere with the formation or administration of any labor organization or contribute financial or other support to it: *Provided,* That subject to rules and regulations made and published by the Board . . . an employer shall not be prohibited from permitting employees to confer with him during work hours without loss of time or pay.

(3) By discrimination in regard to hire or tenure of employment or any term or condition of employment to encourage or discourage membership in any labor organization: *Provided,* That nothing in this Act, or in the National Industrial Recovery Act (U.S.C., Supp. VII, title 15, secs. 701–712), as amended from time to time, or in any code or agreement approved or prescribed thereunder, or in any other statute of the United States, shall preclude an employer from making an agreement with a labor organization (not established, maintained, or assisted by any action defined in this Act as an unfair labor practice) to require as a condition of employment membership therein, if such labor organization is the representative of the employees . . . , in the appropriate collective bargaining unit covered by such agreement when made.

(4) To discharge or otherwise discriminate against an employee because he has filed charges or given testimony under this Act.

(5) To refuse to bargain collectively with the representatives of his employees. . . .

45. Extracts from a Statement by Alfred P. Sloan, President of General Motors Corporation, January 5, 1937

To All Employees of General Motors Corporation:
In view of the fact that several of our manufacturing plants have been forced to close down, possibly necessitating similar closing on the part of others in the not distant future, and realizing that this means a great deal to you and your families, as well as to the business, it seems only fair that I should tell you the circumstances that have brought this about in order that you may better understand and therefore judge more intelligently. . . .

You are being told you had better join a union. You are being told that to bargain collectively you must be a member of a labor organization. You are being told that the automotive industry is to be run as a closed shop. You are being told that if you do not join now it will be impossible for you to work in any automobile plant when the union wins, unless you pay. In other words, you will be without a job, therefore you must sign up, pay dues; or else.

I want to say to you most frankly, that this is positively not so. Do not be misled. Have no fear that any union or any labor dictator will dominate the plants of General Motors Corporation. No General Motors worker need join any organization to get a job or to keep a job.

General Motors grew up on the principle that a worker's job and his promotion depend on his own individual ability—not on the say-so of any labor union dictator. And on that principle, General Motors stands and will continue to stand. . . .

Neither is it necessary for you to join any organization in order to bargain collectively. General Motors is pledged to collective bargaining on the basis of absolute and uninfluenced freedom of choice on the part of any worker to join any organization without coercion, restraint or intimidation. . . .

I mention all this because efforts are being made, in various ways, to make you, as well as the public, believe that General Motors refuses to bargain collectively with its workers and exercises discrimination against men who elect to join one organization or another. Nothing could be further from the truth.

But, after all, this is not the real issue that has brought about the situation that we face today. That real issue is perfectly clear, and here it is:

Will a labor organization run the plants of General Motors Corporation or will the management continue to do so? On this issue depends the question as to whether you have to have a union card to hold a job, or whether your job will depend in the future, as it has in the past, upon your own individual merit?

In other words, will you pay to a private group of labor dictators for the privilege of working, or will you have the right to work as you may desire? Wages, working conditions, honest collective bargaining, have little, if anything, to do with the underlying situation. They are simply a smokescreen to cover the real objective.

Now, you are entitled to know what General Motors position is. That is the real purpose of this message to you. Here it is:

1. General Motors will not recognize any union bargaining agency for its workers, to the exclusion of all others. General Motors will continue to recognize, for the purpose of collective bargaining, the representatives of its workers, whether union or nonunion.

2. Work in General Motors plants will continue to depend on the ability and efficiency of the worker—not on the membership or non-membership in any labor organization whatsoever. This means that you do not have to pay tribute to any one for the right to work.

3. General Motors will continue to pay the highest justifiable wages in the future, as it has in the past, and just as it is doing at present. It believes in high wages. It is justly proud of its record in that respect.

4. General Motors standard work week will continue to be 40 hours. Time and a half will be paid for overtime.

5. Seniority rights will be observed under the rules laid down by the Automobile Labor Board appointed by the President of the United States in March, 1934. These rules are recognized as fair and just to all workers and permit no discrimination against any worker on account of any organization membership.

I tell you all this not only in your own interest, but in the interest of your family and for the future progress and stability of the business, as well. And, let me add, that General Motors will continue to keep its plants going just as long as its workers can safely work, and as long as we are able to obtain the essential materials from other plants on which we are dependent in order to build our various products.

I realize what this situation means to you. It has been brought about through no lack of effort on the part of the management of General Motors Corporation to make the business a good business, not only for the workers and for the stockholders, but likewise a contributing factor to the prosperity of the country, and, after all, that means much to all of us.

46. Instructions issued to strikers at Woolworth stores, New York City, 1937

WHAT TO DO IN CASE OF SIT-DOWN
The strike starts at a signal given by some authorized member of the union. Upon receiving the signal, you will finish whatever you may be doing at the moment. Then you will stay at your post, fold your arms, and inform any customer who may want to be waited on that you are on strike. There will be no more waiting on customers.

After the store has been emptied of customers, some one who has received instructions from the union will explain them to you.
DURING A SIT-DOWN IT IS IMPORTANT TO REMEMBER THE FOLLOWING

1. Maintain rigid discipline.

2. Unity in your ranks.

3. Elect a strike committee, with a chairman. This committee is to be in complete charge while in the store. This committee shall meet daily.

4. Elect a picket committee. This committee is to be in charge of all people entering or leaving the store. They will assign which strikers shall be stationed at the door. This will work in one-hour shifts.

5. No person is allowed to enter the store without an official union credential, or leave without permission of the strike committee. Collect all credentials immediately and hold them.

6. There is to be absolutely no damage done to any of the store's property.

7. Anyone wishing to use any of the merchandise in the store will pay for it as they did ordinarily. Elect one person to be in charge of collecting the money.

8. If any of you are approached by any petty boss or manager do not converse with them, but refer them to the strike committee.

9. If any new problem comes up of which you are in doubt, call the union immediately—Gramercy 5-8875.

47. EXTRACTS FROM "IN THE MATTER OF REPUBLIC STEEL CORPORATION AND STEEL WORKERS ORGANIZING COMMITTEE," DECISION OF THE NATIONAL LABOR RELATIONS BOARD, OCTOBER 1938

The respondent [Republic Steel] in its answer asserts that the strike was called without any cause or justification and solely for the selfish benefit and advantage of the S.W.O.C. and the C.I.O. in an attempt to gain control of the respondent's employees and all steel company employees, and that there was no labor dispute between the respondent and its employees and no difference as to wages, hours, and working conditions. . . .

The record shows that ever since . . . June 1933, the respondent has made plain its policy of complete antagonism to the self-organization of the employees and its determination to forestall or destroy any such organization by all means at its command. On July 2, 1936, shortly after the advent of the S.W.O.C., the respondent reiterated this policy in a public statement, and immediately and ruthlessly put it into effect. Its spies shadowed union organizers; its police attacked and beat them; its superintendent and foremen threatened, laid off and discharged employees for union activities; its officers fostered and supported a whole series of puppet labor organizations which the respondent manipulated to oppose the Union; and its chairman and president publicly vilified the Union's leaders, purposes and policies under circumstances intended to throw the weight of his influence against his employees' efforts at self-organization. Finally in May 1937 there occurred a series of events which precipitated the strike. . . .

The respondent having engaged in unfair labor practices, we shall order it to cease and desist therefrom and to take certain affirmative action which we find necessary to effectuate the policies of the Act and to restore as nearly as possible the situation that existed prior to the commission of the unfair labor practices and which would have existed except for them.

The respondent has unlawfully sponsored and supported various labor organizations. . . . These organizations cannot, in view of the circumstances, operate as a true representative of the employees, and we shall order the respondent to withdraw recognition from them and to disestablish them as such representative.

The respondent has also unlawfully discriminated against its employees by locking them out at the Massillon Works and the Canton tin-plate mill. To remedy this illegal conduct, we shall order the respondent to pay the employees involved back pay for the period during which they were deprived of employment.

We have found that the respondent has unlawfully laid off, discharged, and refused reinstatement to certain employees. In accordance with our usual practice, we shall order the reinstatement of such employees with back pay for losses suffered by reason of the respondent's unlawful acts.

We have also found that the strike at the respondent's plants, which was still in effect at the time of the hearing, was caused fundamentally by the respondent's unfair labor practices. In previous cases of this character we have required the employer to reinstate the striking employees, upon application, to their former or substantially equivalent positions. We find this requirement appropriate and necessary to effectuate the purposes of the Act in this case. In order to protect the right of the respondent's employees to "full freedom of association, self-organization, and designation of representatives," as guaranteed by the Act, it is essential that the respondent be required not only to cease and desist from its unfair labor practices but so far as possible to repair the damage occasioned by such unlawful acts. The most effective method of restoring the situation to that existing prior to the respondent's unfair labor practices, and thereby assuring all the respondent's employees full freedom in self-organization and collective bargaining, is to reinstate to their former positions those employees who have gone out on strike as a consequence of the respondent's unlawful conduct.

48. EXECUTIVE ORDER 8802, JUNE 25, 1941

REAFFIRMING POLICY OF FULL PARTICIPATION IN THE DEFENSE PROGRAM BY ALL PERSONS, REGARDLESS OF RACE, CREED, COLOR, OR NATIONAL ORIGIN, AND DIRECTING CERTAIN ACTION IN FURTHERANCE OF SAID POLICY.

WHEREAS it is the policy of the United States to encourage full participation in the national defense program by all citizens of the United States, regardless of race, creed, color, or national origin, in the firm belief that the democratic way of life within the Nation can be defended successfully only with the help and support of all groups within its borders; and

WHEREAS there is evidence that available and needed workers have been barred from employment in industries engaged in defense production solely because of considerations of race, creed, color, or national origin, to the detriment of workers' morale and of national unity;

NOW, THEREFORE, by virtue of the authority vested in me by the Constitution and the statutes, and as a prerequisite to the successful conduct of our national defense production effort, I do hereby reaffirm the policy of the United States that there shall be no discrimination in the employment of workers in defense industries or government because of race, creed, color, or national origin, and I do hereby declare that it is the duty of employers and of labor organizations, in furtherance of said policy and of this order, to provide for the full and equitable participation of all workers in defense industries, without discrimination because of race, creed, color, or national origin;

And it is hereby ordered as follows:

1. All departments and agencies of the Government of the United States concerned with vocational and training programs for defense production shall take special measures appropriate to assure that such programs are administered without discrimination because of race, creed, color, or national origin;

2. All contracting agencies of the Government of the United States shall include in all defense contracts hereafter negotiated by them a provision obligating the contractor not to discriminate against any worker because of race, creed, color, or national origin;

3. There is established in the Office of Production Management a Committee on Fair Employment Practice, which shall consist of a chairman and four other members to be appointed by the President. The Chairman and members of the Committee shall serve as such without compensation but shall be entitled to actual and necessary transportation, subsistence and other expenses incidental to performance of their duties. The Committee shall receive and investigate complaints of discrimination in violation of the provisions of this order and shall take appropriate steps to redress grievances which it finds to be valid. The Committee shall also recommend to the several departments and agencies of the Government of the United States and to the President all measures which may be deemed by it necessary or proper to effectuate the provisions of this order.

Franklin D. Roosevelt
The White House

49. Extract from the Constitution of the Congress of Industrial Organizations, 1946

Article I Name

This organization shall be known as the "Congress of Industrial Organizations" (CIO).

Article II Objects

The objects of the organization are:

First. To bring about the effective organization of the working men and women of America regardless of race, creed, color, or nationality, and to unite them for common action into labor unions for their mutual aid and protection.

Second. To extend the benefits of collective bargaining and to secure for the workers means to establish peaceful relations with their employers, by forming labor unions capable of dealing with modern aggregates of industry and finance.

Third. To maintain determined adherence to obligations and responsibilities under collective bargaining and wage agreements.

Fourth. To secure legislation safeguarding the economic security and social welfare of the workers of America, to protect and extend our democratic institutions and civil rights and liberties, and thus to perpetuate the cherished traditions of our democracy.

Article III Affiliates

Section 1. The Organization shall be composed of affiliated national and international unions, organizing committees, local industrial unions and industrial union councils.

Sec. 2. Certificates of affiliation shall be issued to national and international unions and organizing committees by the Executive Board.

Sec. 3. Certificates of affiliation shall be issued to local industrial unions by the Executive Board. The

Executive Board shall issue rules governing the conduct, activities, affairs, and the suspension and expulsion of local industrial unions. It shall be the duty of the Executive Board to combine local industrial unions into national or international unions or organizing committees. Any local industrial union or group of local industrial unions may request the Executive Board to authorize such combination. The decision of the Executive Board may be appealed to the convention, provided, however, that pending the appeal the decision shall remain in full force and effect.

Sec. 4. Certificates of affiliation shall be issued to industrial union councils by the Executive Board. Industrial Union Councils shall be organized upon a city, state or other regional basis as may be deemed advisable by the Executive Board and shall be composed of the locals of national unions, international unions and organizing committees, and local industrial unions and local industrial union councils within the territorial limits of such council. It shall be the duty of national and international unions and organizing committees to direct their locals to affiliate with the proper industrial union councils. It shall be the duty of all local industrial unions and local industrial union councils to affiliate with the proper industrial union councils. The Executive Board shall issue rules governing the conduct, activities, affairs, and the suspension and expulsion of industrial union councils. The decision of the Executive Board may be appealed to the convention, provided, however, that pending the appeal the decision shall remain in full force and effect. . . .

Sec. 6. National or international unions and organizing committees may not be suspended or expelled except upon a two-thirds vote at the convention. This provision may not be amended except by a two-thirds vote at the convention.

50. AMENDMENT TO THE CONSTITUTION OF THE CONGRESS OF INDUSTRIAL ORGANIZATIONS PROHIBITING COMMUNISTS, 1949

PAGE 10: Article IV Concerning Officers and Executive Board is amended by the insertion of a new Section 4 which reads as follows: "Section 4. No individual shall be eligible to serve either as an officer or as a member of the Executive Board who is a member of the Communist party, any fascist organization, or other totalitarian movement, or who consistently pursues policies and activities directed toward the achievement of the program or the purposes of the Communist Party, any fascist organization, or other totalitarian movement, rather than the objectives and policies set forth in the constitution of the C.I.O.

51. EXTRACT FROM THE CONSTITUTION OF THE AFL–CIO, 1955

Preamble

The establishment of this Federation through the merger of the American Federation of Labor and the Congress of Industrial Organizations is an expression of the hopes and aspirations of the working people of America.

We seek the fulfillment of these hopes and aspirations through democratic processes within the framework of our constitutional government and consistent with our institutions and traditions.

At the collective bargaining table, in the community, in the exercise of the rights and responsibilities of citizenship, we shall responsibly serve the interests of the American people.

We pledge ourselves to the more effective organization of working men and women; to the securing to them of full recognition and enjoyment of the rights to which they are justly entitled; to the achievement of ever higher standards of living and working conditions; to the attainment of security for all the people; to the enjoyment of the leisure which their skills make possible; and to the strengthening and extension of our way of life and the fundamental freedoms which are the basis of our democratic society.

We shall combat resolutely the forces which seek to undermine the democratic institutions of our nation and to enslave the human soul. We shall strive always to win full respect for the dignity of the human individual whom our unions serve. . . .

Article II Objects and Principles

The objects and principles of this Federation are:

1. To aid workers in securing improved wages, hours and working conditions with due regard for the autonomy, integrity and jurisdiction of affiliated unions.

2. To aid and assist affiliated unions in extending the benefits of mutual assistance and collective

bargaining to workers and to promote the organization of the unorganized into unions of their own choosing for their mutual aid, protection and advancement, giving recognition to the principle that both craft and industrial unions are appropriate, equal and necessary as methods of union organization.

3. To affiliate national and international unions with this Federation and to establish such unions; to form organizing committees and directly affiliated local unions and to secure their affiliation to appropriate national and international unions affiliated with or chartered by the Federation; to establish, assist and promote state and local central bodies composed of local unions of all affiliated organizations and directly affiliated local unions; to establish and assist trade departments composed of affiliated national and international unions and organizing committees.

4. To encourage all workers without regard to race, creed, color, national origin or ancestry to share equally in the full benefits of union organization.

5. To secure legislation which will safeguard and promote the principle of free collective bargaining, the rights of workers, farmers and consumers, and the security and welfare of all the people and to oppose legislation inimical to these objectives.

6. To protect and strengthen our democratic institutions, to secure full recognition and enjoyment of the rights and liberties to which we are justly entitled, and to preserve and perpetuate the cherished traditions of our democracy.

7. To give constructive aid in promoting the cause of peace and freedom in the world and to aid, assist and cooperate with free and democratic labor movements throughout the world.

8. To preserve and maintain the integrity of each affiliated union in the organization to the end that each affiliate shall respect the established bargaining relationships of every other affiliate and that each affiliate shall refrain from raiding the established bargaining relationship of any other affiliate and, at the same time, to encourage the elimination of conflicting and duplicating organizations and jurisdictions through the process of voluntary agreement or voluntary merger in consultation with the appropriate officials of the Federation, to preserve, subject to the foregoing, the organizing jurisdiction of each affiliate.

9. To aid and encourage the sale and use of union made goods and union services through the use of the union label and other symbols; to promote the labor press and other means of furthering the education of the labor movement.

10. To protect the labor movement from any and all corrupt influences and from the undermining efforts of communist agencies and all others who are opposed to the basic principles of our democracy and free and democratic unionism.

11. To safeguard the democratic character of the labor movement and to protect the autonomy of each affiliated national and international union.

12. While preserving the independence of the labor movement from political control, to encourage workers to register and vote, to exercise their full rights and responsibilities of citizenship, and to perform their rightful part in the political life of the local, state, and national communities.

52. Extracts from Title VII of the Civil Rights Act of 1964
DISCRIMINATION BECAUSE OF RACE, COLOR, RELIGION, SEX, OR NATIONAL ORIGIN

Sec. 703. (a) It shall be an unlawful employment practice for an employer—

(1) to fail or refuse to hire or to discharge any individual, or otherwise discriminate against any individual with respect to his compensation, terms, conditions, or privileges of employment, because of such individual's race, color, religion, sex, or national origin; or

(2) to limit, segregate, or classify his employees in any way which would deprive or tend to deprive any individual of employment opportunities or otherwise adversely affect his status as an employee, because of such individual's race, color, religion, sex, or national origin.

(b) It shall be an unlawful employment practice for an employment agency to fail or refuse to refer for employment, or otherwise to discriminate against, any individual because of his race, color, religion, sex, or national origin, or to classify or refer for employment any individual on the basis of his race, color, religion, sex, or national origin.

(c) It shall be an unlawful employment practice for a labor organization—

(1) to exclude or to expel from its membership, or otherwise to discriminate against, any individual because of his race, color, religion, sex, or national origin;

(2) to limit, segregate, or classify its membership, or to classify or fail or refuse to refer for employment any individual, in any way which would deprive or tend to deprive any individual of employment opportunities, or would limit such employment opportunities or otherwise adversely affect his status as an employee or as an applicant for employment, because of such individual's race, color, religion, sex, or national origin; or

(3) to cause or attempt to cause an employer to discriminate against an individual in violation of this section.

(d) It shall be an unlawful employment practice for any employer, labor organization, or joint labor-management committee controlling apprenticeship or other training or retraining, including on-the-job training programs to discriminate against any individual because of his race, color, religion, sex, or national origin in admission to, or employment in, any program established to provide apprenticeship or other training . . .

Sec. 705. (a) There is hereby created a Commission to be known as the Equal Employment Opportunity Commission, which shall be composed of five members, not more than three of whom shall be members of the same political party, who shall be appointed by the President by and with the advice and consent of the Senate. . . .

(g) The Commission shall have power—

(1) to cooperate with and, with their consent, utilize regional, State, local, and other agencies, both public and private, and individuals;

(2) to pay to witnesses whose depositions are taken or who are summoned before the Commission or any of its agents the same witness and mileage fees as are paid to witnesses in the courts of the United States;

(3) to furnish to persons subject to this title such technical assistance as they may request to further their compliance with this title or an order issued thereunder;

(4) upon the request of (i) any employer, whose employees or some of them, or (ii) any labor organization, whose members or some of them, refuse or threaten to refuse to cooperate in effectuating the provisions of this title, to assist in such effectuation by conciliation or such other remedial action as is provided by this title;

(5) to make such technical studies as are appropriate to effectuate the purposes and policies of this title and to make the results of such studies available to the public;

(6) to refer matters to the Attorney General with recommendations for intervention in a civil action brought by an aggrieved party . . . or for the institution of a civil action by the Attorney General . . . and to advise, consult, and assist the Attorney General on such matters.

53. THE EQUAL RIGHTS AMENDMENT, 1972

Section 1. Equality of rights under the law shall not be denied or abridged by the United States or by any state on account of sex.

Section 2. The Congress shall have the power to enforce, by appropriate legislation, the provisions of this article.

Section 3. This amendment shall take effect two years after the date of ratification.

APPENDIX B
Biographies of Major Personalities

Abbott, Edith (1876–1957) *social worker, educator, author*

Abbott was graduated from the University of Nebraska at Lincoln in 1901 and earned a Ph.D. degree from the University of Chicago. In 1924, she became the first woman dean of the School of Social Services at the University of Chicago, and she held that position until 1942. As a social scientist, Abbott studied working women, child labor, and immigration. As an educator, she advocated fieldwork as training for social workers. She advised the federal government on the development of relief programs during the Great Depression and was an adviser to the International Office of the League of Nations. Her books include *Women in Industry* (1910), *Historical Aspects of the Immigration Problem* (1926), *Report on Crime and the Foreign Born* (1931), and *Social Welfare and Professional Education* (1931).

Abbott, Grace (1878–1939) *social worker, activist*

Like her sister, Edith Abbott, Grace Abbott studied at the Universities of Nebraska and Chicago. In 1908, she moved to Hull House, the settlement house founded by Jane Addams and Ellen Gates Starr, where she headed the Immigrants' Protective League. She supported striking garment workers in Chicago in 1910 and 1911. In 1917, she joined the U.S. Children's Bureau, and in 1919 she became its director. In that position, she distributed funding for approximately 3,000 child and maternal health centers that were established nationwide during the 1920s. She helped to draft the Social Security Act of 1935 and contributed suggestions for the Fair Labor Standards Act of 1938. Abbott wrote numerous articles on the exploitation of immigrants, and she lobbied for child-labor legislation.

Abernathy, Ralph David (1926–90) *civil rights leader, clergyman*

Abernathy served in the army in Europe in World War II and was ordained a Baptist minister in 1948. He attended Alabama State College on the G.I. bill and received a degree in mathematics in 1950. In 1951, he received a master of arts degree in sociology from Atlanta University and became pastor of the First Baptist Church in Montgomery, Alabama. He and the Reverend Martin Luther King, Jr., were founders of the Montgomery Improvement Association in 1955 and the Southern Christian Leadership Conference (SCLC) in 1957. Both organizations worked for nonviolent social change. Abernathy was King's closest associate in the civil rights movement and often worked behind the scenes to organize demonstrations. In 1961, he became pastor of the West Hunter Street Baptist Church in Atlanta, Georgia. He assumed the presidency of the SCLC upon King's death in 1968 and held that position until 1977. He continued work that King had begun, marching with striking sanitation workers in Memphis, Tennessee, on April 8, 1969, and leading the Poor People's Campaign in Washington, D.C., in May 1969. His controversial autobiography *And the Walls Came Tumbling Down* was published in 1989.

Adamic, Louis (1899–1951) *author, journalist*

Adamic emigrated from Slovenia to the United States at 13 and worked for a Slovenian newspaper in New York City until joining the army in 1916. He became a U.S. citizen in 1918. In the 1920s, he translated stories by Eastern European writers into English and wrote articles for *American Mercury* magazine. His first book, *Dynamite,* about labor violence, was published in 1931. Other books followed: *Laughing in the Jungle* (1932), an autobiography; *The Native's Return* (1934), a best-selling account of a visit to Slovenia; *Grandsons*

(1935) and *Cradle of Life* (1936), two novels; and *My America* (1938), a collection of short, impressionistic writings. In 1940 Adamic became editor of *Common Ground,* a journal devoted to racial and cultural issues. In the same year he published *From Many Lands,* a book on immigration. His last two books, *My Native Land* (1943) and *The Eagle and the Roots* (1952), concern Yugoslavian politics. Marshal Josip Tito awarded Adamic the Yugoslavian Order of National Unity in 1944.

Addams, Jane ((1860–1935) *social reformer, Nobel laureate*

Addams was born in Illinois and educated at the Rockford Female Seminary (now Rockford College) and in Europe, where she was inspired by the social reform movement. In 1889, she and college classmate Ellen Starr established Hull House, a social welfare center, or settlement house, in Chicago. The Hull House staff was active in child labor reform, education, and community service. A pacifist, Addams became chairperson of the Woman's Peace Party in 1915. The same year, she was elected president of the International Congress of Women at The Hague, Netherlands. She traveled through much of Europe during World War I, urging peace through mediation. Her pacifism following U.S. entry into the war, however, earned her criticism at home. In 1939, she shared the Nobel Peace Prize with American educator Nicholas Murray Butler. Her 10 books include *Democracy and Social Ethics* (1902), *Newer Ideals of Peace* (1907), and *Twenty Years at Hull House* (1910).

Altgeld, John Peter (1847–1902) *governor of Illinois, 1893–97*

Altgeld was born in Germany and traveled to the United States with his parents as an infant. He grew up in Ohio and fought for the Union in the Civil War. He later became an attorney and was elected a judge of the Cook County, Illinois, Superior Court in 1886. In 1893 Altgeld, a Democrat, was elected governor of Illinois. He was widely criticized while governor for pardoning the anarchists convicted of the Haymarket Square bombing. He was also criticized for protesting to President Grover Cleveland against the use of federal troops to control the Pullman strike. An advocate of prison reform, Altgeld wrote *Our Penal Machinery and Its Victims* (1884).

Arkwright, Sir Richard (1732–92) *British cotton manufacturer, inventor of the spinning frame*

Arkwright's machine, which spun cotton fiber into thread, was first used in his hometown of Preston, Lancashire, in 1768. Hand spinners, who feared competition from the machine, pressured Arkwright into leaving the region. He moved to Nottingham and formed a partnership with the cotton spinner Jedediah Strutt. In 1769, Arkwright patented the spinning frame and established his first mill, which was powered by horses. He opened a water-powered mill at Cromford in 1771. There he experimented with the division of labor, which would become standard practice in later factories. Arkwright's patent was annulled in 1785, but he remained a successful cotton manufacturer. He was knighted by King George III of Great Britain.

Auden, Wystan Hugh (1907–73) *poet, playwright, literary critic*

Auden was born in York, England, and attended Oxford University. After graduating in 1928, he had a brief career as a schoolmaster. His first commercially published book, *Poems,* appeared in 1930; he published three verse plays written with Christopher Isherwood between 1935 and 1938. He also wrote two books based on trips to Iceland and China, *Letter from Iceland* (1937) with Isherwood and *Journey to a War* (1939) with Louis MacNeice. In 1937, he traveled to Spain in support of the Loyalists in the Spanish Civil War. The same year, he received the King's Gold Medal for Poetry. Auden moved to the United States in 1939 and became a U.S. citizen in 1946. He was judge and editor of the Yale Series of Younger Poets from 1946 to 1958 and received the 1948 Pulitzer Prize for poetry for *The Age of Anxiety.* His other works include *The Orators* (1932), *The Dance of Death* (1933), *Collected Poetry* (1945), *The Shield of Achilles* (1955), and *Collected Longer Poems* (1969). He also wrote several opera libretti with Chester Kallman. He was professor of poetry at Oxford from 1956 to 1961 and writer in residence beginning in 1972.

Aveling, Eleanor Marx (1855–98) *English socialist, labor organizer*

In 1884, Eleanor Marx married Dr. Edward Aveling and became active in socialist politics. Also in 1884, the couple founded the Socialist League, which was dedicated to bringing socialism to England. By the late 1880s, Eleanor Aveling had turned her attention to labor unions. In 1889, she wrote the "General Statement and Aims of the Gasworkers and General Labourers Union" and formed a women's branch of that organization. She subsequently helped to unionize typists and female tailors. Aveling translated into English some writings by her father, Karl Marx, as well as several literary works. She and her husband wrote several books, including *The Woman Question* (1886) and *The Working-Class Movement in America* (1891).

Baker, Russell Wayne (1925–) *journalist, author*

Baker earned a bachelor of arts degree from Johns Hopkins University in 1947. He was employed by the *Baltimore Sun* from 1947 to 1954, serving as London bureau chief in 1953 and 1954. He joined the staff of the *New York Times* in 1954 and commenced writing his column, "Observer," in 1962. Baker's best-known book is *Growing Up* (1982), a memoir of his youth during the Great Depression; for it he received the Pulitzer Prize for biography in 1983. His other writings include a second memoir, *The Good Times* (1989); a work of fiction, *Our Next President* (1968); and several collections of newspaper articles. He began hosting "Masterpiece Theater" on PBS in 1993.

Beck, David (1894–1993) *president of the International Brotherhood of Teamsters who was jailed for illegal activities*

Following service as an aviation gunner on patrols over the North Sea in World War I, Beck delivered laundry in Seattle. He was also a persuasive and effective union organizer. He worked his way up in the Teamsters, becoming executive vice president in 1947 and president in 1952. In 1957, while testifying before a Senate hearing on union corruption, he invoked Fifth Amendment protection against self-incrimination 117 times. He was convicted in 1959 of federal income-tax evasion and state embezzlement charges, and served 30 months in prison. In 1975, President Gerald Ford granted Beck a full pardon. In retirement, Beck lived on a pension of $50,000 from the union and income from real estate. Holding strict Presbyterian beliefs he neither smoked, drank, nor gambled.

Beecher, Henry Ward (1813–87) *clergyman, orator, abolitionist*

Beecher was born in Litchfield, Connecticut, and educated at Amherst College and the Lane Theological Seminary. As pastor of the Plymouth Church of Pilgrims in Brooklyn, New York, from 1847 until his death, he became one of the most popular preachers and most famous lecturers in U.S. history. Although his religious views tended to be orthodox, he expressed some notably controversial opinions—favoring, for example, Darwin's theory of evolution, as well as scientific scrutiny of biblical texts. Beecher supported the abolitionist movement and women's suffrage. He was editor in chief of the *Independent* from 1861 to 1863 and editor of the *Christian Union* from 1870 to 1881. His 1874 trial on charges of adultery ended in a mistrial, but later investigations exonerated him. In addition to sermons and lectures, Beecher's published writings include a novel, *Norwood; Or, a Tale of Village Life in New England* (1867), and *The Life of Jesus the Christ* (1871–91), a work in four volumes.

Beveridge, Albert Jeremiah (1859–1912) *U.S. senator from Indiana, historian*

Beveridge, a Republican, represented Indiana in the Senate from 1899 until 1911. While in the Senate he worked for passage of the Pure Food Act and the Meat Inspection Act of 1906. He also proposed national child-labor legislation. He was defeated in the election of 1910 and again when he attempted to return to the Senate in 1922. He published a four-volume biography of Chief Justice John Marshall (1919).

Bourke-White, Margaret (1906–71) *photographer, photojournalist*

A graduate of Cornell University, Bourke-White was the first photographer for *Fortune* magazine, holding that job from 1929 to 1933. In 1934, she photographed industrial sites in the Soviet Union and produced two documentary films, *Eyes on Russia* and *Red Republic*. She joined the staff of *Life* magazine in 1936 and documented the lives of southern sharecroppers. The 1937 book *You Have Seen Their Faces,* a collaboration with her future husband, the writer Erskine Caldwell, pursued this subject in greater depth. During World War II, Bourke-White reported from Europe and photographed the Buchenwald concentration camp. Subsequent assignments took her to Korea, India, and Africa. Her later books include *Shooting the Russian War* (1942), *Halfway to Freedom, A Report on the New India* (1949), and *Portrait of Myself* (1963).

Brown, William Wells (1815–84) *African-American writer and orator*

Brown was born in slavery in Kentucky and taken to St. Louis in childhood. He worked in the offices of the *St. Louis Times* and on Mississippi riverboats before escaping to Canada. As a free man, he found employment as a Lake Erie boatman and became known as a public speaker. He spent the years 1849 through 1854 in Europe. His first book, *Narrative of the Life of William W. Brown,* was published in 1847. It was followed by *The Anti-Slavery Harp* (1848), a book of poems; and *Three Years in Europe* (1852), a travelogue. In 1853, Brown's *Clotel, or the President's Daughter* appeared. It was the first novel published by an African American. His other works include *The Escape* (1858), a play; and *The Black Man: His Antecedents, His Genius, and His Achievements* (1863).

Bryant, William Cullen (1794–1878) *poet, journalist*

Bryant wrote the first draft of his most famous poem, "Thanatopsis," at age 16. His first collection of poems was published in 1821 and established him as an important 19th-century American poet. Although trained in law, Bryant left his home state of Massachusetts in 1825 to be an editor of the *New York Review.* In 1826, he became an editor of the *New York Evening Post.*

He was an organizer of the Republican Party and a strong supporter of the Union cause in the Civil War. Bryant's early poetry is considered his best. His work is praised for its beautiful descriptions of the Massachusetts landscape; his translations of Homer's *Iliad* and *Odyssey,* published in 1870 and 1871, respectively, are counted among the finest in English verse.

Carnegie, Andrew (1835–1919) *industrialist, philanthropist*

Carnegie was born in Dunfermline, Scotland, and immigrated to the United States in 1848. At 13 he went to work as a bobbin boy in a Pennsylvania cotton mill, and the following year he became a messenger for a Pittsburgh telegraph office. He was soon promoted to the position of telegraph operator. His next job was as secretary and personal assistant to Thomas Scott, of the Pennsylvania Railroad. Meanwhile, he invested in railroad sleeping cars and subsequently Pennsylvania oil lands. Carnegie left the railroad in 1865 to found the Keystone Bridge Company to build iron railroad bridges. In 1875, he established a steel mill and began buying other large steel mills. In 1883, he acquired the Homestead Works, the site of a violent strike in 1892. When he consolidated his interests in the Carnegie Steel Company, in 1899, he controlled about 25 percent of U.S. iron and steel production. He sold the company to the United States Steel Corporation in 1901 for nearly $500 million. Carnegie was a noted philanthropist who gave more than $350 million to further education, culture, and world peace. In 1911, he established the Carnegie Corporation of New York for "the advancement and diffusion of knowledge and understanding," with an endowment of $125 million.

Chavez, Cesar Estrada (1927–93) *leader of the United Farm Workers (UFW), the first effective union of migrant farm laborers in U.S. history*

Chavez was a migrant farm worker both before and after his service in the Pacific in World War II. Throughout the 1950s, he worked with the Community Service Organization (CSO), first as a volunteer and later as a paid staff member, leading voter-registration drives and assisting Mexican farm laborers with immigration problems. In 1958, Chavez became general director of the CSO. He resigned from that position in 1962 to found the National Farm Workers Association (NFWA), recruiting 1,700 families by 1965. When an AFL-CIO–affiliated farmworkers union went on strike in September 1965, NFWA voted to join it. The unions combined to form the United Farm Workers Organizing Committee (UFWOC), with Chavez as its leader. In 1965, Chavez organized a national boycott of California table grapes to combat the grape growers' practice of importing Mexican laborers and paying them a lower wage than union members were demanding. During the five years of the boycott, U.S. grape consumption declined 20 percent. On April 1, 1970, two major grape producers signed a contract with the UFWOC granting a pay increase and health insurance to their workers. Other growers followed their example.

Child, Lydia Maria Francis (1802–80) *abolitionist, author*

At age 22 she published her first novel, *Hobomok,* about a marriage between a white woman and an American Indian man. In 1825, she began publishing *Juvenile Miscellany,* a bimonthly magazine for children. She married lawyer and abolitionist David Lee Child in 1828 and devoted herself to the antislavery cause. She published *An Appeal in Favor of that Class of Americans Called Africans,* a world history of slavery, in 1833 and began editing the *National Anti-Slavery Standard,* the journal of the American Anti-Slavery Society, in 1840. She withdrew from the society in 1843 to protest the call by its president, William Lloyd Garrison, for "no union with slaveholders." An 1859 letter to a Virginia senator in which Child defended free speech and condemned the use of violence against abolitionists sold more than three million copies when it was printed in pamphlet form by the American Slavery Society. Child's other writings include *The Frugal Housewife* (1829), a book on household management, two additional books on women's work, and three volumes of biographical essays.

Cleveland, Grover (1837–1908) *president of the United States, 1885–1889 and 1893–1897*

After holding a series of minor political offices, Cleveland, a Democrat, was elected mayor of Buffalo, New York, in 1881. In 1882, he was elected governor of New York. Cleveland won the 1884 presidential election with the support of Democrats and reform-minded Republicans known as Mugwumps. During his first term as president, he worked to reform federal agencies and assert the power of the presidency. He denied special favors to any interest group, whether Civil War veterans who wanted pensions for injuries unrelated to war or Texas farmers desiring federal funds for seed distribution following droughts. He investigated land grants to railroads and forced the railroads to return 81 million acres. He signed the Interstate Commerce Act in 1887. Cleveland lost the election of 1888 to Republican Benjamin Harrison, although he won a majority of the popular vote. Public sentiment turned against the Republicans, though, when the protective tariff they passed in 1890 was followed by inflation. Cleveland ran for president in 1892 on an antitariff ticket and won. In 1894, in his second term, he sent federal troops to Chicago to restore order during the Pullman strike and ensure passage of the mail trains. Cleveland was known for his efforts to preserve the public trust and resist partisan influences and political favoritism. He was the only president elected to two nonconsecutive terms, the only president to be married in the White House (in 1886), and the first president to have a child born in the White House (in 1893).

Collinson, Frank (1855–1943) *Texas cowboy*

Collinson was born in Yorkshire, England. In 1872, he immigrated to Castroville, Texas, and went to work on a cattle ranch. He remained in the cattle business for life. He gained a reputation in Texas as a lively storyteller with an excellent memory for details, and he served as a model for numerous paintings and statues with western subjects. In 1963, writer Mary Whatley Clarke collected many of Collinson's letters and first-person writings to create a book, *Life in the Saddle.*

Comstock, Henry Tompkins Paige (1820–70) *western adventurer, miner for whom the Comstock Lode was named*

Comstock was born in Trenton, Ontario, to parents from Connecticut and grew up with a strong desire to see the West. He worked as a fur trader and fought in the Black Hawk War (1832) and the Mexican War (1846–48). He rushed to California following the discovery of gold at Sutter's Mill in 1848, and then to the Washoe mining district of Nevada when precious minerals were found there. Comstock had claimed by right of discovery the site of the Comstock Lode. He sold his holdings for a fraction of their worth, however, and left Nevada in 1862. Historians are unsure of his activities during the next eight years; he is thought to have prospected and built roads in the Northwest. It is known that in 1870 he accompanied the Big Horn exploratory expedition in Wyoming and Montana. His death, which occurred while he was traveling on horseback from Nevada to Montana, was either a murder or a suicide.

Coolidge, John Calvin (1872–1933) *thirtieth president of the United States*

Coolidge was a lawyer in Northampton, Massachusetts, until he became lieutenant governor in 1916. He was elected governor of Massachusetts in 1918. After gaining national attention for putting down a strike by Boston police officers, he became the Republican nominee for vice president in 1920.

His running mate, Warren G. Harding, was elected; Coolidge succeeded to the presidency upon Harding's death in 1923. He was a popular president who easily won the election of 1924. He presided during a time of peace and prosperity, in which the nation was receptive to his philosophy of minimal government intervention in financial and social concerns. He chose not to seek reelection in 1928 and returned to private life.

Coxe, Tench (1755–1824) *statesman, writer*
Coxe was born and educated in Philadelphia and began his career as a merchant. In 1777, he joined the British army. He was arrested by the Americans and subsequently sided with the patriots in the Revolutionary War. He was a member of the Continental Congress in 1789. From 1789 until 1792, he was assistant secretary of the treasury. His later government posts included revenue commissioner and purveyor of public supplies. Coxe also wrote on political and economic subjects.

Debs, Eugene Victor (1855–1926) *socialist leader, labor organizer*
Debs, a native of Terra Haute, Indiana, went to work as a locomotive fireman at 16. He was grand secretary and treasurer of the Brotherhood of Locomotive Firemen from 1880 until 1893, when he resigned to organize the American Railway Union (ARU). As the first ARU president, he led a successful strike on the Great Northern Railway in 1894. In the same year, his union supported striking Pullman workers by shutting down the western railroads. President Grover Cleveland and the federal courts acted to break the strike, citing the right of the government to ensure the transmission of the U.S. mail. In July 1894, Debs and other union officials were arrested and charged with violating an injunction. While serving his six-month sentence in Woodstock, Illinois, he was introduced to socialism. Debs organized the Social Democratic Party of America in 1897 and spent the rest of his life as a socialist lecturer and organizer. His pacifistic teachings earned him a 10-year prison sentence during World War I, but his sentence was commuted in 1921. Debs was the Socialist candidate for president in 1900, 1904, 1908, and 1912, and again in 1920, while he was in prison. Debs's 1911 speech "Industrial Unionism" was widely read. He also wrote a book, *Walls and Bars* (1927).

Deere, John (1804–86) *manufacturer of farm equipment*
Deere, a Vermont blacksmith, went west with his tools in 1837. He opened a shop at Grand Detour, Illinois, and began experimenting to produce a plow that would prove satisfactory on the prairie. He developed three plows with steel shares by 1838 and continued to perfect his designs. Demand steadily increased, and by 1846 Deere and his partner, Leonard Andrus, were producing 1,000 plows annually. In that year, Deere sold his interest in the shop to Andrus and founded a new company in Moline, Illinois, to make plows using a superior grade of steel imported from England. The new plows proved so successful that Deere contracted to have steel plate for plowshares manufactured in Pittsburgh. By 1857, he was producing 10,000 plows a year. He took his son, Charles Deere, and his son-in-law, Stephen H. Velie, into partnership and in 1868 incorporated the firm under the name Deere and Company.

Dickens, Charles John Huffam (1812–70) *English novelist whose writings often dealt with social issues and the conditions of work*
Dickens left school and went to work when his father was imprisoned for debt in 1824. Although he soon returned to school, he was to be largely self-educated. He later worked as a legal clerk and a court reporter. In 1833, he published a series of literary sketches of London life under the pseudonym "Boz." His first novel, *The Pickwick Papers* (1836–37), was initially published in monthly installments, as were subsequent works. *American Notes* (1842) describes his experiences on a lecture tour of the United States, including his visits to factories, schools, and prisons. Among Dickens's major works are *Oliver Twist* (1837–39), the autobiographical novel *David Copperfield* (1849–50), *A Tale of Two Cities* (1859), and *Great Expectations* (1860–61).

Douglass, Frederick (1817–95) *abolitionist, orator, writer*
Douglass was born into slavery in Tuckahoe, Maryland. He escaped in 1838 and went to New Bedford, Massachusetts. After speaking at an abolitionist convention in 1841, he became an agent of the Massachusetts Anti-Slavery Society and spoke throughout the United States. Douglass went to

England in 1845 to prevent his capture under the fugitive slave laws. He returned to the United States in 1847 and founded the abolitionist newspaper *North Star* in Rochester, New York. He edited that paper until 1860. Douglass began working with the Underground Railroad in 1850. He campaigned for Abraham Lincoln in the presidential election of 1860. During the Civil War, he helped to raise two African-American regiments, the Massachusetts 54th and 55th. Following the war, Douglass lobbied for enactment of the 13th, 14th, and 15th Amendments to the Constitution. He was U.S. marshal for the District of Columbia from 1877 to 1881 and recorder of deeds for the District of Columbia from 1881 to 1886. Between 1889 and 1891, he served as U.S. minister to Haiti. Douglass's autobiography, *Narrative of the Life of Frederick Douglass, an American Slave,* was published in 1845. A revised version, *Life and Times of Frederick Douglass,* appeared in 1882.

Du Bois, William Edward Burghardt

(1868–1963) *scholar, writer, a founder of the National Association for the Advancement of Colored People (NAACP)*

In 1895, Du Bois became the first African American to earn a Ph.D. from Harvard University. From 1897 to 1910, he taught history and economics at Atlanta University. He emerged as a spokesperson for African Americans in the early 20th century when he objected in print to Booker T. Washington's advocacy of manual training for young blacks. Du Bois called instead for the education of the "Talented Tenth" of his race to serve as leaders and role models in the African-American community. Du Bois led the Niagara Movement, a group that first met in Niagara Falls, Canada, in 1905 to demand an end to racial inequality. After the NAACP was formed in 1910, he served as director of publications. He also edited *The Crisis,* the journal of the NAACP. Du Bois became an advocate of pan-Africanism after World War I and organized several international pan-African conferences. He worked again with the NAACP from 1944 to 1948. In 1959, the Soviet Union awarded Du Bois the Lenin Peace Prize. In 1961, he joined the Communist Party and moved to Ghana. His 20 books include *The Philadelphia Negro* (1899), *The Souls of Black Folk* (1903), *Black Reconstruction* (1935), and *Worlds of Color* (1961). He died before completing his final project, *Encyclopedia Africana.*

Dubuque, Julien (1762–1810) *miner, trader*

Dubuque was raised in Quebec and went west as a young man. He befriended the Fox Indians, who lived alongside the Mississippi River in present-day Iowa, and in 1788 he obtained their permission to mine lead on their land, which was also under Spanish rule. Spanish authorities granted him title to a plot extending seven leagues (about 21 miles) along the river and three leagues (about nine miles) inland. Employing Canadians and Indians, Dubuque built cabins, a smelting furnace, and a trading post. He came up with the idea of molding the lead into pigs, or oblong bars, for river transport to St. Louis, a practice adopted by later miners in the region. When Dubuque died the Fox people buried him with honors usually reserved for a chief.

Eckert, John Prosper, Jr. (1919–95) *electrical engineer, computer pioneer*

Eckert was graduated from the Moore School of Electrical Engineering at the University of Pennsylvania in 1941. He became an instructor at the school while working toward his master's degree. He also was involved in defense-related research. Eckert teamed up with physicist John Mauchly to build a computer and in 1943 was named chief engineer on the project. The Electrical Numerical Integrator and Calculator (ENIAC), completed in early 1946, was the first general-purpose digital computer. Eckert and Mauchly left the University of Pennsylvania in October 1946 to form the Electronic Controls Company, which built the Binary Automatic Computer (BINAC), a machine that stored data on magnetic tape. After the company became the Eckert-Mauchly Computer Corporation, it built the Universal Automatic Computer (UNIVAC), the first computer sold commercially in the United States. Eckert remained with the corporation after Remington Rand acquired it in 1950 and through mergers with the Sperry Corporation in 1955 and the Burroughs Corporation in 1986. He patented 85 inventions between 1948 and 1966 and retired in 1989. He was elected to the National Academy of Engineering in 1967 and was awarded the National Medal of Science in 1969.

Fletcher, Baylis John (1859–1912) *cowboy, public servant*

Fletcher was born in Lexington, Texas. Because his mother died at the time of his birth, his maternal grandparents and an aunt raised him. He learned to ride horses, rope, and brand calves as a teenager. When he was 19, his neighbor Tom Snyder, a prominent cattleman who owned 173,000 acres, hired him to ride north along the Chisholm Trail with a herd of longhorns. Fletcher recounted his experiences on that trip in *Up the Trail in '79,* first published in serial form in 1966. After completing that trail drive, Fletcher clerked in a general store, taught school, and served as principal of Lexington's public school. In 1896, he was elected to the Texas legislature. In 1900, he was appointed treasurer of Lee County. He held that position until 1911, supplementing his income by trading in cotton.

Fortune, Timothy Thomas (1856–1928) *journalist*

Fortune was born a slave in Florida. He entered Howard University in 1876 but could not afford to remain there to graduate. After a period spent teaching school, he worked as a printer for the *New York Sun* and was soon promoted to the editorial staff. He subsequently edited the *New York Globe* and the *New York Freeman,* which was renamed the *New York Age* in 1887. Fortune's forceful editorials made the *Age* the leading African-American newspaper of its time; in them he called for racial equality and advocated a militant response to racism. His book *Black and White* appeared in 1884. In 1885 he published *The Negro in Politics,* an argument against black support of the Republican Party. In 1889, he helped to form the Afro-American League, a group that combatted discrimination, and served as its secretary until 1893, when the league folded. He was president of a similar organization, the Afro-American Council, from 1902 to 1904. In the 1890s Fortune formed a friendship with Booker T. Washington. He edited Washington's speeches and ghostwrote some on his articles and books. In 1923, he became editor of Marcus Garvey's *Negro World,* holding that position until his death.

Foster, William Zebulon (1881–1961) *communist and labor organizer*

Foster grew up in poverty in Philadelphia and went to work at age 10. As a child he was strongly affected by the Homestead and Pullman strikes of the 1890s. He joined the Socialist Party in 1901 but was expelled for his role in a free-speech dispute in Spokane, Washington, in 1909. He joined the Industrial Workers of the World (IWW) and in 1910

traveled to Europe to study French labor unions. Returning to the United States, Foster broke with the IWW to form two short-lived organizations, the Syndicalist League of North America (1912–14) and the International Trade Union Education League (1915–17). He also joined the Chicago Federation of Labor and worked to organize packinghouse employees and steel workers. Foster joined the American Communist Party in 1921 and was a founder of the Trade Union Education League, which was active in several large strikes in the 1920s. In 1928, he assumed a leadership role in the Trade Union Unity league. He was the Communist Party's presidential candidate in 1924, 1928, and 1932, and party chairperson from 1932 to 1957. Foster died in Moscow. His ashes were placed near the monument to the Haymarket martyrs in Chicago.

Fourier, François Marie Charles (1772–1837) *socialist philosopher*

Fourier studied politics and economics in his native France. In *Theory of the Four Movements and of General Destinies* (1808), he outlined Fourierism, a system for the organization of society into cooperative phalanxes in which wealth and labor were shared. Fourier's ideas generated little interest in Europe; they were of greater influence in the United States.

Frick, Henry Clay (1849–1919) *industrialist, philanthropist*

In 1871, Frick organized the H. C. Frick Coke Company of Pennsylvania; it became one of the world's largest producers of coke. Andrew Carnegie acquired a major interest in Frick's company, while Frick played an important role in Carnegie's organization. He was chairman of the board of Carnegie's firm from 1889 to 1900. His handling of the Homestead strike of 1892 led to an attempt to assassinate him. Frick helped to negotiate the sale of the Carnegie Steel Company to the United States Steel Corporation in 1901. He bequeathed land and an endowment to the city of Pittsburgh to create a park. He also left his home and collection of paintings to the City of New York.

Friedan, Betty Naomi (1921–) *feminist leader and author*

Friedan, who was educated at Smith College, published *The Feminine Mystique* in 1963. This influential book challenged the widely accepted idea that marriage and children were sufficiently fulfilling for most women. In 1966, Friedan was a founding member of the National Organization for Women (NOW), a group that works to achieve equality for women. From 1966 to 1970, she was the first president of NOW. Friedan's other books include *It Changed My Life,* (1976), *The Second Stage* (1981), and *The Fountain of Age* (1994).

Fulton, Robert (1765–1815) *inventor, engineer, designer of the first efficient steamboat*
Fulton was born in Pennsylvania and studied painting in London before turning to engineering and mechanics. In 1800, he tried without success to sell to France and Great Britain a submarine that he had developed. In 1802, Fulton and Robert R. Livingston, then U.S. minister to France, operated a steam-powered paddlewheel boat on the River Seine in Paris, reaching a speed of three miles per hour. Fulton returned to the United States and entered into a business partnership with Livingston to provide steamboat transportation in New York State. On August 18, 1807, his 150-foot *North River Steamboat* (later *Clermont*) made its first trip on the Hudson River from New York City to Albany, New York; traveling at approximately 4.5 miles per hour, it ushered in a new era in water transport. Fulton designed additional steamboats for use on the Raritan, Potomac, and Mississippi Rivers, and ferryboats to service New York City, Philadelphia, and Boston. In 1814 and 1815 he designed the first steam warship, *Fulton the First*.

Garland, Hannibal Hamlin (1860–1940) *writer whose experiences of frontier life inspired his most popular work*
Garland was born on a farm in West Salem, Wisconsin, and worked on farms in Wisconsin, Iowa, and South Dakota. He published two volumes of stories that are critical of American farm life, *Main-Travelled Roads* (1890) and *Other Main Travelled Roads* (1910). He wrote two memoirs, *A Son of the Middle Border* (1917) and *A Daughter of the Middle Border* (1921), winner of the Pulitzer Prize for biography in 1922. His other books include *Crumbling Idols* (1894), a collection of essays on art and literature; *Afternoon Neighbors* (1934), a memoir; and *The Mystery of the Buried Crosses* (1939), an inquiry into psychic research.

Gary, Elbert Henry (1846–1927) *lawyer, corporate executive*
Gary attended the Union College of Law (now part of the University of Chicago) and worked for a time in the Cook County, Illinois, clerk's office. In 1871, he began a successful career as a trial lawyer. He also practiced corporate law and acted as counsel to railroads and steel companies. Beginning in 1862, he served two four-year terms as judge of Du Page County. In 1873, he abandoned the practice of law to enter business. He was founder and first president of the Gary-Wheaton Bank of Wheaton, Illinois. He organized the Consolidated Steel and Wire Company in 1890 and the American Steel and Wire Company in 1898. Also in 1898, he organized the Federal Steel Company, which was to be merged into the United States Steel Corporation in 1901. He became chairman of the board of directors of United States Steel in 1903 and held that position until his death. His Federal Steel Works were constructed alongside Lake Michigan, and the company town built there, Gary, Indiana, was named for him. The works began operations in 1903. Gary resisted the efforts of his workers to unionize, and he refused to grant union demands in the 1919 steel strike. The federal government accused Gary in 1919 of attempting to create a monopoly in steel, but the Supreme Court ruled in his favor.

Gates, William Henry III (1955–) *chairman and chief executive officer of Microsoft Corporation*
Gates, who acquired an in-depth understanding of computers in childhood, dropped out of Harvard University in 1975 after two years of study to form Microsoft Corporation with his friend Paul Allen. Based in Albuquerque, New Mexico, and later near Gates's hometown, Seattle, Washington, the company produced programs for early microcomputers. In 1980, Gates developed the Microsoft Disk Operating System (MS-DOS) for IBM personal computers and compatible models. Microsoft's sales reached $16 million in 1981. By the mid-1980s, the company was one of the leading software developers in the United States. In 1985, Microsoft introduced Windows 3.0, an operating system, operated by a mouse, for IBM-compatible PCs. More than six million copies had been sold by October 1991, and updated versions of Windows followed. In 1986, Gates was the youngest person ever to become a billionaire.

In 1996, Microsoft introduced its World Wide Web browser, Internet Explorer. Evidence that Microsoft Corporation violated federal antitrust laws led to a 1999 lawsuit by the U.S. Justice Department.

Gerry, Elbridge Thomas (1837–1927) *lawyer, children's advocate*
Gerry graduated from Columbia University in 1857 and was admitted to the bar in New York in 1860. In 1867, he was a delegate to the constitutional convention of New York State. He acted as legal counsel to the American Society for the Prevention of Cruelty to Animals and was a founder in 1874 of the New York Society for the Prevention of Cruelty to Children. He became president of the society in 1879. In 1886, Gerry chaired a commission to determine the most humane method of execution; the group advised the New York legislature to adopt electrocution instead of hanging. In 1889, he chaired the committee that planned the centennial celebration of the U.S. government, and in 1892 he led an investigation into the care of the insane in New York State. Gerry moved to Rhode Island and was admitted to the bar in that state in 1889, but by 1896 he had largely retired from the practice of law.

Gilman, Charlotte Anna Perkins Stetson (1860–1935) *writer, feminist*
Gilman was raised in poverty in Rhode Island after her parents divorced. As a teenager she worked as a commercial artist and as a teacher. She settled in California in 1888 following a failed marriage and an episode of mental illness; she wrote to earn a living. Her well-known short story "The Yellow Wall-Paper" (1892) was based on her illness. She became active in the feminist cause in California and supplemented her income by lecturing. Lecture tours took her to New York and, in 1896, to London. Her book *Women and Economics* (1892) discussed the need for women to achieve financial independence. *Concerning Children* (1900) presented the case for common nurseries to free women for paying work; *The Home* (1903) advocated a similar approach to domestic chores. From 1909 to 1916, Gilman published the feminist journal *Forerunner*. She spoke at the 1913 International Suffrage Convention in Budapest and was a founder of the Women's Peace Party in 1915. Her later writings include *Human Work* (1904), *Man-Made World* (1911), and *His Religion and Hers* (1923).

Giovannitti, Arturo (1884–1959) *radical labor leader, poet*
Giovannitti was born in Italy and immigrated to Canada before making his home in New York City in 1904. He involved himself in radical politics while studying at Columbia University and joined the Italian Socialist Federation in 1907. Two years later, he went to work for *Il Proletario,* the Italian publication of the Industrial Workers of the World (IWW). In 1911 he became its editor. As an IWW organizer, Giovannitti went to Lawrence, Massachusetts, in January 1912, when textile workers there went on strike. He and Joseph J. Ettor, another IWW organizer, were falsely accused of murdering a woman striker. Their case gained national attention, and they spent almost a year in jail before a jury found them not guilty. For the rest of his life, Giovannitti devoted his energy to radical politics and organized labor. He protested U.S. involvement in World War I, and in 1921 he reunited with Ettor to speak on behalf of Nicola Sacco and Bartolomeo Vanzetti, immigrants accused of murder and theft in a controversial case. Giovannitti contributed to radical and labor-union publications in both Italian and English, and he helped to organize the Italian Dress Makers Union following World War I. His first book of poems in English, *Arrows in the Gale,* was published in 1914.

Gompers, Samuel (1850–1924) *president of the American Federation of Labor (AFL) from its founding in 1886 until 1924, with the exception of one term, in 1895, when he lost his bid for reelection*
Gompers was born in London, where he learned cigar making, a trade he would practice for 25 years. He immigrated to the United States in 1863 and joined the Cigar Makers International Union the following year. He founded Local 144 of the international union in 1874, becoming its president and a member for life. In 1881, Gompers was a founder and the first president of the Federation of Organized Trades and Labor Unions of the United States and Canada, a lobbying group. Woodrow Wilson appointed him to an Advisory Committee to the National Council of Defense during World War I. Gompers also chaired the Commission on International Labor Legislation for the Peace Conference of 1919. Throughout his career, he advocated cooperation between labor and manage-

ment rather than strikes and antagonism. He used his influence as a nationally recognized labor leader to secure federal and state legislation that was beneficial to labor.

Gould, Jay (Jason Gould) (1836–92) *financier, railroad magnate*
Gould, a native of New York State, left school at 16 to work first as a surveyor, then as a merchant and a banker. He began buying railroad bonds in the 1850s and gained control of the Rensselaer and Saratoga Line. In 1859, he became a stockbroker in New York City, where he and two partners manipulated stock in order to take possession of the Erie Railroad. Gould was sued for transacting a five-million-dollar sale of worthless stock in the railroad; he relinquished his control of the line in 1872. In 1869, he was involved in a scheme to corner the gold market, a stratagem that led to a sudden drop in the price of gold and a severe financial panic. His investments in western railroads were legitimate, and by 1890 he controlled 13,000 miles of track. Gould's other holdings included the *World,* a New York newspaper that he owned from 1879 to 1883, and the Western Union Company.

Gowen, Franklin Benjamin (1836–89) *prosecutor of the Molly Maguires, railroad president*
Gowen was admitted to the bar in Pennsylvania in 1860 and was elected district attorney of Schuylkill County in 1862. At the conclusion of his term, he was hired as counsel to the Philadelphia and Reading Railroad. After winning an important legal battle against the Pennsylvania Railroad in 1870, he was made president of the company. His efforts to buy up coal fields for the company brought him into conflict with the Molly Maguires, a secret society of labor terrorists operating in the Pennsylvania coal mines. He employed labor spies, including James McParlan, to secure the evidence needed to gain the conviction and execution of several Molly Maguires and to destroy their organization. Gowen's business policies caused the railroad to default on its financial obligations. As a result, a U.S. circuit court placed the company in receivership in 1880. Gowen resigned from the presidency of the railroad and returned to the practice of law. His death by suicide occurred in a Washington, D.C., hotel.

Greeley, Horace (1811–72) *journalist, politician, antislavery activist*
Greeley was born in Amherst, New Hampshire, and apprenticed to a printer at age 14. At 18 he was an itinerant journeyman printer. In 1831, he moved to New York City, where he edited the *New Yorker,* the *Jeffersonian,* and then the *Log Cabin.* He also published political articles and promoted progressive government policies. In 1841, he founded the *New York Tribune,* which he edited for 31 years. As the *Tribune's* editor he spoke out against the unequal distribution of wealth and the growth of monopolies. He advocated westward migration and the development of agriculture. Greeley opposed slavery prior to the Civil War, although he was not an abolitionist. He objected to the Mexican War and the Kansas-Nebraska Act, viewing both as means of extending slavery into the West. He criticized Lincoln for hesitating to free the slaves during the Civil War and angered many northerners after the war when he signed a bail bond for Jefferson Davis. In 1872, Greeley was the Democratic candidate for president but was defeated by the incumbent, Ulysses S. Grant.

Green, William (1873–1952) *president of the American Federation of Labor, 1924–52*
Green was born in Coshocton, Ohio, and worked in the bituminous coal mines in that state. He joined the United Mine Workers in 1890 and worked his way up to a position of leadership. Between 1910 and 1913, he served two terms in the Ohio state senate, where he secured passage of a workmen's compensation law and other measures beneficial to labor. In 1913, he was appointed to the Executive Council of the AFL. He became president of the AFL following the death of Samuel Gompers. Green was a member of several government advisory boards, including the Labor Advisory Council of the National Recovery Administration. He also served on the governing board of the International Labor Organization.

Grofé, Ferde (Ferdinand Rudolph von Grofé) (1892–1972) *composer and conductor*
After years of private music study, Grofé played professionally with several orchestras in the early 20th century. About 1920, he became pianist and orchestrator for Paul Whiteman's jazz band. In 1924, he orchestrated *Rhapsody in Blue* by George Gershwin.

Gershwin and Whiteman's band gave the first performance of the piece on February 12, 1924. Grofé's compositions include *Mississippi Suite* (1925) and *Grand Canyon Suite* (1931).

Guthrie, Woodrow Wilson (1912–67) *folksinger, songwriter*

Guthrie, of Oklahoma, traveled the United States during the Great Depression, doing odd jobs and performing to pay his way. In the 1940s he performed with Pete Seeger and the Almanac Singers. He often found subject matter for his songs in the plight of the poor and downtrodden. "Blowin' Down the Long, Dusty Road," "This Land Is Your Land," and other Woody Guthrie songs have influenced younger songwriters, including Bob Dylan. Guthrie's autobiography, *Bound for Glory,* was published in 1947.

Hamilton, Alexander (1755–1804) *statesman, writer, first secretary of the treasury*

Hamilton was born in the West Indies and educated in New Jersey and New York. He involved himself in revolutionary activities before his 20th birthday. He wrote two anonymous political pamphlets, *A Full Vindication of the Measures of Congress from the Calumnies of Their Enemies* (1774) and *The Farmer Refuted* (1775); he gained widespread recognition when his authorship was revealed. Hamilton served as a captain of the artillery in the Revolutionary War and took part in battles in New York and New Jersey. In March 1777, General George Washington made Hamilton his aide-de-camp and personal secretary. Hamilton resigned those posts in 1781 to take command of an infantry regiment, which later gained distinction at Yorktown. After representing New York in Congress from 1782 to 1783, he practiced law in New York City. As a participant in the Annapolis Convention of 1786, he drafted a resolution that resulted in the Constitutional Convention, held in Philadelphia in 1787. At that gathering he called for a strong central government with representation based on wealth and property. The delegates rejected the establishment of a privileged aristocracy, but they voted in favor of a government that strongly resembled Hamilton's proposal in form. In 1789, Hamilton was appointed secretary of the treasury. He used that position to institute policies that have influenced the operation of the federal

government until the present. For example, his concept of the implied powers of the federal government under the Constitution had a strong impact on Supreme Court decisions in later years. In 1775, Hamilton returned to the practice of law. When the 1800 presidential election ended in a tie between Thomas Jefferson and Aaron Burr, Hamilton used his influence to sway the deciding vote in the House of Representatives in favor of Jefferson. A powerful man in New York as well as Washington, Hamilton brought about Burr's defeat in the contest for governor of New York. Burr challenged him to a duel, which took place on July 11, 1804; Hamilton was mortally wounded. Hamilton also was the principal author of the *Federalist Papers,* in which he advocated a strong federal government.

Hawthorne, Nathaniel (1804–64) *American novelist*

A native of Salem, Massachusetts, Hawthorne established himself as an important writer with the publication of *Twice-Told Tales* (1837), a collection of stories and sketches dealing with moral issues and Puritanism. Out of financial necessity he worked as a weigher at the Boston customshouse, a farmer, and a surveyor. He published *Mosses from an Old Manse,* a collection of tales, in 1846; *The Scarlet Letter,* a novel about loyalty and guilt, set among the Puritans, in 1850; and *The House of the Seven Gables,* a novel tracing the decline of a New England family, in 1851. In 1852, President Franklin Pierce appointed him consul to Liverpool, England. Hawthorne held that post until 1857. In 1860, he published *The Marble Faun,* a novel that drew heavily on his trip to Italy in 1857 and 1858. Hawthorne died at Plymouth, New Hampshire, while traveling with Pierce. *American Notes* (1868) was published posthumously.

Haywood, William Dudley (1869–1928) *a founder and national secretary-treasurer of the Industrial Workers of the World (IWW)*

A native of Salt Lake City, Utah, "Big Bill" Haywood first gained national attention in 1904, when he led members of the Western Federation of Miners in a strike at Cripple Creek, Colorado; Haywood was accused, as he would be in other labor disputes, of inciting workers to violence. In 1905, he presided at the founding of the IWW, a militant labor group committed to class struggle and socialism. Haywood and other IWW leaders were implicated in the 1905 murder of Frank R. Steunenberg, a former governor of Idaho. The renowned criminal lawyer Clarence Darrow defended him, and he was acquitted in 1907. Haywood continued to play a role in labor uprisings and was present during the textile workers' strike at Lawrence, Massachusetts, in 1912. His advocacy of violence in labor disputes cost him a position on the national committee of the Socialist Party. During World War I, he was arrested and charged with sedition. Haywood fled to the Soviet Union while free on bail in 1918 and remained there for the rest of his life.

Herman, Alexis M. (1947–) *U.S. secretary of labor*
After graduating from Xavier University in New Orleans in 1969, Herman became a social worker for Catholic Charities. In the 1970s, as national director of the Minority Women Employment Program of R-T-P, Inc., of Atlanta, she expanded employment opportunities for minority women. Herman directed the Women's Bureau of the Department of Labor from 1977 to 1981, during the administration of Jimmy Carter. After leaving government service, she founded A. M. Herman and Associates to advise corporations and state and local governments on human-resource issues. In 1988, Herman became chief of staff and vice chairman of the Democratic National Committee, and in 1991 she was named chief executive officer of the 1992 Democratic National Convention Committee. She was appointed director of public liaison in the Clinton White House in 1993, and on May 9, 1997, she was sworn in as the nation's 23d labor secretary. She is the fourth woman and first African American in that position.

Hill, James Jerome (1838–1916) *railroad entrepreneur, financier*
Hill was born near Rockwood, Ontario, Canada. The loss of an eye in a childhood shooting accident forced him to abandon plans to become a physician. He traveled west as a young man and went into business, operating a steamboat line in Manitoba and forming a fuel company to supply the railroads. He also worked as an agent for the St. Paul and Pacific Railroad. He and three partners bought the railroad in 1878 and extended it to the Canadian border, where it connected to a line serving Winnipeg. Hill extended the railroad to Great Falls, Montana, and

later to Seattle, Washington. In 1890, he consolidated his holdings into one corporation, the Great Northern Railway Company. He was president of the railroad until 1907, when he retired to serve on the board of directors. Hill did much to encourage settlement on lands served by his rail lines. He was known to import thoroughbred bulls from England and distribute them to northwestern farmers free of charge. He helped to organize the Canadian Pacific Railway but resigned in 1883 when the line began to compete with the Great Northern. His involvement in the stock market, mining, and banking in addition to railroads caused him to be called the "Empire Builder."

Hine, Lewis Wickes (1874–1940) *pioneer of social documentary, photographer whose images of working children inspired support for the passage of child-labor legislation*
Hine attended the state normal school at Oshkosh, Wisconsin, and spent a year at the University of Chicago before being hired to teach nature study and geography at the Ethical Culture School in New York City in 1901. In 1904, he began to photograph immigrants arriving at Ellis Island, becoming one of the first photographers to document American social history. He also photographed immigrants in tenements and sweatshops during this period. In 1907, the National Child Labor Committee hired Hine to photograph working children in a variety of settings: in coal mines, on farms, in factories, in canneries, and in sweatshops. Hine spent 11 years at this task. In 1919, he documented Red Cross relief efforts in Europe in the aftermath of World War I. In the 1930s, he focused his camera on the American worker. As part of this effort, he created 1,000 photographs of construction on the Empire State Building. Hine published *Men at Work,* a collection of his industrial photographs, in 1932.

Hoffa, James Riddle (1913–ca. 1975) *president of the International Brotherhood of Teamsters, Chauffeurs, Warehousemen, and Helpers (IBT), 1957–71*
Hoffa undertook his first labor protest as a teenager working for the Kroger grocery chain in Michigan. He formed a small union, which was taken into the IBT in 1931. He then worked as a business agent for the IBT local in the Detroit area. He was elected president of the Michigan Conference of Teamsters in 1942. Ten years later, he became an international vice

president of the IBT. In the late 1950s, a Senate investigation of corruption in organized labor resulted in the expulsion of the IBT from the AFL. Hoffa was tried on charges of racketeering but acquitted. He succeeded Dave Beck as president of the IBT in 1957 and secured the first national contract for union workers. Beginning in 1960, Attorney General Robert Kennedy, convinced that Hoffa had ties to organized crime, became determined to prosecute him. Hoffa was sentenced in 1964 to 13 years in prison for jury tampering and mishandling union funds; he began serving his sentence in 1967. He continued to act as IBT president behind bars until he resigned in 1971. President Richard Nixon commuted Hoffa's sentence in that year, on condition that he refrain from union activity until 1980. Hoffa disappeared after dining at a Detroit restaurant on July 30, 1975; he is believed to have been abducted. A Michigan court declared him to be "presumed dead" in December 1982.

Hoover, Herbert Clark (1874–1964) *thirty-first president of the United States*
Hoover studied mining engineering at Stanford University and spent the first part of his career managing mining properties in Western Australia and China. He performed relief work during World War I, arranging transportation home for 120,000 American tourists stranded in Europe. He also secured food for war-torn Belgium. Returning to the United States in 1917, Hoover headed the Food Administration. Following the war, he led the American Relief Administration, which distributed food, clothing, and medical supplies in Eastern Europe. Between 1921 and 1928, he was secretary of commerce under Presidents Warren G. Harding and Calvin Coolidge. Hoover, a Republican, was elected president in 1928. He took unaccustomed measures when the Great Depression began in 1929, sanctioning government spending for public works and loans to businesses through the Reconstruction Finance Corporation. The public perceived him as unwilling to relieve their distress, however, and he was defeated by Franklin D. Roosevelt in the 1932 election. Hoover headed commissions under Presidents Harry S. Truman and Dwight D. Eisenhower to streamline the executive branch of the federal government. He was the author of *American Individualism* (1922), *The Challenge to Liberty* (1934), and his three-volume *Memoirs* (1951–52).

Hopper, Grace Murray (1906–92) *computer-programming pioneer, naval officer*
Murray received a bachelor of science degree in mathematics and physics from Vassar College in 1928 and a Ph.D. in mathematics from Yale University in 1934. She taught at Vassar until 1943, when she joined the U.S. Naval Reserve. The navy assigned her to the Cruft Laboratory at Harvard University, where she developed programs for the Mark I, Mark II, and Mark III computers. She joined the Eckert-Mauchly Computer Corporation in 1949 and worked on a series of compilers (which translate mathematical code into a form that computers can read). She promoted the concept of English-language compilers to make computers more user friendly, and she was a proponent of such computer languages as COBOL. Hopper had also continued to be a consultant and lecturer for the Naval Reserve, and she returned to active duty in 1967 to lead the Naval Data Automation Command. She was the first American and first woman named a distinguished fellow of the British Computer Society. She retired from the navy in 1986 with the rank of rear admiral and became a senior consultant to the Digital Equipment Corporation. She continued in that capacity until her death.

Howe, Elias (1819–67) *inventor of the sewing machine*
Howe was apprenticed to a manufacturer of textile machinery at 17. He obtained a patent for the sewing machine in 1846 and built four machines before traveling to England, where he sold his patent rights. He returned to the United States in 1849 to discover that sewing machines were being used widely and that several manufacturers were making them. Following lengthy legal proceedings, Howe was ruled to be entitled to receive royalties on all sewing machines manufactured in the United States.

Ickes, Harold LeClair (1874–1952) *U.S. secretary of the interior, 1933–46*
Ickes began practicing law in Chicago in 1907; in 1912 he helped form the Progressive, or Bull Moose, Party. In 1916 he managed the presidential campaign of Republican Charles Evans Hughes. Ickes led the liberal Republican support of Franklin D. Roosevelt's candidacy in 1932. Roosevelt, once elected, appointed Ickes secretary of the interior. Ickes headed the Public Works Administration from 1933 to 1939. He resigned his

cabinet post following a dispute with President Harry S. Truman.

Jackson, Jesse Louis (1941–) *civil rights leader who worked to improve economic opportunities for African Americans as the director of Operation Breadbasket and Operation PUSH*

Jackson first involved himself in the civil rights struggle while a student at North Carolina Agricultural and Technical State College in Greensboro in the early 1960s. The demonstrations and sit-ins that he organized helped to integrate Greensboro. Jackson attended Chicago Theological Seminary on a scholarship and was ordained in 1968. As a seminarian he took part in the 1965 Selma-to-Montgomery march with the Reverend Martin Luther King, Jr. In 1966, King placed him in charge of the Chicago branch of Operation Breadbasket, an organization that sought jobs and business opportunities for African Americans. His accomplishments in Chicago led to his appointment in 1967 as national director of Operation Breadbasket. In 1971, Jackson founded Operation PUSH to further his economic goals. Jackson ran for president of the United States in 1984 and 1988. He gained international recognition in 1990, when he helped to secure the release of American prisoners held in Iraq, and in 1999, when he persuaded Serb leaders to free three American servicemen held captive in Serbia.

Jefferson, Thomas (1743–1826) *third president of the United States and author of the Declaration of Independence*

The son of a Virginia planter, Jefferson was educated at the College of William and Mary and was admitted to the bar in 1857. In 1859, he was elected to the Virginia House of Burgesses. He read extensively on a variety of subjects, including the Enlightenment. His reading informed his *Summary View of the Rights of British America,* which Jefferson wrote for the Virginia delegates to the First Continental Congress in 1774. He drafted the Declaration of Independence in June 1776 for the Second Continental Congress. From 1779 until 1781, Jefferson served as governor of Virginia. Over the years, he spent much of his free time designing and building his Virginia estate, Monticello, where he pursued the occupation of gentleman farmer. The operation of both his farm and his home depended on the labor of enslaved African Americans. Upon ending his term as governor, Jefferson retreated to Monticello to write *Notes on the State of Virginia,* a work describing the social, political, and commercial life of his state. He served as minister to France from 1784 to 1789 and returned to the United States to accept the position of secretary of state under President George Washington. In 1796, he was one of four candidates for president under the electoral system then in use, as recipient of the second-largest number of votes he became vice president under John Adams. Jefferson and Aaron Burr received an equal number of votes in the presidential election of 1800, requiring the House of Representatives to determine the outcome of the election. The House decided in Jefferson's favor. Jefferson's principal achievement as president was to purchase the Louisiana Territory from France, significantly increasing the area of the United States. He dispatched Meriwether Lewis and William Clark to explore this largely unknown territory. Jefferson retired to Monticello in 1809. In 1819, he established the University of Virginia.

Jobs, Steven Paul (1955–) *founder of Apple Computer, Inc.*

Jobs completed one semester of full-time study and additional classes at Reed College in Portland, Oregon, before working for Atari, Inc., a video-game company, in 1974. He left Atari after several months to travel in India. In 1975, at meetings of the Homebrew Computer Club of Palo Alto, California, Jobs befriended computer engineer Stephen Wozniak. Together they built a prototype personal computer (PC) in Jobs's garage. With minimal funding, Jobs and Wozniak formed Apple Computer, Inc., introducing the Apple I computer in 1976. Its read-only memory (ROM) enabled the machine to load programs from an external source, and it displayed information on a video screen. In 1977, Apple began marketing the Apple II, a popular model that brought in earnings of $139 million in three years. The Apple III made its debut in 1981 but was recalled for design corrections. In January 1983, Jobs introduced the enhanced Apple IIe and also Lisa, a high-priced personal computer that was the first to be controlled by a mouse. The Macintosh, with 128 kilobytes of memory, twice that of the IBM PC, soon followed. Jobs left Apple in 1985 to found NeXT Computers. The company introduced its first computer in 1989, but consumers rejected it. NeXT closed its hardware division in 1993. In 1996, Apple acquired NeXT Software, and Jobs returned to Apple.

Johnson, James Weldon (1871–1938) *writer, civil rights leader*

Johnson earned a bachelor of arts degree from Atlanta University in 1894. He spent four years as principal of Staughton High School in Jacksonville, Florida, and was admitted to the bar. In 1898, he went to New York City and formed the successful songwriting team of Cole and Johnson Brothers—with his brother, the composer J. Rosamond Johnson, and performer Bob Cole. He began publishing poetry in national magazines at this time. In 1906, Johnson was appointed U.S. consul at Puerto Cabello, Venezuela, and from 1909 to 1913 he was U.S. consul at Corinto, Nicaragua. In 1916, he became field secretary of the NAACP, and from 1920 to 1930 he held the position of executive secretary. As a writer Johnson was associated with the Harlem Renaissance. His works include *Fifty Years and Other Poems* (1917); a novel, *Autobiography of an Ex-Coloured Man* (1927); a collection of African-American sermons in verse form, *God's Trombones* (1927); a nonfiction book, *Black Manhattan* (1930); an autobiography, *Along This Way* (1933); and anthologies of African-American poetry and spirituals. Johnson died in an automobile accident while vacationing in Maine.

Jones, Mary Harris ("Mother Jones") (1830–1930) *itinerant labor organizer*

Born in Cork, Ireland, and educated at a Toronto, Canada, normal school, she taught school in Michigan and Tennessee and worked as a dressmaker in Chicago before marrying George Jones, an iron molder, in 1861. Mary Jones lost her husband and four children to yellow fever in 1867, and all of her possessions in the Chicago Fire of 1871. From 1880 on, she committed herself to the labor movement, traveling to scenes of labor strife and organizing workers. She was frequently arrested and jailed. Jones assisted loggers, factory workers, and railroad hands and lobbied against child labor. From the 1890s through 1903 she was affiliated with the United Mine Workers (UMW). Her interest in the welfare of miners continued after she broke with the UMW. In 1914, it brought her to Ludlow, Colorado, site of a machine-gun massacre of striking miners and their

families. Jones traveled to Washington, D.C., to persuade President Woodrow Wilson to intervene in that strike. In 1905, she became a founder of the IWW. In 1921, she attended the meeting of the Pan American Federation of Labor in Mexico City.

Kennedy, John Fitzgerald (1917–63) *thirty-fifth president of the United States*

Kennedy was graduated from Harvard University in 1940. His expanded senior thesis, *Why England Slept,* was published in the same year. In August 1943, he was commanding a navy PT boat that was rammed and sunk by a Japanese destroyer off the Solomon Islands. Although severely injured, Kennedy led the surviving crew members to safety. Massachusetts voters elected him to the U.S. House of Representatives as a Democrat in 1946 and to the Senate in 1952. Kennedy wrote *Profiles in Courage* (1956) while recovering from back surgery. In 1960, he was elected president. Early in his presidency, he took responsibility for a failed attempt by Cuban refugees, aided by U.S. agencies, to overthrow Fidel Castro. In October 1962, he responded to the installation of Soviet missiles in Cuba with a naval blockade of the island and forced the Soviets to remove their weapons. Kennedy also responded vigorously to African Americans' call for equality. The civil rights bill that he sent to Congress became law on July 2, 1964, more than seven months after his assassination in Dallas, Texas.

Kennedy, Joseph Patrick (1888–1969) *businessman, government official*

Kennedy, who was born in Boston, became wealthy as a young man by investing in motion pictures, shipbuilding, and real estate, and also by speculating in the stock market. From 1934 to 1935, he was the first chairman of the U.S. Securities and Exchange Commission. In 1937 he became chairman of the Federal Maritime Commission, and from 1938 to 1940 he was ambassador to Great Britain.

Kennedy, Robert Francis (1925–68) *counsel to the McClellan Committee, U.S. attorney general*

Kennedy earned a law degree from the University of Virginia in 1951. The same year, the U.S. Justice Department hired him as an attorney. He resigned in 1952 to manage the campaign of his brother, John F. Kennedy, who sought a U.S. Senate seat from Massachusetts. From 1955 through 1957, he was chief counsel to the Senate subcommittee investigating corruption in organized labor. In 1960, following John Kennedy's election as president, Robert Kennedy was appointed attorney general. He distinguished himself in that position by actively enforcing federal civil rights legislation. In 1964, he resigned his cabinet post and was elected U.S. senator from New York. Kennedy was assassinated in June 1968, while campaigning for the Democratic nomination for president.

King, Martin Luther, Jr. (1929–68) *civil rights leader, Nobel laureate, clergyman*
King was ordained a Baptist minister at 17 and was graduated from Crozer Theological Seminary in 1951. He received a Ph.D. from Boston University in 1954. The same year, he became pastor of the Dexter Avenue Baptist Church in Montgomery, Alabama. He emerged as a national civil rights leader after directing the Montgomery bus boycott in 1955 and 1956. The boycott ended when the U.S. Supreme Court outlawed segregation on municipal transportation. He and other African-American ministers then formed the Southern Christian Leadership Conference, an organization devoted to nonviolent social change, with King as president. In 1959, King traveled to India to study the nonviolent-protest methods of Mohandas K. Gandhi. He became co-pastor of the Ebenezer Baptist Church in Atlanta, Georgia, in 1960. King led civil rights demonstrations in Birmingham, Alabama, in 1963, and a voting-rights drive in Selma, Alabama, in 1965, He was arrested several times, and his home was bombed in 1956. In 1964, King was awarded the Nobel Peace Prize for his efforts in the civil rights movement. He broadened his concerns in later years to include poverty and housing for African Americans in northern cities, and to protest U.S. military involvement in Vietnam. He was assassinated in Memphis, Tennessee, where he was assisting striking sanitation workers. King's writings include *Stride toward Freedom* (1958), about the Montgomery bus boycott; "Letter from a Birmingham Jail" (1963), an essay outlining the need for nonviolent civil disobedience; and *Why We Can't Wait* (1963), on civil rights issues.

Lange, Dorothea (1895–1965) *photographer best known for her documentary work during the Great Depression*
Lange was a commercial photographer in San Francisco in the early 1930s when she began documenting street life with her camera. Working for the Farm Security Administration in the 1930s, she produced haunting, realistic portraits of migrant farm workers. Many of her pictures were published in *An American Exodus* (1939), written with Paul Schuster Taylor.

Larcom, Lucy (1824–93) *writer, teacher*
Upon the death of her father when she was six, Larcom moved with her mother and siblings to Lowell, Massachusetts, where her mother opened a boardinghouse. When she was about 10, Larcom went to work in a Lowell textile mill. She read frequently and contributed to the *Lowell Offering,* which published writing by mill workers. In 1846, she moved to Illinois to teach school and pursue formal education at a private academy. She returned to Massachusetts in 1852 and published *Similitudes,* a book of stories with morals for children, in 1853. In 1854, she began teaching at the Wheaton Female Seminary. Her 1858 poem "Hannah Binding Shoes" was immensely popular and was set to music. Larcom left teaching in 1853 to edit *Our Young Folks,* a children's magazine. In 1868, she published *Poems,* a collection. Her later works include *An Idyl of Work* (1875), a story of Lowell mill workers in verse, and *A New England Girlhood* (1889), an autobiography. She also collaborated on two poetry anthologies with poet John Greenleaf Whittier.

Lemlich, Clara (Clara Lemlich Shavelson) (1886–1982) *political, social activist*
Clara Lemlich came to the United States from Russia in 1905 and worked in a New York City garment sweatshop. She recruited women into the male-dominated International Ladies' Garment Workers Union and led the women in several strikes. In November 1909, she addressed a union meeting in New York City and inspired thousands of garment workers to strike. Following the strike, Lemlich was blacklisted from New York garment shops. She next helped to found the Wage Earners League for Woman Suffrage and worked briefly for that organization, but she was fired for being too radical. In 1913, she married Joe Shavelson, a printer. While raising three children in Brooklyn, New York, she organized mothers' demonstrations for better housing and public education. She led protests against high prices for kosher meats and high rents following World War I. In 1926, Clara Shavelson joined the Communist Party. In 1929, she was a founder of the United Council of Working-Class Women, which became the

Progressive Women's Councils in 1935. This group worked to lower food prices, rents, and utility costs during the Great Depression. In the 1940s, Shavelson was a member of the American Committee to Survey Trade Union Conditions in Europe, and she helped to organize the American League against War and Fascism. In 1951, she testified before the House Committee on Un-American Activities. Shavelson moved to a California nursing home at age 81; there, she helped to unionize the orderlies.

Leonard, Charles McClung (1860–1951) *miner, mechanic*

Leonard was born on a farm in Ohio. He moved to Colorado with his family in 1876 and worked in a flour mill owned by his father. He was later employed by a grocery wholesaler; in 1879 he moved to Leadville. He spent nearly 40 years in Colorado mining camps, where he not only mined but served as master mechanic for the Vindicator Mine. In 1918, he became master mechanic of the Great Western Sugar Company. Leonard and his wife retired to Pasadena, California, in 1926.

Le Sueur, Meridel (1900–96) *writer, political activist*

As a young woman, Le Sueur, the daughter of midwestern radicals, acted in New York and performed in silent films. Government attacks on her parents and other dissidents during World War I confirmed Le Sueur's leftist opinions. In the 1930s, she reported on depression conditions for *New Masses* and the *Daily Worker.* Her experiences among poor women during this period would inspire the novel *The Girl* (1978). Le Sueur was a Communist Party organizer in the 1930s and a teacher in the Writers Project of the WPA. She published a story collection, *Salute to Spring,* in 1940 and a book on midwestern culture and history, *North Star Country,* in 1945. Le Sueur was blacklisted in the 1950s because of her association with communism and was no longer published. In the 1960s, as a result of renewed interest in her writing, her career was revived. Some of her books were reissued, and others were published for the first time.

Lewis, John Llewellyn (1880–1969) *president of the United Mine Workers (UMW), first leader of the Congress of Industrial Organizations (CIO)*

As a coal miner in Illinois, Lewis involved himself in union activities at the local level. His skills as an orga-

nizer and orator caused him to rise in the union ranks until in 1920 he was elected president of the UMW, a post he held until 1960. Lewis presided over the Committee for Industrial Organization when it was founded within the AFL in 1935; he continued in that role when the committee left the AFL and became the Congress of Industrial Organizations. As president of the CIO, Lewis successfully challenged the automobile and steel industries with crippling strikes. In 1942, he withdrew the UMW from the CIO and ended his affiliation with the latter organization. Lewis was a colorful and controversial figure who has been accused of wielding dictatorial control over the UMW yet is credited with bringing about the improvement in miners' standard of living that occurred prior to World War II. Following his retirement as UMW president, Lewis served as a trustee of the union's pension fund.

Lincoln, Abraham (1809–65) *sixteenth president of the United States, commander in chief during the Civil War, author of the Emancipation Proclamation*

Lincoln grew up in the wilderness of Kentucky and Illinois and had little formal education. As a young man he worked as a postmaster and a surveyor and clerked in a store. He also served as a captain in the Black Hawk War of 1832. Lincoln studied law on his own and was admitted to the bar in 1836. He also won a seat in the Illinois legislature in 1834. He became a leader in the Whig Party at the local level. In 1846, he was elected to the U.S. House of Representatives and served one term. In 1858, he was the Republican candidate for the Senate from Illinois, challenging the incumbent, Stephen A. Douglas. Lincoln spoke against slavery during his campaign and gained national recognition but lost the election. In 1860, as the Republican nominee for president, he defeated two democrats and one candidate from the Constitutional Union Party. Following the election, seven southern states seceded from the Union. Four others would later secede as well. When Lincoln attempted to relieve forces stationed at Fort Sumter, South Carolina, in April 1861, the Confederates fired on the fort and thereby started the Civil War. On January 1, 1863, Lincoln issued the Emancipation Proclamation, freeing slaves in regions held by the Confederates. He advocated passage of a constitutional amendment outlawing slavery; it was ratified December 6, 1865. Lincoln was reelected in

November 1864 but was assassinated on April 14, 1865, days after the Confederate surrender.

Love, Nat (Deadwood Dick) (1854–1921) *cowboy*
Love, who was born in slavery, grew up on a farm in Tennessee and left home at 15. He worked as a cowhand in Dodge City, Kansas; in Texas, and in Arizona. He gained some measure of fame as "Deadwood Dick," a skilled gunslinger and Indian fighter. He retired from the trail in 1889, when he married, and worked as a Pullman porter. He published a highly embellished autobiography in 1907.

Lowell, Francis Cabot (1775–1817) *textile manufacturer*
After completing his studies at Harvard in 1793, Lowell joined his uncle in the importing and exporting business. In 1810, he traveled to Great Britain, where he studied textile machinery in use. He returned to the United States in 1812 to open a cotton factory. He purchased land at Waltham, Massachusetts, and in 1812 and 1813 designed and constructed machines based on his memory of ones he had seen in England, adding improvements of his own. By 1814, the mill—the first factory in the world to convert raw cotton into finished cloth—was in full operation.

Malcolm X (Malcolm Little, El-Hajj Malik El-Shabazz) (1925–65) *African-American leader*
Malcolm X, who was born Malcolm Little in Omaha, Nebraska, was arrested for burglary at age 20. While in jail he learned about the Nation of Islam, or Black Muslims. He joined a Black Muslim temple in Detroit following his release from jail in 1952 and took the name Malcolm X. He rose to become the organization's leading spokesperson, preaching that whites are evil. In 1964, he made a pilgrimage to the Islamic holy cities of Mecca and Jiddah, an experience that caused him to renounce his racist teachings. Following his return to the United States, he founded a black-nationalist group, the Organization of Afro-American Unity, and took on a new name. Assassins connected with the Nation of Islam murdered him while he was addressing a gathering in New York City.

Marshall, James Wilson (1810–85) *discoverer of gold in California*
Trained as a wheelwright by his father in New Jersey, Marshall went west as a pioneer. He farmed in Kansas before joining a wagon train for the Far West in 1844. The journey took him to the Willamette Valley of Oregon and then south to California. In July 1845, Marshall arrived at a settlement founded by John Sutter. In 1846, he and Sutter formed a partnership to build and operate a sawmill on Sutter's property at the South Fork of the American River. He discovered gold on January 24, 1848, while excavating the raceway, or water channel, for the mill. The sawmill venture failed, and Marshall earned no profit from the gold rush. The state of California paid him a pension from 1872 to 1878, and he spent his final years as a gardener.

Marx, Karl (1818–83) *political philosopher*
Marx was born and educated in Germany. In 1842, he became editor of *Rheinische Zeitung,* a Cologne newspaper. He resigned when his radical editorials angered local authorities, and in 1843 he went to Paris to continue his studies. While in Paris, he embraced communism. He also engaged in revolutionary activities and was forced to leave France. In 1845, Marx took up residence in Brussels and organized a political network, the Communist Correspondence Committees. The committees were consolidated into the Communist League in 1847. In 1848, with colleague Friedrich Engels, Marx published *The Communist Manifesto,* a statement of socialist doctrine. After the book influenced revolutionaries in France, Germany, and the Austrian Empire, the Belgian government banished Marx. He traveled to Paris and then to Cologne, where he founded a communist journal, *Neue Rheinische Zeitung.* Following his arrest for political activities in 1849, he left Germany for France and then London, his final home. There, he devoted himself to study, writing, and building an international communist movement. His efforts resulted in the establishment in 1864 of the First International. Marx's writings include *Critiques of Political Economy* (1859); the three-volume *Das Kapital* (1867–94), considered by many historians to be his masterpiece; and *The Civil War in France* (1871).

McClellan, John Little (1896–1977) *U.S. representative and senator from Arkansas*
McClellan studied law and was admitted to the bar in Arkansas at age 17. His practice of law was interrupted by service in World War I from 1917 to 1919. Between 1927 and 1930 he was prosecuting attorney

of the seventh judicial district of Arkansas. McClellan represented Arkansas as a Democrat in Congress from 1935 to 1939. He was a U.S. senator from 1943 until his death. He chaired the Senate Select Committee on Labor-Management Relations in the 85th and 86th Congresses.

McCormick, Cyrus Hall (1809–84) *inventor, manufacturer*

McCormick, who was raised in Rockbridge County, Virginia, invented the first successful mechanical reaper in 1831. At first he produced his machines for local customers only. In 1847, he built a factory in Chicago to manufacture and distribute reapers on a large scale. He continued to improve his invention and thus managed to outsell his competitors. McCormick's reaper was essential to the development of modern agriculture.

McCoy, Joseph Geating (1837–1915) *pioneer of the cattle industry*

McCoy first thought of transporting western cattle to markets in the East in 1867, while operating a prosperous farm in Illinois. That same year, he purchased 480 acres in Abilene, Kansas, alongside tracks of the Kansas Pacific Railway, which he had contracted to carry the cattle. He constructed stockyards and a hotel and persuaded Texas ranchers to drive their herds to Abilene. The venture quickly proved highly profitable. McCoy later opened other cattle markets, including one at Wichita, Kansas, in 1872. As one of the best-known people in Kansas, he was the Democratic nominee for Congress in 1890, but he lost the election. His memoir, *Historic Sketches of the Cattle Trade of the West and Southwest,* was published in 1874.

Meany, George (1894–1980) *third president of the AFL, first president of the AFL-CIO*

Meany, a plumber from New York City, became business representative of his local chapter of the Plumbers Union in 1922; he held that position for 12 years. In 1934, he was elected president of the New York State Federation of Labor, and in 1939 he became secretary-treasurer of the AFL. He was a member of the National War Labor Board during World War II, and in 1952 he became AFL president following the death of William Green. He held that position for the rest of his life. Meany exerted enormous influence on national politics and legislation.

Organized labor followed his lead in supporting Democratic candidates for office and, because of his support of the War in Vietnam, in remaining neutral in the 1972 presidential election. He served as a delegate to the United Nations in 1957 and 1959.

Morgan, John Pierpont (1837–1913) *financier, art collector, philanthropist*

Morgan was born in Hartford, Connecticut, and educated in Germany. In 1871 he joined the firm of Drexel, Morgan and Company, which he reorganized in 1895 as J. P. Morgan and Company, with branches in Paris and London. Morgan gained control of private and government finance to a greater degree than any other American of his time and became one of the foremost financial figures in the world. In 1895, he carried out a private bond sale to stabilize the U.S. economy, which had been shaken by the panic of 1893. He acquired and reorganized railroad lines to make them more profitable, and by 1900 he was an influential railroad leader. In 1901, he merged several steel companies to create United States Steel, the largest corporation in the world at that time. In 1912, a committee of the U.S. House of Representatives investigated Morgan. In his testimony Morgan denied engaging in illegal trust activity or exerting any far-reaching financial control. Morgan donated money to art museums, houses of worship, and hospitals. He bequeathed a large portion of his art collection to the Metropolitan Museum of Art in New York City. The Pierpont Library, which was Morgan's private library, was made a public institution in 1924.

Murphy, Edgar Gardner (1869–1913) *clergyman, reformer*

Murphy entered the priesthood of the Episcopal Church in 1893. In 1900, while assigned to a parish in Montgomery, Alabama, he founded a church for African Americans, managed the construction of YMCA and YWCA buildings, and persuaded Andrew Carnegie to donate a public library to the city. Also in that year, he organized a conference to discuss racial and social issues facing the South, including child labor. He founded the Alabama Child Labor Committee in 1901, and he helped to create the National Child Labor Committee (NCLC) in 1904. Murphy left the priesthood in 1903 to continue his social activism outside the church. From 1903 to 1908, he was secretary of the Southern Education

Board. He resigned from the NCLC in 1907 because of the committee's support of proposed federal child-labor legislation, which he viewed as unconstitutional. In 1908, ill health forced Murphy to retire from reform work. Beginning in that year, he studied and wrote about astronomy. His writings include *The Problems of the Present South* (1904) and *A Beginner's Star Book* (1912), the latter published under the pseudonym Kelvin McKready.

Murphy, Frank (1890–1949) *governor of Michigan during the sit-down strike against General Motors in 1937, Supreme Court justice*

Murphy is remembered as a defender of civil liberties. He was assistant U.S. attorney for eastern Michigan in 1919 and 1920. Between 1924 and 1930, he was a judge of the Recorder's Court. In 1930, Murphy was elected mayor of Detroit, and he worked to aid the city's unemployed in the first years of the depression. Franklin D. Roosevelt appointed him governor-general of the Philippine Islands in 1933 and U.S. high commissioner when the Philippine Commonwealth was inaugurated in 1935. Murphy returned to Michigan in 1936 and was elected governor. He had been in office only a short time when auto workers employed by General Motors staged a sit-down strike at Flint, Michigan. He ordered 1,500 National Guardsmen to Flint, but to keep peace there and not to break the strike—an approach that earned him the support of organized labor but the ill will of industry. Murphy served as U.S. attorney general after losing his bid for reelection in 1938 and established the first civil rights unit in the Justice Department. In 1940, Roosevelt appointed him to the Supreme Court. In 1944 Murphy delivered a dissenting opinion in the case of *Korematsu v. United States,* condemning the government's wartime policy of Japanese internment.

Murray, Philip (1886–1952) *labor leader, second president of the CIO*

The Scottish-born Murray came to the United States at age 16 and worked as a coal miner in Pennsylvania; there he started a local chapter of the United Mine Workers of America. In 1920, he was elected international vice president of the union. Murray was named head of the Steel Workers Organizing Committee when the Committee for Industrial Organization was formed in 1935. In 1940, when the United

Steelworkers of America was founded, he became its first president. Murray was a strong supporter of Franklin Roosevelt's policies, while John L. Lewis opposed them. That difference of opinion led Lewis to remove Murray as vice president of the UMW in 1942; Murray, however, replaced Lewis as the leader of the CIO. Because that organization's membership exceeded seven million, he became one of the most powerful figures in the American labor movement. He advocated moderate reform measures and condemned racism.

Newcomen, Thomas (1663–1729) *English engineer and inventor*

Working with another inventor, John Calley, Newcomen perfected a reliable steam engine that was used throughout much of Europe to pump water. Newcomen made improvements to the machine in 1725. It was first used in the United States around 1755, but by 1790 it had been almost completely replaced by James Watt's steam engine.

Nixon, Edgar Daniel (1899–1987) *Pullman porter, civil rights leader*

The son of a tenant farmer, Nixon was raised by an aunt in Montgomery, Alabama. He went to work in a meatpacking plant at 13. In 1923, he was hired as a Pullman porter, and he held that position until he retired in 1964. In 1938, he became president of the Montgomery local of the Brotherhood of Sleeping Car Porters. During the 1940s, he worked to secure voting rights for Montgomery's African Americans. He was elected president of the Montgomery branch of the NAACP in 1945 and of the state NAACP in 1947. In 1952, no longer leading the NAACP, he became president of the Progressive Democratic Association, a black political organization. Nixon bailed out his friend Rosa Parks when she was arrested for violating segregation laws on a Montgomery bus in December 1955. It was he who suggested a boycott as a way to protest seating on city buses according to race. From 1968 until the end of his life, Nixon worked with poor youth in a Montgomery housing project.

Otero, Miguel Antonio (1829–82) *territorial delegate to Congress from New Mexico, railroad executive*

Otero was born in New Mexico and attended St. Louis University in Missouri and Pingree's College in

New York. He studied law in New York and St. Louis, and he was admitted to the bar in Missouri in 1851. In 1852, he became secretary to Governor William C. Lane of New Mexico and was elected to the territorial legislature. In 1854, he was appointed attorney general of New Mexico. Beginning in 1856, Otero represented New Mexico in Congress for six terms. During this period he supported slavery in the territories south of the 36th parallel, including New Mexico. He also persuaded the New Mexico legislature to enact a slave code, in 1859. Following the Civil War, Otero pursued banking and land speculation in New Mexico. He was founder and first president of the San Miguel National Bank. He was a director of the Maxwell Land Grant and Railway Company and of the Atcheson, Topeka, and Santa Fe Railroad.

Parks, Gordon (1912–   ) *photographer, writer, composer*
Parks attended high school in St. Paul, Minnesota. He worked at odd jobs as a young man while experimenting in art, writing, and music. He joined the Civilian Conservation Corps in 1933. Late in the depression, while working as a railroad porter, he discovered photography as an artistic medium. In 1942, he was hired as a correspondent for the U.S. Farm Security Administration; from 1943 to 1945, he was a correspondent for the Office of War Information. In 1948, he became a staff photographer for *Life* magazine and soon gained an international reputation. Although his work encompasses a wide range of subject matter, he is known best for his documentation of African-American life. Parks has published an autobiography, *A Choice of Weapons* (1966); poetry; and books on photographic technique. He has directed and scored several motion pictures.

Parsons, Albert (1848–87) *anarchist hanged for alleged participation in the Haymarket bombing*
Parsons, an apprentice printer in Texas when the Civil War began, served in the Confederate army. The racial conflicts that occurred in the South following the war caused him to become a political radical. As editor of the Waco, Texas, *Spectator,* he worked to further the rights of African Americans, and he was attacked and shot in the leg by white supremacists as a result. Parsons moved to Chicago in 1873 and worked as a printer until he was blacklisted for taking a highly vis-

ible part in the widespread rail strike of 1877. He continued to be active in the Typographical Union and the Knights of Labor, and he was a member of the Socialist Labor Party. In 1883, Parsons joined the International Working People's Association and preached a doctrine of anarchy. He was well known to Chicago authorities when the May 1886 bombing in Haymarket Square occurred. He was one of several anarchists tried, convicted, and executed on scanty evidence.

Pattison, Robert Emory (1850–1904) *governor of Pennsylvania during the Homestead strike*
Pattison was admitted to the bar in Pennsylvania in 1872. He first held public office in 1878, when he was elected comptroller of Philadelphia. A popular figure, he was the Democratic candidate for governor in 1882 and the overwhelming victor in the election. After leaving office in 1887, he became president of the Chestnut Street National Bank. In the same year, President Grover Cleveland appointed him to the Pacific Railroad Commission. Pattison again ran for governor in 1890 and defeated his Republican opponent in a close race. In his second term as governor, he called up the state militia to restore order during the strike at Homestead. He returned to private life in 1895 and resumed the practice of law.

Paul, Alice (1885–1977) *feminist, author of the Equal Rights Amendment*
Paul earned a Ph.D. in social work from the University of Pennsylvania and went to England in 1906 to continue her studies. There she was introduced to the suffragist movement and feminist activism. She was arrested three times in England for taking part in demonstrations. She returned to the United States and in 1913 became affiliated with the American Women's Suffrage Alliance. She left to form a more militant group, the Congressional Union, which became the National Women's Party in 1916. In 1915, she toured the nation to denounce Democratic candidates for office who did not support universal suffrage. A Quaker by birth, Paul demonstrated against U.S. involvement in World War I. When the 19th Amendment gave women the right to vote in 1920, she lobbied for passage of the Equal Rights Amendment. In 1928 she founded the World Party for Equal Rights for Women.

Powderly, Terence (1849–1924) *grand master workman of the Knights of Labor*
Born in Carbondale, Pennsylvania, of Irish immigrant parents, Powderly left school at 13 to be a railroad worker. He learned the machinist's trade at 17, and in 1871 he joined the Machinists' and Blacksmiths' International Union. He became secretary and president of the local chapter in 1872. In 1874, he was initiated into the Knights of Labor, then a secret organization. Powderly helped to draft the organization's constitution. An inspired orator, in 1879 he was elected to the highest position in the Knights of Labor, grand master workman. He did away with secrecy in the organization and increased membership from 9,000 to more than 700,000 by 1886. During his term of leadership, the Knights of Labor was involved in strikes against the Union Pacific and Southwest Railways (1884) and the Wabash Railroad (1885). He also served as mayor of Scranton, Pennsylvania, from 1878 to 1884. His term of leadership in the Knights of Labor ended in 1893. He was admitted to the Pennsylvania bar in 1894 and in 1896 was appointed U.S. commissioner general of immigration by President William McKinley. From 1902 to 1924, he held positions in the U.S. Department of Labor.

Prosser, Gabriel (ca. 1776–1800) *leader of a slave uprising*
Prosser was born of an enslaved African mother near Richmond, Virginia. In the spring of 1800, he conspired with other slaves to take possession of the U.S. arsenal at Richmond and to execute whites. When an army of slaves gathered outside Richmond on August 30, Governor James Monroe dispatched the militia to put down the insurrection. Prosser and 35 others were captured and hanged.

Pullman, George Mortimer (1831–97) *designer of the first modern railroad sleeping car*
Pullman, who was trained as a cabinetmaker, became a building contractor in Chicago in 1885. In 1863, he designed a railroad car with folding upper berths and seats that extended to form lower berths. He formed the Pullman Palace Car Company in 1867 to manufacture sleeping cars, parlor cars, and dining cars. In 1860, he founded a town, Pullman, Illinois (now part of Chicago), for the company's employees. A violent strike occurred in 1894 when the Pullman Company lowered wages without reducing rents and other fees for residents of the town of Pullman.

Randolph, Asa Philip (1889–1979) *president of the Brotherhood of Sleeping Car Porters (BSCP) from its founding in 1925 until 1968*
The BSCP was the first predominantly African-American labor union to be granted a charter by the American Federation of Labor. Randolph spent more than 10 years struggling to win recognition of the union as the employee's bargaining agent with the Pullman Company. His work with the union gained him national prominence and recognition as an early leader in the struggle for civil rights. Randolph began his career as a radical in New York City, where he edited a socialist magazine, *The Messenger,* between 1917 and 1928. He was instrumental in persuading Franklin D. Roosevelt to issue an executive order in 1941 ending discriminatory hiring in the defense industries. In 1947, he led a successful effort to pressure Harry S. Truman to desegregate the U.S. military. In 1957, he was elected a vice president of the AFL-CIO. It was Randolph who conceived of the historic March on Washington of August 1963, a high point of the civil rights movement of the 1950s and 1960s. He was the driving force behind its success.

Reuther, Walter Philip (1907–70) *longtime president of the United Automobile Workers (UAW), president of the Congress of Industrial Organizations (CIO)*
Reuther began his working life as a 16-year-old steel-mill worker but was later employed in various automobile plants in the Detroit area. In 1932, he was fired by the Ford Motor Company for union activity. He then spent three years in Europe observing labor conditions, and in the Soviet Union working in an auto plant. Reuther returned to the United States in 1935 and became an organizer for the UAW. He became UAW vice president in 1942 and president in 1946, stepping into an office that he would hold for the rest of his life. In 1939, the UAW joined the CIO; Reuther was elected president of that organization in 1952. When the CIO merged with the AFL, Reuther continued as president of the CIO division. In 1968, the UAW withdrew from the CIO. In 1969, it joined with the International Brotherhood of Teamsters to form the Alliance for Labor Action, of which Reuther was a leader. Reuther held liberal political beliefs and was active in the civil rights movement of the 1960s.

Robinson, Harriet Jane Henson (1825–1911)
women's suffragist, writer

Like her contemporary, Lucy Larcom, Harriet Henson was the child of a widow who kept a boardinghouse. She went to work in a Lowell, Massachusetts, textile mill at age 10 and took advantage of educational opportunities offered to the mill girls. On one occasion, she led a group of older coworkers in a strike of short duration. She married journalist William Stevens Robinson in 1848, and the couple became active in the abolitionist movement. After the Civil War, Robinson focused her energy on women's suffrage. She published a book, *Massachusetts in the Woman Suffrage Movement,* in 1881. The following year, she helped to found the National Woman Suffrage Association of Massachusetts and testified before a committee of the U.S. Senate. Her writings include a memoir of her years in the mills, *Loom and Spindle* (1898); a novel, *Captain Mary Miller* (1887); and a play in verse form, *The New Pandora* (1889).

Rockefeller, John Davison (1839–1937) *industrialist, philanthropist*

Rockefeller began working as a bookkeeper at age 16 in Cleveland, Ohio. In 1859, he became a partner in a business selling grain, hay, meats, and other commodities. In 1862, he involved himself in the Pennsylvania oil boom by investing in a petroleum refinery. In 1870, Rockefeller, his brother William, and other associates established the Standard Oil Company, with capitalization of one million dollars. Railroads granted the company rebates and reduced rates, a practice not uncommon at the time. In 1872, Rockefeller helped to form the South Improvement Company, an association of the largest oil refineries in Cleveland; the company was designed to control prices and competition and generate large rebates on railroad shipments. This business arrangement ended after three months due to popular protest, but it had forced many of Rockefeller's smaller competitors to sell out. By 1878, Rockefeller controlled 90 percent of the oil refineries in the United States, and in 1882 he formed the Standard Oil Trust, the first corporate trust in the United States. The Ohio Supreme Court declared the trust to be an illegal monopoly in 1892 and ordered it dissolved, but the dissolution was not effected until 1899. In that year, Rockefeller established the Standard Oil Company of New Jersey; he served as its president until his retirement in 1911. In 1911, the U.S. Supreme Court, in deciding a suit brought against the company by the government, ruled that the Standard Oil Company was a monopoly in restraint of trade and ordered its dissolution. At its peak Rockefeller's personal fortune approached a billion dollars. His lifetime philanthropic contributions totaled approximately $550 million, the largest amount ever donated by an individual. Rockefeller made most of his monetary gifts through four charitable organizations that he established: the Rockefeller Foundation, the General Education Board, the Rockefeller Institute for Medical Research (now Rockefeller University), and the Laura Spelman Rockefeller Memorial (incorporated into the Rockefeller Foundation in 1929).

Rogers, Will (William Penn Adair Rogers) (1879–1935) *humorist, actor, writer*

Rogers was born in Indian Territory (now Oklahoma). He first appeared onstage in a vaudeville rope-twirling act in 1905 and achieved wide popularity with his humorous monologues delivered while performing rope tricks. Beginning in 1914, he appeared in several of the annual *Ziegfeld Follies* revues. He also acted in numerous motion pictures and wrote syndicated newspaper articles that found humor in current events and applied homespun philosophy to timely issues. His books include *The Cowboy Philosopher on Prohibition* (1919), *Illiterate Digest* (1924), and *Will Rogers' Political Follies* (1929).

Roosevelt, Anna Eleanor (1884–1962) *social activist, U.S. representative to the United Nations, wife of Franklin D. Roosevelt*

Eleanor Roosevelt became active in Democratic politics in 1920, assisting her husband in his career in New York State. She was influential in his administration after he was elected president in 1932, although she held no official position. She was particularly active in helping the poor during the depression and in furthering civil rights for African Americans. In the 1930s she established an experimental manufacturing program in the impoverished coal-mining community of Arthurdale, West Virginia, and she was a supporter of the National Youth Administration. In 1939, when the Daughters of the American Revolution denied African-American singer Marian Anderson permission to sing in Constitution Hall in Washington, D.C., which the organization owned, Roosevelt arranged for her to sing at the Lincoln

Memorial. Roosevelt visited American service personnel overseas during World War II, and she called for the desegregation of the armed forces. As U.S. delegate to the United Nations from 1945 to 1953, she was instrumental in drafting the Universal Declaration of Human Rights. John F. Kennedy appointed her to the UN again in 1961. Her books include *This Is My Story* (1937), *This I Remember* (1949), and *On My Own* (1958).

Roosevelt, Franklin Delano (1882–1945) *thirty-second president of the United States*
After graduating from Harvard in 1904, Roosevelt studied law at Columbia University. He was admitted to the New York State bar in 1907. In 1905 he married a distant cousin, Eleanor Roosevelt. His political career began with his election to the New York State Senate in 1910. President Woodrow Wilson appointed him secretary of the navy during World War I. In 1920, Roosevelt was the Democratic candidate for vice president, sharing the ticket with James M. Cox, but Cox lost the election to Warren G. Harding. An attack of poliomyelitis in 1921 left Roosevelt unable to walk. Despite his disability, he was elected governor of New York in 1928. In 1932, he defeated the incumbent, Herbert Hoover, in the presidential election. He would be elected to an unprecedented four terms in office. During his first three months in office, Roosevelt prevailed on Congress to pass legislation to combat the economic instability and unemployment of the Great Depression. Among the pieces of legislation constituting the New Deal were measures to provide liquidity for banks and relief to individuals; the Agricultural Adjustment Act (1933) to aid farmers; and the National Industrial Recovery Act (1933) to stabilize industry and promote labor unions. The other crisis of Roosevelt's presidency was World War II. In 1940, although the United States remained neutral, Congress passed Roosevelt's lend-lease legislation to supply Great Britain in its war against Germany. He asked Congress to declare war following the Japanese attack on Pearl Harbor, Hawaii, on December 7, 1941. Roosevelt died before the United States and its allies achieved victory in the war.

Sherman, John (1823–1900) *legislator from Ohio, cabinet officer*
Sherman was admitted to the Ohio bar in 1844. He represented Ohio in the House of Representatives from 1855 to 1861 and in the Senate from 1861 to 1877 and again from 1881 to 1897. Between 1877 and 1881 he served as secretary of the treasury under President Rutherford B. Hayes. As a senator he was the author of two important pieces of legislation, the Sherman Silver Purchase Act (1890), which provided for government purchase of silver bullion and the issuance of treasury notes based on it, and the Sherman Antitrust Act (1890), which outlawed combinations in restrain of trade (monopolies). He became secretary of state under President William McKinley in 1897 but resigned in 1898 due to ill health. Sherman wrote a two-volume memoir, *Recollections of Forty Years in the House, Senate, and Cabinet* (1895).

Slater, Samuel (1768–1835) *founder of the cotton industry in the United States, pioneer of the factory system*
At age 14, the British-born Slater was apprenticed to Sir Richard Arkwright, inventor of cotton-spinning machinery. In 1789, at a time when Great Britain prohibited textile workers from leaving the country, Slater traveled to the United States in disguise. He had memorized techniques of textile manufacture and machinery specifications, and he was able to build and operate Arkwright's machines in Providence, Rhode Island. In 1790, he formed a partnership with Almy and Brown, a textile firm, and opened the first important spinning mills in the United States in Pawtucket, Rhode Island. In 1798, he established his own firm, Samuel Slater and Company, at Rehoboth, Massachusetts. At the time of his death, he operated a number of mills in Massachusetts, Rhode Island, Connecticut, and New Hampshire.

Sloan, Alfred Pritchard, Jr. (1875–1966) *president of General Motors Corporation (GM)*
Sloan earned a degree in engineering from the Massachusetts Institute of Technology in 1895. In 1898, he became president of the Hyatt Roller Bearing Company. In 1916 William Durant, the founder of GM, purchased Sloan's firm and created a subsidiary, United Motors Corporation, with Sloan as president. Sloan was promoted to vice president and director of GM in 1919. From 1923 until 1937, Sloan was president of GM. The period of his presidency included the sit-down strikes of 1936 and 1937. GM under Sloan offered the public a variety of products—in contrast to the Ford Motor Company, which pro-

duced only one—and became the largest auto manufacturer in the world. From 1937 until 1956, Sloan served as chairman of the board of GM.

Spies, August (1855–87) *radical leader executed for alleged participation in the Haymarket bombing*
Spies emigrated from Germany to the United States at 17. He settled in Chicago and worked as an upholsterer. The railroad strike of 1877 inspired him to join the Socialist Labor Party. He became editor of the *Arbeiter-Zeitung,* a socialist newspaper, in 1880. During the next few years, he grew to favor anarchism, and in 1883 he was a delegate to the Pittsburgh Congress, which established the International Working People's Association, an anarchist organization. Spies was one of several anarchists arrested following the May 1886 bombing in Chicago's Haymarket Square. A jury found him guilty, although no evidence linked him to the crime, and he was executed.

Stanford, Amasa Leland (1824–93) *first president of the Central Pacific Railroad, politician, patron of education*
Stanford, who was born in New York State, was admitted to the bar in Wisconsin in 1848. In 1852, he moved to San Francisco and went into business. He supported the building of a transcontinental railroad and served as president of the Central Pacific Company from 1861 until his death. Stanford was governor of California from 1862 to 1863, and he represented California in the U.S. Senate from 1885 to 1893. He and his wife, Jane Lanthrop Stanford, founded Stanford University in Palo Alto, California, in 1885, with an endowment of $20 million.

Steinbeck, John Ernst (1902–68) *Nobel Prize–winning novelist best known for documenting the lives of laborers and displaced southwesterners during the 1930s*
Steinbeck, a California native, was educated at Stanford University and worked as a farmhand in his youth. His earliest work dealing directly with labor issues was the novel *In Dubious Battle* (1936), a fictional account of a strike among migratory farm workers. Steinbeck first reported on the dust bowl migrants for the *San Francisco News.* He captured the nation's attention with *The Grapes of Wrath* (1939, Pulitzer Prize 1940), his stark tale of an Oklahoma family's attempts to survive in California during the Great Depression. Steinbeck's other works include *Of Mice and Men* (1937), a short, tragic novel about itinerant farm workers; *East of Eden* (1952), the interwoven stories of two families spanning several generations; and *Travels with Charley in Search of America* (1962), a nonfiction account of a road trip across the United States with his dog. Steinbeck reported on World War II from Europe for the New York *Herald Tribune;* he spent six weeks in Southeast Asia in 1966 and 1967 covering the Vietnam War for the Long Island, New York, newspaper *Newsday.*

Strobridge, James Harvey (1827–1921) *railroad builder, banker*
Strobridge first worked in railroading in New England, as a track layer on the Boston and Fitchburg line. He migrated west in 1849, following the discovery of gold in California; by 1851, he was raising grain and operating a hotel there. In 1864, he went to work for the Central Pacific Railroad. His level of responsibility increased until he was in charge of 14,000 workers and the entire construction program. He remained with the Central Pacific through its completion. He continued building western railroads until 1909, when he became president of the First National Bank of Hayward, California, a position he held until 1912.

Sutter, John Augustus (1803–80) *pioneer settler of California*
Sutter immigrated to the United States from Germany in 1934 and settled in the Sacramento Valley of California, which was then owned by Mexico. The Mexican government granted him 49,000 acres. He became a Mexican citizen and developed a settlement that attracted newcomers from the United States. Workers building a sawmill on Sutter's land discovered gold on January 24, 1848, days before Mexico ceded California to the U.S. News of the find triggered the California Gold Rush. The many squatters who settled on Sutter's land contested his claim of ownership. The case went to court and eventually reached the U.S. Supreme Court, which found Sutter's title to most of his land invalid. The government of California later granted Sutter a $250 monthly pension in gratitude for his efforts in settling the state.

Sweeney, John Joseph (1934–) *labor-union leader*
As a child, Sweeney attended union activities with his father, a New York City bus driver. He earned a degree

in economics from Iona College in New Rochelle, New York, in 1956, and soon afterward took a job as a researcher with the International Ladies' Garment Workers Union. In 1960, he went to work for Local 32B of the Building Service Employees Union. In 1972, he was elected to the executive board of the union, which was now called the Service Employees International Union (SEIU). He became a vice president in 1973. In 1976, as the new president of Local 32B, he called a surprise strike of New York City building maintenance workers and won an increase in wages. A second strike, in 1980, gained higher pay and greater job security. Sweeney was elected SEIU president in 1980. In that position, he worked to organize office workers and supported research on repetitive-stress injuries in keyboard users. In 1983, he directed organizing efforts among nursing-home workers, and in 1985 he targeted home-healthcare aides. Sweeney then lobbied for federal laws requiring family and medical leave benefits, employer-financed health insurance, and a higher minimum wage. SEIU worked to protect hospital workers from accidental transmission of blood-borne infections. In 1991, as a result of union mergers and recruiting efforts, SEIU had more than a million members. On October 25, 1995, Sweeney was elected president of the AFL-CIO.

Sylvis, William H. (1828–69) *labor leader and reformer*
Sylvis grew up in poverty in Pennsylvania and was apprenticed to an iron molder while in his teens. In 1857, he joined a local iron molders' union and was made secretary of the organization. He soon conceived of an international union for the trade and helped to bring about the first meeting of the Iron-Moulders International Union, held in Philadelphia in July 1859. In 1860 he was elected treasurer of the new union, and in 1863 he became its president. Following the Civil War, Sylvis was a founder of the National Labor Union, the first major labor organization in the United States, which held its initial meeting in Baltimore in 1866. In 1868, he was elected president of that 600,000-member organization. As the best-known labor leader of the mid-19th century, Sylvis worked for reforms that would benefit the American laborer, including the eight-hour day, educational resources for workers, and arbitration of labor-management disputes. He was also active in the temperance movement.

Taft, Robert Alphonso (1889–1953) *Senator from Ohio, coauthor of the Labor-Management Relations Act (Taft-Hartley Act)*
Taft, the son of President William Howard Taft, was educated at Yale and Harvard Universities and began practicing law in his hometown of Cincinnati, Ohio, in 1913. He was an assistant counsel of the U.S. Food Administration in 1917 and 1918; in 1919 he became a member of the American Relief Administration, which coordinated aid for survivors of World War I in Europe. Between 1921 and 1926 Taft served in the Ohio House of Representatives, holding the position of speaker of the house in 1926. He was a member of the Ohio senate from 1931 until 1932, and in 1939 he was elected to the U.S. Senate as a Republican. He held his Senate seat until his death. As a U.S. senator, Taft led the conservative Republican opposition to the policies of Franklin D. Roosevelt and Harry S. Truman, both Democrats. In 1947, he and Representative Fred Allan Hartley of New Jersey drafted the Labor-Management Relations Act, curbing the power of unions. Taft campaigned unsuccessfully for the Republican nomination for president three times, in 1940, 1948, and 1952. His *Foreign Policy for Americans* was published in 1951.

Thoreau, Henry David (1817–62) *naturalist, writer, philosopher*
Thoreau advocated individualism and the quest for new experiences as a path toward personal growth and viewed property ownership and dedication to earning a profit as barriers to that growth. He was educated at Harvard University and spent most of his life in Concord, Massachusetts, the town of his birth. He supported himself by teaching, carpentry, and surveying. In 1843, he built a cabin beside Walden Pond in Concord and lived in it until 1847. His most popular work, *Walden; or, Life in the Woods* (1854), is based on that experience. The book outlines his reasons for adopting a simple, contemplative way of life and describes the details of that life. In his most famous essay, "Civil Disobedience" (1849), Thoreau used his refusal to pay a poll tax to support the Mexican War, and his subsequent jailing, as a vehicle for discussing passive resistance as a form of protest. Thoreau's works also include *A Week on the Concord and Merrimack Rivers* (1849), a narrative of a boat trip taken in 1849.

Townsend, Willard Saxby (1895–1957) *labor union official*
After serving in the military during World War I, Townsend lived in Chicago and worked as a railroad dining-car waiter. He left the railroad to earn a degree in chemistry from the Royal Academy of Toronto, but he was unable to gain employment as a chemist and returned to railroad work in 1932. He organized the "red caps" at the Chicago railroad stations into a union, the International Brotherhood of Red Caps. He was elected vice president of the union in 1936, and president in 1937. The red caps had been paid primarily in tips until the union persuaded the railroads to pay them a salary. The union also welcomed railroad laundry workers and porters; it was renamed the United Transport Service Employees of America in 1940. Townsend then became the only African American to lead a union with white members. He continued his education, earning a law degree from the Blackstone College of Law in Chicago. In 1955, he and A. Philip Randolph were named to the executive council of the AFL-CIO.

Turner, Nat (1800–31) *leader of a slave rebellion in Southampton County, Virginia*
Turner, a religious leader within the slave community of Southampton County, claimed that God had selected him to lead the enslaved population to freedom. The uprising began on August 21, 1831, when Turner and five followers murdered their master and his family. Approximately 60 slaves from nearby plantations joined the revolt. White militia forces and volunteers brought the rebellion under control on August 24, but not before more than 50 whites had been killed and an unknown number of African Americans, many of them innocent, had been lynched. Turner and 15 of his followers were hanged in Jerusalem, Virginia.

Van Kleeck, Mary Abby (1883–1972) *social reformer*
Following her graduation from Smith College in 1904, van Kleeck investigated conditions in New York City factories and tenement sweatshops for the College Settlements Association. While researching women's working conditions for the Alliance Employment Bureau, she began a long association with the Russell Sage Foundation. In 1910, she became director of the Foundation's Department of Industrial Studies. Her books from this period include *Artificial Flower Makers* (1913), *Women in the Bookbinding Trade* (1913), and *Wages in the Millinery Trade* (1914). During World War I, she established policies on the employment of women in wartime for the War Labor Policies Board. She also advised the Department of Labor on issues relating to women in industry. She took part in the President's Conference on Unemployment in 1921 and served on the Committee on Unemployment and Business Cycles from 1922 to 1923. In the 1930s, van Kleeck embraced socialism. In *Creative America* (1936), she advocated collective ownership of the means of production. She traveled to the Soviet Union in the 1940s and wrote for the communist press in the United States. In 1948, she retired from the Russell Sage Foundation and ran unsuccessfully for the New York State Senate as the American Labor Party candidate. In 1953, she was subpoenaed to appear before the Senate subcommittee chaired by Joseph McCarthy to answer questions about her political activities.

Von Neumann, John Louis (1903–57) *mathematician, computer pioneer*
Von Neumann, born in Hungary, was a mathematical prodigy. He earned a degree in chemical engineering from the Swiss Federal Institute of Technology in 1925 and a Ph.D. in mathematics from the University of Budapest in 1926. In 1933, he accepted a professorship at the Institute for Advanced Studies at Princeton University and remained there for life. He became a U.S. citizen prior to the outbreak of World War II and was a consultant to the armed forces during and after the war. Von Neumann's principal interest in developing computers was to create a machine capable of solving complex mathematical problems. His greatest contribution to the development of computers was the "von Neumann architecture," a way of dividing a computer's logical functions among its components.

Vorse, Mary Heaton (1874–1966) *journalist, writer*
Mary Heaton grew up in an affluent family and was educated in Europe. Her first book, *Breaking In of a Yachtsman's Wife,* inspired by the early years of her marriage to Albert White Vorse, appeared in 1908. It was followed by a tribute to her mother, *Autobiography of an Elderly Woman* (1911), and tales of family life, *Stories of the Very Little Person* (1911). In 1912, Vorse reported on the textile workers' strike in Lawrence,

Massachusetts; she was shocked by the destitution of the mill workers. The experience caused her to dedicate herself to reporting on labor issues. Her book *Men and Steel* (1920) describes the steel strike of 1919; the novel *Strike!* (1930) was based on a textile strike in North Carolina. Vorse reported on the General Motors sit-down strike of 1937 and was injured in violence while covering the Little Steel strike later that year. In 1952, she wrote about corruption in the longshoreman's union operating on the New York waterfront. Vorse covered World War I in Europe and reported on conditions in the Soviet Union in 1921 and 1922. A 1939 European trip coincided with the German invasion of Poland, and she described that event for U.S. readers. She was in Europe again from 1945 to 1947, representing the United Nations Relief and Rehabilitation Administration.

Wagner, Robert Ferdinand (1877–1953) *U.S. senator from New York, sponsor of the National Labor Relations Act*
Wagner emigrated from Germany with his parents in 1898. He was graduated from the City College of New York in 1898 and admitted to the bar in 1900. In 1904 he was elected to the New York State Assembly, and in 1908 he won a seat in the New York State Senate. He left it in 1918 to become a justice of the Supreme Court of New York. Wagner, a Democrat, was elected to the U.S. Senate in 1926. He introduced important housing bills and sponsored key pieces of New Deal legislation, including the National Industrial Recovery Act (1933); the National Labor Relations Act (1935), known as the Wagner Act; and the Social Security Act (1935). Wagner retired from the Senate in 1949.

Washington, Booker Taliaferro (1856–1915) *educator, founder of the Tuskegee Institute*
Washington was born to a slave mother in Franklin County, Virginia. His family moved to Malden, West Virginia, following the Civil War. There he worked in a salt furnace and in coal mines. Washington attended the Hampton Normal and Agricultural Institute, a school for African Americans, from 1872 to 1875. He taught for two years in Malden before entering the Wayland Seminary in Washington, D.C. He returned to the Hampton Institute as an instructor in 1879. In 1881, the director of the school, Samuel Chapman

Armstrong, named Washington to organize and direct the Tuskegee Institute in Alabama. The school became a leading center for vocational training for African Americans, and Washington emerged as a spokesperson for his race. In Atlanta, Georgia, in 1895, he delivered a controversial speech in which he advised blacks to accept temporary social inferiority. Washington's books include *The Future of the American Negro* (1899); his autobiography, *Up from Slavery* (1901); *Life of Frederick Douglass* (1907); *The Story of the Negro* (1909); and *My Larger Education* (1911).

Watt, James (1736–1819) *Scottish inventor, mechanical engineer known best for perfecting the steam engine*
Watt began making mathematical instruments at age 19 but soon turned his attention to improving the steam engine (developed by Thomas Newcomen) that was currently in use in British mines. By designing a separate condensing chamber for the steam engine, he significantly increased its efficiency. Watt patented his improvements in 1769. In 1775, he and manufacturer Matthew Boulton began producing steam engines at Birmingham, England. Watt's subsequent inventions include the rotary engine for powering machinery; the steam indicator, a gauge that registers the steam pressure in a pipe or container; and an attachment that allows telescopes to be used for measuring distances. The Watt, a unit of electricity, was named for him.

Weld, Angelina Grimké (1805–79) *abolitionist, feminist*
Angelina Grimké was born into a wealthy slaveholding South Carolina family, yet she and her sister, Sarah Grimké, felt a lifelong abhorrence of slavery. As adults they moved to the North, converted to Quakerism, and joined the abolitionist cause. Their writings and speeches brought them celebrity and notoriety. They were the first women to address a mixed audience of men and women, which was considered improper for women at the time. Grimké's published writings include *An Appeal to Christian Women in the South* (1836), which called on women to influence their husbands on the slavery issue. Her *Appeal to the Women of the Nominally Free States* (1837) claimed many converts to the cause of women's rights. In 1838, she married Theodore Weld, who renounced his legal right as her husband to own and manage her property.

Weld, Theodore Dwight (1803–95) *abolitionist, educator*

Weld studied at Hamilton College in Clinton, New York, but left school in 1825 to travel the state as a revivalist preacher. He also converted to the abolitionist cause. In 1831, he entered Lane Seminary in Cincinnati, Ohio, to complete his theological studies, but he departed in 1834 when the administration objected to his continuous antislavery activities. He and a group of like-minded students relocated to Oberlin College in Oberlin, Ohio. Weld soon joined the American Anti-Slavery Society and lectured throughout the East. He published a number of pamphlets and books, including *American Slavery as It Is* (1839), a collection of news items describing the realities of slavery. Harriet Beecher Stowe consulted this book while writing *Uncle Tom's Cabin.* In 1843, an exhausted Weld retired from public life and settled with his wife and sister-in-law, the abolitionists Angelina Grimké Weld and Sarah Grimké, in Belleville, New Jersey. There he farmed and founded the Weld Institute, a school for children. He was headmaster of Eagleswood, a school in the utopian community of Raritan Bay Union, near Perth Amboy, New Jersey, from 1854 to 1862. In 1862, he moved with his family to the Boston area and taught English at a school for girls.

Whitman, Walter, Jr. (1819–92) *influential poet whose work celebrated the worth of the individual and the unity of all living things*

Whitman was born on Long Island but spent his youth in Brooklyn, New York. As a young man he drifted from one line of work to another, finding employment as a printer, teacher, newspaperman, and carpenter. In 1855, he published the first edition of *Leaves of Grass,* a groundbreaking volume of poetry that departed from the traditions of the 19th century in terms of meter, form, and subject matter. His poems praising the human body were considered scandalous. Whitman spent the rest of his life expanding and revising *Leaves of Grass;* he published numerous editions of the book. During the Civil War, Whitman journeyed to Washington, D.C., where he worked for the federal government and nursed wounded soldiers in the army hospitals. His 1865 collection of poems, *Drum-Taps,* conveyed Whitman's impressions of the war. It also contained two poems written in memory of Abraham Lincoln, "When Lilacs Last in the Dooryard Bloom'd" and "O Captain! My Captain!" In 1873, Whitman suffered a stroke that left him partially paralyzed. He left Washington to live with his brother George in Camden, New Jersey. In 1884, he purchased his own house in Camden, and he lived there until his death. Whitman's prose writings include *Democratic Vistas* (1871), a series of essays on democratic government, and *Specimen Days* (1882), a book of memoirs and observations of nature.

Whitney, Eli (1765–1825) *American inventor best known for the cotton gin*

Whitney was born in Westboro, Massachusetts. After being educated at Yale College, he traveled to Savannah, Georgia, to teach and study law. Staying at a local plantation, he designed and constructed a model of his cotton gin, a machine that separated seeds from the fibers of short-staple cotton. He built his first cotton gin in 1793 and patented it in 1794. With Whitney's invention, workers could clean 50 times the amount of cotton than they could with other methods. Cotton became the principal crop of the South and the basis of a profitable agricultural economy. In 1796, Whitney entered a business partnership with plantation manager Phineas Miller to manufacture cotton gins at New Haven, Connecticut, but a factory fire prevented Whitney and Miller from producing enough gins to meet consumer demand. Manufacturers throughout the South started copying the machine; Whitney sued for copyright infringement, but it was not until 1807 that a decision was rendered protecting his patent. In 1812, when the patent expired, Congress refused to renew it. In all, Whitney earned very little profit from the cotton gin. Whitney also undertook, in 1798, to produce factory-made firearms. He contracted to supply the federal government with 10,000 military muskets and built a plant at the site of present-day Hamden, Connecticut. There he developed the mass-production concept of manufacturing and assembling standardized, interchangeable parts that proved essential to the development of the factory system.

Wilson, Thomas Woodrow (1856–1924) *twenty-eighth president of the United States*

In 1886, Wilson received a Ph.D. in political science from Johns Hopkins University. He joined the faculty at Princeton University in 1890 and became president of Princeton in 1902. In 1910, he was elected governor of New Jersey. He became the Democratic candidate for president in 1912 and was elected. As president, he maneuvered through Congress the Federal Reserve Act and the Clayton Anti-Trust Act. He also secured federal legislation establishing an eight-hour day for railroad workers and prohibiting child labor (later struck down by the U.S. Supreme Court). He was reelected in 1916. When World War I began in Europe, Wilson repeatedly called for "peace without victory" and worked to end the war through mediation. Germany ignored his efforts and warnings, and he asked Congress to declare war on April 2, 1917. In January 1918 he outlined his "Fourteen Points," a peace program that included national self-determination, an end to colonialism, and a League of Nations. The peace treaty he negotiated in Europe following the war failed to win Senate approval, and the United States never joined the League of Nations.

Wilson suffered a severe stroke in October 1919 and never fully recovered.

Wright, Carroll Davidson (1840–1909) *government official and social researcher*
After serving with the 14th New Hampshire Volunteers in the Civil War, Wright practiced law in Boston. He was a member of the Massachusetts Senate from 1871 to 1872. In 1873, he was appointed chief of the Massachusetts Bureau of Labor. In that position he conducted a series of groundbreaking studies of working conditions and workers' lives. The information that he gathered led to improved sanitation in factories and other reforms. From 1885 to 1905, Wright was the first U.S. commissioner of labor. As commissioner, he investigated labor disputes and chaired a commission appointed by President Grover Cleveland to study the Pullman strike of 1894. In 1905, Wright became president of Clark University in Worcester, Massachusetts. He held that position until his death.

APPENDIX C
Maps

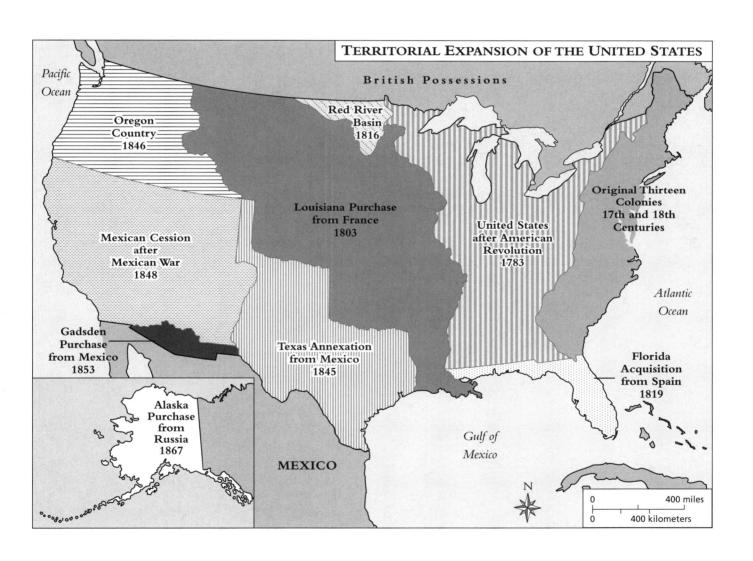

TERRITORIAL EXPANSION OF THE UNITED STATES

British Possessions

Pacific Ocean

Oregon Country 1846

Red River Basin 1816

Louisiana Purchase from France 1803

United States after American Revolution 1783

Original Thirteen Colonies 17th and 18th Centuries

Mexican Cession after Mexican War 1848

Atlantic Ocean

Gadsden Purchase from Mexico 1853

Texas Annexation from Mexico 1845

Florida Acquisition from Spain 1819

Alaska Purchase from Russia 1867

MEXICO

Gulf of Mexico

N

0   400 miles

0   400 kilometers

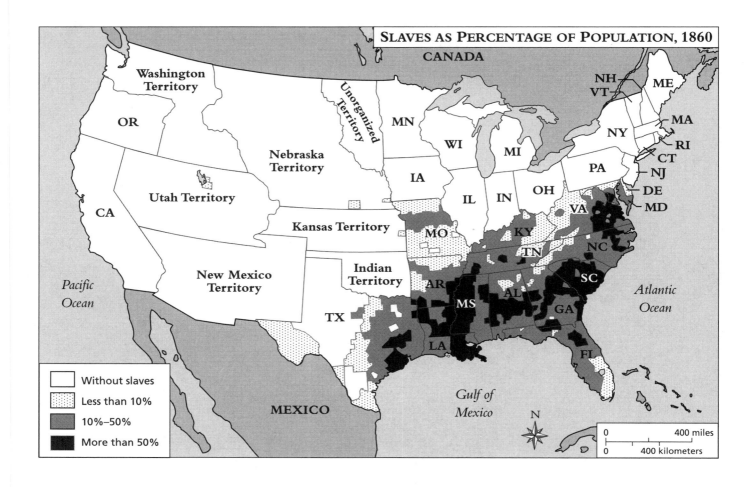

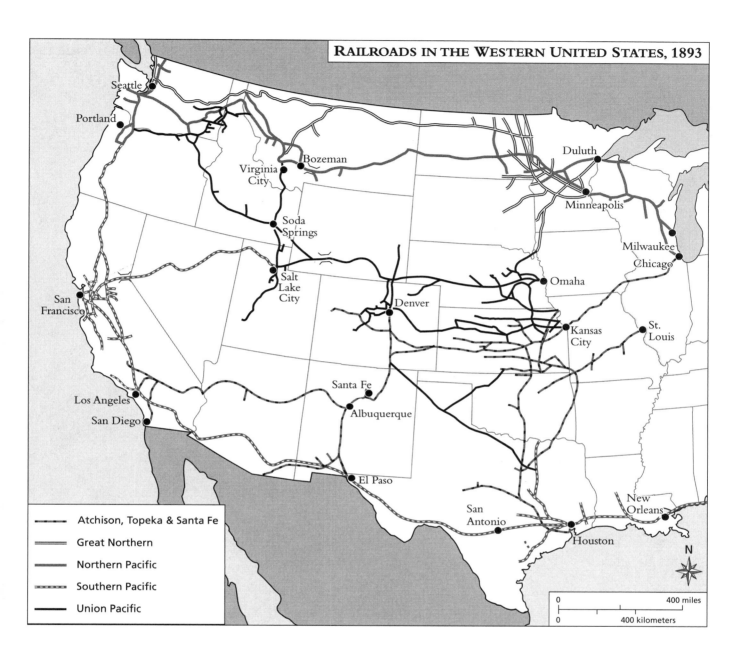

RAILROADS IN THE WESTERN UNITED STATES, 1893

Seattle
Portland
Virginia City
Bozeman
Duluth
Minneapolis
Soda Springs
Milwaukee
Chicago
San Francisco
Salt Lake City
Denver
Omaha
Kansas City
St. Louis
Los Angeles
San Diego
Santa Fe
Albuquerque
El Paso
San Antonio
Houston
New Orleans

Atchison, Topeka & Santa Fe
Great Northern
Northern Pacific
Southern Pacific
Union Pacific

N

0   400 miles
0   400 kilometers

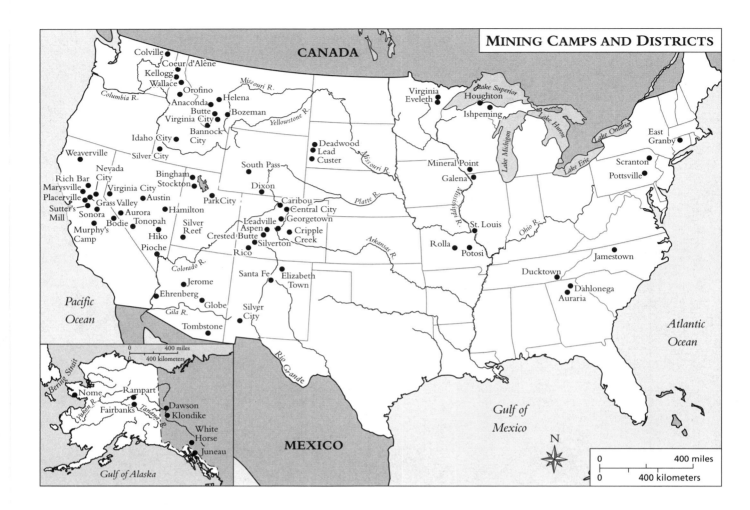

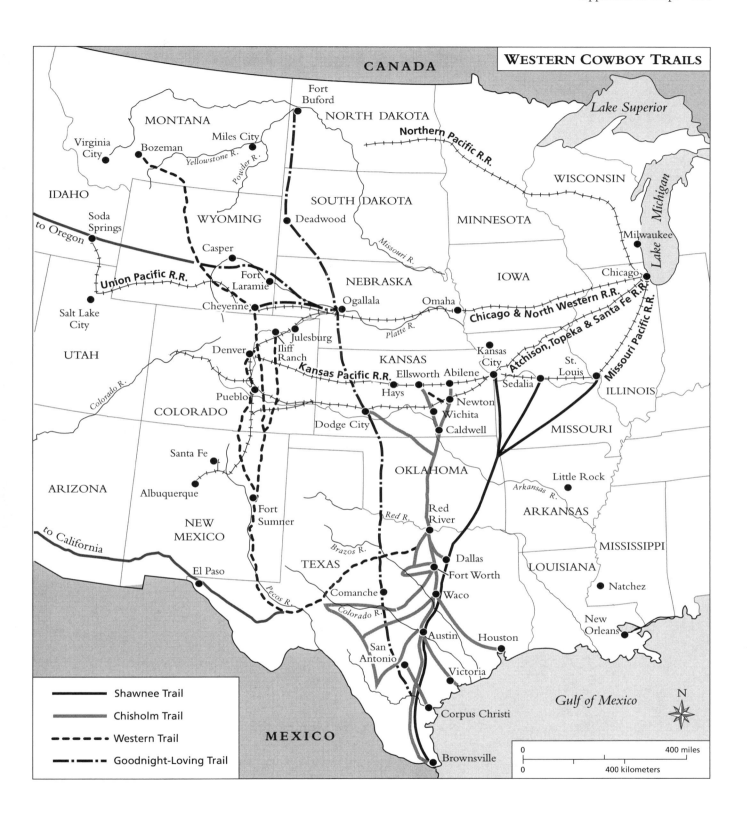

BIBLIOGRAPHY

Abbott, E. C., with Helena Huntington Smith. *We Pointed Them North*. New York: Farrar and Rinehart, 1939.

Abbott, Edith. "A Study of the Early History of Child Labor in America." *American Journal of Sociology* 14, no. 1 (July 1908), pp. 15–37.

———. *Women in Industry: A Study in American Economic History*. New York: D. Appleton, 1910.

Abbott, Grace. *The Child and the State*. Vol. 1, *Legal Status in the Family, Apprenticeship and Child Labor*. Chicago: University of Chicago Press, 1938.

Adamic, Louis. *Dynamite: The Story of Class Violence in America*. New York: Viking Press, 1934.

———. "The Hill-Billies Come to Detroit." *Nation* 140, no. 3632 (February 13, 1935), pp. 177–78.

———. *My America: 1928–1938*. New York: Harper and Brothers, 1938.

Adams, Thomas F. *Typographia: or the Printer's Instructor*. Pittsburgh: James Kay, Jr., and Brother, 1845.

Addams, Jane. *The Spirit of Youth and the City Streets*. New York: Macmillan, 1912.

"Among the Nail-Makers." *Harper's New Monthly Magazine* 21, no. 122 (July 1860), pp. 143–64.

Anderson, Jervis. *A. Philip Randolph: A Biographical Portrait*. New York: Harcourt Brace Jovanovich, 1973.

Anderson, Karen Tucker. "Last Hired, First Fired: Black Women Workers during World War II." *Journal of American History* 69, no. 1 (June 1982), pp. 82–97.

Aveling, Edward, and Eleanor Marx Aveling. *The Working-Class Movement in America*, 2d ed. London: Swan Sonnenschein, 1891.

Bagnall, William R. *Samuel Slater and the Early Development of the Cotton Manufacture in the United States*. Middleton, Conn.: J. S. Stewart, 1890.

———. *The Textile Industries of the United States*. Vol. 1. Cambridge, Mass.: Riverside Press, 1893.

Bain, David Haward. *Empire Express: Building the First Transcontinental Railroad.* New York: Viking, 1999.

Baldwin, W. W., ed. "Driving Cattle from Texas to Iowa, 1866." *Annals of Iowa* 14, no. 4 (April 1924), pp. 243–62.

Barnard, Evan G. *A Rider of the Cherokee Strip.* Boston: Houghton Mifflin, 1936.

Barnum, Gertrude. "The Story of a Fall River Mill Girl." *The Independent* 58, no. 2931 (February 2, 1905), pp. 241–43.

Bausman, R. O., and J. A. Munrow, eds. "James Tilton's Notes on the Agriculture of Delaware in 1788." *Agricultural History* 20, no. 3 (July 1946), pp. 176–87.

Baxandall, Rosalyn, and Linda Gordon, eds. *America's Working Women: A Documentary History, 1600 to the Present.* New York: W. W. Norton, 1995.

Beals, Carlton. *American Earth.* Philadelphia: J. B. Lippincott, 1939.

Beard, Charles A. *America Faces the Future.* Boston: Houghton Mifflin, 1932.

Beatty, Bess. "Lowells of the South: Northern Influences on the Nineteenth-Century North Carolina Textile Industry." *Journal of Southern History* 53, no. 1 (February 1987), pp. 37–62.

Beecher, Henry Ward. "Laboring Together with God." *Christian Union* 12, no. 19 (November 10, 1875), pp. 388–90.

———. *Lectures to Young Men, on Various Important Subjects.* New York: J. B. Ford, 1873.

Beirne, Joseph A. *Challenge to Labor: New Rules for American Trade Unions.* Englewood Cliffs, N.J.: Prentice-Hall, 1969.

Bell, James G. "A Log of the Texas-California Cattle Trail, 1854." *Southwestern Historical Quarterly* 35, no. 3 (January 1932), pp. 208–37.

Bennett, Estelline. *Old Deadwood Days.* New York: J. H. Sears, 1928.

Bennett, Lerone, Jr. *Before the Mayflower: A History of Black America.* Chicago: Johnson, 1987.

Benton, Jesse James. *Cow by the Tail.* Boston: Houghton Mifflin, 1943.

Bibb, Henry. *Narrative of the Life and Adventures of Henry Bibb, an American Slave.* New York: Published by the Author, 1850.

Billington, Ray Allen, and Martin Ridge. *Westward Expansion: A History of the American Frontier.* 5th ed. New York: Macmillan, 1982.

Bird, Isabella L. *A Lady's Life in the Rocky Mountains.* New York: G. P. Putnam's Sons, 1879–80.

Blackwelder, Julia Kirk. *Now Hiring: The Feminization of Work in the United States, 1900–1995.* College Station: Texas A & M University Press, 1997.

———. *Women in the Depression: Caste and Culture in San Antonio, 1929–1939*. College Station: Texas A & M University Press, 1984.

Blassingame, John W. *The Slave Community: Plantation Life in the Antebellum South*. New York: Oxford University Press, 1972.

Blewett, Mary H. *We Will Rise in Our Might: Workingwomen's Voices from Nineteenth-Century New England*. Ithaca, N.Y.: Cornell University Press, 1991.

Blumberg, Barbara. *The New Deal and the Unemployed*. Lewisburg, Pa.: Bucknell University Press, 1979.

Blumberg, Rhoda. *Full Steam Ahead: The Race to Build a Transcontinental Railroad*. Washington, D.C.: National Geographic Society, 1996.

Bogue, Allan G. *From Prairie to Corn Belt: Farming on the Illinois and Iowa Prairies in the Nineteenth Century*. Chicago: University of Chicago Press, 1963.

"The Bonanza Farms of the West." *Atlantic Monthly* 45, no. 67 (January 1880), pp. 33–44.

Booth, William. "By the Sweat of Their Brows, a New Economy." *Washington Post,* July 13, 1998, pp. A1, A10–A11.

Bourke-White, Margaret. "Dust Changes America." *Nation* 140, no. 3646 (May 22, 1935), pp. 597–98.

Bowles, Samuel. *Across the Continent: A Summer's Journey to the Rocky Mountains, the Mormons, and the Pacific States*. Springfield, Mass.: Samuel Bowles, 1865.

Brace, Charles Loring. *The Dangerous Classes of New York*. 3d ed. New York: Wynkoop and Hallenbeck, 1880.

Bratt, John. *Trails of Yesterday*. Chicago: University Publishing, 1921.

Brewer, William H. *Rocky Mountain Letters*. Gunnison, Colo.: James D. Houston, 1992.

———. *Up and Down California in 1860–1864*. Berkeley: University of California Press, 1966.

Brissot de Warville, J. P. *New Travels in the United States of America: 1788*. Cambridge, Mass.: Belknap Press, 1964.

Brooks, Thomas R. *Toil and Trouble: A History of American Labor*. 2d ed. New York: Delacorte Press, 1971.

Brown, Dee. *Hear that Lonesome Whistle Blow*. New York: Holt, Rinehart and Winston, 1977.

Brown, William Wells. *Narrative of the Life of William W. Brown, a Fugitive Slave*. Boston: Anti-Slavery Office, 1847.

———. *The Black Man, His Antecedents, His Genius, and His Achievements*. Boston: Robert F. Wallcut, 1865.

Browne, J. Ross. *J. Ross Browne's Illustrated Mining Adventures: California and Nevada, 1863–1865*. Balboa Island, Calif.: Paisano Press, 1961.

Brownson, Orestes. "The Laboring Classes." *Boston Quarterly* 3, no. 3 (July 1840), pp. 358–95.

Bruce, Robert V. *1877: Year of Violence*. Chicago: Ivan R. Dee, 1987.

Bryant, William Cullen. *Letters of a Traveller; or, Notes of Things Seen in Europe and America*. New York: George P. Putnam, 1851.

Buck, Solon Justis. *Illinois in 1818*. Springfield: Illinois Centennial Commission, 1917.

Buckingham, J. S. *The Slave States of America*. Vol. 1. London: Fisher, Son, 1842.

Buhle, Paul, and Alan Dawley, eds. *Working for Democracy: American Workers from the Revolution to the Present*. Urbana: University of Illinois Press, 1985.

Bullock, Edna D., comp. *Selected Articles on Child Labor*. White Plains, N.Y.: H. W. Wilson, 1915.

Burgoyne, Arthur G. *Homestead: A Complete History of the Struggle of July 1892*. Pittsburgh: Rawsthorne Engraving and Printing, 1893.

Burn, James Dawson. *Three Years Among the Working-Class in the United States During the War*. London: Smith, Elder, 1865.

Burt, Olive W. *The National Road*. New York: John Day, 1968.

Buss, Fran Leeper, comp. *Dignity: Lower Income Women Tell of Their Lives and Struggle*. Ann Arbor: University of Michigan Press, 1985.

Byington, Margaret. *Homestead: The Households of a Mill Town*. Pittsburgh: University Center for International Studies, 1974.

"A California Mining Camp." *Scribner's Monthly* 15, no. 4 (February 1878), pp. 480–93.

Callahan, Tom. "Go to School. AGAIN." *Parade*, August 1, 1999, pp. 4–6.

Candee, Helen Churchill. *How Women May Earn a Living*. New York: Macmillan, 1900.

Carlton, Frank T. "The Workingmen's Party of New York City: 1829–1831." *Political Science Quarterly* 22, no. 3 (September 1907), pp. 401–15.

Carnegie, Andrew. "The Bugaboo of Trusts." *North American Review* 148, no. 2 (February 1889), pp. 141–50.

———. "Wealth." *North American Review* 148, no. 6 (June 1889), pp. 653–64.

Carter, Clarence Edwin, ed. *The Territorial Papers of the United States*. Vol. 2. Washington, D.C.: U.S. Government Printing Office, 1934.

Carter, John Franklin. *The New Dealers*. New York: Simon and Schuster, 1934.

Carwardine, William H. *The Pullman Strike.* Chicago: Charles H. Kerr, 1894.

Casey, Charles. *Two Years on the Farm of Uncle Sam.* London: Richard Bentley, 1852.

Cashman, Sean Dennis. *America in the Gilded Age: From the Death of Lincoln to the Rise of Theodore Roosevelt.* New York: New York University Press, 1984.

Ceplair, Larry. *Charlotte Perkins Gilman: A Nonfiction Reader.* New York: Columbia University Press, 1996.

Chaplin, Ralph. *The Rough-and-Tumble Story of an American Radical.* Chicago: University of Chicago Press, 1948.

Chevalier, Michel. *Society, Manners and Politics in the United States: Being a Series of Letters on North America.* Boston: Weeks, Jordan, 1839.

Child, Lydia Maria, ed. *Incidents in the Life of a Slave Girl.* Boston: Published for the Author, 1861.

Chisholm, James. *South Pass, 1868: James Chisholm's Journal of the Wyoming Gold Rush.* Lincoln: University of Nebraska Press, 1988.

Christian, Charles M. *Black Saga: The African American Experience: A Chronology.* Boston: Houghton Mifflin, 1995.

Clappe, Louise A. *The Shirley Letters: Being Letters Written in 1851–1852 from the California Mines.* Santa Barbara, Calif.: Peregrine Publishers, 1970.

Clawson, Augusta H. *Shipyard Diary of a Woman Welder.* New York: Penguin Books, 1944.

Cochrane, Willard W. *The Development of Agriculture: A Historical Analysis.* Minneapolis: University of Minnesota Press, 1979.

Cohen, Lizabeth. *Making a New Deal: Industrial Workers in Chicago, 1919–1939.* Cambridge, U.K.: Cambridge University Press, 1990.

Coleman, J. Winston, Jr. *Slavery Times in Kentucky.* Chapel Hill: University of North Carolina Press, 1940.

Collinson, Frank. *Life in the Saddle.* Norman: University of Oklahoma Press, 1963.

Commager, Henry Steele, ed. *Documents of American History,* 9th ed. 2 vols. Englewood Cliffs, N.J.: Prentice-Hall, 1973.

Conrat, Richard, and Maisie Conrat. *The American Farm: A Photographic History.* San Francisco: California Historical Society; Boston: Houghton Mifflin, 1977.

A Conversation with the Reverend Jesse Jackson: The Quest for Economic and Educational Parity. Washington, D.C.: American Enterprise Institute for Public Policy Research, 1978.

Coxe, Tench. *A View of the United States of America in a Series of Papers Written at Various Times, in the Years between 1787 and 1794.* New York: Augustus M. Kelley, 1965.

Cronon, E. David, ed. *Labor and the New Deal.* Chicago: Rand McNally, 1963.

Culley, John H. *Cattle, Horses and Men.* Los Angeles: Ward Ritchie Press, 1940.

Dale, Henry, and Rodney Dale. *The Industrial Revolution.* New York: Oxford University Press, 1992.

Danhof, Clarence H. *Change in Agriculture: The Northern United States, 1820–1870.* Cambridge, Mass.: Harvard University Press, 1969.

Daniel, Cletus E. *Bitter Harvest: A History of California Farmworkers, 1870–1941.* Ithaca, N.Y.: Cornell University Press, 1981.

Davis, John P. *The Union Pacific Railway: A Study in Railway Politics, History, and Economics.* Chicago: S. C. Griggs, 1894.

Debs, Eugene V. *Writings and Speeches of Eugene V. Debs.* New York: Hermitage Press, 1948.

Dewees, F. P. *The Molly Maguires: The Origin, Growth, and Character of the Organization.* Philadelphia: J. B. Lippincott, 1877.

Dickens, Charles. *American Notes: A Journey.* New York: Fromm International, 1985.

Dodge, Grenville M. *How We Built the Union Pacific.* Washington, D.C.: U.S. Government Printing Office, 1910.

Dodge, Richard Irving. *Our Wild Indians: Thirty-three Years' Personal Experience among the Red Men of the Great West.* Hartford, Conn.: A. D. Worthington, 1883.

Donovan, Frances R. *The Saleslady.* Chicago: University of Chicago Press, 1929.

Douglass, Frederick. *Narrative of the Life of Frederick Douglass, an American Slave.* New York: Anchor Books, 1989.

Drache, Hiram M. *Legacy of the Land: Agriculture's Story to the Present.* Danville, Ill.: Interstate Publishers, 1996.

"Drought: Field Report from Five of the States Most Seriously Affected." *New Republic* 66, no. 847 (February 25, 1931), pp. 37–41.

Dublin, Louis I. "Home-Making and Careers." *Atlantic Monthly* 138, no. 3 (September 1926), pp. 335–43.

Dublin, Thomas, ed. *Farm to Factory: Women's Letters, 1830–1860.* New York: Columbia University Press, 1981.

Du Bois, W. E. B. "The Black Man and the Unions." *The Crisis* 15, no. 5 (March 1918), pp. 216–17.

————. *The Philadelphia Negro.* Philadelphia: University of Pennsylvania Press, 1996.

————. *Writings.* New York: Library of America, 1986.

Duffield, George C. "Youthtime in Frontier Iowa." *Annals of Iowa* 7, no. 5 (April 1906), pp. 347–60.

Duffus, R. L. *The Valley and Its People: A Portrait of the TVA.* New York: Alfred A. Knopf, 1944.

Dulles, Foster Rhea. *Labor in America: A History.* New York: Thomas Y. Crowell, 1966.

Durham, Philip, and Everett L. Jones. *The Negro Cowboys.* Lincoln: University of Nebraska Press, 1965.

Ebert, Justus. *The Trial of a New Society.* Cleveland: I. W. W. Publishing Bureau, 1912.

Ellis, Anne. *The Life of an Ordinary Woman.* Boston: Houghton Mifflin, 1929.

Ellis, Edward Robb. *A Nation in Torment: The Great American Depression, 1929–1939.* New York: Coward-McCann, 1970.

Faler, Paul G. *Mechanics and Manufacturers in the Early Industrial Revolution: Lynn Massachusetts 1780–1860.* Albany: State University of New York Press, 1981.

The Famous Speeches of the Eight Chicago Anarchists in Court. Chicago: Lucy E. Parsons, 1910.

"Farming Life in New England." *Atlantic Monthly* 2, no. 10 (August 1858), pp. 334–41.

Featherstonhaugh, G. W. *Excursion through the Slave States.* New York: Harper and Brothers, 1844.

"The Fetish of the Job." *Harper's Monthly Magazine* 151, no. 906 (November 1925), pp. 731–36.

Filippelli, Ronald L. *Labor in the USA: A History.* New York: Alfred A. Knopf, 1984.

Fine, Sidney, ed. "John L. Lewis Discusses the General Motors Sit-Down Strike: A Document." *Labor History* 15, no. 4 (Fall 1974), pp. 563–70.

Fisher, Leonard Everett. *Tracks across America: The Story of the American Railroad, 1825–1900.* New York: Holiday House, 1992.

Fite, Gilbert C. *The Farmer's Frontier: 1865–1900.* New York: Holt, Rinehart and Winston, 1966.

Fletcher, Baylis John. *Up the Trail in '79.* Norman: University of Oklahoma Press, 1968.

Flexner, Elizabeth. *Century of Struggle: The Woman's Rights Movement in the United States.* Cambridge, Mass.: Belknap Press, 1975.

Foner, Philip S. *Organized Labor and the Black Worker.* New York: International Publishers, 1981.

———, ed. *The Autobiographies of the Haymarket Martyrs.* New York: Humanities Press, 1968.

Foner, Philip S., and Ronald L. Lewis, eds. *Black Workers: A Documentary History from Colonial Times to the Present.* Philadelphia: Temple University Press, 1989.

Fordham, Elias Pym. *Personal Narrative of Travels in Virginia, Maryland, Pennsylvania, Ohio, Indiana, Kentucky; and of a Residence in the Illinois Territory: 1817–1818.* Cleveland: Arthur H. Clark, 1906.

Fortune, T. Thomas. *Black and White: Land, Labor, and Politics in the South.* New York: Fords, Howard, and Hulbert, 1884.

Foster, William Z. *The Great Steel Strike and Its Lessons.* New York: B. W. Huebsch, 1920.

Franklin, John Hope, and Alfred A. Moss, Jr. *From Slavery to Freedom.* 7th ed. New York: McGraw-Hill, 1994.

Frantz, Joe B., and Julian Ernest Choate, Jr. *The American Cowboy: The Myth and the Reality.* Norman: University of Oklahoma Press, 1955.

Fried, Albert, ed. *Except to Walk Free: Documents and Notes in the History of American Labor.* Garden City, N.Y.: Anchor Books, 1974.

Friedan, Betty. *The Feminine Mystique.* New York: W. W. Norton, 1963.

"Galena and Its Lead Mines." *Harper's New Monthly Magazine* 32, no. 192 (May 1866), pp. 681–96.

Gardner, Joseph. *Labor on the March: The Story of America's Unions.* New York: American Heritage Publishing, 1969.

Garland, Hamlin. *A Son of the Middle Border.* New York: Macmillan, 1917.

Garraty, John A. *The Great Depression.* New York: Anchor Books, 1987.

George, Henry. *Moses and the Crime of Poverty.* New York: International Joseph Fels Commission, 1918.

Gerhard, Fred. *Illinois as It Is.* Chicago: Keen and Lee, 1857.

Gerry, Elbridge T., comp. *Manual of the New York Society for the Prevention of Cruelty to Children.* New York: Published by the Society, 1913.

Giddens, Paul H. "Eastern Kansas in 1869–1870." *Kansas Historical Quarterly* 9, no. 4 (November 1940), pp. 371–83.

Gilman, Charlotte Perkins. *Human Work.* New York: McClure, Phillips, 1904.

———. *Women and Economics.* Boston: Small, Maynard, 1900.

"The Girl Who Comes to the City, Part 1." *Harper's Bazar* 42, no. 2 (February 1908), pp. 170–72.

"The Girl Who Comes to the City, Part 2." *Harper's Bazar* 42, no. 3 (March 1908), pp. 277–79.

Gompers, Samuel. *Seventy Years of Life and Labor.* New York: E. P. Dutton, 1925.

Goulden, Joseph C. *Meany.* New York: Atheneum, 1972.

Greeley, Horace. *Hints toward Reforms, in Lectures, Addresses, and Other Writings.* New York: Harper and Brothers, 1850.

Green, Charles H. *The Headwear Workers: A Century of Trade Unionism.* New York: United Hatters, Cap and Millinery Workers International Union, 1944.

Green, Gil. *What's Happening to Labor.* New York: International Publishers, 1976.

Green, William. "Labor's Opportunity and Responsibility." *American Federationist* 40, no. 6 (June 1933), pp. 692–694.

————. "The Taft–Hartley Act: A Critical View." *Annals of the American Academy of Political and Social Science* 274 (March 1951), pp. 200–05.

Greenberg, Cheryl Lynn. *"Or Does It Explode?" Black Harlem in the Great Depression.* New York: Oxford University Press, 1991.

Greene, Laura Offenhartz. *Child Labor: Then and Now.* New York: Franklin Watts, 1992.

Gregory, James N. *American Exodus: The Dust Bowl Migration and Okie Culture in California.* New York: Oxford University Press, 1989.

Grund, Francis J. *The Americans in their Moral, Social, and Political Relations.* Vol. 2. London: Longman, Rees, Orme, Brown, Green, and Longman, 1837.

Guernsey, Charles A. *Wyoming Cowboy Days.* New York: G. P. Putnam's Sons, 1936.

Guthrie, Woody. *Bound for Glory.* New York: E. P. Dutton, 1968.

Gutman, Herbert G. *Work, Culture, and Society in Industrializing America.* New York: Alfred A. Knopf, 1976.

Hafen, Le Roy R. *Colorado Gold Rush: Contemporary Letters and Reports.* Philadelphia: Porcupine Press, 1974.

Hafen, Le Roy R., W. Eugene Hollon, and Carl Coke Rister. *Western America: The Exploration and Development of the Region beyond the Mississippi.* 3d ed. Englewood Cliffs, N.J.: Prentice-Hall, 1970.

Hall, Mrs. Cecil. *A Lady's Life on a Farm in Manitoba.* London: W. H. Allen, 1884.

Halper, Albert. *Good-bye, Union Square.* Chicago: Quadrangle Books, 1970.

Halsell, H. H. *Cowboys and Cattleland.* Nashville, Tenn.: Parthenon Press, 1937.

Hancock, Ellery M. *Past and Present of Allamakee County, Iowa: A Record of Settlement, Organization, Progress and Achievement.* Chicago: J. J. Clarke, 1913.

Haney, E. D. "The Experiences of a Homesteader in Kansas." In *Collections of the Kansas State Historical Society,* edited by William Esley Connelley. Vol. 17. Topeka: Kansas State Printing Plant, 1928, pp. 305–25.

Harris, Frank. *My Reminiscences as a Cowboy.* New York: Charles Boni, 1930.

Hawthorne, Nathaniel. *American Notebooks.* New Haven, Conn.: Yale University Press, 1932.

Haywood, William D. *Bill Haywood's Book.* New York: International Publishers, 1929.

Henson, Josiah. *Father Henson's Story of His Own Life.* Boston: John P. Jewett, 1858.

Herling, John. "Field Notes from Arkansas." *Nation* 140, no. 3640 (April 10, 1935), pp. 419–20.

Heymann, C. David. *RFK.* New York: Dutton, 1998.

Hill, Frank Ernest. *The School in the Camps: The Education Program of the Civilian Conservation Corps.* New York: American Association for Adult Education, 1935.

Hine, Robert V. *The American West: An Interpretive History.* Boston: Little, Brown, 1973.

Hinkle, James F. *Early Days of a Cowboy on the Pecos.* Roswell, N.M.: Privately published, 1937.

Hoch, Edward Wallace. "Kansas and the Standard Oil Company." *The Independent* 58, no. 2935 (March 2, 1905), pp. 461–63.

Hochschild, Arlie. *The Second Shift.* New York: Viking, 1989.

Holden, W. C. "The Problem of Hands on the Spur Ranch." *Southwestern Historical Quarterly* 35, no. 3 (January 1932), pp. 208–37.

Howbert, Irving. *Memories of a Lifetime in the Pike's Peak Region.* New York: C. P. Putnam's Sons, 1925.

Howells, William Cooper. *Recollections of Life in Ohio from 1813 to 1840.* Cincinnati: Robert Clarke, 1895.

Hughes, Louis. *Thirty Years a Slave.* New York: Negro Universities Press, 1969.

Hurt, R. Douglas. *American Agriculture: A Brief History.* Ames: Iowa State University Press, 1994.

Hutchins, Levi. *The Autobiography of Levi Hutchins.* Cambridge, Mass.: Riverside Press, 1865.

Hutchinson, John. *The Imperfect Union: A History of Corruption in American Trade Unions.* New York: E. P. Dutton, 1972.

Jackson, Andrew. *Narrative and Writings of Andrew Jackson, of Kentucky.* Syracuse, N.Y.: Daily and Weekly Star Office, 1847.

Jackson, Donald Dale. "They Were Poor, Hungry, and They Built to Last." *Smithsonian* 25, no. 9 (December 1994), pp. 66–78.

Jackson, Jesse L. "Three Challenges to Organized Labor." *Freedomways* 12, no. 4 (Fourth Quarter 1972), pp. 307–15.

Jacobson, Julius, ed. *The Negro and the American Labor Movement.* New York: Anchor Books, 1968.

James, Will S. *27 Years a Mavrick, or Life on a Texas Range.* Chicago: Donohue and Henneberry, 1893.

Jefferson, Thomas. *The Life and Selected Writings of Thomas Jefferson.* New York: Modern Library, 1944.

Johnsen, Julia E., comp. *Selected Articles on Child Labor.* New York: H. W. Wilson, 1925.

Johnson, Hugh S. *The Blue Eagle from Egg to Earth.* Garden City, N.Y.: Doubleday, Doran, 1935.

Jones, Jacqueline. *American Work: Four Centuries of Black and White Labor.* New York: W. W. Norton, 1998.

Jones, Mary Harris. *Autobiography of Mother Jones.* Chicago: Charles H. Kerr, 1925.

Josephson, Hannah. *The Golden Threads: New England's Mill Girls and Magnates.* New York: Duell, Sloan and Pearce, 1949.

Kaztauskis, Antanas. "From Lithuania to the Chicago Stockyards: An Autobiography." *Independent* 57, no. 2905 (August 4, 1904), pp. 241–48.

Keating, W. H. *Considerations upon the Art of Mining.* Philadelphia: M. Carey and Sons, 1821.

Keckley, Elizabeth. *Behind the Scenes: Thirty Years a Slave and Four Years in the White House.* New York: G. W. Carleton, 1868.

Kennedy, Joseph P. *I'm for Roosevelt.* New York: Reynal and Hitchcock, 1936.

Kenny, Kevin. *Making Sense of the Molly Maguires.* New York: Oxford University Press, 1998.

Kessler, Sidney H. "Organization of Negroes in the Knights of Labor." *Journal of Negro History* 37, no. 3 (July 1952), pp. 248–76.

Kilbourn, John, comp. *Public Documents Concerning the Ohio Canals.* Columbus, Ohio: I. N. Whiting, 1832.

King, Clarence. *Mountaineering in the Sierra Nevada.* New York: Charles Scribner's Sons, 1902.

King, Frank M. *Longhorn Trail Drivers.* Burbank, Calif.: Privately published, 1940.

———. *Wranglin' the Past.* Los Angeles: Privately published, 1935.

King, Martin Luther, Jr. *Stride toward Freedom.* New York: Harper and Row, 1958.

———. *Why We Can't Wait.* New York: Mentor, 1964.

Kingdon, Frank. *As FDR Said: A Treasury of His Speeches, Conversations, and Writings.* New York: Duell, Sloan and Pearce, 1950.

Klingaman, William K. *1929: The Year of the Great Crash.* New York: Harper and Row, 1989.

Kulick, Gary, Roger Parks, and Theodore Z. Penn, eds. *The New England Mill Village, 1790–1860.* Cambridge, Mass.: MIT Press, 1982.

Lacy, Leslie Alexander. *The Soil Soldiers: The Civilian Conservation Corps in the Great Depression.* Radnor, Pa.: Chilton, 1976.

Lange, Dorothea, and Paul Schuster Taylor. *An American Exodus: A Record of Human Erosion.* New York: Reynal and Hitchcock, 1939.

Lapin, Eva. *Mothers in Overalls.* New York: Workers Library Publishers, 1943.

Larcom, Lucy. *An Idyl of Work.* Boston: James R. Osgood, 1875.

———. *A New England Girlhood.* Boston: Houghton Mifflin, 1889.

Laslett, John. *The Workingman in American Life.* Boston: Houghton Mifflin, 1968.

Lauck, W. Jett, and Edgar Sydenstrecker. *Conditions of Labor in American Industries: A Summarization of the Results of Recent Investigations.* New York: Funk and Wagnalls, 1917.

Lee, Yan Phou. "The Chinese Must Stay." *North American Review* 148, no. 4 (April 1889), pp. 476–83.

Leonard, Charles McClung. "Forty Years in Colorado Mining Camps." *Colorado Magazine* 37, no. 2 (July 1960), pp. 161–84.

Leonard, Jonathan Norton. *Three Years Down.* New York: Carrick and Evans, 1939.

Levinson, Edward. *Labor on the March.* Ithaca, N.Y.: ILR Press, 1995.

Litwack, Leon. *The American Labor Movement.* New York: Simon and Schuster, 1962.

Lloyd, Henry D. "Story of a Great Monopoly." *Atlantic Monthly* 47, no. 28 (March 1881), pp. 317–34.

———. "The Political Economy of Seventy-three Million Dollars." *Atlantic Monthly* 50, no. 297 (July 1882), pp. 69–81.

Lower, Arthur R. M. *Canadians in the Making.* Toronto: Longmans, Green, 1958.

Lyendecker, Liston E. "Young Man Gone West: George M. Pullman's Letters from the Colorado Goldfields." *Chicago History* 7, no. 4 (Winter 1978–79), pp. 208–25.

Lynd, Alice, and Staughton Lynd, eds. *Rank and File: Personal Histories by Working-Class Organizers.* New York: Monthly Review Press, 1988.

Lynd, Staughton, ed. *American Labor Radicalism: Testimonies and Interpretations.* New York: John Wiley and Sons, 1973.

Mailly, William. "The Working Girls' Strike." *Independent* 67, no. 3186 (December 23, 1909), pp. 1416–20.

Malin, James. *Winter Wheat in the Golden Belt of Kansas.* Lawrence: University of Kansas Press, 1944.

Mandel, Bernard. "Samuel Gompers and the Negro Workers." *Journal of Negro History* 40, no. 1 (January 1955), pp. 34–60.

Mangold, George B. *Problems of Child Welfare.* New York: Macmillan, 1924.

Markham, Edwin, Benjamin B. Lindsey, and George Creel. *Children in Bondage: A Complete and Careful Presentation of the Anxious Problem of Child Labor—Its Causes, Its Crimes, and Its Cure.* New York: Hearst's International Library, 1914.

Marshall, Ray. *The Negro Worker.* New York: Random House, 1967.

Martin, Molly. *Hard-Hatted Women.* Seattle: Seal Press, 1988.

Maurer, John G., Joel M. Shulman, Marcia L. Ruwe, and Richard C. Becherer. *Encyclopedia of Business.* Vol. 1. New York: Gale Research, 1995.

Mayer, Lynne Rhodes, and Kenneth E. Vose. *Makin' Tracks: The Story of the Transcontinental Railroad in the Pictures and Words of the Men Who Were There.* New York: Praeger Publishers, 1975.

McCauley, J. E. *A Stove-Up Cowboy's Story.* Austin: Texas Folklore Society, 1943.

McClellan, John L. *Crime without Punishment.* New York: Duell, Sloan and Pearce, 1962.

McClure, A. K. *Three Thousand Miles through the Rocky Mountains.* Philadelphia: J. B. Lippincott, 1869.

McCoy, Donald R. *Calvin Coolidge: The Quiet President.* New York: Macmillan, 1967.

McCoy, Joseph. *Historic Sketches of the Cattle Trade of the West and Southwest.* Kansas City, Mo.: Ramsey, Millet and Hudson, 1874.

McCreesh, Carolyn Daniel. *Women in the Campaign to Organize Garment Workers, 1880–1917.* New York: Garland Publishing, 1985.

McDonald, William. *The Menace of Recovery: What the New Deal Means.* New York: Macmillan, 1934.

McElvaine, Robert S. *Down and Out in the Great Depression.* Chapel Hill: University of North Carolina Press, 1983.

McGill, Nettie P. *Children in Street Work.* Washington, D.C.: U.S. Government Printing Office, 1928.

McIntire, Jim. *Early Days in Texas: A Trip to Hell and Heaven.* Norman: University of Oklahoma Press, 1992.

McLean, Evalyn Walsh. *Father Struck It Rich*. Boston: Little, Brown, 1936.

McNaught, Kenneth. *The Pelican History of Canada*. New York: Penguin Books, 1976.

McNeill, George E. *The Labor Movement: The Problem of To-Day*. New York: M. W. Hazen, 1887.

McWilliams, Carey. *Factories in the Field: The Story of Migratory Farm Labor in California*. N.p.: Archo Books, 1969.

Miller, Kelly. "The Negro as a Workingman." *American Mercury* 6, no. 23 (November 1925), pp. 310–13.

Miller, Marc S., ed. *Working Lives: The Southern Exposure History of Labor in the South*. New York: Pantheon, 1980.

Miller, Perry. *The New England Mind: The Seventeenth Century*. Cambridge, Mass.: Harvard University Press, 1954.

Minnesota Farmers' Diaries: William R. Brown, 1845–46; Mitchell Y. Jackson, 1852–63. St. Paul: Minnesota Historical Society, 1939.

Mishel, Lawrence, and Jared Bernstein. *The State of Working America: 1992–93*. Armonk, N.Y.: M. W. Sharpe, 1993.

Mohkiber, Russell, and Robert Weissman. *Corporate Predators: The Hunt for Mega-Profits and the Attack on Democracy*. Monroe, Maine: Common Courage Press, 1999.

Morris, Richard B., ed. *The U.S. Department of Labor Bicentennial History of the American Worker*. Washington, D.C.: U.S. Government Printing Office, 1976.

Murphy, Edgar Gardner. *Problems of the Present South*. New York: Macmillan, 1904.

———. *The Federal Regulation of Child Labor: A Criticism of the Policy Represented in the Beveridge-Parsons Bill*. Montgomery: Alabama Child Labor Committee, 1907.

National Manpower Council. *Womanpower*. New York: Columbia University Press, 1957.

Nelson, Daniel. *Shifting Fortunes: The Rise and Decline of American Labor, from the 1820s to the Present*. Chicago: Ivan R. Dee, 1997.

Nelson, Oliver. *The Cowman's Southwest, Being the Reminiscences of Oliver Nelson, Freighter, Camp Cook, Cowboy, Frontiersman in Kansas, Indian Territory, Texas and Oklahoma*. Glendale, Calif.: Arthur H. Clark, 1953.

"A New Anvil Chorus." *Scribner's Monthly* 15, no. 3 (January 1878), pp. 386–95.

Newhall, Howard Mudge. "A Pair of Shoes." *Harper's New Monthly Magazine* 70, no. 416 (January 1885), pp. 273–89.

Nimmo, Joseph, Jr. "The American Cow-Boy." *Harper's New Monthly Magazine* 73, no. 438 (November 1886), pp. 880–84.

―――――. *The Insurrection of June and July 1894 Growing Out of the Pullman Strike at Chicago, Ill.* Washington, D.C.: Age Printing, 1894.

Nobile, A. *Vade Mecum, or Guide for the Visitors to the Exposition at Philadelphia on Occasion of the One Hundredth Anniversary of Its Independence.* Philadelphia: Collins, 1876.

Northup, Solomon. *Twelve Years a Slave.* Baton Rouge: Louisiana State University Press, 1968.

"O-Be-Joyful Creek and Poverty Gulch." *Atlantic Monthly* 52, no. 314 (December 1883), pp. 753–62.

Odencrantz, Louise C. *Italian Women in Industry: A Study of Conditions in New York City.* New York: Russell Sage Foundation, 1919.

"The Old National Pike." *Harper's New Monthly Magazine* 59, no. 354 (November 1879), pp. 801–16.

Oliver, William. *Eight Months in Illinois; with Information to Emigrants.* Chicago: W. M. Hill, 1924.

Organized Labor and the Black Worker. New York: United Electrical, Radio, and Machine Workers of America, 1967.

Otero, Miguel Antonio. *My Life on the Frontier, 1864–1882.* New York: Press of the Pioneers, 1935.

Page, Jake. "Writing Got a Lot Easier When the Old 'Manual' Was New." *Smithsonian* 21, no. 9 (December 1990), pp. 54–64.

Patterson, Orlando. "Everything Changes Money." *New York Times Magazine*, May 7, 2000, pp. 90–91

Parsons, George Whitwell. *A Tenderfoot in Tombstone: The Private Journal of George Whitwell Parsons: The Turbulent Years, 1880–82.* Tucson, Ariz.: Westernlore Press, 1996.

Pennington, James W. C. *The Fugitive Blacksmith; or, Events in the Life of James W. C. Pennington, Pastor of a Presbyterian Church in New York, Formerly a Slave in the State of Maryland, United States.* 3d ed. London: Charles Gilpin, 1850.

Porter, Glenn, ed. *Encyclopedia of American Economic History.* New York: Charles Scribner's Sons, 1980.

Porter, Kenneth W. "Negro Labor in the Western Cattle Industry." *Labor* 10, no. 3 (Summer 1969), pp. 346–74.

Powderly, Terence V. *The Path I Trod.* New York: Columbia University Press, 1940.

―――――. *Thirty Years of Labor.* Columbus, Ohio: Excelsior Publishing House, 1890.

Power, Tyrone. *Impressions of America, during the Years 1833, 1834, and 1835.* Vol. 2. London: Richard Bentley, 1836.

President's Council on Civil Rights. *To Secure These Rights.* Washington, D.C.: U.S. Government Printing Office, 1947.

Price, Con. *Trails I Rode.* Pasadena, Calif.: Trail's End Publishing, 1947.

Raitz, Karl, ed. *The National Road.* Baltimore: Johns Hopkins University Press, 1996.

Rantoul, Robert, Jr. "An Address to the Workingmen of the United States." In *Middlesex County Lyceum Publications, 1833–34.* Charlestown, Mass.: N.p., 1834.

Rasmussen, Wayne D., ed. *Readings in the History of American Agriculture.* Urbana: University of Illinois Press, 1960.

Report of the Massachusetts Commission on the Employment Problems of Negroes. Boston: Commonwealth of Massachusetts, 1942.

Reynolds, David S. *Walt Whitman's America: A Cultural Biography.* New York: Alfred A. Knopf, 1995.

Richardson, Dorothy. *The Long Day: The Story of a New York Working Girl as Told by Herself.* New York: Century, 1905.

Richthoven, Walter Baron von. *Cattle-Raising on the Plains of North America.* Norman: University of Oklahoma Press, 1964.

Rickard, T. A. *A History of American Mining.* New York: McGraw-Hill, 1932.

Ricketts, W. P. *50 Years in the Saddle.* Sheridan, Wyo.: Star Publishing, 1942.

Robinson, Harriet H. *Loom and Spindle, or Life among the Early Mill Girls.* New York: Thomas Y. Crowell, 1898.

Rockefeller, John D. *Random Reminiscences of Men and Events.* Garden City, N.Y.: Doubleday, Doran, 1909.

Rodgers, Daniel T. *The Work Ethic in Industrial America: 1850–1920.* Chicago: University of Chicago Press, 1978.

Roosevelt, Franklin D. *The Public Papers and Addresses of Franklin D. Roosevelt.* Vol. 2, *The Year of Crisis, 1932.* New York: Random House, 1938.

Root, Waverly. "Women Have Nothing to Kick About." *American Mercury* 68, no. 304 (April 1949), pp. 400–07.

Rowbotham, Sheila. *A Century of Women: The History of Women in Britain and the United States.* New York: Viking, 1997.

St. Clair, Hillary W. *Mineral Industry in Early America.* Washington, D.C.: U.S. Department of the Interior, Bureau of Mines, 1977.

Salmon, Lucy Maynard. *Domestic Service.* New York: Macmillan, 1897.

Salzman, Jack, ed. *Years of Protest: A Collection of American Writings of the 1930s.* New York: Pegasus, 1970.

Samuelson, Paul A., and William D. Nordhaus. *Economics.* 14th ed. New York: McGraw-Hill, 1992.

Sandler, Corey. "Keeping Up with Grace." *PC Magazine* 2, no. 7 (December 1983), pp. 199–215.

Savage, William W., Jr. *Cowboy Life: Reconstructing an American Myth.* Norman: University of Oklahoma Press, 1975.

Schoolcraft, Henry R. *A View of the Lead Mines of Missouri.* New York: Charles Wiley, 1819.

Schuyler, George S. "Jim Crow in the North." *American Mercury* 68, no. 306 (June 1949), pp. 663–70.

Schwartz, Alvin. *The Unions: What They Are, How They Came to Be, How They Affect Each of Us.* New York: Viking, 1972.

Scoresby, William. *American Factories and Their Female Operatives.* London: Longman, Brown, Green, and Longmans, 1845.

Seldes, Gilbert. *The Years of the Locust (America, 1929–1932).* Boston: Little, Brown, 1933.

Shaw, Ronald. *Erie Water West: A History of the Erie Canal, 1792–1854.* Lexington: University Press of Kentucky, 1966.

Sheriff, Carol. *The Artificial River: The Erie Canal and the Paradox of Progress, 1817–1862.* New York: Hill and Wang, 1996.

Siringo, Charles A. *A Texas Cow Boy, or Fifteen Years on the Hurricane Deck of a Spanish Pony.* Lincoln: University of Nebraska Press, 1950.

Sloane, Howard N., and Lucille L. Sloane. *A Pictorial History of American Mining.* New York: Crown Publishers, 1970.

Smalley, Eugene V. *History of the Northern Pacific Railroad.* New York: G. P. Putnam's Sons, 1883.

Smith, Benjamin, ed. *Twenty-four Letters from Labourers in America to Their Friends in England.* London: Edward Rainford, 1829.

Smith, Duane A. *Mining America: The Industry and the Environment, 1800–1980.* Lawrence: University Press of Kansas, 1987.

Smith, Page. *Redeeming the Time: A People's History of the 1920s and the New Deal.* New York: McGraw-Hill, 1987.

———. *The Rise of Industrial America.* New York: McGraw-Hill, 1984.

Snyder, Louis L., and Richard B. Morris, eds. *A Treasury of Great Reporting.* New York: Simon and Schuster, 1949.

Songs of the Workers. Chicago: Industrial Workers of the World, 1956.

Spargo, John. *The Bitter Cry of the Children.* New York: Macmillan, 1906.

Spero, Sterling D., and Abram L. Harris. *The Black Worker: The Negro and the Labor Movement.* New York: Columbia University Press, 1931.

Stanley, Jerry. *Children of the Dust Bowl: The True Story of the School at Weedpatch Camp.* New York: Crown Publishers, 1992.

Stead, W. T. *Chicago To-Day: The Labour War in America.* London: "Review of Reviews" Office, 1894.

Steel, Edward M., ed. *The Speeches and Writings of Mother Jones.* Pittsburgh: University of Pittsburgh Press, 1988.

Steenerson, Knute. "Knute Steenerson's Recollections: The Story of a Pioneer." *Minnesota History Bulletin* 4, nos. 3–4 (August–November 1921), pp. 130–51.

Stein, Robert, ed. *Why Young Mothers Feel Trapped.* New York: Trident Press, 1965.

Stein, Walter J. *California and the Dust Bowl Migration.* Westport, Conn.: Greenwood Press, 1973.

Steinbeck, John. *The Harvest Gypsies: On the Road to the Grapes of Wrath.* Berkeley, Calif.: Heyday Books, 1988.

———. "A Primer on the 30's." *Esquire* 53, no. 6 (June 1960), pp. 85–93.

Stern, Edith M. "Women Are Household Slaves." *American Mercury* 68, no. 301 (January 1949), pp. 71–76.

Stevens, John. *Documents Tending to Prove the Superior Advantages of Rail-Ways and Steam Carriages over Canal Navigation.* New York: T. and J. Swords, 1812.

Steward, Austin. *Twenty-two Years a Slave, and Forty Years a Freeman.* Rochester, N.Y.: William Alling, 1857.

Stone, William L. *History of New York City from the Discovery to the Present Day.* New York: Virtue and Yorston, 1872.

Stowell, Myron R. *"Fort Frick," or the Siege of Homestead.* Pittsburgh: Pittsburgh Printing, 1893.

Sullivan, William A. *The Industrial Worker in Pennsylvania: 1800–1840.* Harrisburg: Pennsylvania Historical and Museum Commission, 1955.

Sutherland, Edwin H., and Harvey J. Locke. *Twenty Thousand Homeless Men: A Study of Unemployed Men in the Chicago Shelters.* Chicago: J. B. Lippincott, 1936.

Svendsen, Gro. *Frontier Mother: The Letters of Gro Svendsen.* Translated and edited by Pauline Farseth and Theodore C. Bergen. New York: Arno Press, 1979.

Sweeney, John J. *Remarks at the Rainbow/PUSH Labor Breakfast.* AFL–CIO Home Page. URL: http://www.aflcio.org/publ.speech98/sp0813.htm. August 13, 1998.

———. *Tenth Annual Philip Murray Memorial Lecture.* AFL–CIO Home Page. URL: http://www.aflcio.org/publ/speech99/sp0413.htm. April 13, 1999.

Sweeney, John J., and Karen Nussbaum. *Solutions for the New Work Force.* Cabin John, Md.: Seven Locks Press, 1989.

Sweeney, John J., with David Kusnet. *America Needs a Raise.* Boston: Houghton Mifflin, 1996.

Sylvis, James C. *The Life, Speeches, Labors and Essays of William H. Sylvis.* Philadelphia: Claxton, Ramsen and Haffelfinger, 1872.

Taft, Philip. *Organized Labor in American History.* New York: Harper and Row, 1964.

Taft, Robert A. "The Taft–Hartley Act: A Favorable View." *Annals of the American Academy of Political and Social Science* 274 (March 1951), pp. 195–99.

Taylor, Don, and Bradley Dow. *The Rise of Industrial Unionism in Canada: A History of the CIO.* Kingston, Ont.: Industrial Relations Centre, Queen's University, 1988.

Terkel, Studs. *Hard Times.* New York: Pantheon Books, 1970.

———. *Working.* New York: Pantheon Books, 1974.

Thoreau, Henry David. *Reform Papers.* Edited by Wendell Glick. Princeton, N.J.: Princeton University Press, 1973.

———. *Walden and Other Writings by Henry David Thoreau.* New York: Bantam Books, 1962.

Throne, Mildred, ed. "Iowa Farm Letters, 1856–1865." *Iowa Journal of History* 58, no. 1 (1960), pp. 37–88.

Towne, Ezra Thayer. *Social Problems: A Study of Present-Day Social Conditions.* New York: Macmillan, 1924.

Transportation and the Early Nation. Indianapolis: Indiana Historical Society, 1982.

Tussey, Jean Y., ed. *Eugene V. Debs Speaks.* New York: Pathfinder Press, 1970.

Uchitelle, Louis. "The American Middle, Just Getting By." *New York Times,* August 1, 1999, pp. 1, 13.

"Unfinished Jobs." *Atlantic Monthly* 138, no. 5 (November 1926), pp. 639–45.

U.S. Department of Agriculture. *Our American Land.* Washington, D.C.: U.S. Government Printing Office, 1987.

U.S. Department of Labor, Division of Negro Economics. *Negro Migration in 1916–1917.* Washington, D.C.: U.S. Government Printing Office, 1919.

U.S. Strike Commission. *Report of the Chicago Strike of June–July 1894.* Washington, D.C.: U.S. Government Printing Office, 1895.

Van Kleeck, Mary. *Artificial Flower Makers.* New York: Survey Associates, 1913.

Vorse, Mary Heaton. *Labor's New Millions.* New York: Modern Age Books, 1938.

———. "School for Bums." *New Republic* 66, no. 856 (April 29, 1931), pp. 292–94.

Walker, Charles Rumford. *Steel: The Diary of a Furnace Worker.* Boston: Atlantic Monthly Press, 1922.

Warne, Colston E., ed. *The Steel Strike of 1919.* Boston: D. C. Heath, 1963.

Washington, Booker T. *The Booker T. Washington Papers.* Vol. 2, *1860–89.* Louis R. Harlan, ed. Urbana: University of Illinois Press, 1972.

———. *The Future of the American Negro.* Chicago: Afro-Am Press, 1969.

———. "The Negro and the Labor Unions." *Atlantic Monthly* 111, no. 6 (June 1913), pp. 756–767.

———. *Up from Slavery.* New York: Penguin Books, 1986.

Watkins, T. H. *The Great Depression: America in the 1930s.* Boston: Little, Brown, 1993.

Way, Peter. *Common Labour: Workers and the Digging of North American Canals, 1780–1860.* Cambridge, U.K.: Cambridge University Press, 1993.

Weiner, Lynn Y. *From Working Girl to Working Mother: The Female Labor Force in the United States, 1820–1980.* Chapel Hill: University of North Carolina, 1985.

Weir, Robert E. *Beyond Labor's Veil: The Culture of the Knights of Labor.* University Park: Pennsylvania State University Press, 1996.

Weld, Theodore. *American Slavery as It Is: Testimony of a Thousand Witnesses.* New York: American Anti-Slavery Society, 1839.

"What Labor Wants." *U.S. News & World Report,* November 6, 1953, pp. 54–62.

White, Richard. *"It's Your Misfortune and None of My Own": A New History of the American West.* Norman: University of Oklahoma Press, 1991.

Whitman, Walt. *Leaves of Grass.* New York: W. W. Norton, 1973.

Wilentz, Sean. *Chants Democratic: New York City and the Rise of the American Working Class, 1788–1850.* New York: Oxford University Press, 1984.

Woods, John. *Two Years' Residence in the Settlement on the English Prairie, in the Illinois County, United States.* London: 1822.

Worthen, Augusta. *The History of Sutton, New Hampshire.* Concord, N.H.: Republican Press Association, 1890.

Wright, Carroll D. *The Industrial Evolution of the United States.* New York: Meadville Penna, 1895.

———. *The Working Girls of Boston.* Boston: Wright and Potter Printing, 1889.

Wright, William. *History of the Big Bonanza.* San Francisco: Bancroft, 1876.

Wyman, Lillie B. Chance. "Studies of Factory Life: Black-Listing at Fall River." *Atlantic Monthly* 62, no. 373 (November 1888), pp. 605–12.

———. "Studies of Factory Life: The Village System." *Atlantic Monthly* 62, no. 369 (July 1888), pp. 16–29.

Zinn, Howard, ed. *New Deal Thought.* Indianapolis: Bobbs-Merrill, 1966.

INDEX

Page locators in **boldface** indicate main entries.
Page locators in *italic* indicate illustrations. Page locators followed by *m* indicate maps.